The Works of JOHN OWEN

EDITED BY

William H. Goold

VOLUME X

The Banner of Truth Trust

THE BANNER OF TRUTH TRUST

Head Office
3 Murrayfield Road
Edinburgh, EH12 6EL
UK

North America Office
610 Alexander Spring Road
Carlisle, PA 17015
USA

banneroftruth.org

This edition of *The Works Of John Owen* first published by
Johnstone & Hunter, 1850-53

Reprinted by the Banner of Truth Trust, 1967
Reprinted 1976, 1978, 1987, 1993, 2000, 2009, 2018, 2024

VOLUME X

*

ISBN
This volume: 978 0 85151 064 4
16-volume set: 978 0 85151 392 8

*

Printed in the USA by
Versa Press Inc.,
East Peoria, IL.

The Works of John Owen

VOLUME X

CONTENTS OF VOLUME X.

ΘΕΟΜΑΧΙΑ ΑΥΤΕΞΟΥΣΙΑΣΤΙΚΗ·

OR,

A DISPLAY OF ARMINIANISM.

SALUS ELECTORUM, SANGUIS JESU;

OR,

THE DEATH OF DEATH IN THE DEATH OF CHRIST.

BOOK I.

BOOK II.

BOOK III.

BOOK IV.

OF THE DEATH OF CHRIST.

A DISSERTATION ON DIVINE JUSTICE.

PART II.

ΘΕΟΜΑΧΙΑ ΑΥΤΕΞΟΥΣΙΑΣΤΙΚΗ·

OR,

A DISPLAY OF ARMINIANISM:

BEING

A DISCOVERY OF THE OLD PELAGIAN IDOL FREE-WILL, WITH THE NEW GODDESS CONTINGENCY,

ADVANCING THEMSELVES INTO THE THRONE OF THE GOD OF HEAVEN, TO THE PREJUDICE OF HIS GRACE, PROVIDENCE, AND SUPREME DOMINION OVER THE CHILDREN OF MEN;

WHEREIN

THE MAIN ERRORS BY WHICH THEY ARE FALLEN OFF FROM THE RECEIVED DOCTRINE OF ALL THE REFORMED CHURCHES, WITH THEIR OPPOSITION IN DIVERS PARTICULARS TO THE DOCTRINE ESTABLISHED IN THE CHURCH OF ENGLAND, ARE DISCOVERED AND LAID OPEN OUT OF THEIR OWN WRITINGS AND CONFESSIONS, AND CONFUTED BY THE WORD OF GOD.

Produce your cause, saith the LORD: bring forth your strong reasons, saith the King of Jacob.—ISA. xli. 21.

Woe unto him that striveth with his Maker! Let the potsherd strive with the potsherds of the earth.—Chap. xlv. 9

Θές, ὦ Ἀκεσίλαε, κλίμακα καὶ μόνος ἀνάβηθι εἰς τὸν οὐρανόν.—Constant., apud Socrat., lib. i. cap. 10.

PREFATORY NOTE.

The relation of man to his Creator has engaged the attention of earnest and thoughtful minds, from the days of the patriarch of Uz to the most recent controversies of modern times. The entrance of sin into the world has vastly complicated this relationship; so that, considered in its various bearings, it involves some of the most difficult problems with which the human intellect has ever attempted to grapple. The extent to which the intellect itself has been weakened and beclouded by the corruption of our nature, renders us the less able to penetrate into the deep mysteries of human duty and destiny. Whether man sins now as essentially affected with the taint of the first sin, and involved in the responsibilities of the first sinner, or sins wholly on his own account and by his own free act, under the bias of no connection with Adam, except what connection obtains between example on the one hand and imitation on the other? whether, on the supposition of a scheme of saving grace, grace is simply divine and external aid to the will of man, already operating freely in the direction of what is good, and so establishing a meritorious claim upon God for the bestowal of such aid, or a supernatural influence creating in man the very liberty itself to will and to do what is good? and whether, in the latter view of divine grace, as bestowed in divine sovereignty, and therefore according to a divine purpose, it can be reconciled with human responsibility?—are the questions which produced the sharp encounter of keen and conflicting wits between Pelagius and Augustine of old.

Towards the middle of the ninth century, these questions again assumed distinctive prominence in the history of theological speculation. Gottschalc, a monk of Orbais, distinguished himself by his advocacy of the doctrines of Augustine. It was the doctrine of predestination chiefly on which he insisted; and the controversy in his hands assumed this peculiar modification, that not merely the application of gracious influence, but the reference of the atonement, was exhibited as under the limit and regulation of the divine sovereignty and purpose. Not that in this respect he was at variance with Augustine, but the point seems to have been specially and formally mooted in the discussions of this age. His view of predestination embraced an element which may be reckoned an advance on the Augustinian doctrine; for according to him, predestination was twofold, comprehending the punishment of the reprobate as well as the salvation of the elect; but while he held the predestination of men to the punishment of their sin, he was far from holding, as his opponents alleged, that they were predestinated to the commission of sin. Council warred with council in the case of Gottschalc. Gottschalc himself expiated by a death in prison his audacious anticipation of the rights of private judgment and free inquiry in a dark age.

The next revival of the same controversy in substance, though under certain modifications, took place after the Reformation. It is remarkable that at this period discussion on these weighty questions sprang up almost simultaneously in three different parts of Europe, and in three schools of theology, among which a wide diversity existed. The shackles of mediæval ignorance were burst asunder by the awakening intelligence of Europe; and if we except the controversy between Protestantism and Popery, on which the Reformation hinged, no point could more naturally engage the mind, in the infancy of its freedom, than the compatibility of the divine purpose with human responsibility; on the solution of which problem the nature of redemption seemed to depend, and around which, by the spell of the very mystery attaching to it, human speculation in all ages had revolved. When an interdict still lay on theological inquiry, Thomists and Scotists had discussed it in its metaphysical form, and under a cloud of scholastic subtilties, lest the jealousies of a dominant church should be awakened. But now, when a measure of intellectual freedom had been acquired, and the dispute between free-will on the one hand and efficacious grace on the other involved a practical issue between Rome and Geneva, the question received a treatment almost exclusively theological.

First, perhaps, in the order of time, this discussion was revived in Poland, and in connection with the heresies of Socinus. The divinity of Christ, the nature of the atonement, and the corruption of human nature, are all doctrines essentially connected. It is because Christ is divine that an adequate satisfaction has been rendered, in his sufferings, to the claims of divine justice; and such an atonement is indispensable for our salvation, if man, because dead in sin, has no power to achieve salvation by any merit of his own. A denial of the total corruption of our nature seems essential to the Unitarian system; so far there is common ground between the systems of Pelagius and Socinus. It is not wonderful that this measure of identity should develop consequences affecting the doctrine of the divine purposes and of predestination, though it is beyond our limits to trace either the necessary or the historical evolution of these consequences. Spanheim, in his "Elenchus Controversiarum," p. 237, ascribes the origin of the Arminian controversy in Holland to certain emissaries, Ostorodius and Voidovius, despatched by the Polish Socinians into the Low Countries, for the purpose of propagating the tenets of their sect. Their tenets respecting the Trinity and the atonement took no root in these countries; but Spanheim affirms that it was otherwise in regard to certain opinions of Socinus, "quae ille recoxit ex Pelagii disciplinâ," on predestination, free-will, and the ground of justification before God.

About the same time, the Church of Rome was shaken to its centre by the same controversy. The Jesuits had always Pelagian leanings, and in the Council of Trent their influence was triumphant, and, so far as its decrees stereotype the Romish creed, sealed the doom of the waning authority of Augustine. Louis Molina, in 1588, made an attempt, in his lectures on "The Concord of Grace and Free-will," to unite the conflicting theories. The Jesuits regarded his attempt with no favour. A lengthened controversy arose, in which Molinism, as partly a deviation from, and partly a compromise of, the fundamental principles of the Augustinian system, was effectually assailed by the piety of Jansen, the learning of Arnauld, and the genius of Pascal, till the bull Unigenitus secured a lasting triumph for Jesuitism, by the authoritative condemnation of the doctrines of Augustine, as declared in the collection of extracts from his writings which Jansen had published under the title "Augustinus."

But it was in Holland that the controversy on this point arose which had the chief influence on British theology, and reduced the questions at issue to the shape under which they are discussed by Owen in his "Display of Arminianism." On the death of an eminent theologian of the name of Junius, Arminius was called to the vacant chair in the University of Leyden. Gomar, a professor in the same university, and the Presbytery of Amsterdam, opposed his appointment, on the ground of his erroneous principles. On giving a pledge that he would teach nothing at variance with the Belgic Confession and Catechism, he was allowed to enter on his office as professor in 1603. Gomar and he again fell into a dispute on the subject of predestination,—the origin of prolonged troubles and controversies in the Church of Holland. Gomar and his party were supported by the majority of the clergy in the church. Arminius depended upon the political support of the state. The former sought a national synod to adjudicate on the prevailing controversy. The latter, having the ear of the state, contrived to prevent it. Stormy scenes ensued, amid which Arminius died, and Episcopius became the leader of the Remonstrants, as his followers were called, from a remonstrance which they submitted in 1610 to the States of Holland and West Friesland. The Remonstrants levied soldiers to sustain their cause, and the provinces resounded with military preparations. At last, profiting by the confusion, Maurice, the head of the house of Orange, by a series of daring and reckless movements, seized upon the government of the States. In deference to Gomar and his party, he convened a general synod on the 13th November 1618. The doctrines of Arminius were condemned, and five articles were drawn up and published as the judgment of the synod on the points in dispute. The first asserts election by grace, in opposition to election on the ground of foreseen excellence; in the second God is declared to have willed that Christ should *efficaciously* redeem all those, and those only, who from eternity were chosen to salvation; the third and fourth relate to the moral impotence of man, and the work of the Spirit in conversion; and the fifth affirms the doctrine of the perseverance of the saints. The Church of France embodied these articles among her own standards. The Church of Geneva as cordially acquiesced in them.

Four English deputies, Drs Carleton, Hall, Davenant, and Ward, together with Dr Balcanquhal from Scotland, by the command of James VI., repaired to Holland, and took their place in the Synod of Dort, in accordance with a request of the Dutch Church to be favoured with the aid and countenance of some delegates from the British Churches. The proceedings of the Synod of Dort had the sanction of these British divines. No doubt can be entertained that the Thirty-nine Articles of the Church of England were not Arminian; but on the elevation of Laud to the see of Canterbury, Arminianism grew strong within its pale. A royal prohibition was issued against all discussion of the controverted points in the pulpit. All ecclesiastical preferments at the disposal of the Crown were bestowed on those who leaned to Arminian views. "The fates of our church," says Owen, in the note to the reader prefixed to the following treatise, "having of late devolved the government thereof into the hands of men tainted with this poison, Arminianism became backed with the powerful arguments of praise and preferment, and quickly prevailed to beat poor naked truth into a corner." It would, however, be neither fair nor correct if the statement of these facts left an impression that Arminianism made progress solely through the help of royal and prelatic favour. It was embraced and supported by some authors to whom no sinister motives can be imputed; and the cause has never found an abler advocate than John Goodwin, whose name, for his publications against the royal interest, was associated with that of Milton, in the legal proceedings instituted against them both at the Restoration.

At this juncture, Owen felt it his duty to oppose the innovations on the received doctrine of the church, by the publication of a work in which the views of the Arminians are exhibited on all the leading topics of the controversy, with the exception of three points, relating to universal grace, justification, and the perseverance of the saints. He substantiates his statements regarding the Arminian tenets by copious quotations from the works of the Dutch Remonstrants; and contrasts them, at the close of each chapter, with passages from Scripture. Exception may be taken to this course, as the sentence of any author, detached from the context, may convey a meaning which is essentially modified by it. Some of these quotations are so far accommodated by Owen as to present a full statement of a particular opinion, instead of appearing in the parenthetic and incidental form which they present in the original works, as merely parts of a sentence. We did not feel it needful to interfere with them in this shape; for, so far as we can judge, our author evinces perfect integrity in all the quotations to which he has recourse, and the slight alterations occasionally made on them never superinduce a dishonest or mistaken gloss on the views of the authors from whom the passages are selected. It may be questioned if Owen sufficiently discriminates the doctrine of Arminius from the full development which his system, after his death, received in the hands of his followers. Sometimes, moreover, opinions possessing the distinctive features of Pelagianism are confounded with Arminianism, strictly so called. Our author, perhaps, may be vindicated on the ground that it was his object to exhibit Arminianism as current and common in his day; and his quotations seem to prove that his Display of it was not far from the truth, though, from the refinement of modern discrimination on some of the points, many an Arminian would hardly subscribe to some of the statements as a correct representation of his creed, and a Calvinistic author is under obvious temptation to run up Arminian views into what he may esteem their legitimate consequences in the extravagance of the Pelagian theory. The style is simple; some polish appears in the composition; and occasionally a degree of ornament and pleasantry is employed (as when he enters on the question of Free-will, chap. xii.), which is rare with Owen, who perhaps prided himself on the studious rejection of literary elegance. It could be wished that he had risen superior to the vice of the age in such discussions, by manifesting less acerbity of temper and diction in the refutation of the views which he combats in this work. It was Owen's first publication (1642), and immediately brought him into notice. The living of Fordham in Essex was conferred upon him by the Committee of Religion, to whom the work is dedicated. —Ed.

---

2 *Martii, anno Domini* 1642.

It is this day ordered, by the Committee of the House of Commons in Parliament for the Regulating of Printing and Publishing of Books, That this book, entitled "A Display of Arminianism," be printed.

John White.

TO THE RIGHT HONOURABLE

THE LORDS AND GENTLEMEN OF THE COMMITTEE FOR RELIGION.[1]

THE many ample testimonies of zealous reverence to the *providence* of God, as well as affectionate care for the *privileges* of men, which have been given by this honourable assembly of parliament, encourage the adorers of the one, no less than the lovers of the other, to vindicate that also from the encroachments of men. And as it was not, doubtless, without divine disposition that those should be the chiefest agents in robbing men of their privileges who had nefariously attempted to spoil God of his providence; so we hope the same all-ruling hand hath disposed of them to be glorious instruments of re-advancing his right and supreme dominion over the hearts of men whose hearts he hath prepared with courage and constancy to establish men in their inviolated rights, by reducing a sweet harmony between *awful sovereignty* and a *well-moderated liberty*. Now, the first of these being demandated to your particular care, I come unto you with a bill of complaint against no small number in this kingdom, who have wickedly violated our interest in the providence of God, and have attempted to bring in the foreign power of an old idol, to the great prejudice of all the true subjects and servants of the Most High. My accusation I make good by the evidence of the fact, joined with their own confessions. And because, to waive the imputation of violent intrusion into the dominion of another, they lay some claim and pretend some title unto it, I shall briefly show how it is contrary to the express terms of *the great charter of Heaven* to have any such power introduced amongst men. Your known love to truth and the gospel of Christ makes it altogether needless for me to stir you up by any motives to hearken to this just complaint, and provide a timely remedy for this growing evil; especially since experience hath so clearly taught us here, in England, that not only eternal but temporal happiness also dependeth on the flourishing of the truth of Christ's gospel.

Justice and *religion* were always conceived as the main columns and upholders of any state or commonwealth; like two pillars in a building, whereof the one cannot stand without the other, nor the whole fabric without them both. As the philosopher spake of logic and rhetoric, they are *artes* ἀντίστροφαι, mutually aiding each other, and both aiming at the same end, though in different manners; so they, without repugnancy, concur and sweetly fall in one with another, for the reiglement and direction of every person in a commonwealth, to make the whole happy and blessed: and where they are both thus united, there, and only there, is the blessing in assurance whereof Hezekiah rejoiced,—*truth* and *peace*. An agreement without truth is no peace, but a covenant with death, a league with hell, a conspiracy against the kingdom of Christ, a stout rebellion against the God of heaven; and without justice, great commonwealths are but great troops of robbers. Now, the result of the one of these is civil peace; of the other, ecclesiastical: betwixt which

[1] This committee was appointed by the House of Lords, March 12, 1640. It sometimes bears the name of the Committee of Accommodation, and consisted of ten earls, ten bishops, and ten barons. To prepare the subjects of discussion, some bishops and several divines of different persuasions were appointed a sub-committee. The duty of the committee was to examine all innovations in doctrine and discipline, illegally introduced into the church since the Reformation. See Neal's History, vol. ii. 395.—ED.

two there is a great sympathy, a strict connection, having on each other a mutual dependence. Is there any disturbance of the state? it is usually attended with schisms and factions in the church; and the divisions of the church are too often even the subversions of the commonwealth. Thus it hath been ever since that unhappy difference between Cain and Abel; which was not concerning the bounds and limits of their inheritance, nor which of them should be heir to the whole world, but about the dictates of religion, the offering of their sacrifices. This fire, also, of dissension hath been more stirred up since the Prince of Peace hath, by his gospel, sent the sword amongst us; for the preaching thereof, meeting with the strongholds of Satan and the depraved corruption of human nature, must needs occasion a great shaking of the earth. But most especially, *distracted Christendom* hath found fearful issues of this discord, since the proud Romish prelates have sought to establish their hell-broached errors, by inventing and maintaining uncharitable, destructive censures against all that oppose them: which, first causing schisms and distractions in the church, and then being helped forward by the blindness and cruelty of ambitious potentates, have raised war of nation against nation, —witness the Spanish invasion of '88;[1] [and war] of a people within themselves, as in the late civil wars of France, where, after divers horrible massacres, many chose rather to die soldiers than martyrs.

And, oh, that this truth might not, at this day, be written with the blood of almost expiring Ireland! Yea, it hath lastly descended to dissension betwixt private parties,—witness the horrible murder of Diazius, whose brains were chopped out with an axe by his own brother Alphonsus,[2] for forsaking the Romish religion; what rents in [the] State, what grudgings, hatreds, and exasperations of mind among private men, have happened by reason of some inferior differences, we all at this day grieve to behold. "Tantum religio potuit suadere malorum!" Most concerning, then, is it for us to endeavour obedience to our Saviour's precept, of seeking first the kingdom of God, that we may be partakers of the good things comprised in the promise annexed. Were there but this one argument for to seek the peace of the church, because thereon depends the peace of the commonwealth, it were sufficient to quicken our utmost industry for the attaining of it. Now, what peace in the church without truth? All conformity to any thing else is but the agreement of Herod and Pilate to destroy Christ and his kingdom. Neither is it this or that particular truth, but the whole counsel of God revealed unto us, without adding or detracting, whose embracement is required to make our peace firm and stable. No halting betwixt Jehovah and Baal, Christ and Antichrist; as good be all Philistine, and worshippers of Dagon, as to speak part the language of Ashdod and part the language of the Jews: hence, hence hath been the rise of all our miseries, of all our dissensions, whilst factious men laboured every day to commend themselves to them who sat aloft in the temple of God, by introducing new popish-arminian errors, whose patronage they had wickedly undertaken. Who would have thought that our church would ever have given entertainment to these Belgic semi-Pelagians, who have cast dirt upon the faces and raked up the ashes of all those great and pious souls whom God magnified, in using as his instruments to reform his church; to the least of which the whole troop of Arminians shall never make themselves equal, though they swell till they break? What benefit did ever come to this church by attempting to prove that the chief part *in the several degrees of our salvation is to be ascribed unto ourselves, rather than God?*—which is the head and sum of all the controversies between them and us. And must not the introducing and fomenting of a doctrine so opposite to that truth our church hath quietly enjoyed

[1] He alludes to the attempted invasion of England by the Spanish Armada in 1588. In France the civil wars on account of religion were terminated about 1628, when the Protestants secured the confirmation of the Edict of Nantes, but lost possession of the towns that had been given in guarantee for the faithful observance of it.—Ed.

[2] Sleid. Com.

ever since the first Reformation necessarily bring along with it schisms and dissensions, so long as any remain who love the truth, or esteem the gospel above preferment? Neither let any deceive your wisdoms, by affirming that they are differences of an inferior nature that are at this day agitated between the Arminians and the orthodox divines of the reformed church. Be pleased but to cast an eye on the following instances, and you will find them hewing at the very root of Christianity. Consider seriously their denying of that fundamental article of *original sin.* Is this but a small escape in theology?—why, what need of the gospel, what need of Christ himself, if our nature be not guilty, depraved, corrupted? Neither are many of the rest of less importance. Surely these are not things "in quibus possimus dissentire salvâ pace ac charitate," as Austin speaks,—"about which we may differ without loss of peace or charity." One church cannot wrap in her communion Austin and Pelagius, Calvin and Arminius. I have here only given you a taste, whereby you may judge of the rest of their fruit,—"mors in olla, mors in olla;" their doctrine of the *final apostasy of the elect*, of true believers, of a wavering hesitancy concerning our present grace and future glory, with divers others, I have wholly omitted: those I have produced are enough to make their abettors incapable of our church-communion. The sacred bond of peace compasseth only the unity of that Spirit which leadeth into all truth. We must not offer the right hand of fellowship, but rather proclaim ἱερὸν πόλεμον,[1] "a holy war," to such enemies of God's providence, Christ's merit, and the powerful operation of the Holy Spirit. Neither let any object, that all the Arminians do not openly profess all these errors I have recounted. Let ours, then, show wherein they differ from their masters.[2] We see their own confessions; we know their arts, βάθη καὶ μεθοδείας τοῦ Σατανᾶ,—"the depths and crafts of Satan;" we know the several ways they have to introduce and insinuate their heterodoxies into the minds of men. With some they appear only to dislike our doctrine of *reprobation;* with others, to claim an allowable *liberty of the will:* but yet, for the most part,—like the serpent, wherever she gets in her head, she will wriggle in her whole body, sting and all,—give but the least admission, and the whole poison must be swallowed. What was the intention of the maintainers of these strange assertions amongst us I know not,—whether the efficacy of error prevailed really with them or no, or whether it were the better to comply with Popery, and thereby to draw us back again unto Egypt;—but this I have heard, that it was affirmed on knowledge, in a former parliament, that the introduction of Arminianism amongst us was the issue of a Spanish consultation. It is a strange story that learned Zanchius[3] tells us, how, upon the death of the Cardinal of Lorraine there was found in his study a note of the names of divers German doctors and ministers, being Lutherans, to whom was paid an annual pension, by the assignment of the cardinal, that they might take pains to oppose the Calvinists; and so, by cherishing dissension, reduce the people again to Popery. If there be any such amongst us, who, upon such poor inconsiderable motives, would be won to betray the gospel of Christ, God grant them repentance before it be too late! However, upon what grounds, with what intentions, for what ends soever, these tares have been sowed amongst us by envious men, the hope of all the piously learned in the kingdom is, that, by your effectual care and diligence, some means may be found to root them out. Now, God Almighty increase and fill your whole honourable society with wisdom, zeal, knowledge, and all other Christian graces, necessary for your great calling and employments; which is the daily prayer of your most humble and devoted servant,

JOHN OWEN.

[1] Greg. Naz.

[2] Profitentur Remonst. hasce ad promotionem causæ suæ artes adhibere, ut apud vulgus non ulterius progrediantur quam de articulis vulgo notis, ut pro ingeniorum diversitate quosdam lacte diu alant, alios solidiore cibo, etc.—Festus Hom. præstat ad specimen Con. Bel.

[3] Hieron. Zanch. ad Holderum. Res. Miscel.

TO THE CHRISTIAN READER.

Reader,—Thou canst not be such a stranger in our Israel as that it should be necessary for me to acquaint thee with the first sowing and spreading of these tares in the field of the church, much less to declare what divisions and thoughts of heart, what open bitter contentions, to the loss of ecclesiastical peace, have been stirred up amongst us about them. Only some few things, relating to this my particular endeavour, I would willingly premonish thee of:—

First, Never were so many *prodigious errors* introduced into a church, with so high a hand and so little opposition, as these into ours, since the nation of Christians was known in the world. The chief cause I take to be that which Æneas Sylvius gave why more maintained the pope to be above the council than the council above the pope,—because popes gave archbishoprics, bishoprics, &c., but the councils sued "in forma pauperis," and, therefore, could scarce get an advocate to plead their cause. The fates of our church having of late devolved the government thereof into the hands of men tainted with this poison, Arminianism became backed with the powerful arguments of praise and preferment, and quickly prevailed to beat poor naked Truth into a corner. It is high time, then, for all the lovers of the old way to oppose this innovation, prevailing by such unworthy means, before our breach grow great like the sea, and there be none to heal it.

My intention in this weak endeavour (which is but the undigested issue of a few broken hours, too many causes, in these furious malignant days, continually interrupting the course of my studies), is but to stir up such who, having more leisure and greater abilities, will not as yet move a finger to help [to] vindicate oppressed truth.

In the meantime, I hope this discovery may not be unuseful, especially to such who, wanting either will or abilities to peruse larger discourses, may yet be allured by their words, which are smoother than oil, to taste the poison of asps that is under their lips. Satan hath βάθη καὶ μεθοδείας, depths where to hide, and methods how to broach his lies; and never did any of his emissaries employ his received talents with more skill and diligence than our Arminians, labouring earnestly, in the first place, to instil some errors that are most plausible, intending chiefly an introduction of them that are more palpable, knowing that if those be for a time suppressed until these be well digested, they will follow of their own accord. Wherefore, I have endeavoured to lay open to the view of all some of their foundation-errors, not usually discussed, on which the whole inconsistent superstructure is erected, whereby it will appear how, under a most vain pretence of farthering piety, they have prevaricated against the very grounds of Christianity; wherein,—

First, I have not observed the same method in handling each particular controversy, but followed such several ways as seemed most convenient to clear the truth and discover their heresies.

Secondly, Some of their errors I have not touched at all,—as those concerning *universal grace, justification,* the *final apostasy of true believers,*—because they came not within the compass of my proposed method, as you may see chap. i., where you have the sum of the whole discourse.

Thirdly, I have given some instances of their opposing the received doctrine of the church of England, contained in divers of the Thirty-nine Articles; which would it did not yield us just cause of farther complaint against the iniquity of those times whereinto we were lately fallen! Had a poor Puritan offended against half so many canons as they opposed articles, he had forfeited his livelihood, if not endangered his life. I would I could hear any other probable reason why divers prelates were so zealous for the discipline and so negligent of the doctrine of the church, but because the one was reformed by the word of God, the other remaining as we found it in the times of Popery.

Fourthly, I have not purposely undertaken to answer any of their arguments, referring that labour to a farther design, even a clearing of our doctrine of reprobation, and of the administration of God's providence towards the reprobates, and over all their actions, from those calumnious aspersions they cast upon it; but concerning this, I fear the discouragements of these woful days will leave me nothing but a desire that so necessary a work may find a more able pen.

JOHN OWEN.

ΘΕΟΜΑΧΙΑΣ ΑΥΤΕΞΟΥΣΙΑΣΤΙΚΗΣ

Arma:

Ut omnis controversia dirimatur per verbum Dei, consilium hoc suspectum videri debet et non uno nomine perniciosum est.—Remon. Vindic. ad Videl., p. 30.

1. Lib. Arbitrium.
2. Contingentia.
3. Indifferentia ad τὸ velle et nolle.
4. Supremum actûs sui dominium.
5. Ens αὐτὸ ὂν independens in agendo.

} Divinam { 1. Voluntatem mutabilem, 2. Scientiam fallibilem, conjecturalem, 3. Providentiam otiosam. } Constituentia.

Specimen:

Primus Copiarum impetus, in Campo qui de nomine alterius ducis, Lib. Arbit. dicitur seu humanarum actionum ditio.

———

Utrinque autem à voluntate humanâ remota et confossa jacent,—

1. Coactio,
2. Necessitas absoluta interna,
3. Mera seu solitaria sponta-neitas.

Arma:

Ad Legem, ad Prophetas.
Scrutamini Scripturas.—Johan. v. 39.

1. Decretum absolutum immutabile,
2. Præscientia infallibilis,
3. Providentia, per { 1. Sustentationem, 2. Determinationem, 3. Gubernationem, 4. Directionem, summe efficax. } Quibus omnem creaturam, { 1. Essentiam, 2. Subsistentiam, 3. Motionem, 4. Determinationem ad actum, 5. Efficientiam in agendo realem, debere necesse est.

---

1. Lib. Arbit.
2. Integritas naturæ.
3. Lumen naturale.
4. Actus elicitus.
5. Faciens quod in se est.
6. Fædus novum universale.
7. Vires credendi per lapsum non amissæ.
8. Potentia active obedientialis ad bonum morale.
9. Suasio moralis.

} "Linguâ nostra prævalemus; labia nostra penes nos sunt: quis esset nobis Dominus?" Ps. xii.

His tu gradibus Romule Arpin; ascendisti in cœlum.

Dei munus est quod vivimus, nostrum vero, quod bene sanctèque vivimus.

——fortunam a Deo petendam, à seipso sumendam esse sapientiam.

Quia sibi quisque virtutem acquirit nemo de sapientibus de eâ gratias Deo egit.

Impetus copiarum secundus, circa gratiam et naturam, ubi adversis frontibus et cominus pugnatur.

———

Campus autem hic status naturæ post lapsum vocetur, cujus loca præcipua quæ in mappa —τοῦ μικροῦ κόσμου delineantur, sunt,—

1. Reatus primi peccati.
2. Corruptio naturæ.
3. Mors spiritualis, ubi multa mortuorum sepulchra, e quibus resurgente Christo, exierunt pauci.
4. Impotentia credendi.
5. Cæcitas intellectus.
6. Pravitas voluntatis.
7. Obduratio cordis.
8. Aversio à bono incommutabili.
9. Propensio ad bonum commutabile.

1. Prædestinatio gratuita.
2. Meritum Christi.
3. Operatio Spiritus.
4. Gratia efficax.
5. Infusio habituum.
6. Vocatio secundum immutabile dei propositum.
7. Evangelium Jesu Christi.
8. Liber vitæ.

} "Non nobis, Domine, non nobis, sed nomini tuo da honorem," Ps. cxiv.

"Nam quos præscivit, etiam prædestinavit conformandos imagini Filii sui: ut is sit primogenitus inter multos fratres. Quos vero prædestinavit, eos etiam vocavit: et quos vocavit, eos etiam justificavit: et quos justificavit, eos etiam glorificavit," Rom. viii.

Cui soli sapienti gloria sit per Jesum Christum in secula!

A DISPLAY OF ARMINIANISM.

ΣΥΝ ΘΕῼ.

CHAPTER I.

Of the two main ends aimed at by the Arminians, by their innovations in the received doctrine of the reformed churches.

THE soul of man, by reason of the corruption of nature, is not only darkened[1] with a mist of ignorance, whereby he is disenabled for the comprehending of divine truth, but is also armed with prejudice and opposition against some parts thereof,[2] which are either most above or most contrary to some false principles which he hath framed unto himself. As a desire of self-sufficiency was the first cause of this infirmity, so a conceit thereof is that wherewith he still languisheth; nothing doth he more contend for than an independency of any supreme power, which might either help, hinder, or control him in his actions. This is that bitter root from whence have sprung all those heresies[3] and wretched contentions which have troubled the church, concerning the power of man in working his own happiness, and his exemption from the over-ruling providence of Almighty God. All which wrangling disputes of carnal reason against the word of God come at last to this head, Whether the first and chiefest part, in disposing of things in this world, ought to be ascribed to God or man? Men for the most part have vindicated this pre-eminence unto themselves,[4] by exclamations that so it must be, or else that God is unjust, and his ways unequal. Never did any men, "postquam Christiana gens esse cæpit," more eagerly endeavour the erecting of this Babel than the Arminians, the modern blinded patrons of human self-sufficiency; all whose innovations in the received doctrine of the reformed churches aim at and tend to one of these two ends:—

[1] Eph. iv. 18; John i. 5; 1 Cor. ii. 14.

[2] John vi. 42, vii. 52. "Natura sic apparet vitiata ut hoc majoris vitii sit, non videre."—Aug.

[3] Pelag. Semipelag. Scholastic.

[4] "In hac causa non judicant secundum æquitatem, sed secundum affectum commodi sui."—Luth. de Arbit. Serv.

FIRST, To exempt themselves from God's jurisdiction,—to free themselves from the supreme dominion of his all-ruling providence; not to live and move in him, but to have an absolute independent power in all their actions, so that the event of all things wherein they have any interest might have a considerable relation to nothing but chance, contingency, and their own wills;—a most nefarious, sacrilegious attempt! To this end,—

First, They deny the eternity and unchangeableness of God's decrees; for these being established, they fear they should be kept within bounds from doing any thing but what his counsel hath determined should be done. If the purposes of the Strength of Israel be eternal and immutable, their idol free-will must be limited, their independency prejudiced; wherefore they choose rather to affirm that his decrees are temporary and changeable, yea, that he doth really change them according to the several mutations he sees in us: which, how wild a conceit it is, how contrary to the pure nature of God, how destructive to his attributes, I shall show in the second chapter.

Secondly, They question the prescience or foreknowledge of God; for if known unto God are all his works from the beginning, if he certainly foreknew all things that shall hereafter come to pass, it seems to cast an infallibility of event upon all their actions, which encroaches upon the large territory of their new goddess, contingency; nay, it would quite dethrone the queen of heaven, and induce a kind of necessity of our doing all, and nothing but what God foreknows. Now, that to deny this prescience is destructive to the very essence of the Deity, and plain atheism, shall be declared, chapter the third.

Thirdly, They depose the all-governing providence of this King of nations, denying its energetical, effectual power, in turning the hearts, ruling the thoughts, determining the wills, and disposing the actions of men, by granting nothing unto it but a general power and influence, to be limited and used according to the inclination and will of every particular agent; so making Almighty God a desirer that many things were otherwise than they are, and an idle spectator of most things that are done in the world: the falseness of which assertions shall be proved, chapter the fourth.

Fourthly, They deny the irresistibility and uncontrollable power of God's will, affirming that oftentimes he seriously willeth and intendeth what he cannot accomplish, and so is deceived of his aim; nay, whereas he desireth, and really intendeth, to save every man, it is wholly in their own power whether he shall save any one or no; otherwise their idol free-will should have but a poor deity, if God could, how and when he would, cross and resist him in his dominion. Concerning this see chapter the fifth. "His gradibus itur in cœlum." Corrupted nature is still ready, either nefariously, with Adam, to attempt to be like God, or to think foolishly that he is altogether like unto us, Ps. l.; one of which inconveniences all men run into, who have not learned to submit their frail wills to the almighty will of God, and captivate their understandings to the obedience of faith. [See chapter fifth.]

SECONDLY, The second end at which the new doctrine of the Arminians aimeth is, to clear human nature from the heavy imputation of being sinful, corrupted, wise to do evil but unable to do good; and so to vindicate unto themselves a power and ability of doing all that good which God can justly require to be done by them in the state wherein they are,—of making themselves differ from others who will not make so good use of the endowments of their natures; that so the first and chiefest part in the work of their salvation may be ascribed unto themselves;—a proud Luciferian endeavour! To this end,—

First, They deny that doctrine of predestination whereby God is affirmed to have chosen certain men before the foundation of the world, that they should be holy, and obtain everlasting life by the merit of Christ, to the praise of his glorious grace,—any such predestination which may be the fountain and cause of grace or glory, determining the persons, according to God's good pleasure, on whom they shall be bestowed: for this doctrine would make the special grace of God to be the sole cause of all the good that is in the elect more than [in] the reprobates; would make faith the work and gift of God, with divers other things, which would show their idol to be nothing, of no value. Wherefore, what a corrupt heresy they have substituted into the place hereof see chapter the sixth.

Secondly, They deny original sin and its demerit; which being rightly understood, would easily demonstrate that, notwithstanding all the labour of the smith, the carpenter, and the painter, yet their idol is of its own nature but an unprofitable block; it will discover not only the impotency of doing good which is in our nature, but show also whence we have it: see chapter the seventh.

Thirdly, If ye will charge our human nature with a repugnancy to the law of God, they will maintain that it was also in Adam when he was first created, and so comes from God himself: chapter the eighth.

Fourthly, They deny the efficacy of the merit of the death of Christ;—both that God intended by his death to redeem his church, or to acquire unto himself a holy people; as also, that Christ by his death hath merited and procured for us grace, faith, or righteousness, and power to obey God, in fulfilling the condition of the new covenant. Nay, this were plainly to set up an ark to break their Dagon's neck; for, "what praise," say they, "can be due to ourselves for believing, if the blood of Christ hath procured God to bestow faith upon us?" "Increpet te Deus, O Satan!" See chapters nine and ten.

Fifthly, If Christ will claim such a share in saving of his people, of them that believe in him, they will grant some to have salvation quite without him, that never heard so much as a report of a Saviour; and, indeed, in nothing do they advance their idol nearer the throne of God than in this blasphemy: chapter eleven.

Sixthly, Having thus robbed God, Christ, and his grace, they adorn their idol free-will with many glorious properties no way due unto it: discussed, chapter twelve, where you shall find how, "movet cornicula risum, furtivis nudata coloribus."

Seventhly, They do not only claim to their new-made deity a saving power, but also affirm that he is very active and operative in the great work of saving our souls,—

First, In fitly preparing us for the grace of God, and so disposing of ourselves that it becomes due unto us: chapter thirteen.

Secondly, In the effectual working of our conversion together with it: chapter fourteen.

And so at length, with much toil and labour, they have placed an altar for their idol in the holy temple, on the right hand of the altar of God, and on it offer sacrifice to their own net and drag; at least, "nec Deo, nec libero arbitrio, sed dividatur,"—not all to God, nor all to free-will, but let the sacrifice of praise, for all good things, be divided between them.

CHAPTER II.

Of the eternity and immutability of the decrees of Almighty God, denied and overthrown by the Arminians.

It hath been always believed among Christians, and that upon infallible grounds, as I shall show hereafter, that all the decrees of God, as they are internal, so they are eternal, acts of his will; and therefore unchangeable and irrevocable. Mutable decrees and occasional resolutions are most contrary to the pure nature of Almighty God. Such principles as these, evident and clear by their own light, were never questioned by any before the Arminians began ἀκίνητα κινεῖν, and to profess themselves to delight in opposing common notions of reason concerning God and his essence, that they might exalt themselves into his throne. To ascribe the least mutability to the divine essence, with which all the attributes and internal free acts of God are one and the same, was ever accounted ὑπερβολὴ ἀθεότητος, "transcendent atheism," in the highest degree.[1] Now, be this crime of what nature it will, it is no unjust imputation to charge it on the

[1] Phil. lib. quod sit Deus immutabilis.

Arminians, because they confess themselves guilty, and glory in the crime.

First, They undermine and overthrow the eternity of God's purposes, by affirming that, in the order of the divine decrees, *there are some which precede every act of the creature, and some again that follow them:* so Corvinus,[1] the most famous of that sect. Now, all the acts of every creature being but of yesterday, temporary, like themselves, surely those decrees of God cannot be eternal which follow them in order of time; and yet they press this, especially in respect of human actions, as a certain, unquestionable verity. "It is certain that God willeth or determineth many things which he would not, did not some act of man's will go before it," saith their great master, Arminius.[2] The like affirmeth, with a little addition (as such men do always "proficere in pejus"), his genuine scholar, Nic. Grevinchovius. [3]"I suppose," saith he, "that God willeth many things which he neither would nor justly could will and purpose, did not some action of the creature precede." And here observe, that in these places they speak not of God's external works, of those actions which outwardly are of him,—as inflicting of punishments, bestowing of rewards, and other such outward acts of his providence, whose administration we confess to be various, and diversely applied to several occasions,—but of the internal purposes of God's will, his decrees and intentions, which have no present influence upon, or respect unto, any action of the creature; yea, they deny that concerning many things God hath any determinate resolution at all, or any purpose farther than a natural affection towards them. "God doth or omitteth that towards which, in his own nature and his proper inclination, he is affected, as he findeth man to comply or not to comply with that order which he hath appointed," saith Corvinus.[4] Surely these men care not what indignities they cast upon the God of heaven, so they may maintain the pretended endowments of their own wills; for such an absolute power do they here ascribe unto them, that God himself cannot determine of a thing whereunto, as they strangely phrase it, he is well affected, before, by an actual concurrence, he is sure of their compliance. Now, this imputation, that they are temporary, which they cast upon the decrees of God in general, they press home upon that particular which lies most in their way, the

[1] "In ordine volitorum divinorum, quædam sunt quæ omnem actum creaturæ præcedunt, quædam quæ sequuntur."—Corv. ad Molin., cap. v. sect. 1, p. 67.

[2] "Certum est Deum quædam velle, quæ non vellet nisi aliqua volitio humana antecederet."—Armin., Antip., p. 211.

[3] "Multa tamen arbitror Deum velle, quæ non vellet, adeoque nec juste velle posset, nisi aliqua actio creaturæ præcederet."—Ad Ames., p. 24.

[4] "Deus facit vel non facit id ad quod, ex se et natura sua ac inclinatione propria est affectus, prout homo cum isto ordine conspirat, vel non conspirat."—Corv. ad Molin., cap v. ad sect. 3.

decree of election. Concerning this they tell us roundly, that it is [1]false that election is confirmed from eternity: so the Remonstrants in their Apology, notwithstanding that St Paul tells us that it is the "purpose of God," Rom. ix. 11, and that we were "chosen before the foundation of the world," Eph. i. 4. Neither is it any thing material what the Arminians there grant,—namely, that there is a decree preceding this, which may be said to be from everlasting: for seeing that St Paul teacheth us that election is nothing but God's purpose of saving us, to affirm that God eternally decreed that he would elect us is all one as to say that God purposed that in time he would purpose to save us. Such resolutions may be fit for their own wild heads, but must not be ascribed to God only wise.

Secondly, As they affirm them to be temporary and to have had a beginning, so also to expire and have an ending, to be subject to change and variableness. "Some acts of God's will do cease at a certain time," saith Episcopius.[2] What? doth any thing come into his mind that changeth his will? "Yes," saith Arminius, [3]"He would have all men to be saved; but, compelled with the stubborn and incorrigible malice of some, he will have them to miss it." However, this is some recompense,—denying God a power to do what he will, they grant him to be contented to do what he may, and not much repine at his hard condition. Certainly, if but for this favour, he is a debtor to the Arminians. Thieves give what they do not take. Having robbed God of his power, they will leave him so much goodness as that he shall not be troubled at it, though he be sometimes compelled to what he is very loath to do. How do they and their fellows, the Jesuits,[4] exclaim upon poor Calvin, for sometimes using the hard word of *compulsion*, describing the effectual, powerful working of the providence of God in the actions of men; but they can fasten the same term on the will of God, and no harm done! Surely he will one day plead his own cause against them. But yet blame them not, "si violandum est jus, regnandi causâ violandum est." It is to make themselves absolute that they thus cast off the yoke of the Almighty, and that both in things concerning this life and that which is to come. They are much troubled that it should be said that [5]every one of us bring along with us into the world an unchangeable pre-ordination of life and death eternal; for such a supposal

[1] "Falsum est quod electio facta est ab æterno."—Rem. Apol., cap. xviii. p. 190.

[2] "Volitiones aliquæ Dei cessant certo quodam tempore."—Episcop. Disp. de Vol. Dei., thes. 7

[3] "Deus vult omnes salvos fieri, sed compulsus pertinaci et incorrigibili malitia quorundam, vult illos jacturam facere salutis."—Armin. Antip. fol. 195.

[4] Bell. Amiss. Grat.; Armin. Antip. Rem. Apol.

[5] "(Docent) unumquemque invariabilem vitæ, ac mortis προταγὴν una cum ipso ortu, in lucem hanc nobiscum adferre."—Filii Armin. in Epist. Ded. ad Examen Lib. Perk.

would quite overthrow the main foundation of their heresy,—namely, that men can make their election void and frustrate, as they jointly lay it down in their Apology.[1] Nay, it is a dream, saith Dr Jackson,[2] to think of God's decrees concerning things to come as of acts irrevocably finished; which would hinder that which Welsingius lays down for a truth,—to wit, [3]"that the elect may become reprobates, and the reprobates elect." Now, to these particular sayings is their whole doctrine concerning the decrees of God, inasmuch as they have any reference to the actions of men, most exactly conformable; as,—

First, [4]Their distinction of them into peremptory and not peremptory (terms rather used in the citations of litigious courts than as expressions of God's purpose in sacred Scripture), is not, as by them applied, compatible with the unchangeableness of God's eternal purposes. Πρόσκαιροι, say they, or temporary believers, are elected (though not peremptorily) with such an act of God's will as hath a co-existence every way commensurate, both in its original, continuance, and end, with their fading faith; which sometimes, like Jonah's gourd, is but "filia unius noctis,"—in the morning it flourisheth, in the evening it is cut down, dried up, and withereth. A man in Christ by faith, or actually believing (which to do is, as they say, in every one's own power), [5]is, in their opinion, the proper object of election;—of election, I say, not peremptory, which is an act pendent, expecting the final perseverance and consummation of his faith; and therefore immutable, because man having fulfilled his course, God hath no cause to change his purpose of crowning him with reward. Thus also (as they teach), a man according to his infidelity, whether present and removable, or obdurate and final, is the only object of reprobation; which, in the latter case, is peremptory and absolute, in the former conditional and alterable. It is the qualities of faith and unbelief on which their election and reprobation do attend.[6] Now, let a faithful man, elected of God according to his present righteousness, apostate [apostatize] totally from grace (as to affirm that there is any promise of God implying his perseverance is

[1] "Possunt homines electionem suam irritam et frustraneam reddere."—Rem. Apol., cap. ix. p. 105.

[2] Jackson, of the Divine Essence.

[3] "Non mirum videri debet quod aliquando ex electis reprobi et ex reprobis electi fiant."—Welsin. de Of. Ch. Hom.

[4] "Omnia Dei decreta, non sunt peremptoria, sed quædam conditionata ac mutabilia."—Concio. ad Cler. Oxon. ann. 1641, Rem. Decla. Sent. in Synod., alibi passim. "Electio sicut et justificatio, et incerta et revocabilis, utramque vero conditionatam qui negaverit, ipsum quoque evangelium negabit."—Grevinch. ad Ames., pp. 136, 137.

[5] "Ad gloriam participandam pro isto tempore quo credunt electi sunt."—Rem. Apol., p. 190.

[6] "Decreta hypothetica possunt mutari, quia conditio respectu hominis vel præstatur vel non præstatur, atque ita existit vel non existit. Et quum extitit aliquandiu, sæpe existere desinit, et rursus postquam aliquandiu desiit, existere incipit."—Corv. ad Molin., cap. v. sec. 10.

with them to overthrow all religion), and let the unbelieving reprobate depose his incredulity and turn himself unto the Lord; answerable to this mutation of their conditions are the changings of the purpose of the Almighty concerning their everlasting state. Again; suppose these two, by alternate courses (as the doctrine of apostasy maintaineth they may), should return each to their former estate, the decrees of God concerning them must again be changed; for it is unjust with him either not to elect him that believes, though it be but for an hour, or not to reprobate unbelievers. Now, what unchangeableness can we fix to these decrees, which it lies in the power of man to make as inconstant as Euripus; making it, beside, to be possible that all the members of Christ's church, whose names are written in heaven, should within one hour be enrolled in the black book of damnation?

Secondly, As these not-peremptory decrees are mutable, so they make the peremptory decrees of God to be temporal. "Final impenitency," say they, "is the only cause, and the finally unrepenting sinner is the only object, of reprobation, peremptory and irrevocable." As the poet thought none happy,[1] so they think no man to be elected, or a reprobate, before his death. Now, that denomination he doth receive from the decrees of God concerning his eternal estate, which must necessarily then be first enacted. The relation that is between the act of reprobation and the person reprobated importeth a co-existence of denomination. When God reprobates a man, he then becomes a reprobate; which if it be not before he hath actually fulfilled the measure of his iniquity, and sealed it up with the talent of final impenitency in his death, the decree of God must needs be temporal, the just Judge of all the world having till then suspended his determination, expecting the last resolution of this changeable Proteus. Nay, that God's decrees concerning men's eternal estates are in their judgment temporal, and not beginning until their death, is plain from the whole course of their doctrine, especially where they strive to prove that if there were any such determination, God could not threaten punishments or promise rewards. "Who,"[2] say they, "can threaten punishment to him whom, by a peremptory decree, he will have to be free from punishment?" It seems he cannot have determined to save any whom he threatens to punish if they sin, which [it] is evident he doth all so long as they live in this world; which makes God not only mutable, but quite deprives him of his foreknowledge, and makes the form of his decree run thus:—"If man will believe, I determine he shall be saved; if he will not, I determine he shall be

[1] "Dicique beatus—Ante obitum nemo," etc.—Ovid.

[2] "Quis enim comminetur pœnam ei, quem peremptorio decreto a pœna immunem esse vult?"—Rem. Apol., cap. xvii. p. 187.

damned,"—that is, "I must leave him in the meantime to do what he will, so I may meet with him in the end."

Thirdly, They affirm no decree of Almighty God concerning men is so unalterable[1] but that all those who are now in rest or misery might have had contrary lots;—that those which are damned, as Pharaoh, Judas, etc., might have been saved; and those which are saved, as the blessed Virgin, Peter, John, might have been damned: which must needs reflect with a strong charge of mutability on Almighty God, who knoweth who are his. Divers other instances in this nature I could produce, whereby it would be farther evident that these innovators in Christian religion do overthrow the eternity and unchangeableness of God's decrees; but these are sufficient to any discerning man. And I will add, in the close, an antidote against this poison, briefly showing what the Scripture and right reason teach us concerning these secrets of the Most High.

First, "Known unto God," saith St James, "are all his works from the beginning," Acts xv. 18; whence it hath hitherto been concluded that whatever God doth in time bring to pass, that he decreed from all eternity so to do. All his works were from the beginning known unto him. Consider it particularly in the decree of election, that fountain of all spiritual blessings, that a saving sense and assurance thereof (2 Pet. i. 10) being attained, might effect a spiritual rejoicing in the Lord, 1 Cor. xv. 31. Such things are everywhere taught as may raise us to the consideration of it as of an eternal act, irrevocably and immutably established: "He hath chosen us before the foundation of the world," Eph. i. 4: his "purpose according to election," before we were born, must "stand," Rom. ix. 11; for to the irreversible stability of this act of his will he hath set to the seal of his infallible knowledge, 2 Tim. ii. 19. His purpose of our salvation by grace, not according to works, was "before the world began," 2 Tim. i. 9: an eternal purpose, proceeding from such a will as to which none can resist, joined with such a knowledge as to which all things past, present, and to come are open and evident, must needs also be, like the laws of the Medes and Persians, permanent and unalterable.

Secondly, The [2]decrees of God, being conformable to his nature and essence, do require eternity and immutability as their inseparable properties. God, and he only, never was, nor ever can be, what now he is not. Passive possibility to any thing, which is the foun-

[1] Author of "God's Love to Mankind," p. 4, [a treatise written by Hoard. Davenant, professor of divinity in Cambridge, and afterwards bishop of Salisbury, wrote in reply his "Animadversions" on it. Dr Hill, in his Lectures on Divinity, pronounces this work of Davenant to be "one of the ablest defences of the Calvinistic system of predestination."—Ed.]

[2] "Quicquid operatur, operatur ut est."

tain of all change, can have no place in him who is "actus simplex," and purely free from all composition; whence St James affirmeth that "with him is no variableness, neither shadow of turning," James i. 17; with him,—that is, in his will and purposes: and himself by his prophet, "I am the LORD, I change not; therefore ye sons of Jacob are not consumed," Mal. iii. 6; where he proveth the not changing of his gracious purposes, because he is the LORD. The eternal acts of his will not really differing from his unchangeable essence, must needs be immutable.

Thirdly, Whatsoever God hath determined, according to the counsel of his wisdom and good pleasure of his will, to be accomplished, to the praise of his glory, standeth sure and immutable; for "the Strength of Israel will not lie nor repent; for he is not a man, that he should repent," 1 Sam. xv. 29. "He declareth the end from the beginning, and from ancient times the things that are not yet done, saying, My counsel shall stand, and I will do all my pleasure," Isa. xlvi. 10; which certain and infallible execution of his pleasure is extended to particular contingent events, chap. xlviii. 14. Yea, it is an ordinary thing with the Lord to confirm the certainty of those things that are yet for to come from his own decree; as, "The LORD of hosts hath sworn, saying, Surely as I have thought, so it shall come to pass; and as I have purposed, it shall stand, that I will break the Assyrian," etc., chap. xiv. 24, 25;—"It is certain the Assyrian shall be broken, because the Lord hath purposed it;" which were a weak kind of reasoning, if his purpose might be altered. Nay, "He is of one mind, and who can turn him? and what his soul desireth, that he doeth," Job xxiii. 13. "The LORD of hosts hath purposed, and who shall disannul it?" Isa. xiv. 27. So that the purpose of God and immutability of his counsel (Heb. vi. 17) have their certainty and firmness from eternity, and do not depend on the variable lubricity of mortal men; which we must needs grant, unless we intend to set up impotency against omnipotency, and arm the clay against the potter.

Fourthly, If God's determination concerning any thing should have a temporal original, it must needs be either because he then perceived some goodness in it of which before he was ignorant, or else because some accident did affix a real goodness to some state of things which it had not from him; neither of which, without abominable blasphemy, can be affirmed, seeing he knoweth the end from the beginning, all things from everlasting, being always the same, the fountain of all goodness, of which other things do participate in that measure which it pleaseth him to communicate it unto them. Add to this the omnipotency of God: there is "power and might in his hand," [so] that none is able to withstand him, 2 Chron. xx. 6; which will not permit that any of his purposes be frustrate. In all our intentions, if the defect be not in the error of our understandings, which may be rectified by better information, when we cannot do that which we would, we will do that which we can: the alteration of our purpose is for want of power to fulfil it; which impotency cannot be ascribed to Almighty God, who is "in heaven, and hath done whatsoever he pleased," Ps. cxv. 3. So that the immutability of God's nature, his almighty power, the infallibility of his knowledge, his immunity from error in all his counsels, do show that he never faileth in accomplishing any thing that he proposeth for the manifestation of his glory.

To close up this whole discourse, wherein I have not discovered half the poison contained in the Arminian doctrine concerning God's decrees, I will in brief present to your view the opposition that is in this matter betwixt the word of God and the patrons of free-will:—

S. S.	Lib. Arbit.
"He hath chosen us in him before the foundation of the world," Eph. i. 4.	"It is false to say that election is confirmed from everlasting," Rem. Apol.
"He hath called us according to his own purpose and grace, before the world began," 2 Tim. i. 9.	"It is certain that God determineth divers things which he would not, did not some act of man's will go before," Armin.
"Known unto God are all his works from the beginning of the world," Acts xv. 18.	"Some decrees of God precede all acts of the will of the creature, and some follow," Corv.
"Declaring the end from the beginning, and from ancient times the things that are not yet done, saying, My counsel shall stand, and I will do all my pleasure," Isa. xlvi. 10.	"Men may make their election void and frustrate," Rem. Apol.
"For the children being not yet born, neither having done any good or evil, that the purpose of God according to election might stand," as Rom. ix. 11.	"It is no wonder if men do sometimes of elect become reprobate, and of reprobate, elect," Welsin.
"The foundation of God standeth sure, having this seal, The Lord knoweth them that are his," 2 Tim. ii. 19.	"Election is uncertain and revocable, and whoever denies it overthrows the gospel," Grevinch.
"The counsel of the LORD standeth for ever, the thoughts of his heart to all generations," Ps. xxxiii. 11.	"Many decrees of God cease at a certain time," Episcop.

S. S.	Lib. Arbit.
"My counsel shall stand, and I will do all my pleasure," Isa. xlvi. 10.	"God would have all men to be saved, but, compelled with the stubborn malice of some, he changeth his purpose, and will have them to perish," Armin.
"I am the LORD, I change not," Mal. iii. 6.	"As men may change themselves from believers to unbelievers, so God's determination concerning them changeth," Rem.
"With the Father of lights is no variableness, neither shadow of turning," James i. 17; Exod. iii. 13, 14; Ps. cii. 27; 2 Tim. ii. 13; 1 Sam. xv. 29; Isa. xiv. 27; Job xxiii. 13; Ps. cxv. 3.	"All God's decrees are not peremptory, but some conditionate and changeable," Sermon at Oxford.

CHAPTER III.

Of the prescience or foreknowledge of God, and how it is questioned and overthrown by the Arminians.

THE prescience or foreknowledge of God hath not hitherto, in express terms, been denied by the Arminians, but only questioned and overthrown by consequence, inasmuch as they deny the certainty and unchangeableness of his decrees, on which it is founded. It is not a foreknowledge of all or any thing which they oppose, but only of things free and contingent, and that only to comply with their formerly-exploded error, that the purposes of God concerning such things are temporal and mutable; which obstacle being once removed, the way is open how to ascribe the presidentship of all human actions to omnipotent contingency, and her sire free-will. Now, we call that contingent which, in regard of its next and immediate cause, before it come to pass, may be done or may be not done; as, that a man shall do such a thing to-morrow, or any time hereafter, which he may choose whether ever he will do or no. Such things as these are free and changeable, in respect of men, their immediate and second causes; but if we, as we ought to do, [1]look up unto Him who foreseeth and hath ordained the event of them or their omission, they may be said necessarily to come to pass or to be omitted. It could not be but as it was. Christians hitherto, yea, and heathens,[2] in all things of this nature, have usually, upon their event, reflected

[1] James iv. 13–15.

[2] Διὸς δ' ἐτελείετο βουλή, Hom;—"God's will was done."

on God as one whose determination was passed on them from eternity, and who knew them long before; as the killing of men by the fall of a house, who might, in respect of the freedom of their own wills, have not been there. Or if a man fall into the hands of thieves, we presently conclude it was the will of God. It must be so; he knew it before.

Divines, for distinction's sake, [1]ascribe unto God a twofold knowledge; one, intuitive or intellective, whereby he foreknoweth and seeth all things that are possible,—that is, all things that can be done by his almighty power,—without any respect to their future existence, whether they shall come to pass or no. Yea, infinite things, whose actual being eternity shall never behold, are thus open and naked unto him; for was there not strength and power in his hand to have created another world? was there not counsel in the storehouse of his wisdom to have created this otherwise, or not to have created it at all? Shall we say that his providence extends itself every way to the utmost of its activity? or can he not produce innumerable things in the world which now he doth not. Now, all these, and every thing else that is feasible to his infinite power, he foresees and knows, "scientiâ," as they speak, "simplicis intelligentiæ," by his essential knowledge.

Out [2]of this large and boundless territory of things possible, God by his decrees freely determineth what shall come to pass, and makes them future which before were but possible. After this decree, as they commonly speak, followeth, or together with it, as [3]others more exactly, taketh place, that prescience of God which they call "visionis," "of vision," [4]whereby he infallibly seeth all things in their proper causes, and how and when they shall come to pass. Now, these two sorts of knowledge differ, [5]inasmuch as by the one God knoweth what

1 "Quæcunque possunt per creaturam fieri, vel cogitari, vel dici, et etiam quæcunque ipse facere potest, omnia cognoscit Deus, etiamsi neque sunt, neque erunt, neque fuerunt, scientiâ simplicis intelligentiæ."—Aquin. p. q. 14, a. 9, c. Ex verbis apostoli, Rom. iv., "Qui vocat ea quæ non sunt tanquam ea quæ sunt." Sic scholastici omnes. Fer. Scholast. Orthod. Speci. cap. iii., alii passim. Vid. Hieron. Zanch. de Scientia Dei, lib. diatrib. iii., cap. 2, q. 5.

2 Vid. Sam. Rhætorfort. Exercit. de Grat., ex. i. cap. 4.

3 "Res ipsæ nullo naturæ momento possibiles esse dicendæ sunt priusquam a Deo intelliguntur, scientiâ quæ dicitur simplicis intelligentiæ, ita etiam scientiâ quæ dicitur visionis, et fertur in res futuras, nullo naturæ momento, posterior statuenda videtur, ista futuritione, rerum; cum scientia," etc.—Dr Twiss. ad Errat. Vind. Grat.

4 "Scientia visionis dicitur, quia ea quæ videntur, apud nos habent esse distinctum extra videntem."—Aq. p. q. 14, a. 9, c.

5 "In eo differt præscientia intuitionis, ab ea, quæ approbationis est, quod illa præsciat, quod evenire possibile est; hoc vero quod impossibile est non evenire."—Ferrius. Orthod. Scholast. Speci. cap. xxiii. Cæterum posterior ista scientia non proprie dicitur a Ferrio scientia approbationis, illa enim est, qua Deus dicitur nosse quæ amat et approbat; ab utraque altera distincta. Matt. vii. 23; Rom. xi. 2; 2 Tim. ii. 19. "Quamvis infinitorum numerorum, nullus sit numerus, non tamen est incomprehensibilis ei, cujus scientiæ non est numerus."—Aug. de Civit. Dei, lib. xii. cap. 18.

it is possible may come to pass; by the other, only what it is impossible should not come to pass. Things are possible in regard of God's power, future in regard of his decree. So that (if I may so say) the measure of the first kind of science is God's omnipotency, what he can do; of the other his purpose, what certainly he will do, or permit to be done. With this prescience, then, God foreseeth all, and nothing but what he hath decreed shall come to pass.

For every thing to be produced next and under him, [1]God hath prepared divers and several kinds of causes, diversely operative in producing their effects, some whereof are said to work necessarily, the institution of their nature being to do as they do, and not otherwise; so the sun giveth light, and the fire heat. And yet, in some regard, their effects and products may be said to be contingent and free, inasmuch as the concurrence of God, the first cause, is required to their operation, who doth all things most freely, according to the counsel of his will. Thus the sun stood still in the time of Joshua, and the fire burned not the three children; but ordinarily such agents working "necessitate naturæ," their effects are said to be necessary. Secondly, To some things God hath fitted free and contingent causes, which either apply themselves to operation in particular, according to election, choosing to do this thing rather than that; as angels and men, in their free and deliberate actions, which they so perform as that they could have not done them;—or else they produce effects κατὰ τὸ συμβεβηκός, merely by accident, and the operation of such things we say to be casual; as if a hatchet, falling out of the hand of a man cutting down a tree, should kill another whom he never saw. Now, nothing in either of these ways comes to pass but God hath determined it, both for the matter and manner, [2]even so as is agreeable to their causes,—some necessarily, some freely, some casually or contingently, yet also, as having a certain futurition from his decree, he infallibly foreseeth that they shall so come to pass. But yet that he doth so in respect of things free and contingent is much questioned by the Arminians in express terms, and denied by consequence, notwithstanding St Jerome affirmeth [3]that so to do is destructive to the very essence of the Deity.

First, Their doctrine of the mutability of God's decrees, on whose firmness is founded the infallibility of this prescience, doth quite overthrow it. God thus foreknowing only what he hath so decreed shall come to pass, if that be no firmer settled but that it may [be] and

[1] "Quibusdam effectibus præparavit causas necessarias, ut necessario eveniret, quibusdam vero causas contingentes ut evenirent contingenter, secundum conditionem proximarum causarum."—Aquin. p. q. 23, a. 4, in Cor. Zanch. de Natur. Dei, lib. v., qu. 4, thes.

[2] "Res et modos rerum."—Aquin.

[3] "Cui præscientiam tollis, aufers divinitatem."—Hieron. ad Pelag., lib. v.

is often altered, according to the divers inclinations of men's wills, which I showed before they affirm, he can have at best but a conjectural foreknowledge of what is yet for to come, not founded on his own unchangeable purpose, but upon a guess at the free inclination of men's wills. For instance, [1]God willeth that all men should be saved. This act of his will, according to the Arminian doctrine, is his conditionate decree to save all men if they will believe. Well, among these is Judas, as [2]equal a sharer in the benefit of this decree as Peter. God, then, will have him to be saved, and to this end allows him all those means which are necessary to beget faith in him, and are every way sufficient to that purpose, and do produce that effect in others; what can God foresee, then, but that Judas as well as Peter will believe? He intendeth he should, he hath determined nothing to the contrary. Let him come, then, and act his own part. Why, he proves so obstinately malicious, [3]that God, with all his omnipotency, as they speak, by any way that becomes him, which must not be by any irresistible efficacy, cannot change his obdurate heart. Well, then, he determineth, according to the exigence of his justice, that he shall be damned for his impenitency, and foreseeth that accordingly. But now, suppose this wretch, even at his last moment, should bethink himself and return to the Lord, which in their conceit he may, notwithstanding his former reprobation (which, [4]as they state it, seems a great act of mercy), [5]God must keep to the rules of his justice, and elect or determine to save him; by which the varlet hath twice or thrice deceived his expectation.

Secondly, [6]They affirm that God is said properly to expect and desire divers things which yet never come to pass. "We grant," saith Corvinus, "that there are desires in God that never are fulfilled." Now, surely, to desire what one is sure will never come to pass is not an act regulated by wisdom or counsel; and, therefore, they must grant that before he did not know but perhaps so it might be. "God wisheth and desireth some good things, which yet come not to pass,"[7] say they, in their Confession; whence one of these two things must needs follow,—either, first, that there is a great deal of imperfec-

[1] "Deus ita omnium salutem ex æquo vult, ut illam ex æquo optet et desideret."—Corv. ad Molin., cap. xxxi. sect. 1.

[2] "Talis gratia omnibus datur quæ sufficiat ad fidem generandam."—Idem, ibid, sect. 15.

[3] "Pertinaci quorundam malitia compulsus."—Armin., ubi sup.

[4] "Reprobatio populi Judaici fuit actio temporaria et quæ bono ipsorum Judæorum si modo sanabiles adhuc essent, animumque advertere vellent, servire poterat, utque ei fini serviret a Deo facta erat."—Rem. Apol., cap. xx. p. 221.

[5] "Injustum est apud Deum vel non credentem eligere, vel credentem non eligere."—Rem. Apol.

[6] "Concedimus in Deo desideria, quæ nunquam implentur."—Corv. ad Molin., cap. v. sect. 2.

[7] "Bona quædam Deus optat et desiderat."—Rem. Confes., cap. ii. sect. 9.

tion in his nature, to desire and expect what he knows shall never come to pass; or else he did not know but it might, which overthrows his prescience. Yea, and say they expressly, [1] "That the hope and expectation of God is deceived by man;" and confess, "that the strength of their strongest argument lies in this, that God hoped and expected obedience from Israel." Secondly, That he complaineth that his hope is deluded, which, being taken properly, and as they urge it, cannot consist with his eternal prescience; for they disesteem the usual answer of divines, that hope, expectation, and such like passions, which include in them any imperfection, are ascribed unto God per ἀνθρωποπάθειαν,—in regard of that analogy his actions hold with such of ours as we perform having those passions.

Thirdly, [2] They teach that God hath determined nothing concerning such things as these in question. "That God hath determined future contingent things unto either part (I mean such as issue from the free-will of the creature), I abominate, hate, and curse, as false, absurd, and leading us on unto blasphemy," saith Arminius. To determine of them to either part is to determine and ordain whether they shall be, or whether they shall not be; as, that David shall or shall not go up to-morrow against the Philistines, and prevail. Now, the infallibility of God's foreknowing of such things depending on the certainty of his decree and determination, if there be no such thing as this, that also must needs fall to the ground.

Fourthly, [3] See what positively they write concerning this everlasting foreknowledge of God:—First, They call it a troublesome question; secondly, They make it a thing disputable whether there be any such thing or no; and though haply it may be ascribed unto God, yet, thirdly, They think it no motive to the worship of him; fourthly, They say, better it were quite exploded, because the difficulties that attend it can scarcely be reconciled with man's liberty, God's threatenings and promises; yea, fifthly, It seems rather to be invented to crucify poor mortals than to be of any moment in religion. So Episcopius. It may be excepted that this is but one

[1] "Dei spes et expectatio est ab hominibus elusa."—Rem. Scrip. Syn. in cap. v., Isa. v. 1. "In eo vis argumenti est, quod Deus ab Israele obedientiam et sperarit, et expectarit."—Idem, ibid. "Quod Deus de elusa spe sua conqueratur."—Idem, ubi supra.

[2] "Deum futura contingentia, decreto suo determinasse ad alterutram partem (intellige quæ a libera creaturæ voluntate patrantur), falsum, absurdum, et multiplicis blasphemiæ prævium abominor et exsecror."—Armin. Declarat. Senten.

[3] "Disquiri permittimus:—1. Operosam illam quæstionem, de scientia futurorum contingentium absoluta et conditionata; 2. Etsi non negemus Deo illam scientiam attribui posse; 3. Tamen an necessarium saluti sit ad hoc ut Deus recte colatur examinari permittimus; 4. Tum merito facessere debent a scholis et ecclesiis, intricatæ et spinosæ istæ quæstiones quæ de ea agitari solent,—quomodo illa cum libertate arbitrii, cum seriis Dei comminationibus, aliisque actionibus, consistere possit: quæ omnia crucem potius miseris mortalibus fixerunt, quam ad religionem cultumque divinum, momenti aliquid inquisitoribus suis attulerunt."—Episcopius, Disput. iv. sect. 10.; Rem. Apol., pp. 43, 44.

doctor's opinion. It is true, they are one man's words; but the thing itself is countenanced by the whole sect. As, first, in the large prolix declaration of their opinions, they speak not one word of it; and being taxed for this omission by the professors of Leyden, they vindicate themselves so coldly in their Apology, that some learned men do from hence conclude,[1] that certainly, in their most secret judgments, all the Arminians do consent with Socinus in ascribing unto God only a conjectural foreknowledge. And one great prophet of their own affirms roundly, [2]"That God, after his manner, oftentimes feareth, that is, suspecteth, and that not without cause, and prudently conjectureth, that this or that evil may arise," Vorstius. And their chiefest patriarchs, [3]"That God doth often intend what he doth not foresee will come to pass," Armin., Corv. Now, whether this kind of atheism be tolerable among Christians or no, let all men judge who have their senses exercised in the word of God; which, I am sure, teaches us another lesson. For,—

First, It is laid down as a firm foundation, that "known unto God are all his works from the beginning of the world," Acts xv. 18. Every thing, then, that in any respect may be called his work, is known unto him from all eternity. Now, what in the world, if we may speak as he hath taught us, can be exempted from this denomination? Even actions in themselves sinful are not; though not as sinful, yet in some other regard, as punishments of others. "Behold," saith Nathan to David, in the name of God, "I will take thy wives before thine eyes, and give them unto thy neighbour, and he shall lie with thy wives in the sight of this sun; for thou didst it secretly, but I will do this thing before all Israel," 2 Sam. xii. 11, 12. So, also, when wicked robbers had nefariously spoiled Job of all his substance, the holy man concludeth, "The LORD gave, and the LORD hath taken away," chap. i. 21. Now, if the working of God's providence be so mighty and effectual, even in and over those actions wherein the devil and men do most maliciously offend, as did Absalom and the Sabean with the Chaldean thieves, that it may be said to be his work, and he may be said to "do it" (I crave liberty to use the Scripture phrase), then certainly nothing in the world, in some respect or other, is independent of his all-disposing hand; yea, Judas himself betraying our Saviour did nothing but "what his hand and counsel determined before should be done,"[4] Acts iv. 28, in respect of the

[1] Ames. Antisynod, p. 10.

[2] "Deus suo modo aliquando metuit, hoc est, merito suspicatur et prudenter conjicit, hoc vel illud malum oriturum."—Vorsti. de Deo, p. 451.

[3] "Deus non semper ex præscientia finem intendit."—Armin., Antip., p. 667; Corv. ad Molin., cap. v. sect. 5.

[4] "Cum et pater tradiderit filium suum, et ipse Christus corpus suum: et Judas dominum suum: cur in hac traditione Deus est pius, et homo reus, nisi quia in re una quam fecerunt, causa non fuit una propter quam fecerunt."—Aug., Epist. xlviii.

event of the thing itself. And if these actions, notwithstanding these two hinderances,—first, that they were contingent, wrought by free agents, working according to election and choice; secondly, that they were sinful and wicked in the agents,—had yet their dependence on his purpose and determinate counsel, surely he hath an interest of operation in the acts of every creature. But his works, as it appears before, are all known unto him from the beginning, for he worketh nothing by chance or accidentally, but all things determinately, according to his own decree, or "the counsel of his own will," Eph. i. 11.

Secondly, The manner of God's knowing of things doth evidently show that nothing that is, or may be, can be hid from him; [1]which is not by discourse and collection of one thing out of another, conclusions out of principles, but altogether and at once, evidently, clearly, and distinctly, both in respect τοῦ ὅτι and τοῦ διότι. By one most pure act of his own essence he discerneth all things: for there is "no creature that is not manifest in his sight, but all are naked and opened unto his eyes," Heb. iv. 13. So that those things concerning which we treat [2]he knoweth three ways:—First, In himself and his own decree, as the first cause; in which respect they may be said to be necessary, in respect of the certainty of their event. Secondly, In their immediate causes, wherein their contingency doth properly consist. Thirdly, In their own nature as future, but to his infinite knowledge ever present.

Thirdly, The Scripture[3] is full of expressions to this purpose,—to wit, "That God knoweth all secrets, and revealeth hidden things. he searcheth the reins and the heart: he knoweth the number of the stars, and the birds of the air, the lilies of the field, the falling of sparrows, the number of the hairs of our heads." Some places are most remarkable, as that of the Psalmist, "He knoweth my thoughts long before;" even before ever they come into our minds, before their first rising. And yet many actions that are most contingent depend upon those thoughts known unto God from eternity; nay,—which breaketh the very neck of the goddess contingency,—those things wherein her greatest power is imagined to consist are directly ascribed unto God, as our words, "the answer of the tongue," Prov. xvi. 1; and the directing of an arrow, shot by chance, to a mark not aimed at, 1 Kings xxii. 34. Surely God must needs foreknow the event of that contingent action; he must needs know the man would so

[1] "Deus non particulatim, vel singillatim omnia videt, velut alternanter concepta, hinc illuc, inde huc, sed omnia videt simul."—Aug., lib. xv. de Trinit., cap. 14. "In scientia divina nullus est discursus, sed omnia perfecte intelligit."—Tho., p. q. 14, a. 7. c.

[2] Tilen. Syntag. de Attrib. Dei, thes. 22; Zanch. de Nat. Dei. Unumquodque quod est, dum est, necesse est, ut sit.

[3] Ps. xliv. 21; Job xi. 11; Dan. ii. 47; Ps. vii. 9, xxvi. 2, cxlvii. 4; Luke xii. 27; Matt. x. 29, 30; Ps. cxxxix. 2.

shoot who had determined his arrow should be the death of a king. He maketh men poor and rich, Prov. xxii. 2; He lifteth up one, and pulleth down another, Ps. lxxv. 7. How many contingencies did γοργὸν ὄμμα τοῦ δεσπότου, his piercing eye run through to foresee the crowning of Esther for the deliverance of his people! In a word, "Known unto God are all his works." Now, what can possibly be imagined to be more contingent than the killing of a man by the fall of an axe from out of his hand who intended no such thing? Yet this God assumeth as his own work, Deut. xix. 5, Exod. xxi. 13; and so surely was by him foreknown.

Fourthly, Do but consider the prophecies in Scripture, especially those concerning our Saviour, how many free and contingent actions did concur for the fulfilling of them; as Isa. vii. 14, ix. 6, liii.; Gen. iii. 15, etc. The like may be said of other predictions; as of the wasting of Jerusalem by the Babylonians, which though, in regard of God's prescience, it was certainly to come to pass, yet they did it most freely, not only following the counsel of their own wills, but also using divination, or chanceable lots, for their direction, Ezek. xxi. 21. Yet he who made the eye seeth all these things, Ps. xciv. 9.

Divers other reasons and testimonies might be produced to confirm our doctrine of God's everlasting prescience; which, notwithstanding Episcopius' blasphemy, that it serves for nought but to cruciate poor mortals, we believe to be a good part of the foundation of all that consolation which God is pleased to afford us in this vale of tears. Amidst all our afflictions and temptations, under whose pressure we should else faint and despair, it is no small comfort to be assured that we do nor can suffer nothing but what his hand and counsel guides unto us, what is open and naked before his eyes, and whose end and issue he knoweth long before; which is a strong motive to patience, a sure anchor of hope, a firm ground of consolation. Now, to present in one view how opposite the opinions of the worshippers of the great goddess contingency are to this sacred truth, take this short antithesis:—

S. S.	Lib. Arbit.
"Known unto God are all his works from the beginning of the world," Acts xv. 18.	"God sometimes feareth, and prudently conjectureth, that this or that evil may arise," Vorsti.
"Neither is there any creature that is not manifest in his sight: but all things are naked and opened unto the eyes of him with whom we have to do," Heb. iv. 13.	"God doth not always foresee the event of what he intendeth," Corvin. ad Mol.

S. S.	Lib. Arbit.
"He that formed the eye, shall he not see?" Ps. xciv. 9. "When a man goeth into the wood with his neighbour to hew wood, and his hand fetcheth a stroke with the axe to cut down the tree, and the head slippeth from the helve, and lighteth upon his neighbour, that he die," Deut. xix. 5. "God delivers him into his hand," Exod. xxi. 13.	"Future contingencies are not determined unto either part," Armin. That is, God hath not determined, and so, consequently, doth not foreknow, whether they shall come to pass or no.
"Take no thought, saying, What shall we eat? or, What shall we drink? or, Wherewithal shall we be clothed? for your heavenly Father knoweth that ye have need of all these things," Matt. vi. 31, 32.	"God hopeth and expecteth divers things that shall never come to pass," Rem.
"Take away God's prescience and you overthrow his deity," Jerome.	"The doctrine of prescience seems to be invented only to vex and cruciate poor mortal men," Episcop.

CHAPTER IV.

Of the providence of God in governing the world diversely, thrust from this pre-eminence by the Arminian idol of free-will.

I COME now to treat of that betwixt which and the Pelagian idol there is *bellum* ἄσπονδον, implacable war and immortal hatred, absolutely destructive to the one side,—to wit, the providence of God. For this, in that notion Christianity hath hitherto embraced it, and that, in such a sense as the Arminians maintain it, can no more consist together than fire and water, light and darkness, Christ and Belial, and he that shall go to conjoin them ploughs with an ox and an ass; they must be tied together with the same ligament "quo ille mortua jungebat corpora vivis,"—wherewith the tyrant tied dead bodies to living men. This strange advancement of the clay against the potter, not by the way of repining, and to say, "Why hast thou made me thus?" but by the way of emulation, "I will not be so, I will advance myself to the sky, to the sides of thy throne," was heretofore unknown to the more refined Paganism.[1] As these of contingency, so

[1] "Θεία πάντων ἀρχὴ δι' ἧς ἅπαντα καὶ ἔστι καὶ διαμένει."—Theophrastus, apud Picum. Vid. Senecam de Provid. et Plotinum.

they, with a better error, made a goddess of providence, because, as they feigned, she helped Latona to bring forth in the isle of Delos; intimating that Latona, or nature, though big and great with sundry sorts of effects, could yet produce nothing without the interceding help of divine providence: which mythology of theirs seems to contain a sweeter gust of divine truth than any we can expect from their towering fancies [1] who are inclinable to believe that God for no other reason is said to sustain all things, but because he doth not destroy them. Now, that their proud, God-opposing errors may the better appear, according to my former method, I will plainly show what the Scripture teacheth us concerning this providence, with what is agreeable to right and Christian reason, not what is dictated by tumultuating affections.

Providence is a word which, in its proper signification, may seem to comprehend all the actions of God that outwardly are of him, that have any respect unto his creatures, all his works that are not *ad intra*, essentially belonging unto the Deity. Now, because God "worketh all things according to his decree, or the counsel of his will," Eph. i. 11, for whatsoever he doth now it pleased him from the beginning, Ps. cxv. 3; seeing, also, that known unto God are all his works from eternity; therefore, three things concerning his providence are considerable:—1. His *decree* or *purpose*, [2] whereby he hath disposed of all things in order, and appointed them for certain ends, which he hath fore-ordained. 2. His *prescience*, whereby he certainly foreknoweth all things that shall come to pass. 3. His *temporal operation*, or working in time,—"My Father worketh hitherto," John v. 17,—whereby he actually executeth all his good pleasure. The first and second of these have been the subject of the former chapters; the latter only now requireth our consideration.

This, then, we may conceive as an ineffable act or work of Almighty God, *whereby he cherisheth, sustaineth, and governeth the world, or all things by him created, moving them, agreeably to those natures which he endowed them withal in the beginning, unto those ends which he hath proposed.* To confirm this, I will first prove this position, That the whole world is cared for by God, and by him governed, and therein all men, good or bad, all things in particular, be they never so small and in our eyes inconsiderable. Secondly, show the manner how God worketh all, in all things, and according to the diversity of secondary causes which he hath created; whereof

1 "An actus divinæ providentiæ omnium rerum conservatrix, sit affirmativus potentiæ, an tantum negativus voluntatis, quo nolit res creatas perdere."—Rem. Apol., cap. vi.

2 "Providentia seu ratio ordinis ad finem duo præcipue continet: principium decernens seu ipsam rationem ordinis in mente divina, ipsi Deo coæternum, et principium exequens, quo suo modo, per debita media, ipsa in ordine et numero disponit."—Thom.

some are necessary, some free, others contingent, which produce their effects *nec* πάντως, *nec* ἐπὶ τὸ πολύ, *sed* κατὰ συμβεβηκός, merely by accident.

The providence of God in governing the world is plentifully made known unto us, both by his works and by his word. I will give a few instances of either sort:—1. In general, that the almighty Δημιουργός, and Framer of this whole universe, should propose unto himself no end in the creation of all things,—that he should want either power, goodness, will, or wisdom, to order and dispose the works of his own hands,—is altogether impossible. 2. Take a particular instance in one concerning accident, the knowledge whereof by some means or other, in some degree or other, hath spread itself throughout the world,—and that is that almost universal destruction of all by the flood, whereby the whole world was well-nigh reduced to its primitive confusion. Is there nothing but chance to be seen in this? was there any circumstance about it that did not show a God and his providence? Not to speak of those revelations whereby God foretold that he would bring such a deluge, what chance, what fortune, could collect such a small number of individuals of all sorts, wherein the whole kind might be preserved? What hand guided that poor vessel from the rocks and gave it a resting-place on the mountains? Certainly, the very reading of that story, Gen. vii., viii., having for confirmation the catholic tradition of all mankind, were enough to startle the stubborn heart of an atheist.

The word of God doth not less fully relate it than his works do declare it, Ps. xix. "My Father worketh hitherto," saith our Saviour, John v. 17. But did not God end his work on the seventh day, and did he not then "rest from all his work?" Gen. ii. 2. True, from his work of creation by his omnipotence; but his work of gubernation by his providence as yet knows no end. Yea, and divers particular things he doth besides the ordinary course, only to make known "that he thus worketh," John ix. 3. As he hath framed all things by his wisdom, so he continueth them by his providence in excellent order, as is at large declared in that golden Psalm civ.: and this is not bounded to any particular places or things, but "his eyes are in every place, beholding the evil and the good," Prov. xv. 3; so that "none can hide himself in secret places that he shall not see him," Jer. xxiii. 24; Acts xvii. 24; Job v. 10, 11; Exod. iv. 11. And all this he saith that men "may know from the rising of the sun, and from the west, that there is none beside him. He is the LORD, and there is none else. He formeth the light, and createth darkness: he maketh peace, and createth evil: he doeth all these things," Isa. xlv. 6, 7. In these and innumerable like places doth the Lord declare that there is nothing which he hath made, that with the good hand of his providence he doth not govern and sustain.

Now, this general extent of his common providence to all doth no way hinder but that he may exercise certain special acts thereof towards some in particular, even by how much nearer than other things they approach unto him and are more assimilated unto his goodness. I mean his church here on earth, and those whereof it doth consist; "for what nation is there so great, who hath God so nigh unto them?" Deut. iv. 7. In the government hereof he most eminently showeth his glory, and exerciseth his power. Join here his works with his word, what he hath done with what he hath promised to do for the conservation of his church and people, and you will find admirable issues of a more special providence. Against this he promiseth "the gates of hell shall not prevail," Matt. xvi. 18;—amidst of these he hath promised to remain, chap. xxviii. 20; supplying them with an addition of all things necessary, Matt. vi. 33; desiring that "all their care might be cast upon him, who careth for them," 1 Pet. v. 7; forbidding any to "touch his anointed ones," Ps. cv. 15, and that because they are unto him as "the apple of his eye," Zech. ii. 8. Now, this special providence hath respect unto a supernatural end, to which that, and that alone, is to be conveyed.

For wicked men, as they are excepted from this special care and government, so they are not exempted from the dominion of his almighty hand. He who hath created them "for the day of evil," Prov. xvi. 4, and provided a "place of their own" for them to go unto, Acts i. 25, doth not in this world suffer them to live without the verge of his all-ruling providence; but by suffering and enduring their iniquities with great patience and "long-suffering," Rom. ix. 22, defending them oftentimes from the injuries of one another, Gen. iv. 15, by granting unto them many temporal blessings, Matt. v. 45, disposing of all their works to the glory of his great name, Prov. xxi. 1, 2, he declareth that they also live, and move, and have their being in him, and are under the government of his providence. Nay, there is not the least thing in this world to which his care and knowledge doth not descend. Ill would it become his wisdom not to sustain, order, and dispose of all things by him created, but leave them to the ruin of uncertain chance. Jerome[1] then was injurious to his providence, and cast a blemish on his absolute perfection, whilst he thought to have cleared his majesty from being defiled with the knowledge and care of the smallest reptiles and vermin every moment; and St Austin is express to the contrary: [2]"Who," saith he, "hath

[1] "Majestatem Dei dedecet scire per momenta singula, quot nascantur culices, quæ pulicum et muscarum in terra multitudo."—Hieron. in cap. i., Hab.

[2] "Quis disposuit membra pulicis ac culicis, ut habeant ordinem suum, habeant vitam suam, habeant motum suum," etc. "Qui fecit in cœlo angelum, ipse fecit in terra vermi-

disposed the several members of the flea and gnat, that hath given unto them order, life, and motion?" etc.,—even most agreeable to holy Scriptures: so Ps. civ. 20, 21, cxlv. 15; Matt. vi. 26, 30, "He feedeth the fowls, and clotheth the grass of the field;" Job xxxix. 1, 2; Jonah iv. 6, 7. Sure it is not troublesome to God to take notice of all that he hath created. Did he use that great power in the production of the least of his creatures, so far beyond the united activity of men and angels, for no end at all? Doubtless, even they also must have a well-disposed order, for the manifestation of his glory. "Not a sparrow falleth on the ground without our Father;" even "the hairs of our head are all numbered," Matt. x. 29, 30. "He clotheth the lilies and grass of the field, which is to be cast into the oven," Luke xii. 27, 28. Behold his knowledge and care of them! Again, he used frogs and lice for the punishment of the Egyptians, Exod. viii.; with a gourd and a worm he exercised his servant Jonah, chap. iv.; yea, he calls the locusts his "terrible army;"—and shall not God know and take care of the number of his soldiers, the ordering of his dreadful host?

That God by his providence governeth and disposeth of all things by him created is sufficiently proved; the manner how he worketh all in all, how he ordereth the works of his own hands, in what this governing and disposing of his creatures doth chiefly consist, comes now to be considered. And here four things are principally to be observed:—First, The sustaining, preserving, and upholding of all things by his power; for "he upholdeth all things by the word of his power," Heb. i. 3. Secondly, His working together with all things, by an influence of causality into the agents themselves; "for he also hath wrought all our works in us," Isa. xxvi. 12. Thirdly, His powerful overruling of all events, both necessary, free, and contingent, and disposing of them to certain ends for the manifestation of his glory. So Joseph tells his brethren, "As for you, ye thought evil against me; but God meant it unto good, to bring to pass, as it is at this day, to save much people alive," Gen. l. 20. Fourthly, His determining and restraining second causes to such and such effects: "The king's heart is in the hand of the LORD, as the rivers of water: he turneth it whithersoever he will," Prov. xxi. 1.

First, His sustentation or upholding of all things is his powerful continuing of their being, natural strength, and faculties, bestowed on them at their creation: "In him we live, and move, and have our being," Acts xvii. So that he doth neither work all himself in them, without any co-operation of theirs, which would not only turn all

culum, sed angelum in cœlo pro habitatione cœlesti, vermiculum in terra pro habitatione terrestri, nunquid angelum fecit repere in cœno, aut vermiculum in cœlo," etc. —Aug., tom. viii., in Ps. cxlviii.

things into stocks, yea, and take from stocks their own proper nature, but also is contrary to that general blessing he spread over the face of the whole world in the beginning, "Be fruitful, and multiply," Gen. i. 22;—nor yet leave them to a self-subsistence, he in the meantime only not destroying them;[1] which would make him an idle spectator of most things in the world, not to "work hitherto," as our Saviour speaks, and grant to divers things here below an absolute being, not derivative from him: the first whereof is blasphemous, the latter impossible.

Secondly, For God's working in and together with all second causes for producing of their effects, what part or portion in the work punctually to assign unto him, what to the power of the inferior causes, seems beyond the reach of mortals; neither is an exact comprehension thereof any way necessary, so that we make every thing beholding to his power for its being, and to his assistance for its operation.

Thirdly, His supreme dominion exerciseth itself in disposing of all things to certain and determinate ends for his own glory, and is chiefly discerned advancing itself over those things which are most contingent, and making them in some sort necessary, inasmuch as they are certainly disposed of to some proposed ends. Between the birth and death of a man, how many things merely contingent do occur! how many chances! how many diseases! in their own nature all evitable, and, in regard of the event, not one of them but to some proves mortal; yet, certain it is that a man's "days are determined, the number of his months are with the Lord, he hath appointed his bounds that he cannot pass," Job xiv. 5. And oftentimes by things purely contingent and accidental he executeth his purposes,—bestoweth rewards, inflicteth punishments, and accomplisheth his judgments; as when he delivereth a man to be slain by the head of an axe, flying from the helve in the hand of a man cutting a tree by the way. But in nothing is this more evident than in the ancient casting of lots, a thing as casual and accidental as can be imagined, huddled in the cap at a venture. Yet God overruleth them to the declaring of his purpose, freeing truth from doubts, and manifestation of his power: Prov. xvi. 33, "The lot is cast into the lap, but the whole disposing thereof is of the LORD;"—as you may see in the examples of Achan, Josh. vii. 16–18; Saul, 1 Sam. x. 20, 21; Jonathan, chap. xiv. 41, 42; Jonah, chap. i. 7; Matthias, Acts i. 26. And yet this overruling act of God's providence (as no other decree or act of his) doth not rob things contingent of their proper nature; for cannot he who effectually causeth that they shall come to pass, cause also that they shall come to pass contingently?

Fourthly, God's predetermination of second causes (which I name not last as though it were the last act of God's providence about his

[1] Rem. Apol., cap. vi.

creatures, for indeed it is the first that concerneth their operation) is that effectual working of his, according to his eternal purpose, whereby, though some agents, as the wills of men, are causes most free and indefinite, or unlimited lords of their own actions, in respect of their internal principle of operation (that is, their own nature), [they] are yet all, in respect of his decree, and by his powerful working, determined to this or that effect in particular; not that they are compelled to do this, or hindered from doing that, but are inclined and disposed to do this or that, according to their proper manner of working, that is, most freely: for truly such testimonies are everywhere obvious in Scripture, of the stirring up of men's wills and minds, of bending and inclining them to divers things, of the governing of the secret thoughts and motions of the heart, as cannot by any means be referred to a naked permission, with a government of external actions, or to a general influence, whereby they should have power to do this or that, or any thing else; wherein, as some suppose, his whole providence consisteth.

Let us now jointly apply these several acts to free agents, working according to choice, or relation, such as are the wills of men, and that will open the way to take a view of Arminian heterodoxies, concerning this article of Christian belief. And here two things must be premised:—First, That they be not deprived of their own radical or original internal liberty; secondly, That they be not exempt from the moving influence and gubernation of God's providence;—the first whereof would leave no just room for rewards and punishments; the other, as I said before, is injurious to the majesty and power of God. St Augustine[1] judged Cicero worthy of special blame, even among the heathens, for so attempting to make men free that he made them sacrilegious, by denying them to be subject to an overruling providence: which gross error was directly maintained by Damascen,[2] a learned Christian, teaching, "Things whereof we have any power, not to depend on providence, but on our own free will;" an opinion fitter for a hog of the Epicurus herd than for a scholar in the school of Christ. And yet this proud, prodigious error is now, though in other terms, stiffly maintained: for what do they else who ascribe such an absolute independent liberty to the will of man, that it should have in its own power every circumstance, every condition whatsoever, that belongs to operation, so that all things required on the part of God, or otherwise, to the performance of an action being accomplished, it remaineth solely in the power of a man's own will whether he will do it or no? which supreme and plainly divine liberty, joined with such an absolute uncontrollable power and dominion over all his

[1] "Qui sic homines voluit esse liberos ut fecit sacrilegos."—Aug.

[2] Τὰ ἐφ' ὑμῖν οὐ τῆς προνοίας ἀλλὰ τοῦ ἡμετέρου αὐτεξουσίου.—Damascen.

actions, would exempt and free the will of man, not only from all fore-determining to the production of such and such effects, but also from any effectual working or influence of the providence of God into the will itself, that should sustain, help, or co-operate with it in doing or willing any thing; and, therefore, the authors of this imaginary liberty have wisely framed an imaginary concurrence of God's providence, answerable unto it,—namely, a general and indifferent influence, always waiting and expecting the will of man to determine itself to this or that effect, good or bad; God being, as it were, always ready at hand to do that small part which he hath in our actions, whensoever we please to use him, or, if we please to let him alone, he no way moveth us to the performance of any thing. Now, God forbid that we should give our consent to the choice of such a captain, under whose conduct we might go down again unto Paganism,—to the erecting of such an idol into the throne of the Almighty. No, doubtless, let us be most indulgent to our wills, and assign them all the liberty that is competent unto a created nature, to do all things freely according to election and foregoing counsel, being free from all natural necessity and outward compulsion; but for all this, let us not presume to deny God's effectual assistance, his particular powerful influence into the wills and actions of his creatures, directing of them to a voluntary performance of what he hath determined: which the Arminians opposing in the behalf of their darling free-will, do work in the hearts of men an overweening of their own power, and an absolute independence of the providence of God; for,—

First, they deny that God (in whom we live, and move, and have our being) doth any thing by his providence, [1]"whereby the creature should be stirred up, or helped in any of his actions." That is, God wholly leaves a man in the hand of his own counsel, to the disposal of his own absolute independent power, without any respect to his providence at all; whence, as they do, they may well conclude, [2]"that those things which God would have to be done of us freely" (such as are all human actions), "he cannot himself will or work more powerfully and effectually than by the way of wishing or desiring," as Vorstius speaks; which is no more than one man can do concerning another, perhaps far less than an angel. I can wish or desire that another man would do what I have a mind he should; but, truly, to describe the providence of God by such expressions seems to me intolerable blasphemy. But thus it must be; without such helps as these, Dagon cannot keep on his head, nor the idol of uncontrollable free-will enjoy his dominion.

[1] "Deus influxu suo nihil confert creaturæ, quo ad agendum incitetur ac adjuvetur." —Corv. ad Molin., cap. iii. sect. 15, p. 35.

[2] "Quæ Deus libere prorsus et contingenter a nobis fieri vult, ea potentius aut efficacius quam per modum voti aut desiderii, velle non potest.—Vorst. Parasc., p. 4.

Hence Corvinus will grant[1] that the killing of a man by the slipping of an axe's head from the helve, although contingent, may be said to happen according to God's counsel and determinate will; but *on no terms will he yield that this may be applied to actions wherein the counsel and freedom of man's will do take place, as though that they also should have dependence on any such overruling power;*—whereby he absolutely excludeth the providence of God from having any sovereignty within the territory of human actions, which is plainly to shake off the yoke of his dominion, and to make men lords paramount within themselves: so that they may well ascribe unto God (as they do[2]) *only a deceivable expectation of those contingent things that are yet for to come,* there being no act of his own in the producing of such effects on which he can ground any certainty; only, he may take a conjecture, according to his guess at men's inclinations. And, indeed, this is the Helen for whose enjoyment, these thrice ten years, they have maintained warfare with the hosts of the living God; their whole endeavour being to prove, that, notwithstanding the performance of all things, on the part of God, required for the production of any action, [3]yet *the will of man remains absolutely free, yea, in respect of the event, as well as its manner of operation, to do it or not to do it.* That is, notwithstanding God's decree that such an action shall be performed, and his foreknowledge that it will so come to pass; notwithstanding his co-operating with the will of man (as far as they will allow him) for the doing of it, and though he hath determined by that act of man to execute some of his own judgments; [4]yet there is no kind of necessity but that he may as well omit as do it: which is all one as if they should say, "Our tongues are our own; we ought to speak: who is lord over us? We will vindicate ourselves into a liberty of doing what and how we will, though for it we cast God out of his throne." And, indeed, if we mark it, we shall find them undermining and pulling down the actual providence of God, at the root and several branches thereof; for,—

First, For his conservation or sustaining of all things, they affirm[5]

[1] "Deinde etsi in isto casu destinatum aliquod consilium ac voluntas Dei determinata consideranda esset, tamen in omnibus actionibus et in iis quidem quæ ex deliberato hominum consilio et libera voluntate et male quidem fiunt, ita se rem habere inde concludi non possit, puta, quia hic nullum consilium et arbitrii libertas locum habent."—Corv. ad. Molin., cap. iii. sect. 14, p. 33.

[2] "Respectu contingentiæ quam res habent in se, tum in divina scientia Deo expectatio tribuitur."—Rem. Defen. Sent. in Act. Syn., p. 107.

[3] "Potentia voluntatis, ab omni interna et externa necessitate immunis debet manere."—Rem. Confes., cap. vi. sect. 3. Vid. plura. Rem. Apol., cap. vi. p. 69, a.

[4] "In arbitrio creaturæ semper est vel influere in actum vel influxum suum suspendere, et vel sic, vel aliter influere."—Corv. ad. Molin., cap. iii. sect. 15.

[5] "An conservatio ista sit vis sive actus potentiæ an actus merus voluntatis negativus, quo vult res creatas non destruere aut annihilare,—posterius non sine magna

it to be very likely that this is nothing but *a negative act of his will, whereby he willeth or determineth not to destroy the things by him created;* and when we produce places of Scripture which affirm that it is an act of his power, they say *they are foolishly cited.* So that, truly, let the Scripture say what it will, (in their conceit,) God doth no more sustain and uphold all his creatures than I do a house when I do not set it on fire, or a worm when I do not tread upon it.

Secondly, For God's concurring with inferior causes in all their acts and working, they affirm it to be only [1]*a general influence, alike upon all and every one, which they may use or not use at their pleasure,* and in the use determine it to this or that effect, be it good or bad (so Corvinus), as it seems best unto them. In a word, to the will of man [2]it is nothing but what suffers it to play its own part freely, according to its inclination; as they jointly speak in their Confession. Observe, also, that they account this influence of his providence not to be into the agent, the will of man, whereby that should be helped or enabled to do any thing (no, that would seem to grant a self-sufficiency), [3]but *only into the act itself for its production:* as if I should help a man to lift a log, it becomes perhaps unto him so much the lighter, but he is not made one jot the stronger; which takes off the proper work of providence, consisting in an internal assistance.

Thirdly, For God's determining or circumscribing the will of man to do this or that in particular, they absolutely explode it, as a thing destructive to their adored liberty. [4]"It is no way consistent with it," say they, in their Apology. So also Arminius: [5]"The providence of God doth not determine the will of man to one part of the contradiction." That is, "God hath not determined that you shall, nor doth by any means overrule your wills, to do this thing rather than that, to do this or to omit that." So that the sum of their endeavour is, to prove that the will of man is so absolutely free, independent, and uncontrollable, that God doth not, nay, with all his power cannot, determine it certainly and infallibly to the performance of this or

veri specie affirmatur: locus ad Heb. i. 3 inepte adducitur."—Rem. Apol., cap. vi. sect. 1, p. 68, a.

[1] "Curandum diligenter, ut Deo quidem universalis, homini vero particularis influxus in actus tribuatur, quo universalem Dei influxum, ad particularem actum determinet."—Corv. ad Molin., cap. iii. sect. 5.

[2] "Ita concurrit Deus in agendo, cum hominis voluntate, ut istam pro genio suo agere et libere suas partes obire sinat."—Rem. Confes., cap. vi. sect. 3.

[3] "Influxus divinus est in ipsum actum non in voluntatem."—Armin. Antip., alii passim.

[4] "Determinatio cum libertate vera nullo modo consistere potest."—Rem. Apol., cap. vii. fol. 82.

[5] "Providentia divina non determinat voluntatem liberam ad unam contradictionis vel contrarietatis partem."—Armin. Artic. Perpen.

that particular action, thereby to accomplish his own purposes, to attain his own ends. Truly, it seems to me the most unfortunate attempt that ever Christians lighted on; which, if it should get success answerable to the greatness of the undertaking, the providence of God, in men's esteem, would be almost thrust quite out of the world. "Tantæ molis erat." The new goddess contingency could not be erected until the God of heaven was utterly despoiled of his dominion over the sons of men, and in the room thereof a home-bred idol of self-sufficiency set up, and the world persuaded to worship it. But that the building climb no higher, let all men observe how the word of God overthrows this Babylonian tower.

First, then, In innumerable places it is punctual that his providence doth not only bear rule in the counsels of men and their most secret resolutions, (whence the prophet declareth that he knoweth that "the way of man is not in himself,"—that "it is not in man that walketh to direct his steps," Jer. x. 23; and Solomon, that "a man's heart deviseth his way, but the LORD directeth his steps," Prov. xvi. 9; David, also, having laid this ground, that "the LORD bringeth the counsel of the heathen to nought," and "maketh the devices of the people of none effect," but "his own counsel standeth for ever, the thoughts of his heart to all generations," Ps. xxxiii. 10, 11, proceedeth accordingly, in his own distress, to pray that the Lord would infatuate and make [1] "foolish the counsel of Ahithophel," 2 Sam. xv. 31,—which also the Lord did, by working in the heart of Absalom to hearken to the cross counsel of Hushai); but also, secondly, That the working of his providence is effectual even in the hearts and wills of men to turn them which way he will, and to determine them to this or that in particular, according as he pleaseth: "The preparations of the heart in man, and the answer of the tongue, is from the LORD," saith Solomon, Prov. xvi. 1;—which Jacob trusted and relied on when he prayed that the Lord would grant his sons to find favour and mercy before that man whom then he supposed to be some atheistical Egyptian, Gen. xliii. 14; whence we must grant, either that the good old man believed that it was in the hand of God to incline and unalterably turn and settle the heart of Joseph to favour his brethren, or else his prayer must have had such a senseless sense as this: "Grant, O Lord, such a general influence of thy providence, that the heart of that man may be turned to good towards my sons, or else that it may not, being left to its own freedom." A strange request! yet how it may be bettered by one believing the Arminian doctrine I cannot conceive. Thus So-

[1] "Dominus dissipavit consilium quod dederat Achitophel agendo in corde Absolon, ut tale consilium repudiaret, et aliud quod ei non expediebat eligeret."—Aug. de Grat., et Lib. Arbit., cap. xx.

lomon affirmeth that "the king's heart is in the hand of the LORD, like the rivers of water: he turneth it whithersoever he will," Prov. xxi. 1. If the heart of a king, who hath an inward natural liberty equal with others, and an outward liberty belonging to his state and condition above them, be yet so in the hand of the Lord as that he always turneth it to what he pleaseth in particular, then certainly other men are not excepted from the rule of the same providence; which is the plain sense of these words, and the direct thesis which we maintain in opposition to the Arminian idol of absolute independent free-will. So Daniel, also, reproving the Babylonian tyrant, affirmeth that he "glorified not the God in whose hand was his breath, and whose were all his ways," chap. v. 23. Not only his breath and life, but also all his ways, his actions, thoughts, and words, were in the hand of God.

Yea, thirdly, sometimes the saints of God, as I touched before, do pray that God would be pleased thus to determine their hearts, and bend their wills, and wholly incline them to some one certain thing, and that without any prejudice to their true and proper liberty: so David, Ps. cxix. 36, "Incline my heart unto thy testimonies, and not to covetousness." This prayer being his may also be ours, and we may ask it in faith, relying on the power and promise of God in Christ that he will perform our petitions, John xiv. 14. Now, I desire any Christian to resolve, whether, by these and the like requests, he intendeth to desire at the hand of God nothing but such an indifferent motion to any good as may leave him to his own choice whether he will do it or no, which is all the Arminians will grant him; or rather, that he would powerfully bend his heart and soul unto his testimonies, and work in him an actual embracing of all the ways of God, not desiring more liberty, but only enough to do it willingly. Nay, surely the prayers of God's servants, requesting, with Solomon, that the Lord would be with them, and "incline their heart unto him, to keep his statutes and walk in his commandments," 1 Kings viii. 57, 58; and with David, to "create in them a clean heart, and renew a right spirit within them," Ps. li. 10; when, according to God's promises, they entreat him "to put his fear into their hearts," Jer. xxxii. 40, "to unite their hearts to fear his name," Ps. lxxxvi. 11, to work in them both the will and the deed, an actual obedience unto his law;—cannot possibly aim at nothing but a general influence, enabling them alike either to do or not to do what they so earnestly long after.

Fourthly, The certainty of divers promises and threatenings of Almighty God dependeth upon his powerful determining and turning the wills and hearts of men which way he pleaseth; thus, to them that fear him he promiseth that they shall find favour in the sight of men, Prov. iii. 4. Now, if, notwithstanding all God's powerful operation in their hearts, it remaineth absolutely in the hands of men whether they will favour them that fear him or no, it is wholly in their power whether God shall be true in his promises or no. Surely when Jacob wrestled with God on the strength of such promise, Gen. xxxii. 12, he little thought of any question whether it were in the power of God to perform it. Yea, and the event showed that there ought to be no such question, chap. xxxiii.; for the Lord turned the heart of his brother Esau, as he doth of others when he makes them pity his servants when at any time they have carried them away captives, Ps. cvi. 46. See, also, the same powerful operation required to the execution of his judgments, Job xii. 17, xx. 21, etc. In brief, there is no prophecy nor prediction in the whole Scripture, no promise to the church or faithful, to whose accomplishment the free actions and concurrence of men are required, but evidently declareth that God disposeth of the hearts of men, ruleth their wills, inclineth their affections, and determines them freely to choose and do what he in his good pleasure hath decreed shall be performed;—such as were the prophecies of deliverance from the Babylônish captivity by Cyrus, Isa. xlv.; of the conversion of the Gentiles; of the stability of the church, Matt. xvi.; of the destruction of Jerusalem by the Romans, chap. xxiv.; with innumerable others. I will add only some few reasons for the close of this long discourse.

This opinion, that God hath nothing but a general influence into the actions of men, not effectually moving their wills to this or that in particular,—

First, Granteth a goodness of *entity*, or being, unto divers things, whereof God is not the author, as those special actions which men perform without his special concurrence; which is blasphemous. The apostle affirms that "of him are all things."

Secondly, It denieth God to be the author of all moral goodness, for an action is good inasmuch as it is such an action in particular;[1] which that any is so, according to this opinion, is to be attributed merely to the will of man. The general influence of God moveth him no more to prayer than to evil communications tending to the corruption of good manners.

Thirdly, It maketh all the decrees of God, whose execution dependeth on human actions, to be altogether uncertain, and his foreknowledge of such things to be fallible and easily to be deceived; so that there is no reconciliation possible to be hoped for betwixt these following and the like assertions:—

[1] "Qui aliquid boni a Deo non effici affirmat, ille Deum esse negat: si namque vel tantillum boni a Deo non est: jam non omnis boni effector est eoque nec Deus."—Bucer. in cap. ix. ad Rom.

S. S.	Lib. Arbit.
"In him we live, and move, and have our being," Acts xvii. 28.	"God's sustaining of all things is not an affirmative act of his power, but a negative act of his will."
"He upholdeth all things by the word of his power," Heb. i. 3.	—— "Whereby he will not destroy them," Rem. Apol.
"Thou hast wrought all our works in us," Isa. xxvi. 12. "My Father worketh hitherto," John v. 17.	"God by his influence bestoweth nothing on the creature whereby it may be incited or helped in its actions," Corvinus.
"The preparations of the heart in man, and the answer of the tongue, is from the LORD," Prov. xvi. 1. "The king's heart is in the hand of the LORD, like the rivers of water: he turneth it whithersoever he will," Prov. xxi. 1.	"Those things God would have us freely do ourselves; he can no more effectually work or will than by the way of wishing," Vorstius.
"Incline my heart unto thy testimonies, and not to covetousness," Ps. cxix. 36. "Unite my heart to fear thy name," Ps. lxxxvi. 11. "The God in whose hand thy breath is, and whose are all thy ways, thou hast not glorified," Dan. v. 23.	"The providence of God doth not determine the free-will of man to this or that particular, or to one part of the contradiction," Arminius.
See Matt. xxvii. 1, compared with Acts ii. 23, and iv. 27, 28; Luke xxiv. 27; John xix. 31–36. For the necessity of other events, see Exod. xxi. 17; Job xiv. 5; Matt. xix. 7, etc.	"The will of man ought to be free from all kind of internal and external necessity in its actions," Rem. That is, God cannot lay such a necessity upon any thing as that it shall infallibly come to pass as he intendeth. See the contrary in the places cited.

CHAPTER V.

Whether the will and purpose of God may be resisted, and he be frustrate of his intentions.

BY the former steps is the altar of Ahaz set on the right hand of the altar of God,—the Arminian idol, in a direct opposition, exalted to an equal pitch with the power and will of the Most High. I shall now present unto you the Spirit of God once more contending with the towering imaginations of poor mortals, about a transcendent privilege of greatness, glory, and power: for having made his decrees mutable, his prescience fallible, and almost quite divested him of his providence, as the sum and issue of all their endeavours, they affirm that his will may be resisted, he may fail of his intentions, be frustrate of his ends,—he may and doth propose such things as he neither doth nor can at any time accomplish, and that because the execution of such acts of his will might haply clash against the freedom of the will of men; which, if it be not an expression of spiritual pride above all that ever the devil attempted in heaven, divines do not well explicate that sin of his. Now, because there may seem some difficulty in this matter, by reason of the several acceptations of the *will* of God, especially in regard of that whereby it is affirmed that his law and precepts are his will, which, alas! we all of us too often resist or transgress, I will unfold one distinction of the will of God, which will leave it clear what it is that the Arminians oppose, for which we count them worthy of so heavy a charge.

"Divinum velle est ejus esse," say the schoolmen,[1] "The will of God is nothing but God willing;" not differing from his essence "secundem rem," in the thing itself, but only "secundem rationem," in that it importeth a relation to the thing willed. The essence of God, then, being a most absolute, pure, simple act or substance, his will consequently can be but simply one; whereof we ought to make neither division nor distinction. If that whereby it is signified were taken always properly and strictly for the eternal will of God, the differences hereof that are usually given are rather distinctions of the signification of the word than of the thing.

In which regard they are not only tolerable, but simply necessary, because without them it is utterly impossible to reconcile some places of Scripture seemingly repugnant. In the 22d chapter of Genesis, verse 2, God commandeth Abraham to take his only son Isaac, and offer him for a burnt-offering in the land of Moriah. Here the words of God are declarative of some will of God unto Abraham, who knew it ought to be, and little thought but that it should be, performed; but yet, when he actually addressed himself to his duty, in obedience to the will of God, he receiveth a countermand, verse 12, that he should not lay his hand upon the child to sacrifice him. The event plainly manifesteth that it was the will of God that Isaac should not be sacrificed; and yet notwithstanding, by reason of his command, Abraham seems before bound to believe that it was well-pleasing unto God that he should accomplish what he was enjoined. If the will of God in the Scripture be used but in one ac-

[1] Aquin., p. q. 19, ar. ad. 1.

ceptation, here is a plain contradiction. Thus God commands Pharaoh to let his people go. Could Pharaoh think otherwise, nay, was he not bound to believe that it was the will of God that he should dismiss the Israelites at the first hearing of the message? Yet God affirms that he would harden his heart, that he should not suffer them to depart until he had showed his signs and wonders in the land of Egypt. To reconcile these and the like places of Scripture, both the ancient fathers and schoolmen, with modern divines, do affirm that the one will of God may be said to be divers or manifold, in regard of the sundry manners whereby he willeth those things to be done which he willeth, as also in other respects, and yet, taken in its proper signification, is simply one and the same. The vulgar distinction of God's secret and revealed will is such as to which all the others may be reduced; and therefore I have chosen it to insist upon.

The secret will of God is his eternal, unchangeable purpose concerning all things which he hath made, to be brought by certain means to their appointed ends: of this himself affirmeth, that "his counsel shall stand, and he will do all his pleasure," Isa. xlvi. 10. This some call the absolute, efficacious will of God, the will of his good pleasure, always fulfilled; and indeed this is the only proper, eternal, constant, immutable will of God, whose order can neither be broken nor its law transgressed, so long as with him there is neither change nor shadow of turning.

The revealed will of God containeth not his purpose and decree, but our duty,—not what *he* will do according to his good pleasure, but what *we* should do if we will please him; and this, consisting in his word, his precepts and promises, belongeth to us and our children, that we may do the will of God. Now this, indeed, is rather τὸ θελητόν than τὸ θέλημα, that which God willeth, rather than his will, but termed so as we call that the will of a man which he hath determined shall be done: "This is the will of him that sent me, that every one which seeth the Son, and believeth on him, may have everlasting life," saith our Saviour, John vi. 40; that is, this is that which his will hath appointed. Hence it is called "voluntas signi," or the sign of his will, metaphorically only called his will, saith Aquinas;[1] for inasmuch as our commands are the signs of our wills, the same is said of the precepts of God. This is the rule of our obedience, and whose transgression makes an action sinful; for ἡ ἁμαρτία ἐστὶν ἡ ἀνομία, "sin is the transgression of a law," and that such a law as is given to the transgressor to be observed. Now, God hath not imposed on us the observation of his eternal decree and intention; which, as it is utterly impossible for us to transgress or frustrate, so were we un-

[1] Aquin., q. g. 19, a. 11, c.

blamable if we should. A master requires of his servant to do what he commands, not to accomplish what he intends, which perhaps he never discovered unto him; nay, the commands of superiors are not always signs that the commander will have the things commanded actually performed (as in all precepts for trial), but only that they who are subjects to this command shall be obliged to obedience, as far as the sense of it doth extend. "Et hoc clarum est in præceptis divinis," saith Durand,[1] etc.,—"And this is clear in the commands of God," by which we are obliged to do what he commandeth; and yet it is not always his pleasure that the thing itself, in regard of the event, shall be accomplished, as we saw before in the examples of Pharaoh and Abraham.

Now, the will of God in the first acceptation is said to be hid or secret, not because it is so always, for it is in some particulars revealed and made known unto us two ways:—

First, By his word; as where God affirmeth that the dead shall rise. We doubt not but that they shall rise, and that it is the absolute will of God that they shall do so. Secondly, By the effects; for when any thing cometh to pass, we may cast the event on the will of God as its cause, and look upon it as a revelation of his purpose. Jacob's sons little imagined that it was the will of God by them to send their brother into Egypt; yet afterward Joseph tells them plainly it was not they, but God that sent him thither, Gen. xlv. 5. But it is said to be secret for two causes:—First, Because for the most part it is so. There is nothing in divers issues declarative of God's determination but only the event, which, while it is future, is hidden to them who have faculties to judge of things past and present, but not to discern things for to come. Hence St James bids us not be too peremptory in our determinations that we will do this or that, not knowing how God will close with us for its performance. Secondly, It is said to be secret in reference to its cause, which for the most part is past our finding out: "His path is in the great waters, and his footsteps are not known."

It appeareth, then, that the secret and revealed will of God are diverse in sundry respects, but chiefly in regard of their acts and their objects. First, In regard of their acts, the secret will of God is his eternal decree and determination concerning any thing to be done in its appointed time; his revealed will is an act whereby he declareth himself to love or approve any thing, whether ever it be done or no. Secondly, They are diverse in regard of their objects. The object of God's purpose and decree is that which is good in any kind, with reference to its actual existence, for it must infallibly be performed; but the object of his revealed will is that only which is morally good (I

[1] Durand, Dist. c. 48, q. 3.

speak of it inasmuch as it approveth or commandeth), agreeing to the law and the gospel, and that considered only inasmuch as it is good; for whether it be ever actually performed or no is accidental to the object of God's revealed will.

Now, of these two differences the first is perpetual, in regard of their several acts; but not so the latter. They are sometimes coincident in regard of their objects. For instance, God commandeth us to believe; here his revealed will is that we should so do: withal, he intendeth we shall do so; and therefore ingenerateth faith in our hearts that we may believe. Here his secret and revealed will are coincident; the former[1] being his precept that we should believe, the latter his purpose that we shall believe. In this case, I say, the object of the one and the other is the same,—even what we ought to do, and what he will do. And this inasmuch as he hath "wrought all our works in us," Isa. xxvi. 12. They are our own works which he works in us; his act in us and by us is ofttimes our duty towards him. He commands us by his revealed will to walk in his statutes, and keep his laws; upon this he also promiseth that he will so effect all things, that of some this shall be performed: Ezek. xxxvi. 26, 27, "A new heart also will I give you, and a new spirit will I put within you: and I will take away the stony heart out of your flesh, and I will give you an heart of flesh. And I will put my Spirit within you, and cause you to walk in my statutes, and ye shall keep my judgments and do them." So that the self-same obedience of the people of God is here the object of his will, taken in either acceptation. And yet the precept of God is not here, as some learned men suppose, declarative of God's intention, for then it must be so to all to whom it is given; which evidently it is not, for many are commanded to believe on whom God never bestoweth faith. It is still to be looked upon as a mere declaration of our duty, its closing with God's intention being accidental unto it. There is a wide difference betwixt "Do such a thing," and, "You shall do it." If God's command to Judas to believe imported as much as, "It is my purpose and intention that Judas shall believe," it must needs contradict that will of God whereby he determined that Judas, for his infidelity, should go to his "own place." His precepts are in all obedience of us to be performed, but do not signify his will that we shall actually fulfil his commands. Abraham was not bound to believe that it was God's intention that Isaac should be sacrificed, but that it was his duty. There was no obligation on Pharaoh to think it was God's purpose the people should depart at the first summons; he

[1] The words "former" and "latter" evidently refer to the previous sentence,—"former" corresponding with the revealed will, "latter" with the secret will of God. The order is reversed in the first clause of this sentence, and hence the author's meaning might be mistaken.—Ed.

had nothing to do with that: but there was one to believe that if he would please God, he must let them go. Hence divers things of good use in these controversies may be collected:—

First, That God may command many things by his word which he never decreed that they should actually be performed; because, in such things, his words are not a revelation of his eternal decree and purpose, but only a declaration of some thing wherewith he is well-pleased, be it by us performed or no. In the fore-cited case he commanded Pharaoh to let his people go, and plagued him for refusing to obey his command. Hence we may not collect that God intended the obedience and conversion of Pharaoh by this his precept, but was frustrated of his intention,—for the Scripture is evident and clear that God purposed by his disobedience to accomplish an end far different, even a manifestation of his glory by his punishment,—but only that obedience unto his commands is pleasing unto him; as 1 Sam. xv. 22.

Secondly, That the will of God to which our obedience is required is the revealed will of God contained in his word; whose compliance with his decree is such, that hence we learn three things tending to the execution of it:—First, That it is the condition of the word of God, and the dispensation thereof, instantly to persuade to faith and obedience. Secondly, That it is our duty by all means to aspire to the performance of all things by it enjoined, and our fault if we do not. Thirdly, That God by these means will accomplish his eternal decree of saving his elect; and that he willeth the salvation of others, inasmuch as he calleth them unto the performance of the condition thereof. Now, our obedience is so to be regulated by this revealed will of God, that we may sin either by omission against its precepts or commission against its prohibitions; although by our so omitting or committing of any thing the secret will or purpose of God be fulfilled. Had Abraham disobeyed God's precept, when he was commanded to sacrifice his son Isaac, though God's will had been accomplished thereby, who never intended it, yet Abraham had grievously sinned against the revealed will of God, the rule of his duty. The holiness of our actions consisteth in a conformity unto his precepts, and not unto his purposes. On this ground Gregory affirmeth,[1] "That many fulfil the will of God" (that is, his intentions) "when they think to change it" (by transgressing his precepts); "and by resisting imprudently, obey God's purpose." And to show how merely we in our actions are tied to this rule of our duty, St Austin[2] shows how a man may do good in a thing cross to God's secret will, and evil in that which complieth with it, which he illustrates by the example of a

1 "Multi voluntatem Dei faciunt, cum illam nituntur vitare, et resistendo imprudenter obsequuntur divino consilio."—Greg. Moral., lib. vi. cap. 11.

2 Aug. Enchirid. ad Lauren., cap. ci.

sick parent having two children, the one wicked, who desires his father's death, the other godly, and he prays for his life. But the will of God is he shall die, agreeably to the desire of the wicked child; and yet it is the other who hath performed his duty, and done what is pleasing unto God.

Thirdly, To return from this not unnecessary digression, that which we have now in agitation is the secret will of God, which we have before unfolded; and this it is that we charge the Arminians for affirming that it may be resisted,—that is, that *God may fail in his purposes, come short of what he earnestly intendeth, or be frustrated of his aim and end:* as if, [when] he should determinately resolve the faith and salvation of any man, it is in the power of that man to make void his determination, and not believe, and not be saved. Now, it is only in cases of this nature, wherein our own free wills have an interest, that they thus limit and circumscribe the power of the Most High. In other things they grant his omnipotence to be of no less extent than others do; but in this case they are peremptory and resolute, without any colouring or tergiversation: for whereas there is a question proposed by the apostle, Rom. ix. 19, "Who hath resisted his will?" which that none hath or can he grants in the following verses, Corvinus affirms, [1]"It is only an objection of the Jews, rejected by the apostle;"—which is much like an answer young scholars usually give to some difficult place in Aristotle, when they cannot think of a better, "Loquitur ex aliorum sententia;" for there is no sign of any such rejection of it by the apostle in the whole following discourse; yea, and it is not the Jews that St Paul disputeth withal here, but weaker brethren concerning the Jews, which is manifest from the first verse of the next chapter, where he distinguisheth between "brethren" *to* whom and "Israel" *of* whom he spake. Secondly, He speaks of the Jews in the whole treatise in the third person, but of the disputer in the second. Thirdly, It is taken for a confessed principle between St Paul and the disputer, as he calls him, that the Jews were rejected, which surely themselves would not readily acknowledge. So that Corvinus rejects, as an objection of the Jews, a granted principle of St Paul and the other Christians of his time. With the like confidence the same author affirmeth, [2]"That they nothing doubt but that many things are not done which God would have to be done." Vorstius goes farther, teaching [3]"that not only many things are [not] done which he would have done, but also that many things are done which he would not have done." He means not

[1] "Ea sententia non continet apostoli verba, sed Judæorum objectionem ab apostolo rejectam."—Corv. ad Molin., cap. iii. per. 19.

[2] "Multa non fieri quæ Deus fieri vult, vel non dubitamus."—Ibid, cap. v. p. 5.

[3] "Multa fiunt quæ Deus fieri non vult: nec semper fiunt quæ ipse fiere vult."—Vorst. de Deo, p. 64.

our transgressing of his law, but God's failing in his purpose, as Corvinus clears it, acknowledging that the execution of God's will is suspended or hindered by man; to whom Episcopius subscribes.[1] As, for example, God purposeth and intendeth the conversion of a sinner,—suppose it were Mary Magdalene;—can this intention of his be crossed and his will resisted? "Yea," say the Arminians, "for God converts sinners by his grace." "But we can resist God when he would convert us by his grace,"[2] say six of them jointly in their meeting at the Hague. "But some one may here object," say they, "that thus God faileth of his intention, doth not attain the end at which he aims. We answer, This we grant." Or be it the salvation of men, they say, [3]"they are certain that God intendeth that for many which never obtain it;" that end he cannot compass.

And here, methinks, they place God in a most unhappy condition, by affirming that they are often damned whom he would have to be saved, though he desires their salvation with a most vehement desire and natural affection,[4]—such, I think, as crows have to the good of their young ones: for that there are in him such desires as are never fulfilled,[5] because not regulated by wisdom and justice, they plainly affirm; for although by his infinite power, perhaps, he might accomplish them, yet it would not become him so to do.

Now, let any good-natured man, who hath been a little troubled for poor Jupiter in Homer, mourning for the death of his son Sarpedon, which he could not prevent, or hath been grieved for the sorrow of a distressed father, not able to remove the wickedness and inevitable ruin of an only son, drop one tear for the restrained condition of the God of heaven, who, when he would have all and every man in the world to come to heaven, to escape the torments of hell, and that with a serious purpose and intention that it shall be so, a vehement affection and fervent natural desire that it should be so, yet, being not in himself alone able to save one, must be forced to lose his desire, lay down his affection, change his purpose, and see the greatest part of them to perish everlastingly,[6] yea, *notwith-*

[1] "Ab homine esse agnoscimus, quod voluntatis (divinæ) executio sæpe suspendatur."—Corv., ubi sup. parag. 12; Episcop. Disput. Pri. de Volun. Dei, corol. 5.

[2] "Possumus Deo resistere, cum nos vult per gratiam suam convertere."—Rem. Coll. Hag., p. 193. "Objiciet quis, ergo illum suum finem Deus non est assecutus, respondemus, nos hoc concedere."—Rem. Defens. Sent. in Synod., p. 256.

[3] "Nobis certum est, Deum multorum salutem intendere, in quibus eam non assequitur."—Grevinch. ad Ames., p. 271.

[4] "Vehemens est in Deo affectus ad homini benefaciendum."—Corv. ad Molin., cap. v. sect. 8.

[5] "Esse in Deo desideria quæ non implentur concedimus."—Idem, sect. 9. "Non decet ut Deus infinita sua potentia utatur ad id efficiendum, quo desiderio suo naturali fertur."—Armin. Antip., p. 584.

[6] "Deus eo fine et intentione remedium præparavit, ut omnes ejus actu fierent participes, quamvis id non actu evenit."—Rem. Apol., cap. vii. fol. 86.

standing that he had provided a sufficient means for them all to escape, with a purpose and intention that they should so do.

In brief, their whole doctrine on this point is laid down by Corvinus, chap. iii., against Moulin, and the third section; where, first, he alloweth of the distinction of the will of God into that whereby *he will have us do something, and that whereby he will do any thing himself.* The first is nothing but his law and precepts; which we with him affirm may be said to be resisted, inasmuch as it is transgressed. The latter, he saith, if it respect any act of man's, may be considered as preceding that act, or following it; if preceding it, then it may be resisted, if man will not co-operate. Now, this is the will of God, whereby himself intendeth to do any thing; the sum of which distinction is this, "The will of God concerning the future being of any thing may be considered as it goeth before the actual existence of the thing itself, and in this regard it may be hindered or resisted; but as it is considered to follow any act of man, it is always fulfilled:" by which latter member, striving to mollify the harshness of the former, he runs himself into inexplicable nonsense, affirming that that act of the will of God whereby he intendeth men shall do any thing cannot be hindered after they have done it,—that is, God hath irresistibly purposed they shall do it, provided they do it! In his following discourse, also, he plainly grants that there is no act of God's will about the salvation of men that may not be made void and of none effect, but only that general decree whereby he hath established an inseparable connection between faith and salvation, or whereby he hath appointed faith in Christ to be the means of attaining blessedness, which is only an immanent act of God's will, producing no outward effect; so that every act thereof that hath an external issue by human co-operation is frustrable and may fall to the ground: which in what direct opposition it stands to the word of God, let these following instances declare:—

First, "Our God is in the heavens," saith the psalmist: "he hath done whatsoever he hath pleased," Ps. cxv. 3. Not only part, but all, whatsoever he pleased should come to pass, by any means. "He ruleth in the kingdom of men, and giveth it to whomsoever he will," Dan. iv. 17. The transposition of kingdoms is not without the mixture of divers free and voluntary actions of men, and yet in that great work God doth all that he pleaseth. Yea, before him "all the inhabitants of the earth are reputed as nothing: and he doeth according to his will in the army of heaven, and among the inhabitants of the earth: and none can stay his hand, or say unto him, What doest thou?" verse 35. "My counsel," saith he, "shall stand, and I will do all my pleasure," Isa. xlvi. 10; "I have purposed, I will also do it," verse 11. Nay, so certain is he of accomplishing all his purposes, that he confirms it with an oath: "The LORD of hosts hath sworn, Surely as I have thought, so it shall come to pass; and as I have purposed, so shall it stand," Isa. xiv. 24. And indeed it were a very strange thing, that God should intend what he foreseeth will never come to pass. But I confess this argument will not be pressing against the Arminians, who question that prescience; but yet, would they also would observe from the Scripture, that the failing of wicked men's counsels and intentions is a thing that God is said to "deride in heaven," as Ps. ii. 4. He threatens them with it. "Take counsel together," saith he, "and it shall come to nought; speak the word, and it shall not stand," Isa. viii. 10. See also chap. xxix. 7, 8. And shall they be enabled to recriminate, and cast the like aspersion on the God of heaven? No, surely. Saith St Austin, [1]"Let us take heed we be not compelled to believe that Almighty God would have any thing done which doth not come to pass." To which truth, also, that the schoolmen have universally consented is showed by Alvarez, Disput. xxxii. pro. 3. And these few instances will manifest the Arminian opposition to the word of God in this particular:—

S. S.	Lib. Arbit.
"Our God is in the heavens: he hath done whatsoever he hath pleased," Ps. cxv. 3.	"We nothing doubt but many things which God willeth, or that it pleaseth him to have done, do yet never come to pass," Corvinus. "We grant that some of God's desires are never fulfilled," Idem.
"I will do all my pleasure." Isa. xlvi. 10. "None can stay his hand, or say unto him, What doest thou?" Dan. iv. 35.	"It is in the power of man to hinder the execution of God's will," Idem.
"I have purposed, I will also do it," Isa. xlvi. 11.	"It is ridiculous to imagine that God doth not seriously will any thing but what taketh effect," Episcopius.
"As I have purposed, so shall it stand," Isa. xiv. 24.	"It may be objected that God faileth of his end: this we readily grant," Rem. Synod.

[1] "Ne credere cogamur aliquid omnipotentem Deum voluisse factumque non esse."—Aug. En., cap. ciii.

CHAPTER VI.

How the whole doctrine of predestination is corrupted by the Arminians.

THE cause of all these quarrels, wherewith the Arminians and their abettors have troubled the church of Christ, comes next unto our consideration. The eternal predestination of Almighty God, that fountain of all spiritual blessings, of all the effects of God's love derived unto us through Christ, the demolishing of this rock of our salvation hath been the chief endeavour of all the patrons of human self-sufficiency; so to vindicate unto themselves a power and independent ability of doing good, of making themselves to differ from others, of attaining everlasting happiness, without going one step from without themselves. And this is their first attempt, to attain their second proposed end, of building a tower from the top whereof they may mount into heaven, whose foundation is nothing but the sand of their own free-will and endeavours. Quite on a sudden (what they have done in effect) to have taken away this divine predestination, name and thing, had been an attempt as noted as notorious, and not likely to attain the least success amongst men professing to believe the gospel of Christ; wherefore, suffering the name to remain, they have abolished the thing itself, and substituted another so unlike it in the room thereof, that any one may see they have gotten a blear-eyed Leah instead of Rachel, and hug a cloud instead of a Deity. The true doctrine itself hath been so excellently delivered by divers learned divines, so freed from all objections, that I shall only briefly and plainly lay it down, and that with special reference to the seventeenth article of our church, where it is clearly avowed; showing withal,—which is my chief intention,—how it is thwarted, opposed, and overthrown by the Arminians. *Predestination, in the usual sense [in which] it is taken, is a part of God's providence concerning his creatures, distinguished from it by a double restriction:—*

First, In respect of their *objects;* for whereas the decree of providence comprehendeth his intentions towards all the works of his hands, predestination respecteth only rational creatures.

Secondly, In regard of their *ends;* for whereas his providence directeth all creatures in general to those several ends to which at length they are brought, whether they are proportioned unto their nature or exceeding the sphere of their natural activity, predestination is exercised only in directing rational creatures to supernatural ends: so that, in general, it is *the counsel, decree, or purpose of Almighty God concerning the last and supernatural end of his rational crea-*

tures, to be accomplished for the praise of his glory. But this also must receive a double restriction before we come precisely to what we in this place aim at: and these again in regard of the objects or the ends thereof.

The object of predestination is all rational creatures. Now, these are either angels or men. Of angels I shall not treat. Secondly, The end by it provided for them is either eternal happiness or eternal misery. I speak only of the former,—the act of God's predestination transmitting men to everlasting happiness: and in this restrained sense it differs not at all from election, and we may use them as *synonyma,* terms of the same importance; though, by some affirming that God predestinateth them to faith whom he hath chosen, they seem to be distinguished as the decrees of the end, and the means conducing thereunto, whereof the first is election, intending the end, and then takes place predestination, providing the means. But this exact distinction appeareth not directly in the Scripture.

This election the word of God proposeth unto us as the gracious, immutable decree of Almighty God, whereby, *before the foundation of the world, out of his own good pleasure, he chose certain men, determining to free them from sin and misery, to bestow upon them grace and faith, to give them unto Christ, to bring them to everlasting blessedness, for the praise of his glorious grace;* or, as it is expressed in our church articles, "Predestination to life is the everlasting purpose of God, whereby, before the foundations of the world were laid, he hath constantly decreed by his counsel, secret to us, to deliver from curse and damnation those whom he hath chosen in Christ out of mankind, and to bring them by Christ unto everlasting salvation, as vessels made unto honour; wherefore, they who are endued with so excellent a benefit of God be called according to God's purpose," etc.

Now, to avoid prolixity, I will annex only such annotations as may clear the sense and confirm the truth of the article by the Scriptures, and show briefly how it is overthrown by the Arminians in every particular thereof:—

First, The article, consonantly to the Scripture, affirmeth that *it is an eternal decree, made before the foundations of the world were laid;* so that by it we must needs be chosen before we were born, before we have done either good or evil. The words of the article are clear, and so also is the Scripture: "He hath chosen us in him before the foundation of the world," Eph. i. 4; "The children being not yet born, neither having done any good or evil, it was said," etc., Rom. ix. 11, 12; "We are called with an holy calling, not according to our works, but according to his own purpose and grace, which was given us in Christ Jesus before the world began," 2 Tim. i. 9.

Now, from hence it would undoubtedly follow that no good thing in us can be the cause of our election, for every cause must in order precede its effect; but all things whereof we by any means are partakers, inasmuch as they are ours, are temporary, and so cannot be the cause of that which is eternal. Things with that qualification must have reference to the sole will and good pleasure of God; which reference would break the neck of the Arminian election. Wherefore, to prevent such a fatal ruin, they deny the principle,—to wit, that election is eternal.[1] So the Remonstrants, in their Apology: [2]"Complete election regardeth none but him that is dying; for this peremptory election decreeth the whole accomplishment and consummation of salvation, and therefore requireth in the object the finished course of faith and obedience," saith Grevinchovius; which is to make God's election nothing but an act of his justice, approving our obedience, and such an act as is incident to any weak man, who knows not what will happen in the next hour that is yet for to come. And is this post-destination that which is proposed to us in the Scripture as the unsearchable fountain of all God's love towards us in Christ? "Yea,"[3] say they, "we acknowledge no other predestination to be revealed in the gospel besides that whereby God decreeth to save them who should persevere in faith;" that is, God's determination concerning their salvatión is pendulous, until he find by experience that they will persevere in obedience. But I wonder why, seeing election is confessedly one of the greatest expressions of God's infinite goodness, love, and mercy towards us, if it follow our obedience, we have it not, like all other blessings and mercies, promised unto us. Is it not because such propositions as these, "Believe, Peter, and continue in the faith unto the end, and I will choose thee before the foundation of the world," are fitter for the writings of the Arminians than the word of God? Neither will we be their rivals in such an election, as from whence no fruit,[4] no effect, no consolation can be derived to any mortal man, whilst he lives in this world.

Secondly, The article affirmeth that it is *constant*,—that is, one immutable decree; agreeably also to the Scriptures, teaching but one purpose, but one foreknowledge, one good pleasure, one decree of God, concerning the infallible ordination of his elect unto glory; although of this decree there may be said to be two acts,—one con-

[1] "Electio non est ab æterno."—Rem. Apol.

[2] "Electio alia completa est, quæ neminem spectat nisi immorientem. Electio peremptoria totum salutis complementum et consummationem decernit, ideoque in objecto requirit totam consummatam fidei obedientiam."—Grevinch. ad Ames. p. 136, passim. dis.

[3] "Non agnoscimus aliam prædestinationem in evangelio patefactam, quam qua Deus decrevit credentes et qui in eadem fide perseverarent, salvos facere."—Rem. Coll. Hag., p. 34.

[4] "Electionis fructum aut sensum in hac vita nullum agnosco."—Grevinch.

cerning the means, the other concerning the end, but both knit up in the "immutability of God's counsel," Heb. vi. 17. "The foundation of God standeth sure, having this seal, The Lord knoweth them that are his," 2 Tim. ii. 19; "His gifts and calling are without recalling," not to be repented of, Rom. xi. 29. Now, what say our Arminians to this? Why, a whole multitude of notions and terms have they invented to obscure the doctrine. "Election," say they,[1] "is either legal or evangelical, general or particular, complete or incomplete, revocable or irrevocable, peremptory or not peremptory," with I know not how many more distinctions of one single eternal act of Almighty God, whereof there is neither "vola nec vestigium," sign or token, in the whole Bible, or any approved author. And to these quavering divisions they accommodate their doctrine, or rather they purposely invented them to make their errors unintelligible. Yet something agreeably thus they dictate: [2]"There is a complete election, belonging to none but those that are dying; and there is another, incomplete, common to all that believe: as the good things of salvation are incomplete which are continued whilst faith is continued, and revoked when that is denied, so election is incomplete in this life, and revocable." Again: "There are," they say in their Confession, [3]"three orders of believers and repenters in the Scripture, whereof some are beginners, others having continued for a time, and some perseverants. The first two orders are chosen *verè*, truly, but not *absolutè prorsus*, absolutely, but only for a time,—so long as they will remain as they are; the third are chosen finally and peremptorily: for this act of God is either continued or interrupted, according as we fulfil the condition." But whence learned the Arminians this doctrine? Not one word of it from the word of truth; no mention there of any such desultory election, no speech of faith, but such as is consequent to one eternal irrevocable decree of predestination: They "believed" who were "ordained to eternal life," Acts xiii. 48. No distinction of men half and wholly elected, where it is affirmed that it is impossible the elect should be seduced, Matt. xxiv. 24,—that none should snatch Christ's sheep out of his Father's hand, John x. 28, 29. What would they have more? God's purpose of election is sealed up, 2 Tim. ii. 19, and therefore cannot be revoked; it must stand firm, Rom. ix. 11, in spite of all opposition. Neither will reason allow us to think any

[1] Episcop. Thes., p. 35; Epist. ad Walach., p. 38; Grevinch. ad Ames., p. 133.

[2] "Electio alia completa est, quæ neminem spectat nisi morientem, alia incompleta, quæ omnibus fidelibus communis est; ut salutis bona sunt incompleta quæ continuantur, fide continuatâ, et abnegatâ revocantur, sic electio est incompleta in hac vita, non peremptoria, revocabilis."—Grevinch. ad Ames.

[3] "Tres sunt ordines credentium et resipiscentium in Scripturis, novitii, credentes aliquandiu, perseverantes. Duo priores ordines credentium eliguntur vere quidem, at non prorsus absolute, nec nisi ad tempus, puta quamdiu et quatenus tales sunt," etc. —Rem. Confess., cap. xviii. sect. 6, 7.

immanent act of God to be incomplete or revocable, because of the mere alliance it hath with his very nature. But reason, Scripture, God himself, all must give place to any absurdities, if they stand in the Arminian way, bringing in their idol with shouts, and preparing his throne, by claiming the cause of their predestination to be in themselves.

Thirdly, The article is clear that the object of this predestination is *some particular men chosen out of mankind;* that is, it is such an act of God as concerneth some men in particular, taking them, as it were, aside from the midst of their brethren, and designing them for some special end and purpose. The Scripture also aboundeth in asserting this verity, calling them that are so chosen a "few," Matt. xx. 16, which must needs denote some certain persons; and the "remnant according to election," Rom. xi. 5; those whom "the Lord knoweth to be his," 2 Tim. ii. 19; men "ordained to eternal life," Acts xiii. 48; "us," Rom. viii. 39; those that are "written in the Lamb's book of life," Rev. xxi. 27;—all which, and divers others, clearly prove that the number of the elect is certain, not only materially, as they say,[1] that there are so many, but formally also, that these particular persons, and no other, are they, which cannot be altered. Nay, the very nature of the thing itself doth so demonstratively evince it, that I wonder it can possibly be conceived under any other notion. To apprehend an election of men not circumscribed with the circumstance of particular persons is such a conceited, Platonical abstraction, as it seems strange that any one dares profess to understand that there should be a predestination, and none predestinated; an election, and none elected; a choice amongst many, yet none left or taken; a decree to save men, and yet thereby salvation destinated to no one man, either "re aut spe," in deed or in expectation. In a word, that there should be a purpose of God to bring men unto glory, standing inviolable, though never any one attained the purposed end, is such a riddle as no Œdipus can unfold. Now, such an election, such a predestination, have the Arminians substituted in the place of God's everlasting decree. "We deny,"[2] say they, "that God's election extendeth itself to any singular persons as singular persons;" that is, that any particular persons, as Peter, Paul, John, are by it elected. No; how, then? Why, [3]"God hath appointed, without difference, to dispense the means of faith; and as he seeth these persons to believe or not to believe by the use of those means, so at length he deter-

[1] Aquinas.

[2] "Nos negamus Dei electionem ad salutem extendere sese ad singulares personas, qua singulares personas."—Rem. Coll. Hag., fol. 76.

[3] "Deus statuit indiscriminatim media ad fidem administrare, et prout has, vel illas personas, istis mediis credituras vel non credituras videt, ita tandem de illis statuit."—Corv. ad Tilen., 76.

mineth of them," as saith Corvinus. Well, then, God chooseth no particular man to salvation, but whom he seeth believing by his own power, with the help only of such means as are afforded unto others who never believe; and as he maketh himself thus differ from them by a good use of his own abilities, so also he may be reduced again unto the same predicament, and then his election, which respecteth not him in his person, but only his qualification, quite vanisheth. But is this God's decree of election? "Yes," say they; and make a doleful complaint that any other doctrine should be taught in the church. [1]"It is obtruded," say the true-born sons of Arminius, "on the church as a most holy doctrine, that God, by an absolute, immutable decree, from all eternity, out of his own good pleasure, hath chosen certain persons, and those but few in comparison, without any respect had to their faith and obedience, and predestinated them to everlasting life." But what so great exception is this doctrine liable unto, what wickedness doth it include, that it should not be accounted most holy? Nay, is not only the matter but the very terms of it contained in the Scripture? Doth it not say the elect are few, and they chosen before the foundation of the world, without any respect to their obedience or any thing that they had done, out of God's mere gracious good pleasure, that his free purpose according to election might stand, even because so it pleased him; and this that they might be holy, believe, and be sanctified, that they might come unto Christ, and by him be preserved unto everlasting life? Yea, this is that which galls them: [2]"No such will can be ascribed unto God, whereby he so willeth any one to be saved as that thence their salvation should be sure and infallible," saith the father of those children.

Well, then, let St Austin's definition be quite rejected, [3]"That predestination is a preparation of such benefits whereby some are most certainly freed and delivered from sin and brought to glory;" and that also of St Paul, "That (by reason of this) nothing can separate us from the love of God, which is in Christ." What is this election in your judgment? [4]"Nothing but a decree whereby God hath appointed to save them that believe in Christ," saith Corvinus, be they who they will; or a general purpose of God, whereby he hath ordained faith in Christ to be the means of salvation. Yea, but this belongs

[1] "Ecclesiæ tanquam sacrosancta doctrina obtruditur, Deum absolutissimo et immutabili decreto ab omni retro æternitate, pro puro suo beneplacito, singulares quosdam homines, eosque, quoad cæteros, paucissimos, citra ullius obedientiæ aut fidei in Christum intuitum prædestinasse ad vitam."—Præfat. Lib. Armin. ad Perk.

[2] "Nulla Deo tribui potest voluntas, qua ita velit hominem ullum salvari, ut salus inde illis constet certo et infallibiliter."—Armin. Antip., p. 583.

[3] "Prædestinatio est præparatio beneficiorum quibus certissime liberantur quicunque liberantur."—Aug. de Bono Per. Sen., cap. xiv.

[4] "Decretum electionis nihil aliud est quam decretum quo Deus constituit credentes in Christo justificare et salvare."—Corv. ad Tilen., p. 13.

to Judas as well as to Peter. This decree carrieth as equal an aspect to those that are damned as to those that are saved. Salvation, under the condition of faith in Christ, was also proposed to them; but was Judas and all his company elected? How came they, then, to be seduced and perish? That any of God's elect go to hell is as yet a strange assertion in Christianity. Notwithstanding this decree, none may believe, or all that do may fall away, and so none at all be saved; which is a strange kind of predestination: or all may believe, continue in faith, and be saved; which were a more strange kind of election.

We, poor souls, thought hitherto that we might have believed, according unto Scripture, that some by this purpose were in a peculiar manner made the Father's ("Thine they were"), and by him given unto Christ, that he might bring them unto glory; and that these men were so certain and unchangeable a number, that not only God "knoweth them" as being "his," but also that Christ "calleth them by name," John x. 3, and looketh that none taketh them out of his hand. We never imagined before that Christ hath been the mediator of an uncertain covenant, because there are no certain persons covenanted withal but such as may or may not fulfil the condition. We always thought that some had been separated before by God's purpose from the rest of the perishing world, that Christ might lay down his life for his "friends," for his "sheep," for them that were "given him" of his Father. But now it should seem he was ordained to be a king when it was altogether uncertain whether he should ever have any subjects, to be a head without a body, or to such a church whose collection and continuance depend wholly and solely on the will of men.

These are doctrines that I believe searchers of the Scripture had scarce ever been acquainted withal, had they not lighted on such expositors as teach, [1]"That the only cause why God loveth" (or chooseth) "any person is, because the honesty, faith, and piety wherewith, according to God's command and his own duty, he is endued, are acceptable to God;" which, though we grant it true of God's consequent or approving love, yet surely there is a divine love wherewith he looks upon us otherwise, when he gives us unto Christ, else either our giving unto Christ is not out of love, or we are pious, just, and faithful before we come unto him,—that is, we have no need of him at all. Against either way, though we may blot these testimonies out of our hearts, yet they will stand still recorded in holy Scripture,—namely, that God so loved us when we were his "enemies," Rom. v. 10, "sinners," verse 8, of no "strength," verse 6; that "he gave his only-begotten Son" to die, "that we should not perish, but have everlasting life," John iii. 16. But of this enough.

[1] "Ratio dilectionis personæ est, quod probitas, fides, vel pietas, qua ex officio suo et præscripto Dei ista persona prædita est, Deo grata sit."—Rem. Apol., p. 13.

Fourthly, Another thing that the article asserteth according to the Scripture is, that *there is no other cause of our election but God's own counsel.* It recounteth no motives in us, nothing impelling the will of God to choose some out of mankind, rejecting others, but his own decree,—that is, his absolute will and good pleasure; so that as there is no cause, in any thing without himself, why he would create the world or elect any at all,—for he doth all these things for himself, for the praise of his own glory,—so there is no cause in singular elected persons why God should choose them rather than others. He looked upon all mankind in the same condition, vested with the same qualifications, or rather without any at all; for *it is the children not yet born, before they do either good or evil, that are chosen or rejected,* his free grace embracing the one and passing over the other. Yet here we must observe, that although God freely, without any desert of theirs, chooseth some men to be partakers both of the end and the means, yet he bestoweth faith, or the means, on none but for the merit of Christ; neither do any attain the end or salvation but by their own faith, through that righteousness of his. The free grace of God notwithstanding, choosing Jacob when Esau is rejected, the only antecedent cause of any difference between the elect and reprobates, remaineth firm and unshaken; and surely, unless men were resolved to trust wholly to their own bottoms, to take nothing gratis at the hands of God, they would not endeavour to rob him of his glory, of having mercy on whom he will have mercy, of loving us without our desert before the world began. If we must claim an interest in obtaining the temporal acts of his favour by our own endeavours, yet, oh, let us grant him the glory of being good unto us, only for his own sake, when we were in his hand as the clay in the hand of the potter. What made this piece of clay fit for comely service, and not a vessel wherein there is no pleasure, but the power and will of the Framer? It is enough, yea, too much, for them to repine and say, "Why hast thou made us thus?" who are vessels fitted for wrath. Let not them who are prepared for honour exalt themselves against him, and sacrifice to their own nets, as the sole providers of their glory. But so it is: human vileness will still be declaring itself, by claiming a worth no way due unto it; of a furtherance of which claim if the Arminians be not guilty, let the following declaration of their opinions in this particular determine:—

"We confess," say they,[1] "roundly, that faith, in the consideration of God choosing us unto salvation, doth precede, and not follow as a fruit of election." So that whereas Christians have hitherto believed that God bestoweth faith on them that are chosen, it seems now it is

[1] "Rotunde fatemur, fidem in consideratione Dei in eligendo ad salutem antecedere, et non tanquam fructum electionis sequi."—Rem. Hag. Coll., p. 35.

no such matter, but that those whom God findeth to believe, upon the stock of their own abilities, he afterward chooseth. Neither is faith, in their judgment, only required as a necessary condition in him that is to be chosen, but as a cause moving the will of God to elect him that hath it, [1]" as the will of the judge is moved to bestow a reward on him who according to the law hath deserved it," as Grevinchovius speaks: which words of his, indeed, Corvinus strives to temper, but all in vain, though he wrest them contrary to the intention of the author; for with him agree all his fellows. [2]" The one only absolute cause of election is, not the will of God, but the respect of our obedience," saith Episcopius. At first they required nothing but faith, and that as a condition, not as a cause;[3] then perseverance in faith, which at length they began to call obedience, comprehending all our duty to the precepts of Christ: for the cause, say they, of this love to any person, is the righteousness, faith, and piety wherewith he is endued; which being all the good works of a Christian, they, in effect, affirm a man to be chosen for them,—that our good works are the cause of election; which whether it were ever so grossly taught, either by Pelagians or Papists, I something doubt.

And here observe, that this doth not thwart my former assertion, where I showed that they deny the election of any particular persons, which here they seem to grant upon a foresight of their faith and good works; for there is not any one person, as such a person, notwithstanding all this, that in their judgment is in this life elected, but only as he is considered with those qualifications of which he may at any time divest himself, and so become again to be no more elected than Judas.

The sum of their doctrine in this particular is laid down by one of ours in a tract entitled " God's Love to Mankind," etc.; a book full of palpable ignorance, gross sophistry, and abominable blasphemy, whose author seems to have proposed nothing unto himself but to rake all the dunghills of a few of the most invective Arminians, and to collect the most filthy scum and pollution of their railings to cast upon the truth of God; and, under I know not what self-coined pretences, belch out odious blasphemies against his holy name.

The sum, saith he, of all these speeches (he cited to his purpose) is, [4]" That there is no decree of saving men but what is built on God's foreknowledge of the good actions of men." No decree? No, not that whereby God determineth to give some unto Christ, to ingraft

[1] Grevinch. ad Ames., p. 24; Corv. ad Molin., p. 260.

[2] " Electionis et reprobationis causa unica vera et absoluta non est Dei voluntas, sed respectus obedientiæ et inobedientiæ."—Epis. Disput. viii.

[3] " Cum peccatum pono causam meritoriam reprobationis, ne existimato e contra me ponere justitiam causam meritoriam electionis."—Armin. Antip.; Rem. Apol., p. 73.

[4] God's Love, p. 6.

them in him by faith, and bring them by him unto glory; which giveth light to that place of Arminius, where he affirmeth, [1]"That God loveth none precisely to eternal life but considered as just, either with legal or evangelical righteousness." Now, to love one to eternal life is to destinate one to obtain eternal life by Christ, and so it is coincident with the former assertion, that our election, or choosing unto grace and glory, is upon the foresight of our good works; which contains a doctrine so contradictory to the words and meaning of the apostle, Rom. ix. 11, condemned in so many councils, suppressed by so many edicts and decrees of emperors and governors, opposed as a pestilent heresy, ever since it was first hatched, by so many orthodox fathers and learned schoolmen, so directly contrary to the doctrine of this church, so injurious to the grace and supreme power of Almighty God, that I much wonder any one, in this light of the gospel and flourishing time of learning, should be so boldly ignorant or impudent as to broach it amongst Christians. To prove this to be a heresy exploded by all orthodox and catholic antiquity were to light a candle in the sun; for it cannot but be known to all and every one who ever heard or read any thing of the state of Christ's church after the rising of the Pelagian tumults.[2]

To accumulate testimonies of the ancients is quite beside my purpose. I will only add the confession of Bellarmine,[3] a man otherwise not over-well affected to truth. "Predestination," saith he, "from the foresight of works, cannot be maintained unless we should suppose something in the righteous man, which should make him differ from the wicked, that he doth not receive from God; which truly all the fathers with unanimous consent do reject." But we have a more sure testimony, to which we will take heed, even the holy Scripture, pleading strongly for God's free and undeserved grace.

First, our Saviour Christ, Matt. xi. 26, declaring how God revealeth the gospel unto some, which is hidden from others (a special fruit of election), resteth in his will and good pleasure as the only cause thereof: "Even so, Father; for so it seemed good in thy sight." So, comforting his "little flock," Luke xii. 32, he bids them fear not, "for it is your Father's good pleasure to give you the kingdom;"—"His good pleasure is the only cause why his kingdom is prepared for you rather than others." But is there no other reason of this discrimination? No; he doth it all "that his purpose according to election might stand" firm, Rom. ix. 11; for we are "predestinated

[1] "Deum nullam creaturam præcise ad vitam æternam amare, nisi consideratam ut justam sive justitia legali sive evangelica."—Armin. Artic. Perpend., fol. 21.

[2] Vid. Prosp. ad Excep. Gen. ad Dub., 8, 9. Vid. Car. de Ingratis., c. 2, 3.

[3] "Non potest defendi prædestinatio ex operibus prævisis, nisi aliquid boni ponatur in homine justo, quo discernatur ab impio, quod non sit illi a Deo, quod sane patres omnes summa consensione rejiciunt."—Bellar. de Grat., et Lib. Arbit., cap. xiv.

according to the purpose of him who worketh all things after the counsel of his own will," Eph. i. 11. But did not this counsel of God direct him to choose us rather than others because we had something to commend us more than they? No; "The LORD did not set his love upon you, nor choose you, because ye were more in number than any people; but because the LORD loved you," Deut. vii. 7, 8. "He hath mercy on whom he will have mercy;" yea, "the children being not yet born, neither having done any good or evil, that the purpose of God according to election might stand, not of works, but of him that calleth, it was said unto her, The elder shall serve the younger: as it is written, Jacob have I loved, but Esau have I hated," Rom. ix. 11–13. In brief, wherever there is any mention of election or predestination, it is still accompanied with the purpose, love, or will of God; his foreknowledge, whereby he knoweth them that are his; his free power and supreme dominion over all things. Of our faith, obedience, or any thing importing so much, not one syllable, no mention, unless it be as the fruit and effect thereof. It is the sole act of his free grace and good pleasure, that "he might make known the riches of his glory on the vessels of mercy," Rom. ix. 23. For this only end hath he "saved us, and called us with an holy calling, not according to our works, but according to his own purpose and grace, which was given us in Christ Jesus before the world began," 2 Tim. i. 9. Even our calling is free and undeserved, because flowing from that most free grace of election, whereof we are partakers before we are [*i.e.*, exist]. It were needless to heap up more testimonies in a thing so clear and evident. When God and man stand in competition who shall be accounted the cause of an eternal good, we may be sure the Scripture will pass the verdict on the part of the Most High. And the sentence, in this case, may be derived from thence by these following reasons:—

First, If final perseverance in faith and obedience be the cause of, or a condition required unto, election, then none can be said in this life to be elected; for no man is a final perseverer until he be dead, until he hath finished his course and consummated the faith. But certain it is that it is spoken of some in the Scripture that they are even in this life elected: "Few are chosen," Matt. xx. 16; "For the elect's sake those days shall be shortened," chap. xxiv. 22; "And shall, if it were possible, deceive the very elect," verse 24,—where it is evident that election is required to make one persevere in the faith, but nowhere is perseverance in the faith required to election; yea, and Peter gives us all a command that we should give all diligence to get an assurance of our "election," even in this life, 2 Pet. i. 10: and, therefore, surely it cannot be a decree presupposing consummated faith and obedience.

Secondly, Consider two things of our estate, before the first temporal act of God's free grace (for grace is no grace if it be not free), which is the first effect of our predestination, comprehendeth us:—*First*, "Were we better than others? No, in no wise: both Jews and Gentiles were all under sin," Rom. iii. 9. "There is no difference; for all have sinned, and come short of the glory of God," verse 23;—being all "dead in trespasses and sins," Eph. ii. 1; being "by nature the children of wrath, even as others," verse 3; "far off," until we are "made nigh by the blood of Christ," verse 13. We were "enemies" against God, Rom. v. 10; Titus iii. 3. And look what desert there is in us with these qualifications, when our vocation, the first effect of our predestination, as St Paul showeth, Rom. viii. 30, and as I shall prove hereafter, separateth us from the world of unbelievers. So much there is in respect of predestination itself; so that if we have any way deserved it, it is by being sinners, enemies, children of wrath, and dead in trespasses. These are our deserts; this is the glory, whereof we ought to be ashamed. But, *secondly*, When they are in the same state of actual alienation from God, yet then, in respect of his purpose to save them by Christ, some are said to be his: "Thine they were, and thou gavest them me," John xvii. 6;—they were his before they came unto Christ by faith; the sheep of Christ before they are called, for he "calleth his sheep by name," chap. x. 3; before they come into the flock or congregation, for "other sheep," saith he, "I have, which are not of this fold, them also must I bring," chap. x. 16;—to be beloved of God before they love him: "Herein is love, not that we loved God, but that he loved us," 1 John iv. 10. Now, all this must be with reference to God's purpose of bringing them unto Christ, and by him unto glory; which we see goeth before all their faith and obedience.

Thirdly, Election is an eternal act of God's will: "He hath chosen us before the foundation of the world," Eph. i. 4; consummated antecedently to all duty of ours, Rom. ix. 11. Now, every cause must, in order of nature, precede its effect; nothing hath an activity in causing before it hath a being. Operation in every kind is a second act, flowing from the essence of a thing which is the first. But all our graces and works, our faith, obedience, piety, and charity, are all temporal, of yesterday, the same standing with ourselves, and no longer; and therefore cannot be the cause of, no, nor so much as a condition necessarily required for, the accomplishment of an eternal act of God, irrevocably established before we are.

Fourthly, If predestination be for faith foreseen, these three things, with divers such absurdities, will necessarily follow:—*First*, That election is not of "him that calleth," as the apostle speaks, Rom. ix. 11,—that is, of the good pleasure of God, who calleth us with a holy calling,—but of him that is called; for, depending on faith, it must be his whose faith is, that doth believe. *Secondly,* God cannot have mercy on whom he will have mercy, for the very purpose of it is thus tied to the qualities of faith and obedience, so that he must have mercy only on believers antecedently to his decree. Which, *thirdly,* hinders him from being an absolute free agent, and doing of what he will with his own,—of having such a power over us as the potter hath over his clay; for he finds us of different matter, one clay, another gold, when he comes to appoint us to different uses and ends.

Fifthly, God sees no faith, no obedience, perseverance, nothing but sin and wickedness, in any man, but what himself intendeth graciously and freely to bestow upon him; for "faith is not of ourselves, it is the gift of God;" it is "the work of God, that we believe," John vi. 29; he "blesseth us with all spiritual blessings in Christ," Eph. i. 3. Now, all these gifts and graces God bestoweth only upon those whom he hath antecedently ordained to everlasting life: for "the election obtained it, and the rest were blinded," Rom. xi. 7; "The Lord added to the church daily such as should be saved," Acts ii. 47. Therefore, surely, God chooseth us not because he foreseeth those things in us, seeing he bestoweth those graces because he hath chosen us. "Wherefore,"[1] saith Austin, "doth Christ say, 'Ye have not chosen me, but I have chosen you,' but because they did not choose him that he should choose them; but he chose them that they might choose him." We choose Christ by faith; God chooseth us by his decree of election. The question is, Whether we choose him because he hath chosen us, or he chooseth us because we have chosen him, and so indeed choose ourselves? We affirm the former, and that because our choice of him is a gift he himself bestoweth only on them whom he hath chosen.

Sixthly, and principally, The effects of election, infallibly following it, cannot be the causes of election, certainly preceding it. This is evident, for nothing can be the cause and the effect of the same thing, before and after itself. But all our faith, our obedience, repentance, good works, are the effects of election, flowing from it as their proper fountain, erected on it as the foundation of this spiritual building; and for this the article of our church is evident and clear. "Those," saith it, "that are endued with this excellent benefit of God are called according to God's purpose, are justified freely, are made the sons of God by adoption; they be made like the image of Christ; they walk religiously in good works," etc. Where, *first,* they are said to be partakers of this benefit of election, and then by virtue thereof to be entitled to the fruition of all those graces. *Secondly,* it

[1] "Non ob aliud dicit, 'Non vos me eligistis, sed ego vos elegi,' nisi quia non elegerunt eum ut eligeret eos; sed ut eligerent eum elegit eos."—Aug. de Bono Perse., cap. xvi.

saith, "Those who are endued with this benefit enjoy those blessings;" intimating that election is the rule whereby God proceedeth in bestowing those graces, restraining the objects of the temporal acts of God's special favour to them only whom his eternal decree doth embrace. Both these, indeed, are denied by the Arminians; which maketh a farther discovery of their heterodoxies in this particular. [1]"You say," saith Arminius to Perkins, "that election is the rule of giving or not giving of faith; and, therefore, election is not of the faithful, but faith of the elect: but by your leave this I must deny." But yet, whatever it is the sophistical heretic here denies, either antecedent or conclusion, he falls foul on the word of God. "They 'believed,'" saith the Holy Ghost, "who were 'ordained to eternal life,'" Acts xiii. 48; and, "The Lord added to the church daily such as should be saved," chap. ii. 47. From both which places it is evident that God bestoweth faith only on them whom he hath pre-ordained to eternal life; but most clearly, Rom. viii. 29, 30, "For whom he did foreknow, he also did predestinate to be conformed to the image of his Son. Moreover whom he did predestinate, them he also called: and whom he called, them he also justified: and whom he justified, them he also glorified." St Austin interpreted this place by adding in every link of the chain, "Only those." However, the words directly import a precedency of predestination before the bestowing of other graces, and also a restraint of those graces to them only that are so predestinated. Now, the inference from this is not only for the form logical, but for the matter also; it containeth the very words of Scripture, "Faith is of God's elect," Tit. i. 1.

For the other part of the proposition, that faith and obedience are the fruits of our election, they cannot be more peremptory in its denial than the Scripture is plentiful in its confirmation: "He hath chosen us in Christ, that we should be holy," Eph. i. 4; not because we were holy, but that we should be so. Holiness, whereof faith is the root and obedience the body, is that whereunto, and not for which, we are elected. The end and the meritorious cause of any one act cannot be the same; they have divers respects, and require repugnant conditions. Again; we are "predestinated unto the adoption of children by Jesus Christ," verse 5. Adoption is that whereby we are assumed into the family of God, when before we are "foreigners, aliens, strangers, afar off;" which we see is a fruit of our predestination, though it be the very entrance into that estate wherein we begin first to please God in the least measure. Of the same nature are all those places of holy writ which speak of God's giving some unto

[1] "Dicis electionem divinam esse regulam fidei dandæ vel non dandæ; ergo, electio non est fidelium, sed fides electorum: sed liceat mihi tua bona venia hoc negare."—Armin. Antip., p. 221.

Christ, of Christ's sheep hearing his voice, and others not hearing, because they are not of his sheep; all which, and divers other invincible reasons, I willingly omit, with sundry other false assertions and heretical positions of the Arminians about this fundamental article of our religion, concluding this chapter with the following scheme:—

S. S.	Lib. Arbit.
"Whom he did foreknow, he also did predestinate to be conformed to the image of his Son, that he might be the first-born among many brethren. Moreover whom he did predestinate, them he also called: and whom he called, them he also justified: and whom he justified, them he also glorified." So that "nothing shall be able to separate us from the love of God, which is in Christ Jesus," Rom. viii. 29, 30, 39.	"No such will can be ascribed unto God, whereby he so would have any to be saved, that from thence his salvation should be sure and infallible," Armin. "I acknowledge no sense, no perception of any such election in this life," Grevinch. "We deny that God's election unto salvation extendeth itself to singular persons," Rem. Coll. Hag.
"He hath chosen us in him before the foundation of the world, that we should be holy," Eph. i. 4.	"As we are justified by faith, so we are not elected but by faith," Grevinch.
"Not according to our works, but according to his own purpose and grace, which was given us in Christ Jesus before the world began," 2 Tim. i. 9.	"We profess roundly that faith is considered by God as a condition preceding election, and not following as a fruit thereof," Rem. Coll. Hag.
"For the children being not yet born, neither having done any good or evil, that the purpose of God according to election might stand, not of works, but of him that calleth," etc., Rom. ix. 11. "All that the Father giveth me shall come to me," John vi. 37.	"The sole and only cause of election is not the will of God, but the respect of our obedience," Episcop. "For the cause of this love to any person is, [that] the goodness, faith, and piety, wherewith, according to God's command and his own duty, he is endued, are pleasing to God," Rem. Apol.
"Many are called, but few are chosen," Matt. xxii. 14. "Fear not, little flock; for it is your Father's good pleasure to give you the kingdom," Luke xii. 32.	"God hath determined to grant the means of salvation unto all without difference; and according as he foreseeth men will use those means, so he determineth of them," Corv.

S. S.

"What hast thou that thou didst not receive?" 1 Cor. iv. 7. "Are we better than they? No, in no wise," Rom. iii. 9. But we are "predestinated to the adoption of children by Jesus Christ, according to the good pleasure of his will," Eph. i. 5; John vi. 37–39, x. 3, xiii. 18, xvii. 6; Acts xiii. 48; Tit. i. 1; 2 Tim. ii. 19; James i. 17, 18, etc.

Lib. Arbit.

The sum of their doctrine is: God hath appointed the obedience of faith to be the means of salvation. If men fulfil this condition, he determineth to save them, which is their election; but if, after they have entered the way of godliness, they fall from it, they lose also their predestination. If they will return again, they are chosen anew; and if they can hold out to the end, then, and for that continuance, they are peremptorily elected, or postdestinated, after they are saved. Now, whether these positions may be gathered from those places of Scripture which deliver this doctrine, let any man judge.

CHAPTER VII.

Of original sin and the corruption of nature.

HEROD the Great, imparting his counsel of rebuilding the temple unto the Jews, they much feared he would never be able to accomplish his intention,[1] but, like an unwise builder, having demolished the old before he had sat down and cast up his account whether he were able to erect a new, they should (by his project) be deprived of a temple. Wherefore, to satisfy their jealousies, he resolved, as he took down any part of the other, presently to erect a portion of the new in the place thereof. Right so the Arminians, determining to demolish the building of divine providence, grace, and favour, by which men have hitherto ascended into heaven, and fearing lest we should be troubled, finding ourselves on a sudden deprived of that wherein we reposed our confidence for happiness, they have, by degrees, erected a Babylonish tower in the room thereof, whose top, they would persuade us, shall reach unto heaven. First, therefore, the foundation-stones they bring forth, crying, "Hail, hail," unto

[1] Joseph. Antiq. Judæ., lib. xv. cap. 11, sect. 6.

them, and pitch them on the sandy, rotten ground of our own natures. Now, because heretofore some wise master-builders had discovered this ground to be very unfit to be the basis of such a lofty erection, by reason of a corrupt issue of blood and filth arising in the midst thereof, and overspreading the whole platform, to encourage men to an association in this desperate attempt, they proclaim to all that there is no such evil fountain in the plain which they have chosen for the foundation of their proud building, setting up itself against the knowledge of God in plain terms. Having rejected the providence of God from being the original of that goodness of entity which is in our actions, and his predestination from being the cause of that moral and spiritual goodness wherewith any of them are clothed, they endeavour to draw the praise of both to the rectitude of their nature and the strength of their own endeavours. But this attempt, in the latter case, being thought to be altogether vain, because of the disability and corruption of nature, by reason of original sin, propagated unto us all by our first parents, whereby it is become wholly void of integrity and holiness, and we all become wise and able to do evil, but to do good have no power, no understanding; therefore, they utterly reject this imputation of an inherent, original guilt, and demerit of punishment, as an enemy to our upright and well-deserving condition. And oh, that they were as able to root it out of the hearts of all men, that it should never more be there, as they have been to persuade the heads of divers that it was never there at all!

If any would know how considerable this article concerning original sin hath ever been accounted in the church of Christ, let him but consult the writings of St Augustine, Prosper, Hilary, Fulgentius, any of those learned fathers whom God stirred up to resist, and enabled to overcome, the spreading Pelagian heresy, or look on those many councils, edicts, decrees of emperors, wherein that heretical doctrine of denying this original corruption is condemned, cursed, and exploded. Now, amongst those many motives they had to proceed so severely against this heresy, one especially inculcated deserves our consideration, namely,—

That it overthrew the necessity of Christ's coming into the world to redeem mankind. It is sin only that makes a Saviour necessary; and shall Christians tolerate such an error as, by direct consequence, infers the coming of Jesus Christ into the world to be needless? My purpose for the present is not to allege any testimonies of this kind; but, holding myself close to my first intention, to show how far in this article, as well as others, the Arminians have apostated from the pure doctrine of the word of God, the consent of orthodox divines, and the confession of this church of England.

In the ninth article of our church, which is concerning original sin, I observe especially four things:—First, That it is an inherent evil, the fault and corruption of the nature of every man. Secondly, That it is a thing not subject or conformable to the law of God, but hath in itself, even after baptism, the nature of sin. Thirdly, That by it we are averse from God, and inclined to all manner of evil. Fourthly, That it deserveth God's wrath and damnation. All which are frequently and evidently taught in the word of God, and every one denied by the Arminians, as it may appear by these instances, in some of them:—

First, That it *is an inherent sin and pollution of nature, having a proper guilt of its own, making us responsible to the wrath of God,* and not a bare imputation of another's fault to us his posterity: which, because it would reflect upon us all with a charge of a native imbecility and insufficiency to good, is by these self-idolizers quite exploded.

[1]"Infants are simply in that estate in which Adam was before his fall," saith Venator. [2]"Neither is it at all considerable whether they be the children of believers or of heathens and infidels; for infants, as infants, have all the same innocency," say they jointly, in their Apology: nay, more plainly, [3]"It can be no fault wherewith we are born." In which last expression these bold innovators, with one dash of their pens, have quite overthrown a sacred verity, an apostolic, catholic, fundamental article of Christian religion. But, truly, to me there are no stronger arguments of the sinful corruption of our nature than to see such nefarious issues of unsanctified hearts. Let us look, then, to the word of God confounding this Babylonish design.

First, That the nature of man, which at first was created pure and holy, after the image of God, endowed with such a rectitude and righteousness as was necessary and due unto it, to bring it unto that supernatural end to which it was ordained, is now altogether corrupted and become abominable, sinful, and averse from goodness, and that this corruption or concupiscence is originally inherent in us and derived from our first parents, is plentifully delivered in holy writ, as that which chiefly compels us to a self-denial, and drives us unto Christ. "Behold, I was shapen in iniquity; and in sin did my mother conceive me," saith David, Ps. li. 5. Where, for the praise of God's goodness towards him, he begins with the confession of his native perverseness, and of the sin wherein

[1] "Infantes sunt simplices, et stantes in eodem statu in quo Adamus fuit ante lapsum."—Venat. Theol. re. et me., fol. 2.

[2] "Nec refert an infantes isti sint fidelium, an ethnicorum liberi, infantium enim, qua infantium, eadem est innocentia."—Rem. Apol., p. 87.

[3] "Malum culpæ non est, quia nasci plane est involuntarium," etc.—Ibid, p. 84.

he was wrapped before he was born. Neither was this peculiar to him alone; he had it not from the particular iniquity of his next progenitors, but by an ordinary propagation from the common parent of us all; though in some of us, Satan, by this Pelagian attempt for hiding the disease, hath made it almost incurable: for even those infants of whose innocency the Arminians boast are unclean in the verdict of St Paul, 1 Cor. vii. 14, if not sanctified by an interest in the promise of the covenant; and no unclean thing shall enter into the kingdom of heaven. [1]"The weakness of the members of infants is innocent, and not their souls;" they want nothing, but that the members of their bodies are not as yet ready instruments of sin. They are not sinful only by external denomination,—accounted so because of the imputation of Adam's actual transgression unto them; for they have all an uncleanness in them by nature, Job xiv. 4, from which they must be "cleansed with the washing of water by the word," Eph. v. 20. Their whole nature is overspread with such a pollution as is proper only to sin inherent, and doth not accompany sin imputed; as we may see in the example of our Saviour, who was pure, immaculate, holy, undefiled, and yet "the iniquity of us all" was imputed unto him. Hence are those phrases of "washing away sin," Acts xxii. 16; of "cleansing filth," 1 Pet. iii. 21, Tit. iii. 5. Something there is in them, as soon as they are born, excluding them from the kingdom of heaven; for except they also be born again of the Spirit, they shall not enter into it, John iii. 5.

Secondly, The opposition that is made between the righteousness of Christ and the sin of Adam, Rom. v., which is the proper seat of this doctrine, showeth that there is in our nature an inbred sinful corruption; for the sin of Adam holds such relation unto sinners, proceeding from him by natural propagation, as the righteousness of Christ doth unto them who are born again of him by spiritual regeneration. But we are truly, intrinsically, and inherently sanctified by the Spirit and grace of Christ; and therefore there is no reason why, being so often in this chapter called sinners, because of this original sin, we should cast it off, as if we were concerned only by an external denomination, for the right institution of the comparison and its analogy quite overthrows the solitary imputation.

Thirdly, All those places of Scripture which assert the proneness of our nature to all evil, and the utter disability that is in us to do any good, that wretched opposition to the power of godliness, wherewith from the womb we are replenished, confirms the same truth. But of these places I shall have occasion to speak hereafter.

[1] "Imbecillitas membrorum infantilium innocens est, non animus."—Aug.

Fourthly, The flesh, in the Scripture phrase, is a quality (if I may so say) inherent in us; for *that*, with its concupiscence, is opposed to the Spirit and his holiness, which is certainly inherent in us. Now, the whole man by nature is flesh; for "that which is born of the flesh is flesh," John iii. 6;—it is an inhabiting thing, a thing that "dwelleth" within us, Rom. vii. 17. In brief, this vitiosity, sinfulness, and corruption of our nature is laid open,—*First*, By all those places which cast an aspersion of guilt, or desert of punishment, or of pollution, on nature itself; as Eph. ii. 1, 3, we are "dead in trespasses and sins," being "by nature the children of wrath, even as others," being wholly encompassed by a "sin that doth easily beset us." *Secondly*, By them which fix this original pravity in the heart, will, mind, and understanding, Eph. iv. 18; Rom. xii. 2; Gen. vi. 5. *Thirdly*, By those which positively decipher this natural depravation, 1 Cor. ii. 14; Rom. viii. 7;—or, *Fourthly*, That place it in the flesh, or old man, Rom. vi. 6; Gal. v. 16. So that it is not a bare imputation of another's fault, but an intrinsical adjacent corruption of our nature itself, that we call by this name of original sin. But, alas! it seems we are too large carvers for ourselves, in that wherewith we will not be contented.

The Arminians deny all such imputation, as too heavy a charge for the pure, unblamable condition wherein they are brought into this world. They deny, I say, that they are guilty of Adam's sin, as sinning in him, or that his sin is any way imputed unto us; which is their second assault upon the truth of this article of faith.

[1]"Adam sinned in his own proper person, and there is no reason why God should impute that sin of his unto infants," saith Boræus. The nature of the first covenant, the right and power of God, the comparison instituted by the apostle between Adam and Christ, the divine constitution, whereby Adam was appointed to be the head, fountain, and origin of all human kind, are with him no reasons at all to persuade it. [2]"For it is against equity," saith their Apology, "that one should be accounted guilty for a sin that is not his own,—that he should be reputed nocent who, in regard of his own will, is truly innocent." And here, Christian reader, behold plain Pelagianism obtruded on us without either welt[3] or guard; men on a sudden made pure and truly innocent, notwithstanding all that natural pollution and corruption the Scripture everywhere proclaims them to be

[1] Adamus in propria persona peccavit, et nulla est ratio cur Deus peccatum illud infantibus imputet."—Bor. in Artic. xxxi.

[2] "Contra æquitatem est, ut quis reus agatur propter peccatum non suum, ut vere nocens judicetur, qui quoad propriam suam voluntatem innocens est."—Rem. Apol., c. vii. p. 84.

[3] An old Saxon word denoting *a fence* or *border*.—Ed.

replenished withal. Neither is the reason they intimate of any value, that their wills assented not to it, and which a little before they plainly urge. "It is," say they, [1]"against the nature of sin that that should be counted a sin to any by whose own proper will it was not committed:" which being all they have to say, they repeat it over and over in this case,—"It must be voluntary, or it is no sin." But I say this is of no force at all; for,—first, St John, in his most exact definition of sin, requires not voluntariness to the nature of it, but only an obliquity, a deviation from the rule. It is an anomy,—a discrepancy from the law, which whether voluntary or no it skills not much; but sure enough there is in our nature such a repugnancy to the law of God. So that, secondly, if originally we are free from a voluntary actual transgression, yet we are not from an habitual voluntary digression and exorbitancy from the law. But, thirdly, in respect of our wills, we are not thus innocent neither; for we all sinned in Adam, as the apostle affirmeth. Now, all sin is voluntary, say the Remonstrants, and therefore Adam's transgression was our voluntary sin also, and that in divers respects,—first, in that *his voluntary act is imputed to us as ours*, by reason of the covenant which was made with him on our behalf. But because this, consisting in an imputation, must needs be extrinsical unto us, therefore, secondly, we say that Adam, being the root and head of all human kind, and we all branches from that root, all parts of that body whereof he was the head, *his will may be said to be ours. We were then all that one man*,[2]—we were all in him, and had no other will but his; so that though that be extrinsical unto us, considered as particular persons, yet it is intrinsical, as we are all parts of one common nature. As in him we sinned, so in him we had a will of sinning. Thirdly, *original sin is a defect of nature, and not of this or that particular person:*[3] whereon Alvarez grounds this difference of actual and original sin,—that the one is always committed by the proper will of the sinner; to the other is required only the will of our first parent, who was the head of human nature. Fourthly, It is hereditary, natural, and no way involuntary, or put into us against our wills. It possesseth our wills and inclines us to voluntary sins.

I see no reason, then, why Corvinus should affirm, as he doth, [4]"That it is absurd, that by one man's disobedience many should be made actually disobedient," unless he did it purposely to contradict

[1] "Contra naturam peccati est, ut censeatur peccatum, aut ut proprie in peccatum imputetur, quod propria voluntate commissum non est."—Rem. Apol., c. vii. p. 84.

[2] "Omnes eramus unus ille homo."—Aug.

[3] "Est voluntarium, voluntate primi originantis, non voluntate contrahentis: ratione naturæ, non personæ."—Thom. i. ii., q. 81, a.

[4] "Absurdum est ut ex unius inobedientia multi actu inobedientes, facti essent."—Corv. ad Molin., cap. vii. sect. 8.

St Paul, teaching us that "by one man's disobedience many were made sinners," Rom. v. 19. *Paulus ait, Corvinus negat; eligite cui credatis;*—Choose whom you will believe, St Paul or the Arminians. The sum of their endeavour in this particular is, to clear the nature of man from being any way guilty of Adam's actual sin, as being then in him a member and part of that body whereof he was the head, or from being obnoxious unto an imputation of it by reason of that covenant which God made with us all in him. So that, denying, as you saw before, all inherent corruption and pravity of nature, and now all participation, by any means, of Adam's transgression, methinks they cast a great aspersion on Almighty God, however he dealt with Adam for his own particular, yet for casting us, his most innocent posterity, out of paradise. It seems a hard case, that having no obliquity or sin in our nature to deserve it, nor no interest in his disobedience whose obedience had been the means of conveying so much happiness unto us, we should yet be involved in so great a punishment as we are; for that we are not now by birth under a great curse and punishment, they shall never be able to persuade any poor soul who ever heard of paradise, or the garden where God first placed Adam. And though all the rest, in their judgment, be no great matter, but an infirmity and languor of nature, or some such thing, yet, whatever it be, they confess it lights on us as well as him. [1]"We confess," say they, "that the sin of Adam may be thus far said to be imputed to his posterity, inasmuch as God would have them all born obnoxious to that punishment which Adam incurred by his sin, or permitted that evil which was inflicted on him to descend on them." Now, be this punishment what it will, never so small, yet if we have no demerit of our own, nor interest in Adam's sin, it is such an act of injustice as we must reject from the Most Holy, with a "God forbid." Far be it from the Judge of all the world to punish the righteous with the ungodly. If God should impute the sin of Adam unto us, and thereon pronounce us obnoxious to the curse deserved by it,—if we have a pure, sinless, unspotted nature,—even this could scarce be reconciled with that rule of his proceeding in justice with the sons of men, "The soul that sinneth it shall die;" which clearly granteth an impunity to all not tainted with sin. Sin and punishment, though they are sometimes separated by his mercy, pardoning the one and so not inflicting the other, yet never by his justice, inflicting the latter where the former is not. Sin imputed, by itself alone, without an inherent guilt, was never

[1] "Fatemur peccatum Adami, a Deo posse dici imputatum posteris ejus, quatenus Deus posteros Adami eidem malo, cui Adamus per peccatum obnoxium se reddidit, obnoxios nasci voluit; sive quatenus Deus, malum, quod Adamo inflictum erat in pœnam, in posteros ejus dimanare et transire permisit."—Rem. Apol., p. 84.

punished in any but Christ. The unsearchableness of God's love and justice, in laying the iniquity of us all upon him who had no sin, is an exception from that general rule he walketh by in his dealing with the posterity of Adam. So that if punishment be not due unto us for a solely imputed sin, much less, when it doth not stand with the justice and equity of God to impute any iniquity unto us at all, can we justly be wrapped in such a curse and punishment as woful experience teaches us that we lie under. Now, in this act of injustice, wherewith they charge the Almighty, the Arminians place the whole nature of original sin. [1]"We account not," say they, "original sin for a sin properly so called, that should make the posterity of Adam to deserve the wrath of God, nor for an evil that may properly be called a punishment, but only for an infirmity of nature;" which they interpret to be a kind of evil that, being inflicted on Adam, God suffereth to descend upon his posterity. So all the depravation of nature, the pollution, guilt, and concupiscence we derive from our first parents, the imputation of Adam's actual transgression, is all straitened to a small infirmity inflicted on poor innocent creatures.

But let them enjoy their own wisdom, which is earthly, sensual, and devilish. The Scripture is clear that the sin of Adam is the sin of us all, not only by propagation and communication (whereby not his singular fault, but something of the same nature, is derived unto us), but also by an imputation of his actual transgression unto us all, his singular disobedience being by this means made ours. The grounds of this imputation I touched before, which may be all reduced to his being a common person and head of all our nature; which investeth us with a double interest in his demerits, whilst so he was:—1. As we were then in him and parts of him; 2. As he sustained the place of our whole nature in the covenant God made with him;—both which, even according to the exigence of God's justice, require that his transgression be also accounted ours. And St Paul is plain, not only that "by one man's disobedience many were made sinners," Rom. v. 19, by the derivation of a corrupted nature, but also that "by one man's offence judgment came upon all," verse 18. Even for his one sin all of us are accounted to have deserved judgment and condemnation; and therefore, verse 12, he affirmeth that by one man sin and death entered upon all the world; and that because we have all sinned in him: which we no otherwise do but that his transgression in God's estimation is accounted ours. And the opposition the apostle there maketh between Christ and his righte-

[1] "Peccatum itaque originale nec habent pro peccato proprie dicto, quod posteros Adami odio Dei dignos faciat, nec pro malo, quod per modum proprie dictæ pœnæ ab Adamo in posteros dimanet sed pro infirmitate," etc.—Rem. Apol., fol. 84.

ousness, and Adam and his disobedience, doth sufficiently evince it; as may appear by this figure:—[1]

Sicut	ex	Adamo,	in omnes	κρίμα,	redundavit, eis	κατάκριμα,	per unum	παράπτωμα Adami,
sic		Christo,		χάρις Θεοῦ,		δικαίωσιν ζωῆς,		δικαίωμα Christi.

The whole similitude chiefly consists in the imputation of Adam's sin and Christ's righteousness, unto the seed of the one by nature, and of the other by grace. But that we are counted righteous for the righteousness of Christ is, among Protestants (though some differ in the manner of their expressions), as yet without question; and, therefore, are no less undoubtedly accounted sinners by, or guilty of, the first sin of Adam.

I shall not show their opposition unto the truth in many more particulars concerning this article of original sin, having been long ago most excellently prevented, even in this very method, by the way of antithesis to the Scripture and the orthodox doctrine of our church, by the famously learned Master Reynolds, in his excellent treatise, "Of the Sinfulness of Sin;" where he hath discovered their errors, fully answered their sophistical objections, and invincibly confirmed the truth from the word of God. Only, as I have showed already how they make this we call original sin no sin at all, neither inherent in us nor imputed unto us, nor no punishment truly so called; so, because our church saith directly that it meriteth damnation, I will briefly show what they conceive to be the desert thereof.

First, For Adam himself, they affirm "that the death threatened unto him if he transgressed the covenant, and due unto him for it,[2] was neither death temporal, for that before he was subject unto, by the primary constitution of his nature; nor yet such an eternal death as is accompanied with damnation or everlasting punishment." No! why, then, let us here learn some new divinity. Christians have hitherto believed that whatsoever may be comprised under the name of death, together with its antecedents, consequents, and attendants, was threatened to Adam in this commination; and divines, until this day, can find but these two sorts of death in the Scripture, as penal unto men, and properly so called; and shall we now be persuaded that it was neither of these that was threatened unto Adam? It must be so, if we will believe the Arminians; it was neither the one nor the other of the former; but whereas he was created mortal, and subject to a temporal death, the sanction of his obedience was a threatening of the utter dissolution of his soul and body, or a reduc-

[1] Paræus., ad Rom. v.

[2] "Cum de æterna morte loquuntur Remonstrantes in hac de Adamo quæstione, non intelligunt mortem illam, quæ æterna pœna sensus—dicitur," etc.—Rem. Apol., cap. iv. p. 57.

tion to their primitive nothing. But what if a man will not here take them at their words, but believe, according to St Paul, That death entered by sin; that if we had never sinned, we had never died; that man, in the state of innocency, was, by God's constitution, free even from temporal death, and all things directly conducing thereunto? secondly, That this death, threatened to our first parents, comprehended damnation also of soul and body for evermore, and that of their imaginary dissolution there is not the least intimation in the word of God?—why, I confess they have impudence enough, in divers places, to beg that we would believe their assertions, but never confidence enough to venture once to prove them true. Now, they who make so slight of the desert of this sin in Adam himself will surely scarce allow it to have any ill merit at all in his posterity.

[1]"Whether ever any one were damned for original sin, and adjudged to everlasting torments, is deservedly doubted of. Yea, we doubt not to affirm that never any was so damned," saith Corvinus. And that this is not his sole opinion he declares by telling you no less of his master, Arminius. [2]" It is most true," saith he, "that Arminius teacheth that it is perversely said that original sin makes a man guilty of death." Of any death, it should seem, temporal, eternal, or that annihilation they dream of. And he said true enough. Arminius doth affirm it, adding this reason, [3]" Because it is only the punishment of Adam's actual sin." Now, what kind of punishment they make this to be I showed you before. But truly I wonder, seeing they are everywhere so peremptory that the same thing cannot be a sin and a punishment, why they do so often nickname this " infirmity of nature," and call it a sin; which they suppose to be as far different from it as fire from water. Is it because they are unwilling, by new naming it, to contradict St Paul in express terms, never proposing it under any other denomination? or, if they can get a sophistical elusion for him, is it lest, by so doing, Christians should the more plainly discern their heresy? Or whatever other cause it be, in this I am sure they contradict themselves, notwithstanding in this they agree full well, [4]" That God rejecteth none for original sin only," as Episcopius speaks. And here, if you tell them that the question is not " de facto," what God doth, but " de jure," what such sin-

[1] " An ullus omnino homo, propter peccatum originis solum damnetur, ac æternis cruciatibus addicatur, merito dubitari potest: imo nullum ita damnari affirmare non veremur."—Corv. ad Molin., cap. ix. sect. 5.

[2] " Verissimum est Arminium docere, perverse dici peccatum originis reum facere mortis."—Corv. ad Tilen., p. 388.

[3] " Perverse dicitur peccatum originis, reum facere mortis, quum peccatum illud pœna sit peccati actualis Adami."—Armin. Resp. ad Quæst. ix. a. 3.

[4] " Deus neminem ob solum peccatum originis rejecit."—Episcop., disp. ix. thes. 2.

ners deserve, they tell us plainly, [1]"That God will not destinate any infants to eternal punishment for original sin, without their own proper actual sins; neither can he do so by right or in justice." So that the children of Turks, Pagans, and the like infidels, strangers from the covenant of grace, departing in their infancy, are far happier than any Christian men, who must undergo a hard warfare against sin and Satan, in danger to fall finally away at the last hour, and through many difficulties entering the kingdom of heaven, when they, without farther trouble, are presently assumed thither for their innocency; yea, although they are neither elected of God (for, as they affirm, he chooseth none but for their faith, which they have not); nor redeemed by Christ (for he died only for sinners, "he saveth his people from their sins," which they are not guilty of); nor sanctified by the Holy Ghost, all whose operations they restrain to a moral suasion, whereof infants are not a capable subject;—which is not much to the honour of the blessed Trinity, that heaven should be replenished with them whom the Father never elected, the Son never redeemed, nor the Holy Ghost sanctified.

And thus you see what they make of this original pravity of our nature, at most an infirmity or languor thereof,—neither a sin, nor the punishment of sin properly so called, nor yet a thing that deserves punishment as a sin; which last assertion, whether it be agreeable to holy Scripture or no, these three following observations will declare:—

First, There is no confusion, no disorder, no vanity in the whole world, in any of God's creatures, that is not a punishment of our sin in Adam. That great and almost universal ruin of nature, proceeding from the curse of God overgrowing the earth, and the wrath of God revealing itself from heaven, is the proper issue of his transgression. It was of the great mercy of God that the whole frame of nature was not presently rolled up in darkness, and reduced to its primitive confusion. Had we ourselves been deprived of those remaining sparks of God's image in our souls, which vindicate us from the number of the beasts that perish,—had we been all born fools and void of reason,—by dealing so with some in particular, he showeth us it had been but justice to have wrapped us in the same misery, all in general. All things, when God first created them, were exceeding good, and thought so by the wisdom of God himself; but our sin even compelled that good and wise Creator to hate and curse the work of his own hands. "Cursed is the ground," saith he to Adam, "for thy sake; in sorrow shalt thou eat of it all the days of thy life; thorns also and thistles shall it bring forth to thee," Gen. iii. 17, 18.

[1] "Pro certo statuunt Deum nullos infantes, sine actualibus ac propriis peccatis morientes, æternis cruciatibus destinare velle, aut jure destinare posse ob peccatum quod vocatur originis."—Rem. Apol., p. 87.

Hence was that heavy burden of "vanity," that "bondage of corruption," under which to this day "the whole creation groaneth and travaileth in pain" until it be delivered, Rom. viii. 20–22. Now, if our sin had such a strange malignant influence upon those things which have no relation unto us but only as they were created for our use, surely it is of the great mercy of God that we ourselves are not quite confounded; which doth not yet so interpose itself, but that we are all compassed with divers sad effects of this iniquity, lying actually under divers pressing miseries, and deservedly obnoxious to everlasting destruction. So that,—

Secondly, Death temporal, with all its antecedents and attendants,—all infirmities, miseries, sicknesses, wasting destroying passions, casualties that are penal, all evil conducing thereunto or waiting on it,—is a punishment of original sin; and this not only because the first actual sin of Adam is imputed to us, but most of them are the proper issues of that native corruption and pollution of sin which is stirring and operative within us for the production of such sad effects, our whole nature being by it thoroughly defiled. Hence are all the distortures and distemperatures of the soul by lusts, concupiscence, passions, blindness of mind, perverseness of will, inordinateness of affections, wherewith we are pressed and turmoiled, even proper issues of that inherent sin which possesseth our whole souls.

Upon the body, also, it hath such an influence, in disposing it to corruption and mortality, as it is the original of all those infirmities, sicknesses, and diseases, which make us nothing but a shop of such miseries for death itself. As these and the like degrees are the steps which lead us on apace in the road that tends unto it, so they are the direct, internal, efficient causes thereof, in subordination to the justice of Almighty God, by such means inflicting it as a punishment of our sins in Adam. Man before his fall, though not in regard of the matter whereof he was made, nor yet merely in respect of his quickening form, yet in regard of God's ordination, was immortal, a keeper of his own everlastingness. Death, to which before he was not obnoxious, was threatened as a punishment of his sin: "In the day thou eatest thereof thou shalt surely die;" the exposition of which words, given by God at the time of his inflicting this punishment, and pronouncing man subject to mortality, clearly showeth that it comprehended temporal death also: "Dust thou art, and unto dust shalt thou return." Our return to dust is nothing but the soul leaving the body, whereby before it was preserved from corruption. Farther, St Paul opposeth that death we had by the sin of Adam to the resurrection of the body by the power of Christ: "For since by man came death, by man came also the resurrection of the dead. For as in Adam all die, even so in Christ shall all be made alive," 1 Cor. xv. 21, 22. The life which all shall receive by the power of Christ at the last day is essentially a reunion of soul and body; and therefore their separation is a thing we incurred by the sin of Adam. The same apostle also, Rom. v., describeth a universal reign of death over all, by reason of the first transgression. Even diseases, also, in the Scripture, are attributed unto sin, as their meritorious cause, John v. 14; 1 Cor. xi. 30; Rev. ii. 22. And, in respect of all these, the mercy of God doth not so interpose itself but that all the sons of men are in some sort partakers of them.

Thirdly, The final desert of original sin, as our article speaketh, is damnation,—the wrath of God, to be poured on us in eternal torments of body and soul. To this end, also, many previous judgments of God are subservient,—as the privation of original righteousness (which he took and withheld upon Adam's throwing it away), spiritual desertion, permission of sin, with all other destroying depravations of our nature, as far as they are merely penal; some of which are immediate consequents of Adam's singular actual transgression, as privation of original righteousness; others, as damnation itself, the proper effects of that derived sin and pollution that is in us. There is none damned but for his own sin. When divines affirm that by Adam's sin we are guilty of damnation, they do not mean that any are actually damned for this particular fact; but that by his sin, and our sinning in him, by God's most just ordination, we have contracted that exceeding pravity and sinfulness of nature which deserveth the curse of God and eternal damnation. It must be an inherent uncleanness that actually excludes out of the kingdom of heaven, Rev. xxi. 27; which uncleanness the apostle shows to be in infants not sanctified by an interest in the covenant. In brief, we are baptized unto the "remission of sins," that we may be saved, Acts ii. 38. That, then, which is taken away by baptism is that which hinders our salvation; which is not the first sin of Adam imputed, but our own inherent lust and pollution. We cannot be washed, and cleansed, and purged from an imputed sin; which is done by the laver of regeneration. From that which lies upon us only by an external denomination, we have no need of cleansing; we may be said to be freed from it, or justified, but not purged. The soul, then, that is guilty of sin shall die, and that for its own guilt. If God should condemn us for original sin only, it were not by reason of the imputation of Adam's fault, but of the iniquity of that portion of nature in which we are proprietaries.

Now here, to shut up all, observe, that in this inquiry of the desert of original sin, the question is not, What shall be the certain lot of those that depart this life under the guilt of this sin only? but, What this hereditary and native corruption doth deserve in all those in whom it is? for, as St Paul saith, "We judge not them that are without" (especially infants), 1 Cor. v. 13. But for the demerit of it in the justice of God, our Saviour expressly affirmeth, that "except a man be born again, he cannot enter into the kingdom of God," John iii. 3, 5; and let them that can, distinguish between a not going to heaven and a going to hell: a third receptacle of souls in the Scripture we find not. St Paul also tells us that "by nature we are the children of wrath," Eph. ii. 3. Even originally and actually we are guilty of and obnoxious unto that wrath, which is accompanied with fiery indignation, that shall consume the adversaries. Again, we are assured that no unclean thing shall enter into heaven, Rev. xxi. 27; with which hell-deserving uncleanness children are polluted: and, therefore, unless it be purged with the blood of Christ, they have no interest in everlasting happiness. By this means sin is come upon all to condemnation; and yet do we not peremptorily censure to hell all infants departing this world without the laver of regeneration,—the ordinary means of waiving the punishment due to this pollution. That is the question "de facto," which we before rejected. Yea, and two ways there are whereby God saveth such infants, snatching them like brands out of the fire:—

First, By interesting them in the covenant, if their immediate or remote parents have been believers. He is a God of them and of their seed, extending his mercy unto a thousand generations of them that fear him.

Secondly, By his grace of election, which is most free, and not tied to any conditions; by which I make no doubt but God taketh many unto him in Christ whose parents never knew, or had been despisers of, the gospel. And this is the doctrine of our church, agreeable to the Scripture, affirming the desert of original sin to be God's wrath and damnation. To both which how opposite is the Arminian doctrine may thus appear:—

S. S.	Lib. Arbit.
"By the offence of one judgment came upon all men to condemnation," Rom. v. 18.	"Adam sinned in his own proper person only, and there is no reason why God should impute that sin unto infants," Boræus.
"By one man's disobedience many were made sinners," Rom. v. 19.	"It is absurd that by one man's disobedience many should be made actually disobedient," Corvinus.
"Behold, I was shapen in iniquity; and in sin did my mother conceive me," Ps. li. 5.	"Infants are simply in that estate in which Adam was before his fall," Venator.

S. S.	Lib. Arbit.
"Else were your children unclean; but now are they holy," 1 Cor. vii. 14. "Who can bring a clean thing out of an unclean? not one," Job xiv. 4. "Except a man be born again, he cannot see the kingdom of God," John iii. 3. "That which is born of the flesh is flesh," John iii. 6.	"Neither is it considerable whether they be the children of believers or of heathens; for all infants have the same innocency," Rem. Apol. "That which we have by birth can be no evil of sin, because to be born is plainly involuntary," Idem.
"By nature the children of wrath, even as others," Eph. ii. 3. "By one man sin entered into the world, and death by sin; and so death passed upon all men, for that all have sinned," to wit, in him, Rom. v. 12. "For I know that in me (that is, in my flesh,) dwelleth no good thing," chap. vii. 18.	"Original sin is neither a sin properly so called, which should make the posterity of Adam guilty of God's wrath, nor yet a punishment of any sin on them," Rem. Apol. "It is against equity that one should be accounted guilty of a sin that is not his own, that he should be judged nocent who in regard of his own will is truly innocent," Idem.
"In the day that thou eatest thereof thou shalt surely die," Gen. ii. 17. "For as in Adam all die, even so," etc., 1 Cor. xv. 22. "By nature the children of wrath," Eph. ii. 3. "And there shall in no wise enter into it any thing that defileth," Rev. xxi. 27.	"God neither doth nor can in justice appoint any to hell for original sin," Rem. Apol. "It is perversely spoken, that original sin makes any one guilty of death," Armin. "We no way doubt to affirm, that never any one was damned for original sin," Corv.

CHAPTER VIII.

Of the state of Adam before the fall, or of original righteousness.

In the last chapter we discovered the Arminian attempt of re-advancing the corrupted nature of man into that state of innocency and holiness wherein it was at first by God created; in which design, because they cannot but discern that the success is not answerable to their desires, and not being able to deny but that for so much good as we want (having cast it away), or evil of sin that we are subject unto more than we were at our first creation, we must be responsible to the justice of God, they labour to draw down our first parents, even from the instant of their forming, into the same condition wherein we are engaged by reason of corrupted nature. But, truly, I fear they will scarce obtain so prosperous an issue of their endeavour as Mohammed had when he promised the people he would call a mountain unto him; which miracle when they assembled to behold, but the mountain would not stir for all his calling, he replied, "If the mountain will not come to Mohammed, Mohammed will go to the mountain," and away he packed towards it. For we shall find that our Arminians can neither themselves climb the high mountain of innocency, nor yet call it down into the valley of sin and corruption wherein they are lodged. We have seen already how vain and frustrate was their former attempt: let us now take a view of their aspiring insolence, in making the pure creatures of God, holy and undefiled with any sin, to be invested with the same wretchedness and perverseness of nature with ourselves.

It is not my intention to enter into any curious discourse concerning the state and grace of Adam before his fall, but only to give a faithful assent to what God himself affirmed of all the works of his hands,—they were exceeding good. No evil, no deformity, or anything tending thereunto, did immediately issue from that Fountain of goodness and wisdom; and therefore, doubtless, man, the most excellent work of his hands, the greatest glory of his Creator, was then without spot or blemish, endued with all those perfections his nature and state of obedience was capable of. And careful we must be of casting any aspersions of defect on him that we will not with equal boldness ascribe to the image of God.

Nothing doth more manifest the deviation of our nature from its first institution, and declare the corruption wherewith we are polluted, than that propensity which is in us to every thing that is evil; that inclination of the flesh which lusteth always against the Spirit; that lust and concupiscence which fomenteth, conceiveth, hatcheth, bringeth forth, and nourisheth sin; that perpetual proneness that is in unregenerate nature to every thing that is contrary to the pure and holy law of God. Now, because neither Scripture nor experience will suffer Christians quite to deny this pravity of our nature, this averseness from all good and propensity to sin, the Arminians extenuate as much as they are able, affirming that it is no great matter, no more than Adam was subject unto in the state of innocency. But, what! did God create in Adam a proneness unto evil? was that a part of his glorious image in whose likeness he was framed? Yea, saith Corvinus, [1]"By reason of his creation, man had an affection to

[1] "Ex ratione creationis homo habebat affectum ad ea quæ vetabantur."—Corv. ad Molin., cap. vi. sect. 1.

what was forbidden by the law." But yet this seems injustice, that [1]"God should give a man a law to keep, and put upon his nature a repugnancy to that law;" as one of them affirmed at the synod of Dort. "No," saith the former author; [2]"man had not been fit to have had a law given unto him, had he not been endued with a propension and natural inclination to that which is forbidden by the law." But why is this so necessary in men rather than angels? No doubt there was a law, a rule for their obedience, given unto them at their first creation, which some transgressed, when others kept it inviolate. Had they also a propensity to sin concreated with their nature? had they a natural affection put upon them by God to that which was forbidden by the law? Let them only who will be wise beyond the word of God affix such injustice on the righteous Judge of all the earth. But so it seems it must be. [3]"There was an inclination in man to sin before the fall, though not altogether so vehement and inordinate as it is now," saith Arminius. Hitherto we have thought that the original righteousness wherein Adam was created had comprehended the integrity and perfection of the whole man; not only that whereby the body was obedient unto the soul, and all the affections subservient to the rule of reason for the performance of all natural actions, but also a light, uprightness, and holiness of grace in the mind and will, whereby he was enabled to yield obedience unto God for the attaining of that supernatural end whereunto he was created. No; but [4]"original righteousness," say our new doctors, "was nothing but a bridle to help to keep man's inordinate concupiscence within bounds:" so that the faculties of our souls were never endued with any proper innate holiness of their own. [5]"In the spiritual death of sin there are no spiritual gifts properly wanting in the will, because they were never there," say the six collocutors at the Hague.

The sum is, man was created with a nature not only weak and imperfect, unable by its native strength and endowments to attain that supernatural end for which he was made, and which he was commanded to seek, but depraved also with a love and desire of things repugnant to the will of God, by reason of an inbred inclination to sinning. It doth not properly belong to this place to show how they extenuate those gifts also with which they cannot deny but that he

[1] "Deus homini repugnantiam indidit adversus legem."—Joh. Gest. in Synod. Confes.

[2] "Homo non est idoneus cui lex feratur, quando in eo, ad id quod lege vetatur, non est propensio, ac inclinatio naturalis."—Corv. ad Molin., cap. x. sect. 15.

[3] "Inclinatio ad peccandum ante lapsum in homine fuit, licet non ita vehemens ac inordinata ut nunc est."—Armin. ad Artic. Respon.

[4] "Justitia originalis instar fræni fuit, quod præstabat internæ concupiscentiæ ordinationem."—Corv. ad Molin., cap. viii. sect. 1.

[5] "In spirituali morte non separantur proprie dona spiritualia a voluntate, quia illa nunquam fuerunt ei insita."—Rem. Coll. Hag., p. 250.

was endued, and also deny those which he had, as a power to believe in Christ, or to assent unto any truth that God should reveal unto him; and yet they grant this privilege to every one of his posterity, in that depraved condition of nature whereinto by sin he cast himself and us. We have all now a power of believing in Christ; that is, Adam, by his fall, obtained a supernatural endowment far more excellent than any he had before. And let them not here pretend the universality of the new covenant until they can prove it; and I am certain it will be long enough. But this, I say, belongs not to this place; only, let us see how, from the word of God, we may overthrow the former odious heresy:—

God in the beginning "created man in his own image," Gen. i. 27, —that is, "upright," Eccles. vii. 29, endued with a nature composed to obedience and holiness. That habitual grace and original righteousness wherewith he was invested was in a manner due unto him for the obtaining of that supernatural end whereunto he was created. A universal rectitude of all the faculties of his soul, advanced by supernatural graces, enabling him to the performance of those duties whereunto they were required, is that which we call the innocency of our first parents. Our nature was then inclined to good only, and adorned with all those qualifications that were necessary to make it acceptable unto God, and able to do what was required of us by the law, under the condition of everlasting happiness. Nature and grace, or original righteousness, before the fall, ought not to be so distinguished as if the one were a thing prone to evil, resisted and quelled by the other; for both complied, in a sweet union and harmony, to carry us along in the way of obedience to eternal blessedness. [There was] no contention between the flesh and the Spirit; but as all other things at theirs, so the whole man jointly aimed at his own chiefest good, having all means of attaining it in his power. That there was then no inclination to sin, no concupiscence of that which is evil, no repugnancy to the law of God, in the pure nature of man, is proved, because,—

First, The Scripture, describing the condition of our nature at the first creation thereof, intimates no such propensity to evil, but rather a holy perfection, quite excluding it. We were created "in the image of God," Gen. i. 27,—in such a perfect uprightness as is opposite to all evil inventions, Eccles. vii. 29; to which image when we are again in some measure "renewed" by the grace of Christ, Col. iii. 10, we see by the first-fruits that it consisted in "righteousness and true holiness,"—in truth and perfect holiness, Eph. iv. 24.

Secondly, An inclination to evil, and a lusting after that which is forbidden, is that inordinate concupiscence wherewith our nature is now infected; which is everywhere in the Scripture condemned as a sin; St Paul, in the seventh to the Romans, affirming expressly that it is a sin, and forbidden by the law, verse 7, producing all manner of evil, and hindering all that is good,—a "body of death," verse 24; and St James maketh it even the womb of all iniquity, James i. 14, 15. Surely our nature was not at first yoked with such a troublesome inmate. Where is the uprightness and innocency we have hitherto conceived our first parents to have enjoyed before the fall? A repugnancy to the law must needs be a thing sinful. An inclination to evil, to a thing forbidden, is an *anomy*,—a deviation and discrepancy from the pure and holy law of God. We must speak no more, then, of the state of innocency, but only of a short space wherein no outward actual sins were committed. Their proper root, if this be true, was concreated with our nature. Is this that obediential harmony to all the commandments of God which is necessary for a pure and innocent creature, that hath a law prescribed unto him? By which of the ten precepts is this inclination to evil required? Is it by the last, "Thou shalt not covet?" or by that sum of them all, "Thou shalt love the LORD thy God with all thy heart," etc.? Is this all the happiness of paradise,—to be turmoiled with a nature swelling with abundance of vain desires, and with a main stream carried headlong to all iniquity, if its violent appetite be not powerfully kept in by the bit and bridle of original righteousness? So it is we see with children now;[1] and so it should have been with them in paradise, if they were subject to this rebellious inclination to sin.

Thirdly, and principally, Whence had our primitive nature this affection to those things that were forbidden it,—this rebellion and repugnancy to the law, which must needs be an anomy, and so a thing sinful? There was as yet no demerit, to deserve it as a punishment. What fault is it to be created? [2]The operation of any thing which hath its original with the being of the thing itself must needs proceed from the same cause as doth the essence or being itself; as the fire's tending upwards relates to the same original with the fire: and, therefore, this inclination or affection can have no other author but God; by which means he is entitled not only to the first sin, as the efficient cause, but to all the sins in the world arising from thence. Plainly, and without any strained consequences, he is made the author of sin; for even those positive properties which can have no other fountain but the author of nature, being set on evil, are directly sinful. And here the idol of free-will may triumph in this victory over the God of heaven. Heretofore all the

[1] "Vidi ego zelantem parvulum qui nondum loquebatur, et intuebatur pallidus, amaro aspectu colluctaneum suum."—Aug.

[2] "Operatio quæ simul incipit cum esse rei, est ei ab agente, a quo habet esse, sicut moveri sursum inest igni a generante."—Alvar., p. 199.

blame of sin lay upon his shoulders, but now he begins to complain, Οὐκ ἐγὼ αἴτιός εἰμι ἀλλὰ Ζεὺς καὶ μοῖρα. "It is God and the fate of our creation that hath placed us in this condition of naturally affecting that which is evil. Back with all your charges against the ill government of this new deity within his imaginary dominion; what hurt doth he do but incline men unto evil, and God himself did no less at the first?" But let them that will, rejoice in these blasphemies: it sufficeth us to know that "God created man upright," though he "hath sought out many inventions;" so that in this following dissonancy we cleave to the better part:—

S. S.	Lib. Arbit.
"So God created man in his own image, in the image of God created he him; male and female created he them," Gen. i. 27. "Put on the new man, which is renewed in knowledge after the image of him that created him," Col. iii. 10. "—— which after God is created in righteousness and true holiness," Eph. iv. 24.	"There was in man before the fall an inclination to sinning, though not so vehement and inordinate as now it is," Armin. "God put upon man a repugnancy to his law," Gesteranus in the Synod. "Man, by reason of his creation, had an affection to those things that are forbidden by the law," Corv.
"Lo, this only have I found, that God hath made man upright; but he hath sought out many inventions," Eccles. vii. 29. "By one man sin entered into the world, and death by sin," Rom. v. 12.	"The will of man had never any spiritual endowments," Rem. Apol.
"Let no man say when he is tempted, I am tempted of God: for God tempteth no man: but every man is tempted when he is drawn away of his own lust," James i. 13, 14.	"It was not fit that man should have a law given him, unless he had a natural inclination to what was forbidden by the law," Corv.

CHAPTER IX.

Of the death of Christ, and of the efficacy of his merits.

THE sum of those controversies, wherewith the Arminians and their abettors have troubled the church, about the death of Christ, may be reduced to two heads:—First, Concerning the object of his merit, or whom he died for; secondly, Concerning the efficacy and end of his death, or what he deserved, procured, merited, and obtained, for them for whom he died. In resolution of the first, they affirm that he died for all and every one; of the second, that he died for no one man at all in that sense Christians have hitherto believed that he laid down his life, and submitted himself to bear the burden of his Father's wrath for their sakes. It seems to me a strange extenuation of the merit of Christ, to teach that no good at all by his death doth redound to divers of them for whom he died. What participation in the benefit of his suffering had Pharaoh or Judas? Do they not at this hour, and shall they not to eternity, feel the weight and burden of their own sins? Had they either grace in this world, or glory in the other, that they should be said to have an interest in the death of our Saviour? Christians have hitherto believed, that for whom Christ died, for their sins he made satisfaction, that they themselves should not eternally suffer for them. Is God unjust to punish twice for the same fault? his own Son once, and again the poor sinners for whom he suffered? I cannot conceive an intention in God that Christ should satisfy his justice for the sin of them that were in hell some thousands of years before, and yet be still resolved to continue their punishment on them to all eternity. No, doubtless: Christ giveth life to every one for whom he gave his life; he loseth not one of them whom he purchased with his blood.

The first part of this controversy may be handled under these two questions:—First, Whether God giving his Son, and Christ making his soul a ransom for sin, intended thereby to redeem all and every one from their sins, that all and every one alike, from the beginning of the world to the last day, should all equally be partakers of the fruits of his death and passion; which purpose of theirs is in the most frustrate? Secondly, Whether God had not a certain infallible intention of gathering unto himself a "chosen people," of collecting a "church of first-born," of saving his "little flock," of bringing some certainly to happiness, by the death of his only Son; which in the event he doth accomplish?

The second part also may be reduced to these two heads:—First, Whether Christ did not make full satisfaction for all their sins for whom he died, and merited glory, or everlasting happiness, to be bestowed on them upon the performance of those conditions God should require? Secondly (which is the proper controversy I shall chiefly insist upon), Whether Christ did not procure for his own people a power to become the sons of God, merit and deserve at the hands of God for them, grace, faith, righteousness, and sanctification, whereby they may be enabled infallibly to perform the conditions of the new covenant, upon the which they shall be admitted to glory?

To the first question of the first part of the controversy, the Arminians answer affirmatively,—to wit, that Christ died for all alike; the benefit of his passion belongs equally to all the posterity of Adam. And to the second negatively,—that God had no such intention of bringing many chosen sons unto salvation by the death of Christ, but determined of grace and glory no more precisely to one than to another, to John than Judas, Abraham than Pharaoh? Both which, as the learned Moulin observed,[1] seemed to be invented to make Christianity ridiculous, and expose our religion to the derision of all knowing men: for who can possibly conceive that one by the appointment of God should die for another, and yet that other, by the same justice, be allotted unto death himself, when one's death only was due; that Christ hath made a full satisfaction for their sins who shall everlastingly feel the weight of them themselves; that he should merit and obtain reconciliation with God for them who live and die his enemies, grace and glory for them who are graceless in this life and damned in that which is to come; that he should get remission of sins for them whose sins were never pardoned? In brief, if this sentence be true, either Christ by his death did not reconcile us unto God, make satisfaction to his justice for our iniquities, redeem us from our sins, purchase a kingdom, an everlasting inheritance for us,—which I hope no Christian will say; or else all the former absurdities must necessarily follow,—which no rational man will ever admit.

Neither may we be charged as straiteners of the merit of Christ; for we advance the true value and worth thereof (as hereafter will appear) far beyond all the Arminians ascribe unto it. We confess that that "blood of God," Acts xx. 28, of the "Lamb without blemish and without spot," 1 Pet. i. 19, was so exceedingly precious, of that infinite worth and value, that it might have saved a thousand believing worlds, John iii. 16; Rom. iii. 22. His death was of sufficient dignity to have been made a ransom for all the sins of every one in the world. And on this internal sufficiency of his death and passion is grounded the universality of evangelical promises; which have no such restriction in their own nature as that they should not be made to all and every one, though the promulgation and knowledge of them are tied only to the good pleasure of God's special providence, Matt. xvi. 17; as also that economy and dispensation of the new covenant whereby, the partition-wall being broken down, there remains no more difference between Jew and Gentile, the utmost borders of the earth being given in for Christ's inheritance. So that, in some

[1] Molin. Suffrag. ad. Synod. Dordra.

sense, Christ may be said to die for "all," and "the whole world;"—first, Inasmuch as the worth and value of his death was very sufficient to have been made a price for all their sins; secondly, Inasmuch as this word "all" is taken for some of all sorts (not for every one of every sort), as it is frequently used in the holy Scripture: so Christ being lifted up, "drew all unto him," John xii. 32; that is, believers out of all sorts of men. The apostles cured all diseases, or some of all sorts: they did not cure every particular disease, but there was no kind of disease that was exempted from their power of healing. So that where it is said that Christ "died for all," it is meant either,—first, All the faithful; or, secondly, Some of all sorts; thirdly, Not only Jews, but Gentiles. For,—

Secondly, The proper counsel and intention of God in sending his Son into the world to die was, that thereby he might confirm and ratify the new covenant to his elect, and purchase for them all the good things which are contained in the tenure of that covenant,—to wit, grace and glory; that by his death he might bring many (yet some certain) children to glory, obtaining for them that were given unto him by his Father (that is, his whole church) reconciliation with God, remission of sins, faith, righteousness, sanctification, and life eternal. That is the end to which they are to be brought, and the means whereby God will have them attain it. He died that he might gather the dispersed children of God, and make them partakers of everlasting glory,—to "give eternal life to as many as God gave him," John xvii. 2. And on this purpose of himself and his Father is founded the intercession of Christ for his elect and chosen people; performed partly on the earth, John xvii., partly in heaven, before the throne of grace: which is nothing but a presentation of himself and his merits, accompanied with the prayers of his mediatorship before God, that he would be pleased to grant and effectually to apply the good things he hath by them obtained to all for whom he hath obtained them. His intercession in heaven is nothing but a continued oblation of himself. So that whatsoever Christ impetrated, merited, or obtained by his death and passion, must be infallibly applied unto and bestowed upon them for whom he intended to obtain it; or else his intercession is vain, he is not heard in the prayers of his mediatorship. An actual reconciliation with God, and communication of grace and glory, must needs betide all them that have any such interest in the righteousness of Christ as to have it accepted for their good. The sole end why Christ would so dearly purchase those good things is, an actual application of them unto his chosen: God set forth the propitiation of his blood for the remission of sins, that he might be the justifier of him which believeth on Jesus, Rom. iii. 25, 26. But this part of the controversy is not that which I principally intend; only, I will give you a brief sum of those reasons which overthrow their heresy in this particular branch thereof:—

First, The death of Christ is in divers places of the Scripture restrained to his "people," and "elect," his "church," and "sheep," Matt. i. 21; John x. 11–13; Acts xx. 28; Eph. v. 25; John xi. 51, 52; Rom. viii. 32, 34; Heb. ii. 9, 14; Rev. v. 9; Dan. ix. 26;—and therefore the good purchased thereby ought not to be extended to "dogs," "reprobates," and "those that are without."

Secondly, For whom Christ died, he died as their sponsor, in their room and turn, that he might free them from the guilt and desert of death; which is clearly expressed Rom. v. 6–8. "He was wounded for our transgressions, he was bruised for our iniquities: the chastisement of our peace was upon him; and with his stripes we are healed," Isa. liii. 5, 6, etc. "He hath redeemed us from the curse of the law, being made a curse for us," Gal. iii. 13. "He hath made him to be sin for us, who knew no sin," 2 Cor. v. 21. Evidently he changeth turns with us, "that we might be made the righteousness of God in him." Yea, in other things, it is plain in the Scripture that to die for another is to take his place and room, with an intention that he should live, 2 Sam. xviii. 33; Rom. v. So that Christ dying for men made satisfaction for their sins, that they should not die. Now, for what sins he made satisfaction, for them the justice of God is satisfied; which surely is not done for the sins of the reprobates, because he justly punisheth them to eternity upon themselves, Matt. v. 26.

Thirdly, For whom Christ "died," for them also he "rose again," to make intercession for them: for whose "offences he was delivered," for their "justification he was raised," Rom. iv. 25, v. 10. He is a high priest "to make intercession for them" in the holy of holies for whom "by his own blood he obtained eternal redemption," Heb. ix. 11, 12. These two acts of his priesthood are not to be separated; it belongs to the same mediator for sin to sacrifice and pray. Our assurance that he is our advocate is grounded on his being a propitiation for our sins. He is an "advocate" for every one for whose sins his blood was a "propitiation," 1 John ii. 1, 2. But Christ doth not intercede and pray for all, as himself often witnesseth, John xvii.; he "maketh intercession" only for them who "come unto God by him," Heb. vii. 25. He is not a mediator of them that perish, no more than an advocate of them that fail in their suits; and therefore the benefit of his death also must be restrained to them who are finally partakers of both. We must not so disjoin the offices of Christ's mediatorship, that one of them may be versated about some towards whom he exerciseth not the other; much less ought we so to separate the several acts of the same office. For whom Christ is a priest, to offer himself a sacrifice for their sins, he is surely a king, to apply the good things purchased by his death unto them, as Arminius himself confesseth; much more to whom he is a priest by sacrifice, he will be a priest by intercession. And, therefore, seeing he doth not intercede and pray for every one, he did not die for every one.

Fourthly, For whom Christ died he merited grace and glory, faith and salvation, and reconciliation with God; as I shall show hereafter. But this he hath not done for all and every one. Many do never believe; the wrath of God remaineth upon some; the wrath of God abideth on them that do not believe, John iii. 36. To abide argueth a continued, uninterrupted act. Now, to be reconciled to one, and yet to lie under his heavy anger, seem to me ἀσύστατα,—things that will scarce consist together. The reasons are many; I only point at the heads of some of them.

Fifthly, Christ died for them whom God gave unto him to be saved: "Thine they were, and thou gavest them me," John xvii. 6. He layeth down his life for the sheep committed to his charge, chap. x. 11. But all are not the sheep of Christ, all are not given unto him of God to be brought to glory; for of those that are so given there is not one that perisheth, for "he giveth eternal life to as many as God hath given him," chap. xvii. 2. "No man is able to pluck them out of his Father's hand," chap. x. 28, 29.

Sixthly, Look whom, and how many, that love of God embraced that was the cause of sending his Son to redeem them; for them, and so many, did Christ, according to the counsel of his Father, and in himself, intentionally lay down his life. Now, this love is not universal, being his "good pleasure" of blessing with spiritual blessings and saving some in Christ, Eph. i. 4, 5; which good pleasure of his evidently comprehendeth some, when others are excluded, Matt. xi. 25, 26. Yea, the love of God in giving Christ for us is of the same extent with that grace whereby he calleth us to faith, or bestoweth faith on us: for "he hath called us with an holy calling, according to his own purpose and grace, which was given us in Christ Jesus," 2 Tim. i. 9; which, doubtless, is not universal and common unto all.

Innumerable other reasons there are to prove, that seeing God hath given his elect only, whom only he loved, to Christ to be redeemed; and seeing that the Son loveth only those who are given him of his Father, and redeemeth only whom he loveth; seeing, also, that the Holy Spirit, the love of the Father and the Son, sanctifieth all, and only them, that are elected and redeemed,—it is not our part, with a preposterous liberality, against the witness of Christ himself, to assign the salvation attained by him as due to them that are without the congregation of them whom the Father hath loved and chosen, without that church which the Son loved and gave his life for, nor none of the members of that sanctified body whereof Christ is the Head and Saviour. I urge no more, because this is not that part of the controversy that I desire to lay open.

I come now to consider the main question of this difference, though sparingly handled by our divines, concerning what our Saviour merited and purchased for them for whom he died. And here you shall find the old idol playing his pranks, and quite divesting the merit of Christ from the least ability or power of doing us any good; for though the Arminians pretend, very speciously, that Christ died for all men, yet, in effect, they make him die for no one man at all, and that by denying the effectual operation of his death, and ascribing the proper issues of his passion to the brave endeavours of their own Pelagian deity.

We, according to the Scriptures, plainly believe that Christ hath, by his righteousness, merited for us grace and glory; that we are blessed with all spiritual blessings, in, through, and for him; that he is made unto us righteousness, and sanctification, and redemption; that he hath procured for us, and that God for his sake bestoweth on us, every grace in this life that maketh us differ from others, and all that glory we hope for in that which is to come; he procured for us remission of all our sins, an actual reconciliation with God, faith, and obedience. Yea, but this is such a desperate doctrine as stabs at the very heart of the idol, and would make him as altogether useless as if he were but a fig-tree log. What remaineth for him to do, if all things in this great work of our salvation must be thus ascribed unto Christ and the merit of his death? Wherefore the worshippers of this great god, Lib. Arbit., oppose their engines against the whole fabric, and cry down the title of Christ's merits to these spiritual blessings, in the behalf of their imaginary deity.

Now, because they are things of a twofold denomination about which we contend before the King of heaven, each part producing their evidence, the first springing from the favour of God towards us, the second from the working of his grace actually within us, I shall handle them severally and apart;—especially because to things of this latter sort, gifts, as we call them, enabling us to fulfil the condition required for the attaining of glory, we lay a double claim on God's behalf; first, As the death of Christ is the meritorious cause procuring them of him; secondly, As his free grace is their efficient cause working them in us;—they also producing a double title, whereby they would invest their beloved darling with a sole propriety in causing these effects; first, In regard that they are our own acts, performed in us and by us; secondly, As they are parts of our duty which we are enjoined to do. So that the quarrel is directly between Christ's merits and our own free-will about procuring the favour of

God, and obtaining grace and righteousness. Let us see what they say to the first.

They affirm that [1]"the immediate and proper effect or end of the death and passion of Christ is, not an actual ablation of sin from men, not an actual remission of iniquities, justification and redemption of any soul;" that is, Christ's death is not the meritorious cause of the remission of our sins, of redemption and justification. The meritorious cause, I say: for of some of them, as of justification, as it is terminated in us, we confess there are causes of other kinds, as faith is the instrument and the Holy Spirit the efficient thereof; but for the sole meritorious procuring cause of these spiritual blessings, we always took it to be the righteousness and death of Christ, believing plainly that the end why Christ died, and the fruit of his sufferings, was our reconciliation with God, redemption from our sins, freedom from the curse, deliverance from the wrath of God and power of hell,—though we be not actual partakers of these things, to the pacification of our own consciences, without the intervening operation of the Holy Spirit, and faith by him wrought in us.

But if this be not, pray what is obtained by the death of Christ? Why, [2]"a potential, conditionate reconciliation, not actual and absolute," saith Corvinus. But yet this potential reconciliation being a new expression, never intimated in the Scripture, and scarce of itself intelligible, we want a farther explanation of their mind, to know what it is that directly they assign to the merits of Christ. Wherefore they tell us that the fruit of his death was [3]"such an impetration or obtaining of reconciliation with God, and redemption for us, that God thereby hath a power, his justice being satisfied, and so not compelling him to the contrary, to grant remission of sins to sinful men on what condition he would;" or, as another speaketh it, [4]"There was, by the effusion of Christ's blood, a right obtained unto and settled in God, of reconciling the world, and of opening unto all a gate of repentance and faith in Christ." But now, whereas the Scripture everywhere affirmeth that Christ died for our good, to obtain blessings for us, to purchase our peace, to acquire and merit for us the good things contained in the promise of the

[1] "Immediata mortis Christi effectio, ac passionis, illa est non actualis peccatorum ab his aut illis ablatio, non actualis remissio, non justificatio, non actualis horum aut illorum redemptio."—Armin. Antip., p. 76.

[2] "Reconciliatio potentialis et conditionata non actualis et absoluta, per mortem Christi impetratur."—Corv. ad Molin., cap. xxviii. sect. 11.

[3] "Remissionis, justificationis, et redemptionis, apud Deum impetratio, qua factum est, ut Deus jam possit, utpote justitia cui satisfactum est non obstante, hominibus peccatoribus peccata remittere."—Armin., ubi sup.

[4] "Autoris mens non est alia, quam effuso sanguine Christi reconciliandi mundum Deo jus impetratum fuisse, et inito novo fœdere et gratioso cum hominibus, Deum gratiæ ostium omnibus denuo, pœnitentiæ ac veræ in Christum fidei lege, adaperuisse."—Epistol. ad Wal., p. 93.

covenant, this opinion seems to restrain the end and fruit thereof to the obtaining of a power and liberty unto God of prescribing us a condition whereby we may be saved. But yet, it may be, thus much at least Christ obtained of God in our behalf, that he should assign faith in him to be this condition, and to bestow it upon us also. No; neither the one nor the other. [1]"After all this, had it so seemed good unto his wisdom, God might have chosen the Jews, and others, following the righteousness of the law, as well as believers; because he might have assigned any other condition of salvation besides faith in Christ," saith Grevinchovius. Notwithstanding, then, the death of Christ for us, we might have been held to the old rule, "Do this, and live." But if this be true, I cannot perceive how it may be said that Christ died to redeem us from our sins, to save our souls, and bring us unto glory. Neither, perhaps, do they think this to be any great inconvenience; for the same author affirmeth that [2]"Christ cannot be said properly to die to save any one." And a little after he more fully declares himself, that [3]"after Christ had obtained all that he did obtain by his death, the right remained wholly in God to apply it, or not to apply it, as it should seem good unto him; the application of grace and glory to any man was not the end for which Christ obtained them, but to get a right and power unto God of bestowing those things on what sort of men he would;"—which argues no redemption of us from our sins, but a vindication of God from such a condition wherein he had not power to forgive them; not an obtaining of salvation for us, but of a liberty unto God of saving us on some condition or other.

But now, after God hath got this power by the death of Christ, and out of his gracious good pleasure assigned faith to be the means for us to attain those blessings, he hath procured himself a liberty to bestow. Did Christ obtain this faith for us of him, if it be a thing not in our own power? No; [4]"faith is not obtained by the death of Christ," saith Corvinus. So that there is no good thing, no spiritual blessing, into which any man in the world hath any interest by the death of Christ: which is not so great an absurdity but that they are most ready to grant it. Arnoldus confesseth, [5]"that he believes that the death of Christ might have enjoyed its end, or his

[1] "Potuisset Deus, si ita sapientiæ suæ visum fuisset, operarios, Judæos, vel alios etiam præter fideles eligere, quia potuit aliam salutis conditionem, quam fidem in Christum exigere."—Grevinch. ad Ames., p. 415.

[2] "Christus non est proprie mortuus ad aliquem salvandum."—Idem, ibid, p. 8.

[3] "Postquam impetratio præstita ac peracta esset, Deo jus suum integrum mansit, pro arbitrio suo, eam applicare, vel non applicare; nec applicatio finis impetrationis propriè fuit, sed jus et potestas applicandi, quibus et qualibus vellet."—P. 9.

[4] "Fides non est impetrata merito Christi," etc.—Corv. ad Molin., cap. xxviii. p. 419.

[5] "Se omnino credere, futurum fuisse, ut finis mortis Christi constaret, etiamsi nemo credidisset."—Idem, cap. xxvii. sect. 3, 4.

merit its full force, although never any had believed:" and again, [1]"The death and satisfaction of Christ being accomplished, it might come to pass that, none fulfilling the condition of the new covenant, none should be saved." So also saith Grevinchovius. O Christ! that any pretending to profess thy holy name should thus slight the precious work of thy death and passion! Surely never any before, who counted it their glory to be called Christians, did ever thus extenuate (their friends the Socinians only excepted) the dignity of his merit and satisfaction. Take but a short view of what benefit they allow to redound to us by the effusion of his precious blood, and you may see what a pestilent heresy these men have laboured to bring into the church. Neither faith nor salvation, grace nor glory, hath he purchased for us,—not any spiritual blessing, that by our interest in his death we can claim to be ours! It is not such a reconciliation with God as that he thereupon should be contented again to be called our God; it is not justification, nor righteousness, nor actual redemption from our sins; it did not make satisfaction for our iniquities, and deliver us from the curse; [2]"only it was a means of obtaining such a possibility of salvation, as that God, without wronging of his justice, might save us if he would, one way or other." So that, when Christ had done all that he could, there was not one man in the world immediately the better for it; notwithstanding the utmost of his endeavour, every one might have been damned with Judas to the pit of hell; for [3]"he died as well for Simon Magus and Judas as he did for Peter and Paul," say the Arminians. Now, if no more good redound to us by the death of Christ than to Simon Magus, we are not much obliged to him for our salvation. Nay, he may be rather said to have redeemed God than us; for he procured for him immediately a power to redeem us if he would; for us only, by virtue of that power, a possibility to be redeemed;—which leaves nothing of the nature of merit annexed to his death, for that deserveth that something be done, not only that it *may* be done; the workman deserveth that his wages be given him, and not that it *may* be given him. And then what becomes of all the comfort and consolation that is proposed to us in the death of Christ? But it is time to see how this stubble is burned and consumed by the word of God, and that established which they thought to overthrow.

First, It is clear that Christ died to procure for us an actual

[1] "Posita et præstita Christi morte et satisfactione, fieri potest, ut, nemine novi fœderis conditionem præstante, nemo salvaretur."—Idem. Grevinch. ad Ames. p. 9.

[2] "Impetratio salutis pro omnibus, est acquisitio possibilitatis, ut nimirum Deus, illæsa sua justitia, hominem peccatorem possit recipere in gratiam."—Rem. Coll. Hag., p. 172.

[3] "Pro Juda ac Petro mortuus est Christus, et pro Simone Mago et Juda tam quam pro Paulo et Petro."—Rem. Synod, p. 320.

reconciliation with God, and not only a power for us to be reconciled unto him; for "when we were enemies, we were reconciled to God by the death of his Son," Rom. v. 10. We enjoy an actual reconciliation unto God by his death. He is content to be called "our God" when we are enemies, without the intervening of any condition on our part required; though the sweetness, comfort, and knowledge of this reconciliation do not compass our souls before we believe in him. Again, we have remission of sins by his blood, and justification from them; not a sole vindication into such an estate wherein, if it please God and ourselves, our sins are pardonable: for we are "justified freely by his grace, through the redemption that is in Christ Jesus: whom God hath set forth to be a propitiation through faith in his blood, to declare his righteousness for the remission of sins," Rom. iii. 24, 25. Yea, he obtained for us by his death righteousness and holiness. "He gave himself for the church, that he might sanctify and cleanse it," Eph. v. 25, 26; "that he might present it to himself a glorious church, not having spot or wrinkle;" that we should be "holy and without blemish," verse 27. Where, first, we have whom Christ died or gave himself for, even his church; secondly, what he obtained for it,—holiness and righteousness, a freedom from the spots and blemishes of sin, that is, the grace of justification and sanctity: "He made him to be sin for us, who knew no sin; that we might be made the righteousness of God in him," 2 Cor. v. 21. And, lastly, he died to purchase for us "an eternal inheritance," Heb. ix. 15. So that both grace and glory are bestowed on them for whom he died, as the immediate fruits of his death and passion.

Secondly, See what the Scripture ῥητῶς, "expressly," assigneth as the proper end and immediate effect (according to the purpose of God and his own intention) of the effusion of the blood of Jesus Christ, and you shall find that he intended by it to take away the sins of many; to "make his soul an offering for sin," that he might "see his seed," that "the pleasure of the LORD might prosper in his hand," Isa. liii. 10; to be "a ransom for many," Matt. xx. 28; to "bear the sins of many," Heb. ix. 28. He "bare our sins in his own body on the tree, that we should live unto righteousness," 1 Pet. ii. 24; that "we might be made the righteousness of God in him," 2 Cor. v. 21; thereby reconciling us unto God, verse 19. He died to "reconcile us unto God, in the body of his flesh through death," that we might be "holy and unblamable," Col. i. 21, 22; to "purge our sins," Heb. i. 3; to "obtain eternal redemption for us," chap. ix. 12. So that if Christ by his death obtained what he did intend, he hath purchased for us not only a possibility of salvation, but holiness, righteousness, reconciliation with God, justification freedom from the guilt and condemning power of sin, everlasting redemption, eternal life and glory in heaven.

Thirdly, I appeal unto the conscience of all Christians,—*First*, Whether they do not suppose the very foundation of all their consolation to be stricken at, when they shall find those places of Scripture[1] that affirm Christ to have died to take away our sins, to reconcile us unto God, to put away or abolish our transgressions, to wash and regenerate us, perfectly to save us, and purchase for us an everlasting redemption, whereby he is become unto us righteousness, and redemption, and sanctification, the Lord our righteousness, and we become the righteousness of God in him, to be so wrested as if he should be said only to have done something from which these things might happily follow?

Secondly, Whether they think it not a ready way to impair their love and to weaken their faith in Christ, when they shall be taught that Christ hath done no more for them than for those that are damned in hell; that, be their assurance never so great that Christ died for them, yet there is enough to be laid to their charge to condemn them; that though God is said to have reconciled them unto himself in Christ, Col. i. 19, 20, yet indeed he is as angry with them as with any reprobate in the world; that God loveth us not first, but so long as we continue in a state of enmity against him, before our conversion, he continues our enemy also, so that the first act of friendship or love must be performed on our part, notwithstanding that the Scripture saith, "When we were enemies, we were reconciled unto God," Rom. v. 10?

Thirdly, Whether they have not hitherto supposed themselves bound to believe that Christ died for their sins, and rose for their justification? Do they not think it lawful to pray that God would bestow upon them grace and glory for Christ's sake? and to believe that Jesus Christ was such a mediator of the new covenant as procured for the persons covenanted withal all the good things comprehended in the promise of that covenant?

I will not farther press upon this prevarication against Christian religion; only, I would desire all the lovers of Jesus Christ seriously to consider whether these men do truly aim at his honour and advancing the dignity of his merit, and not rather at the crying up of their own endeavours, seeing the sole cause of their denying these glorious effects of the blood of Christ is to appropriate the praise of them unto themselves; as we shall see in the next chapter.

These charges are never to be waived by the vanity of their sophistical distinctions, as of that of impetration and application; which, though it may be received in an orthodox meaning, yet not in that

[1] Heb. ix. 12, 14, 15, 24, 28; Isa. liii. 10; 1 John ii. 2, etc.

sense, or rather nonsense, whereunto they abuse it;—namely, as though Christ had obtained that for some which shall never be imparted unto them; that all the blessings procured by his death are proper to none, but pendent in the air for them that can or will catch them: whereupon, when we object [1]that by this means all the efficacy of the merit of Christ is in our own power, they readily grant it, and say it cannot otherwise be. Let them that can, receive these monsters in Christianity; for my part, in these following contradictory assertions I will choose rather to adhere to the authority of the word of God than of Arminius and his sectaries:—

S. S.	Lib. Arbit.
"He made him to be sin for us, who knew no sin; that we might be made the righteousness of God in him," 2 Cor. v. 21. "He loved the church, and gave himself for it; that he might present it unto himself a glorious church, not having spot, or wrinkle, or any such thing," Eph. v. 25, 27.	"The immediate effect of the death of Christ is not the remission of sins, or the actual redemption of any," Armin. "Christ did not properly die to save any one," Grevinch.
"God was in Christ, reconciling the world unto himself," 2 Cor. v. 19.	"A potential and conditionate reconciliation, not actual and absolute, is obtained by the death of Christ," Corv.
"When thou shalt make his soul an offering for sin, he shall see his seed, he shall prolong his days, and the pleasure of the LORD shall prosper in his hand," Isa. liii. 10. "By his knowledge shall my righteous servant justify many; for he shall bear their iniquities," Isa. liii. 11.	"I believe it might have come to pass that the death of Christ might have had its end, though never any man had believed," Corv. "The death and satisfaction of Christ being accomplished, yet it may so come to pass that, none at all fulfilling the condition of the new covenant, none might be saved," Idem.
"Christ was once offered to bear the sins of many," Heb. ix. 28. "By his own blood he entered in once into the holy place, having obtained eternal redemption	"The *impetration* of salvation for all, by the death of Christ, is nothing but the obtaining of a possibility thereof; that God, without wronging his justice, may open

1 "Sic efficacia meriti Christi tota penes nos stabit, qui vocationem alioqui inefficacem, efficacem reddimus; sane, fieri aliter non potest."—Rem. Apol., p. 93.

S. S.	Lib. Arbit.
for us," chap. ix. 12. "He hath reconciled you in the body of his flesh through death, to present you holy, and unblamable, and unreprovable," Col. i. 21, 22.	unto them a gate of mercy, to be entered on some condition," Rem. Coll. Hag.
"Whom God hath set forth to be a propitiation through faith in his blood, to declare his righteousness for the remission of sins," etc.: "that he might be just, and the justifier of him which believeth in Jesus," Rom. iii. 25, 26.	"Notwithstanding the death of Christ, God might have assigned any other condition of salvation as well as faith, or have chosen the Jews following the righteousness of the law," Grevinch.
"Who his own self bare our sins in his own body on the tree, that we, being dead to sins, should live unto righteousness: by whose stripes we were healed," 1 Pet. ii. 24.	"Why, then, the efficacy of the death of Christ depends wholly on us." "True; it cannot otherwise be," Rem. Apol.

CHAPTER X.

Of the cause of faith, grace, and righteousness.

THE second part of this controversy is in particular concerning grace, faith, and holiness, sincere obedience to the precepts of the new covenant, all whose praise we appropriate to the Most High by reason of a double interest,—first, Of the merit of Christ, which doth procure them for us; secondly, Of the Holy Spirit, which works them in us. The death of Christ is their meritorious cause; the Spirit of God and his effectual grace their efficient, working instrumentally with power by the word and ordinances. Now, because this would deprive the idol of his chiefest glory, and expose him to open shame, like the bird "furtivis nudata coloribus," the Arminians advance themselves in his quarrel, and in behalf of their darling quite exclude both merit of Christ and Spirit of God from any title to their production.

First, For the merit of Christ. Whereas we affirm that God "blesseth us with all spiritual blessings in him," or for his sake, Eph. i. 3, amongst which, doubtless, faith possesseth not the lowest room; that "he is made unto us righteousness, and sanctification, and redemption;" that "he was made sin for us, that we might be made the righteousness of God in him;" that he is "the Lord our righteousness," and glories to be called by that name (and whatever he is unto us, it is chiefly by the way of merit); that "to us it is given ὑπὲρ Χριστοῦ, for Christ's sake, to believe on him," Phil. i. 29, where ὑπὲρ Χριστοῦ is plainly referred to δίδοται, [ἐχαρίσθη,?] "is given,"—as if the apostle should have said, "Christ is the meritorious cause of the bestowing of those good gifts, faith and constancy unto martyrdom, upon you;"—when, I say, we profess all these to be the proper and immediate products of the passion and blood of Christ, these turbulent Davusses come in with a prohibition, and quite expel it from having any interest therein.

[1] "There is nothing more vain, nothing more foolish," say they in their Apology, "than to attribute our regeneration and faith unto the death of Christ; for if Christ may be said to have merited for us faith and regeneration, then faith cannot be a condition whose performance God should require at the hands of sinners under the pain of eternal damnation." And again, [2] "If faith be the effect of the merit of Christ, it cannot be our duty." No? Suppose, then, that the church should pray that it would please God, for Christ's sake, to call home those sheep that belong to his fold not as yet collected, —that he would grant faith and repentance, for the merit of his Son, to them that are as yet afar off,—were this an altogether vain and foolish prayer? Let others think as they please, it is such a vanity as I desire not to be weaned from; nor any one else, I believe, that loves the Lord Jesus in sincerity. Oh, that Christians should patiently endure such a diminution of their Saviour's honour, as with one dash of an Arminian pen to have the chief effects of his death and passion quite obliterated! If this be a motive to the love and honour of the Son of God, if this be a way to set forth the preciousness of his blood, by denying the efficacy thereof in enabling us by faith to get an interest in the new covenant, most Christians in the world are under a necessity of being new catechised by these seraphical doctors. Until when, they must give us leave to believe, with the apostle, that God "blesseth us with all spiritual blessings in Christ," Eph. i. 3; and we will take leave to account faith a spiritual blessing, and, therefore, bestowed on us for Christ's sake. Again; since our regeneration is nothing but a "purging of our consciences from dead works that we may serve the living God," which being done by "the blood of Christ," as the apostle witnesseth, Heb. ix. 14, we will ascribe our new birth, or forming anew, to the virtue of that grace which is purchased by his blood; that "precious blood" it is which "redeemeth us from our vain conversation," 1 Pet. i. 18, 19, by whose efficacy we are vindicated from the state of sin and corrupted nature wherein we are born.

[1] "Nihil ineptius, nihil vanius, quam regenerationem et fidem merito Christi tribuere; si enim Christus nobis meritus dicatur fidem et regenerationem, tum fides conditio esse non poterat quam a peccatoribus Deus sub comminatione mortis æternæ exigeret." —Rem. Apol., cap. viii. p. 95.

[2] "Si fides sit effectum meriti Christi, non potest esse actus officii nostri."—Idem.

The Arminians have but one argument, that ever I could meet with, whereby they strive to rob Christ of this glory of meriting and procuring for us faith and repentance; and that is, because they are such acts of ours as in duty and obedience to the precepts of the gospel we are bound to perform;[1] and this they everywhere press at large, "usque et usque." In plain terms, they will not suffer their idol to be accounted defective in any thing that is necessary to bring us unto heaven. Now, concerning this argument, that nothing which God requireth of us can be procured for us by Christ, I would have two things noted:—*First*, That the strength of it consists in this, that no gift of God bestowed upon us can be a thing well-pleasing to him, as being in us, for all his precepts and commands signify only what is well-pleasing unto him that we should be or do; and it is not the meriting of any thing by Christ, but God's bestowing of it as the effect thereof, which hinders it from being a thing requirable of us as a part of our duty: which I shall consider hereafter. Only now observe, that there being nothing in us, by the way of habit or act, from the beginning of our faith to the consummation thereof, from our new birth until we become perfect men in Christ by the finishing of our course, that is not required of us in the gospel, all and every grace whereof we are in this life partakers are, by this means, denied to be the gifts of God. *Secondly*, Consider the extent of this argument itself. Nothing whose performance is our duty can be merited for us by Christ. When the apostle beseecheth us to be "reconciled unto God," I would know whether it be not a part of our duty to yield obedience to the apostle's exhortation? If not, his exhortation is frivolous and vain: if so, then to be reconciled unto God is a part of our duty; and yet the Arminians sometimes seem to confess that Christ hath obtained for us a reconciliation with God. The like may be said in divers other particulars. So that this argument either proveth that we enjoy no fruit of the death of Christ in this life, or (which is most true) it proveth nothing at all; for neither the merit of Christ procuring nor God bestowing any grace in the habit doth at all hinder but that, in the exercise thereof, it may be a duty of ours, inasmuch as it is done in us and by us. Notwithstanding, then, this exception,—which cannot stand by itself alone without the help of some other not as yet discovered,—we will continue our prayers, as we are commanded, in the name of Christ; that is, that God would bestow upon us those things we ask for Christ's sake, and that by an immediate collation, yea, even then when we cry with the poor penitent, "Lord, help our unbelief," or with the apostles, "Lord, increase our faith."

Secondly, The second plea on God's behalf, to prove him the

[1] Rem. Apol., ubi sup.; Corv. ad Molin., cap. xxviii. sect. 9.

author and finisher of all those graces whereof in this life we are partakers, ariseth from what the Scripture affirmeth concerning his working these graces in us, and that powerfully, by the effectual operation of his Holy Spirit. To which the Arminians oppose a seeming necessity that they must needs be our own acts, contradistinct from his gifts, because they are in us and commanded by him. The head, then, of this contention betwixt our God and their idol about the living child of grace is, whether he can work that in us which he requireth of us. Let us hear them pleading their cause:—

[1]"It is most certain that that ought not to be commanded which is wrought in us; and that cannot be wrought in us which is commanded. He foolishly commandeth that to be done of others who will work in them what he commandeth," saith their Apology. O foolish St Prosper, who thought that it was the whole Pelagian heresy to say, [2]"That there is neither praise nor worth, as ours, in that which Christ bestoweth upon us!" Foolish St Augustine, praying, [3]"Give us, O Lord, what thou commandest, and command what thou wilt!" Foolish Benedict, bishop of Rome, who gave such a form to his prayer as must needs cast an aspersion of folly on the Most High! [4]"O Lord," saith he, "teach us what we should do; show us whither we should go; work in us what we ought to perform." O foolish fathers of the second Arausican council, affirming, [5]"That many good things are done in man which he doth not himself; but a man doth no good which God doth not so work that he should do it!" And again, "As often as we do good, God worketh in us and with us, that we may so work." In one word, this makes fools of all the doctors of the church who ever opposed the Pelagian heresy, inasmuch as they all unanimously maintained that we are partakers of no good thing in this kind without the effectual powerful operation of the almighty grace of God, and yet our faith and obedience, so wrought in us, to be most acceptable unto him. Yea, what shall we say to the Lord himself, in one place commanding us to fear him, and in another promising that he will put his fear into our hearts, that we shall not depart from him? Is his command foolish, or his promise false? The Arminians must affirm the one or

[1] "Illud certissimum est, nec jubendum esse quod efficitur, nec efficiendum quod jubetur. Stulte jubet et vult ab alio fieri aliquid, qui ipse quod jubet in eo efficere vult."—Rem. Apol., cap. ix. p. 105, a.

[2] "At exigua conclusione pene tu totum Pelagianum dogma confirmas, dicendo, nullius laudis esse ac meriti; si id in eo Christus quod ipse donaverat prætulisset."—Prosp. ad Collat., cap. xxxvi.

[3] "Da, Domine, quod jubes, et jube quod vis."—Aug.

[4] "O Domine, doce nos quid agamus; quo gradiamur ostende; quid efficiamus operare."—Ben. Pap. in Concil. Legunstad.

[5] "Multa in homine bona fiunt, quæ non facit homo: nulla vero facit homo bona, quæ non Deus præstet ut faciat."—Consil. Arau. ii. can. 20. "Quoties enim bona agimus, Deus in nobis et nobiscum, ut operemur, operatur."—Can. 9.

renounce their heresy. But of this, after I have a little farther laid open this monstrous error from their own words and writings.

[1]"Can any one," say they, "wisely and seriously prescribe the performance of a condition to another, under the promise of a reward and threatening of punishment, who will effect it in him to whom it is prescribed? This is a ridiculous action, scarce worthy of the stage." That is, seeing Christ hath affirmed that "he that believeth shall be saved; but he that believeth not shall be damned," Mark xvi. 16, whereby faith is established the condition of salvation, and unbelief threatened with hell, if God should by his Holy Spirit ingenerate faith in the hearts of any, causing them so to fulfil the condition, it were a mere mockery, to be exploded from a theatre as an unlikely fiction; which, what an aspersion it casts upon the whole gospel of Christ, yea, on all God's dealings with the children of men ever since, by reason of the fall, they became unable of themselves to fulfil his commands, I leave to all men's silent judgment. Well, then, seeing they must be accounted ἀσύστατα, things inconsistent, that God should be so righteous as to show us our duty, and yet so good and merciful as to bestow his graces on us, let us hear more of this stuff. [2]"Faith and conversion cannot be our obedience, if they are wrought in us by God," say they at the Hague; and Episcopius, [3]"That it is a most absurd thing to affirm that God either effects by his power, or procureth by his wisdom, that the elect should do those things that he requireth of them." So that where the Scripture calls faith the gift and work of God, they say it is an improper locution, inasmuch as he commands it; properly, it is an act or work of our own. And for that renowned saying of St Augustine, that [4]"God crowneth his own gifts in us," "it is not to be received without a grain of salt;" that is, some such gloss as wherewith they corrupt the Scripture. The sum at which they aim is, that to affirm that God bestoweth any graces upon us, or effectually worketh them in us, contradicteth his word requiring them as our duty and obedience. By which means they have erected their idol into the throne of God's free grace and mercy, and attribute unto it all the praise due to those many heavenly qualifications the servants of God are endowed withal, for they never have more good in them, no, nor so much, as is

[1] "Anne conditionem quis serio et sapienter præscribet alteri, sub promisso præmii et pœnæ gravissimæ comminatione, qui eam, in eo cui præscribit efficere vult? Hæc actio tota ludicra, et vix scenâ digna est."—Rem. Apol., cap. ix. p. 105, a.

[2] "Fides et conversio non possunt esse obedientia, si tantum ab aliquo, in alio, efficiantur."—Rem. Coll. Hag., p. 196.

[3] "Absurdem est statuere Deum aut efficere per potentiam, aut procurare per sapientiam, ut electi ea faciant, quæ ab ipsis, ut ipsi ea faciant, exigit et postulat."—Episcop., Disp. Pri. viii. thes. 7.

[4] Apol., cap. ix. ubi. sup.—"Deum dona sua in nobis coronare, dictum hoc Augustini nisi cum grano salis accipiatur, neutiquam est admittendum."—Idem, ibid p. 115.

required; all that they have or do is but their duty;—which, how derogatory it is to the merit of Christ, themselves seem to acknowledge, when they affirm that he is no otherwise said to be a Saviour than are all they who confirm the way to salvation by preaching, miracles, martyrdom, and example. So that, having quite overthrown the merits of Christ,[1] "they grant us to be our own saviours in a very large sense," Rem. Apol., fol. 96. All which assertions, how contrary they are to the express word of God, I shall now demonstrate.

There is not one of all those plain texts of Scripture, not one of those innumerable and invincible arguments, whereby the effectual working of God's grace in the conversion of a sinner, his powerful translating us from death to life, from the state of sin and bondage to the liberty of the sons of God, which doth not overthrow this prodigious error. I will content myself with instancing in some few of them which are directly opposite unto it, even in terms:—

First, Deut. x. 16, The Lord commandeth the Israelites to "circumcise the foreskin of their hearts, and to be no more stiff-necked;" so that the circumcising of their hearts was a part of their obedience,—it was their duty so to do, in obedience to God's command. And yet, in the 30th chapter, verse 6, he affirmeth that "he will circumcise their hearts, that they might love the LORD their God with all their hearts." So that, it seems, the same thing, in diverse respects, may be God's act in us and our duty towards him. And how the Lord will here escape that Arminian censure, that if his words be true in the latter place, his command in the former is vain and foolish, "ipse viderit,"—let him plead his cause, and avenge himself on those that rise up against him.

Secondly, Ezek. xviii. 31, "Make you a new heart and a new spirit: for why will ye die, O house of Israel?" The making of a new heart and a new spirit is here required under a promise of a reward of life, and a great threatening of eternal death; so that so to do must needs be a part of their duty and obedience. And yet, chap. xxxvi. 26, 27, he affirmeth that he will do this very thing that here he requireth of them: "A new heart will I give you, and a new spirit will I put within you: and I will take away the stony heart out of your flesh, and I will give you an heart of flesh; and I will cause you to walk in my statutes," etc. In how many places, also, are we commanded to "fear the Lord!" which, when we do, I hope none will deny it to be a performance of our duty; and yet, Jer. xxxii. 40, God promiseth that "he will put his fear in our hearts, that we shall not depart from him."

Thirdly, Those two against which they lay particular exceptions,

[1] "Atqui dices, sic servatores nostri essent omnes,"—eodem sensu quo Christus,—"saltem ex parte qui præconio, miraculis, et exemplo salutis viam, confirmant; esto, quid tum?"—Rem. Apol., cap. viii. [p. 94.]

faith and repentance, are also expressly attributed to the free donation of God: He "granteth unto the Gentiles repentance unto life," Acts xi. 18; and of faith directly, "It is not of ourselves, it is the gift of God," Eph. ii. 8. To which assertion of the Holy Spirit I shall rather fasten my belief than to the Arminians, affirming that it is no gift of God because it is of ourselves; and yet this hindereth not but that it may be styled, "Our most holy faith," Jude 20. Let them that will, deny that any thing can properly be ours which God bestoweth on us; the prophet accounted them not inconsistent when he averred that "the LORD worketh all our works in us," Isa. xxvi. 12. They are our works, though of his working. The apostle laboured; though it was not he, but "the grace of God that was with him," 1 Cor. xv. 10. He "worketh in us καὶ τὸ θέλειν καὶ τὸ ἐνεργεῖν of his good pleasure," Phil. ii. 13; and yet the performance of our duty may consist in those acts of our wills and those good deeds whereof he is the author. So that, according to St Austin's counsel,[1] we will still pray that he would bestow what he commandeth us to have.

Fourthly, 1 Cor. iv. 7, "Who maketh thee to differ from another? and what hast thou that thou didst not receive?" Every thing that makes us differ from others is received from God; wherefore, the foundation of all difference in spiritual things between the sons of Adam being faith and repentance, they must also of necessity be received from above. In brief, God's "circumcising our hearts," Col. ii. 11, his "quickening us when we are dead," Eph. ii. 1, 2, begetting us anew, John i. 13, making us in all things such as he would have us to be, is contained in that promise of the new covenant, Jer. xxxii. 40, "I will make an everlasting covenant with them, that I will not turn away from them, to do them good; but I will put my fear in their hearts, that they shall not depart from me;" and is no way repugnant to the holy Scripture, declaring our duty to be all this that the Lord would have us. And now, let all men judge whether, against so many and clear testimonies of the Holy Ghost, the Arminian reasons, borrowed from the old philosophers, be of any value. The sum of them all you may find in Cicero, his third book De Natura Deorum. [2]"Every one," saith he, "obtaineth virtue for himself; never any wise man thanked God for that: for our virtue we are praised; in virtue we glory, which might not be were it a gift of God." And truly this, in softer terms, is the sum of the Remonstrants' arguments in this particular.

Lastly, Observe, that this error is that which, of all others, the orthodox fathers did most oppose in the Pelagian heretics; yea, and

[1] "Petamus ut det quod ut habeamus jubet."—Aug.

[2] "Virtutem autem nemo unquam acceptam deo retulit. Nimirum rectè: propter virtutem enim jure laudamur, et in virtute rectè gloriamur. Quod non contingeret, si id donum à Deo, non à nobis haberemus."—Cicero De Nat. Deor. iii. 36.

to this day, [1]the more learned schoolmen stoutly maintain the truth herein against the innovating Jesuits. With some few of the testimonies of the ancients I will shut up this discourse. [2]"It is certain that when we do any thing, we do it," saith St Augustine; "but it is God that causeth us so to do." And in another place, [3]"Shall we not account that to be the gift of God, because it is required of us under the promise of eternal life? God forbid that this should seem so, either to the partakers or defenders of grace;" where he rejecteth both the error and the sophism wherewith it is upholden. So also Cœlestius, bishop of Rome, in his epistle to the bishops of France. [4]"So great," saith he, "is the goodness of God towards men, that he will have those good things to be our good duties" (he calls them merits, according to the phrase of those days) "which are his own gifts;" to which purpose I cited before two canons out of the Arausican council. And St Prosper, in his treatise against Cassianus the semi-Pelagian, affirmeth it to be a foolish complaint of proud men [5]"that free-will is destroyed, if the beginning, progress, and continuance in good be said to be the gifts of God." And so the imputation of folly, wherewith the Arminians in my first quotation charge their opposers, being retorted on them by this learned father, I refer you to these following excerpta for a close:—

S. S.

"Circumcise the foreskin of your heart, and be no more stiff-necked," Deut. x. 16. "And the LORD thy God will circumcise thine heart, and the heart of thy seed," chap. xxx. 6.—"Make you a new heart and a new spirit, for why will ye die, O house of Israel?" Ezek. xviii. 31. "A new heart will I give you, and a new spirit will I put within you," chap. xxxvi. 26.

"If ye will fear the LORD, and

Lib. Arbit.

"This is most certain, that that ought not to be commanded which is wrought in us. He foolishly commandeth that to be done of others who will work in them what he commandeth," Rem. Apol.

"It is absurd to affirm that

[1] Alvarez, Disput. lxxxvi., ubi Aug., Thom., alios, citat.

[2] "Certum est nos facere cum facimus; sed ille facit ut faciamus."—Aug. de Grat., et Lib. Arbit., cap. xvi.

[3] "—— Neque id donum Dei esse fateamur, quoniam exigi audivimus a nobis, præmio vitæ si hoc fecerimus oblato? Absit, ut hoc placeat participibus et defensoribus gratiæ."—Aug. de Prædest. Sanc., cap. xx.

[4] "Tanta est erga homines bonitas Dei, ut nostra velit esse merita quæ sunt ipsius dona."—Cœlest. Epist. ad Ep. Gal., cap. xii.

[5] "Non enim conturbat nos superbientium inepta querimonia; quia liberum arbitrium causantur auferri: si et principia, et profectus, et perseverantia in bonis usque ad finem Dei dona esse dicantur."—Prosp. ad Collat., p. 404.

S. S.	Lib. Arbit.
serve him, then shall ye continue following the LORD your God," 1 Sam. xii. 14. "I will put my fear in their hearts, that they shall not depart from me," Jer. xxxii. 40.	God either worketh by his power, or procureth by his wisdom, that the elect should do those things which God requireth of them," Episcop.
"Thou hast wrought all our works in us," Isa. xxvi. 12. "God worketh in you both to will and to do of his good pleasure," Phil. ii. 13.	"Faith and conversion cannot be acts of our obedience if they are wrought by God in us," Rem. Coll. Hag. "That God should require that of us which himself will work in us is a ridiculous action, scarce fit for a stage," Rem. Apol.
"He hath blessed us with all spiritual blessings in Christ," Eph. i. 3.	"That saying of Augustine, that 'God crowneth his own gifts in us,' is not easily to be admitted," Ibid.
"Unto you it is given in the behalf of Christ to believe on him," Phil. i. 29. "The blood of Christ purgeth our consciences from dead works to serve the living God," Heb. ix. 14.	"There is nothing more vain and foolish than to ascribe faith and regeneration to the merit of Christ," Idem.

CHAPTER XI.

Whether salvation may be attained without the knowledge of, or faith in, Christ Jesus.

I SHALL shut up all this discourse concerning the meritorious cause of salvation, with their shutting out of Christ from being the only one and absolutely necessary means to bring us unto heaven, to make us happy. This is the last pile they erect upon their Babylonish foundation, which makes the idol of human self-sufficiency every way perfect, and fit to be sacrificed unto. Until these proud builders, to get materials for their own temple, laid the axe to the root of Christianity, we took it for granted that "there is no salvation in any other," because "there is none other name under heaven given unto men whereby we must be saved," Acts iv. 12. Neither yet shall their nefarious attempts frighten us from our creed, nor make us be wanting to the defence of our Saviour's honour. But I shall be very brief in the consideration of this heterodoxy, nothing doubting but that to have repeated it is fully to have confuted it, in the judgment of all pious Christians.

First, then, They grant salvation to the ancient patriarchs and Jews, before the coming of Christ, without any knowledge of or faith in him at all; nay, they deny that any such faith in Christ was ever prescribed unto them or required of them. [1]"It is certain that there is no place in the Old Testament from whence it may appear that faith in Christ as a Redeemer was ever enjoined or found in any of them," say they jointly in their Apology; the truth of which assertion we shall see hereafter. Only they grant a general faith, involved under types and shadows, and looking on the promise as it lay hid in the goodness and providence of God, which indirectly might be called a faith in Christ: from which kind of faith I see no reason why thousands of heathen infidels should be excluded. Agreeable unto these assertions are the dictates of their patriarch Arminius, affirming, [2]"that the whole description of the faith of Abraham, Rom. iv., makes no mention of Jesus Christ, either expressly or so implicitly as that it may be of any one easily understood." And to the testimony of Christ himself to the contrary, John viii. 56, "Your father Abraham rejoiced to see my day; and he saw it, and was glad," he answereth, "He rejoiced to see the birth of Isaac, who was a type of me,"—a goodly gloss, corrupting the text.

Secondly, What they teach of the Jews, that also they grant concerning the Gentiles living before the incarnation of Christ; they also might attain salvation, and be justified without his knowledge. [3]"For although," saith Corvinus, "the covenant was not revealed unto them by the same means that it was unto the Jews, yet they are not to be supposed to be excluded from the covenant" (of grace), "nor to be excluded from salvation; for some way or other they were called."

Thirdly, They are come at length to that perfection in setting out this stain of Christianity, that Bertius, on good consideration, denied this proposition, [4]"That no man can be saved that is not ingrafted into Christ by a true faith;" and Venator to this question, [5]"Whe-

[1] "Certum est locum nullum esse, unde appareat fidem istam, sub Vet. Test., præceptam fuisse aut viguisse."—Rem. Apol., cap. vii. p. 91.

[2] "Consideretur omnis descriptio fidei Abrahæ, Rom. iv. et apparebit in illa Jesu Christi non fieri mentionem, expresse, sed illa tantum implicatione, quam explicare cuivis non est facile."—Armin. "Gavisus est videre natalem Isaac, qui fuit typus mei."—Idem.

[3] "Gentes sub Veteri Testamento viventes licet ipsis ista ratione qua Judæis non fuit revelatum, non tamen inde continuo ex fædere absolute exclusæ sunt, nec a salute præcise exclusi judicari debent, quia aliquo saltem modo vocantur."—Corv. Defens. Armin. ad Tilen., p. 107.

[4] "Nego hanc propositionem: neminem posse salvari, quam qui Jesu Christo per veram fidem sit insitus."—Bert. ad Sibrand., p. 133.

[5] "Ad hanc quæstionem an unica via salutis, sit vita, passio, mors, resurrectio, et ascensio Jesu Christi? respondeo, Non."—Venat., apud Fest. Hom. et Peltium.

ther the only means of salvation be the life, passion, death, resurrection, and ascension of Jesus Christ?" answereth, "No." Thus they lay men in Abraham's bosom who never believed in the Son of Abraham; make them overcome the serpent who never heard of the Seed of the woman; bring goats into heaven, who never were of the flock of Christ, never entered by him, the door; make men please God without faith, and obtain the remission of sins without the sprinkling of the blood of the Lamb,—to be saved without a Saviour, redeemed without a Redeemer,—to become the sons of God, and never know their elder Brother;—which prodigious error might yet be pardoned, and ascribed to human imbecility, had it casually slipped from their pens, as it did from some others.[1] But seeing it hath foundation in all the grounds of their new doctrine, and is maintained by them on mature deliberation,[2] it must be looked on by all Christians as a heresy to be detested and accursed. For, first, deny the contagion and demerit of original sin; then make the covenant of grace to be universal, and to comprehend all and every one of the posterity of Adam; thirdly, grant a power in ourselves to come unto God by any such means as he will appoint, and affirm that he doth assign some means unto all,—and it will naturally follow that the knowledge of Christ is not absolutely necessary to salvation, and so down falls the pre-eminence of Christianity; its heaven-reaching crown must be laid level with the services of dunghill gods.[3]

It is true, indeed, some of the ancient fathers, before the rising of the Pelagian heresy,—who had so put on Christ, as Lipsius speaks, that they had not fully put off Plato,—have unadvisedly dropped some speeches seeming to grant that divers men before the incarnation, living μετὰ λόγου, "according to the dictates of right reason," might be saved without faith in Christ; as is well showed by learned Casaubon in his first exercitation on Baronius. But let this be accounted part of that stubble which shall burn at the last day, wherewith the writings of all men not divinely inspired may be stained. It hath also since (as what hath not?) been drawn into dispute among the wrangling schoolmen; and yet, which is rarely seen, their verdict in this particular almost unanimously passeth for the truth. Aquinas[4] tells us a story of the corpse of a heathen, that should be taken up in the time of the Empress Irene and her son Constantine, with a golden plate on his breast, wherein was this inscription:—"Christ is born of a virgin, and I believe in him. O

[1] Zuing. Profes. Fid. ad Reg. Gall.

[2] Art. of the Church of Eng., art. xvii.

[3] "Nihil magis repugnat fidei, quam sine fide salvum esse posse quempiam hominum."—Acost. de Indo. Salu. Proc.

[4] Aquin. 2, 2æ q. 2, a. 7, c.—"Christus nascitur ex virgine, et ego credo in eum. O sol, sub Irenæ et Constantini temporibus iterum me videbis."

sun, thou shalt see me again in the days of Irene and Constantine." But the question is not, Whether a Gentile believing in Christ may be saved? or whether God did not reveal himself and his Son extraordinarily to some of them? for shall we straiten the breast and shorten the arm of the Almighty, as though he might not do what he will with his own; but, Whether a man by the conduct of nature, without the knowledge of Christ, may come to heaven? the assertion whereof we condemn as a wicked, Pelagian, Socinian heresy, and think that it was well said of Bernard, [1]"That many labouring to make Plato a Christian, do prove themselves to be heathens." And if we look upon the several branches of this Arminian novel doctrine, extenuating the precious worth and necessity of faith in Christ, we shall find them hewed off by the two-edged sword of God's word.

FIRST, For their denying the patriarchs and Jews to have had faith "in Christum exhibendum et moriturum," as we in him "exhibitum et mortuum," it is disproved,—

First, By all evangelical promises made from the beginning of the world to the birth of our Saviour; as that, Gen. iii. 15, "The seed of the woman shall break the serpent's head;" and chap. xii. 3, xlix. 10; Ps. ii. 7, 8, cx.; with innumerable others concerning his life, office, and redeeming of his people: for surely they were obliged to believe the promises of God.

Secondly, By those many clear expressions of his death, passion, and suffering for us, as Gen. iii. 15; Isa. liii. 6–10, etc., lxiii. 1–3; Dan. ix. 26. But what need we reckon any more? Our Saviour taught his disciples that all the prophets from Moses spake concerning him, and that the sole reason why they did not so readily embrace the faith of his passion and resurrection was because they believed not the prophets, Luke xxiv. 25, 26; showing plainly that the prophets required faith in his death and passion.

Thirdly, By the explicit faith of many Jews, as of old Simeon, Luke ii. 34; of the Samaritan woman, who looked for a Messiah, not as an earthly king, but as one that should "tell them all things,"—redeem them from sin, and tell them all such things as Christ was then discoursing of, concerning the worship of God, John iv. 25.

Fourthly, By the express testimony of Christ himself. "Abraham," saith he, "rejoiced to see my day; and he saw it, and was glad," John viii. 56. His day, his hour, in the Scripture, principally denote his passion. And that which he saw surely he believed, or else the father of the faithful was more diffident than Thomas, the most incredulous of his children.

[1] "Dum multum sudant nonnulli, quomodo Platonem faciant Christianum, se probant esse ethnicos."—Bern. Epist.

Fifthly, By these following, and the like places of Scripture: Christ is a "Lamb slain from the foundation of the world," Rev. xiii. 8; slain in promises, slain in God's estimation and in the faith of believers. He is "the same yesterday, and to-day, and for ever," Heb. xiii. 8, under the law and the gospel. "There is none other name under heaven given unto men, whereby we must be saved," Acts iv. 12. Never any, then, without the knowledge of a Redeemer, participation of his passion, communication of his merits, did ever come to the sight of God; no man ever came to the Father but by him. Hence St Paul tells the Ephesians that they were "without Christ," because they were "aliens from the commonwealth of Israel," Eph. ii. 12; intimating that God's covenant with the Jews included Christ Jesus and his righteousness no less than it doth now with us. On these grounds holy Ignatius called Abel [1]"A martyr of Christ;" he died for his faith in the promised Seed. And in another place, [2]"All the saints were saved by Christ; hoping in him, and waiting on him, they obtained salvation by him." So Prosper, also, [3]"We must believe that never any man was justified by any other faith, either before the law or under the law, than by faith in Christ coming to save that which was lost." Whence Eusebius contendeth [4]that all the old patriarchs might properly be called Christians; they all ate of the same spiritual meat, and all drank of the same spiritual drink, even of the rock that followed them, which rock was Christ.

SECONDLY, If the ancient people of God, notwithstanding divers other especial revelations of his will and heavenly instructions, obtained not salvation without faith in Christ, much less may we grant this happiness without him to them who were deprived of those other helps also. So that though we confess the poor natural endeavours of the heathen not to have wanted their reward (either positive in this life, by outward prosperity, and inward calmness of mind, in that they were not all perplexed and agitated with furies, like Nero and Caligula; or negative in the life to come, by a diminution of the degrees of their torments,—they shall not be beaten with so many stripes), yet we absolutely deny that there is any saving mercy of God towards them revealed in the Scripture, which should give us the least intimation of their attaining everlasting happiness.

[1] *Παραδοθείς γε, τῶν διὰ Χριστὸν ἀναιρουμένων, ἀπὸ τοῦ αἵματος Ἄβελ τοῦ δικαίου.*—Ignat. Epist. ad Ephes. [cap. xii.]

[2] *Πάντες οὖν οἱ ἅγιοι ἐν Χριστῷ ἐσώθησαν, ἐλπίσαντες εἰς αὐτὸν καὶ αὐτὸν ἀναμείναντες, καὶ δι' αὐτοῦ σωτηρίας ἔτυχον.*—Epist. ad Phil. [cap. v.]

[3] "Non alia fide quemquam hominum, sive ante legem sive legis tempore, justificatum esse, credendum est, quam hac eadem qua Dominus Jesu," etc.—Prosp. ad Ob. viii., Gallorum.

[4] "Omnes ergo illos qui ab Abraham sursum versus ad primum hominem, generationis ordine conscribuntur, etsi non nomine, rebus tamen, et religione Christianos fuisse, si quis dicat, non mihi videtur errare."—Euseb. Hist. Eccles., lib. i. cap. 4.

For, not to consider the corruption and universal disability of nature to do any thing that is good ("without Christ we can do nothing," John xv. 5), nor yet the sinfulness of their best works and actions, the "sacrifice of the wicked being an abomination unto the LORD," Prov. xv. 8 ("Evil trees cannot bring forth good fruit; men do not gather grapes of thorns, nor figs of thistles," Matt. vii. 16, 17);—the word of God is plain, that "without faith it is impossible to please God," Heb. xi. 6; that "he that believeth not is condemned," Mark xvi. 16; that no nation or person can be blessed but in the Seed of Abraham, Gen. xii. 3. And the "blessing of Abraham" comes upon the Gentiles only "through Jesus Christ," Gal. iii. 14. He is "the way, the truth, and the life," John xiv. 6. "None cometh to the Father but by him." He is the "door," by which those that do not enter are "without," with "dogs and idolaters," Rev. xxii. 15. So that "other foundation" of blessedness "can no man lay than that is laid, which is Jesus Christ," 1 Cor. iii. 11. In brief, do but compare these two places of St Paul, Rom. viii. 30, where he showeth that none are glorified but those that are called; and chap. x. 14, 15, where he declares that all calling is instrumentally by the preaching of the word and gospel; and it will evidently appear that no salvation can be granted unto them on whom the Lord hath so far poured out his indignation as to deprive them of the knowledge of the sole means thereof, Christ Jesus. And to those that are otherwise minded, I give only this necessary caution,—Let them take heed, lest, whilst they endeavour to invent new ways to heaven for others, by so doing they lose the true way themselves.

S. S.	Lib. Arbit.
"O fools, and slow of heart to believe all that the prophets have spoken: ought not Christ to have suffered these things?" Luke xxiv. 25, 26.	"There is no place in the Old Testament whence it may appear that faith in Christ as a Redeemer was either enjoined or found in any then," Rem. Apol.
"Abraham rejoiced to see my day; and he saw it, and was glad," John viii. 56. "By his knowledge shall my righteous servant justify many; for he shall bear their iniquities," Isa. liii. 11. See the places before cited.	"Abraham's faith had no reference to Christ," Armin.
"At that time ye were without Christ, being aliens from the commonwealth of Israel, and strangers from the covenants of	"The Gentiles living under the Old Testament, though it was not revealed unto them as unto the Jews, yet were not excluded from

S. S.	Lib. Arbit.
promise, having no hope, and without God in the world," Eph. ii. 12.	the covenant of grace, and from salvation," Corv.
"There is none other name under heaven given unto men, whereby we must be saved," but only by Christ, Acts iv. 12.	"I deny this proposition, That none can be saved that is not ingrafted into Christ by a true faith," Bert.
"The blessing of Abraham cometh on the Gentiles through Jesus Christ," Gal. iii. 14. "He that believeth not is condemned," Mark xvi. 16. "Without faith it is impossible to please God," Heb. xi. 6. "Other foundation can no man lay than that is laid, which is Jesus Christ," 1 Cor. iii. 11.	"To this question, Whether the only way of salvation be the life, passion, death, resurrection, and ascension of Jesus Christ? I answer, No," Venat.

CHAPTER XII.

Of free-will, the nature and power thereof.

OUR next task is to take a view of the idol himself, of this great deity of free-will, whose original being not well known, he is pretended, like the Ephesian image of Diana, to have fallen down from heaven, and to have his endowments from above. But yet, considering what a nothing he was at his first discovery in comparison of that vast giant-like hugeness to which now he is grown, we may say of him as the painter said of his monstrous picture, which he had mended or rather marred according to every one's fancy, "Hunc populus fecit,"—it is the issue of the people's brain. Origen[1] is supposed to have brought him first into the church; but among those many sincere worshippers of divine grace, this setter forth of new demons found but little entertainment. It was looked upon but like the stump of Dagon, with his head and hands laid down before the ark of God, without whose help he could neither know nor do that which is good in any kind, still accounted but "truncus ficulnus, inutile lignum,"—"a fig-tree log, an unprofitable piece of wood." "Incerti patres scamnum facerentne?" The fathers of the succeeding ages had much debate to what use they should put it, and though some exalted it a degree or two above its merits, yet the most con-

[1] Hieron. ad Ruf.

cluded to keep it a block still; until at length there arose a stout champion,[1] challenging on his behalf the whole church of God, and, like a knight-errant, wandered from the west to the east to grapple with any that should oppose his idol; who, though he met with divers adversaries,[2] one especially,[3] who in the behalf of the grace of God continually foiled him and cast him to the ground, and that in the judgment of all the lawful judges assembled in councils,[4] and in the opinion of most of the Christian bystanders,[5] yet, by his cunning insinuation, he planted such an opinion of his idol's deity and self-sufficiency in the hearts of divers, that to this day it could never be rooted out.

Now, after the decease of his Pelagian worshippers, some of the corrupter schoolmen, seeing him thus from his birth exposed without shelter to wind and weather, to all assaults, out of mere charity and self-love built him a temple, and adorned it with natural lights, merits, uncontrolled independent operations, with many other gay attendances. But in the beginning of the Reformation,—that fatal time for idolatry and superstition, together with abbeys and monasteries,—the zeal and learning of our forefathers, with the help of God's word, demolished this temple, and brake this building down to the ground; in the rubbish whereof we well hoped the idol himself had been so deeply buried as that his head should never more have been exalted, to the trouble of the church of God, until not long since some curious wits, whose weak stomachs were clogged with manna and loathed the sincere milk of the word, raking all dunghills for novelties, lighted unhappily upon this idol, and presently, with no less joy than did the mathematician at the discovery of a new geometrical proportion, exclaim, " We have found it! we have found

1 "Pelagius: Dogma quod—Pestifero vomuit coluber sermone Britannus."—Prosper. de Ingrat., cap. i.

2 "Adfuit, exhortante Deo provisa per orbem, Sanctorum pia cura patrum :—1. Pestem subeuntem Prima recidit, Sedes Roma Petri. 2. Non segnior inde, orientis Rectorum cura emicuit. Synod. Palest. 3. Hieronymus libris valde excellentibus hostem Dissecuit. 4. Atticus Constantinop. 5. Duæ Synodi Africanæ."—Prosper. de Ingrat.

3 "Concilium cui dux Aurelius ingeniumque Augustinus erat. Quem Christi gratia cornu Uberiore rigans, nostro lumen dedit ævo."—Prosp., ibid.

4 "Dixit Pelagius, quis est mihi Augustinus? Universi acclamabant blasphemantem in episcopum, ex cujus ore, dominus universæ Africæ, unitatis indulserit felicitatem, non solum a conventu illo, sed ab omni ecclesia pellendum."—Oros. Apologet., p. 621, de Synod. Palest. "Præ omnibus studium gerite libros. S. Aug. quos ad Prosp. et Hilar. scripsit, memoratis fratribus legendos ingerere," etc.—Epist. Synod. Byzac.

5 "Imo noverunt, non solum Romanam Africanamque ecclesiam, sed per omnes mundi partes, universæ promissionis filios, cum doctrina hujus viri, sicut in tota fide, ita in gratiæ confessione congruere."—Prosp. ad Rufin. " Augustinum sanctæ recordationis virum pro vita sua, et meritis, in nostra communione semper habuimus, nec unquam hunc sinistræ suspicionis saltem rumor suspexit."—Cœlest., Epist. ad Gal. Episcop. These I have cited to show what a heavy prejudice the Arminian cause lies under, being professedly opposite to the doctrine of St Austin, and they continually slighting of his authority.

it!" And without more ado, up they erected a shrine, and until this day continue offering of praise and thanks for all the good they do to this work of their own hands.

And that the idol may be free from ruin, to which in himself they have found by experience that he is subject, they have matched him to contingency, a new goddess of their own creation, who, having proved very fruitful in monstrous births upon their conjunctions, they nothing doubt they shall never want one to set on the throne and make president of all human actions: so that after he hath, with various success, at least twelve hundred years, contended with the providence and grace of God, he boasteth now as if he had obtained a total victory. But yet all his prevailing is to be attributed to the diligence and varnish of his new abettors, with (to our shame be it spoken!) the negligence of his adversaries. In him and his cause there is no more real worth than was when by the ancient fathers he was exploded and cursed out of the church: so that they who can attain, through the many winding labyrinths of curious distinctions, to look upon the thing itself, shall find that they have been, like Egyptian novices, brought through many stately frontispieces and goodly fabrics, with much show of zeal and devotion, to the image of an ugly ape.

Yet here observe, that we do not absolutely oppose free-will, as if it were "nomen inane," a mere figment, when there is no such thing in the world, but only in that sense the Pelagians and Arminians do assert it. About words we will not contend. We grant man, in the substance of all his actions, as much power, liberty, and freedom as a mere created nature is capable of. We grant him to be free in his choice from all outward coaction, or inward natural necessity, to work according to election and deliberation, spontaneously embracing what seemeth good unto him. Now, call this power free-will, or what you please, so you make it not supreme, independent, and boundless, we are not at all troubled. The imposition of names depends upon the discretion of their inventers. Again; even in spiritual things, we deny that our wills are at all debarred, or deprived of their proper liberty: but here we say, indeed, that we are not properly free until the Son makes us free;—no great use of freedom in that wherein we can do nothing at all. We do not claim such a liberty as should make us despise the grace of God,[1] whereby we may attain true liberty indeed; which addeth to, but taketh nothing from, our original freedom. But of this after I have showed what an idol the Arminians make of free-will. Only take notice in the entrance that we speak of it now, not as it was at first by God created, but as it is now by sin corrupted; yet, being considered in that estate also, they ascribe more

[1] "Homo non libertate gratiam, sed gratia libertatem, assequitur."—Aug.

unto it than it was ever capable of. As it now standeth, according to my formerly-proposed method, I shall show,—first, what inbred native virtue they ascribe unto it, and with how absolute a dominion and sovereignty over all our actions they endow it; secondly, what power they say it hath in preparing us for the grace of God; thirdly, how effectually operative it is in receiving the said grace, and with how little help thereof it accomplisheth the great work of our conversion;—all briefly, with so many observations as shall suffice to discover their proud errors in each particular.

[1]"Herein," saith Arminius, "consisteth the liberty of the will, that all things required to enable it to will any thing being accomplished, it still remains indifferent to will or not." And all of them at the synod: [2]"There is," say they, "accompanying the will of man an inseparable property, which we call liberty, from whence the will is termed a power, which, when all things pre-required as necessary to operation are fulfilled, may will any thing, or not will it;" that is, our free-wills have such an absolute and uncontrollable power in the territory of all human actions, that no influence of God's providence, no certainty of his decree, no unchangeableness of his purpose, can sway it at all in its free determinations, or have any power with his highness to cause him to will or resolve on any such act as God by him intendeth to produce. Take an instance in the great work of our conversion. [3]"All unregenerate men," saith Arminius, "have, by virtue of their free-will, a power of resisting the Holy Spirit, of rejecting the offered grace of God, of contemning the counsel of God concerning themselves, of refusing the gospel of grace, of not opening the heart to him that knocketh." What a stout idol is this, whom neither the Holy Spirit, the grace and counsel of God, the calling of the gospel, the knocking at the door of the heart, can move at all, or in the least measure prevail against him! Woe be unto us, then, if when God calls us our free-will be not in good temper, and well disposed to hearken unto him! for it seems there is no dealing with it by any other ways, though powerful and almighty. [4]"For grant," saith Corvinus, "all the operations of grace which God can use in our conversion, yet conversion remaineth so in our own free power

[1] "Libertas Arbitrii consistit in eo, quod homo, positis omnibus requisitis ad volendum, indifferens tamen sit, ad volendum vel nolendum, hoc vel illud."—Armin. Art. Perpend., p. 11.

[2] "Voluntatem comitatur proprietas quædam inseparabilis, quam libertatem vocamus; a qua voluntas dicitur potentia, quæ positis omnibus prærequisitis ad agendum necessariis, potest velle et nolle, aut velle et non velle."—Remon. in Act. Synod, p. 16.

[3] "Omnes irregeniti habent Lib. Arbit. et potentiam Spiritui Sancto resistendi, gratiam Dei oblatam repudiandi, consilium Dei adversus se contemnendi, evangelium gratiæ repudiandi, ei qui cor pulsat non aperiendi."—Armin. Artic. Perpend.

[4] "Positis omnibus operationibus gratiæ, quibus Deus in conversione nostri uti possit, manet tamen conversio ita in nostra potestate libera, ut possimus non converti; hoc est, nosmet ipsos convertere vel non convertere."—Corv. ad Bog., p. 263.

that we can be not converted; that is, we can either turn or not turn ourselves;"—where the idol plainly challengeth the Lord to work his utmost, and tells him that after he hath so done he will do what he please. His infallible prescience, his powerful predetermination, the moral efficacy of the gospel, the infusion of grace, the effectual operation of the Holy Spirit, all are nothing, not at all available in helping or furthering our independent wills in their proceedings. Well, then, in what estate will you have the idol placed? [1]"In such a one wherein he may be suffered to sin, or to do well, at his pleasure," as the same author intimates. It seems, then, as to sin, so nothing is required for him to be able to do good but God's permission? No! For the Remonstrants[2] (as they speak of themselves) "do always suppose a free power of obeying or not obeying, as well in those who do obey as in those who do not obey;"—that he that is obedient may therefore be counted obedient, because he obeyeth when he could not obey, and so on the contrary:" where all the praise of our obedience, whereby we are made to differ from others, is ascribed to ourselves alone, and that free power that is in us. Now, this they mean not of any one act of obedience, but of faith itself, and the whole consummation thereof. [3]"For if a man should say, that every man in the world hath a power of believing if he will, and of attaining salvation, and that this power is settled in his nature, what argument have you to confute him?" saith Arminius triumphantly to Perkins; where the sophistical innovator as plainly confounds grace and nature as ever did Pelagius. That, then, which the Arminians claim here in behalf of their free-will is, an absolute independence on God's providence in doing any thing, and of his grace in doing that which is good,—a self-sufficiency in all its operations, a plenary indifferency of doing what we will, this or that, as being neither determined to the one nor inclined to the other by any overruling influence from heaven. So that the good acts of our wills have no dependence on God's providence as they are acts, nor on his grace as they are good; but in both regards proceed from such a principle within us as is no way moved by any superior agent. Now, the first of these we deny unto our wills, because they are created; and the second, because they are corrupted. Their creation hinders them from doing any thing of themselves without the assistance of

[1] "Non potest Deus Lib. Arbit. integrum servare, nisi tam peccare hominem sineret, quam bene agere."—Corv. ad Molin., cap. vi.

[2] "Semper Remonstrantes supponunt liberam obediendi potentiam et non obediendi; ut qui obediens est idcirco obediens censeatur, quia cum possit non obedire obedit tamen, et e contra."—Rem. Apol., p. 70.

[3] "Quod si quis dicat omnes in universum homines, habere potentiam credendi si velint, et salutem consequendi: et hanc potentiam esse naturæ hominum divinitus collatam, quo tuo argumento eum confutabis?"—Armin. Antip., p. 272.

God's providence; and their corruption, from doing any thing that is good without his grace. A self-sufficiency for operation, without the effectual motion of Almighty God, the first cause of all things, we can allow neither to men nor angels, unless we intend to make them gods; and a power of doing good, equal unto that they have of doing evil, we must not grant to man by nature, unless we will deny the fall of Adam, and fancy ourselves still in paradise. But let us consider these things apart.

FIRST, I shall not stand to decipher the nature of human liberty, which perhaps would require a larger discourse than my proposed method will bear. It may suffice that, according to my former intimation, we grant as large a freedom and dominion to our wills over their own acts as a creature, subject to the supreme rule of God's providence, is capable of. Endued we are with such a liberty of will as is free from all outward compulsion and inward necessity, having an elective faculty of applying itself unto that which seems good unto it, in which it is a free choice; notwithstanding, it is subservient to the decree of God, as I showed before, chap. iv. Most free it is in all its acts, both in regard of the object it chooseth and in regard of that vital power and faculty whereby it worketh, infallibly complying with God's providence, and working by virtue of the motion thereof; but surely to assert such a supreme independency and every way unbounded indifferency as the Arminians claim, whereby, all other things requisite being pre-supposed, it should remain absolutely in our own power to will or not to will, to do any thing or not to do it, is plainly to deny that our wills are subject to the rule of the Most High. It is granted that in such a chimerical, fancied consideration of free-will, wherein it is looked upon as having no relation to any act of God's but only its creation, abstracting from his decree, it may be said to have such a liberty in regard of the object; but the truth is, this divided sense is plain nonsense, a mere fiction of such an estate as wherein it never was, nor ever can be, so long as men will confess any deity but themselves, to whose determinations they must be subject. Until, then, more significant terms may be invented for this free power in our nature, which the Scripture never once vouchsafed to name, I shall be content to call it with Prosper, a [1]"spontaneous appetite of what seemeth good unto it," free from all compulsion, but subservient to the providence of God. And against its exaltation to this height of independency, I oppose,—

First, Every thing that is independent of any else in operation is purely active, and so consequently a god; for nothing but a divine will

[1] "Lib. Arbit. est rei sibi placitæ spontaneus appetitus."—Prosp. ad Collat., cap. xviii. p. 379.

can be a pure act, possessing such a liberty by virtue of its own essence. Every created will must have a liberty by participation, which includeth such an imperfect potentiality as cannot be brought into act without some premotion (as I may so say) of a superior agent. Neither doth this motion, being extrinsical, at all prejudice the true liberty of the will, which requireth, indeed, that the internal principle of operation be active and free, but not that that principle be not moved to that operation by an outward superior agent. Nothing in this sense can have an independent principle of operation which hath not an independent being. It is no more necessary to the nature of a free cause, from whence a free action must proceed, that it be the first beginning of it, than it is necessary to the nature of a cause that it be the first cause.

Secondly, If the free acts of our wills are so subservient to the providence of God as that he useth them to what end he will, and by them effecteth many of his purposes, then they cannot of themselves be so absolutely independent as to have in their own power every necessary circumstance and condition, that they may use or not use at their pleasure. Now, the former is proved by all those reasons and texts of Scripture I before produced to show that the providence of God overruleth the actions and determineth the wills of men freely to do that which he hath appointed. And, truly, were it otherwise, God's dominion over the most things that are in the world were quite excluded; he had not power to determine that any one thing should ever come to pass which hath any reference to the wills of men.

Thirdly, All the acts of the will being positive entities, were it not previously moved by God himself, "in whom we live, move, and have our being," must needs have their essence and existence solely from the will itself; which is thereby made αὐτὸ ὄν, a first and supreme cause, endued with an underived being. And so much to that particular.

Let us now, in the SECOND place, look upon the power of our free-will in doing that which is morally good; where we shall find not only an essential imperfection, inasmuch as it is created, but also a contracted effect, inasmuch as it is corrupted. The ability which the Arminians ascribe unto it in this kind, of doing that which is morally and spiritually good, is as large as themselves will confess to be competent unto it in the state of innocency, even a power of believing and a power of resisting the gospel, of obeying and not obeying, of turning or of not being converted.

The Scripture, as I observed before, hath no such term at all, nor any thing equivalent unto it. But the expressions it useth concerning our nature and all the faculties thereof, in this state of sin and unregeneration, seem to imply the quite contrary; as, that we are in "bondage," Heb. ii. 15; "dead in sins," Eph. ii. 1, and so "free from righteousness," Rom. vi. 20; "servants of sin," verse 17; under the "reign" and "dominion" thereof, verses 12, 14; all "our members being instruments of unrighteousness," verse 13; not "free indeed," until "the Son make us free." So that this idol of free-will, in respect of spiritual things, is not one whit better than the other idols of the heathen. Though it look like "silver and gold," it is the "work of men's hands." "It hath a mouth, but it speaketh not; it hath eyes, but it seeth not; it hath ears, but it heareth not; a nose, but it smelleth not; it hath hands, but it handleth not; feet, but it walketh not; neither speaketh it through its throat. They that made it are like unto it; and so is every one that trusteth in it. O Israel, trust thou in the LORD," etc., Ps. cxv. 4–9. That it is the work of men's hands, or a human invention, I showed before. For the rest, it hath a mouth unacquainted with the "mystery of godliness," "full only of cursing and bitterness," Rom. iii. 14; "speaking great swelling words," Jude 16; "great things, and blasphemies," Rev. xiii. 5; a "mouth causing the flesh to sin," Eccles. v. 6;—his eyes are blind, not able to perceive those things that are of God, nor to know those things that are "spiritually discerned," 1 Cor. ii. 14; "eyes before which there is no fear of God," Rom. iii. 18;—his "understanding is darkened, because of the blindness of his heart," Eph. iv. 18; "wise to do evil, but to do good he hath no knowledge," Jer. iv. 22; so that without farther light, all the world is but a mere "darkness," John i. 5;—he hath ears, but they are like the ears of the "deaf adder" to the word of God, "refusing to hear the voice of charmers, charming never so wisely," Ps. lviii. 5; being "dead" when his voice first calls it, John v. 25; "ears stopped that they should not hear," Zech. vii. 11; "heavy ears" that cannot hear, Isa. vi. 10;—a nose, to which the gospel is "the savour of death unto death," 2 Cor. ii. 16;—"hands full of blood," Isa. i. 15; and "fingers defiled with iniquity," chap. lix. 3;—feet, indeed, but, like Mephibosheth, lame in both by a fall, so that he cannot at all walk in the path of goodness; but "swift to shed blood, destruction and misery are in his ways, and the way of peace hath he not known," Rom. iii. 15–17. These, and divers other such endowments and excellent qualifications, doth the Scripture attribute to this idol, which it calls "The old man," as I shall more fully discover in the next chapter. And is not this a goodly reed whereon to rely in the paths of godliness? a powerful deity whereunto we may repair for a power to become the sons of God, and attain eternal happiness? The abilities of free-will in particular I shall consider hereafter; now only I will, by one or two reasons, show that it cannot be the sole and proper cause of any truly good and spiritual act, well-pleasing unto God.

First, All spiritual acts well-pleasing unto God, as faith, repentance, obedience, are supernatural; flesh and blood revealeth not these things: "Not of blood, nor of the will of the flesh, nor of the will of man; but of God," John i. 13; "That which is born of the flesh is flesh; and that which is born of the Spirit is spirit," chap. iii. 6. Now, to the performance of any supernatural act it is required that the productive power thereof be also supernatural; for nothing hath an activity in causing above its own sphere. "Nec imbelles generant feroces aquilas columbæ." But our free-will is a merely natural faculty, betwixt which and those spiritual, supernatural acts there is no proportion, unless it be advanced above its own orb, by inherent, habitual grace. Divine, theological virtues, differing even in the substance of the act from those moral performances about the same things to which the strength of nature may reach (for the difference of acts ariseth from their formal objects, which to both these are diverse), must have another principle and cause above all the power of nature in civil things and actions morally good, inasmuch as they are subject to a natural perception, and do not exceed the strength of our own wills. This faculty of free-will may take place, but yet not without these following limitations:—*First*, That it always requireth the general concurrence of God, whereby the whole *suppositum* in which free-will hath its subsistence may be sustained, Matt. x. 29, 30. *Secondly*, That we do all these things imperfectly and with much infirmity; every degree, also, of excellency in these things must be counted a special gift of God, Isa. xxvi. 12. *Thirdly*, That our wills are determined by the will of God to all their acts and motions in particular; but to do that which is spiritually good we have no knowledge, no power.

Secondly, That concerning which I gave one special instance, in whose production the Arminians attribute much to free-will, is faith. This they affirm (as I showed before) to be inbred in nature, every one having in him from his birth a natural power to believe in Christ and his gospel; for Episcopius denies that [1]"any action of the Holy Spirit upon the understanding or will is necessary, or promised in the Scripture, to make a man able to believe the word preached unto him." So that it seems every man hath at all times a power to believe, to produce the act of faith upon the revelation of its object: which gross Pelagianism is contrary,—

First, To the doctrine of the church of England, affirming that a man cannot so much as prepare himself by his own strength to faith

[1] "An ulla actio S. S. immediata in mentem aut voluntatem necessaria sit, aut in Scriptura promittatur ad hoc, ut quis credere possit verbo extrinsecus proposito, negativam tuebimur."—Episcop., Disput. Privat.

and calling upon God, until the grace of God by Christ prevent him, that he may have a good will.—Artic. x.

Secondly, To the Scripture, teaching that it is "the work of God that we do believe," John vi. 29. It is "not of ourselves; it is the gift of God," Eph. ii. 8. To some "it is given to know the mysteries of the kingdom of heaven," Matt. xiii. 11. And what is peculiarly given to some cannot be in the power of every one: "To you it is given in the behalf of Christ to believe on him," Phil. i. 29. Faith is our access or coming unto Christ; which none can do "except the Father draw him," John vi. 44; and he so draweth, or "hath mercy, on whom he will have mercy," Rom. ix. 18. And although Episcopius rejects any immediate action of the Holy Spirit for the ingenerating of faith, yet St Paul affirmeth that there is no less effectual power required to it than that which raised Christ from the dead; which, sure, was an action of the almighty Godhead. "That ye may know," saith he, "what is the exceeding greatness of his power to us-ward who believe, according to the working of his mighty power, which he wrought in Christ, when he raised him from the dead," Eph. i. 18–20. So that, let the Arminians say what they please, recalling that I write to Christians, I will spare my labour of farther proving that faith is the free gift of God; and their opposition to the truth of the Scripture in this particular is so evident to the meanest capacity that there needs no recapitulation to present the sum of it to their understandings.

CHAPTER XIII.

Of the power of free-will in preparing us for our conversion unto God.

THE judgment of the Arminians concerning the power of free-will about spiritual things in a man unregenerate, merely in the state of corrupted nature, before and without the help of grace, may be laid open by these following positions:—

First, That every man in the world, reprobates and others, have in themselves power and ability of believing in Christ, of repenting and yielding due obedience to the new covenant; and that because they lost not this power by the fall of Adam. [1]"Adam after his fall," saith Grevinchovius, "retained a power of believing; and so did all reprobates in him." [2]"He did not lose" (as they speak at the synod)

[1] "Adamus post lapsum potentiam credendi retinuit, et reliqui reprobi etiam in illo." —Grevinch. ad Ames., p. 183.

[2] "Adamus non amisit vires eam obedientiam præstandi quæ in novo fœdere exigitur, prout puta ea consideratur formaliter, hoc est, prout novo fœdere exacta est, nec potentiam credendi amisit; nec amisit potentiam, per resipiscentiam, ex peccato resurgendi."—Rem. Declar. Sent. in Synod., p. 107.

"the power of performing that obedience which is required in the new covenant considered formally, as it is required by the new covenant; he lost not a power of believing, nor a power of forsaking sin by repentance." And those graces that he lost not are still in our power. Whence they affirm, that [1]"faith is called the work of God only because he requireth us to do it." Now, having appropriated this power unto themselves, to be sure that the grace of God be quite excluded, which before they had made needless, they teach,—

Secondly, That for the reducing of this power into act, that men may become actual believers, there is no infused habit of grace, no spiritual vital principle, necessary for them, or bestowed upon them; but every one, by the use of his native endowments, doth make himself differ from others. [2]"Those things which are spoken concerning the infusion of habits before we can exercise the act of faith, we reject," saith the epistle to the Walachians. [3]"That the internal principle of faith required in the gospel is a habit divinely infused, by the strength and efficacy whereof the will should be determined, I deny," saith another of them. Well, then, if we must grant that the internal vital principle of a supernatural spiritual grace is a mere natural faculty, not elevated by any divine habit,—if it be not God that begins the good work in us, but our own free-wills,—let us see what more goodly stuff will follow. One man by his own mere endeavours, without the aid of any received gift, makes himself differ from another. [4]"What matter is it in that, that a man should make himself differ from others? There is nothing truer; he who yieldeth faith to God commanding him, maketh himself differ from him who will not have faith when he commandeth." They are the words of their Apology, which, without question, is an irrefragable truth, if faith be not a gift received from above; for on that ground only the apostle proposeth these questions, "Who maketh thee to differ from another? and what hast thou that thou didst not receive? now if thou didst receive, why dost thou glory, as if thou hadst not received?" The sole cause why he denies any one by his own power to make himself differ from another is, because that wherein the difference consisteth is "received," being freely bestowed upon him. Deny this, and I confess the other will fall of itself. But until their authority be equal

[1] "Fides vocatur opus Dei, quia Deus ipse id a nobis fieri postulat."—Rem. Apol., cap. x. p. 112.

[2] "Ea quæ de habituum infusione dicuntur, ante omnem fidei actum, rejiciuntur a nobis."—Epist. ad Wal., p. 67.

[3] "Principium internum fidei a nobis in evangelio requisitum, esse habitum quendam divinitus infusum, cujus vi ac efficacitate voluntas determinetur; hoc negavi."—Grevinch. ad Ames., p. 324.

[4] "Quid in eo positum est, quod homo discriminare seipsum dicitur? Nihil verius; qui fidem Deo præcipienti habet, is discriminat se ab eo qui Deo præcipienti fidem habere non vult."—Rem. Apol., cap. xiv. p. 144.

with the apostles', they would do well to forbear the naked obtrusion of assertions so contradictory to theirs; and so they would not trouble the church. Let them take all the glory unto themselves, as doth Grevinchovius. [1]"I make myself," saith he, "differ from another when I do not resist God and his divine predetermination; which I could have resisted. And why may I not boast of this as of mine own? That I could is of God's mercy" (endowing his nature with such an ability as you heard before); "but that I would, when I might have done otherwise, is of my power." Now, when, after all this, they are forced to confess some evangelical grace, though consisting only in a moral persuasion by the outward preaching of the word, they teach,—

Thirdly, That God sendeth the gospel, and revealeth Christ Jesus unto men, according as they well dispose themselves for such a blessing. [2]"Sometimes," say they in their synodical writings, "God calleth this or that nation, people, city, or person, to the communion of evangelical grace, whom he himself pronounceth worthy of it, in comparison of others." So that whereas, Acts xviii. 10, God encourageth Paul to preach at Corinth by affirming that he had "much people in that city" (which, doubtless, were his people then only by virtue of their election), in these men's judgments [3]"they were called so because that even then they feared God, and served him with all their hearts, according to that knowledge they had of him, and so were ready to obey the preaching of St Paul." Strange doctrine, that men should fear God, know him, serve him in sincerity, before they ever heard of the gospel, and by these means deserve that it should be preached unto them! This is that pleasing of God before faith that they plead for, Act. Synod., p. 66; that [4]"preparation and disposition to believe, which men attain by the law and virtuous education;" that "something which is in sinners,[5] whereby though they are not justified, yet they are made worthy of justification." For [6]"conversion and the performance of

[1] "Ego meipsum discerno, cum enim Deo ac divinæ prædeterminationi resistere possem, non restiti tamen. Atqui in eo quidni liceat mihi tanquam de meo gloriari? Quod enim potui Dei miserentis est, quod autem volui cum possem nolle, id meæ potestatis est."—Grevinch. ad Ames., p. 253.

[2] "Interdum Deus hanc vel illam gentem, civitatem, personam, ad evangelicæ gratiæ communionem vocat, quam ipse dignam pronuntiat comparative," etc.—Rem. Declarat. Sent. Synod.

[3] "Illi, in quorum gratiam, Dominus Paulum in Corinthum misit, dicuntur Dei populus, quia Deum tum timebant, eique, secundum cognitionem quam de eo habebant, serviebant ex animo, et sic ad prædicationem Pauli," etc.—Corv. ad Molin. iii. sect. 27.

[4] "Per legem, vel per piam educationem vel per institutionem—per hæc enim hominem præparari et disponi ad credendum, planissimum est."—Rem. Act. Synod.

[5] "Præcedit aliquid in peccatoribus, quo quamvis nondum justificati sunt, digni efficiantur justificatione."—Grevinch. ad Ames., p. 434.

[6] "Tenendum est, veram conversionem præstationemque bonorum operum esse conditionem prærequisitam ante justificationem."—Filii Arm. Præf. ad cap. vii. ad Rem.

good works is," in their apprehension, "a condition pre-required to justification," for so speak the children of Arminius; which if it be not an expression not to be paralleled in the writings of any Christian, I am something mistaken. The sum of their doctrine, then, in this particular concerning the power of free-will in the state of sin and unregeneration, is, *That every man having a native, inbred power of believing in Christ upon the revelation of the gospel, hath also an ability of doing so much good as shall procure of God that the gospel be preached unto him; to which, without any internal assistance of grace, he can give assent and yield obedience; the preparatory acts of his own will always proceeding so far as to make him excel others who do not perform them, and are therefore excluded from farther grace;*—which is more gross Pelagianism than Pelagius himself would ever justify. Wherefore we reject all the former positions, as so many monsters in Christian religion, in whose room we assert these that follow:—

First, That we, being by nature dead in trespasses and sins, have no power to prepare ourselves for the receiving of God's grace, nor in the least measure to believe and turn ourselves unto him. Not that we deny that there are any conditions pre-required in us for our conversion, dispositions preparing us in some measure for our new birth or regeneration; but we affirm that all these also are the effects of the grace of God, relating to that alone as their proper cause, for of ourselves, "without him, we can do nothing," John xv. 5. "We are not sufficient of ourselves to think any thing as of ourselves," 2 Cor. iii. 5, much less do that which is good. In respect of that, "every one of our mouths must be stopped;" for "we have all sinned and come short of the glory of God," Rom. iii. 19, 23. We are "by nature the children of wrath, dead in trespasses and sins," Eph. ii. 1–3; Rom. viii. 6. Our new birth is a resurrection from death, wrought by the greatness of God's power. And what ability, I pray, hath a dead man to prepare himself for his resurrection? Can he collect his scattered dust, or renew his perished senses? If the leopard can change his spots, and the Ethiopian his skin, then can we do good who by nature are taught to do evil, Jer. xiii. 23. We are all "ungodly," and "without strength" considered, when Christ died for us, Rom. v. 6; "wise to do evil," but "to do good we have no strength, no knowledge." Yea, all the faculties of our souls, by reason of that spiritual death under which we are detained by the corruption of nature, are altogether useless, in respect of any power for the doing of that which is truly good. Our understandings are blind or "darkened, being alienated from the life of God through the ignorance that is in us, because of the blindness of our hearts," Eph. iv. 18; whereby we become even "darkness" itself, chap. v. 8. So void is the understanding of true knowledge, that "the natural man receiveth not the things of the Spirit of God; they are foolishness unto him," 1 Cor. ii. 14. [He is] nothing but confounded and amazed at spiritual things; and, if he doth not mock, can do nothing but wonder, and say, "What meaneth this?" Acts ii. 12, 13. Secondly, we are not only blind in our understandings, but captives also to sin in our wills, Luke iv. 18; whereby "we are servants of sin," John viii. 34; "free" only in our obedience to that tyrant, Rom. vi. 20. Yea, thirdly, all our affections are wholly corrupted, for "every imagination of the thoughts of the heart of man is only evil continually," Gen. vi. 5. While we are "in the flesh, the motions of sin do work in our members to bring forth fruit unto death," Rom. vii. 5.

These are the endowments of our nature, these are the preparations of our hearts for the grace of God, which we have within ourselves. Nay,—

Secondly, There is not only an *impotency* but an *enmity* in corrupted nature to any thing spiritually good: The things that are of God are "foolishness unto a natural man," 1 Cor. ii. 14. And there is nothing that men do more hate and contemn than that which they account as folly. They mock at it as a ridiculous drunkenness, Acts ii. 13. And would to God our days yielded us not too evident proofs of that universal opposition that is between light and darkness, Christ and Belial, nature and grace,—that we could not see every day the prodigious issues of this inbred corruption swelling over all bounds, and breaking forth into a contempt of the gospel and all ways of godliness! So true it is that "the carnal mind is enmity against God: it is not subject to the law of God, neither indeed can be," Rom. viii. 7. So that,—

Thirdly, As a natural man, by the strength of his own free-will, neither knoweth nor willeth, so it is utterly impossible he should do any thing pleasing unto God. "Can the Ethiopian change his skin, or the leopard his spots? then can he do good," Jer. xiii. 23. "An evil tree cannot bring forth good fruit." "Without faith it is impossible to please God," Heb. xi. 6; and "that is not of ourselves, it is the gift of God," Eph. ii. 8. So that though Almighty God, according to the unsearchableness of his wisdom, worketh divers ways and in sundry manners, for the translating of his chosen ones from the power of darkness into his marvellous light,—calling some powerfully in the midst of their march in the way of ungodliness, as he did Paul,—preparing others by outward means and helps of common restraining grace, moralizing nature before it be begotten anew by the immortal seed of the word,—yet this is certain, that all good in this kind is from his free grace; there is nothing in ourselves, as of ourselves, but sin. Yea, and all those previous dispositions wherewith our hearts are prepared, by virtue of common grace, do not at all enable us to concur, by any vital operation, with that powerful, blessed, renewing grace of regeneration whereby we become the sons of God. Neither is there any disposition unto grace so remote as that possibly it can proceed from a mere faculty of nature, for every such disposition must be of the same order with the form that is to be introduced; but nature, in respect of grace, is a thing of an inferior alloy, between which there is no proportion. A good use of gifts may have a promise of an addition of more, provided it be in the same kind. There is no rule, law, or promise that should make grace due upon the good use of natural endowments. But you will say, here I quite overthrow free-will, which before I seemed to grant. To which I answer, that in regard of that object concerning which now we treat, a natural man hath no such thing as free-will at all, if you take it for a power of doing that which is good and well-pleasing unto God in things spiritual, for an ability of preparing our hearts unto faith and calling upon God, as our church article speaks, a home-bred self-sufficiency, preceding the change of our wills by the almighty grace of God, whereby any good should be said to dwell in us; and we utterly deny that there is any such thing in the world. The will, though in itself radically free, yet in respect of the term or object to which in this regard it should tend, is corrupted, inthralled, and under a miserable bondage; tied to such a necessity of sinning in general, that though unregenerate men are not restrained to this or that sin in particular, yet for the main they can do nothing but sin. All their actions wherein there is any morality are attended with iniquity: "An evil tree cannot bring forth good fruit;" even "the sacrifice of the wicked is an abomination to the LORD." These things being thus cleared from the Scripture, the former Arminian positions will of themselves fall to the ground, having no foundation but their own authority; for any pretence of proof they make none from the word of God. The first two I considered in the last chapter, and now add only concerning the third,—that the sole cause why the gospel is sent unto some and not unto others is, not any dignity, worth, or desert of it in them to whom it is sent, more than in the rest that are suffered to remain in the shadow of death, but only the sole good pleasure of God, that it may be a subservient means for the execution of his decree of election: "I have much people in this city," Acts xviii. 20; "I thank thee, O Father, Lord of heaven and earth, because thou hast hid these things from the wise and prudent, and hast revealed them unto babes. Even so, Father; for so it seemed good in thy sight," Matt. xi. 25, 26. So that the Arminian opposition to the truth of the gospel in this particular is clearly manifest:—

S. S.	Lib. Arbit.
"Of ourselves we can do nothing," John xv. 5. "We are not sufficient of ourselves to think any thing as of ourselves," 2 Cor. iii. 5. "We are by nature the children of wrath, dead in trespasses and sins," Eph. ii. 1–3.	"We retain still after the fall a power of believing and of repentance, because Adam lost not this ability," Rem. Declar. Sen. in Synod.
"Faith is not of ourselves: it is the gift of God," Eph. ii. 8.	"Faith is said to be the work of God, because he commandeth us to perform it," Rem. Apol. "There is no infusion of any habit or spiritual vital principle necessary to enable a man to believe," Corv.
"Who maketh thee to differ from another? and what hast thou that thou didst not receive? now if thou didst receive, why dost thou glory as if thou hadst not received?" 1 Cor. iv. 7.	"There is nothing truer than that one man maketh himself differ from another. He who believeth when God commandeth, maketh himself differ from him who will not," Rem. Apol.
"Can the Ethiopian change his skin, or the leopard his spots? then may ye also do good, who are taught to do evil," Jer. xiii. 23.	"I may boast of mine own, when I obey God's grace, which it was in my power not to obey, as well as to obey," Grevinch.
"Believing on him that justifieth the ungodly," Rom. iv. 5. "Being justified freely by his grace," chap. iii. 24.	"True conversion and the performance of good works is a condition required on our part before justification," Filii Armin.
"I thank thee, O Father, Lord of heaven and earth, because thou hast hid these things from the wise and prudent, and hast revealed them unto babes. Even so, Father; for so it seemed good in thy sight," Matt. xi. 25, 26.	"God sendeth the gospel to such persons or nations, that in comparison of others may be said to be worthy of it," Rem. Apol.

CHAPTER XIV.

Of our conversion to God.

How little or nothing at all it is that the Arminians assign to the *grace of God*, in performing the great work of our conversion, may plainly appear from what I have showed already that they ascribe to *our own free-will*, so that I shall briefly pass that over, which otherwise is so copiously delivered in holy Scripture that it would require a far larger discussion. A prolix confirmation of the truth we profess will not suit so well with my intention; which is merely to make a discovery of their errors, by not knowing the depths whereof so many are deceived and inveigled.

Two things, in this great conjunction of grace and nature, the Arminians ascribe unto free-will:—first, *A power of co-operation* and working with grace, to make it at all effectual; secondly, *A power of resisting* its operation, and making it altogether ineffectual; God in the meantime bestowing no grace but what awaits an act issuing from one of these two abilities, and hath its effect accordingly. If a man will co-operate, then grace attains its end; if he will resist, it returns empty. To this end they feign all the grace of God bestowed upon us for our conversion to be but a moral persuasion by his word, not an infusion of a new vital principle by the powerful working of the Holy Spirit. And, indeed, granting this, I shall most willingly comply with them in assigning to free-will one of the endowments before recited,—a power of resisting the operation of grace; but instead of the other, must needs ascribe to our whole corrupted nature, and every one that is partaker of it, a universal disability of obeying it, or coupling in that work which God by his grace doth intend. If the grace of our conversion be nothing but a moral persuasion, we have no more power of obeying it in that estate wherein we are dead in sin, than a man in his grave hath in himself to live anew and come out at the next call. God's promises and the saints' prayers in the holy Scripture seem to design such a kind of grace as should give us a real internal ability of doing that which is spiritually good. But it seems there is no such matter; for if a man should persuade me to leap over the Thames, or to fly in the air, be he never so eloquent, his sole persuasion makes me no more able to do it than I was before ever I saw him. If God's grace be nothing but a sweet persuasion (though never so powerful), it is a thing extrinsical, consisting in the proposal of a desired object, but gives us no new strength at all to do any thing we had not before a power to do. But let us hear them pleading themselves to each of these particulars concerning grace and nature. And,—

First, for the nature of grace: [1]"God hath appointed to save believers by grace,—that is, a soft and sweet persuasion, convenient and agreeing to their free-will,—and not by any almighty action," saith

[1] "Deus statuit salvare credentes per gratiam, id est, lenem ac suavem liberoque ipsorum arbitrio convenientem seu congruam suasionem, non per omnipotentem actionem seu motionem."—Armin. Antip., p. 211.

Arminius. It seems something strange, that "the carnal mind being enmity against God," and the will inthralled to sin, and full of wretched opposition to all his ways, yet God should have no other means to work them over unto him but some persuasion that is sweet, agreeable, and congruous unto them in that estate wherein they are. And a small exaltation it is of the dignity and power of grace, when the chief reason why it is effectual, as Alvarez observes, may be reduced to a well-digested supper or an undisturbed sleep, whereby some men may be brought into better temper than ordinary to comply with this congruous grace. But let us for the present accept of this, and grant that God doth call some by such a congruous persuasion, at such a time and place as he knows they will assent unto it. I ask whether God thus calleth all men, or only some? If all, why are not all converted? for the very granting of it to be congruous makes it effectual. If only some, then why them, and not others? Is it out of a special intention to have them obedient? But let them take heed, for this will go near to establish the decree of election; and out of what other intention it should be they shall never be able to determine. Wherefore [1]Corvinus denies that any such congruity is required to the grace whereby we are converted, but only that it be a moral persuasion; which we may obey if we will, and so make it effectual. Yea, and Arminius himself, after he had defended it as far as he was able, puts it off from himself, and falsely fathers it upon St Austin. So that, as they jointly affirm, [2]"they confess no grace for the begetting of faith to be necessary, but only that which is moral;" which one of them interpreteth to be [3]"a declaration of the gospel unto us;"—right like their old master, Pelagius. "God," saith he, [4]"worketh in us to will that which is good and to will that which is holy, whilst he stirs us up with promise of rewards and the greatness of the future glory, who before were given over to earthly desires, like brute beasts, loving nothing but things present, stirring up our stupid wills to a desire of God by a revelation of wisdom, and persuading us to all that is good." Both of them affirm the grace of God to be nothing but a *moral persuasion*, working by the way of powerful, convincing arguments; but yet herein Pelagius seems to ascribe a greater efficacy to

[1] Corv. ad Molin.—"His ita expositis ex mente Augustini," etc.—Armin. Antip. De Elec.

[2] "Fatemur, aliam nobis ad actum fidei eliciendum necessariam gratiam non agnosci quam moralem."—Rem. Act. Synod. ad Art. iv.

[3] "Annuntiatio doctrinæ evangelicæ."—Popp. August. Port. p. 110.

[4] "Operatur in nobis velle quod bonum est, velle quod sanctum est, dum nos terrenis cupiditatibus deditos mutorum more animalium, tantummodo præsentia diligentes, futuræ gloriæ magnitudine et præmiorum pollicitatione, succendit: dum revelatione sapientiæ in desiderium Dei stupentem suscitat voluntatem, dum nobis suadet omne quod bonum est."—Pelag., ap. Aug. de Grat. Ch. cap. x.

it than the Arminians, granting that it works upon us when, after the manner of brute beasts, we are set merely on earthly things. But these, as they confess that, for the production of faith,[1] it is necessary that such arguments be proposed on the part of God to which nothing can probably be opposed why they should not seem credible; so there is, say they, required on our part a pious docility and probity of mind. So that all the grace of God bestowed on us consisteth in persuasive arguments out of the word; which, if they meet with teachable minds, may work their conversion.

Secondly, Having thus extenuated the grace of God, they affirm, [2]"that in operation the efficacy thereof dependeth on free-will:" so the Remonstrants in their Apology. [3]"And to speak confidently," saith Grevinchovius, "I say that the effect of grace, in an ordinary course, dependeth on some act of our free-will." Suppose, then, that of two men made partakers of the same grace,—that is, [who] have the gospel preached unto them by the same means,—one is converted and the other is not, what may be the cause of this so great a difference? Was there any intention or purpose in God that one should be changed rather than the other? "No; he equally desireth and intendeth the conversion of all and every one." Did, then, God work more powerfully in the heart of the one by his Holy Spirit than of the other? "No; the same operation of the Spirit always accompanieth the same preaching of the word." But was not one, by some almighty action, made partaker of real infused grace, which the other attained not unto? "No; for that would destroy the liberty of his will, and deprive him of all the praise of believing." How, then, came this extreme difference of effects? who made the one differ from the other? or what hath he that he did not receive? "Why, all this proceedeth merely from the strength of his own free-will yielding obedience to God's gracious invitation, which, like the other, he might have rejected: this is the immediate cause of his conversion, to which all the praise thereof is due." And here the old idol may glory to all the world, that if he can but get his worshippers to prevail in this, he hath quite excluded the grace of Christ, and made it "nomen inane," a mere title, whereas there is no such thing in the world.

Thirdly, They teach, that notwithstanding any purpose and intention of God to convert, and so to save, a sinner,—notwithstanding the most powerful and effectual operation of the blessed Spirit, with

[1] "Ut autem assensus hic eliciatur in nobis, duo in primis necessaria sunt:—1. Argumenta talia ex parte Dei, quibus nihil verisimiliter opponi potest cur credibilia non sint. 2. Pia docilitas animique probitas."—Rem. Declar., cap. xvii. sect. 1.

[2] "Ut gratia sit efficax in actu secundo pendet a libera voluntate."—Rem. Apol., p. 164.

[3] "Imo ut confidentius agam, dico effectum gratiæ, ordinaria lege, pendere ab actu aliquo arbitrii."—Grevinch. ad Ames., p. 198.

the most winning, persuasive preaching of the word,—yet it is in the power of a man to frustrate that purpose, resist that operation, and reject that preaching of the gospel. I shall not need to prove this, for it is that which, in direct terms, they plead for; which also they must do, if they will comply with their former principles. For granting all these to have no influence upon any man but by the way of moral persuasion, we must not only grant that it may be resisted, but also utterly deny that it can be obeyed. We may resist it, I say, as having both a disability to good and repugnancy against it; but for obeying it, unless we will deny all inherent corruption and depravation of nature, we cannot attribute any such sufficiency unto ourselves.

Now, concerning this weakness of grace, that it is not able to overcome the opposing power of sinful nature, one testimony of Arminius shall suffice: [1]"It always remaineth in the power of free-will to reject grace that is given and to refuse that which followeth; for grace is no almighty action of God, to which free-will cannot resist." Not that I would assert, in opposition to this, such an operation of grace as should, as it were, violently overcome the will of man, and force him to obedience, which must needs be prejudicial unto our liberty; but only consisting in such a sweet effectual working as doth infallibly promote our conversion, make us willing who before were unwilling, and obedient who were not obedient, that createth clean hearts and reneweth right spirits within us.

That, then, which we assert, in opposition to these Arminian heterodoxies, is, That *the effectual grace which God useth in the great work of our conversion, by reason of its own nature,—being also the instrument of and God's intention for that purpose,—doth surely produce the effect intended, without successful resistance, and solely, without any considerable co-operation of our own wills, until they are prepared and changed by that very grace.* The infallibility of its effect depends chiefly on the purpose of God. When by any means he intends a man's conversion, those means must have such an efficacy added unto them as may make them fit instruments for the accomplishment of that intention, that the counsel of the Lord may prosper, and his word not return empty. But the manner of its operation,—that it requires no human assistance, and is able to overcome all repugnance,—is proper to the being of such an act as wherein it doth consist. Which nature and efficacy of grace, in opposition to an indifferent influence of the Holy Spirit, a metaphorical motion, a working by the way of moral persuasion, only proposing a

[1] "Manet semper in potestate Lib. Arbit. gratiam datam rejicere et subsequentem repudiare, quæ gratia non est omnipotentis Dei actio, cui resisti a libero hominis arbitrio non possit."—Armin. Antip., p. 243.

desirable object, easy to be resisted, and not effectual unless it be helped by an inbred ability of our own (which is the Arminian grace), I will briefly confirm, having premised these few things:—

First, Although God doth not use the wills of men, in their conversion, as malign spirits use the members of men in enthusiasms, by a violent wrested motion, but sweetly and agreeably to their own free nature; yet in the first act of our conversion the will is merely passive, as a capable subject of such a work, not at all concurring co-operatively to our turning. It is not, I say, the cause of the work, but the subject wherein it is wrought, having only a passive capability for the receiving of that supernatural being, which is introduced by grace. The beginning of this "good work" is merely from God, Phil. i. 6. Yea, faith is ascribed unto grace, not by the way of conjunction with, but of opposition unto, our wills: "Not of ourselves; it is the gift of God," Eph. ii. 8. "Not that we are sufficient of ourselves; our sufficiency is of God," 2 Cor. iii. 5. "Turn thou us unto thee, O LORD, and we shall be turned," Lam. v. 21.

Secondly, Though the will of man conferreth nothing to the infusion of the first grace, but a subjective receiving of it, yet in the very first act that is wrought in and by the will, it most freely co-operateth (by the way of subordination) with the grace of God; and the more effectually it is moved by grace, the more freely it worketh with it. Man being converted, converteth himself.

Thirdly, We do not affirm grace to be *irresistible*, as though it came upon the will with such an overflowing violence as to beat it down before it, and subdue it by compulsion to what it is no way inclinable [unto.] But if that term must be used, it denoteth, in our sense, only such an unconquerable efficacy of grace as always and infallibly produceth its effect; for who is it that can "withstand God?" Acts xi. 17. As also, it may be used on the part of the will itself, which will not resist it: "All that the Father giveth unto Christ shall come to him," John vi. 37. The operation of grace is resisted by no hard heart; because it mollifies the heart itself. It doth not so much take away a power of resisting as give a will of obeying, whereby the *powerful impotency* of resistance is removed.

Fourthly, Concerning grace itself, it is either common or special. Common or general grace consisteth in the external revelation of the will of God by his word, with some illumination of the mind to perceive it, and correction of the affections not too much to contemn it; and this, in some degree or other, to some more, to some less, is common to all that are called. Special grace is the grace of regeneration, comprehending the former, adding more spiritual acts, but especially presupposing the purpose of God, on which its efficacy doth chiefly depend.

Fifthly, This saving grace, whereby the Lord converteth or regenerateth a sinner, translating him from death to life, is either external or internal. External consisteth in the preaching of the word, etc., whose operation is by the way of moral persuasion, when by it we beseech our hearers "in Christ's stead that they would be reconciled unto God," 2 Cor. v. 20; and this in our conversion is the instrumental organ thereof, and may be said to be a sufficient cause of our regeneration, inasmuch as no other in the same kind is necessary. It may also be resisted *in sensu diviso*, abstracting from that consideration wherein it is looked on as the instrument of God for such an end.

Sixthly, Internal grace is by divines distinguished into the first or preventing grace, and the second following co-operating grace. The first is that spiritual vital principle that is infused into us by the Holy Spirit, that new creation and bestowing of new strength, whereby we are made fit and able for the producing of spiritual acts, to believe and yield evangelical obedience: "For we are the workmanship of God, created in Christ Jesus unto good works," Eph. ii. 10. By this God "gives us a new heart, and a new spirit he puts within us;" he "takes the stony heart out of our flesh, and gives us an heart of flesh;" he "puts his Spirit within us, to cause us to walk in his statutes," Ezek. xxxvi. 26, 27.

Now, this first grace is not properly and formally a vital act, but *causaliter* only, in being a principle moving to such vital acts within us. It is the habit of faith bestowed upon a man, that he may be able to eliciate and perform the acts thereof, giving new light to the understanding, new inclinations to the will, and new affections unto the heart: for the infallible efficacy of which grace it is that we plead against the Arminians. And amongst those innumerable places of holy Scripture confirming this truth, I shall make use only of a very few, reduced to these three heads:—

First, Our conversion is wrought by a divine, almighty action, which the will of man will not, and therefore cannot resist. The impotency thereof ought not to be opposed to this omnipotent grace, which will certainly effect the work for which it is ordained, being an action not inferior to the greatness of his "mighty power, which he wrought in Christ when he raised him from the dead," Eph. i. 19, 20. And shall not that power which could overcome hell, and loose the bonds of death, be effectual for the raising of a sinner from the death of sin, when by God's intention it is appointed unto that work? He accomplisheth "the work of faith with power," 2 Thess. i. 11. It is "his divine power that giveth unto us all things that pertain unto life and godliness," 2 Pet. i. 3. Surely a moral, resistible persuasion would not be thus often termed the "power" of God, which denoteth an actual efficacy to which no creature is able to resist.

Secondly, That which consisteth in a real efficiency, and is not at all but when and where it actually worketh what it intendeth, cannot without a contradiction be said to be so resisted that it should not work, the whole nature thereof consisting in such a real operation. Now, that the very essence of divine grace consisteth in such a formal act may be proved by all those places of Scripture that affirm God by his grace, or the grace of God, actually to accomplish our conversion: as Deut. xxx. 6, "And the LORD thy God will circumcise thine heart, and the heart of thy seed, to love the LORD thy God with all thine heart, and with all thy soul, that thou mayest live." The circumcision of our hearts, that we may love the Lord with all our hearts, and with all our souls, is our conversion, which the Lord affirmeth here that he himself will do; not only enable us to do it, but he himself really and effectually will accomplish it. And again, "I will put my law in their inward parts, and write it in their hearts," Jer. xxxi. 33. "I will put my fear in their hearts, that they shall not depart from me," chap. xxxii. 40. He will not *offer* his fear unto them, but actually *put* it into them. And most clearly, Ezek. xxxvi. 26, 27: "A new heart also will I give you, and a new spirit will I put within you: and I will take away the stony heart out of your flesh, and I will give you an heart of flesh. And I will put my Spirit within you, and cause you to walk in my statutes." Are these expressions of a moral persuasion only? Doth God affirm here he will *do* what he intends only to *persuade* us to, and which we may refuse to do if we will? Is it in the power of a stony heart to remove itself? What an active stone is this, in mounting upwards! What doth it at all differ from that heart of flesh that God promiseth? Shall a stony heart be said to have a power to change itself into such a heart of flesh as shall cause us to walk in God's statutes? Surely, unless men were wilfully blind, they must needs here perceive such an action of God denoted, as effectually, solely, and infallibly worketh our conversion; "opening our hearts, that we may attend unto the word," Acts xvi. 14; "giving us in the behalf of Christ to believe on him," Phil. i. 29. Now, these and the like places prove both the nature of God's grace to consist in a real efficiency, and the operation thereof to be certainly effectual.

Thirdly, Our conversion is a "new creation," a "resurrection," a "new birth." Now, he that createth a man doth not persuade him to create himself, neither can he if he should, nor hath he any power to resist him that will create him,—that is, as we now take it, translate him from something that he is to what he is not. What arguments do you think were sufficient to persuade a dead man to rise?

or what great aid can he contribute to his own resurrection? Neither doth a man beget himself; a new real form was never yet introduced into any matter by subtle arguments. These are the terms the Scripture is pleased to use concerning our conversion:—"If any man be in Christ, he is a new creature," 2 Cor. v. 17. The "new man after God is created in righteousness and true holiness," Eph. iv. 24. It is our new birth: "Except a man be born again, he cannot see the kingdom of God," John iii. 3. "Of his own will begat he us with the word of truth," James i. 18. And so we become "born again, not of corruptible seed, but of incorruptible, by the word of God, which liveth and abideth for ever," 1 Pet. i. 23. It is our vivification and resurrection: "The Son quickeneth whom he will," John v. 21, even those "dead," who "hear his voice and live," verse 25. "When we were dead in sins," we are "quickened together with Christ by grace," Eph. ii. 5; for "being buried with him by baptism, we are also risen with him through the faith of the operation of God," Col. ii. 12. And "blessed and holy is he that hath part in that first resurrection; on such the second death hath no power, but they shall be priests of God and of Christ, and shall reign with him a thousand years."

Τῷ Θεῷ ἀριστομεγίστῳ δόξα.

SALUS ELECTORUM, SANGUIS JESU;

OR,

THE DEATH OF DEATH IN THE DEATH OF CHRIST:

A TREATISE OF THE REDEMPTION AND RECONCILIATION THAT IS IN THE BLOOD OF CHRIST;

WITH

THE MERIT THEREOF, AND THE SATISFACTION WROUGHT THEREBY:

WHEREIN

THE PROPER END OF THE DEATH OF CHRIST IS ASSERTED; THE IMMEDIATE EFFECTS AND FRUITS THEREOF ASSIGNED, WITH THEIR EXTENT IN RESPECT OF ITS OBJECT;

AND THE

WHOLE CONTROVERSY ABOUT UNIVERSAL REDEMPTION FULLY DISCUSSED.

IN FOUR PARTS.

I. DECLARING THE ETERNAL COUNSEL AND DISTINCT ACTUAL CONCURRENCE OF THE HOLY TRINITY UNTO THE WORK OF REDEMPTION IN THE BLOOD OF CHRIST; WITH THE COVENANTED INTENDMENT AND ACCOMPLISHED END OF GOD THEREIN.

II. REMOVING FALSE AND SUPPOSED ENDS OF THE DEATH OF CHRIST, WITH THE DISTINCTIONS INVENTED TO SOLVE THE MANIFOLD CONTRADICTIONS OF THE PRETENDED UNIVERSAL ATONEMENT; RIGHTLY STATING THE CONTROVERSY.

III. CONTAINING ARGUMENTS AGAINST UNIVERSAL REDEMPTION FROM THE WORD OF GOD; WITH AN ASSERTION OF THE SATISFACTION AND MERIT OF CHRIST.

IV. ANSWERING ALL CONSIDERABLE OBJECTIONS AS YET BROUGHT TO LIGHT, EITHER BY THE ARMINIANS OR OTHERS (THEIR LATE FOLLOWERS AS TO THIS POINT), IN THE BEHALF OF UNIVERSAL REDEMPTION; WITH A LARGE UNFOLDING OF ALL THE TEXTS OF SCRIPTURE BY ANY PRODUCED AND WRESTED TO THAT PURPOSE.

The Son of man came not to be ministered unto, but to minister, and to give his life a ransom for many.—MATT. xx. 28.

In whom we have redemption through his blood, the forgiveness of sins, according to the riches of his grace.—EPH. i. 7.

Imprimatur,

Jan. 22, 1647. JOHN CRANFORD.

PREFATORY NOTE.

In the testimonies from the ancient fathers, which Owen appends to the following treatise, he quotes Augustine and Prosper as authorities in support of his own view of a definite and effectual atonement. Though these fathers, in opposition to the Pelagians and semi-Pelagians of their day, held this view, the point did not emerge into commanding prominence in the controversy with which their names are chiefly and honourably associated. It was by no means a subject of special controversy, or the key of their position in the field on which their polemical laurels were won. It was otherwise in the dispute which prevailed between Hincmar and Gottschalc, exactly four centuries later. The discussion on the extent of the atonement then assumed a distinct and positive shape. The decisions of the different councils which sat in judgment upon their conflicting principles will be found in the appendix to this treatise. The same controversy was renewed in Holland between the Gomarists and the Arminians, when the Synod of Dort, in one of its articles, condemned the Remonstrant doctrine of a universal atonement. Cameron, the accomplished professor of divinity at Saumur, originated the last important discussion on this point before Owen wrote his treatise on it. The views of Cameron were adopted and urged with great ability by two of his scholars, Amyraut and Testard; and in the year 1634 a controversy arose, which agitated the French Church for many years. Amyraut had the support of Daillé and Blondell. He was ably opposed by Rivet, Spanheim, and Des Marets.

In the last two instances in which discussion on the extent of the atonement revived in the Reformed Churches, there was an essential distinction, very commonly overlooked, between the special points upon which the controversies respectively turned. The object of the article on the death of Christ, emitted by the Synod of Dort, was to counteract the tenet that Christ by the atonement only acquired for the Father a plenary right and freedom to institute a new procedure with all men, by which, on condition of their own obedience, they might be saved. The divines of Saumur would not have accepted this tenet as a correct representation of their sentiments. Admitting that, by the purpose of God, and through the death of Christ, the elect are infallibly secured in the enjoyment of salvation, they contended for an antecedent decree, by which God is free to give salvation to all men through Christ, on the *condition* that they believe on him. Hence their system was termed *hypothetic universalism.* The vital difference between it and the strict Arminian theory lies in the absolute security asserted in the former for the spiritual recovery of the elect. They agree, however, in attributing some kind of universality to the atonement, and in maintaining that, on a certain *condition,* within the reach of fulfilment by all men,—obedience generally, according to the Arminians, and faith, according to the divines of Saumur,—all men have access to the benefits of Christ's death. To impart consistency to the theory of Amyraut, faith must, in some sense, be competent to all men; and he held, accordingly, the doctrine of *universal grace:* in which respect his theory differs essentially from the doctrine of universal atonement, as embraced by eminent Calvinistic divines, who held the necessity of the *special operation* of grace in order to the exercise of faith. The readers of Owen will understand, from this cursory explanation, why he dwells with peculiar keenness and reiteration of statement upon a refutation of the conditional system, or the system of *universal grace,* according to the name it bore in subsequent discussions. It was plausible; it had many learned men for its advocates; it had obtained currency in the foreign churches; and it seems to have been embraced by More, or Moore, to whose work on "The Universality of God's Free Grace," our author replies at great length.

Thomas Moore is described by Edwards, in his "Gangræna," part ii. p. 86, as "a great sectary, that did much hurt in Lincolnshire, Norfolk, and Cambridgeshire; who was famous also in Boston, Lynn, and even in Holland, and was followed from place to place by many." His work, in a quarto volume, was published in 1643; and in the same year a reply to it appeared from the pen of

Thomas Whitefield, "Minister of the Gospel at Great Yarmouth." Mr Orme remarks, "He takes care to inform us on the title-page that 'Thomas Moore was late a weaver at Wills, near Wisbitch.'" And he adds, in regard to Moore's production, "Without approving of the argument of the work, I have no hesitation in saying that it is creditable to the talents of the weaver, and not discreditable to his piety." The weaver, it should be added, was the author of some other works: "Discovery of Seducers that Creep into Houses," "On Baptism," "A Discourse about the Precious Blood and Sacrifice of Christ," etc.

In 1650, Mr Horne, minister at Lynn in Norfolk, a man, according to Palmer (Nonconf. Mem., iii. pp. 6, 7), "of exemplary and primitive piety," and author of several works, published a reply to Owen's work, under the title, "The Open Door for Man's Approach to God; or, a vindication of the record of God concerning the extent of the death of Christ, in answer to a treatise on that subject by Mr John Owen." Horne had considerable reputation for skill in the oriental languages, and "some of his remarks and interpretations of Scripture," in the judgment of Mr Orme, "were not unworthy of Owen's attention." Owen, however, in his epistle prefixed to his "Vindiciæ Evangelicæ," expresses his opinion that the work of Horne did not deserve a reply.

Two years after the following work had been published, its author had to defend some of the views he had maintained in it against a more formidable and celebrated adversary. Richard Baxter, in an appendix to his "Aphorisms on Justification," took exception to some of the views of Owen on redemption. Owen answered him in a treatise which may be regarded as an appendix to his "Death of Death." In the discussions between them, so much of scholastic subtilty appears on both sides that little interest is likely to be felt in that department of the general question on which they were at variance.

It may be necessary to state precisely what opinion Owen really held on the subject of the extent of the atonement. All opinions on this point may, in general terms, be reduced to four. There are a few who hold that Christ died so as ultimately to secure the salvation of all men. There are others who maintain the view condemned by the Synod of Dort, that by the death of Christ God is enabled to save all or any, on condition of their obedience. There is a third party, who, while they believe that Christ died so as infallibly to secure the salvation of the elect, hold that inasmuch as Christ, in his obedience and sufferings, did what all men were under obligation to do, and suffered what all men deserved to suffer, his atonement has a general as well as a special aspect and reference, in virtue of which the offer of the gospel may be freely tendered to them. Lastly, there are those, and Owen amongst the number, who advocate a limited or definite atonement, such an atonement as implies a necessary connection between the death of Christ and the salvation of those for whom he died, while the actual bearing of the atonement on the lost is left among the things unrevealed, save only that their guilt and punishment are enhanced by the rejection of that mercy offered in the gospel. Hagenbach, in his "History of Doctrines," vol. ii. p. 255, strangely asserts, that "as regards the extent of the atonement, all denominations, with the exception of the Calvinists, hold that salvation was offered to all." It would be difficult to specify any Calvinists worthy of the name who hold that salvation should not be offered to all; and it seems needful to state that Owen at least, a very Calvinist of Calvinists, held no such view. On the contrary, among Calvinists that adhere to the doctrine of a definite atonement, it has been matter of debate, not whether the gospel should be universally offered, but on what basis,—the simple command and warrant of the Word, or the intrinsic and infinite sufficiency of the atonement,—the universal offer of the gospel proceeds. Perhaps this point was never formally before the mind of our author, but he intimates that the "innate sufficiency of the death of Christ is the foundation of its promiscuous proposal to the elect and reprobate."

Among the editions of this valuable work, that printed in Edinburgh, 1755, under the superintendence of the Rev. Adam Gib, deserves honourable mention. It is printed with some care; considerable attention is paid to the numeration; and a valuable analysis of the whole work is prefixed to it. We have not felt at liberty to adopt the numeration in all respects, as rather more of freedom is used with the original than is consistent with the principles on which this edition of Owen's works has been issued. We acknowledge our obligations to it in the preparation of the subjoined analysis, which is mostly taken from it.

ANALYSIS.

BOOK I. declares the eternal counsel and distinct actual concurrence of the holy Trinity unto the work of redemption in the blood of Christ; with the covenanted intendment and accomplished end of God therein.

CHAPTER I. treats in general of the end of the death of Christ, as it is in the Scripture proposed:—I. What his Father and himself intended in it. II. What was effectually fulfilled and accomplished by it:—1. Reconciliation; 2. Justification; 3. Sanctification; 4. Adoption; 5. Glorification. III. A general view of the opposite doctrine.

CHAPTER II. Of the nature of an end in general, and some distinctions about it:—I. The general distinction of end and means. II. Their mutual relation:—1. In a moral sense; 2. In a natural sense. III. A twofold end noticed, viz.:—1. Of the work; 2. Of the worker. IV. The end of every free agent is either that which he effects, or that for the sake of which it is effected. V. The means of two sorts, viz.:—1. Such as have a goodness in themselves; 2. Such as have no goodness, but as conducing to the end. VI. An application of these distinctions to the business in hand.

CHAPTER III. considers,—I. The FATHER as the chief author of the work of our redemption; II. The acts ascribed to the person of the Father:—1. The Father sending his Son into the world for the work of redemption:—(1.) By an authoritative imposition of the office of mediator upon him:—[1.] The purposed imposition of his counsel; [2.] The actual inauguration of Christ as mediator. (2.) By furnishing him with a fulness of all gifts and graces:—[1.] Christ had a natural all-sufficient perfection of his deity; [2.] He had a communicated fulness. (3.) By entering into covenant with him about his work:—[1.] With a promise of assistance; [2.] With a promise of success. 2. The Father laying upon him the punishment of sin.

CHAPTER IV. Of those things which, in the work of redemption, are peculiarly ascribed to the person of the SON:—I. His incarnation; II. His oblation; III. His intercession.

CHAPTER V. The peculiar actings of the HOLY SPIRIT in this business:—I. As to the incarnation of Christ; II. As to the oblation or passion of Christ; III. As to the resurrection of Christ.

CHAPTER VI. The means used by the fore-recounted agents in this work:—I. The means used is that whole dispensation from whence Christ is called a Mediator:—1. His oblation; 2. His intercession. II. His oblation not a mean good in itself, but only as conducing to its end, and inseparable from his intercession; as,—1. Both intended for the same end; 2. Both of the same extent, as respecting the same objects; 3. His oblation the foundation of his intercession.

CHAPTER VII. contains reasons to prove the oblation and intercession of Christ to be one entire mean respecting the accomplishment of the same proposed end, and to have the same personal object:—I. From their conjunction in Scripture; II. From their being both acts of the same priestly office; III. From the nature of his intercession; IV. From the identity of what he procured in his oblation with what results from his intercession; V. From their being conjoined by himself, John xvii.; VI. From the sad consequence of separating them, as cutting off all consolation by his death.

CHAPTER VIII. Objections are answered, being a consideration of Thomas More's reply to the former arguments for the inseparable conjunction of Christ's oblation and intercession, viz.:—I. As to Christ being a double mediator, both general and special, alleged from 1 Tim. ii. 5, iv. 10; Heb. ix. 15. II. As to the tenor of Christ's intercession, according to Isa. liii. 12; Luke xxiii. 34; John xvii. 21-23; Matt. v. 14-16; John i. 9. III. As to Christ being a priest for all in respect of one end, and for some only in respect of all ends, alleged from Heb. ii. 9, ix. 14, 15, 26; John i. 29; 1 John ii. 2; Matt. xxvi. 28.

BOOK II. removes false and supposed ends of the death of Christ, with the distinctions invented to salve the manifold contradictions of the pretended universal atonement, rightly stating the controversy.

CHAPTER I. Some previous considerations to a more particular inquiry after the proper end and effect of the death of Christ:—I. The supreme end of Christ's death in respect of God; II. The subordinate end of his death in respect of us.

CHAPTER II. removes some mistaken ends assigned to the death of Christ:—I. It was not his own good. II. It was not his Father's good, to secure for him a right to save sinners.

CHAPTER III. More particularly of the immediate end of the death of Christ, with the several ways whereby it is designed. The immediate end of the death of Christ particularly asserted from the Scriptures, viz.:—I. From those scriptures which hold out the intention and counsel of God with our Saviour's own mind in this work, Matt. xviii. 11, etc. II. From those scriptures which state the actual accomplishment or effect of his oblation, Heb. ix. 12, 14, 26, etc. III. From those scriptures that point out the persons for whom Christ died, viz., Matt. xxvi. 28; Isa. liii. 11, etc. The force of the word "many" in several of these texts, and the argument taken from them, in comparison with other texts, vindicated from the exceptions of Thomas More. Who are meant by Christ's sheep, and who not, John x. 15; and his objections answered.

CHAPTER IV. Of the distinction between impetration and application:—I. The sense wherein this distinction is used by the adversaries, and their various expressions about it. II. The distinction itself handled:—1. The true nature, meaning, and use thereof:—(1.) It has no place in the intention of Christ; (2.) The will of God in this business is not at all conditional; (3.) All the things obtained by Christ are not bestowed upon condition, and the condition on which some things are bestowed is absolutely purchased; (4.) Impetration and application have the same persons for their objects. 2. The meaning of those who seek to maintain universal redemption by that distinction; with a discovery of their various opinions on this head. III. The main question rightly stated.

CHAPTER V. Farther of application and impetration:—I. That these, though they may admit of a distinction, cannot admit of a separation, as to the objects thereof, is proved by sundry arguments. II. The defence made by the Arminians on this head (alleging that Christ purchased all good things for all, to be bestowed upon condition; which condition not being performed, these good things are not bestowed), overthrown by sundry arguments.

BOOK III. contains arguments against universal redemption from the word of God; with an assertion of the satisfaction and merit of Christ.

CHAPTER I. Arguments against the universality of redemption. The first two from the nature of the new covenant, and the dispensation thereof:—Arg. I. From the nature of the covenant of grace, as being made in Christ, not with all, but only some. Arg. II. From the dispensation of the covenant of grace, as not extended to all, but only some.

CHAPTER II. Three other arguments:—Arg. III. From the absolute nature of Christ's purchase for all the objects thereof. Arg. IV. From the distinction of men into two sorts by God's eternal purpose. Arg. V. From the Scripture nowhere saying that Christ died for all men.

CHAPTER III. Two other arguments, from the person which Christ sustained in this business:—Arg. VI. From Christ having died as a sponsor. Arg. VII. From Christ being a mediator.

CHAPTER IV. Of sanctification, and of the cause of faith, and the procurement thereof by the death of Christ:—Arg. VIII. From the efficacy of Christ's death for sanctification. Arg. IX. From the procurement of faith by the death of Christ. Arg. X. From the antitype of the people of Israel.

CHAPTER V. Continuance of arguments from the nature and description of the thing in hand; and, first, of redemption:—I. Arg. XI. From *redemption* by the death of Christ.

CHAPTER VI. Of the nature of reconciliation, and the argument taken from thence:—II. Arg. XII. From *reconciliation* by the death of Christ.

CHAPTER VII. Of the nature of the satisfaction of Christ, with arguments from thence:—III. Arg. XIII. From *satisfaction* by the death of Christ:—1. What satisfaction is:—(1.) Christ made satisfaction, and how; against Grotius. (2.) Acts exercised by God in this business:—[1.] Of severe justice, as a creditor; against Grotius. [2.] Of supreme sovereignty and dominion. Consequences of these acts as to those for whom Christ satisfied. 2. Inconsistency of all this with universal redemption.

CHAPTER VIII. A digression, containing the substance of an occasional conference concerning the satisfaction of Christ:—I. Its consistency with God's eternal love to his elect. II. Necessity of it for executing the purposes of that love.

CHAPTER IX. Being a second part of the former digression, containing arguments to prove the satisfaction of Christ:—Arg. I. From Christ bearing sin, and the punishment thereof. Arg. II. From his paying a ransom for sinners. Arg. III. From his making atonement and reconciliation. Arg. IV. From the nature of his priestly office as exercised on earth. Arg. V. From the necessity thereof unto faith and consolation. Arg. VI. From 2 Cor. v. 21, and Isa. liii. 5.

CHAPTER X. Of the merit of Christ, with arguments from thence:—IV. Arg. XIV. From the *merit* ascribed to the death of Christ. V. Arg. XV. From the phrases "dying for us," "bearing our sins," being our "surety," etc.

CHAPTER XI. The last general argument:—VI. Arg. XVI. From some particular places of Scripture, viz.:—1. Gen. iii. 15; 2. Matt. vii. 23, etc.

BOOK IV.—All considerable objections are answered as yet brought to light, either by the Arminians or others, in the behalf of universal redemption, with a large unfolding of all the texts of Scripture by any produced and wrested to that purpose.

CHAPTER I. Things to be considered previously to the solution of objections:—I. The infinite value of the blood of Christ. II. The administration of the new covenant under the gospel. III. The distinction between man's duty and God's purpose. IV. The error of the Jews about the extent of redemption. V. The nature and signification of general terms used:—1. The word "world" of various significations. 2. The word "all" of various extent. VI. Persons and things often spoken of according to their appearance. VII. Difference between the judgment of charity and verity. VIII. The infallible connection of faith and salvation. IX. The mixture of elect and reprobates in the world. X. The different acts and degrees of faith.

CHAPTER II. An entrance to the answer unto particular objections. Answer to objections from Scripture, viz.:—I. From the word "world" in several scriptures:—1. John iii. 16 largely opened and vindicated.

CHAPTER III. An unfolding of the remaining texts of Scripture produced for the confirmation of the first general objection or argument for universal redemption. 2. 1 John ii. 1, 2, largely opened and vindicated. 3. John vi. 51 explained. 4. A vindication of other texts produced by Thomas More, viz.:—(1.) 2 Cor. v. 19. (2.) John i. 9. (3.) John i. 29. (4.) John iii. 17. (5.) John iv. 42; 1 John iv. 14; John vi. 51.

CHAPTER IV. Answer to the second general objection or argument for the universality of redemption. II. From the word "all" in several scriptures, viz.:—1. 1 Tim. ii. 4, 6. 2. 2 Pet. iii. 9. 3. Heb. ii. 9. 4. 2 Cor. v. 14, 15. 5. 1 Cor. xv. 22. 6. Rom. v. 18.

CHAPTER V. The last objection or argument from Scripture answered. III. From texts which seem to hold out a perishing of some for whom Christ died, viz.:—1. Rom. xiv. 15. 2. 1 Cor. viii. 11. 3. 2 Pet. ii. 1. 4. Heb. x. 29.

CHAPTER VI. An answer to the twentieth chapter of the book entitled "The Universality of God's Free Grace," etc., being a collection of all the arguments used by the author (Thomas More) throughout the whole book, to prove the universality of redemption:—Answers to Arg. I. From the absolute literal sense of Scripture. Arg. II. From an alleged unlimitedness of Scripture phrases. Arg. III. From Christ's exaltation to be Lord and Judge of all, Rom. xiv. 9, 11, 12. Arg. IV. From the proposal of Christ's death to all by the gospel. Arg. V. From the confession to be made of Christ by all. Arg. VI. From Scripture assertions and consequences. Answers to the proofs of this sixth argument:—1. From 1 John iv. 14; John i. 4, 7; 1 Tim. ii. 4. 2. From some texts before vindicated. 3. From Ps. xix. 4; Rom. x. 18; Acts xiv. 17, etc. 4. From John xvi. 7–11, etc. 5. From Ezek. xviii. 23, 32, xxxiii. 11, etc. 6. From Matt. xxviii. 19, 20; Mark xvi. 15; Isa. xlv. 22, etc. 7. From Acts ii. 38, 39, etc. 8. From 1 Cor. xv. 21, 22, 45–47; Rom. iii. 22–25, etc. 9. From Matt. xxviii. 19, 20; 2 Cor. v. 19, etc. 10. From Matt. v. 44, 48; 1 Tim. ii. 1–4, etc. 11. From 1 Tim. ii. 3, 8, etc. 12. From 1 Cor. vi. 10, 11, etc. 13. From Tit. ii. 11, 13, iii. 4, 5, etc. 14. From John iii. 19, etc, 15. From Scripture expostulations with men. 16. From Jude 4, 12, 13, etc. 17. From Rom. xiv. 9–12, etc. 18. From Jude 3–5.

CHAPTER VII. Other objections from reason are removed:—Answers to Objection I. From men being bound to believe that Christ died for them. Obj. II. Alleging that the doctrine of particular redemption fills the minds of sinners with doubts and scruples whether they ought to believe or not; the objection retorted. Obj. III. That this doctrine disparages the freedom of grace; the objection retorted. Obj. IV. That this doctrine disparages the merit of Christ; the objection retorted. Obj. V. That this doctrine mars gospel consolation; in answer whereto it is proved that,—1. The doctrine of universal redemption affords no ground of consolation; 2. That it quite overthrows the true ground of consolation; 3. That the doctrine of particular redemption is not liable to any just exception as to this matter; 4. That this doctrine is the true, solid foundation of all durable consolation.—ED.

TO THE RIGHT HONOURABLE

ROBERT, EARL OF WARWICK,[1] ETC.

MY LORD,

IT is not for the benefit of any protection to the ensuing treatise,—let it stand or fall as it shall be found in the judgments of men; nor that I might take advantage to set forth any of that worth and honour which, being personal, have truly ennobled your lordship, and made a way for the delivering over of your family unto posterity with an eminent lustre added to the roll of your worthy progenitors,—which, if by myself desired, my unfitness to perform must needs render unacceptable in the performance; neither yet have I the least desire to attempt a farther advancement of myself into your lordship's favour, being much beneath what I have already received, and fully resolved to own no other esteem among the sons of men but what shall be accounted due (be it more or less) to the discharge of my duty to my master, Jesus Christ, whose wholly I would be;—it is not all, nor one of these, nor any such as these, the usual subjects and ends of dedications, real or pretended, that prevailed upon me unto this boldness of prefixing your honoured name to this ensuing treatise (which yet, for the matter's sake contained in it, I cannot judge unworthy of any Christian eye); but only that I might take the advantage to testify (as I do) to all the world the answering of my heart unto that obligation which your lordship was pleased to put upon me, in the undeserved, undesired favour of opening that door wherewith you are intrusted, to give me an entrance to that place for the preaching of the gospel whither I was directed by the providence of the Most High, and where I was sought by his people. In which place this I dare say, by the grace of God, that such a stock of prayers and thankfulness as your heart, which hath learned to value the least of Christ, in whomsoever it be, will not despise, is tendered to and for your lordship, even on his behalf who is less than the least of all the saints of God, and unworthy the name which yet he is bold to subscribe himself by,—Your honour's most obliged servant in the service of Jesus Christ,

JOHN OWEN.

1 This nobleman is represented by Neal as having been "the greatest patron of the Puritans." He was admiral of the parliamentary fleet. He seized on the ships belonging to the king, and during the whole course of the war made use of them against the royal interest. Owen had received the presentation to Coggeshall from this nobleman, whose upright and amiable character was celebrated long after his death under the designation of THE GOOD EARL OF WARWICK.—ED.

TWO ATTESTATIONS

TOUCHING THE ENSUING TREATISE.

READER,

THERE are two rotten pillars on which the fabric of late Arminianism (an egg of the old Pelagianism, which we had well hoped had been long since chilled, but is sit upon and brooded by the wanton wits of our degenerate and apostate spirits) doth principally stand.

The one is, That *God loveth all alike,* Cain as well as Abel, Judas as the rest of the apostles.

The other is, That *God giveth* (nay is bound, "ex debito," so to do) *both Christ, the great gift of his eternal love, for all alike to work out their redemption, and* "vires credendi," *power to believe in Christ to all alike to whom he gives the gospel;* whereby that redemption may effectually be applied for their salvation, if they please to make right use of that which is so put into their power.

The former destroys the *free* and *special* grace of God, by making it *universal;* the latter gives cause to man of glorying in himself rather than in God,—God concurring no farther to the salvation of a believer than a reprobate. Christ died for both alike;—God giving power of accepting Christ to both alike, men themselves determining the whole matter by their free-will; Christ making both savable, themselves make them to be saved.

This cursed doctrine of theirs crosseth the main drift of the holy Scripture; which is to abase and pull down the pride of man, to make him even to despair of himself, and to advance and set up the glory of God's free grace from the beginning to the end of man's salvation. His hand hath laid the foundation of his spiritual house; his hand shall also finish it.

The reverend and learned author of this book hath received strength from God (like another Samson) to pull down this rotten house upon the head of those Philistines who would uphold it. Read it diligently, and I doubt not but you will say with me, there is such variety of choice matter running through every vein of each discourse here handled, and carried along with such strength of sound and deep judgment, and with such life and power of a heavenly spirit, and all expressed in such pithy and pregnant words of wisdom, that you will both delight in the reading and praise God for the writer. That both he and it may be more and more profitable shall be my hearty prayers.—The unworthiest of the ministers of the gospel,

STANLEY GOWER.[1]

CHRISTIAN READER,

UNTO such alone are these directed. If all and every one in the world in this gospel-day did bear this precious name of Christian, or if the name of Christ were known to all, then were this compellation very improper, because it is distinguish-

[1] A Puritan divine of considerable eminence, and a member of the Westminster Assembly. He was at first minister of Brampton Bryan, Herefordshire. Latterly he was a minister at Dorchester, where he seems to have been alive about 1660.—ED.

ing. But if God distinguish men and men, choose we or refuse we, so it is, and so it will be; there is a difference,—a difference which God and Christ doth make of mere good pleasure.

This book contends earnestly for this truth against the error of *universal redemption.* With thy leave I cannot but call it an error; unless it had been, it were, and while the world continueth it should be, found indeed that Adam and all that come of him, in a natural way of generation, are first set by Christ, the second Adam, in an estate of redeemed ones and made Christians, and then they fall, whole nations of them, and forfeit that estate also, and lose their Christendom, and thereby it is come to pass that they are become atheists, without God in the world, and heathen, Jews, and Turks, as we see they are at this day.

The author of this book I know not so much as by name; it is of the book itself that I take upon me the boldness to write these few lines. It being delivered unto me to peruse, I did read it with delight and profit:—with delight, in the keenness of argument, clearness and fulness of answers, and candour in language; —with profit, in the vindication of abused Scriptures, the opening of obscure places, and chiefly in disclosing the hid mystery of God and the Father and of Christ, in the glorious and gracious work of redemption. The like pleasure and profit this tractate promiseth to all diligent readers thereof, for the present controversy is so managed that the doctrine of faith, which we ought to believe, is with dexterity plentifully taught; yea, the glory of each person in the unity of the Godhead about the work of redemption is distinctly held forth with shining splendour, and the error of the Arminians smitten in the jaw-bone, and the broachers of it bridled with bit and curb.

When, on earth, the blood can be without the water and the Spirit,—can witness alone, or can witness there where the water and the Spirit agree not to the record; when, in heaven, the Word shall witness without the Father and the Holy Ghost,—when the Father, the Word, and the Holy Ghost shall not be one, as in *essence,* so in *willing, working, witnessing the redemption of sinners;*—then shall universal redemption of all and every sinner by Christ be found a truth, though the Father elect them not, nor the Spirit of grace neither sanctify nor seal them. The glory of God's free and severing grace, and the salvation of the elect through the redemption that is in Jesus Christ (which is external, or none at all), are the unfeigned desires and utmost aims of all that are truly Christian. In pursuit of which desire and aims, I profess myself to be for ever to serve thee.—Thine in Christ Jesus,

RICHARD BYFIELD.[1]

1 Richard Byfield was ejected by the Act of Uniformity from Long Ditton, in the county of Surrey. Besides some sermons and tracts, he was the author of a quarto volume, "The Doctrine of the Sabbath Vindicated," etc. He suffered suspension and sequestration for four years for not reading the Book of Sports. He was a member of the Westminster Assembly. During the time of Cromwell, a difference occurred between him and the patron of the parish, Sir John Evelyn, about the repairs of the church. Cromwell brought them together, succeeded in reconciling them, and, to cement the reconciliation, generously advanced £100, one-half of the sum needed for the repairs. Byfield did not know Owen, even by name, when he gave his recommendation to this work. It was then of some importance to our author that he should have the sanction of Byfield's name; and the favour is requited when the latter owes most of his own reputation with posterity to the countenance which he gave to the young and rising theological author of his day.—ED.

TO THE READER.

READER,

IF thou intendest to go any farther, I would entreat thee to stay here a little. If thou art, as many in this pretending age, *a sign or title gazer*, and comest into books as Cato into the theatre, to go out again,—thou hast had thy entertainment; farewell! With him that resolves a serious view of the following discourse, and really desireth satisfaction from the word and Christian reason, about the great things contained therein, I desire a few words in the portal. Divers things there are of no small consideration to the business we have in hand, which I am persuaded thou canst not be unacquainted with; and therefore I will not trouble thee with a needless repetition of them.

I shall only crave thy leave to preface a little to the point in hand, and my present undertaking therein, with the result of some of my thoughts concerning the whole, after a more than seven-years' serious inquiry (bottomed, I hope, upon the strength of Christ, and guided by his Spirit) into the mind of God about these things, with a serious perusal of all which I could attain that the wit of man, in former or latter days, hath published in opposition to the truth; which I desire, according to the measure of the gift received, here to assert. Some things, then, as to the chief point in hand I would desire the reader to observe; as,—

First, That the assertion of *universal redemption*, or the general ransom, so as to make it in the least measure beneficial for the end intended, goes not *alone*. Election of free grace, as the fountain of all following dispensations, all discriminating purposes of the Almighty, depending on his own good pleasure and will, must be removed out of the way. Hence, those who would for the present ("populo ut placerent, quas fecere fabulas,") desirously retain some show of asserting the liberty of eternally distinguishing free grace, do themselves utterly raze, in respect of any fruit or profitable issue, the whole imaginary fabric of general redemption, which they had before erected. Some of these make the decree of election to be "antecedaneous to the death of Christ" (as themselves absurdly speak), or the decree of the death of Christ: then frame a twofold election;[1]—one, of some to be the sons; the other, of the rest to be servants. But this election of some to be servants the Scripture calls reprobation, and speaks of it as the issue of hatred, or a purpose of rejection, Rom. ix. 11–13. To be a servant, in opposition to children and their liberty, is as high a curse as can be expressed, Gen. ix. 25. Is this Scripture election? Besides, if Christ died to bring those he died for unto the adoption and inheritance of children, what good could possibly redound to them thereby who were predestinated before to be only servants? Others[2] make a general conditionate decree of redemption to be antecedaneous to election; which they assert to be the first discriminating purpose concerning the sons of men, and to depend on the alone good pleasure of God. That any others shall partake of the death of Christ or the fruits thereof, either unto grace or glory, but only those persons so elected, that they deny. "Cui bono" now? To what purpose serves the general ransom, but only to assert that Almighty God would have the precious blood of his dear Son poured out for innumerable souls whom he will not have to share in any drop thereof, and so, in respect of them, to be spilt in vain, or else to be shed for them only that they might be the deeper damned? This fountain, then, of free grace, this foundation of

1 T. M., Universality of Free Grace. [He refers to an author of the name of Thomas More. See page 153 of this preface.—ED.]

2 Camero, Amirald, etc.

the new covenant, this bottom of all gospel dispensations, this fruitful womb of all eternally distinguishing mercies, the purpose of God according to election, must be opposed, slighted, blasphemed, that the figment of the sons of men may not appear to be "truncus ficulnus, inutile lignum,"—an unprofitable stock; and all the thoughts of the Most High, differencing between man and man, must be made to take "occasion," say some, to be "caused," say others, by their holy, self-spiritual endeavours. "Gratum opus agricolis,"—a savoury sacrifice to the Roman Belus, a sacred orgie to the long-bewailed manes of St Pelagius.

And here, secondly, free-will, "amor et deliciæ humani generis," corrupted nature's deformed darling, the Pallas or beloved self-conception of darkened minds, finds open hearts and arms for its adulterous embraces; yea, the die being cast, and Rubicon passed over, "eo devenere fata ecclesiæ," that having opposed the free distinguishing grace of God as the sole sworn enemy thereof, it advanceth itself, or an inbred native ability in every one to embrace a portion of generally exposed mercy, under the name of free grace. "Tantane nos tenuit generis fiducia vestri?" This, this is Universalists' free grace, which in the Scripture phrase is cursed, corrupted nature. Neither can it otherwise be. A general ransom without free-will is but "phantasiæ inutile pondus,"—"a burdensome fancy;" the merit of the death of Christ being to them as an ointment in a box, that hath neither virtue nor power to act or reach out its own application unto particulars, being only set out in the gospel to the view of all, that those who will, by their own strength, lay hold on it and apply it to themselves may be healed. Hence the dear esteem and high valuation which this old idol free-will hath attained in these days, being so useful to the general ransom that it cannot live a day without it. Should it pass for true what the Scripture affirms, namely, that we are by nature "dead in trespasses and sins," etc., there would not be left of the general ransom a shred to take fire from the hearth. Like the wood of the vine, it would not yield a pin to hang a garment upon: all which you shall find fully declared in the ensuing treatise. But here, as though all the undertakings and Babylonish attempts of the old Pelagians, with their varnished offspring, the late Arminians, were slight and easy, I shall show you greater abominations than these, and farther discoveries of the imagery of the hearts of the sons of men. In pursuance of this persuasion of universal redemption, not a few have arrived (whither it naturally leads them) to deny the satisfaction and merit of Christ. Witness P—— H——, who, not being able to untie, ventured boldly to cut this Gordian knot, but so as to make both ends of the chain useless. To the question, Whether Christ died for all men or no? he answers, "That he died neither for all nor any, so as to purchase life and salvation for them." Ὦ πᾶν ποῖόν σε ἔπος φύγεν ἕρκος ὀδόντων; Shall cursed Socinianism be worded into a glorious discovery of free grace? Ask now for proofs of this assertion, as you might justly expect Achillean arguments from those who delight ἀκίνητα κινεῖν, and throw down such foundations (as shall put all the righteous in the world to a loss thereby), "Projicit ampullas et sesquipedalia verba," ὑπέρογκα ματαιότητος, great swelling words of vanity, drummy expressions, a noise from emptiness, the usual language of men who know not what they speak, nor whereof they do affirm, is all that is produced. Such contemptible products have our tympanous mountains! Poor creatures, whose souls are merchandised by the painted faces of novelty and vanity, whilst these Joabs salute you with the kisses of free grace, you see not the sword that is in their hands, whereby they smite you under the fifth rib, in the very heart-blood of faith and all Christian consolation. It seems our blessed Redeemer's deep humiliation, in bearing the chastisement of our peace and the punishment of our transgressions, being made a curse and sin, deserted under wrath and the power of death, procuring redemption and the remission of sins through the effusion of his blood, offering himself up a sacrifice to God, to make reconciliation and purchase an atonement, his pursuing this undertaking with continued intercession in the holy of holies, with all the benefits of his mediatorship, do no way procure either life and salvation or remission of sins, but only serve to declare that we are not indeed what his word affirms we are,—namely, cursed, guilty, defiled, and only not actually cast into hell. "Judas, betrayest thou the Son of man with a kiss?" See this at large confuted, lib. iii. Now, this last assertion, thoroughly fancied, hath opened a door and given an inlet to all those pretended heights and new-named glorious attainments which have metamorphosed the person and mediation of Christ into an imaginary diffused goodness and love, communicated from the Creator unto the new creation; than which familistical fables Cerdon's two principles were not more absurd; the Platonic numbers nor the Valentinian Æones,[1] flowing from the teeming wombs of Πλήρωμα, Αἰών, Τέλειος, Βυθός, Σιγή, and the rest, vented for high glorious attainments in Christian religion, near fifteen hundred years ago, were not less intelligible. Neither did the corroding of Scriptures by that Pontic vermin Marcion equalize the contempt and scorn cast upon them by these impotent impostors, exempting their whispered discoveries from their trial, and exalting their revelations above their authority. Neither do some stay here; but "his gradibus itur in cœlum," heaven itself is broke open for all. From universal redemption, through universal justification, in a general covenant, they have arrived ("haud ignota loquor") at universal salvation; neither can any forfeiture be made of the purchased inheritance.

> "Quare agite, ô juvenes, tantarum in munere laudum,
> Cingite fronde comas, et pocula porgite dextris,
> Communemque vocate Deum, et date vina volentes."[2]

> "March on, brave youths, i' th' praise of such free grace,
> Surround your locks with bays; and full cups place
> In your right hands: drink freely on, then call
> O' th' common hope, the ransom general."

These and the like persuasions I no way dislike, because wholly new to the men of this generation; that I may add this by the way:—Every age hath its employment in the discovery of truth. We are not come to the bottom of vice or virtue. The whole world hath been employed in the practice of iniquity five thousand years and upwards, and yet "aspice hoc novum" may be set on many villanies. Behold daily new inventions! No wonder, then, if all truth be not yet discovered. Something may be revealed to them who as yet sit by. Admire not if Saul also be among the prophets, for who is their father? Is he not free in his dispensations? Are all the depths of Scripture, where the elephants may swim, just fathomed to the bottom? Let any man observe the progress of the last century in unfolding the truths of God, and he will scarce be obstinate that no more is left as yet undiscovered. Only the itching of corrupted fancies, the boldness of darkened minds and lascivious wanton wits, in venting new-created nothings, insignificant vanities, with an intermixed dash of blasphemy, is that which I desire to oppose; and that especially considering the genius (if I may so speak) of the days wherein we live; in which, what by one means, what by another, there is almost a general deflection after novelty grown amongst us. [3]"Some are credulous, some negligent, some fall into errors, some seek them." A great suspicion also every day grows upon me, which I would thank any one upon solid grounds to free me from, that pride of spirit, with an Herostratus-like design to grow big in the mouths of men, hath acted many in the conception and publication of some easily-invented false opinions. Is it not to be thought, also, that it is from the same humour possessing many, that every one of them almost strives to put on beyond his companions in framing some singular artifice? To be a follower of others, though in desperate engagements, is too mean an undertaking.

> "Aude[4] aliquod brevibus Gyaris, et carcere dignum,
> Si vis esse aliquis: probitas laudatur et alget."[5]

1 Iren. lib. ii., cap. 6, 7, 14, 15, etc.; Clem. Strom. iii.; Epiph. Hæres. xxxi.; Tertul. ad Valen.
2 Virg. Æn. viii. 273, et seq.
3 "Quidam creduli, quidam negligentes sunt, quibusdam mendacium obrepit, quibusdam placet."
4 "In tam occupata civitate fabulas vulgaris nequitia non invenit."—Sen. Ep. 120.
5 Juv. Sat. i. 74.

And let it be no small peccadillo, no underling opinion, friends, if in these busy times you would have it taken notice of. Of ordinary errors you may cry,—

> "Quis leget hæc?——nemo hercule nemo,
> Vel duo, vel nemo."[1]

They must be glorious attainments, beyond the understanding of men, and above the wisdom of the word, which attract the eyes of poor deluded souls. The great shepherd of the sheep, our Lord Jesus Christ, recover his poor wanderers to his own fold! But to return thither from whence we have digressed:—

This is that fatal Helena, a useless, barren, fruitless fancy, for whose enthroning such irksome, tedious contentions have been caused to the churches of God; a mere Rome, a desolate, dirty place of cottages, until all the world be robbed and spoiled to adorn it. Suppose Christ died for all, yet if God in his free purpose hath chosen some to obtain life and salvation, passing by others, will it be profitable only to the *former*, or unto *all?* Surely the purpose of God must stand, and he will do all his pleasure. Wherefore, election either, with Huberus, by a wild contradiction, must be made universal, or the thoughts of the Most High suspended on the free-will of man. Add this borrowed feather to the general ransom, that at least it may have some colour of pompous ostentation. Yet if the free grace of God work effectually in some, not in others, can those others, passed by in its powerful operation, have any benefit by universal redemption? No more than the Egyptians had in the angel's passing over those houses whose doors were not sprinkled with blood, leaving some dead behind him. Almighty, powerful, free grace, then, must strike its sail, that free-will, like the Alexandrian ships to the Roman havens, may come in with top and top-gallant; for without it the whole territory of universal redemption will certainly be famished. But let these doctrines of God's eternal election, the free grace of conversion, perseverance, and their necessary consequents, be asserted, "movet cornicula risum, furtivis nudata coloribus;" it hath not the least appearance of profit or consolation but what it robs from the sovereignty and grace of God. But of these things more afterward.

Some flourishing pretences are usually held out by the abettors of the general ransom; which by thy patience, courteous reader, we will a little view in the entrance, to remove some prejudice that may lie in the way of truth:—

First, The glory of God, they say, is exceedingly exalted by it; his *good-will and kindness towards men abundantly manifested in this enlargement of its extent;* and his free grace, by others restrained, set out with a powerful endearment. This they say; which is, in effect, "All things will be well when God is contented with that portion of glory which is of our assigning." The princes of the earth account it their greatest wisdom to varnish over their favours, and to set out with a full mouth what they have done with half a hand; but will it be acceptable to lie for God, by extending his bounty beyond the marks and eternal bounds fixed to it in his word? Change first a hair of your own heads, or add a cubit to your own statures, before you come in with an addition of glory, not owned by him, to the Almighty. But so, for the most part, is it with corrupted nature in all such mysterious things; discovering the baseness and vileness thereof. If God be apprehended to be as large in grace as that is in offence (I mean in respect of particular offenders, for in respect of his he is larger), though it be free, and he hath proclaimed to all that he may do what he will with his own, giving no account of his matters, all shall be well,—he is gracious, merciful, etc; but if once the Scripture is conceived to hold out his sovereignty and free distinguishing grace, suited in its dispensation to his own purpose according to election, he is "immanis, truculentus, diabolo, Tiberio tetrior (horresco referens)." The learned know well where to find this language, and I will not be instrumental to propagate their blasphemies to others. "Si deus homini non placuerit, deus non erit," said Ter-

[1] Pers. Sat. i. 2.

tullian of the heathen deities; and shall it be so with us? God forbid! This pride is inbred;[1] it is a part of our corruption to defend it. If we maintain, then, the glory of God, let us speak in his own language, or be for ever silent. That is glorious in him which he ascribes unto himself. Our inventions, though never so splendid in our own eyes, are unto him an abomination, a striving to pull him down from his eternal excellency, to make him altogether like unto us. God would never allow that the will of the creature should be the measure of his honour. The obedience of paradise was to have been regulated. God's prescription hath been the bottom of his acceptation of any duty ever since he had a creature to worship him. The very heathen knew that that service alone was welcome to God which himself required, and that glory owned which himself had revealed that he would appear glorious in it. Hence, as Epimenides[2] advised the Athenians in a time of danger to sacrifice Θεῷ προσήκοντι, "to him to whom it was meet and due,"—which gave occasion to the altar which Paul saw bearing the superscription of Ἀγνώστῳ Θεῷ, "To the unknown God,"—so Socrates tells us in Plato,[3] that every god will be worshipped τῷ μάλιστα αὐτῷ ἀρέσκοντι τρόπῳ, "in that way which pleaseth best his own mind;" and in Christianity, Hierome sets it down for a rule, that "honos præter mandatum est dedecus," God is dishonoured by that honour which is ascribed to him beyond his own prescription: and one wittily on the second commandment, "Non imago, non simulachrum damnatur, sed non facies tibi." Assigning to God any thing by him not assumed is a *making to ourselves*, a deifying of our own imaginations. Let all men, then, cease squaring the glory of God by their own corrupted principles and more corrupted persuasions. The word alone is to be arbitrator in the things of God; which also I hope will appear, by the following treatise, to hold out nothing in the matter in hand contrary to those natural notions of God and his goodness which in the sad ruins of innocency have been retained. On these grounds we affirm, that all that glory of God which is pretended to be asserted by the general ransom, however it may seem glorious to purblind nature, is indeed a sinful flourish, for the obscuring of that glory wherein God is delighted.

Secondly, It is strongly pretended that the worth and value of the satisfaction of Christ, by the opposite opinion limited to a few, are exceedingly magnified in this extending of them to all; when, besides what was said before unto human extending of the things of God beyond the bounds by himself fixed unto them, the merit of the death of Christ, consisting in its own internal worth and sufficiency, with that obligation which, by his obedience unto death, was put upon the justice of God for its application unto them for whom he died, is quite enervated and overthrown by it, made of no account, and such as never produced of itself absolutely the least good to any particular soul: which is so fully manifested in the following treatise, as I cannot but desire the reader's sincere consideration of it, it being a matter of no small importance.

Thirdly, A seeming smile cast upon the opinion of universal redemption by many texts of Scripture, with the ambiguity of some words, which though in themselves either figurative or indefinite, yet seem to be of a universal extent, maketh the abettors of it exceedingly rejoice. Now, concerning this I shall only desire the reader not to be startled at the multitude of places of Scripture which he may find heaped up by some of late about this business (especially by Thomas More, in his "Universality of Free Grace"), as though they proved and confirmed that for which they are produced, but rather prepare himself to admire at the confidence of men, particularly of him now named, to make such a flourish with colours and drums, having indeed no soldiers at all; for, notwithstanding all their pretences, it will appear that they hang the whole weight of their building on

1 "Natura sic apparet vitiata ut hoc majoris vitii sit non videre."—Aug.
2 Laert. in Vit. Epimen. 3 Plato de Legib., lib. vii.

three or four texts of Scripture,—namely, 1 Tim. ii. 5, 6; John iii. 16, 17; Heb. ii. 9; 1 John ii. 2, with some few others,—and the ambiguity of two or three words, which themselves cannot deny to be of exceeding various acceptations. All which are at large discussed in the ensuing treatise, no one place that hath with the least show or colour been brought forth by any of our adversaries, in their own defence, or for the opposing of the effectual redemption of the elect only, being omitted, the book of Thomas More being in all the strength thereof fully met withal and enervated.

Fourthly, Some men have, by I know not what misprision,[1] entertained a persuasion that the opinion of the Universalists serves exceedingly to set forth the love and free grace of God; yea, they make free grace, that glorious expression, to be that alone which is couched in their persuasion,—namely, that "God loves all alike, gave Christ to die for all, and is ready to save all if they will lay hold on him;"—under which notion how greedily the hook as well as the bait is swallowed by many we have daily experience, when the truth is, it is utterly destructive to the free distinguishing grace of God in all the dispensations and workings thereof. It evidently opposeth God's free grace of election, as hath been declared, and therein that very love from which God sent his Son. His free distinguishing grace, also, of effectual calling must be made by it to give place to nature's darling, free-will; yea, and the whole covenant of grace made void, by holding it out no otherwise but as a general removing of the wrath which was due to the breach of the covenant of works: for what else can be imagined (though this certainly they have not, John iii. 36) to be granted to the most of those "all" with whom they affirm this covenant to be made? Yea, notwithstanding their flourish of free grace, as themselves are forced to grant, that after all that was effected by the death of Christ, it was possible that none should be saved, so I hope I have clearly proved that if he accomplished by his death no more than they ascribe unto it, it is utterly impossible that any one should be saved. "Quid dignum tanto?"

Fifthly, The opinion of universal redemption is not a little advantaged by presenting to convinced men a seeming ready way to extricate themselves out of all their doubts and perplexities, and to give them all the comfort the death of Christ can afford before they feel any power of that death working within them, or find any efficacy of free grace drawing their hearts to the embracing of Christ in the promise, or obtaining a particular interest in him; which are tedious things to flesh and blood to attend unto and wait upon. Some boast that, by this persuasion, that hath been effected in an hour which they waited for before seven years without success. To dispel this poor empty flourish, I shall show, in the progress, that it is very ready and apt to deceive multitudes with a plausible delusion, but really undermines the very foundations of that strong unfailing consolation which God hath showed himself abundantly willing that the heirs of promise should receive.

These and the like are the general pretences wherewith the abettors of a general ransom do seek to commend themselves and opinion to the affections of credulous souls; through them making an open and easy passage into their belief, for the swallowing and digesting of that bitter potion which lurks in the bottom of their cup. Of these I thought meet to give the reader a brief view in the entrance, to take off his mind from empty generals, that he might be the better prepared to weigh all things carefully in an equal balance, when he shall come to consider those particulars afterward insisted on, wherein the great strength of our adversaries lies. It remaineth only that I give the Christian reader a brief account of my call unto, and undertaking in, this work, and so close this preface. First, then, I will assure thee it is not the least thirst in my affections to be drinking of the waters of Meribah, nor the least desire to have a share in Ishmael's portion,

[1] The word is here used in the obsolete sense of "*mistake*," and has no reference to the legal offence of evasion or concealment now understood by the term.—Ed.

to have my hand against others, and theirs against me, that put me upon this task. I never like myself worse than when faced with a vizard of disputing in controversies. The complexion of my soul is much more pleasant unto me in the waters of Shiloah:—

> "—— Nuper me in littore vidi,
> Cum placidum ventis staret mare." [1]

What invitation there can be in itself for any one to lodge, much less abide, in this quarrelsome, scrambling territory, where, as Tertullian[2] says of Pontus, "omne quod flat Aquilo est," no wind blows but what is sharp and keen, I know not. Small pleasure in those walks which are attended with dangerous precipices and unpleasing difficulties on every side:—

> "Utque viam teneas, nulloque errore traharis;
> Per tamen adversi gradieris cornua Tauri,
> Hæmoniosque arcus, violentique ora Leonis." [3]

No quiet nor peace in these things and ways, but continual brawls and dissensions:—

> "—— Non hospes ab hospite tutus,
> Non socer a genero: fratrum quoque gratia rara est." [4]

The strongest bonds of nearest relations are too commonly broken by them. Were it not for that precept, Jude 3, and the like, of "contending earnestly for the faith once delivered unto the saints," with the sounding of my bowels for the loss of poor seduced souls, I could willingly engage myself into an unchangeable resolution to fly all wordy battles and paper combats for the residue of my few and evil days.

It is not, then (that I may return), any salamandrian complexion that was the motive to this undertaking. Neither, secondly, was it any conceit of my own abilities for this work, as though I were the fittest among many to undertake it. I know that as in all things I am "less than the least of all saints," so in these I am

> —— οὔτε τρίτος οὔτε τέταρτος
> Οὔτε δυωδέκατος οὐδ' ἐν λόγῳ οὐδ' ἐν ἀριθμῷ.

Abler[5] pens have had, within these few years, the discussing and ventilating of some of these questions in our own language. Some have come to my hands, but none of weight, before I had well-nigh finished this heap of mine own, which was some twelve months since and upwards. In some of these, at least, in all of them, I had rested fully satisfied, but that I observed they had all tied up themselves to some certain parts of the controversy, especially the removing of objections, neither compassing nor methodizing the whole; whereby I discerned that the nature of the things under debate,—namely, satisfaction, reconciliation, redemption, and the like,—was left exceedingly in the dark, and the strong foundation of the whole building not so much as once discovered. It was always upon my desires that some one would undertake the main, and unfold out of the word, from the bottom, the whole dispensation of the love of God to his elect in Jesus Christ, with the conveyance of it through the promises of the gospel, being in all the fruits thereof purchased and procured by the oblation and intercession of Jesus Christ; by which it could not but be made apparent what was the great design of the blessed Trinity in this great work of redemption, with how vain an attempt and fruitless endeavour it must needs be to extend it beyond the bounds and limits assigned unto it by the principal agents therein. That arguments also might be produced for the confirmation of the truth we assert, in opposition to the error opposed, and so the weak established and dissenters convinced, was much in my wishes. The doctrine of the satisfaction of Christ, his merit, and the reconciliation wrought thereby, understood aright by few, and of late oppugned by some, being so nearly related to the point of redemption, I desired also to have seen cleared, unfolded,

1 Virg. Buc. Ecl. ii. 25. 2 Ad. Mar. 3 Ovid. Met. ii. 79. 4 Ovid. Met. i. 144.
5 Vindic. Redempt., by my reverend and learned brother, Mr John Stalham; Mr Rutherford, Christ Drawing Sinners.

vindicated, by some able pen. But now, after long waiting, finding none to answer my expectation, although of myself I can truly say, with him in the Comedian, "Ego me neque tam astutum esse, neque ita perspicacem id scio," that I should be fit for such an undertaking, the counsel of the poet also running much in my mind,—

> "Sumite materiam vestris, qui scribitis, æquam
> Viribus; et versate diu, quid ferre recusent,
> Quid valeant humeri."[1]

Yet, at the last, laying aside all such thoughts, by looking up to Him who supplieth seed to the sower, and doth all our works for us, I suffered myself to be overcome unto the work with that of another, "Ab alio quovis hoc fieri mallem quam a me; sed a me tamen potius quam a nemine;"—"I had rather it should have been done by any than myself, of myself only rather than of none;" especially considering the industrious diligence of the opposers of truth in these days:—

> "Scribimus indocti doctique,——
> Ut jugulent homines, surgunt de nocte latrones;
> Ut teipsum serves non expergisceris?"[2]

Add unto the former desire a consideration of the frequent conferences I had been invited unto about these things, the daily spreading of the opinions here opposed about the parts where I live, and a greater noise concerning their prevailing in other places, with the advantage they had obtained by some military abettors, with the stirring up of divers eminent and learned friends, and you have the sum of what I desire to hold forth as the cause of my undertaking this task. What the Lord hath enabled me to perform therein must be left to the judgment of others. Altogether hopeless of success I am not; but fully resolved that I shall not live to see a solid answer given unto it. If any shall undertake to vellicate and pluck some of the branches, rent from the roots and principles of the whole discourse, I shall freely give them leave to enjoy their own wisdom and imaginary conquest. If any shall seriously undertake to debate the whole cause, if I live to see it effected, I shall engage myself, by the Lord's assistance, to be their humble convert or fair antagonist. In that which is already accomplished by the good hand of the Lord, I hope the learned may find something for their contentment, and the weak for their strengthening and satisfaction; that in all some glory may redound to Him whose it is, and whose truth is here unfolded by the unworthiest labourer in his vineyard,

J. O.

[1] Hor. De Art. Poet., ver. 38.

[2] Hor. Epist. lib. ii. Epist. i. 117; lib. i. Epist. ii. 32.

THE

DEATH OF DEATH IN THE DEATH OF CHRIST.

A TREATISE OF THE REDEMPTION AND RECONCILIATION THAT IS IN THE BLOOD OF CHRIST, WITH THE MERIT THEREOF, AND SATISFACTION WROUGHT THEREBY.

BOOK I.

CHAPTER I.

In general of the end of the death of Christ, as it is in the Scripture proposed.

BY the end of the death of Christ, we mean in general, both,—first, that which his Father and himself intended *in* it; and, secondly, that which was effectually fulfilled and accomplished *by* it. Concerning either we may take a brief view of the expressions used by the Holy Ghost:—

I. For the first. Will you know the *end* wherefore, and the intention wherewith, Christ came into the world? Let us ask himself (who knew his own mind, as also all the secrets of his Father's bosom), and he will tell us that the "Son of man came to save that which was lost," Matt. xviii. 11,—to recover and save poor lost sinners; that was his intent and design, as is again asserted, Luke xix. 10. Ask also his apostles, who know his mind, and they will tell you the same. So Paul, 1 Tim. i. 15, "This is a faithful saying, and worthy of all acceptation, that Christ Jesus came into the world to save sinners." Now, if you will ask who these sinners are towards whom he hath this gracious intent and purpose, himself tells you, Matt. xx. 28, that he came to "give his life a ransom for *many;*" in other places called *us*, believers, distinguished from the world: for he "gave himself for *our* sins, that he might deliver *us* from this present evil *world*, according to the will of God and our Father," Gal. i. 4. That was the will and intention of God, that he should give himself for *us*, that we might be saved, being separated from the world. They are his *church:* Eph. v. 25–27, "He loved the church, and gave himself for it; that he might sanctify and cleanse it with the washing of water by the word, that he might present it to himself a glorious church, not having spot, or wrinkle, or any such thing; but that it should be holy and without blemish:" which last words express also the very aim and end of Christ in giving himself for any, even that they may be made *fit* for God, and brought nigh unto him;—the like whereof is also asserted, Tit. ii. 14, "He gave himself for us, that he might redeem us from all iniquity, and purify unto himself a peculiar people, zealous of good works." Thus clear, then, and apparent, is the intention and design of Christ and his Father in this great work, even what it was, and towards whom,—namely, to save us, to deliver us from the evil world, to purge and wash us, to make us holy, zealous, fruitful in good works, to render us acceptable, and to bring us unto God; for through him "we have access into the grace wherein we stand," Rom. v. 2.

II. The effect, also, and actual product of the work itself, or what is accomplished and fulfilled by the death, blood-shedding, or oblation of Jesus Christ, is no less clearly manifested, but is as fully, and very often more distinctly, expressed;—as, first, *Reconciliation* with God, by removing and slaying the enmity that was between him and us; for "when we were enemies we were reconciled to God by the death of his Son," Rom. v. 10. "God was in him reconciling the world unto himself, not imputing their trespasses unto them," 2 Cor. v. 19; yea, he hath "reconciled us to himself by Jesus Christ," verse 18. And if you would know how this reconciliation was effected, the apostle will tell you that "he abolished in his flesh the enmity, the law of commandments consisting in ordinances; for to make in himself of twain one new man, so making peace; and that he might reconcile both unto God in one body by the cross, having slain the enmity thereby," Eph. ii. 15, 16: so that "he is our peace," verse 14. Secondly, *Justification*, by taking away the guilt of sins, procuring remission and pardon of them, redeeming us from their power, with the curse and wrath due unto us for them; for "by his own blood he entered into the holy place, having obtained eternal redemption for us," Heb. ix. 12. "He redeemed us from the curse, being made a curse for us," Gal. iii. 13; "his own self bearing our sins in his own body on the tree," 1 Pet. ii. 24. We have "all sinned, and come short of the glory of God;" but are "justified freely by his grace through the redemption that is in Christ Jesus, whom God hath set forth to be a propitiation through faith in his blood, to declare his righteousness for the remission of sins," Rom. iii. 23–25: for "in him we have redemption through his blood, even the forgiveness of sins," Col. i. 14. Thirdly, *Sanctification*, by the purging away of the uncleanness and pollution of our sins, renewing in us the image of God, and supplying us with the graces of the Spirit of holiness: for "the blood of Christ, who through the eternal Spirit offered himself to God, purgeth our consciences from dead works, that we may serve the living God," Heb. ix. 14; yea, "the blood of Jesus Christ cleanseth us from all sin," 1 John i. 7. "By himself he purged our sins,"

Heb. i. 3. To "sanctify the people with his own blood, he suffered without the gate," chap. xiii. 12. "He gave himself for the church to sanctify and cleanse it, that it should be holy and without blemish," Eph. v. 25–27. Peculiarly amongst the graces of the Spirit, "it is given to us," ὑπὲρ Χριστοῦ, "for Christ's sake, to believe on him," Phil. i. 29; God "blessing us in him with all spiritual blessings in heavenly places," Eph. i. 3. Fourthly, *Adoption*, with that evangelical liberty and all those glorious privileges which appertain to the sons of God; for "God sent forth his Son, made of a woman, made under the law, to redeem them that were under the law, that we might receive the adoption of sons," Gal. iv. 4, 5. Fifthly, Neither do the effects of the death of Christ rest here; they leave us not until we are settled in heaven, in glory and immortality for ever. Our inheritance is a "purchased possession," Eph. i. 14. "And for this cause he is the mediator of the new testament, that by means of death, for the redemption of the transgressions that were under the first testament, they which are called might receive the promise of eternal inheritance," Heb. ix. 15. The sum of all is,—The death and blood-shedding of Jesus Christ hath wrought, and doth effectually procure, for all those that are concerned in it, eternal redemption, consisting in grace here and glory hereafter.

III. Thus full, clear, and evident are the expressions in the Scripture concerning the *ends* and *effects* of the death of Christ, that a man would think every one might run and read. But we must stay: among all things in Christian religion, there is scarce any thing more questioned than this, which seems to be a most fundamental principle. A spreading persuasion there is of *a general ransom* to be paid by Christ for all; that he died to redeem *all and every one*,—not only for *many*, his *church*, the *elect* of God, but for every one also of the posterity of Adam. Now, the masters of this opinion do see full well and easily, that if *that* be the *end* of the death of Christ which we have from the Scripture asserted, if those before recounted be the immediate *fruits* and *products* thereof, then one of these two things will necessarily follow:—that either, first, God and Christ failed of their end proposed, and did not accomplish that which they intended, the death of Christ being not a fitly-proportioned *means* for the attaining of that end (for any cause of failing cannot be assigned); which to assert seems to us blasphemously injurious to the wisdom, power, and perfection of God, as likewise derogatory to the worth and value of the death of Christ;—or else, that all men, all the posterity of Adam, must be saved, purged, sanctified, and glorified; which surely they will not maintain, at least the Scripture and the woful experience of millions will not allow. Wherefore, to cast a tolerable colour upon their persuasion, they must and do deny that God or his Son had any such absolute aim or end in the death or blood-shedding of Jesus Christ, or that any such thing was immediately procured and purchased by it, as we before recounted; but that God intended nothing, neither was any thing effected by Christ,—that no benefit ariseth to any immediately by his death but what is common to all and every soul, though never so cursedly unbelieving here and eternally damned hereafter, until an act of some, not procured for them by Christ, (for if it were, why have they it not all alike?) to wit, faith, do distinguish them from others. Now, this seeming to me to enervate the virtue, value, fruits and effects of the satisfaction and death of Christ,—serving, besides, for a basis and foundation to a dangerous, uncomfortable, erroneous persuasion,—I shall, by the Lord's assistance, declare what the Scripture holds out in both these things, both that assertion which is intended to be proved, and that which is brought for the proof thereof; desiring the Lord by his Spirit to lead us into all truth, to give us understanding in all things, and if any one be otherwise minded, to reveal that also unto him.

CHAPTER II.

Of the nature of an end in general, and some distinctions about it.

I. The *end* of any thing is that which the *agent* intendeth to accomplish in and by the operation which is proper unto its nature, and which it applieth itself unto,—that which any one aimeth at, and designeth in himself to attain, as a thing good and desirable unto him in the state and condition wherein he is. So the end which Noah proposed unto himself in the building of the ark was the preservation of himself and others. According to the will of God, he made an ark to preserve himself and his family from the flood: "According to all that God commanded him, so did he," Gen. vi. 22. That which the agent doth, or whereto he applieth himself, for the compassing his proposed *end*, is called the *means;* which two do complete the whole reason of working in free *intellectual* agents, for I speak only of such as work according to choice or election. So Absalom intending a revolt from his father, to procure the crown and kingdom for himself, "he prepared him horses and chariots, and fifty men to run before him," 2 Sam. xv. 1; and farther, by fair words and glossing compliances, "he stole the hearts of the men of Israel," verse 6; then pretends a sacrifice at Hebron, where he makes a strong conspiracy, verse 12;—all which were the *means* he used for the attaining of his fore-proposed end.

II. Between both these, *end* and *means*, there is this relation, that (though in sundry kinds) they are mutually causes one of another. The end is the first, principal, *moving cause* of the whole. It is that for whose sake the whole work is. No agent applies itself to action but for an end; and were it not by that determined to some certain effect, thing, way, or manner of working, it would no more do one thing than another. The inhabitants of the old world desiring and intending unity and cohabitation, with perhaps some reserves to provide for their safety against a second storm, they cry, "Go to, let us build us a city, and a tower whose top may reach unto heaven; and let us make us a name, lest we be scattered abroad upon the face of the whole earth," Gen. xi. 4. First, They lay down their *aim* and *design*, and then let out the *means* in their apprehension conducing thereunto. And manifest, then, it is, that the whole reason and method of affairs that a wise worker or agent, according to the counsel, proposeth to himself, is taken from the *end* which he aims at; that is, in intention and contrivance, the beginning of all that order which is in working. Now, the *means* are all those things which are used for the attaining of the end proposed,—as meat for the preservation of life, sailing in a ship for him that would pass the sea, laws for the quiet continuance of human society; and they are the procuring cause of the end, in one kind or another. Their existence is for the end's sake, and the end hath its rise out of them, following them either *morally* as their desert, or *naturally* as their fruit and product. First, In a *moral* sense. When the action and the end are to be measured or considered in reference to a moral rule, or *law* prescribed to the agent, then the *means* are the deserving or meritorious cause of the end; as, if Adam had continued in his innocency, and done all things according to the law given unto him, the end procured thereby had been a blessed life to eternity; as now the end of any sinful act is death, the curse of the law. Secondly, When the means are considered only in their *natural* relation, then they are the instrumentally efficient cause of the end. So Joab intending the death of Abner, "he smote him with his spear under the fifth rib, that he died," 2 Sam. iii. 27. And when Benaiah, by the command of Solomon, fell upon Shimei, the wounds he gave him were the efficient of his death, 1 Kings ii. 46. In which regard there is no difference between the murdering of an innocent man and the executing of an offender; but as they are under a moral consideration, their ends follow their deservings, in respect of conformity to the rule, and so there is χάσμα μέγα between them.

III. The former consideration, by reason of the defect and perverseness of some agents (for otherwise these things are coincident), holds out a twofold end of things,—first, of the work, and, secondly, of the workman; of the act and the agent: for when the means assigned for the attaining of any end are not proportioned unto it, nor, fitted for it, according to that rule which the agent is to work by, then it cannot be but that he must aim at one thing and another follow, in respect of the morality of the work. So Adam is enticed into a desire to be like God; this now he makes his aim, which to effect he eats the forbidden fruit, and that contracts a guilt which he aimed not at. But when the agent acts aright, and as it should do,—when it aims at an end that is proper to it, belonging to its proper perfection and condition, and worketh by such means as are fit and suitable to the end proposed,—the end of the work and the workman are one and the same; as when Abel intended the worship of the Lord, he offered a sacrifice through faith, acceptable unto him; or as a man, desiring salvation through Christ, applieth himself to get an interest in him. Now, the sole reason of this diversity is, that secondary agents, such as men are, have an end set and appointed to their actions by Him which giveth them an external rule or law to work by, which shall always attend them in their working, whether they will or no. God only, whose will and good pleasure is the sole rule of all those works which outwardly are of him, can never deviate in his actions, nor have any end attend or follow his acts not precisely by him intended.

IV. Again; the end of every free agent is either that which he effecteth, or that for whose sake he doth effect it. When a man builds a house to let to hire, that which he effecteth is the building of a house; that which moveth him to do it is love of gain. The physician cures the patient, and is moved to it by his reward. The end which Judas aimed at in his going to the priests, bargaining with them, conducting the soldiers to the garden, kissing Christ, was the betraying of his Master; but the end for whose sake the whole undertaking was set on foot was the obtaining of the thirty pieces of silver: "What will ye give me, and I will do it?" The end which God effected by the death of Christ was the satisfaction of his justice: the end for whose sake he did it was either supreme, or his own glory; or subordinate, ours with him.

V. Moreover, the *means* are of two sorts:—First, Such as have a true goodness in themselves without reference to any farther kind; though not so considered as we use them for means. No means, as a means, is considered as good in itself, but only as conducible to a farther end; it is repugnant to the nature of means, as such, to be considered as good in themselves. Study is in itself the most noble employment of the soul; but, aiming at wisdom or knowledge, we consider it as good only inasmuch as it conducteth to that end, otherwise as "a weariness of the flesh," Eccl. xii. 12. Secondly, Such as have no good at all in any kind, as in themselves considered, but merely as conducing to that end which they are fit to attain. They receive all their goodness (which is but relative) from that whereunto they are appointed, in themselves no way desirable; as the cutting off a leg or an arm for the preservation of life, taking a bitter potion for health's sake, throwing corn and lading into the sea to prevent shipwreck. Of which nature is the death of Christ, as we shall afterward declare.

VI. These things being thus proposed in general, our next task must be to accommodate them to the present business in hand; which we shall do in order, by laying down the *agent* working, the *means* wrought, and the *end* effected, in the great work of our redemption; for these three must be orderly considered and distinctly, that we may have a right apprehension of the whole: into the first whereof, σὺν Θεῷ, we make an entrance in [chapter third.]

CHAPTER III.

Of the agent or chief author of the work of our redemption, and of the first thing distinctly ascribed to the person of the Father.

I. THE agent in, and chief author of, this great work of our redemption is the whole blessed Trinity; for all the works which outwardly are of the Deity are undivided and belong equally to each person, their distinct manner of subsistence and order being observed. It is true, there were sundry other instrumental causes in the oblation, or rather passion of Christ, but the work cannot in any sense be ascribed unto them;—for in respect of God the Father, the issue of their endeavours was exceeding contrary to their own intentions, and in the close they did nothing but what the "hand and counsel of God had before determined should be done," Acts iv. 28; and in respect of Christ they were no way able to accomplish what they aimed at, for he himself laid down his life, and none was able to take it from him, John x. 17, 18: so that they are to be excluded from this consideration. In the several persons of the holy Trinity, the joint author of the whole work, the Scripture proposeth distinct and sundry acts or operations peculiarly assigned unto them; which, according to our weak manner of apprehension, we are to consider severally and apart; which also we shall do, beginning with them that are ascribed to the Father.

II. Two peculiar acts there are in this work of our redemption by the blood of Jesus, which may be and are properly assigned to the person of the FATHER:—First, The sending of his Son into the world for this employment. Secondly, A laying the punishment due to our sin upon him.

1. The Father loves the world, and sends his Son to die: He "sent his Son into the world that the world through him might be saved," John iii. 16, 17. He "sending his Son in the likeness of sinful flesh, and for sin, condemned sin in the flesh, that the righteousness

of the law might be fulfilled in us," Rom. viii. 3, 4. He "set him forth to be a propitiation through faith in his blood," chap. iii. 25. For "when the fulness of the time was come, God sent forth his Son, made of a woman, made under the law, to redeem them that were under the law, that we might receive the adoption of sons," Gal. iv. 4, 5. So more than twenty times in the Gospel of John there is mention of this sending; and our Saviour describes himself by this periphrasis, "Him whom the Father hath sent," John x. 36; and the Father by this, "He who sent me," chap. v. 37. So that this action of sending is appropriate to the Father, according to his promise that he would "send us a Saviour, a great one, to deliver us," Isa. xix. 20; and to the profession of our Saviour, "I have not spoken in secret from the beginning; from the time that it was, there am I: and now the Lord God, and his Spirit, hath sent me," Isa. xlviii. 16. Hence the Father himself is sometimes called our Saviour: 1 Tim. i. 1, "According to the commandment Θεοῦ σωτῆρος ἡμῶν,"—"of God our Saviour." Some copies, indeed, read it, Θεοῦ καὶ σωτῆρος ἡμῶν,—"of God and our Saviour;" but the interposition of that particle καὶ arose, doubtless, from a misprision that Christ alone is called Saviour. But directly this is the same with that parallel place of Tit. i. 3, Κατ' ἐπιταγὴν τοῦ σωτῆρος ἡμῶν Θεοῦ,—"According to the commandment of God our Saviour," where no interposition of that conjunctive particle can have place; the same title being also in other places ascribed to him, as Luke i. 47, "My spirit hath rejoiced in God my Saviour." As also 1 Tim. iv. 10, "We trust in the living God, who is the Saviour of all men, specially of them that believe;" though in this last place it be not ascribed unto him with reference to his redeeming us by Christ, but his saving and preserving all by his providence. So also Tit. ii. 10, iii. 4; Deut. xxxii. 15; 1 Sam. x. 19; Ps. xxiv. 5, xxv. 5; Isa. xii. 2, xl. 10, xlv. 15; Jer. xiv. 8; Micah vii. 7; Hab. iii. 18; most of which places have reference to his sending of Christ, which is also distinguished into three several acts, which in order we must lay down:—

(1.) An authoritative imposition of the office of Mediator, which Christ closed withal by his voluntary susception of it, willingly undergoing the office, wherein by dispensation the Father had and exercised a kind of superiority, which the Son, though "in the form of God," humbled himself unto, Phil. ii. 6–8. And of this there may conceived two parts:—

[1.] The *purposed imposition of his counsel*, or his eternal counsel for the setting apart of his Son incarnate to this office, saying unto him, "Thou art my Son; this day have I begotten thee. Ask of me, and I shall give thee the nations for thine inheritance, and the uttermost parts of the earth for thy possession," Ps. ii. 7, 8. He said unto him, "Sit thou at my right hand until I make thine enemies thy footstool;" for "the LORD sware, and will not repent, Thou art a priest for ever after the order of Melchizedek," Ps. cx. 1, 4. He appointed him to be "heir of all things," Heb. i. 2, having "ordained him to be Judge of quick and dead," Acts x. 42; for unto this he was "ordained before the foundation of the world," 1 Pet. i. 20, and "determined, ὁρισθείς, to be the Son of God with power," Rom. i. 4, "that he might be the first-born among many brethren," chap. viii. 29. I know that this is an act eternally established in the mind and will of God, and so not to be ranged in order with the others, which are all temporary, and had their beginning in the fulness of time, of all which this first is the spring and fountain, according to that of James, Acts xv. 18, "Known unto God are all his works from the beginning of the world;" but yet, it being no unusual form of speaking that the purpose should also be comprehended in that which holds out the accomplishment of it, aiming at truth and not exactness, we pass it thus.

[2.] The actual *inauguration* or solemn admission of Christ into his office; "committing all judgment unto the Son," John v. 22; "making him to be both Lord and Christ," Acts ii. 36; "appointing him over his whole house," Heb. iii. 1–6;—which is that "anointing of the most Holy," Dan. ix. 24; God "anointing him with the oil of gladness above his fellows," Ps. xlv. 7: for the actual setting apart of Christ to his office is said to be by unction, because all those holy things which were types of him, as the ark, the altar, etc., were set apart and consecrated by anointing, Exod. xxx. 25–28, etc. To this also belongs that public testification by innumerable angels from heaven of his nativity, declared by one of them to the shepherds. "Behold," saith he, "I bring you good tidings of great joy, which shall be unto all people; for unto you is born this day in the city of David a Saviour, which is Christ the Lord," Luke ii. 10, 11;—which message was attended by and closed with that triumphant exultation of the host of heaven, "Glory be to God on high, on earth peace, towards men good-will," verse 14: with that redoubled voice which afterward came from the excellent glory, "This is my beloved Son, in whom I am well-pleased," Matt. iii. 17, xvii. 5; 2 Pet. i. 17. If these things ought to be distinguished and placed in their own order, they may be considered in these three several acts:—First, The glorious proclamation which he made of his nativity, when he "prepared him a body," Heb. x. 5, bringing his First-begotten into the world, and saying, "Let all the angels of God worship him," chap. i. 6, sending them to proclaim the message which we before recounted. Secondly, Sending the Spirit visibly, in the form of a dove, to light upon him at the time of his baptism, Matt. iii. 16, when he was endued with a fulness thereof, for the accomplishment of the work and discharge of the office whereunto he was designed, attended with that voice whereby he owned him from heaven as his only-beloved. Thirdly, The "crowning of him with glory and honour," in his resurrection, ascension, and sitting down "on the right hand of the Majesty on high," Heb. i. 3; setting "him as his king upon his holy hill of Zion," Ps. ii. 6; when "all power was given unto him in heaven and in earth," Matt. xxviii. 18, "all things being put under his feet," Heb. ii. 7, 8; himself highly exalted, and "a name given him above every name, that at," etc., Phil. ii. 9–11. Of which it pleased him to appoint witnesses of all sorts;—angels from heaven, Luke xxiv. 4, Acts i. 10; the dead out of the graves, Matt. xxvii. 52; the apostles among and unto the living, Acts ii. 32; with those more than five hundred brethren, to whom he appeared at once, 1 Cor. xv. 6. Thus gloriously was he inaugurated into his office, in the several acts and degrees thereof, God saying unto him, "It is a light thing that thou shouldest be my servant to raise up the tribes of Jacob, and to restore the preserved of Israel: I will also give thee for a light to the Gentiles, that thou mayest be my salvation unto the end of the earth," Isa. xlix. 6.

Between these two acts I confess there intercedes a twofold promise of God;—one, of giving a Saviour to his people, a Mediator, according to his former purpose, as Gen. iii. 15, "The seed of the woman shall break the serpent's head;" and, "The sceptre shall not depart from Judah, nor a lawgiver from between his feet, till Shiloh come; and unto him shall the gathering of the people be," chap. xlix. 10. Which he also foresignified by many sacrifices and other types, with prophetical predictions: "Of which salvation the prophets have inquired and searched diligently, who prophesied of the grace that should come unto you; searching what or what manner of time the Spirit of Christ which was in them did signify, when it testified beforehand the sufferings of Christ, and the glory that should follow. Unto whom it was revealed, that not unto themselves, but unto us they did minister the things which are now reported unto you by them that have preached the gospel unto you with the Holy Ghost sent down from heaven; which things the angels desire to look into," 1 Pet. i. 10–12. The other is a promise of applying the benefits purchased by this Saviour so designed to them that should believe on him, to be given in fulness of time, according to the former promises; telling Abraham, that "in his seed all the families of the earth should be blessed," and justifying himself by the same faith, Gen. xii. 3, xv. 6. But these things belong rather to the application wholly, which was equal both before and after his actual mission.

(2.) The second act of the Father's sending the Son is the furnishing of him in his sending with a fulness of all gifts and graces that might any way be requisite for the office he was to undertake, the work he was to undergo, and the charge he had over the house of God. There was, indeed, in Christ a twofold fulness and perfection of all spiritual excellencies:—

First, the *natural* all-sufficient perfection of his Deity, as one with his Father in respect of his divine nature: for his glory was "the glory of the only-begotten of the Father," John i. 14. He was "in the form of God, and thought it not robbery to be equal with God," Phil. ii. 6; being the "fellow of the LORD of hosts," Zech. xiii. 7. Whence that glorious appearance, Isa. vi. 3, 4, when the seraphims cried one to another, and said, "Holy, holy, holy, is the LORD of hosts: the whole earth is full of his glory. And the posts of the door moved at the voice of him that cried, and the house was filled with smoke." And the prophet cried, "Mine eyes have seen the King, the LORD of hosts," verse 5. Even concerning this vision the apostle saith, "Isaiah saw him, and spake of his glory," John xii. 41. Of which glory ἐκένωσε, he as it were emptied himself for a season, when he was "found in the form" or condition "of a servant, humbling himself unto death," Phil. ii. 7, 8; laying aside that glory which attended his Deity, outwardly appearing to have "neither form, nor beauty, nor comeliness, that he should be desired," Isa. liii. 2. But this fulness we do not treat of, it being not communicated to him, but essentially belonging to his person, which is eternally begotten of the person of his Father.

The second fulness that was in Christ was a *communicated* fulness, which was in him by dispensation from his Father, bestowed upon him to fit him for his work and office as he was and is the "Mediator between God and men, the man Christ Jesus," 1 Tim. ii. 5; not as he is the "LORD of hosts," but as he is "Emmanuel, God with us," Matt. i. 23; as he was a "son given to us, called Wonderful, Counsellor, The mighty God, The everlasting Father, The Prince of Peace, upon whose shoulder the government was to be," Isa. ix. 6. It is a fulness of grace; not that essential which is of the nature of the Deity, but that which is habitual and infused into the humanity as personally united to the other; which, though it be not absolutely infinite, as the other is, yet it extends itself to all perfections of grace, both in respect of parts and degrees. There is no grace that is not in Christ, and every grace is in him in the highest degree: so that whatsoever the perfection of grace, either for the several kinds or respective advancements thereof, requireth, is in him habitually, by the collation of his Father for this very purpose, and for the accomplishment of the work designed; which, though (as before) it cannot properly be said to be infinite, yet it is boundless and endless. It is in him as the light in the beams of the sun, and as water in a living fountain which can never fail. He is the "candlestick" from whence the "golden pipes do empty the golden oil out of themselves," Zech. iv. 12, into all that are his; for he is "the beginning, the first-born from the dead, in all things having the pre-eminence; for it pleased the Father that in him should all fulness dwell," Col. i. 18, 19. In him he caused to be "hid all the treasures of wisdom and knowledge," chap. ii. 3; and "in him dwelt all the fulness of the Godhead σωματικῶς," substantially or personally, verse 9; that "of his fulness we might all receive grace for grace," John i. 16, in a continual supply. So that, setting upon the work of redemption, he looks upon this in the first place. "The Spirit of the Lord GOD," saith he, "is upon me; because the LORD hath anointed me to preach good tidings unto the meek; he hath sent me to bind up the broken-hearted, to proclaim liberty to the captives, and the opening of the prison to them that are bound; to proclaim the acceptable year of the LORD, and the day of vengeance of our God; to comfort all that mourn," Isa. lxi. 1, 2. And this was the "anointing with the oil of gladness" which he had "above his fellows," Ps. xlv. 7; "it was upon his head, and ran down to his beard, yea, down to the skirts of his garments," Ps. cxxxiii. 2, that every one covered with the garment of his righteousness might be made partaker of it. "The Spirit of the LORD did rest upon him, the spirit of wisdom and understanding, the spirit of counsel and might, the spirit of knowledge and of the fear of the LORD," Isa. xi. 2; and that not in parcels and beginnings as in us, proportioned to our measure and degrees of sanctification, but in a fulness, for "he received not the Spirit by measure," John iii. 34; —that is, it was not so with him when he came to the full measure of the stature of his age, as Eph. iv. 13; for otherwise it was manifested in him and collated on him by degrees, for he "increased in wisdom and stature, and in favour with God and man," Luke ii. 52. Hereunto was added "all power in heaven and earth, which was given unto him," Matt. xxviii. 18; "power over all flesh, to give eternal life to as many as he would," John xvii. 2. Which we might branch into many particulars, but so much shall suffice to set forth the second act of God in sending his Son.

(3.) The third act of this sending is his entering into covenant and compact with his Son concerning the work to be undertaken, and the issue or event thereof; of which there be two parts:—

First, His promise to protect and assist him in the accomplishment and perfect fulfilling of the whole business and dispensation about which he was employed, or which he was to undertake. The Father engaged himself, that for his part, upon his Son's undertaking this great work of redemption, he would not be wanting in any assistance in trials, strength against oppositions, encouragement against temptations, and strong consolation in the midst of terrors, which might be any way necessary or requisite to carry him on through all difficulties to the end of so great an employment;—upon which he undertakes this heavy burden, so full of misery and trouble: for the Father before this engagement requires no less of him than that he should "become a Saviour, and be afflicted in all the affliction of his people," Isa. lxiii. 8, 9: yea, that although he were "the fellow of the LORD of hosts," yet he should endure the "sword" that was drawn against him as the "shepherd" of the sheep, Zech. xiii. 7; "treading the wine-press alone, until he became red in his apparel," Isa. lxiii. 2, 3: yea, to be "stricken, smitten of God, and afflicted; wounded for our transgressions, and bruised for our iniquities; to be bruised and put to grief; to make his soul an offering for sin, and to bear the iniquity of many," Isa. liii.; to be destitute of comfort so far as to cry, "My God, my God, why hast thou forsaken me?" Ps. xxii. 1. No wonder, then, if upon this undertaking the Lord promised to make "his mouth like a sharp sword, to hide him in the shadow of his hand, to make him a polished shaft, and to hide him in his quiver, to make him his servant in whom he would be glorified," Isa. xlix. 2, 3; that though "the kings of the earth should set themselves, and the rulers take counsel together, against him, yet he would laugh them to scorn, and set him as king upon his holy hill of Zion," Ps. ii. 2, 4, 6; though the "builders did reject him," yet he should "become the head of the corner," to the amazement and astonishment of all the world, Ps. cxviii. 22, 23, Matt. xxi. 42, Mark xii. 10, Luke xx. 17, Acts iv. 11, 12, 1 Pet. ii. 4; yea, he would "lay him for a foundation, a stone, a tried stone, a precious corner-stone, a sure foundation," Isa. xxviii. 16, that "whosoever should fall upon him should be broken, but upon whomsoever he should fall he should grind him to powder," Matt. xxi. 44. Hence arose that confidence of our Saviour in his greatest and utmost trials, being assured, by virtue of his Father's engagement in this covenant, upon a treaty with him about the redemption of man, that he would never leave him nor forsake him. "I gave," saith he, "my back to the smiters, and my cheeks to them that plucked off the hair: I hid not my face from shame and spitting," Isa. l. 6. But with what confidence, blessed Saviour, didst thou undergo all this shame and sorrow! Why, "The Lord GOD will help me; therefore shall I not be confounded: therefore have I set my face like a flint, and I know that I shall not be ashamed. He is near that justifieth me; who will contend with me? let us stand together: who is mine adversary? let him come near to me. Behold, the Lord GOD will help me; who is he that shall condemn me? lo! they shall all wax old as a garment; the moth shall eat them up," verses 7–9. With this assurance he was brought as a "lamb to the slaughter, and as a sheep before her shearers is dumb, so he opened not his mouth," Isa. liii. 7: for "when he was reviled, he reviled not again; when he suffered, he threatened not; but committed himself to him that judgeth righteously," 1 Pet. ii. 23. So that the ground of our Saviour's confidence and assurance in this great undertaking, and a strong motive to exercise his graces received in the utmost endurings, was this engagement of his Father upon this compact of assistance and protection.

Secondly, [His promise] of success, or a good issue out of all his sufferings, and a happy accomplishment and attainment of the end of his great undertaking. Now, of all the rest this chiefly is to be considered, as directly conducing to the business proposed, which yet would not have been so clear without the former considerations; for whatsoever it was that God promised his Son should be fulfilled and attained by him, that certainly was it at which the Son aimed in the whole undertaking, and designed it as the end of the work that was committed to him, and which alone he could and did claim upon the accomplishment of his Father's will. What this was, and the promises whereby it is at large set forth, ye have Isa. xlix.: "Thou shalt be my servant," saith the Lord, "to raise up the tribes of Jacob, and to restore the preserved of Israel: I will also give thee for a light to the Gentiles, that thou mayest be my salvation to the end of the earth. Kings shall see and arise, princes also shall worship, because of the LORD that is faithful." And he will certainly accomplish this engagement: "I will preserve thee, and give thee for a covenant of the people, to establish the earth, to cause to inherit the desolate heritages; that thou mayest say to the prisoners, Go forth; to them that are in darkness, Show yourselves. They shall feed in the ways, and their pastures shall be in all high places. They shall not hunger nor thirst; neither shall the heat nor sun smite them: for he that hath mercy on them shall lead them, even by the springs of water shall he guide them. And I will make all my mountains a way, and my highways shall be exalted. Behold, these shall come from far: and, lo, these from the north and from the west; and these from the land of Sinim," verses 6–12. By all which expressions the Lord evidently and clearly engageth himself to his Son, that he should gather to himself a glorious church of believers from among Jews and Gentiles, through all the world, that should be brought unto him, and certainly fed in full pasture, and refreshed by the springs of water, all the spiritual springs of living water which flow from God in Christ for their everlasting salvation. This, then, our Saviour certainly aimed at, as being the promise upon which he undertook the work,—the gathering of the sons of God together, their bringing unto God, and passing to eternal salvation; which being well considered, it will utterly overthrow the general ransom or universal redemption, as afterward will appear. In the 53d chapter of the same prophecy, the Lord is more express and punctual in these promises to his Son, assuring him that when he "made his soul an offering for sin, he should see his seed, and prolong his days, and the pleasure of the LORD should prosper in his hand; that he should see of the travail of his soul, and be satisfied; by his knowledge he should justify many; that he should divide a portion with the great, and the spoil with the strong," verses 10–12. He was, you see, to see his seed by covenant, and to raise up a spiritual seed unto God, a faithful people, to be prolonged and preserved throughout all generations; which, how well it consists with their persuasion who in terms have affirmed "that the death of Christ might have had its full and utmost effect and yet none be saved," I cannot see, though some have boldly affirmed it, and all the assertors of universal redemption do tacitly grant, when they come to the assigning of the proper ends and effects of the death of Christ. "The pleasure of the LORD," also, was to "prosper in his hand;" which what it was he declares, Heb. ii. 10, even "bringing of many sons unto glory;" for "God sent his only-begotten Son into the world that we might live through him," 1 John iv. 9; as we shall afterward more abundantly declare. But the promises of God made unto him in their agreement, and so, consequently, his own aim and intention, may be seen in nothing more manifestly than in the request that our Saviour makes upon the accomplishment of the work about which he was sent; which certainly was neither for more nor less than God had engaged himself to him for. "I have," saith he, "glorified thee on earth, I have finished the work which thou gavest me to do," John xvii. 4. And now, what doth he require after the manifestation of his eternal glory, of which for a season he had emptied himself, verse 5? Clearly a full confluence of the love of God and fruits of that love upon all his elect, in faith, sanctification, and glory. God gave them unto him, and he sanctified himself to be a sacrifice for their sake, praying for their sanctification, verses 17–19; their preservation in peace, or communion one with another, and union with God, verses 20, 21, "I pray not for these alone" (that is, his apostles), "but for them also which shall believe on me through their word; that they all may be one; as thou, Father, art in me, and I in thee, that they also may be one in us;" and lastly, their glory, verse 24, "Father, I will that they also, whom thou hast given me, be with me where I am; that they may behold my glory, which thou hast given me." All which several *postulata* are no doubt grounded upon the fore-cited promises, which by his Father were made unto him. And in this, not one word concerning all and every one, but expressly the contrary, verse 9. Let this, then, be diligently observed, that the promise of God unto his Son, and the request of the Son unto his Father, are directed to this peculiar end of bringing sons unto God. And this is the first act, consisting of these three particulars.

2. The second is of laying upon him the punishment of sins, everywhere ascribed unto the Father: "Awake, O sword, against my shepherd, against the man that is my fellow, saith the LORD of

hosts: smite the shepherd, and the sheep shall be scattered," Zech. xiii. 7. What here is set down imperatively, by way of command, is in the gospel indicatively expounded: "I will smite the shepherd, and the sheep of the flock shall be scattered abroad," Matt. xxvi. 31. "He was stricken, smitten of God, and afflicted;" yea, "the LORD laid upon him the iniquity of us all;" yea, "it pleased the LORD to bruise him, and to put him to grief," Isa. liii. 4, 6, 10. "He made him to be sin for us, who knew no sin; that we might be made the righteousness of God in him," 2 Cor. v. 21. The adjunct in both places is put for the subject, as the opposition between his being made sin and our being made righteousness declareth. "Him who knew no sin,"—that is, who deserved no punishment,—"him hath he made to be sin," or laid the punishment due to sin upon him. Or perhaps, in the latter place, sin may be taken for an offering or sacrifice for the expiation of sin, ἁμαρτία answering in this place to the word חַטָּאת in the Old Testament, which signifieth both sin and the sacrifice for it. And this the Lord did; for as for Herod, Pontius Pilate, with the Gentiles, and the people of Israel, when they were gathered together, they did nothing but "what his hand and counsel had determined before to be done," Acts iv. 27, 28. Whence the great shakings of our Saviour were in his close conflict with his Father's wrath, and that burden which by himself he immediately imposed on him. When there was no hand or instrument outwardly appearing to put him to any suffering or cruciating torment, then he "began to be sorrowful, even unto death," Matt. xxvi. 37, 38; to wit, when he was in the garden with his three choice apostles, before the traitor or any of his accomplices appeared, then was he "sore amazed, and very heavy," Mark xiv. 33. That was the time, "in the days of his flesh, when he offered up prayers and supplications with strong crying and tears unto him that was able to save him from death," Heb. v. 7; which how he performed the evangelist describeth, Luke xxii. 43, 44: "There appeared an angel unto him from heaven, strengthening him. But being in an agony he prayed more earnestly: and his sweat was as it were great drops of blood falling down to the ground." Surely it was a close and strong trial, and that immediately from his Father, he now underwent; for how meekly and cheerfully doth he submit, without any regret or trouble of spirit, to all the cruelty of men and violence offered to his body, until this conflict being renewed again, he cries, "My God, my God, why hast thou forsaken me?" And this, by the way, will be worth our observation, that we may know with whom our Saviour chiefly had to do, and what was that which he underwent for sinners; which also will give some light to the grand query concerning the persons of them for whom he undertook all this. His sufferings were far from consisting in mere corporal perpessions and afflictions, with such impressions upon his soul and spirit as were the effects and issues only of them. It was no more nor less than the curse of the law of God which he underwent for us: for he freed us from the curse "by being made a curse," Gal. iii. 13; which contained all the punishment that was due to sin, either in the severity of God's justice, or according to the exigence of that law which required obedience. That the execration of the law should be only *temporal death*, as the law was considered to be the instrument of the Jewish polity, and serving that economy or dispensation, is true; but that it should be no more, as it is the universal rule of obedience, and the bond of the covenant between God and man, is a foolish dream. Nay, but in dying for us Christ did not only aim at our good, but also directly died in our stead. The punishment due to our sin and the chastisement of our peace was upon him; which that it was the pains of hell, in their nature and being, in their weight and pressure, though not in tendence and continuance (it being impossible that he should be detained by death), who can deny and not be injurious to the justice of God, which will inevitably inflict those pains to eternity upon sinners? It is true, indeed, there is a relaxation of the law in respect of the persons suffering, God admitting of commutation; as in the old law, when in their sacrifices the life of the beast was accepted (in respect to the carnal part of the ordinances) for the life of the man. This is fully revealed, and we believe it; but for any change of the punishment, in respect of the nature of it, where is the least intimation of any alteration? We conclude, then, this second act of God, in laying the punishment on him for us, with that of the prophet, "All we like sheep have gone astray; we have turned every one to his own way; and the LORD hath laid on him the iniquity of us all," Isa. liii. 6: and add thereunto this observation, that it seems strange to me that Christ should undergo the pains of hell in their stead who lay in the pains of hell before he underwent those pains, and shall continue in them to eternity; for "their worm dieth not, neither is their fire quenched." To which I may add this dilemma to our Universalists:—God imposed his wrath due unto, and Christ underwent the pains of hell for, either all the sins of all men, or all the sins of some men, or some sins of all men. If the last, some sins of all men, then have all men some sins to answer for, and so shall no man be saved; for if God enter into judgment with us, though it were with all mankind for one sin, no flesh should be justified in his sight: "If the LORD should mark iniquities, who should stand?" Ps. cxxx. 3. We might all go to cast all that we have "to the moles and to the bats, to go into the clefts of the rocks, and into the tops of the ragged rocks, for fear of the LORD, and for the glory of his majesty," Isa. ii. 20, 21. If the second, that is it which we affirm, that Christ in their stead and room suffered for all the sins of all the elect in the world. If the first, why, then, are not all freed from the punishment of all their sins? You will say, " Because of their unbelief; they will not believe." But this unbelief, is it a sin, or not? If not, why should they be punished for it? If it be, then Christ underwent the punishment due to it, or not. If so, then why must that hinder them more than their other sins for which he died from partaking of the fruit of his death? If he did not, then did he not die for all their sins. Let them choose which part they will.

CHAPTER IV.

Of those things which in the work of redemption are peculiarly ascribed to the person of the Son.

SECONDLY, The SON was an *agent* in this great work, concurring by a voluntary susception, or willing undertaking of the office imposed on him; for when the Lord said, " Sacrifice and offering he would not: in burnt-offerings and sacrifices for sin he had no pleasure," then said Christ, " Lo, I come, (in the volume of the book it is written of me,) to do thy will, O God," Heb. x. 6, 7. All other ways being rejected as insufficient, Christ undertaketh the task, " in whom alone the Father was well pleased," Matt. iii. 17. Hence he professeth that " he came not to do his own will, but the will of him that sent him," John vi. 38; yea, that it was his meat and drink to do his Father's will, and to finish his work, chap. iv. 34. The first words that we find recorded of him in the Scripture are to the same purpose, " Wist ye not that I must be about my Father's business?" Luke ii. 49. And at the close of all he saith, " I have glorified thee on the earth; I have finished the work which thou gavest me to do," John xvii. 4; calling it everywhere his Father's work that he did, or his Father's will which he came to accomplish, with reference to the imposition which we before treated of. Now, this undertaking of the Son may be referred to three heads. The first being a common foundation for both the others, being as it were the means in respect of them as the end, and yet in some sort partaking of the nature of a distinct action, with a goodness in itself in reference to the main end proposed to all three, we shall consider it apart; and that is,—

First, His *incarnation*, as usually it is called, or his *taking of flesh*, and pitching his tent amongst us, John i. 14. His " being made of a woman," Gal. iv. 4, is usually called his ἐνσάρκωσις, or incarnation; for this was " the mystery of godliness, that God should be manifested in the flesh," 1 Tim. iii. 16, thereby assuming not any singular person, but our human nature, into personal union with himself. For, " forasmuch as the children are partakers of flesh and blood, he also himself likewise took part of the same; that through death he might destroy him that had the power of death, that is, the devil," Heb. ii. 14. It was the children that he considered, the "children whom the Lord gave him," verse 13. Their participation in flesh and blood moved him to partake of the same,—not because all the world, all the posterity of Adam, but because the *children* were in that condition; for their sakes he sanctified himself. Now, this emptying of the Deity, this humbling of himself, this dwelling amongst us, was the sole act of the second person, or the divine nature in the second person, the Father and the Spirit having no concurrence in it but by liking, approbation, and eternal counsel.

Secondly, His *oblation*, or "offering himself up to God for us without spot, to purge our consciences from dead works," Heb. ix. 14; "for he loved us, and washed us from our sins in his own blood," Rev. i. 5. "He loved the church, and gave himself for it, that he might sanctify and cleanse it," Eph. v. 25, 26; taking the cup of wrath at his Father's hands due to us, and drinking it off, "but not for himself," Dan. ix. 26: for, "for our sakes he sanctified himself," John xvii. 19, that is, to be an offering, an oblation for sin; for "when we were yet without strength, in due time Christ died for the ungodly," Rom. v. 6;—this being that which was typified out by all the institutions, ordinances, and sacrifices of old; which when they were to have an end, then said Christ, "Lo, I come to do thy will." Now, though the perfecting or consummating of this oblation be set out in the Scripture chiefly in respect of what Christ suffered, and not so much in respect of what he did, because it is chiefly considered as the means used by these three blessed agents for the attaining of a farther end, yet in respect of his own voluntary giving up himself to be so an oblation and a sacrifice, without which it would not have been of any value (for if the will of Christ had not been in it, it could never have purged our sins), therefore, in that regard, I refer it to his actions. He was the "Lamb of God, which taketh away the sin of the world," John i. 29; the Lamb of God, which himself had provided for a sacrifice. And how did this Lamb behave himself in it? with unwillingness and struggling? No; he opened not his mouth: "He was brought as a lamb to the slaughter, and as a sheep before her shearers is dumb, so he opened not his mouth," Isa. liii. 7. Whence he saith, "I lay down my life. No man taketh it from me, but I lay it down of myself. I have power to lay it down, and I have power to take it again," John x. 17, 18. He might have been cruciated on the part of God; but his death could not have been an oblation and offering had not his will concurred. "But he loved me," saith the apostle, "and gave himself for me," Gal. ii. 20. Now, that alone deserves the name of a gift which is from a free and a willing mind, as Christ's was when "he loved us, and gave himself for us an offering and a sacrifice to God for a sweet-smelling savour," Eph. v. 2. He does it cheerfully: "Lo, I come to do thy will, O God," Heb. x. 9; and so "his own self bare our sins in his own body on the tree," 1 Pet. ii. 24. Now, this oblation or offering of Christ I would not tie up to any one thing, action, or passion, performance, or suffering; but it compriseth the whole economy and dispensation of God manifested in the flesh and conversing among us, with all those things which he performed in the days of his flesh, when he offered up prayers and supplications, with strong cries and tears, until he had fully "by himself purged our sins, and sat down on the right hand of the Majesty on high," Heb. i. 3, "expecting till his enemies be made his footstool," chap. x. 13,—all the whole dispensation of his coming and ministering, until he had given his soul a price of redemption for many, Matt. xxvi. 28. But for his entering into the holy of holies, sprinkled with his own blood, and appearing so for us before the majesty of God, by some accounted as the continuation of his oblation, we may refer unto,—

Thirdly, His *intercession* for all and every one of those for whom he gave himself for an oblation. He did not suffer for them, and then refuse to intercede for them; he did not do the greater, and omit the less. The price of our redemption is more precious in the eyes of God and his Son than that it should, as it were, be cast away on perishing souls, without any care taken of what becomes of them afterward. Nay, this also is imposed on Christ, with a promise annexed: "Ask of me," saith the Lord, "and I will give thee the nations for thine inheritance, and the uttermost parts of the earth for thy possession," Ps. ii. 8; who accordingly tells his disciples that he had more work to do for them in heaven. "I go," saith he, "to prepare a place for you, that I may come again and receive you unto myself," John xiv. 2, 3. For as "the high priest went into the second [tabernacle] alone once every year, not without blood, which he offered for himself and the errors of the people," Heb. ix. 7; so "Christ being come an high priest of good things to come, by his own blood entered once into the holy place, having obtained eternal redemption for us," verses 11, 12. Now, what was this holy place whereinto he entered thus sprinkled with the blood of the covenant? and to what end did he enter into it? Why, "he is not entered into the holy places made with hands, which are the figures of the true; but into heaven itself, now to appear in the presence of God for us," verse 24. And what doth he there appear for? Why, to be our advocate, to plead our cause with God, for the application of the good things procured by his oblation unto all them for whom he was an offering; as the apostle tells us, "If any man sin, we have an advocate with the Father, Jesus Christ the righteous," 1 John ii. 1. Why, how comes that to pass? "He is the propitiation for our sins," verse 2. His being ἱλασμός, a propitiatory sacrifice for our sins, is the foundation of his interceding, the ground of it; and, therefore, they both belong to the same persons. Now, by the way, we know that Christ refused to pray for the world, in opposition to his elect. "I pray for them," saith he: "I pray not for the world, but for them thou hast given me," John xvii. 9. And therefore there was no foundation for such an interceding for them, because he was not ἱλασμός for them. Again; we know the Father always heareth the Son ("I knew," saith he, "that thou hearest me always," chap. xi. 42), that is, so to grant his request, according to the fore-mentioned engagement, Ps. ii. 8; and, therefore, if he should intercede for all, all should undoubtedly be saved, for "he is able to save them to the uttermost that come unto God by him, seeing he ever liveth to make intercession for them," Heb. vii. 25. Hence is that confidence of the apostle, upon that intercession of Christ, "Who shall lay any thing to the charge of God's elect? It is God that justifieth. Who is he that condemneth? It is Christ that died, yea rather, that is risen again, who is even at the right hand of God, who also maketh intercession for us," Rom. viii. 33, 34. Where, also, we cannot but observe that those for whom he died may assuredly conclude he maketh intercession for them, and that none shall lay any thing to their charge,—which breaks the neck of the general ransom; for according to that, he died for millions that have no interest in his intercession, who shall have their sins laid to their charge, and perish under them: which might be farther cleared up from the very nature of this intercession, which is not a humble, dejected supplication, which beseems not that glorious state of advancement which he is possessed of that sits at the right hand of the Majesty on high, but an authoritative presenting himself before the throne of his Father, sprinkled with his own blood, for the making out to his people all spiritual things that are procured by his oblation, saying, "Father, I will that those whom thou hast given me be with me where I am," John xvii. 24. So that for whomsoever he suffered, he appears for them in heaven with his satisfaction and merit. Here, also, we must call to mind what the Father promised his Son upon his undertaking of this employment; for there is no doubt but that for that, and that alone, doth Christ, upon the accomplishment of the whole, intercede with him about: which was in sum that he might be the captain of salvation to all that believe on him, and effectually bring many sons to glory. And hence it is, having such an high priest over the house of God, we may draw near with the full assurance of faith, for by one offering he hath perfected for ever them that are sanctified, Heb. x. 14. But of this more must be said afterward.

CHAPTER V.

The peculiar actions of the Holy Spirit in this business.

THIRDLY, IN few words we may consider the actions of that agent, who in order is the *third* in that blessed *One,* whose all is the whole, the HOLY SPIRIT, who is evidently concurring, in his own distinct operation, to all the several chief or grand parts of this work. We may refer them to three heads:—

First, The incarnation of the Son, with his plenary assistance in the course of his conversation whilst he dwelt amongst us; for his mother was found ἐν γαστρὶ ἔχουσα, "to have conceived in her womb of the Holy Ghost," Matt. i. 18. If you ask, with Mary, how that could be? the angel resolves both her and us, as far as it is lawful for us to be acquainted with these mysterious things: Luke i. 35, "The Holy Ghost shall come upon thee, and the power of the Highest shall overshadow thee: therefore also that holy thing which shall be born of thee shall be called the Son of God." It was an overshadowing power in the Spirit: so called by an allusion taken from fowls that cover their eggs, that so by their warmth young may be hatched; for by the sole power of the Spirit was this conception, who did "incubare fœtui," as in the beginning of the world. Now, in process, as this child was conceived by the power, so he was filled with the Spirit, and "waxed strong" in it, Luke i. 80; until, having received a fulness thereof, and not by any limited measure, in the gifts and graces of it, he was thoroughly furnished and fitted for his great undertaking.

Secondly, In his *oblation,* or passion (for they are both the same, with several respects,—one to what he suffered, the other to what he did with, by, and under those sufferings), how "by the Eternal Spirit he offered himself without spot to God," Heb. ix. 14: whether it be meant of the offering himself a bloody sacrifice on the cross, or his presentation of himself continually before his Father,—it is by the Eternal Spirit. The willing offering himself through that Spirit was the eternal fire under this sacrifice, which made it acceptable unto God. That which some contend, that by the eternal Spirit is here meant our Saviour's own Deity, I see no great ground for. Some Greek and Latin copies read, not, as we commonly, Πνεύματος αἰωνίου, but Πνεύματος ἁγίου, and so the doubt is quite removed: and I see no reason why he may not as well be said to offer himself through the Holy Spirit, as to be "declared to be the Son of God, according to the Spirit of holiness, by the resurrection from the dead," as Rom. i. 4; as also to be "quickened by the Spirit," 1 Pet. iii. 18. The working of the Spirit was required as well in his oblation as resurrection, in his dying as quickening.

Thirdly, In his *resurrection;* of which the apostle, Rom. viii. 11, "But if the Spirit of him that raised up Jesus from the dead dwell in you, he that raised up Christ from the dead shall also quicken your mortal bodies by his Spirit that dwelleth in you."

And thus have we discovered the blessed agents and undertakers in this work, their several actions and orderly concurrence unto the whole; which, though they may be thus distinguished, yet they are not so divided but that every one must be ascribed to the whole nature, whereof each person is "in solidum" partaker. And as they begin it, so they will jointly carry along the application of it unto its ultimate issue and accomplishment; for we must "give thanks to the Father, which hath made us meet" (that is, by his Spirit) "to be partakers of the inheritance of the saints in light: who hath delivered us from the power of darkness, and hath translated us into the kingdom of his dear Son: in whom we have redemption through his blood, even the forgiveness of sins," Col. i. 12, 13.

CHAPTER VI.

The means used by the fore-recounted agents in this work.

OUR next employment, following the order of execution, not intention, will be the discovery or laying down of the *means* in this work; which are, indeed, no other but the several actions before recounted, but now to be considered under another respect,—as they are a means ordained for the obtaining of a proposed end; of which afterward. Now, because the several actions of Father and Spirit were all exercised towards Christ, and terminated in him, as God and man, he only and his performances are to be considered as the means in this work, the several concurrences of both the other persons before mentioned being presupposed as necessarily antecedent or concomitant.

The means, then, used or ordained by these agents for the end proposed is that whole *economy* or dispensation carried along to the end, from whence our Saviour Jesus Christ is called a Mediator; which may be, and are usually, as I mentioned before, distinguished into two parts:—First, his *oblation;* secondly, his *intercession.*

By his *oblation* we do not design only the particular offering of himself upon the cross an offering to his Father, as the Lamb of God without spot or blemish, when he bare our sins or carried them up with him in his own body on the tree, which was the sum and complement of his oblation and that wherein it did chiefly consist; but also his whole humiliation, or state of emptying himself, whether by yielding voluntary obedience unto the law, as being made under it, that he might be the end thereof to them that believe, Rom. x. 4, or by his subjection to the curse of the law, in the antecedent misery and suffering of life, as well as by submitting to death, the death of the cross: for no action of his as mediator is to be excluded from a concurrence to make up the whole means in this work. Neither by his *intercession* do I understand only that heavenly appearance of his in the most holy place for the applying unto us all good things purchased and procured by his oblation; but also every act of his exaltation conducing thereunto, from his resurrection to his "sitting down at the right hand of the Majesty on high, angels, and principalities, and powers, being made subject unto him." Of all which his resurrection, being the basis, as it were, and the foundation of the rest ("for if he is not risen, then is our faith in vain," 1 Cor. xv. 13, 14; and then are we "yet in our sins," verse 17; "of all men most miserable," verse 19), is especially to be considered, as that to which a great part of the effect is often ascribed; for "he was delivered for our offences, and was raised again for our justification," Rom. iv. 25;—where, and in such other places, by his resurrection the whole following dispensation and the perpetual intercession of Christ for us in heaven is intended; for "God raised up his son Jesus to bless us, in turning every one of us from our iniquities," Acts iii. 26.

Now, this whole dispensation, with especial regard to the death and blood-shedding of Christ, is the means we speak of, agreeably to what was said before of such in general; for it is not a thing in itself desirable for its own sake. The death of Christ had nothing in it (we speak of his sufferings distinguished from his obedience) that was good, but only as it conduced to a farther end, even the end proposed for the manifestation of God's glorious grace. What good was it, that Herod and Pontius Pilate, with the Gentiles and people of Israel, should, with such horrid villany and cruelty, gather themselves together against God's holy child, whom he had anointed? Acts iv. 27: or what good was it, that the Son of God should be made sin and a curse, to be bruised, afflicted, and to undergo such wrath as the whole frame of nature, as it were, trembled to behold? What good, what beauty and form is in all this, that it should be desired in itself and for itself? Doubtless none at all. It must, then, be looked upon as a means conducing to such an end; the glory and lustre thereof must quite take away all the darkness and confusion that was about the thing itself. And even so it was intended by the blessed agents in it, by "whose determinate counsel and foreknowledge he was delivered and slain," Acts ii. 23; there being done unto him "whatsoever his hand and counsel had determined," chap. iv. 28: which what it was must be afterward declared. Now, concerning the whole some things are to be observed:—

That though the *oblation* and *intercession* of Jesus Christ are distinct acts in themselves, and have distinct immediate products and issues assigned ofttimes unto them (which I should now have laid down, but that I must take up this in another place), yet they are not in any respect or regard to be divided or separated, as that the one should have any respect to any persons or any thing which the other also doth not in its kind equally respect. But there is this manifold union between them:—

First, In that they are both alike intended for the obtaining and accomplishing the same entire and complete end proposed,—to wit, the effectual bringing of many sons to glory, for the praise of God's grace; of which afterward.

Secondly, That what persons soever the one respecteth, in the good things it obtaineth, the same, all, and none else, doth the other respect, in applying the good things so obtained; for "he was delivered for our offences, and was raised again for our justification," Rom. iv. 25. That is, in brief, the object of the one is of no larger extent than the object of the other; or, for whom Christ offered himself, for all those, and only those, doth he intercede, according to his own word, "For their sake I sanctify myself" (to be an oblation), "that they also might be sanctified through the truth," John xvii. 19.

Thirdly, That the *oblation* of Christ is, as it were, the foundation of his intercession, inasmuch as by the oblation was procured every thing that, by virtue of his intercession, is bestowed; and that because the sole end why Christ procured any thing by his death was that it might be applied to them for whom it was so procured. The sum is, that the oblation and intercession of Jesus Christ are one entire means for the producing of the same effect, the very end of the oblation being that all those things which are bestowed by the intercession of Christ, and without whose application it should certainly fail of the end proposed in it, be effected accordingly; so that it cannot be affirmed that the death or offering of Christ concerned any one person or thing more, in respect of procuring any good, than his intercession doth for the collating of it: for, interceding there for all good purchased, and prevailing in all his intercessions (for the Father always hears his Son), it is evident that every one for whom Christ died must actually have applied unto him all the good things purchased by his death; which, because it is evidently destructive to the adverse cause, we must a little stay to confirm it, only telling you the main proof of it lies in our following proposal of assigning the proper end intended and effected by the death of Christ, so that the chief proof must be deferred until then. I shall now only propose those reasons which may be handled apart, not merely depending upon that.

CHAPTER VII.

Containing reasons to prove the oblation and intercession of Christ to be one entire means respecting the accomplishment of the same proposed end, and to have the same personal object.

I. OUR first reason is taken from that perpetual union which the Scripture maketh of both these, almost always joining them together, and so manifesting those things to be most inseparable which are looked upon as the distinct fruits and effects of them: "By his knowledge shall my righteous servant justify many, for he shall bear their iniquities," Isa. liii. 11. The actual justification of sinners, the immediate fruit of his *intercession*, certainly follows his bearing of their iniquities. And in the next verse they are of God so put together that surely none ought to presume to put them asunder: "He bare the sin of many" (behold his *oblation!*), "and made intercession for the transgressors;" even for those many transgressors whose sin he bears. And there is one expression in that chapter, verse 5, which makes it evident that the utmost application of all good things for which he *intercedes* is the immediate effect of his passion: "With his stripes we are healed." Our total healing is the fruit and procurement of his stripes, or the *oblation* consummated thereby. So also, Rom. iv. 25, "He was delivered for our offences, and was raised again for our justification." For whose offences he died, for their justification he rose;—and therefore, if he died for all, all must also be justified, or the Lord faileth in his aim and design, both in the death and resurrection of his Son; which though some have boldly affirmed, yet for my part I cannot but abhor the owning of so blasphemous a fancy. Rather let us close with that of the apostle, grounding the assurance of our eternal glory and freedom from all accusations upon the death of Christ, and that because his intercession also for us doth inseparably and necessarily follow it. "Who," saith he, "shall lay any thing to the charge of God's elect?" (It seems, also, that it is only they for whom Christ died.) "It is God that justifieth. Who is he that condemneth? It is Christ that died," (shall none, then, be condemned for whom Christ died? what, then, becomes of the general ransom?) "yea rather, who is risen again, who is even at the right hand of God, who also maketh intercession for us," Rom. viii. 33, 34. Here is an equal extent of the one and the other; those persons who are concerned in the one are all of them concerned in the other. That he died for *all* and intercedeth only for *some* will scarcely be squared to this text, especially considering the foundation of all this, which is (verse 32) that love of God which moved him to give up Christ to death for us all; upon which the apostle infers a kind of impossibility in not giving us all good things in him; which how it can be reconciled with their opinion who affirm that he gave his Son for millions to whom he will give neither grace nor glory, I cannot see. But we rest in that of the same apostle: "When we were yet without strength, in due time Christ died for the ungodly;" so that, "being now justified by his blood, we shall be saved from wrath through him," Rom. v. 6, 9;—the same between the oblation and intercession of Christ, with their fruits and effects, being intimated in very many other places.

II. To offer and to intercede, to sacrifice and to pray, are both acts of the same sacerdotal office, and both required in him who is a *priest;* so that if he omit either of these, he cannot be a faithful *priest* for them: if either he doth not offer for them, or not intercede for the success of his oblation on their behalf, he is wanting in the discharge of his office by him undertaken. Both these we find conjoined (as before) in Jesus Christ: 1 John ii. 1, 2, "If any man sin, we have an *advocate* with the Father, Jesus Christ the righteous: and he is the *propitiation* for our sins." He must be an *advocate* to intercede, as well as offer a propitiatory sacrifice, if he will be such a merciful *high priest* over the house of God as that the children should be encouraged to go to God by him. This the apostle exceedingly clears and evidently proves in the Epistle to the Hebrews, describing the priesthood of Christ, in the execution thereof, to consist in these two acts, of offering up himself in and by the shedding of his blood, and interceding for us to the utmost; upon the performance of both which he presseth an exhortation to draw near with confidence to the throne of grace, for he is " come an high priest of good things to come, not by the blood of goats and calves, but by his own blood he entered into the holy place, having obtained eternal redemption for us," chap. ix. 11, 12. His bloody oblation gave him entrance into the holy place not made with hands, there to accomplish the remaining part of his office, the apostle comparing his entrance into heaven for us with the entrance of the high priest into the holy place, with the blood of bulls and goats upon him, verses 12, 13 (which, doubtless, was to pray for them in whose behalf he had offered, verse 7); so presenting himself before his Father that his former oblation might have its efficacy. And hence he is said to have ἀπαράβατον ἱερωσύνην, because he continueth for ever, chap. vii. 24; so being " able to save to the uttermost them that come unto God by him, verse 25: wherefore we have " boldness to enter into the holiest by the blood of Jesus," chap. x. 19–22. So, then, it is evident that both these are acts of the same priestly office in Christ: and if he perform either of them for any, he must of necessity perform the other for them also; for he will not exercise any act or duty of his priestly function in their behalf for whom he is not a priest: and for whom he is a priest he must perform both, seeing he is faithful in the discharge of his function to the utmost in the behalf of the sinners for whom he undertakes. These two, then, oblation and intercession, must in respect of their objects be of equal extent, and can by no means be separated. And here, by the way (the thing being by this argument, in my apprehension, made so clear), I cannot but demand of those who oppose us about the death of Christ, whether they will sustain that he intercedeth for all or no;—if not, then they make him but half a priest; if they will, they must be necessitated either to defend this error, that all shall be saved, or own this blasphemy, that Christ is not heard of his Father, nor can prevail in his intercession, which yet the saints on earth are sure to do when they make their supplications according to the will of God, Rom. viii. 27, 1 John v. 14. Besides that, of our Saviour it is expressly said that the Father always heareth him, John xi. 42; and if that were true when he was yet in the *way*, in the days of his flesh, and had not finished the great work he was sent about, how much more then *now*, when, having done the will and finished the work of God, he is set down on the right hand of the Majesty on high, desiring and requesting the accomplishing of the promises that were made unto him upon his undertaking this work! of which before.

III. The *nature* of the intercession of Christ will also prove no less than what we assert, requiring an inseparable conjunction between it and its oblation: for as it is now perfected in heaven, it is not a humble dejection of himself, with cries, tears, and supplications; nay, it cannot be conceived to be *vocal*, by the way of entreaty, but merely *real*, by the presentation of himself, sprinkled with the blood of the covenant, before the throne of grace in our behalf. "For Christ," saith the apostle, "is not entered into the holy places made with hands, but into heaven itself, now to *appear* in the presence of God for us," Heb. ix. 24. His intercession there is an *appearing* for us in heaven in the presence of God, a demonstration of his sacred body, wherein for us he suffered: for (as we said before) the apostle, in the ninth to the Hebrews, compares his entrance into heaven for us unto the entrance of the high priest into the holy place, which was with the blood of bulls and goats upon him, verses 12, 13; our Saviour's being with his own blood, so presenting himself that his former oblation might have its perpetual efficacy, until the many sons given unto him are brought to glory. And herein his intercession consisteth, being nothing, as it were, but his oblation continued. He was a "Lamb slain from the foundation of the world," Rev. xiii. 8. Now, his intercession before his actual oblation in the fulness of time being nothing but a presenting of the engagement that was upon him for the work in due time to be accomplished, certainly that which follows it is nothing but a presenting of what according to that engagement is fulfilled; so that it is nothing but a continuation of his oblation in postulating, by remembrance and declaration of it, those things which by it were procured. How, then, is it possible that the one of these should be of larger compass and extent than the other? Can he be said to *offer* for them for whom he doth not *intercede*, when his *intercession* is nothing but a presenting of his oblation in the behalf of them for whom he suffered, and for the bestowing of those good things which by that were purchased.

IV. Again: if the *oblation* and death of Christ procured and obtained that every good thing should be bestowed which is actually conferred by the intervening of his *intercession*, then they have both of them the same aim, and are both means tending to one and the same end. Now, for the proof of this supposal, we must remember that which we delivered before concerning the *compact* and *agreement* that was between the Father and the Son, upon his voluntary engaging of himself unto this great work of redemption; for upon that engagement, the Lord proposed unto him as the end of his sufferings, and promised unto him as the reward of his labours, the fruit of his deservings, every thing which he afterward intercedeth for. Many particulars I before instanced in, and therefore now, to avoid repetition, will wholly omit them, referring the reader to chapter iii. for satisfaction: only, I shall demand what is the ground and foundation of our Saviour's *intercession*, understanding it to be by the way of entreaty, either virtual or formal, as it may be conceived to be either real or oral, for the obtaining of any thing. Must it not rest upon some promise made unto him? or is there any good bestowed that is not promised? Is it not apparent that the intercession of Christ doth rest on such a promise as Ps. ii. 8, "Ask of me, and I will give thee the heathen for thine inheritance," etc.? Now, upon what consideration was this promise and engagement made unto our Saviour? Was it not for his undergoing of that about which "the kings set themselves, and the rulers took counsel together against him," verse 2? which the apostles interpret of Herod and Pontius Pilate, with the people of the Jews, persecuting him to death, and doing to him "whatsoever the hand and counsel of God had before determined to be done," Acts iv. 27, 28. The intercession of Christ, then, being founded on promises made unto him, and these promises being nothing but an engagement to bestow and actually collate upon them for whom he suffered all those good things which his death and *oblation* did merit and purchase, it cannot be but that he intercedeth for all for whom he died, that his death procured all and every thing which upon his *intercession* is bestowed; and until they are bestowed, it hath not its full fruits and effects. For that which some say, namely, that the death of Christ doth procure that which is never granted, we shall see afterward whether it do not contradict Scripture, yea, and common sense.

V. Farther: what Christ hath put together let no man presume to put asunder; distinguish between them they may, but separate them they may not. Now, these things concerning which we treat (the oblation and intercession of Christ) are by himself conjoined, yea united, John xvii.; for there and then he did both offer and intercede. He did then as perfectly offer himself, in respect of his own will and intention, verse 4, as on the cross; and as perfectly intercede as now in heaven: who, then, can divide these things, or put them asunder? especially considering that the Scripture affirmeth that the one of them without the other would have been unprofitable, 1 Cor. xv. 17; for complete remission and redemption could not be obtained for us without the entering of our high priest into the most holy place, Heb. ix. 12.

VI. Lastly, A separating and dividing of the death and intercession of Christ, in respect to the objects of them, cuts off all that consolation which any soul might hope to attain by an assurance that Christ died for him. That the doctrine of the general ransom is an uncomfortable doctrine, cutting all the nerves and sinews of that strong consolation which God is so abundantly willing that we should receive, shall be afterward declared. For the present, I will only show how it trencheth upon our comfort in this particular. The main foundation of all the confidence and assurance whereof in this life we may be made partakers (which amounts to "joy unspeakable, and full of glory") ariseth from this strict connection of the *oblation* and *intercession* of Jesus Christ;—that by the one he hath procured all good things for us, and by the other he will procure them to be actually bestowed, whereby he doth never leave our sins, but follows them into every court, until they be fully pardoned and clearly expiated, Heb. ix. 26. He will never leave us until he hath saved to the uttermost them that come unto God by him. His death without his resurrection would have profited us nothing; all our faith in him had been in vain, 1 Cor. xv. 17. So that separated from it, with the intercession following, either in his own intention or in the several procurements of the one or the other, it will yield us but little consolation; but in this connection it is a sure bottom for a soul to build upon, Heb. vii. 25. "What good will it do me to be persuaded that Christ died for my sins, if, notwithstanding that, my sins may appear against me for my condemnation, where and when Christ will not appear for my justification?" If you will ask, with the apostle, "Who is he that condemneth?" "It is Christ that died," it may easily be answered, Rom. viii. 34. "Why, God by his law may condemn me, notwithstanding Christ died for me!" Yea, but saith the apostle, "He is risen again, and sitteth at the right hand of God, making intercession for us." He rests not in his death, but he will certainly make intercession for them for whom he died: and this alone gives firm consolation. Our sins dare not appear, nor any of our accusers against us, where he appeareth for us. Cavilling objections against this text shall be afterward considered; and so I hope I have sufficiently confirmed and proved what in the beginning of this chapter I did propose about the identity of the object of the oblation and intercession of Jesus Christ.

CHAPTER VIII.

Objections against the former proposal answered.

BY what was said in the last chapter, it clearly appeareth that the oblation and intercession of Christ are of equal compass and extent in respect of their objects, or the persons for whom he once offered himself and doth continually intercede, and so are to be looked on as one joint *means* for the attaining of a certain proposed *end;* which what it is comes next to be considered. But because I find some objections laid by some against the former truth, I must remove them before I proceed; which I shall do "as a man removeth dung until it be all gone."

The sum of one of our former arguments was,—That to sacrifice and intercede belong both to the same person, as high priest; which name none can answer, neither hath any performed that office, until both by him be accomplished. Wherefore, our Saviour being the most absolute, and, indeed, the only true high priest, in whom were really all those perfections which in others received a weak typical representation, doth perform both these in the behalf of them for whose sakes he was such.

I. An argument not unlike to this I find by some to be undertaken to be answered, being in these words proposed, "The ransom and mediation of Christ is no larger than his office of priest, prophet, and king; but these offices pertain to his church and chosen: therefore his ransom pertains to them only."

The intention and meaning of the argument is the same with what we proposed,—namely, that Christ offered not for them for whom he is no priest, and he is a priest only for them for whom he doth also intercede. If afterward I shall have occasion to make use of this argument, I shall, by the Lord's assistance, give more weight and strength to it than it seems to have in their proposal, whose interest it is to present it as slightly as possible, that they may seem fairly to have waived it. But the evasion, such as it is, let us look upon.

"This," saith the answerer, "is a sober objection;" which friendly term I imagined at first he had given for this reason, because he found it kind and easy to be satisfied. But reading the answer and finding that, so wide from yielding any colour or appearance of what was pretended, it only served him to vent some new, weak, false conceptions, I imagined that it must be some other kindness that caused him to give this "objection," as he calls it, so much milder an entertainment than those others, which equally gall him, which hear nothing but, "This is horrid, that blasphemy, that detestable, abominable, and false," as being, indeed, by those of his persuasion neither to be endured nor avoided. And at length I conceived that the reason of it was intimated in the first words of his pretended answer; which are, that "this objection doth not deny the death of Christ for all men, but only his ransom and mediation for all men." Now, truly, if it be so, I am not of his judgment, but so far from thinking it a "sober objection," that I cannot be persuaded that any man in his right wits would once propose it. That Christ should die for all, and yet not be a ransom for all, himself affirming that he came to "give his life a ransom for many," Matt. xx. 28, is to me a plain contradiction. The death of Christ, in the first most general notion and apprehension thereof, is a *ransom*. Nay, do not this answerer and those who are of the same persuasion with him make the ransom of as large extent as any thing in, or about, or following the death of Christ? Or have they yet some farther distinction to make, or rather division about the ends of the death of Christ? as we have had already: "For some he not only paid a ransom, but also intercedeth for them; which he doth not for all for whom he paid a ransom." Will they now go a step backward, and say that for some he not only died, but also paid a ransom for them; which he did not for all for whom he died? Who, then, were those that he thus died for? They must be some beyond all and every man; for, as they contend, for them he paid a ransom. But let us see what he says farther; in so easy a cause as this it is a shame to take advantages.

"The answer to this objection," saith he, "is easy and plain in the Scripture, for the mediation of Christ is both more general and more special;—more general, as he is the 'one mediator between God and men,' 1 Tim. ii. 5; and more special, as he is 'the mediator of the new testament, that they which are called might receive the promise of eternal inheritance,' Heb. ix. 15. According to that it is said, 'He is the Saviour of all men, specially of those that believe,' 1 Tim. iv. 10. So in all the offices of Christ, the priest, the prophet, the king, there is that which is more general, and that which is more special and peculiar."

And this is that which he calls a clear and plain answer from the Scripture, leaving the application of it unto the argument to other men's conjecture; which, as far as I can conceive, must be thus:—It is true Christ paid a ransom for none but those for whom he is a mediator and priest; but Christ is to be considered two ways:

First, As a general mediator and priest for all; secondly, As a special mediator and priest for some. Now, he pays the ransom as a general mediator. This I conceive may be some part of his meaning; for in itself the whole is in expression so barbarous and remote from common sense,—in substance such a wild, unchristian madness, as contempt would far better suit it than a reply. The truth is, for sense and expression in men who, from their manual trades, leap into the office of preaching and employment of writing, I know no reason why we should expect. Only, it can never enough be lamented that wildness, in such tattered rags, should find entertainment, whilst sober truth is shut out of doors; for what, I pray you, is the meaning of this distinction, "Christ is either a general mediator between God and man, or a special mediator of the new testament?" Was it ever heard before that Christ was any way a mediator but as he is so of the new testament? A mediator is not of one; all mediation respects an agreement of several parties; and every mediator is the mediator of a covenant. Now, if Christ be a mediator more generally than as he is so of the new covenant, of what covenant, I beseech you, was that? Of the covenant of works? Would not such an assertion overthrow the whole gospel? Would it not be derogatory to the honour of Jesus Christ that he should be the mediator of a cancelled covenant? Is it not contrary to Scripture, affirming him a "surety" (not of the first, but) "of a better testament?" Heb. vii. 22. Are not such bold assertors fitter to be catechised than to preach? But we must not let it pass thus. The man harps upon something that he hath heard from some Arminian doctor, though he hath had the ill-hap so poorly to make out his conceptions. Wherefore, being in some measure acquainted with their occasions, which they colour with those texts of Scripture which are here produced, I shall briefly remove the poor shift, that so our former argument may stand unshaken.

The poverty of the answer, as before expressed, hath been sufficiently already declared. The fruits of Christ's mediation have been distinguished by some into those that are more general and those which are more peculiar, which, in some sense, may be tolerable; but that the offices of Christ should be said to be either general or peculiar, and himself in relation to them so considered, is a gross, unshapen fancy. I answer, then, to the thing intended, that we deny any such general mediation, or function of office in general, in Christ, as should extend itself beyond his church or chosen. It was his "church" which he "redeemed with his own blood," Acts xx. 28; his "church" that "he loved and gave himself for it, that he might sanctify and cleanse it with the washing of water by the word, that he might present it to himself a glorious church," Eph. v. 25–27. They were his "sheep" he "laid down his life for," John x. 15; and "appeareth in heaven for us," Heb. ix. 24. Not one word of mediating for any other in the Scripture. Look upon his *incarnation.* It was "because the *children* were partakers of flesh and blood," chap. ii. 14; not because all the world were so. Look upon his *oblation:* "For *their sakes,*" saith he, ("those whom thou hast given me,") "do I sanctify myself," John xvii. 19; that is, to be an oblation, which was the work he had then in hand. Look upon his *resurrection:* "He was delivered for *our* offences, and was raised again for *our* justification," Rom. iv. 25. Look upon his *ascension:* "I go," saith he, "to my Father and *your* Father, and that to prepare a place for *you,*" John xiv. 2. Look upon his *perpetuated intercession.* Is it not to "save to the uttermost *them that come unto God by him?*" Heb. vii. 25. Not one word of this general mediation for all. Nay, if you will hear himself, he denies in plain terms to mediate for all: "I pray not," saith he, "for the world, but for them which thou hast given me," John xvii. 9.

But let us see what is brought to confirm this distinction. 1 Tim. ii. 5 is quoted for the maintenance thereof: "For there is one God, and one mediator between God and men, the man Christ Jesus." What then, I pray? what will be concluded hence? Cannot Christ be a mediator between God and men, but he must be a mediator for all men? Are not the elect men? do not the children partake of flesh and blood? doth not his church consist of men? What reason is there to assert, out of an indefinite proposition, a universal conclusion? Because Christ was a mediator for men (which were true had he been so only for his apostles), shall we conclude therefore he was so for all men? "Apage nugas!"

But let us see another proof, which haply may give more strength to the uncouth distinction we oppose, and that is 1 Tim. iv. 10, "Who is the Saviour of all men, specially of those that believe." Had it been, "Who is the *Mediator* of all men, specially of them that believe," it had been more likely. But the consciences, or at least the foreheads of these men! Is there any word here spoken of Christ as mediator? Is it not the "living God" in whom we trust that is the Saviour here mentioned, as the words going before in the same verse are? And is Christ called so in respect of his mediation? That God the Father is often called Saviour I showed before, and that he is here intended, as is agreed upon by all sound interpreters, so also it is clear from the matter in hand, which is the protecting providence of God, general towards all, special and peculiar towards his church. Thus he is said to "save man and beast," Ps. xxxvi. 6, 'Ανθρώπους καὶ κτήνη σώσεις κύριε, rendering the Hebrew תּוֹשִׁיעַ by σώσεις, "Thou shalt save or preserve." It is God, then, that is here called the "Saviour of all," by deliverance and protection in danger, of which the apostle treats, and that by his providence, which is peculiar towards believers; and what this makes for a universal mediation I know not.

Now, the very context in this place will not admit of any other interpretation; for the words render a reason why, notwithstanding all the injury and reproaches wherewith the people of God are continually assaulted, yet they should cheerfully go forward to run with joy the race that is set before them; even because as God preserveth all (for "in him we live, and move, and have our being," Acts xvii. 28; Ps. cxlv. 14–16), so that he will not suffer any to be injured and unrevenged, Gen. ix. 5, so is he especially the preserver of them that do believe; for they are as the apple of his eye, Zech. ii. 8; Deut. xxxii. 10. So that if he should suffer them to be pressed for a season, yet let them not let go their hope and confidence, nor be weary of well-doing, but still rest on and trust in him. This encouragement being that which the apostle was to lay down, what motive would it be hereunto to tell believers that God would have those saved who neither do nor ever will or shall believe?—that I say nothing how strange it seems that Christ should be the Saviour of them who are never saved, to whom he never gives grace to believe, for whom he denies to intercede, John xvii. 9; which yet is no small part of his mediation whereby he saves sinners. Neither the subject, then, nor the predicate proposition, "He is the Saviour of all men," is rightly apprehended by them who would wrest it to the maintenance of *universal redemption*. For the subject, "He," it is God the Father, and not Christ the mediator; and for the predicate, it is a *providential* preservation, and not a purchased salvation that is intimated;—that is, the providence of God protecting and governing all, but watching in an especial manner for the good of them that are his, that they be not always unjustly and cruelly traduced and reviled, with other pressures, that the apostle here rests upon; as also he shows that it was his course to do, 2 Cor. i. 9, 10: "But we had the sentence of death in ourselves, that we should not trust in ourselves, but in God which raiseth the dead: who delivered us from so great a death, and doth deliver us: in whom we trust that he will yet deliver us;" for "he is the Saviour of all men, specially of those that believe." If any shall conceive that these words ("Because we hope in the living God, who is," etc.) do not render an account of the ground of Paul's confidence in going through with his labours and afflictions, but rather are an expression of the head and sum of that doctrine for which he was so turmoiled and afflicted, I will not much oppose it; for then, also, it includes nothing but an assertion of the true God and dependence on him, in opposition to all the idols of the Gentiles, and other vain conceits whereby they exalted themselves into the throne of the Most High. But that Christ should be said to be a Saviour of,—1. Those who are never saved from their sins, as he saves his people, Matt. i. 21; 2. Of those who never hear one word of saving or a Saviour; 3. That he should be a Saviour in a twofold sense,—(1.) For all, (2.) For believers; 4. That to believe is the condition whereby Christ becomes a Saviour in an especial manner unto any, and that condition not procured nor purchased by him;—that this, I say, is the sense of this place, "credat Judæus Apella." To me nothing is more certain than that to whom Christ is in any sense a Saviour in the work of redemption, he saves them to the uttermost from all their sins of infidelity and disobedience, with the saving of grace here and glory hereafter.

II. Farther attempts, also, there are to give strength to this evasion, and so to invalidate our former argument, which I must also remove.

"Christ," say they,[1] "in some sort intercedeth and putteth in for transgressors, even the sons of men, yet in and of the world, that the Spirit may so still unite and bless those that believe on him, and so go forth in their confessions and conversations, and in the ministration of the gospel by his servants, that those among whom they dwell and converse might be convinced and brought to believe the report of the gospel, Isa. liii. 12; as once, Luke xxiii. 34; as himself left a pattern to us, John xvii. 21–23; that so the men of the world might be convinced, and the convinced allured to Christ and to God in him, Matt. v. 14–16; yea, so as that he doth in some measure enlighten every man that cometh into the world, John i. 9. But in a more special manner doth he intercede," etc.

Here is a twofold intercession of Christ as mediator:—1. For all sinners, that they may believe (for that is it which is intended by the many cloudy expressions wherein it is involved). 2. For believers, that they may be saved. It is the first member of the distinction which we oppose; and therefore must insist a little upon it.

First, Our author saith, "It is an interceding in *some sort.*" I ask, in what sort? Is it directly, or indirectly? Is it by virtue of his blood shed for them, or otherwise? Is it with an intention and desire to obtain for them the good things interceded for, or with purpose that they shall go without them? Is it for all and every man, or only for those who live in the outward pale of the church? Is faith the thing required for them, or something else? Is that desired absolutely, or upon some condition? All which queries must be clearly answered before this general intercession can be made intelligible.

First, Whether it be directly or indirectly, and by consequence only, that this intercession after a sort is used, for that thing interceded for is represented not as the immediate issue or aim of the prayer of Christ, but as a reflex arising from a blessing obtained by others; for the prayer set down is that God would so bless believers, that those amongst whom they dwell may believe the report of the gospel. It is believers that are the direct object of this intercession, and others are only glanced at through them. The good also so desired

[1] More's Universality of Grace.

for them is considered either as an accident that may come to pass, or follow the flourishing of believers, κατὰ συμβεβηκός, or as an end intended to be accomplished by it. If the first, then their good is no more intended than their evil. If the latter, why is it not effected? why is not the intention of our Saviour accomplished? Is it for want of wisdom to choose suitable and proportionable means to the end proposed? or is it for want of power to effect what he intendeth?

Secondly, Is it by virtue of his blood shed for them, or otherwise? —If it be, then Christ intercedeth for them that they may enjoy those things which for them by his oblation he did procure; for this it is to make his death and blood-shedding to be the foundation of his intercession; then it follows that Christ by his death procured faith for all, because he intercedeth that all may believe, grounding that intercession upon the merit of his death. But, first, this is more than the assertors of universal redemption will sustain; among all the ends of the death of Christ by them assigned, the effectual and infallible bestowing of faith on those for whom he died is none: secondly, if by his death he hath purchased it for all, and by intercession entreateth for it, why is it not actually bestowed on them? is not a concurrence of both these sufficient for the making out of that one spiritual blessing?—But, secondly, If it be not founded on his death and blood-shedding, then we desire that they would describe unto us this intercession of Christ, differing from his appearing for us in heaven sprinkled with his own blood.

Thirdly, Doth he intercede for them that they should believe, with an intention or desire that they should do so, or no? If not, it is but a mock intercession, and an entreaty for that which he would not have granted. If so, why is it not accomplished? why do not all believe? Yea, if he died for all, and prayed for all, that they might believe, why are not all saved? for Christ is always heard of his Father, John xi. 42.

Fourthly, Is it for all and every one in the world that Christ makes this intercession, or only for those who live within the pale of the church? If only for these latter, then this doth not prove a general intercession for all, but only one more large than that for believers; for if he leaves out any one in the world, the present hypothesis falls to the ground. If for all, how can it consist in that petition, "that the *Spirit would so lead, guide, and bless believers*, and so go forth in the ministration of the gospel by his servants, that others (that is, all and every one in the world) may be convinced and brought to believe?" How, I say, can this be spoken with any reference to those millions of souls that never see a believer, that hear no report of the gospel?

Fifthly, If his intercession be for faith, then either Christ intercedeth for it *absolutely*, that they may certainly have it, or upon *condition*, and that either on the part of God or man.—If *absolutely*, then all do actually believe; or that is not true, the Father always hears him, John xi. 42. If upon condition *on the part of God*, it can be nothing but this, *if he will or please*. Now, the adding of this condition may denote in our Saviour two things:—1. A nescience of what is his Father's will in the thing interceded for: which, first, cannot stand with the unity of his person as now in glory; and, secondly, cannot be, because he hath the assurance of a promise to be heard in whatever he asketh, Ps. ii. 8. Or, 2. An advancement of his Father's will, by submission to that as the prime cause of the good to be bestowed; which may well stand with absolute intercession, by virtue whereof all must believe.—Secondly, Is it a condition *on the part of those for whom he doth intercede?* Now, I beseech you, what condition is that? where in the Scripture assigned? where is it said that Christ doth intercede for men that they may have faith if they do such and such things? Nay, what condition can rationally be assigned of this desire? "Some often intimate that it is, if they suffer the Spirit to have his work upon their hearts, and obey the grace of God." Now, what is it to obey the grace of God? Is it not to believe? Therefore, it seems that Christ intercedeth for them that they may believe, upon condition that they do believe. Others, more cautiously, assert the good using of the means of grace that they do enjoy to be the condition upon which the benefit of this intercession doth depend. But again,—1. What is the good using of the means of grace but submitting to them, that is, believing? and so we are as before. 2. All have not the means of grace, to use well or ill. 3. Christ prays that they may use the means of grace well, or he doth not. If not, then how can he pray that they may believe, seeing to use well the means of grace, by yielding obedience unto them, is indeed to believe? If he do, then he doth it absolutely, or upon condition, and so the argument is renewed again as in the entrance. Many more reasons might be easily produced to show the madness of this assertion, but those may suffice. Only we must look upon the proof and confirmations of it.

First, then, the words of the prophet Isaiah, chap. liii. 12, "He made intercession for the transgressors," are insisted on.—*Ans.* The transgressors here, *for whom* our Saviour is said to make intercession, are either all the transgressors for whom he suffered, as is most likely from the description we have of them, verse 6, or the transgressors only *by whom* he suffered, that acted in his sufferings, as some suppose. If the first, then this place proves that Christ intercedes for all those for whom he suffered; which differs not from that which we contend for. If the latter, then we may consider it as accomplished. How he then did it, so it is here foretold that he should, which is the next place urged, namely,—

Luke xxiii. 34, "Then said Jesus, Father, forgive them; for they know not what they do."—*Ans.* The conclusion which from these words is inferred being, "Therefore there is a general intercession for all, that they may believe," I might well leave the whole argument to the silent judgment of men, without any farther opening and discovery of its invalidity and weakness; but because the ablest of that side have usually insisted much on this place for a general successless intercession, I will a little consider the inference in its dependence on these words of the gospel, and search whether it have any appearance of strength in it. To which end we must observe,—

Secondly, That this prayer is not for all men, but only for that handful of the Jews by whom he was crucified. Now, from a prayer for them to infer a prayer for all and every man that ever were, are, or shall be, is a wild deduction.

It doth not appear that he prayed for all his crucifiers neither, but only for those who did it out of ignorance, as appears by the reason annexed to his supplication: "For they know not what they do." And though, Acts iii. 17, it is said that the rulers also did it ignorantly, yet that all of them did so is not apparent; that some did is certain from that place; and so it is that some of them were converted, as afterward. Indefinite propositions must not in such things be made universal. Now, doth it follow that because Christ prayed for the pardon of their sins who crucified him out of ignorance, as some of them did, that therefore he intercedeth for all that they may believe; crucifiers who never once heard of his crucifying?

Thirdly, Christ in those words doth not so much as pray for those men that they might believe, but only that that sin of them in crucifying of him might be forgiven, not laid to their charge. Hence to conclude, therefore he intercedeth for all men that they may believe, even because he prayed that the sin of crucifying himself might be forgiven them that did it, is a strange inference.

Fourthly, There is another evident limitation in the business; for among his crucifiers he prays only for them that were present at his death, amongst whom, doubtless, many came more out of curiosity, to see and observe, as is usual in such cases, than out of malice and despite. So that whereas some urge that notwithstanding this prayer, yet the chief of the priests continued in their unbelief, it is not to the purpose, for it cannot be proved that they were present at his crucifying.

Fifthly, It cannot be affirmed with any probability that our Saviour should pray for all and every one of them, supposing some of them to be finally impenitent: for he himself *knew* full well "what was in man," John ii. 25; yea, he "knew from the beginning who they were that believed not," chap. vi. 64. Now, it is contrary to the rule which we have, 1 John v. 16, "There is a sin unto death," etc., to pray for them whom we know to be finally impenitent, and to sin unto death.

Sixthly, It seems to me that this supplication was effectual and successful, that the Son was heard in this request also, faith and forgiveness being granted to them for whom he prayed; so that this makes nothing for a general, ineffectual intercession, it being both special and effectual: for, Acts iii., of them whom Peter tells, that they "denied the Holy One, and desired a murderer," verse 14, "and killed the Prince of Life," verse 15,—of these, I say, five thousand believed: chap. iv. 4, "Many of them which heard the word believed, and the number of them was about five thousand." And if any others were among them whom our Saviour prayed for, they might be converted afterward. Neither were the rulers without the compass of the fruits of this prayer; for "a great company of the priests were obedient to the faith," chap. vi. 7. So that nothing can possibly be hence inferred for the purpose intended.

Seventhly, We may, nay we must, grant a twofold praying in our Saviour;—one, by virtue of his office as he was mediator; the other, in answer of his duty, as he was subject to the law. It is true, he who was mediator was made subject to the law; but yet those things which he did in obedience to the law as a private person were not acts of mediation, nor works of him as mediator, though of him who was mediator. Now, as he was subject to the law, our Saviour was bound to forgive offences and wrongs done unto him, and to pray for his enemies; as also he had taught us to do, whereof in this he gave us an example: Matt. v. 44, "I say unto you, Love your enemies, bless them that curse you, do good to them that hate you, and pray for them which despitefully use you, and persecute you;" which doubtless he inferreth from that law, Lev. xix. 18, "Thou shalt not avenge, nor bear any grudge against the children of thy people, but thou shalt love thy neighbour as thyself,"—quite contrary to the wicked gloss put upon it by the Pharisees. And in this sense our Saviour here, as a private person, to whom revenge was forbidden, pardon enjoined, prayer commanded, prays for his very enemies and crucifiers; which doth not at all concern his interceding for us as mediator, wherein he was always heard, and so is nothing to the purpose in hand.

Again, John xvii. 21–23 is urged to confirm this general intercession, which we have exploded; our Saviour praying that, by the unity, concord, and flourishing of his servants, the world might believe and know that God had sent him. From which words, though some make a seeming flourish, yet the thing pretended is no way confirmed; for,—

First, If Christ really intended and desired that the whole world, or all men in the world, should believe, he would also, no doubt, have prayed for more effectual means of grace to be granted unto them than only a beholding of the blessed condition of his (which yet is granted only to a small part of the world); at least for the preaching of the word to them all, that by it, as the only ordinary way, they might come to the knowledge of him. But this we do not find that ever he prayed for, or that God hath granted it; nay, he blessed his Father that so it was not, because so it seemed good in his sight, Matt. xi. 25, 26.

Secondly, Such a gloss or interpretation must not be put upon the place as should run cross to the express words of our Saviour, verse 9, "I pray not for the world;" for if he here prayed that the world should have true, holy, saving faith, he prayed for as great a blessing and privilege for the world as any he procured or interceded for for his own. Wherefore,—

Thirdly, Say some, the world is here taken for the world of the elect, the world to be saved,—God's people throughout the world. Certain it is that the world is not here taken properly *pro mundo continente,* for the world *containing,* but figuratively *pro mundo contento,* for the world *contained,* or men in the world. Neither can it be made appear that it must be taken universally, for all the men in the world, as seldom it is in the Scripture, which afterward we shall make appear; but it may be understood indefinitely, for men in the world, few or more, as the elect are in their several generations. But this exposition, though it hath great authors, I cannot absolutely adhere unto, because through this whole chapter the world is taken either for the world of reprobates, opposed to them that are given to Christ by his Father, or for the world of unbelievers (the same men under another notion), opposed to them who are committed to his Father by Christ. Wherefore I answer,—

Fourthly, That by *believing,* verse 21, and *knowing,* verse 23, is not meant believing in a strict sense, or a saving comprehension and receiving of Jesus Christ, and so becoming the sons of God,—which neither ever was, nor ever will be, fulfilled in every man in the world, nor was ever prayed for,—but a conviction and acknowledgment that the Lord Christ is not, what before they had taken him to be, a seducer and a false prophet, but indeed what he said, one that came out from God, able to protect and do good for and to his own: which kind of conviction and acknowledgment that it is often termed believing in the Scripture is more evident than that it should need to be proved; and that this is here meant the evidence of the thing is such as that it is consented unto by expositors of all sorts. Now, this is not for any good of the world, but for the vindication of his people and the exaltation of his own glory; and so proves not at all the thing in question. But of this word "world" afterward.

The following place of Matthew, chap. v. 15, 16 (containing some instructions given by our Saviour to his apostles, so to improve the knowledge and light which of him they had, and were farther to receive, in the preaching of the word and holiness of life, that they might be a means to draw men to glorify God) is certainly brought in to make up a show of a number, as very many other places are, the author not once considering what is to be proved by them, nor to what end they are used; and therefore without farther inquiry may well be laid aside, as not at all belonging to the business in hand, nor to be dragged within many leagues of the conclusion, by all the strength and skill of Mr More.

Neither is that other place of John, chap. i. 9, any thing more advisedly or seasonably urged, though wretchedly glossed, and rendered, "In some measure enlightening every one that comes into the world." The Scripture says that "Christ is the true Light, that lighteth every man that cometh into the world; "In some measure," says Mr More. Now, I beseech you, in what measure is this? How far, unto what degree, in what measure, is illumination from Christ? by whom or by what means, separated from him, independent of him, is the rest made up? who supplies the defect of Christ? I know your aim is to hug in your illumination by the light of nature, and I know not what common helps that you dream of, towards them who are utterly deprived of all gospel means of grace, and that not only for the knowledge of God as Creator, but also of him as in Christ the Redeemer: but whether the calves of your own setting up should be thus sacrificed unto, with wresting and perverting the word of God, and undervaluing of the grace of Christ, you will one day, I hope, be convinced. It sufficeth us that Christ is said to enlighten every one, because he is the only true light, and every one that is enlightened receiveth his light from him, who is the sum, the fountain thereof. And so the general defence of this general, ineffectual intercession is vanished. But yet farther, it is particularly replied, concerning the priesthood of Christ, that,—

III. "As a priest in respect of one end, he offered sacrifice,—that is, propitiation for all men, Heb. ii. 9, ix. 26; John i. 29; 1 John ii. 2; —in respect of all the ends, propitiation, and sealing the new testament, and testification to the truth;—and of the uttermost end in all, for his called and chosen ones, Heb. ix. 14, 15; Matt. xxvi. 28." (What follows after, being repeated out of another place, hath been already answered.)

Ans. First, These words, as here placed, have no tolerable sense in them, neither is it an easy thing to gather the mind of the author out of them, so far are they from being a clear answer to the argument, as was pretended. Words of Scripture, indeed, are used, but wrested and corrupted, not only to the countenance of error, but to bear a part in unreasonable expressions. For what, I pray, is the meaning of these words: "He offered sacrifice in respect of one end, then of all ends, then of the uttermost end in all?" To inquire backwards:—1. What is this "uttermost end in all?" Is that "in all," in or among all the ends proposed and accomplished? or in all those for whom he offered sacrifice? or is it the uttermost end and proposal of God and Christ in his oblation? If this latter, that is the glory of God; now there is no such thing once intimated in the places of Scripture quoted, Heb. ix. 14, 15; Matt. xxvi. 28. 2. Do those places hold out the uttermost end of the death of Christ (subordinate to God's glory)? Why, in one of them it is the obtaining of redemption, and in the other the shedding of his blood for the remission of sins is expressed! Now, all this you affirm to be the first end of the death of Christ, in the first words used in this place, calling it "propitiation,"—that is, an atonement for the remission of sins; which remission of sins and redemption are for the substance one and the same, both of them the immediate fruits and first end of the death of Christ, as is apparent, Eph. i. 7; Col. i. 14. So here you have confounded the first and last end of the death of Christ, spoiling, indeed, and casting down (as you may lawfully do, for it is your own), the whole frame and building, whose foundation is this, that there be several and diverse ends of the death of Christ towards several persons, so that some of them belong unto all, and all of them only to some; which is the πρῶτον ψεῦδος of the whole book. 3. Christ's offering himself to put away sin, out of Heb. ix. 26, [you make to be] the place for the first end of the death of Christ, and his shedding of his blood for the remission of sins, from Matt. xxvi. 28, to be the last! Pray, when you write next, give us the difference between these two. 4. You say, "He offered sacrifice in respect of one end,—that is, propitiation for all men." Now, truly, if ye know the meaning of sacrifice and propitiation, this will scarce appear sense unto you upon a second view.

But, [secondly,] to leave your words and take your meaning, it seems to be this, in respect of one end that Christ proposed to himself in his sacrifice, he is a priest for all, he aimed to attain and accomplish it for them; but in respect of other ends, he is so only for his chosen and called. Now, truly, this is an easy kind of answering, which, if it will pass for good and warrantable, you may easily disappoint all your adversaries, even first by laying down their arguments, then saying your own opinion is otherwise; for the very thing that is here imposed on us for an answer is the τὸ κρινόμενον, the chief matter in debate. We absolutely deny that the several ends of the death of Christ, or the good things procured by his death, are thus distributed as is here pretended. To prove our assertion, and to give a reason of our denial of this dividing of these things in respect of their objects, we produce the argument above proposed concerning the priesthood of Christ; to which the answer given is a bare repetition of the thing in question.

But you will say divers places of Scripture are quoted for the confirmation of this answer. But these, as I told you before, are brought forth for pomp and show, nothing at all being to be found in them to the business in hand; such are Heb. ix. 26; John i. 29. For what consequence is there from an affirmation indefinite, that Christ bare or took away sin, to this, that he is a priest for all and every one in respect of propitiation? Besides, in that of John i. 29 there is a manifest allusion to the paschal lamb, by which there was a typical, ceremonial purification and cleansing of sin; which was proper only to the people of Israel, the type of the elect of God, and not of all in the world, of all sorts, reprobates and unbelievers also. Those other two places of Heb. ii. 9, 1 John ii. 2, shall be considered apart, because they seem to have some strength for the main of the cause; though apparently there is no word in them that can be wrested to give the least colour to such an uncouth distinction as that which we oppose. And thus our argument from the *equal objective extent of the oblation* and *intercession* of Jesus Christ is confirmed and vindicated, and, withal, the *means* used by the blessed Trinity for the accomplishment of the *proposed end unfolded; which end, what it was, is next to be considered.*

BOOK II.

CHAPTER I.

Some previous considerations to a more particular inquiry after the proper end and effect of the death of Christ.

THE main thing upon which the whole controversy about the death of Christ turneth, and upon which the greatest weight of the business dependeth, comes next to our consideration, being that which we have prepared the way unto by all that hath been already said. It is about the proper end of the death of Christ; which whoso can rightly constitute and make manifest may well be admitted for a day's-man and umpire in the whole contestation: for if it be the end of Christ's death which most of our adversaries assign, we will not deny but that Christ died for all and every one; and if that be the end of it which we maintain so to be, they will not extend it beyond the elect, beyond believers. This, then, must be fully cleared and solidly confirmed by them who hope for any success in their undertakings. The end of the death of Christ we asserted, in the beginning of our discourse, to be our approximation or drawing nigh unto God; that being a general expression for the whole reduction and recovery of sinners from the state of alienation, misery, and wrath, into grace, peace, and eternal communion with him. Now, there being a twofold end in things, one of the worker, the other of the work wrought, we have manifested how that, unless it be either for want of wisdom and certitude of mind in the agent, in choosing and using unsuitable means for the attaining of the end proposed, or for want of skill and power to make use of and rightly to improve well-proportioned means to the best advantage, these things are always coincident; the work effecteth what the workman intendeth. In the business in hand, the agent is the blessed Three in One, as was before declared; and the means whereby they collimed and aimed at the end proposed were the oblation and intercession of Jesus Christ, which are united, intending the same object, as was also cleared. Now, unless we will blasphemously ascribe want of wisdom, power, perfection, and sufficiency in working unto the agent, or affirm that the death and intercession of Christ were not suitable and proportioned for the attaining the end proposed by it to be effected, we must grant that the end of these is one and the same. Whatsoever the blessed Trinity intended by them, that was effected; and whatsoever we find in the issue ascribed unto them, that by them the blessed Trinity intended. So that we shall have no cause to consider these apart, unless it be sometimes to argue from the one to the other;—as, where we find any thing ascribed to the death of Christ, as the fruit thereof, we may conclude that *that* God intended to effect by it; and so also on the contrary.

Now, the end of the death of Christ is either *supreme* and ultimate, or *intermediate* and subservient to that last end.

1. The first is the glory of God, or the manifestation of his glorious attributes, especially of his justice, and mercy tempered with justice, unto us. The Lord doth necessarily aim at himself in the first place, as the chiefest good, yea, indeed, that alone which is good; that is, absolutely and simply so, and not by virtue of communication from another: and therefore in all his works, especially in this which we have in hand, the chiefest of all, he first intends the manifestation of his own glory; which also he fully accomplisheth in the close, to every point and degree by him intended. He "maketh all things for himself," Prov. xvi. 4; and every thing in the end must "redound to the glory of God," 2 Cor. iv. 15; wherein Christ himself is said to be "God's," 1 Cor. iii. 23, serving to his glory in that whole administration that was committed to him. So, Eph. i. 6, the whole end of all this dispensation, both of choosing us from eternity, redeeming us by Christ, blessing us with all spiritual blessings in him, is affirmed to be "the praise of the glory of his grace;" and, verse

12, "That we should be to the praise of his glory." This is the end of all the benefits we receive by the death of Christ; for "we are filled with the fruits of righteousness, which are by Jesus Christ, unto the glory and praise of God," Phil. i. 11;—which also is fully asserted, chap. ii. 11, "That every tongue should confess that Jesus Christ is Lord, to the glory of God the Father." This the apostle fully clears in the ninth to the Romans, where he so asserts the supreme dominion and independency of God in all his actions, his absolute freedom from taking rise, cause, or occasion to his purposes, from any thing among us sons of men, doing all things for his own sake, and aiming only at his own glory. And this is that which in the close of all shall be accomplished, when every creature shall say, "Blessing, and honour, and glory, and power, be unto him that sitteth upon the throne, and unto the Lamb for ever and ever," Rev. v. 13. But this is ἀναμφισβήτητον.

2. There is an *end* of the death of Christ which is *intermediate* and subservient to that other, which is the last and most supreme, even the effects which it hath in respect of us, and that is it of which we now treat; which, as we before affirmed, is the *bringing of us unto God.* Now, this, though in reference to the oblation and intercession of Christ it be one entire end, yet in itself, and in respect of the relation which the several acts therein have one to another, may be considered distinctly in two parts, whereof one is the *end* and the other the *means* for the attaining of that end; both the complete end of the mediation of Christ in respect of us. The ground and cause of this is the appointment of the Lord that there should be such a connection and coherence between the things purchased for us by Jesus Christ, that the one should be a means and way of attaining the other,—the one the condition, and the other the thing promised upon that condition, but both equally and alike procured for us by Jesus Christ; for if either be omitted in his purchase, the other would be vain and fruitless, as we shall afterward declare. Now, both these consist in a communication of God and his goodness unto us (and our participation of him by virtue thereof); and that either to *grace* or *glory*, holiness or blessedness, *faith* or *salvation.* In this last way they are usually called, *faith* being the means of which we speak, and *salvation* the end; *faith* the condition, *salvation* the promised inheritance. Under the name of *faith* we comprise all saving grace that accompanies it; and under the name of *salvation*, the whole "glory to be revealed," the liberty of the glory of the children of God, Rom. viii., 18, 21,—all that blessedness which consisteth in an eternal fruition of the blessed God. With *faith* go all the effectual means thereof, both external and internal;—the word and almighty sanctifying Spirit; all advancement of state and condition attending it, as justification, reconcilia-

tion, and adoption into the family of God; all fruits flowing from it in sanctification and universal holiness; with all other privileges and enjoyments of believers here, which follow the redemption and reconciliation purchased for them by the oblation of Christ. A real, effectual, and infallible bestowing and applying of all these things,—as well those that are the means as those that are the end, the condition as the thing conditioned about, faith and grace as salvation and glory,—unto all and every one for whom he died, do we maintain to be the end proposed and effected by the blood-shedding of Jesus Christ, with those other acts of his mediatorship which we before declared to be therewith inseparably conjoined: so that every one for whom he died and offered up himself hath, by virtue of his death or oblation, a right purchased for him unto all these things, which in due time he shall certainly and infallibly enjoy; or (which is all one), the end of Christ's obtaining grace and glory with his Father was, that they might be certainly bestowed upon all those for whom he died, some of them upon condition that they do believe, but faith itself absolutely upon no condition at all. All which we shall farther illustrate and confirm, after we have removed some false ends assigned.

CHAPTER II.

Containing a removal of some mistakes and false assignations of the end of the death of Christ.

THAT the death, oblation, and blood-shedding of Jesus Christ is to be considered as the *means* for the compassing of an appointed *end* was before abundantly declared; and that such a *means* as is not in itself any way desirable but for the attaining of that end. Now, because that which is the end of any thing must also be good, for unless it be so it cannot be an end (for *bonum et finis convertuntur*), it must be either his Father's good, or his own good, or our good, which was the end proposed.

I. That it was not merely *his own* is exceedingly apparent. For in his divine nature he was eternally and essentially partaker of all that glory which is proper to the Deity; which though in respect of us it be capable of more or less manifestation, yet in itself it is always alike eternally and absolutely perfect. And in this regard, at the close of all, he desires and requests no other glory but that which he had with his Father "before the world was," John xvii. 5. And in respect of his human nature, as he was eternally predestinated, without any foresight of doing or suffering, to be personally united, from the instant of his conception, with the second person of the Trinity, so neither while he was in the way did he merit any thing for himself by his death and oblation. He needed not to suffer for himself, being perfectly and legally righteous; and the glory that he aimed at, by "enduring the cross, and despising the shame," was not so much his own, in respect of possession, by the exaltation of his own nature, as the bringing of many children to glory, even as it was in the promise set before him, as we before at large declared. His own exaltation, indeed, and power over all flesh, and his appointment to be Judge of the quick and the dead, was a consequent of his deep humiliation and suffering; but that it was the effect and product of it, procured *meritoriously* by it, that it was the end aimed at by him in his making satisfaction for sin, that we deny. Christ hath a power and dominion over all, but the foundation of this dominion is not in his death for all; for he hath dominion over all things, being appointed "heir of them, and upholding them all by the word of his power," Heb. i. 2, 3. "He is set over the works of God's hands, and all things are put in subjection under him," chap. ii. 7, 8. And what are those "all things," or what are amongst them, you may see in the place of the psalmist from whence the apostle citeth these words, Ps. viii. 5–8. And did he die for all these things? Nay, hath he not power over the angels? are not principalities and powers made subject to him? Shall he not at the last day judge the angels? for with him the saints shall do it, by giving attestation to his righteous judgments, 1 Cor. vi. 2, 3;—and yet, is it not expressly said that the angels have no share in the whole dispensation of God manifested in the flesh, so as to die for them to redeem them from their sins? of which some had no need, and the others are eternally excluded: Heb. ii. 16, "He took not on him the nature of angels; but he took on him the seed of Abraham." God setting him "king upon his holy hill of Zion," in despite of his enemies, to bruise them and to rule them "with a rod of iron," Ps. ii. 6, 9, is not the immediate effect of his death for them, but rather all things are given into his hand out of the immediate love of the Father to his Son, John iii. 35; Matt. xi. 27. That is the foundation of all this sovereignty and dominion over all creatures, with this power of judging that is put into his hand.

Besides, be it granted (which cannot be proved) that Christ by his death did procure this power of judging, would any thing hence follow that might be beneficial to the proving of the general ransom for all? No, doubtless; this dominion and power of judging is a power of condemning as well as saving; it is "all judgment" that is committed to him, John v. 22. "He hath authority given unto him to execute judgment, because he is the Son of man;" that is, at that hour "when all that are in their graves shall hear his voice and come forth; they that have done good, unto the resurrection of life; and they that have done evil, to the resurrection of condemnation," verses 27–29; 2 Cor. v. 10. Now, can it be reasonably asserted that Christ died for men to redeem them, that he might have power to condemn? Nay, do not these two overthrow one another? If he redeemed thee by his death, then he did not aim at the obtaining of any power to condemn thee; if he did the latter, then that former was not in his intention.

II. Nor, secondly, was it *his Father's good.* I speak now of the proximate and immediate end and product of the death of Christ, not of the ultimate and remote, knowing that the supreme end of Christ's oblation, and all the benefits purchased and procured by it, was "the praise of his glorious grace;" but for this other, it doth not directly tend to the obtaining of any thing unto God, but of all good things from God to us. Arminius, with his followers, with the other Universalists of our days, affirm this to be the end proposed, that God might, his justice being satisfied, save sinners, the hinderance being removed by the satisfaction of Christ. He had by his death obtained a right and liberty of pardoning sin upon what condition he pleased: so that, after the satisfaction of Christ yielded and considered, "integrum Deo fuit" (as his words are), it was wholly in God's free disposal whether he would save any or no; and upon what condition he would, whether of faith or of works. "God," say they, "had a good mind and will to do good to human kind, but could not by reason of sin, his justice lying in the way; whereupon he sent Christ to remove that obstacle, that so he might, upon the prescribing of what condition he pleased, and its being by them fulfilled, have mercy on them." Now, because in this they place the chief, if not the sole, end of the oblation of Christ, I must a little show the falseness and folly of it; which may be done plainly by these following reasons:—

First, The foundation of this whole assertion seems to me to be false and erroneous,—namely, that God could not have mercy on mankind unless satisfaction were made by his Son. It is true, indeed, supposing the decree, purpose, and constitution of God that so it should be, that so he would manifest his glory, by the way of vindicative justice, it was impossible that it should otherwise be; for with the Lord there is "no variableness, neither shadow of turning," James i. 17; 1 Sam. xv. 29: but to assert positively, that absolutely and antecedently to his constitution he could not have done it, is to me an unwritten tradition, the Scripture affirming no such thing, neither can it be gathered from thence in any good consequence. If any one shall deny this, we will try what the Lord will enable us to say unto it, and in the meantime rest contented in that of Augustine: "Though other ways of saving us were not wanting to his infinite wisdom, yet certainly the way which he did proceed in was the most convenient, because we find he proceeded therein."[1]

[1] The reader may be referred to the treatise by the author at the end of this volume, "De Divinâ Justitiâ," for the full and mature expression of his views on the necessity

Secondly, This would make the cause of sending his Son to die to be a common love, or rather wishing that he might do good or show mercy to all, and not an entire act of his will or purpose, of knowing, redeeming, and saving his elect; which we shall afterward disprove.

Thirdly, If the end of the death of Christ were to acquire a right to his Father, that notwithstanding his justice he might save sinners, then did he rather die to redeem a liberty unto God than a liberty from evil unto us,—that his Father might be enlarged from that estate wherein it was impossible for him to do that which he desired, and which his nature inclined him to, and not that we might be freed from that condition wherein, without this freedom purchased, it could not be but we must perish. If this be so, I see no reason why Christ should be said to come and redeem his people from their sins; but rather, plainly, to purchase this right and liberty for his Father. Now, where is there any such assertion, wherein is any thing of this nature in the Scripture? Doth the Lord say that he sent his Son out of love to himself, or unto us? Is God or are men made the immediate subject of good attained unto by this oblation? *Rep.* But it is said, that although immediately, and in the first place, this right did arise unto God by the death of Christ, yet that that also was to tend to our good, Christ obtaining that right, that the Lord might now bestow mercy on us, if we fulfilled the condition that he would propose. But I answer, that this utterly overthrows all the merit of the death of Christ towards us, and leaves not so much as the nature of merit unto it; for that which is truly meritorious indeed deserves that the thing merited, or procured and obtained by it, *shall* be done, or *ought* to be bestowed, and not only that it *may* be done. There is such a habitude and relation between merit and the thing obtained by it, whether it be absolute or arising on contract, that there ariseth a real right to the thing procured by it in them by whom or for whom it is procured. When the labourer hath wrought all day, do we say, "Now his wages *may* be paid," or rather, "Now they *ought* to be paid"? Hath he not a right unto it? Was ever such a merit heard of before, whose nature should consist in this, that the thing procured by it *might* be bestowed, and not that it *ought* to be? And shall Christ be said now to purchase by his meritorious oblation this only at his Father's hand, that he *might* bestow upon and apply the fulness of his death to some or all, and not that he *should* so do? "To him that worketh," saith the apostle, "is the reward not reckoned of grace, but of debt," Rom. iv. 4. Are not the fruits of the death of Christ by his death as truly procured for us as if they had been obtained by

of the atonement. In the statements above, it is implied that salvation might have been accomplished without the absolute necessity of such a satisfaction to the claims of justice as the death of Christ afforded. Dr Owen, it will be found in the treatise referred to, latterly changed his views on this point, and held the necessity for the satisfaction of divine justice by an atonement, in order to salvation, to be absolute.—ED.

our own working? And if so, though in respect of the persons on whom they are bestowed they are of free grace, yet in respect of the purchase, the bestowing of them is of debt.

Fourthly, That cannot be assigned as the complete end of the death of Christ, which being accomplished, it had not only been possible that not one soul might be saved, but also impossible that by virtue of it any sinful soul should be saved; for sure the Scripture is exceedingly full in declaring that through Christ we have remission of sins, grace, and glory (as afterward). But now, notwithstanding this, that Christ is said to have procured and purchased by his death such a right and liberty to his Father, that he might bestow eternal life upon all upon what conditions he would, it might very well stand that not one of those should enjoy eternal life: for suppose the Father would not bestow it, as he is by no engagement, according to this persuasion, bound to do (he had a right to do it, it is true, but that which is any one's right he may use or not use at his pleasure); again, suppose he had prescribed a condition of works which it had been impossible for them to fulfil;—the death of Christ might have had its full end, and yet not one been saved. Was this his coming to save sinners, to "save that which was lost?" or could he, upon such an accomplishment as this, pray as he did, "Father, I will that those whom thou hast given me be with me where I am; that they may behold my glory?" John xvii. 24. Divers other reasons might be used to evert this fancy, that would make the purchase of Christ, in respect of us, not to be the remission of sins, but a possibility of it; not salvation, but a salvability; not reconciliation and peace with God, but the opening of a door towards it;—but I shall use them in assigning the right end of the death of Christ.

Ask now of these, what it is that the Father can do, and will do, upon the death of Christ; by which means his justice, that before hindered the execution of his good-will towards them, is satisfied? and they tell you it is the entering into a new covenant of grace with them, upon the performance of whose condition they shall have all the benefits of the death of Christ applied to them. But to us it seemeth that Christ himself, with his death and passion, is the chief promise of the new covenant itself, as Gen. iii. 15; and so the covenant cannot be said to be procured by his death. Besides, the nature of the covenant overthrows this proposal, that they that are covenanted withal shall have such and such good things if they fulfil the condition, as though that all depended on this obedience, when that obedience itself, and the whole condition of it, is a promise of the covenant, Jer. xxxi. 33, which is confirmed and sealed by the blood of Christ. We deny not but that the death of Christ hath a proper end in respect of God,—to wit, the manifestation of his glory; whence he calls him "his servant, in whom he will be glorified," Isa. xlix. 3. And the bringing of many sons to glory, wherewith he was betrusted, was to the manifestation and praise of his glorious grace; that so his love to his elect might gloriously appear, his salvation being borne out by Christ to the utmost parts of the earth. And this full declaration of his glory, by the way of mercy tempered with justice (for "he set forth Christ to be a propitiation through faith in his blood, that he might be just, and the justifier of him that believeth in Jesus," Rom. iii. 25, 26), is all that which accrued to the Lord by the death of his Son, and not any right and liberty of doing that which before he would have done, but could not for his justice. In respect of us, the end of the oblation and blood-shedding of Jesus Christ was, not that God might if he would, but that he should, by virtue of that compact and covenant which was the foundation of the merit of Christ, bestow upon us all the good things which Christ aimed at and intended to purchase and procure by his offering of himself for us unto God; which is in the next place to be declared.

CHAPTER III.

More particularly of the immediate end of the death of Christ, with the several ways whereby it is designed.

WHAT the Scripture affirms in this particular we laid down in the entrance of the whole discourse; which now, having enlarged in explication of our sense and meaning therein, must be more particularly asserted, by an application of the particular places (which are very many) to our thesis as before declared, whereof this is the sum:—"Jesus Christ, according to the counsel and will of his Father, did offer himself upon the cross, to the procurement of those things before recounted; and maketh continual intercession with this intent and purpose, that all the good things so procured by his death might be actually and infallibly bestowed on and applied to all and every one for whom he died, according to the will and counsel of God." Let us now see what the Scripture saith hereunto, the sundry places whereof we shall range under these heads:—First, Those that hold out the *intention and counsel of God*, with our Saviour's own mind; whose will was one with his Father's in this business. Secondly, Those that lay down the *actual accomplishment or effect* of his oblation, what it did really procure, effect, and produce. Thirdly, Those that point out the *persons* for whom Christ died, as designed peculiarly to be the object of this work of redemption in the end and purpose of God.

I. For the first, or those which hold out the counsel, purpose, mind, intention, and will of God and our Saviour in this work: Matt. xviii.

11, "The Son of man is come to save that which was lost;" which words he repeateth again upon another occasion, Luke xix. 10. In the first place, they are in the front of the parable of seeking the lost sheep; in the other, they are in the close of the recovery of lost Zaccheus; and in both places set forth the end of Christ's coming, which was to do the will of his Father by the recovery of lost sinners: and that as Zaccheus was recovered by conversion, by bringing into the free covenant, making him a son of Abraham, or as the lost sheep which he lays upon his shoulder and bringeth home; so unless he findeth that which he seeketh for, unless he recover that which he cometh to save, he faileth of his purpose.

Secondly, Matt. i. 21, where the angel declareth the end of Christ's coming in the flesh, and consequently of all his sufferings therein, is to the same purpose. He was to "save his people from their sins." Whatsoever is required for a complete and perfect saving of his peculiar people from their sins was intended by his coming. To say that he did but in part or in some regard effect the work of salvation, is of ill report to Christian ears.

Thirdly, The like expression is that also of Paul, 1 Tim. i. 15, evidently declaring the end of our Saviour's coming, according to the will and counsel of his Father, namely, to "save sinners;"—not to open a door for them to come in if they will or can; not to make a way passable, that they may be saved; not to purchase reconciliation and pardon of his Father, which perhaps they shall never enjoy; but actually to save them from all the guilt and power of sin, and from the wrath of God for sin: which, if he doth not accomplish, he fails of the end of his coming; and if that ought not to be affirmed, surely he came for no more than towards whom that effect is procured. The compact of his Father with him, and his promise made unto him, of "seeing his seed, and carrying along the pleasure of the Lord prosperously," Isa. liii. 10–12, I before declared; from which it is apparent that the decree and purpose of giving actually unto Christ a believing generation, whom he calleth "The children that God gave him," Heb. ii. 13, is inseparably annexed to the decree of Christ's "making his soul an offering for sin," and is the end and aim thereof.

Fourthly, As the apostle farther declareth, Heb. ii. 14, 15, "Forasmuch as the children are partakers of flesh and blood, he also himself likewise took part of the same; that through death he might destroy him that had the power of death, that is, the devil; and deliver them who through fear of death," etc. Than which words nothing can more clearly set forth the entire end of that whole dispensation of the incarnation and offering of Jesus Christ,—even a deliverance of the children whom God gave him from the power of death, hell, and the devil, so bringing them nigh unto God. Nothing at all of the purchasing of a possible deliverance for all and every one; nay, all are not those children which God gave him, all are not delivered from death and him that had the power of it: and therefore it was not all for whom he then took flesh and blood.

Fifthly, The same purpose and intention we have, Eph. v. 25–27, "Christ loved the church, and gave himself for it; that he might sanctify and cleanse it with the washing of water by the word, that he might present it to himself a glorious church, not having spot, or wrinkle, or any such thing; but that it should be holy and without blemish:" as also, Tit. ii. 14, "He gave himself for us, that he might redeem us from all iniquity, and purify unto himself a peculiar people, zealous of good works." I think nothing can be clearer than these two places; nor is it possible for the wit of man to invent expressions so fully and livelily to set out the thing we intend, as it is in both these places by the Holy Ghost. What did Christ do? "He gave himself," say both these places alike: "For his church," saith one; "For us," saith the other; both words of equal extent and force, as all men know. To what end did he this? "To sanctify and cleanse it, to present it to himself a glorious church, not having spot or wrinkle," saith he to the Ephesians; "To redeem us from all iniquity, and to purify unto himself a peculiar people, zealous of good works," saith he to Titus. I ask now, Are all men of this church? Are all in that rank of men among whom Paul placeth himself and Titus? Are all purged, purified, sanctified, made glorious, brought nigh unto Christ? or doth Christ fail in his aim towards the greatest part of men? I dare not close with any of these.

Sixthly, Will you hear our Saviour Christ himself expressing this more evidently, restraining the object, declaring his whole design and purpose, and affirming the end of his death? John xvii. 19, "For their sakes I sanctify myself, that they also might be sanctified through the truth." "For their sakes." Whose, I pray? "The men whom thou hast given me out of the world," verse 6. Not the whole world, whom he prayed not for, verse 9. "I sanctify myself." Whereunto? "To the work I am now going about, even to be an oblation." And to what end? Ἵνα καὶ αὐτοὶ ὦσιν ἡγιασμένοι ἐν ἀληθείᾳ·—"That they also may be truly sanctified." That ἵνα there, "*that* they," signifies the intent and purpose of Christ,—it designs out the end he aimed at,—which our hope is (and that is the hope of the gospel), that he hath accomplished ("for the Deliverer that cometh out of Sion turneth away ungodliness from Jacob," Rom. xi. 26);—and that herein there was a concurrence of the will of his Father, yea, that this his purpose was to fulfil the will of his Father, which he came to do.

Seventhly, And that this also was his counsel is apparent, Gal. i. 4; for our Lord Jesus "gave himself for our sins, that he might deliver us from this present evil world, according to the will of God and our

Father;" which will and purpose of his the apostle farther declares, chap. iv. 4–6, "God sent forth his Son, made of a woman, made under the law, to redeem them that were under the law, that we might receive the adoption of sons;" and, because sons, our deliverance from the law, and thereby our freedom from the guilt of sin. Our adoption to sons, receiving the Spirit, and drawing nigh unto God, are all of them in the purpose of the Father giving his only Son for us.

Eighthly, I shall add but one place more, of the very many more that might be cited to this purpose, and that is 2 Cor. v. 21, "He hath made him to be sin for us, who knew no sin, that we might be made the righteousness of God in him." The purpose of God in making his Son to be sin is, that those for whom he was made sin might become righteousness; that was the end of God's sending Christ to be so, and Christ's willingness to become so. Now, if the Lord did not purpose what is not fulfilled, yea, what he knew should never be fulfilled, and what he would not work at all that it might be fulfilled (either of which are most atheistical expressions), then he made Christ sin for no more than do in the effect become actually righteousness in him: so that the counsel and will of God, with the purpose and intention of Christ, by his oblation and blood-shedding, was to fulfil that will and counsel, is from these places made apparent.

From all which we draw this argument:—That which the Father and the Son intended to accomplish in and towards all those for whom Christ died, by his death that is most certainly effected (if any shall deny this proposition, I will at any time, by the Lord's assistance, take up the assertion of it;) but the Father and his Son intended by the death of Christ to redeem, purge, sanctify, purify, deliver from death, Satan, the curse of the law, to quit of all sin, to make righteousness in Christ, to bring nigh unto God, all those for whom he died, as was above proved: therefore, Christ died for all and only those in and towards whom all these things recounted are effected;—which, whether they are all and every one, I leave to all and every one to judge that hath any knowledge in these things.

II. The second rank contains those places which lay down the actual accomplishment and effect of this oblation, or what it doth really produce and effect in and towards them for whom it is an oblation. Such are Heb. ix. 12, 14, "By his own blood he entered in once into the holy place, having obtained eternal redemption for us. . . . . The blood of Christ, who through the eternal Spirit offered himself without spot to God, purge your consciences from dead works to serve the living God." Two things are here ascribed to the blood of Christ;—one referring to God, "It obtains eternal redemption;" the other respecting us, "It purgeth our consciences from dead works:" so that justification with God, by procuring for us an eternal redemption from the guilt of our sins and his wrath due unto them, with sanctification in ourselves (or, as it is called, Heb. i. 3, a "purging our sins"), is the immediate product of that blood by which he entered into the holy place, of that oblation which, through the eternal Spirit, he presented unto God. Yea, this meritorious purging of our sins is peculiarly ascribed to his offering, as performed before his ascension: Heb. i. 3, "When he had by himself purged our sins, he sat down on the right hand of the Majesty on high;" and again, most expressly, chap. ix. 26, "He hath appeared to put away sin by the sacrifice of himself:" which expiation, or putting away of sin by the way of sacrifice, must needs be the actual sanctification of them for whom he was a sacrifice, even as "the blood of bulls and goats, and the ashes of an heifer sprinkling the unclean, sanctifieth to the purifying of the flesh," verse 13. Certain it is, that whosoever was either polluted or guilty, for whom there was an expiation and sacrifice allowed in those carnal ordinances, "which had a shadow of good things to come," had truly;—first, A legal cleansing and sanctifying, to the purifying of the flesh; and, secondly, Freedom from the punishment which was due to the breach of the law, as it was the rule of conversation to God's people: so much his sacrifice carnally accomplished for him that was admitted thereunto. Now, these things being but "shadows of good things to come," certainly the sacrifice of Christ did effect spiritually, for all them for whom it was a sacrifice, whatever the other could typify out; that is, spiritual cleansing by sanctification, and freedom from the guilt of sin: which the places produced do evidently prove. Now, whether this be accomplished in all and for them all, let all that are able judge.

Again; Christ, by his death, and in it, is said to "bear our sins:" so 1 Pet. ii. 24, "His own self bare our sins;"—where you have both what he did, "Bare our sins" (ἀνήνεγκε, he carried them up with him upon the cross); and what he intended, "That we, being dead unto sins, should live unto righteousness." And what was the effect? "By his stripes we are healed:" which latter, as it is taken from the same place of the prophet where our Saviour is affirmed to "bear our iniquities, and to have them laid upon him" (Isa. liii. 5, 6, 10–12), so it is expository of the former, and will tell us what Christ did by "bearing our sins;" which phrase is more than once used in the Scripture to this purpose. 1. Christ, then, so bare our iniquities by his death, that, by virtue of the stripes and afflictions which he underwent in his offering himself for us, this is certainly procured and effected, that we should go free, and not suffer any of those things which he underwent for us. To which, also, you may refer all those places which evidently hold out a commutation in this point of suffering between Christ and us: Gal. iii. 13, "He delivered us from the curse of the law, being made a curse for us;" with divers others which we shall have occasion afterward to mention.

Peace, also, and reconciliation with God,—that is, actual peace by the removal of all enmity on both sides, with all the causes of it,—is fully ascribed to this oblation: Col. i. 21, 22, "And you, that were sometime alienated and enemies in your mind by wicked works, yet now hath he reconciled in the body of his flesh through death, to present you holy and unblamable and unreprovable in his sight;" as also Eph. ii. 13–16, "Ye who sometimes were far off are made nigh by the blood of Christ: for he is our peace; having abolished in his flesh the enmity, even the law of commandments, that he might reconcile both unto God in one body by the cross, having slain the enmity thereby." To which add all those places wherein plenary deliverances from anger, wrath, death, and him that had the power of it, is likewise asserted as the fruit thereof, as Rom. v. 8–10, and ye have a farther discovery made of the immediate effect of the death of Christ. Peace and reconciliation, deliverance from wrath, enmity, and whatever lay against us to keep us from enjoying the love and favour of God,—a redemption from all these he effected for his church "with his own blood," Acts xx. 28. Whence all and every one for whom he died may truly say, "Who shall lay any thing to our charge? It is God that justifieth. Who is he that condemneth? It is Christ that died, yea rather, that is risen again, who is even at the right hand of God, who also maketh intercession for us," Rom. viii. 33, 34. Which that they are procured for all and every one of the sons of Adam, that they all may use that rejoicing in full assurance, cannot be made appear. And yet evident it is that so it is with all for whom he died,—that these are the effects of his death in and towards them for whom he underwent it: for by his being slain "he redeemed them to God by his blood, out of every kindred, and tongue, and people, and nation; and made them unto our God kings and priests," Rev. v. 9, 10; for "he made an end of their sins, he made reconciliation for their iniquity, and brought in everlasting righteousness," Dan. ix. 24.

Add also those other places where our life is ascribed to the death of Christ, and then this enumeration will be perfect: John vi. 33, He "came down from heaven to give life to the world." Sure enough he giveth life to that world for which he gave his life. It is the world of "his sheep, for which he layeth down his life," chap. x. 15, even that he might "give unto them eternal life, that they might never perish," verse 28. So he appeared "to abolish death, and to bring life and immortality to light," 2 Tim. i. 10; as also Rom. v. 6–10.

Now, there is none of all these places but will afford a sufficient strength against the general ransom, or the universality of the merit of Christ. My leisure will not serve for so large a prosecution of the subject as that would require, and, therefore, I shall take from the whole this general argument:—If the death and oblation of Jesus Christ (as a sacrifice to his Father) doth sanctify all them for whom it was a sacrifice; doth purge away their sin; redeem them from wrath, curse, and guilt; work for them peace and reconciliation with God; procure for them life and immortality; bearing their iniquities and healing all their diseases;—then died he only for those that are in the event sanctified, purged, redeemed, justified, freed from wrath and death, quickened, saved, etc.; but that all are not thus sanctified, freed, etc., is most apparent: and, therefore, they cannot be said to be the proper object of the death of Christ. The supposal was confirmed before; the inference is plain from Scripture and experience, and the whole argument (if I mistake not) solid.

III. Many places there are that point out the persons for whom Christ died, as designed peculiarly to be the object of this work of redemption, according to the aim and purpose of God; some of which we will briefly recount. In some places they are called *many:* Matt. xxvi. 28, "The blood of the new testament is shed for many, for the remission of sins." "By his knowledge shall my righteous servant justify many, for he shall bear their iniquities," Isa. liii. 11. "The Son of man came not to be ministered unto, but to minister, and give his life a ransom for many," Mark x. 45; Matt. xx. 28. He was to "bring many sons unto glory;" and so was to be the "captain of their salvation, through sufferings," Heb. ii. 10. And though perhaps the word *many* itself be not sufficient to restrain the object of Christ's death unto *some,* in opposition to *all,* because *many* is sometimes placed absolutely for *all,* as Rom. v. 19, yet these *many* being described in other places to be such as it is most certain all are not, so it is a full and evident restriction of it: for these many are the "sheep" of Christ, John x. 15; the "children of God that were scattered abroad," chap. xi. 52; those whom our Saviour calleth "brethren," Heb. ii. 11; "the children that God gave him," which were "partakers of flesh and blood," verses 13, 14; and frequently, "those who were given unto him of his Father," John xvii. 2, 6, 9, 11, who should certainly be preserved; the "sheep" whereof he was the "Shepherd, through the blood of the everlasting covenant," Heb. xiii. 20; his "elect," Rom. viii. 33; and his "people," Matt. i. 21; farther explained to be his "visited and redeemed people," Luke i. 68; even the people which he "foreknew," Rom. xi. 2; even such a people as he is said to have had at Corinth before their conversion; his people by election, Acts xviii. 10; the people that he "suffered for without the gate, that he might sanctify them," Heb. xiii. 12; his "church, which he redeemed by his own blood," Acts xx. 28, which "he loved and gave himself for," Eph. v. 25; the "many" whose sins he took away, Heb. ix. 28, with whom he made a covenant, Dan. ix. 27. Those many being thus described, and set forth with such qualifications as by no means are common to all, but proper only to the elect, do most evidently appear to be all and only those that are chosen of God to obtain eternal life through the offering and blood-shedding of Jesus Christ. Many things are here excepted with much confidence and clamour, that may easily be removed. And so you see the end of the death of Christ, as it is set out in the Scripture.

That we may have the clearer passage, we must remove the hinderances that are laid in the way by some pretended answers and evasions used to escape the force of the argument drawn from the Scripture, affirming Christ to have died for "many," his "sheep," his "elect," and the like. Now, to this it is replied, that this "reason," as it is called, is "weak and of no force, equivocal, subtile, fraudulent, false, ungodly, deceitful, and erroneous;" for all these several epithets are accumulated to adorn it withal, ("Universality of Free Grace," page xvi.) Now, this variety of terms (as I conceive) serves only to declare with what *copia verborum* the unlearned eloquence of the author is woven withal; for such terrible names imposed on that which we know not well how to gainsay is a strong argument of a weak cause. When the Pharisees were not able to resist the spirit whereby our Saviour spake, they call him "devil and Samaritan." Waters that make a noise are usually but shallow. It is a proverb among the Scythians, that the "dogs which bark most bite least." But let us see "quid dignum tanto feret hic responsor hiatu," and hear him speak in his own language. He says then,—

"First, This reason is weak and of no force: for the word *many* is oft so used, that it both signifies all and every man, and also amplifieth or setteth forth the greatness of that number; as in Dan. xii. 2, Rom. v. 19, and in other places, where *many* cannot, nor is by any Christian understood for less than all men."

Rep. 1. That if the proof and argument were taken merely from the word *many*, and not from the annexed description of those many, with the presupposed distinction of all men into several sorts by the purpose of God, this exception would bear some colour; but for this see our arguments following. Only by the way observe, that he that shall divide the inhabitants of any place, as at London, into poor and rich, those that want and those that abound, afterward affirming that he will bestow his bounty on many at London, on the poor, on those that want, will easily be understood to give it unto and bestow it upon them only. 2. Neither of the places quoted proves directly that *many* must necessarily in them be taken for *all*. In Dan. xii. 2, a distribution of the word to the several parts of the affirmation must be allowed, and not an application of it to the whole, as such; and so the sense is, the dead shall arise, many to life, and many to shame, as in another language it would have been expressed. Neither are such Hebraisms unusual. Besides, perhaps, it is not improbable that many are said to rise to life, because, as the apostle says, "All shall not die." The like, also, may be said of Rom. v. 19. Though the *many* there seem to be *all*, yet certainly they are not called so with any intent to denote all, "with an amplification" (which that *many* should be to *all* is not likely): for there is no comparison there instituted at all between number and number, of those that died by Adam's disobedience and those that were made alive by the righteousness of Christ, but only in the effects of the sin of Adam and the righteousness of Christ, together with the way and manner of communicating death and life from the one and the other; whereunto any consideration of the number of the participators of those effects is not inserted. 3. The other places whereby this should be confirmed, I am confident our author cannot produce, notwithstanding his free inclination of such a reserve, these being those which are in this case commonly urged by Arminians; but if he could, they would be no way material to infringe our argument, as appeareth by what was said before.

"Secondly, This reason," he adds, "is equivocal, subtile, and fraudulent; seeing where *all* men and *every* man is affirmed of, the death of Christ, as the ransom and propitiation, and the fruits thereof, only is assumed for them; but where the word *many* is in any place used in this business, there are more ends of the death of Christ than this one affirmed of."

Rep. 1. It is denied that the death of Christ, in any place of Scripture, is said to be for "all men" or for "every man;" which, with so much confidence, is supposed, and imposed on us as a thing acknowledged. 2. That there is any other end of the death of Christ, besides the fruit of his ransom and propitiation, directly intended, and not by accident attending it, is utterly false. Yea, what other end the ransom paid by Christ and the atonement made by him can have but the fruits of them, is not imaginable. The end of any work is the same with the fruit, effect, or product of it. So that this wild distinction of the ransom and propitiation of Christ, with the fruits of them, to be for all, and the other ends of his death to be only for many, is an assertion neither equivocal, subtile, nor fraudulent! But I speak to what I conceive the meaning of the place; for the words themselves bear no tolerable sense. 3. The observation, that where the word *many* is used many ends are designed, but where *all* are spoken of there only the ransom is intimated, is,—(1.) Disadvantageous to the author's persuasion, yielding the whole argument in hand, by acknowledging that where *many* are mentioned, there *all* cannot be understood, because more ends of the death of Christ than do belong to all are mentioned; and so confessedly all the other answers to prove that by *many*, *all* are to be understood, are against the author's own light. (2.) It is frivolous; for it cannot be proved that there are more ends of the death of Christ besides the fruit of his ransom. (3.) It is false; for where the death of Christ is spoken of as for *many,* he is said to "give his life a ransom" for them, Matt. xx. 28, which are the very words where he is said to die for *all,* 1 Tim. ii. 6. What difference is there in these? what ground for this observation? Even such as these are divers others of that author's observations, as his whole tenth chapter is spent to prove that whereever there is mention of the redemption purchased by the oblation of Christ, there they for whom it is purchased are always spoken of in the third person, as by "all the world," or the like; when yet, in chap. i. of his book, himself produceth many places to prove this general redemption where the persons for whom Christ is said to suffer are mentioned in the first or second person, 1 Pet. ii. 24, iii. 18; Isa. liii. 5, 6; 1 Cor. xv. 3; Gal. iii. 13, etc.

Thirdly, He proceeds, "This reason is false and ungodly; for it is nowhere in Scripture said that Christ died or gave himself a ransom but for many, or only for many, or only for his sheep; and it is ungodliness to add to or diminish from the word of God in Scripture."

Rep. To pass by the loving terms of the author, and allowing a grain to make the sense current, I say,—*First,* That Christ affirming that he gave his life for "many," for his "sheep," being said to die for his "church," and innumerable places of Scripture witnessing that all men are not of his sheep, of his church, we argue and conclude, by just and undeniable consequence, that he died not for those who are not so. If this be adding to the word of God (being only an exposition and unfolding of his mind therein), who ever spake from the word of God and was guiltless? *Secondly,* Let it be observed, that in the very place where our Saviour says that he "gave his life for his sheep," he presently adds, that some are not of his sheep, John x. 26; which, if it be not equivalent to his sheep only, I know not what is. *Thirdly,* It were easy to recriminate; but,—

Fourthly, "But," says he, "the reason is deceitful and erroneous, for the Scripture doth nowhere say,—2. [a][1]Those many he died for are his sheep (much less his elect, as the reason intends it). As for the place, John x. 15, usually instanced to this end, it is therein much abused: for our Saviour, John x., did not set forth the difference between such as he died for and such as he died not for, [b]or such as he died for so and so, and not so and so; [c]but the difference between those that believe on him and those who believe not on him, verses 4, 5, 14, 26, 27. One hear his voice and follow him, the other not. [d]Nor did our Saviour here set forth the privileges of all he died for, or for whom he died so and so, but of those that believe on him

[1] These figures are designed by the author to connect each argument which he is refuting with the answer he supplies to it in the succeeding paragraphs.—Ed.

through the ministration of the gospel, and so do know him, and approach to God, and enter the kingdom by him, verses 3, 4, 9, 27. [e] Nor was our Saviour here setting forth the excellency of those for whom he died, or died for so only, wherein they are preferred before others; but the excellency of his own love, with the fruits thereof to those not only that he died for, but also that are brought in by his ministration to believe on him, verses 11, 27. [f] Nor was our Saviour here treating so much of his ransom-giving and propitiation-making as of his ministration of the gospel, and so of his love and faithfulness therein; wherein he laid down his life for those ministered to, and therein gave us example, not to make propitiation for sin, but to testify love in suffering."

Rep. I am persuaded that nothing but an acquaintedness with the condition of the times wherein we live can afford me sanctuary from the censure of the reader to be lavish of precious hours, in considering and transcribing such canting lines as these last repeated. But yet, seeing better cannot be afforded, we must be content to view such evasions as these, all whose strength is in incongruous expressions, in incoherent structure, cloudy, windy phrases, all tending to raise such a mighty fog as that the business in hand might not be perceived, being lost in this smoke and vapour, cast out to darken the eyes and amuse the senses of poor seduced souls. The argument undertaken to be answered being, that Christ is said to die for "many," and those many are described and designed to be his "sheep," as John x., what answer, I pray, or any thing like thereunto, is there to be picked out of this confused heap of words which we have recited? So that I might safely pass the whole evasion by without farther observation on it, but only to desire the reader to observe how much this one argument presseth, and what a nothing is that heap of confusion which is opposed to it! But yet, lest any thing should adhere, I will give a few annotations to the place, answering the marks wherewith we have noted it, leaving the full vindication of the place until I come to the pressing of our arguments.

I say then, First, [a] That the many Christ died for were his sheep, was before declared. Neither is the place of John x. at all abused, our Saviour evidently setting forth a difference between them for whom he died and those for whom he would not die, calling the first his "sheep," verse 15,—those to whom he would "give eternal life," verse 28,—those "given him by his Father," chap. xvii. 9; evidently distinguishing them from others who were not so. Neither is it material what was the primary intention of our Saviour in this place, from which we do not argue, but from the intention and aim of the words he uses, and the truth he reveals for the end aimed at; which was the consolation of believers.

Secondly, [b] For the difference between them he "died for so and so," and those he "died for so and so," we confess he puts none; for we suppose that this "*so and so*" doth neither express nor intimate any thing that may be suitable to any purpose of God, or intent of our Saviour in this business. To us for whom he died, he died in the same manner, and for the same end.

Thirdly, [c] We deny that the primary difference that here is made by our Saviour is between believers and not believers, but between elect and not elect, sheep and not sheep; the thing wherein they are thus differenced being the believing of the one, called "hearing of his voice and knowing him," and the not believing of the other; the foundation of these acts being their different conditions in respect of God's purpose and Christ's love, as is apparent from the antithesis and opposition which we have in verses 26 and 27, "Ye believe not, because ye are not of my sheep," and, "My sheep hear my voice." First, there is a distinction put,—in the act of believing and hearing (that is, therewithal to obey); and then is the foundation of this distinction asserted, from their distinguished state and condition,—the one being not his sheep, the other being so, even them whom he loved and gave his life for.

Fourthly, [d] *First,* It is nothing to the business before us what privileges our Saviour here expresseth; our question is, for whom he says he would give his life? and that only. *Secondly,* This frequent repetition of that useless *so and so* serves for nothing but to puzzle the poor ignorant reader. *Thirdly,* We deny that Christ died for any but those who shall certainly be brought unto him by the ministration of the gospel. So that there is not a "Not only those whom he died for, but also those that are brought in unto him;" for he died for his sheep, and his sheep hear his voice. They for whom he died, and those that come in to him, may receive different qualifications, but they are not several persons.

Fifthly, [e] *First,* The question is not at all, to what end our Saviour here makes mention of his death? but for whom he died? who are expressly said to be his "sheep;" which all are not. *Secondly,* His intention is, to declare the giving of his life for a ransom, and that according to the "commandment received of his Father," verse 18.

Sixthly, [f] *First,* "The love and faithfulness of Jesus Christ in the ministration of the gospel,"—that is, his performing the office of the mediator of the new covenant,—are seen in nothing more than in giving his life for a ransom, John xv. 13. *Secondly,* Here is not one word of giving us an "example;" though in laying down his life he did that also, yet here it is not improved to that purpose. From these brief annotations, I doubt not but that it is apparent that that long discourse before recited is nothing but a miserable mistaking of the text and question; which the author perhaps perceiving, he adds divers other evasions, which follow.

"Besides," saith he, "the opposition appears here to be not so much between elect and not elect, as between Jews called and Gentiles uncalled."

Rep. The opposition is between sheep and not sheep, and that with reference to their election, and not to their vocation. Now, whom would he have signified by the "not sheep"? those that were not called,—the Gentiles? That is against the text terming them sheep, that is in designation, though not as yet called, verse 16. And who are the called? the Jews? True, they were then outwardly called; yet many of them were not sheep, verse 26. Now, truly, such evasions from the force of truth as this, by so foul corrupting of the word of God, is no small provocation of the eye of his glory. But he adds,—

"Besides, there is in Scripture great difference between sheep, and sheep of his flock and pasture, of which he here speaketh, verses 4, 5, 11, 15, 16."

Rep. 1. This unrighteous distinction well explained must needs, no doubt (if any know how), give a great deal of light to the business in hand. 2. If there be a distinction to be allowed, it can be nothing but this, that the "sheep" who are simply so called are those who are only so to Christ from the donation of his Father; and the "sheep of his pasture," those who, by the effectual working of the Spirit, are actually brought home to Christ. And then of both sorts we have mention in this chapter, verses 16, 27, both making up the number of those sheep for whom he gave his life, and to whom he giveth life. But he proceeds:—

"Besides, sheep, verses 4, 5, 11, 15, are not mentioned as all those for whom he died, but as those who by his ministration are brought in to believe and enjoy the benefit of his death, and to whom he ministereth and communicateth spirit."

Rep. 1. The substance of this and other exceptions is, that by sheep is meant believers; which is contrary to verse 16, calling them sheep who are not as yet gathered into his fold. 2. That his sheep are not mentioned as those for whom he died is in terms contradictory to verse 15, "I lay down my life for my sheep." 3. Between those for whom he died and those whom he brings in by the ministration of his Spirit, there is no more difference than is between Peter, James, and John, and the three apostles that were in the mount with our Saviour at his transfiguration. This is childish sophistry, to beg the thing in question, and thrust in the opinion controverted into the room of an answer. 4. That bringing in which is here mentioned, to believe and enjoy the benefit of the death of Christ, is a most special fruit and benefit of that death, certainly to be conferred on all them for whom he died, or else most certainly his death will do them no good at all. Once more, and we have done:—

"Besides, here are more ends of his death mentioned than ransom or propitiation only, and yet it is not said, 'Only for his sheep;' and when the ransom or propitiation only is mentioned, it is said, 'For all men.' So that this reason appears weak, fraudulent, ungodly, and erroneous."

Rep. 1. Here is no word mentioned nor intimated of the death of Christ, but only that which was accomplished by his being a propitiation, and making his death a ransom for us, with the fruits which certainly and infallibly spring therefrom. 2. If more ends than one of the death of Christ are here mentioned, and such as belong not unto all, why do you deny that he speaks here of his sheep only? Take heed, or you will see the truth. 3. Where it is said, "Of all men," I know not; but this I am sure, that Christ is said to "give his life a ransom," and that is only mentioned where it is not said for all; as Matt. xx. 28, Mark x. 45.

And so, from these brief annotations, I hope any indifferent reader will be able to judge whether the reason opposed, or the exceptions against it devised, be to be accounted "weak, fraudulent, ungodly, and erroneous."

Although I fear that in this particular I have already intrenched upon the reader's patience, yet I cannot let pass the discourse immediately following in the same author to those exceptions which we last removed, laid by him against the arguments we had in hand, without an obelisk; as also an observation of his great abilities to cast down a man of clouds, which himself had set up to manifest his skill in its direction. To the preceding discourse he adds another exception, which he imposeth on those that oppose universal redemption, as though it were laid by them against the understanding of the general expressions in the Scripture, in that way and sense wherein he conceives them; and it is, "That those words were fitted for the time of Christ and his apostles, having another meaning in them than they seem to import." Now, having thus gaily trimmed and set up this man of straw,—to whose framing I dare boldly say not one of his adversaries did ever contribute a penful of ink,—to show his rare skill, he chargeth it with I know not how many errors, blasphemies, lies, set on with exclamations and vehement outcries, until it tumble to the ground. Had he not sometimes answered an argument, he would have been thought a most unhappy disputant. Now, to make sure that for once he would do it, I believe he was very careful that the objection of his own framing should not be too strong for his own defacing. In the meantime, how blind are they who admire him for a combatant who is skilful only at fencing with his own shadow! and yet with such empty janglings as these, proving what none denies, answering what none objects, is the greatest part of Mr More's book stuffed.

CHAPTER IV.

Of the distinction of impetration and application—The use and abuse thereof; with the opinion of the adversaries upon the whole matter in controversy unfolded; and the question on both sides stated.

THE farther reasons whereby the precedent discourse may be confirmed, I defer until I come to oppose some argument to the general ransom. For the present, I shall only take away that general answer which is usually given to the places of Scripture produced, to waive the sense of them; which is φάρμακον πάνσοφον to our adversaries, and serves them, as they suppose, to bear up all the weight wherewith in this case they are urged:—

I. They say, then, that in the oblation of Christ, and concerning the good things by him procured, two things are to be considered:— First, The *impetration*, or obtaining of them; and, secondly, The *application* of them to particular persons. "The first," say they, "is general, in respect to all. Christ obtained and procured all good things by his death of his Father,—reconciliation, redemption, forgiveness of sins,—for all and every man in the world, if they will believe and lay hold upon him: but in respect of *application*, they are actually bestowed and conferred but on a few; because but a few believe, which is the condition on which they are bestowed. And in this latter sense are the texts of Scripture which we have argued, all of them, to be understood. So that they do no whit impeach the *universality of merit*, which they assert; but only the *universality of application*, which they also deny." Now, this answer is commonly set forth by them in various terms and divers dresses, according as it seems best to them that use it, and most subservient to their several opinions; for,—

First, Some of them say that Christ, by his death and passion, did absolutely, according to the intention of God, purchase for all and every man, dying for them, remission of sins and reconciliation with God, or a restitution into a state of grace and favour; all which shall be actually beneficial to them, provided that they do believe. So the Arminians.

Secondly, Some,[1] again, that Christ died for all indeed, but *conditionally* for some, if they do believe, or will so do (which he knows they cannot of themselves); and *absolutely* for his own, even them on whom he purposeth to bestow faith and grace, so as actually to be made possessors of the good things by him purchased. So Camero, and the divines of France, which follow a new method by him devised.

Thirdly, Some[2] distinguish of a twofold reconciliation and redemp-

[1] Camero, Testardus, Amyraldus. [2] More, with some others of late.

tion;—one wrought by Christ with God for man, which, say they, is general for all and every man; secondly, a reconciliation wrought by Christ in man unto God, bringing them actually into peace with him.

And sundry other ways there are whereby men express their conceptions in this business. The sum of all comes to this, and the weight of all lies upon that distinction which we before recounted;—namely, that in respect of *impetration,* Christ obtained redemption and reconciliation for all; in respect of *application,* it is bestowed only on them who do believe and continue therein.

II. Their arguments whereby they prove the generality of the ransom and universality of the reconciliation must afterward be considered: for the present, we handle only the distinction itself, the meaning and misapplication whereof I shall briefly declare; which will appear if we consider,—

FIRST, The true nature and meaning of this distinction, and the true use thereof; for we do acknowledge that it may be used in a sound sense and right meaning, which way soever you express it, either by impetration and application, or by procuring reconciliation with God and a working of reconciliation in us. For by *impetration* we mean the meritorious purchase of all good things made by Christ for us with and of his Father; and by *application,* the actual enjoyment of those good things upon our believing;—as, if a man pay a price for the redeeming of captives, the paying of the price supplieth the room of the *impetration* of which we speak; and the freeing of the captives is as the application of it. Yet, then, we must observe,—

First, That this distinction hath no place in the *intention* and purpose of Christ, but only in respect of the things procured by him; for in his purpose they are both united, his full end and aim being to deliver us from all evil, and procure all good actually to be bestowed upon us. But in respect of the *things themselves,* they may be considered either as procured by Christ, or as bestowed on us.

Secondly, That the will of God is not at all *conditional* in this business, as though he gave Christ to obtain peace, reconciliation, and forgiveness of sins, upon condition that we do believe. There is a condition in the things, but none in the will of God; that is absolute that such things should be procured and bestowed.

Thirdly, That all the things which Christ obtained for us are not bestowed upon *condition,* but some of them *absolutely.* And as for those that are bestowed upon condition, the condition on which they are bestowed is actually purchased and procured for us, upon no condition but only by virtue of the purchase. For instance: Christ hath purchased remission of sins and eternal life for us, to be enjoyed on our believing, upon the condition of faith. But faith itself, which is the condition of them, on whose performance they are bestowed, that he hath procured for us absolutely, on no condition at all; for what condition soever can be proposed, on which the Lord should bestow faith, I shall afterward show it vain, and to run into a circle.

Fourthly, That both these, *impetration* and *application*, have for their objects the same individual persons; that, look, for whomsoever Christ obtained any good thing by his death, unto them it shall certainly be applied, upon them it shall actually be bestowed: so that it cannot be said that he obtained any thing for any one, which that one shall not or doth not in due time enjoy. For whomsoever he wrought reconciliation *with* God, in them doth he work reconciliation *unto* God. The one is not extended to some to whom the other doth not reach. Now, because this being established, the opposite interpretation and misapplication of this distinction vanisheth, I shall briefly confirm it with reasons:—

First, If the *application* of the good things procured be the end why they are procured, for whose sake alone Christ doth obtain them, then they must be applied to all for whom they are obtained; for otherwise Christ faileth of his end and aim, which must not be granted. But that this *application* was the end of the obtaining of all good things for us appeareth,—*First,* Because if it were otherwise, and Christ did not aim at the *applying* of them, but only at their *obtaining,* then might the death of Christ have had its full effect and issue without the application of redemption and salvation to any one soul, that being not aimed at, and so, notwithstanding all that he did for us, every soul in the world might have perished eternally; which, whether it can stand with the dignity and sufficiency of his oblation, with the purpose of his Father, and his own intention, who "came into the world to save sinners,—that which was lost," and to "bring many sons unto glory," let all judge. *Secondly,* God, in that action of sending his Son, laying the weight of iniquity upon him, and giving him up to an accursed death, must be affirmed to be altogether uncertain what event all this should have in respect of us. For, did he intend that we should be saved by it?—then the application of it is that which he aimed at, as we assert: did he not?—certainly, he was uncertain what end it should have; which is blasphemy, and exceeding contrary to Scripture and right reason. Did he appoint a Saviour without thought of them that were to be saved? a Redeemer, not determining who should be redeemed? Did he resolve of a means, not determining the end? It is an assertion opposite to all the glorious properties of God.

Secondly, If that which is obtained by any do, by virtue of that action whereby it is obtained, become his in right for whom it is obtained, then for whomsoever any thing is by Christ obtained, it is to them *applied;* for that must be made theirs in fact which is theirs in right. But it is most certain that whatsoever is obtained for any is theirs by right for whom it is obtained. The very sense of the word, whether you call it *merit, impetration, purchase, acquisition,* or *obtaining,* doth bespeak a right in them for whose good the merit is effected and the purchase made. Can that be said to be obtained for me which is no wise mine? When I obtain any thing by prayer or entreaty of any one, it being obtained, it is mine own. That which is *obtained* by one is *granted* by him of whom it is obtained; and if granted, it is granted by him to *them* for whom it is obtained. But they will say, "It is obtained upon condition; and until the condition be fulfilled no right doth accrue." I answer, If this condition be equally purchased and obtained, with other things that are to be bestowed on that condition, then this hinders not but that every thing is to be applied that is procured. But if it be uncertain whether this condition will be fulfilled or not, then,—*first,* This makes God uncertain what end the death of his Son will have; *secondly,* This doth not answer but deny the thing we are are in proving, which is confirmed.

Thirdly, Because the Scripture, perpetually conjoining these two things together, will not suffer us so to sever them as that the one should belong to some and not to others, as though they could have several persons for their objects: as Isa. liii. 11, "By his knowledge shall my righteous servant justify many,"—there is the application of all good things; "for he shall bear their iniquities,"—there is the impetration. He justifieth all whose iniquities he bore. As also verse 5 of that chapter, "But he was wounded for our transgressions, he was bruised for our iniquities: the chastisement of our peace was upon him; and by his stripes we are healed." His wounding and our healing, impetration and application, his chastisement and our peace, are inseparably associated. So Rom. iv. 25, "He was delivered for our offences, and was raised again for our justification." So chap. v. 18, "By the righteousness of one" (that is, his impetration), "the free gift came upon all men unto justification of life," in the application. See there who are called "All men," most clearly. Chap. viii. 32–34, "He that spared not his own Son, but delivered him up for us all, how shall he not with him also freely give us all things? Who shall lay any thing to the charge of God's elect? It is God that justifieth. Who is he that condemneth? It is Christ that died, yea rather, that is risen again, who is even at the right hand of God, who also maketh intercession for us." From which words we have these several reasons of our assertion:—*First,* That for whom God gives his Son, to them, in him, he freely gives all things; therefore, all things obtained by his death must be bestowed, and are, on them for whom he died, verse 32. *Secondly,* They for whom Christ died are justified, are God's elect, cannot be condemned, nor can any thing be laid to their charge; all that he hath purchased for them must be applied to them, for by virtue thereof it is that they are so saved, verses 33, 34. *Thirdly*, For whom Christ died, for them he maketh intercession. Now, his intercession is for the application of those things, as is confessed, and therein he is always heard. Those to whom the one belongs, theirs also is the other. So, John x. 10, the coming of Christ is, that "his might have life, and have it abundantly;" as also 1 John iv. 9. Heb. x. 10, "By the which will we are sanctified,"—that is the application; "through the offering of the body of Jesus Christ,"—that is the means of impetration: "for by one offering he hath perfected for ever them that are sanctified," verse 14. In brief, it is proved by all those places which we produced rightly to assign the end of the death of Christ. So that this may be rested on, as I conceive, as firm and immovable, that the impetration of good things by Christ, and the application of them, respect the same individual persons.

SECONDLY, We may consider the meaning of those who seek to maintain universal redemption by this distinction in it, and to what use they do apply it. "Christ," say they, "died for all men, and by his death purchased reconciliation with God for them and forgiveness of sins: which to some is applied, and they become actually reconciled to God, and have their sins forgiven them; but to others not, who, therefore, perish in the state of irreconciliation and enmity, under the guilt of their sins. This application," say they, "is not procured nor purchased by Christ,—for then, he dying for all, all must be actually reconciled and have their sins forgiven them and be saved,—but it attends the fulfilling of the condition which God is pleased to prescribe unto them, that is, believing:" which, say some, they can do by their own strength, though not in terms, yet by direct consequence; others not, but God must give it. So that when it is said in the Scripture, Christ hath reconciled us to God, redeemed us, saved us by his blood, underwent the punishment of our sins, and so made satisfaction for us, they assert that no more is meant but that Christ did that which upon the fulfilling of the condition that is of us required, these things will follow. To the death of Christ, indeed, they assign many glorious things; but what they give on the one hand they take away with the other, by suspending the enjoyment of them on a condition by us to be fulfilled, not by him procured; and in terms assert that the proper and full end of the death of Christ was the doing of that whereby God, his justice being satisfied, might save sinners if he would, and on what condition it pleased him,—that a door of grace might be opened to all that would come in, and not that actual justification and remission of sins, life, and immortality were procured by him, but only a possibility of those things, that so it might be. Now, that all the venom that lies under this exposition and abuse of this distinction may the better appear, I shall set down the whole mind of them that use it in a few assertions, that it may be clearly seen what we do oppose.

First, "God," say they, "considering all mankind as fallen from that grace and favour in Adam wherein they were created, and excluded utterly from the attainment of salvation by virtue of the covenant of works which was at the first made with him, yet by his infinite goodness was inclined to desire the happiness of them, all and every one, that they might be delivered from misery, and be brought unto himself;" which inclination of his they call his universal love and antecedent will, whereby he would desirously have them all to be saved; out of which love he sendeth Christ.

Obs. 1. That God hath any natural or necessary inclination, by his goodness, or any other property, to do good to us, or any of his creatures, we do deny. Every thing that concerns us is an act of his free will and good pleasure, and not a natural, necessary act of his Deity, as shall be declared.

Obs. 2. The ascribing an antecedent conditional will unto God, whose fulfilling and accomplishment should depend on any free, contingent act or work of ours, is injurious to his wisdom, power, and sovereignty, and cannot well be excused from blasphemy; and is contrary to Rom. ix. 19, "Who hath resisted his will?" I say,—

Obs. 3. A common affection and inclination to do good to all doth not seem to set out the freedom, fulness, and dimensions of that most intense love of God which is asserted in the Scripture to be the cause of sending his Son; as John iii. 16, "God so loved the world, that he gave his only-begotten Son." Eph. i. 9, "Having made known unto us the mystery of his will, according to his good pleasure which he hath purposed in himself." Col. i. 19, "It pleased the Father that in him should all fulness dwell." Rom. v. 8, "God commendeth his love toward us, in that, while we were yet sinners, Christ died for us." These two[1] I shall, by the Lord's assistance, fully clear, if the Lord give life and strength, and his people encouragement, to go through with the second part of this controversy.

Obs. 4. We deny that all mankind are the object of that love of God which moved him to send his Son to die; God having "made some for the day of evil," Prov. xvi. 4; "hated them before they were born," Rom. ix. 11, 13; "before of old ordained them to condemnation," Jude 4; being "fitted to destruction," Rom. ix. 22; "made to be taken and destroyed," 2 Pet. ii. 12; "appointed to wrath," 1 Thess. v. 9; to "go to their own place," Acts i. 25.

Secondly, "The justice of God being injured by sin, unless something might be done for the satisfaction thereof, that love of God whereby he wouldeth good to all sinners could no way be brought

[1] See book iv., chap. ii. and chap. iv., where John iii. 16, and Rom. v. 8, are very fully considered. These must be the two passages to which he refers.—ED.

forth into act, but must have its eternal residence in the bosom of God without any effect produced."

Obs. 1. That neither Scripture nor right reason will enforce nor prove an utter and absolute want of power in God to save sinners by his own absolute will, without satisfaction to his justice, supposing his purpose that so it should be; indeed, it could not be otherwise. But, without the consideration of that, certainly he could have effected it. It doth not imply any violating of his holy nature.

Obs. 2. An actual and necessary *velleity*, for the doing of any thing which cannot possibly be accomplished without some work fulfilled outwardly of him, is opposite to his eternal blessedness and all-sufficiency.

Thirdly, "God, therefore, to fulfil that general love and good-will of his towards all, and that it might put forth itself in such a way as should seem good to him, to satisfy his justice, which stood in the way, and was the only hinderance, he sent his Son into the world to die."

The failing of this assertion we shall lay forth, when we come to declare that love whereof the sending of Christ was the proper issue and effect.

Fourthly, "Wherefore, the proper and immediate end and aim of the purpose of God in sending his Son to die for all men was, that he might, what way it pleased him, save sinners, his justice which hindered being satisfied,"—as Arminius; or, "That he might will to save sinners,"—as Corvinus. "And the intention of Christ was, to make such satisfaction to the justice of God as that he might obtain to himself a power of saving, upon what conditions it seemed good to his Father to prescribe."

Obs. 1. Whether this was the intention of the Father in sending his Son or no, let it be judged. Something was said before, upon the examination of those places of Scripture which describe his purpose; let it be known from them whether God, in sending of his Son, intended to procure to himself a liberty to save us if he would, or to obtain certain salvation for his elect.

Obs. 2. That such a possibility of salvation, or, at the utmost, a velleity or willing of it, upon an uncertain condition, to be by us fulfilled, should be the full, proper, and only immediate end of the death of Christ, will yet scarcely down with tender spirits.

Obs. 3. The expression, of procuring to himself *ability* to save, upon a condition to be prescribed, seems not to answer that certain purpose of our Saviour in laying down his life, which the Scripture saith was to "save his sheep," and to "bring many sons to glory," as before; nor hath it any ground in Scripture.

Fifthly, "Christ, therefore, obtained for all and every one reconciliation with God, remission of sins, life and salvation; not that they should actually be partakers of these things, but that God (his justice now not hindering) might and would prescribe a condition to be by them fulfilled, whereupon he would actually apply it, and make them partake of all those good things purchased by Christ." And here comes their distinction of impetration and application, which we before intimated; and thereabout, in the explication of this assertion, they are wondrously divided.

Some say that this proceeds so far, that all men are thereby received into a new covenant, in which redemption Adam was a common person as well as in his fall from the old, and all we again restored in him; so that none shall be damned that do not sin actually against the condition wherein they are born, and fall from the state whereinto all men are assumed through the death of Christ. So Boræus, Corvinus; and one of late, in plain terms, that all are reconciled, redeemed, saved, and justified in Christ; though how he could not understand (More, p. 10). But others, more warily, deny this, and assert that *by nature we are all children of wrath,* and that until we come to Christ *the wrath of God abideth on all,* so that it is not actually removed from any: so the assertors of the efficacy of grace in France.

Again, some say that Christ by this satisfaction removed *original sin in all,* and, by consequent, that only; so that all infants, though of Turks and Pagans, out of the covenant, dying before they come to the use of reason, must undoubtedly be saved, that being removed in all, even the calamity, guilt, and alienation contracted by our first fall, whereby God may save all upon a new condition. But others of them, more warily, observing that the blood of Christ is said to "cleanse from all sin," (1 John i. 7; 1 Pet. i. 18, 19; Isa. liii. 6), say he died for all sinners alike; absolutely for none, but conditionally for all. Farther, some of them affirm that after the satisfaction of Christ, or the consideration of it in God's prescience, it was absolutely undetermined what condition should be prescribed, so that the Lord might have reduced all again to the law and covenant of works; so Corvinus: others, that a procuring of a new way of salvation by faith was a part of the fruit of the death of Christ; so More, p. 35.

Again, some of them, that the condition prescribed is by our own strength, with the help of such means as God at all times, and in all places, and unto all, is ready to afford, to be performed; others deny this, and affirm that effectual grace flowing peculiarly from election is necessary to believing: the first establishing the *idol* of *free-will* to maintain their own assertion; others overthrowing their own assertion for the establishment of grace. So Amyraldus, Camero, etc.

Moreover, some say that the love of God in the sending of Christ is equal to all: others go a strain higher, and maintain an inequality in the love of God, although he send his Son to die for all, and though greater love there cannot be than that whereby the Lord sent his Son to die for us, as Rom. viii. 32; and so they say that

Christ purchased a greater good for some, and less for others. And here they put themselves upon innumerable uncouth *distinctions*, or rather (as one calleth them), *extinctions*, blotting out all sense, and reason, and true meaning of the Scripture. Witness Testardus, Amyraldus, and, as every one may see that can but read English, in T. M[ore.] Hence that multiplicity of the several ends of the death of Christ,—some that are the fruits of his ransom and satisfaction, and some that are I know not what; besides his dying for some so and so, for others so and so, this way and that way;—hiding themselves in innumerable unintelligible expressions, that it is a most difficult thing to know what they mean, and harder to find out their mind than to answer their reasons.

In one particular they agree well enough,—namely, in denying that faith is procured or merited for us by the death of Christ. So far they are all of them constant to their own principles, for once to grant it would overturn the whole fabric of universal redemption; but in assigning the cause of faith they go asunder again.

Some say that God sent Christ to die for all men, but only conditionally, if they did and would believe;—as though, if they believed, Christ died for them; if not, he died not; and so make the act the cause of its own object: other some, that he died absolutely for all, to procure all good things for them, which yet they should not enjoy until they fulfil the condition that was to be prescribed unto them. Yet all conclude that in his death Christ had no more respect unto the elect than others, to sustain their persons, or to be in their room, but that he was a public person in the room of all mankind.

III. Concerning the close of all this, in respect of the event and immediate product of the death of Christ, divers have diversely expressed themselves; some placing it in the power, some in the will, of God; some in the opening of a door of grace; some in a right purchased to himself of saving whom he pleased; some that in respect of us he had no end at all, but that all mankind might have perished after he had done all. Others make divers and distinct ends, not almost to be reckoned, of this one act of Christ, according to the diversity of the persons for whom he died, whom they grant to be distinguished and differenced by a foregoing decree; but to what purpose the Lord should send his Son to die for them whom he himself had determined not to save, but at least to pass by and leave to remediless ruin for their sins, I cannot see, nor the meaning of the twofold destination by some invented. Such is the powerful force and evidence of truth that it scatters all its opposers, and makes them fly to several hiding-corners; who, if they are not willing to yield and submit themselves, they shall surely lie down in darkness and error. None of these, or the like intricate and involved impedite distinctions, hath [truth] itself need of; into none of such poor shifts and devices doth it compel its abettors; it needeth not any windings and turnings to bring itself into a defensible posture; it is not liable to contradictions in its own fundamentals: for, without any farther circumstances, the whole of it in this business may be thus summed up:—

"*God, out of his infinite love to his elect, sent his dear Son in the fulness of time, whom he had promised in the beginning of the world, and made effectual by that promise, to die, pay a ransom of infinite value and dignity, for the purchasing of eternal redemption, and bringing unto himself all and every one of those whom he had before ordained to eternal life, for the praise of his own glory.*" So that freedom from all the evil from which we are delivered, and an enjoyment of all the good things that are bestowed on us, in our traduction from death to life, from hell and wrath to heaven and glory, are the proper issues and effects of the death of Christ, as the meritorious cause of them all; which may, in all the parts of it, be cleared by these few assertions:—

First, The fountain and cause of God's sending Christ is his eternal love to his elect, and to them alone; which I shall not now farther confirm, reserving it for the second general head of this whole controversy.

Secondly, The *value, worth,* and *dignity* of the ransom which Christ gave himself to be, and of the price which he paid, was infinite and immeasurable; fit for the accomplishing of any end and the procuring of any good, for all and every one for whom it was intended, had they been millions of men more than ever were created. Of this also afterward. See Acts xx. 28, "God purchased his church with his own blood." 1 Pet. i. 18, 19, "Redeemed not with silver and gold, but with the precious blood of Christ;" and that answering the mind and intention of Almighty God, John xiv. 31, "As the Father gave me commandment, even so I do;" who would have such a price paid as might be the foundation of that economy and dispensation of his love and grace which he intended, and of the way whereby he would have it dispensed. Acts xiii. 38, 39, "Through this man is preached unto you the forgiveness of sins; and by him all that believe are justified from all things, from which ye could not be justified by the law of Moses." 2 Cor. v. 20, 21, "We are ambassadors for Christ, as though God did beseech you by us: we pray you in Christ's stead, be ye reconciled to God. For he hath made him to be sin for us, who knew no sin; that we might be made the righteousness of God in him."

Thirdly, The intention and aim of the Father in this great work was, a bringing of those many sons to glory,—namely, his elect, whom by his free grace he had chosen from amongst all men, of all sorts, nations, and conditions, to take them into a new covenant of grace with himself, the former being as to them, in respect of the event, null and abolished; of which covenant Jesus Christ is the first and chief promise, as he that was to procure for them all other good things promised therein, as shall be proved.

Fourthly, The *things purchased* or procured for those persons,—which are the proper effects of the death and ransom of Christ, in due time certainly to become theirs in possession and enjoyment,—are, remission of sin, freedom from wrath and the curse of the law, justification, sanctification, and reconciliation with God, and eternal life; for the will of his Father sending him for these, his own intention in laying down his life for them, and the truth of the purchase made by him, is the foundation of his intercession, begun on earth and continued in heaven; whereby he, whom his Father always hears, desires and demands that the good things procured by him may be actually bestowed on them, all and every one, for whom they were procured. So that the whole of what we assert in this great business is exceedingly clear and apparent, without any intricacy or the least difficulty at all; not clouded with strange expressions and unnecessary divulsions and tearings of one thing from another, as is the opposite opinion: which in the next place shall be dealt withal by arguments confirming the one and everting the other. But because the whole strength thereof lieth in, and the weight of all lieth on, that one distinction we before spoke of, by our adversaries diversely expressed and held out, we will a little farther consider that, and then come to our arguments, and so to the answering of the opposed objections.

CHAPTER V.

Of application and impetration.

THE allowable use of this distinction, how it may be taken in a sound sense, the several ways whereby men have expressed the thing which in these words is intimated, and some arguments for the overthrowing of the false use of it, however expressed, we have before intimated and declared. Now, seeing that this is the πρῶτον ψεῦδος of the opposite opinion, understood in the sense and according to the use they make of it, I shall give it one blow more, and leave it, I hope, a-dying.

I shall, then, briefly declare, that although these two things may admit of a distinction, yet they cannot of a separation, but that for whomsoever Christ obtained good, to them it might be applied; and for whomsoever he wrought reconciliation with God, they must actually unto God be reconciled. So that the blood of Christ, and his death in the virtue of it, cannot be looked on, as some do, as a medicine in a box, laid up for all that shall come to have any of it, and so applied now to one, then to another, without any respect or difference, as though it should be intended no more for one than for another; so that although he hath obtained all the good that he hath purchased for us, yet it is left indifferent and uncertain whether it shall ever be ours or no: for it is well known, that notwithstanding those glorious things that are assigned by the Arminians to the death of Christ, which they say he purchased for all, as remission of sins, reconciliation with God, and the like, yet they for whom this purchase and procurement is made may be damned, as the greatest part are, and certainly shall be. Now, that there should be such a distance between these two,—

First, It is contrary to common sense or our usual form of speaking, which must be wrested, and our understandings forced to apprehend it. When a man hath obtained an office, or any other obtained it for him, can it be said that it is uncertain whether he shall have it or no? If it be obtained for him, is it not his in right, though perhaps not in possession? That which is impetrated or obtained by petition is his by whom it is obtained. It is to offer violence to common sense to say a thing may be a man's, or it may not be his, when it is obtained for him; for in so saying we say it is his. And so it is in the purchase made by Jesus Christ, and the good things obtained by him for all them for whom he died.

Secondly, It is contrary to all reason in the world, that the death of Christ, in God's intention, should be applied to any one that shall have no share in the merits of that death. God's will that Christ should die for any, is his intention that he shall have a share in the death of Christ, that it should belong to him,—that is, be applied to him; for that is, in this case, said to be applied to any that is his in any respect, according to the will of God. But now the death of Christ, according to the opinion we oppose, is so applied to all, and yet the fruits of this death are never so much as once made known to far the greatest part of those all.

Thirdly, [It is contrary to reason] that a ransom should be paid for captives, upon compact for their deliverance, and yet upon the payment those captives not be made free and set at liberty. The death of Christ is a ransom, Matt. xx. 28, paid by compact for the deliverance of captives for whom it was a ransom; and the promise wherein his Father stood engaged to him at his undertaking to be a Saviour, and undergoing the office imposed on him, was their deliverance, as was before declared, upon his performance of these things: on that [being done, that] the greatest number of these captives should never be released, seems strange and very improbable.

Fourthly, It is contrary to Scripture, as was before at large declared. See [also book iii.] chap. x.

But now, all this our adversaries suppose they shall wipe away with one slight distinction, that will make, as they say, all we affirm in this kind to vanish; and that is this: "It is true," say they, "all things that are absolutely procured and obtained for any do presently become theirs in right for whom they are obtained; but things that are obtained upon condition become not theirs until the condition be fulfilled. Now, Christ hath purchased, by his death for all, all good things, not absolutely, but upon condition; and until that condition come to be fulfilled, unless they perform what is required, they have neither part nor portion, right unto nor possession of them." Also, what this condition is they give in, in sundry terms; some call it a *not resisting* of this redemption offered to them; some, a *yielding* to the invitation of the gospel; some, in plain terms, *faith*. Now, be it so that Christ purchaseth all things for us, to be bestowed on this condition, that we do believe it, then I affirm that,—

First, Certainly this condition ought to be revealed to all for whom this purchase is made, if it be intended for them in good earnest. All for whom he died must have means to know that his death will do them good if they believe; especially it being in his power alone to grant them these means who intends good to them by his death. If I should entreat a physician that could cure such a disease to cure all that came unto him, but should let many rest ignorant of the grant which I had procured of the physician, and none but myself could acquaint them with it, whereby they might go to him and be healed, could I be supposed to intend the healing of those people? Doubtless no. The application is easy.

Secondly, This condition of them to be required is in their power to perform, or it is not. If it be, then have all men power to believe; which is false: if it be not, then the Lord will grant them grace to perform it, or he will not. If he will, why then do not all believe? why are not all saved? if he will not, then this impetration, or obtaining salvation and redemption for all by the blood of Jesus Christ, comes at length to this:—*God intendeth that he shall die for all, to procure for them remission of sins, reconciliation with him, eternal redemption and glory; but yet so that they shall never have the least good by these glorious things, unless they perform that which he knows they are no way able to do, and which none but himself can enable them to perform, and which concerning far the greatest part of them he is resolved not to do.* Is this to intend that Christ should die for them for their good? or rather, that he should die for them to expose them to shame and misery? Is it not all one as if a man should promise a blind man a thousand pounds upon condition that he will see.

Thirdly, This condition of faith is procured for us by the death of Christ, or it is not. If they say it be not, then the chiefest grace, and without which redemption itself (express it how you please) is of no value, doth not depend on the grace of Christ as the meritorious procuring cause thereof;—which, *first*, is exceedingly injurious to our blessed Saviour, and serves only to diminish the honour and love due to him; *secondly*, is contrary to Scripture: Tit. iii. 5, 6; 2 Cor. v. 21, "He became sin for us, that we might be made the righteousness of God in him." And how we can become the righteousness of God but by believing, I know not. Yea, expressly saith the apostle, "It is given to us for Christ's sake, on the behalf of Christ, to believe in him," Phil. i. 29; "God blessing us with all spiritual blessings in him," Eph. i. 3, whereof surely faith is not the least. If it be a fruit of the death of Christ, why is it not bestowed on all, since he died for all, especially since the whole impetration of redemption is altogether unprofitable without it? If they do invent a condition upon which this is bestowed, the vanity of that shall be afterward discovered. For the present, if this condition be, *So they do not refuse or resist the means of grace*, then I ask, if the fruit of the death of Christ shall be applied to all that fulfil this condition of not refusing or not resisting the means of grace? If not, then why is that produced? If so, then all must be saved that have not, or do not resist, the means of grace; that is, all pagans, infidels, and those infants to whom the gospel was never preached.

Fourthly, This whole assertion tends to make Christ but a half mediator, that should procure the end, but not the means conducing thereunto. So that, notwithstanding this exception and new distinction, our assertion stands firm,—That the fruits of the death of Christ, in respect of impetration of good and application to us, ought not to be divided; and our arguments to confirm it are unshaken.

For a close of all; that which in this cause we affirm may be summed up in this: Christ did not die for any upon condition, *if they do believe;* but he died for all God's elect, *that they should believe*, and believing have eternal life. Faith itself is among the principal effects and fruits of the death of Christ; as shall be declared. It is nowhere said in Scripture, nor can it reasonably be affirmed, that if we believe, Christ died for us, as though our believing should make that to be which otherwise was not,—the act create the object; but Christ died for us that we might believe. Salvation, indeed, is bestowed conditionally; but faith, which is the condition, is absolutely procured. The question being thus stated, the difference laid open, and the thing in controversy made known, we proceed, in the next place, to draw forth some of those arguments, demonstrations, testimonies, and proofs, whereby the truth we maintain is established, in which it is contained, and upon which it is firmly founded: only desiring the reader to retain some notions in his mind of those fundamentals which in general we laid down before; they standing in such relation to the arguments which we shall use, that I am confident not one of them can be thoroughly answered before they be everted.

BOOK III.

CHAPTER I.

Arguments against the universality of redemption—The two first; from the nature of the new covenant, and the dispensation thereof.

Argument I. The first argument may be taken from the nature of the covenant of grace, which was established, ratified, and confirmed in and by the death of Christ; that was the testament whereof he was the testator, which was ratified in his death, and whence his blood is called "The blood of the new testament," Matt. xxvi. 28. Neither can any effects thereof be extended beyond the compass of this covenant. But now this covenant was not made universally with all, but particularly only with some, and therefore those alone were intended in the benefits of the death of Christ.

The assumption appears from the nature of the covenant itself, described clearly, Jer. xxxi. 31, 32, "I will make a new covenant with the house of Israel, and with the house of Judah: not according to the covenant that I made with their fathers in the day that I took them by the hand to bring them out of the land of Egypt; which my covenant they brake, though I was an husband to them, saith the Lord;"—and Heb. viii. 9–11, "Not according to the covenant that I made with their fathers in the day when I took them by the hand to lead them out of the land of Egypt; because they continued not in my covenant, and I regarded them not, saith the Lord. For this is the covenant that I will make with the house of Israel after those days, saith the Lord; I will put my laws in their mind, and write them in their hearts: and I will be to them a God, and they shall be to me a people: and they shall not teach every man his neighbour, and every man his brother, saying, Know the Lord: for all shall know me, from the least to the greatest." Wherein, first, the condition of the covenant is not said to be required, but it is absolutely promised: "I will put my fear in their hearts." And this is the main difference between the old covenant of works and the new one of grace, that in that the Lord did only require the fulfilling of the condition prescribed, but in this he promiseth to effect it in them himself with whom the covenant is made. And without this spiritual efficacy, the truth is, the new covenant would be as weak and unprofitable, for the end of a covenant (the bringing of us and binding of us to God), as the old. For in what consisted the weakness and unprofitableness of the old covenant, for which God in his mercy abolished it? Was it not in this, because, by reason of sin, we were no way able to fulfil the condition thereof, "Do this, and live?" Otherwise the connection is still true, that "he that doeth these things shall live." And are we of ourselves any way more able to fulfil the condition of the new covenant? Is it not as easy for a man by his own strength to fulfil the whole law, as to repent and savingly believe the promise of the gospel? This, then, is one main difference of these two covenants,—that the Lord did in the old only require the condition; now, in the new, he will also effect it in all the federates, to whom this covenant is extended. And if the Lord should only exact the obedience required in the covenant of us, and not work and effect it also in us, the new covenant would be a show to increase our misery, and not a serious imparting and communicating of grace and mercy. If, then, this be the nature of the new testament,—as appears from the very words of it, and might abundantly be proved,—that the condition of the covenant should certainly, by free grace, be wrought and accomplished in all that are taken into covenant, then no more are in this covenant than in whom those conditions of it are effected.

But thus, as is apparent, it is not with all; for "all men have not faith,"—it is "of the elect of God:" therefore, it is not made with all, nor is the compass thereof to be extended beyond the remnant that are according to election. Yea, every blessing of the new covenant being certainly common, and to be communicated to all the covenantees, either faith is none of them, or all must have it, if the covenant itself be general. But some may say that it is true God promiseth to write his law in our hearts, and put his fear in our inward parts; but it is upon condition. Give me that condition, and I will yield the cause. Is it if they do believe? Nothing else can be imagined. That is, if they have the law written in their hearts (as every one that believes hath), then God promiseth to write his law in their hearts! Is this probable, friends? is it likely? I cannot, then, be persuaded that God hath made a covenant of grace with all, especially those who never heard a word of covenant, grace, or condition of it, much less received grace for the fulfilling of the condition; without which the whole would be altogether unprofitable and useless. The covenant is made with Adam, and he is acquainted with it, Gen. iii. 15,—renewed with Noah, and not hidden from him,—again established with Abraham, accompanied with a full and rich declaration of the chief promises of it, Gen. xii.; which is most certain not to be effected towards all, as afterwards will appear.

Yea, that first distinction between the seed of the woman and the seed of the serpent is enough to overthrow the pretended universality of the covenant of grace; for who dares affirm that God entered into a covenant of grace with the seed of the serpent?

Most apparent, then, it is that the new covenant of grace, and the promises thereof, are all of them of distinguishing mercy, restrained to the people whom God did foreknow; and so not extended universally to all. Now, the blood of Jesus Christ being the blood of this covenant, and his oblation intended only for the procurement of the good things intended and promised thereby,—for he was the surety thereof, Heb. vii. 22, and of that only,—it cannot be conceived to have respect unto all, or any but only those that are intended in this covenant.

ARG. II. If the Lord intended that he should, and [he] by his death did, procure pardon of sin and reconciliation with God for all and every one, to be actually enjoyed upon condition that they do believe, then ought this good-will and intention of God, with this purchase in their behalf by Jesus Christ, to be made known to them by the word, that they might believe; "for faith cometh by hearing, and hearing by the word of God," Rom. x. 17: for if these things be not made known and revealed to all and every one that is concerned in them, namely, to whom the Lord intends, and for whom he hath procured so great a good, then one of these things will follow;—either, first, That they may be saved without faith in, and the knowledge of, Christ (which they cannot have unless he be revealed to them), which is false, and proved so; or else, secondly, That this good-will of God, and this purchase made by Jesus Christ, is plainly in vain, and frustrate in respect of them, yea, a plain mocking of them, that will neither do them any good to help them out of misery, nor serve the justice of God to leave them inexcusable, for what blame can redound to them for not embracing and well using a benefit which they never heard of in their lives? Doth it become the wisdom of God to send Christ to die for men that they might be saved, and never cause these men to hear of any such thing; and yet to purpose and declare that unless they do hear of it and believe it, they shall never be saved? What wise man would pay a ransom for the delivery of those captives which he is sure shall never come to the knowledge of any such payment made, and so never be the better for it? Is it answerable to the goodness of God, to deal thus with his poor creatures? to hold out towards them all in pretence the most intense love imaginable, beyond all compare and illustration,—as his love in sending his Son is set forth to be,—and yet never let them know of any such thing, but in the end to damn them for not believing it? Is it answerable to the love and kindness of Christ to us, to assign unto him at his death such a resolution as this:—"I will now, by the oblation of myself, obtain for all and every one peace and reconciliation with God, redemption and everlasting salvation, eternal glory in the high heavens, even for all those poor, miserable, wretched worms, condemned caitiffs, that every hour ought to expect the sentence of condemnation; and all these shall truly and really be communicated to them if they will believe. But yet, withal, I will so order things that innumerable souls shall never hear one word of all this that I have done for them, never be persuaded to believe, nor have the object of faith that is to be believed proposed to them, whereby they might indeed possibly partake of these things?" Was this the mind and will, this the design and purpose, of our merciful high priest? God forbid. It is all one as if a prince should say and proclaim, that whereas there be a number of captives held in sore bondage in such a place, and he hath a full treasure, he is resolved to redeem them every one, so that every one of them shall come out of prison that will thank him for his good-will, and in the meantime never take care to let these poor captives know his mind and pleasure; and yet be fully assured that unless he effect it himself it will never be done. Would not this be conceived a vain and ostentatious flourish, without any good intent indeed towards the poor captives? Or as if a physician should say that he hath a medicine that will cure all diseases, and he intends to cure the diseases of all, but lets but very few know his mind, or any thing of his medicine; and yet is assured that without his relation and particular information it will be known to very few. And shall he be supposed to desire, intend, or aim at the recovery of all?

Now, it is most clear, from the Scripture and experience of all ages, both under the old dispensation of the covenant and the new, that innumerable men, whole nations, for a long season, are passed by in the declaration of this mystery. The Lord doth not procure that it shall, by any means, in the least measure be made out to all; they hear not so much as a rumour or report of any such thing. Under the Old Testament, "In Judah was God known, and his name was great in Israel; in Salem was his tabernacle, and his dwelling-place in Zion," Ps. lxxvi. 1, 2. "He showed his word unto Jacob, and his statutes and his judgments unto Israel. He hath not dealt so with any nation: and as for his judgments, they have not known them," Ps. cxlvii. 19, 20. Whence those appellations of the heathen, and imprecations also: as Jer. x. 25, "Pour out thy fury upon the heathen that know thee not, and upon the families that call not upon thy name;" of whom you have a full description, Eph. ii. 12, "Without Christ, aliens from the commonwealth of Israel, and strangers from the covenants of promise, having no hope, and without God in the world." And under the New Testament, though the church have "lengthened her cords, and strengthened her stakes," and "many nations are come up to the mountain of the LORD,"—so many as to be called "all people," "all nations," yea, the "world," the "whole world," in comparison of the small precinct of the church of the Jews,—yet now also Scripture and experience do make it clear that many are passed by, yea, millions of souls, that never hear a word of Christ, nor of reconciliation by him; of which we can give no other reason, but, "Even so, Father, for so it seemed good in thy sight," Matt. xi. 26. For the Scripture, ye have the Holy Ghost expressly forbidding the apostles to go to sundry places with the word, but sending them another way, Acts xvi. 6, 7, 9, 10; answerable to the former dispensation in some particulars, wherein "he suffered all nations to walk in their own ways," chap. xiv. 16. And for experience, not to multiply particulars, do but ask any of our brethren who have been but any time in the Indies, and they will easily resolve you in the truth thereof.

The exceptions against this argument are poor and frivolous, which we reserve for reply. In brief; how is it revealed to those thousands of the offspring of infidels, whom the Lord cuts off in their infancy, that they may not pester the world, persecute his church, nor disturb human society? how to their parents, of whom Paul affirms, that by the works of God they might be led to the knowledge of his eternal power and Godhead, but that they should know any thing of redemption or a Redeemer was utterly impossible?

CHAPTER II.

Containing three other arguments.

ARG. III. If Jesus Christ died for all men,—that is, purchased and procured for them, according to the mind and will of God, all those things which we recounted, and the Scripture setteth forth, to be the effects and fruits of his death, which may be summed up in this one phrase, "*eternal redemption*,"—then he did this, and that according to the purpose of God, either *absolutely* or upon some *condition* by them to be fulfilled. If *absolutely*, then ought all and every one, absolutely and infallibly, to be made actual partakers of that eternal redemption so purchased; for what, I pray, should hinder the enjoyment of that to any which God absolutely intended, and Christ absolutely purchased for them? If upon *condition*, then he did either procure this condition for them, or he did not? If he did procure this condition for them,—that is, that it should be bestowed on them and wrought within them,—then he did it either absolutely again, or upon a condition. If *absolutely*, then are we as we were before; for to procure any thing for another, to be conferred on him upon such a condition, and withal to procure that condition absolutely to be bestowed on him, is equivalent to the absolute procuring of the thing itself. For so we affirm, in this very business: Christ procured salvation for us, to be bestowed conditionally, if we do believe; but faith itself, *that* he hath absolutely procured, without prescribing of any condition. Whence we affirm, that the purchasing of salvation for us is equivalent to what it would have been if it had been so purchased as to have been absolutely bestowed, in respect of the event and issue. So that thus also must all be absolutely saved. But if this *condition* be procured upon *condition*, let that be assigned, and we will renew our *quære* concerning the procuring of that, whether it were absolute or conditional, and so never rest until they come to fix somewhere, or still run into a circle.

But, on the other side, is not this *condition* procured by him on whose performance all the good things purchased by him are to be actually enjoyed? Then, first, This condition must be made known to all, as Arg. ii. Secondly, All men are able of themselves to perform this condition, or they are not. If they are, then, seeing that condition is faith in the promises, as is on all sides confessed, are all men of themselves, by the power of their own free-will, able to believe; which is contrary to the Scriptures, as, by the Lord's assistance, shall be declared. If they cannot, but that this faith must be bestowed on them and wrought within them by the free grace of God, then when God gave his Son to die for them, to procure eternal redemption for them all, upon condition that they did believe, he either purposed to work faith in them all by his grace, that they might believe, or he did not? If he did, why doth not he actually perform it, seeing "he is of one mind, and who can turn him?" why do not all believe? why have not all men faith? Or doth he fail of his purpose? If he did not purpose to bestow faith on them all, or (which is all one) if he purposed not to bestow faith on all (for the will of God doth not consist in a pure negation of any thing,—what he doth not will that it should be, he wills that it should not be), then the sum of it comes to this:—That God gave Christ to die for all men, but upon this condition, that they perform that which of themselves without him they cannot perform, and purposed that, for his part, he would not accomplish it in them.

Now, if this be not extreme madness, to assign a will unto God of doing that which himself knows and orders that it shall never be done, of granting a thing upon a condition which without his help cannot be fulfilled, and which help he purposed not to grant, let all judge. Is this any thing but to delude poor creatures? Is it possible that any good at all should arise to any by such a purpose as this, such a giving of a Redeemer? Is it agreeable to the goodness of God to intend so great a good as is the redemption purchased by Christ, and to pretend that he would have it profitable for them, when he knows that they can no more fulfil the condition which he requires, that it may be by them enjoyed, than Lazarus could of himself come out of the grave? Doth it beseem the wisdom of God, to purpose that which he knows shall never be fulfilled? If a man should promise to give a thousand pounds to a blind man upon condition that he will open his eyes and see,—which he knows well enough he cannot do,—were that promise to be supposed to come from a heart-pitying of his poverty, and not rather from a mind to illude and mock at his misery? If the king should promise to pay a ransom for the captives at Algiers, upon condition that they would conquer their tyrants and come away,—which he knows full well they cannot do,—were this a kingly act? Or, as if a man should pay a price to redeem captives, but not that their chains may be taken away, without which they cannot come out of prison; or promise dead men great rewards upon condition they live again of themselves;—are not these to as much end as the obtaining of salvation for men upon condition that they do believe, without obtaining that condition for them? Were not this the assigning such a will and purpose as this to Jesus Christ:—"I will obtain eternal life to be bestowed on men, and become theirs, by the application of the benefits of my death; but upon this condition, that they do believe. But as I will not reveal my mind and will in this business, nor this condition itself, to innumerable of them, so concerning the rest I know they are no ways able of themselves,—no more than Lazarus was to rise, or a blind man is to see,—to perform the condition that I do require, and without which none of the good things intended for them can ever become theirs; neither will I procure that condition ever to be fulfilled in them. That is, I do will that that shall be done which I do not only know shall never be done, but that it cannot be done, because I will not do that without which it can never be accomplished"? Now, whether such a will and purpose as this beseem the wisdom and goodness of our Saviour, let the reader judge. In brief; an intention of doing good unto any one upon the performance of such a condition as the intender knows is absolutely above the strength of him of whom it is required,—especially if he know that it can no way be done but by his concurrence, and he is resolved not to yield that assistance which is necessary to the actual accomplishment of it,—is a vain fruitless flourish. That Christ, then, should obtain of his Father eternal redemption, and the Lord should through his Son intend it for them who shall never be made partakers of it, because they cannot perform, and God and Christ have purposed not to bestow, the condition on which alone it is to be made actually theirs, is unworthy of Christ, and unprofitable to them for whom it is obtained; which that any thing that Christ obtained for the sons of men should be unto them, is a hard saying indeed. Again; if God through Christ purpose to save all if they do believe, because he died for all, and this faith be not purchased by Christ, nor are men able of themselves to believe, how comes it to pass that any are saved?

[If it be answered], "God bestows faith on some, not on others," I reply, Is this distinguishing grace purchased for those some comparatively, in respect of those that are passed by without it? If it be, then did not Christ die equally for all, for he died that some might have faith, not others; yea, in comparison, he cannot be said to die for those other some at all, not dying that they might have faith, without which he knew that all the rest would be unprofitable and fruitless. But is it *not* purchased for them by Christ? Then have those that be saved no more to thank Christ for than those that are damned; which were strange, and contrary to Rev. i. 5, 6, "Unto him that loved us, and washed us from our sins in his own blood, and hath made us kings and priests unto God and his Father," etc. For my part, I do conceive that Christ hath obtained salvation for men, not upon condition if they *would* receive it, but so fully and perfectly that certainly they *should* receive it. He purchased *salvation*, to be bestowed on them that do believe; but withal *faith*, that they might believe. Neither can it be objected, that, according to our doctrine, God requires any thing of men that they cannot do, yea, faith to believe in Christ: for,—First, Commands do not signify what is God's intention should be done, but what is our duty to do; which may be made known to us whether we be able to perform it or not: it signifieth no intention or purpose of God. Secondly, For the promises which are proposed together with the command to believe:—*First*, they do not hold out the intent and purpose of God, that Christ should die for us if we do believe; which is absurd,—that the act should be the constituter of its own object, which must be before it, and is presupposed to be before we are desired to believe it: nor, *secondly*, the purpose of God that the death of Christ should be profitable to us if we do believe; which we before confuted: but, *thirdly*, only that faith is the way to salvation which God hath appointed; so that all that do believe shall undoubtedly be saved, these two things, faith and salvation, being inseparably linked together, as shall be declared.

ARG. IV. If all mankind be, in and by the eternal purpose of God, distinguished into two sorts and conditions, severally and distinctly described and set forth in the Scripture, and Christ be peculiarly affirmed to die for one of these sorts, and nowhere for them of the other, then did he not die for all; for of the one sort he dies for all and every one, and of the other for no one at all. But,—

First, There is such a discriminating distinguishment among men, by the eternal purpose of God, as those whom he "loves" and those whom he "hates," Rom. ix. 13; whom he "knoweth," and whom he "knoweth not:" John x. 14, "I know my sheep;" 2 Tim. ii. 19, "The Lord knoweth them that are his;" Rom. viii. 29, "Whom he did foreknow;" chap. xi. 2, "His people which he foreknew;" "I know you not," Matt. xxv. 12: so John xiii. 18, "I speak not of you all; I know whom I have chosen." Those that are appointed to life and glory, and those that are appointed to and fitted for destruction,—"elect" and "reprobate;" those that were "ordained to eternal life," and those who "before were of old ordained to condemnation:" as Eph. i. 4, "He hath chosen us in him;" Acts xiii. 48, "Ordained to eternal life;" Rom. viii. 30, "Whom he did predestinate, them he also called: and whom he called, them he also justified: and whom he justified, them he also glorified." So, on the other side, 1 Thess. v. 9, "God hath not appointed us to wrath, but to obtain salvation;" Rom. ix. 18–21, "He hath mercy on whom he will have mercy, and whom he will he hardeneth. Thou wilt say then unto me, Why doth he yet find fault? For who hath resisted his will? Nay but, O man, who art thou that repliest against God? Shall the thing formed say to him that formed it, Why hast thou made me thus? Hath not the potter power over the clay, of the same lump to make one vessel to honour, and another to dishonour?" Jude 4, "Ordained to this condemnation;" 2 Pet. ii. 12, "Made to be taken and destroyed;" "Sheep and goats," Matt. xxv. 32; John x. passim. Those on whom he hath "mercy," and those whom he "hardeneth," Rom. ix. 18. Those that are his "peculiar people" and "the children of promise," that are "not of the world," his "church;" and those that, in opposition to them, are "the world," "not prayed for," "not his people:" as Tit. ii. 14; Gal. iv. 28; John xv. 19, xvii. 9; Col. i. 24; John xi. 52; Heb. ii. 10, 12, 13. Which distinction of men is everywhere ascribed to the purpose, will, and good pleasure of God: Prov. xvi. 4, "The LORD hath made all things for himself, even the wicked for the day of evil." Matt. xi. 25, 26, "I thank thee, O Father, because thou hast hid these things from the wise and prudent, and hast revealed them unto babes. Even so, Father; for so it seemed good in thy sight." Rom. ix. 11, 12, "The children being not yet born, neither having done any good or evil, that the purpose of God according to election might stand, not of works, but of him that calleth; it was said unto her, The elder shall serve the younger." Verses 16, 17, "So then it is not of him that willeth, nor of him that runneth, but of God that showeth mercy. For the scripture saith unto Pharaoh, Even for this same purpose have I raised thee up, that I might show my power in thee, and that my name might be declared throughout all the earth." chap. viii. 28–30, "Who are the called according to his purpose. For whom he did foreknow, he also did predestinate to be conformed to the image of his Son, that he might be the first-born among many brethren. Moreover, whom he did predestinate, them he also called:

and whom he called, them he also justified: and whom he justified them he also glorified." So that the first part of the proposition is clear from the Scripture.

Now, Christ is said expressly and punctually to die for them on the one side: for his "people," Matt. i. 21; his "sheep," John x. 11, 14; his "church," Acts xx. 28, Eph. v. 25, as distinguished from the world, Rom. v. 8, 9, John xi. 51, 52; his "elect," Rom. viii. 32–34; his "children," Heb. ii. 12, 13;—as before more at large. Whence we may surely conclude that Christ died not for all and every one,—to wit, not for those he "never knew," whom he "hateth," whom he "hardeneth," on whom he "will not show mercy," who "were before of old ordained to condemnation;" in a word, for a reprobate, for the world, for which he would not pray. That which some except, that though Christ be said to die for his "sheep," for his "elect," his "chosen," yet he is not said to die for them only,—that term is nowhere expressed, is of no value; for is it not, without any forced interpretation, in common sense, and according to the usual course of speaking, to distinguish men into two such opposite conditions as elect and reprobate, sheep and goats, and then affirm that he died for his elect, [is it not] equivalent to this, he died for his elect only? Is not the sense as clearly restrained as if that restrictive term had been added? Or is that term always added in the Scripture in every indefinite assertion, which yet must of necessity be limited and restrained as if it were expressly added? as where our Saviour saith, "I am the way, the truth, and the life," John xiv. 6;—he doth not say that he *only* is so, and yet of necessity it must be so understood. As also in that, Col. i. 19, "It pleased the Father that in him should all fulness dwell;"—he doth not express the limitation "only," and yet it were no less than blasphemy to suppose a possibility of extending the affirmation to any other. So that this exception, notwithstanding this argument, is, as far as I can see, unanswerable; which also might be farther urged by a more large explication of God's purpose of election and reprobation, showing how the death of Christ was a means set apart and appointed for the saving of his elect, and not at all undergone and suffered for those which, in his eternal counsel, he did determine should perish for their sins, and so never be made partakers of the benefits thereof. But of this more must be spoken, if the Lord preserve us, and give assistance for the other part of this controversy, concerning the cause of sending Christ.

ARG. V. That is not to be asserted and affirmed which the Scripture doth not anywhere go before us in; but the Scripture nowhere saith Christ died *for all men*, much less for all and every man (between which two there is a wide difference, as shall be declared): therefore, this is not to be asserted. It is true, Christ is said to give his life "a ransom for all," but nowhere for all men. And because it is affirmed expressly in other places that he died for *many*, for his *church*, for them that *believe*, for the *children* that God gave him, for *us*, some of all sorts, though not expressly, yet clearly in terms equivalent, Rev. v. 9, 10, it must be clearly proved that where *all* is mentioned, it cannot be taken for all believers, all his elect, his whole church, all the children that God gave him, some of all sorts, before a universal affirmative can be thence concluded. And if men will but consider the particular places, and contain themselves until they have done what is required, we shall be at quiet, I am persuaded, in this business.

CHAPTER III.

Containing two other arguments from the person Christ sustained in this business.

ARG. VI. For whom Christ died, he died as a *sponsor*, in their stead, as is apparent, Rom. v. 6–8, "For when we were yet without strength, in due time Christ died for the ungodly. For scarcely for a righteous man will one die: yet peradventure for a good man some would even dare to die. But God commendeth his love toward us, in that, while we were yet sinners, Christ died for us." Gal. iii. 13, "He was made a curse for us." 2 Cor. v. 21, "He hath made him to be sin for us." All which places do plainly signify and hold out a change or commutation of persons, one being accepted in the room of the other. Now, if he died as the sponsor or surety of them for whom he died, in their stead, then these two things at least will follow:—First, That he freed them from that anger, and wrath, and guilt of death, which he underwent for them, that they should in and for him be all reconciled, and be freed from the bondage wherein they are by reason of death; for no other reason in the world can be assigned why Christ should undergo any thing in another's stead, but that that other might be freed from undergoing that which he underwent for him. And all justice requires that so it should be; which also is expressly intimated, when our Saviour is said to be ἔγγυος, "a surety of a better testament," Heb. vii. 22; that is, by being our priest, undergoing the "chastisement of our peace," and the burden of our "iniquities," Isa. liii. 5, 6. He was "made sin for us, that we might be made the righteousness of God in him," 2 Cor. v. 21. But now all are not freed from wrath and the guilt of death, and actually reconciled to God,—which is to be justified through an imputation of righteousness, and a non-imputation of iniquities;—for until men come to Christ "the wrath of God abideth on them," John iii. 36; which argueth and intimateth a non-removal of wrath, by reason of not believing. He doth not say, it *comes* on them, as though by Christ's death they were freed from being under a state and condition of wrath, which we are all in by nature, Eph. ii. 3; but μένει, "it remaineth," or abideth: it was never removed. And to them the gospel is a savour of death unto death,—bringing a new death and a sore condemnation, by its being despised, unto that death the guilt whereof they before lay under. Some have, indeed, affirmed that all and every one are redeemed, restored, justified, and made righteous in Christ, and by his death; but truly this is so wretched, I will not say perverting of the Scriptures, which give no colour to any such assertion, but so direct an opposition to them, as I judge it fruitless, and lost labour, to go about to remove such exceptions (More, p. 45). Secondly, It follows that Christ made satisfaction for the sins of all and every man, if he died for them; for the reason why he underwent death for us as a surety was, to make satisfaction to God's justice for our sins, so to redeem us to himself, neither can any other be assigned. But Christ hath not satisfied the justice of God for all the sins of all and every man: which may be made evident by divers reasons; for,—

First, For whose sins he made satisfaction to the justice of God, for their sins justice is satisfied, or else his satisfaction was rejected as insufficient, for no other reason can be assigned of such a fruitless attempt; which to aver is blasphemy in the highest degree. But now the justice of God is not satisfied for all the sins of all and every man; which also is no less apparent than the former: for they that must undergo eternal punishment themselves for their sins, that the justice of God may be satisfied for their sins, the justice of God was not satisfied without their own punishment, by the punishment of Christ; for they are not healed by his stripes. But that innumerable souls shall to eternity undergo the punishment due to their own sins, I hope needs, with Christians, no proving. Now, how can the justice of God require satisfaction of them for their sins, if it were before satisfied for them in Christ? To be satisfied, and to require satisfaction that it may be satisfied, are contradictory, and cannot be affirmed of the same in respect of the same; but that the Lord will require of some "the uttermost farthing" is most clear, Matt. v. 26.

Secondly, Christ, by undergoing death for us, as our surety, satisfied for no more than he intended so to do. So great a thing as satisfaction for the sins of men could not accidentally happen besides his intention, will, and purpose; especially considering that his intention and good-will, sanctifying himself to be an oblation, was of absolute necessity to make his death an acceptable offering. But now Christ did not intend to satisfy for the sins of all and every man for innumerable souls were in hell, under the punishment and weight of their own sins; from whence there is no redemption before, nor actually then when our Saviour made himself an oblation for sin. Now, shall we suppose that Christ would make himself an offering for their sins whom he knew to be past recovery, and that it was utterly impossible that ever they should have any fruit or benefit by his offering? Shall we think that the blood of the covenant was cast away upon them for whom our Saviour intended no good at all? To intend good to them he could not, without a direct opposition to the eternal decree of his Father, and therein of his own eternal Deity. Did God send his Son, did Christ come to die, for Cain and Pharaoh, damned so many ages before his suffering? "Credat Apella?" The exception, that Christ died for them, and his death would have been available to them if they had believed and fulfilled the condition required, is, in my judgment, of no force at all; for,—*First,* For the most part they never heard of any such condition. *Secondly,* Christ at his death knew full well that they had not fulfilled the *condition,* and were actually cut off from any possibility ever so to do, so that any intention to do them good by his death must needs be vain and frustrate; which must not be assigned to the Son of God. *Thirdly,* This redemption, *conditionate, if they believe,* we shall reject anon.

Neither is that other exception, that Christ might as well satisfy for them that were eternally damned at the time of his suffering (for whom it could not be useful), as for them that were then actually saved (for whom it was not needful), of any more value. For,—*First,* Those that were saved were saved upon this ground, that Christ should certainly suffer for them in due time; which suffering of his was as effectual in the purpose and promise as in the execution and accomplishment. It was in the mind of God accounted for them as accomplished, the compact and covenant with Christ about it being surely ratified upon mutual, unchangeable promises (according to our conception); and so our Saviour was to perform it, and so it was needful for them that were actually saved: but for those that were actually damned, there was no such inducement to it, or ground for it, or issue to be expected out of it. *Secondly,* A simile will clear the whole:—If a man should send word to a place where captives were in prison, that he would pay the price and ransom that was due for their delivery, and to desire the prisoners to come forth, for he that detains them accepts of his word and engagement; when he comes to make payment, according to his promise, if he find some to have gone forth according as was proposed, and others continued obstinate in their dungeon, some hearing of what he had done, others not, and that according to his own appointment, and were now long since dead; doth he, in the payment of his promised ransom, intend it for them that died stubbornly and obstinately in the prison, or only for them who went forth? Doubtless, only for these last. No more can the passion of Christ be supposed to be a price paid for them that died in the prison of sin and corruption before the payment of his ransom; though it might full well be for them that were delivered by virtue of his engagement for the payment of such a ransom. *Thirdly*, If Christ died in the stead of all men, and made satisfaction for their sins, then he did it for all their sins, or only for some of their sins. If for some only, who then can be saved? If for all, why then are all not saved? They say it is because of their unbelief; they will not believe, and therefore are not saved. That unbelief, is it a sin, or is it not? If it be not, how can it be a cause of damnation? If it be, Christ died for it, or he did not. If he did not, then he died not for all the sins of all men. If he did, why is this an obstacle to their salvation? Is there any new shift to be invented for this? or must we be contented with the old, namely, because they do not believe? that is, Christ did not die for their unbelief, or rather, did not by his death remove their unbelief, because they would not believe, or because they would not themselves remove their unbelief; or he died for their unbelief conditionally, that they were not unbelievers. These do not seem to me to be sober assertions.

Arg. VII. For whom Christ died, for them he is a *mediator:* which is apparent; for the oblation or offering of Christ, which he made of himself unto God, in the shedding of his blood, was one of the chiefest acts of his mediation. But he is not a mediator for all and every one; which also is no less evident, because as mediator he is the priest for them for whom he is a mediator. Now, to a priest it belongs, as was declared before, to sacrifice and intercede, to procure good things, and to apply them to those for whom they are procured; as is evident, Heb. ix., and was proved before at large: which, confessedly, Christ doth not for all. Yea, that Christ is not a mediator for every one needs no proof. Experience sufficiently evinceth it, besides innumerable places of Scripture. It is, I confess, replied by some, that Christ is a mediator for some in respect of some acts, and not in respect of others; but truly, this, if I am able to judge, is a dishonest subterfuge, that hath no ground in Scripture, and would make our Saviour a half mediator in respect of some, which is an unsavoury expression. But this argument was vindicated before.

CHAPTER IV.

Of sanctification, and of the cause of faith, and the procurement thereof by the death of Christ.

Arg. VIII. Another argument may be taken from the *effect* and *fruit* of the death of Christ unto *sanctification*, which we thus propose:—If the blood of Jesus Christ doth *wash, purge, cleanse,* and *sanctify* them for whom it was shed, or for whom he was a sacrifice, then certainly he died, shed his blood, or was a sacrifice, only for them that in the event are *washed, purged, cleansed,* and *sanctified;*—which that all or every one is not is most apparent, faith being the first principle of the heart's purification, Acts xv. 9, and "all men have not faith," 2 Thess. iii. 2; it is "of the elect of God," Tit. i. 1. The consequence, I conceive, is undeniable, and not to be avoided with any distinctions. But now we shall make it evident that the blood of Christ is effectual for all those ends of washing, purging, and sanctifying, which we before recounted. And this we shall do;—first, from the *types* of it; and, secondly, by plain *expressions* concerning the thing itself:—

First, For the *type*, that which we shall now consider is the sacrifice of expiation, which the apostle so expressly compareth with the sacrifice and oblation of Christ. Of this he affirmeth, Heb. ix. 13, that it legally sanctified them for whom it was a sacrifice. "For," saith he, "the blood of bulls and goats, and the ashes of an heifer sprinkling the unclean, sanctifieth to the purifying of the flesh." Now, that which was done carnally and legally in the type must be spiritually effected in the antitype,—the sacrifice of Christ, typified by that bloody sacrifice of beasts. This the apostle asserteth in the verse following. "How much more," saith he, "shall the blood of Christ, who through the eternal Spirit offered himself without spot to God, purge your conscience from dead works to serve the living God?" If I know any thing, that answer of Arminius and some others to this,—namely, that the sacrifice did sanctify, not as offered but as sprinkled, and the blood of Christ, not in respect of the oblation, but of its application, answereth it,—is weak and unsatisfactory; for it only asserts a division between the *oblation* and *application* of the blood of Christ, which, though we allow to be distinguished, yet such a division we are now disproving. And to weaken our argument, the same division which we disprove is proposed; which, if any, is an easy, facile way of answering. We grant that the blood of Christ sanctifieth in respect of the application of the good things procured by it, but withal prove that it is so applied to all for whom it was an oblation; and that because it is said to sanctify and purge, and must answer the type, which did sanctify to the purifying of the flesh.

Secondly, It is expressly, in divers places, *affirmed* of the blood-shedding and death of our Saviour, that it doth effect these things, and that it was intended for that purpose. Many places for the clearing of this were before recounted. I shall now repeat so many of them as shall be sufficient to give strength to the argument in hand, omitting those which before were produced, only desiring that all those places which point out the end of the death of Christ may be considered as of force to establish the truth of this argument.

Rom. vi. 5, 6, "For if we have been planted together in the likeness of his death, we shall be also in the likeness of his resurrection: knowing this, that our old man is crucified with him, that the body of sin might be destroyed, that henceforth we should not serve sin." The words of the latter verse yield a reason of the former assertion in verse 5,—namely, that a participation in the death of Christ shall certainly be accompanied with conformity to him in his resurrection; that is, both to life spiritual, as also to eternal: "Because our old man is crucified with him, that the body of sin might be destroyed." That is, our sinful corruption and depravation of nature are, by his death and crucifying, effectually and meritoriously slain, and disabled from such a rule and dominion over us as that we should be servants any longer unto them; which is apparently the sense of the place, seeing it is laid as a foundation to press forward unto all degrees of sanctification and freedom from the power of sin.

The same apostle also tells us, 2 Cor. i. 20, that "all the promises of God are in him yea, and in him Amen, unto the glory of God by us." "Yea, and Amen,"—confirmed, ratified, unchangeably established, and irrevocably made over to us. Now, this was done "in him,"—that is, in his death and blood-shedding for the confirmation of the testament, whereof these promises are the conveyance of the legacies to us,—confirmed by the "death of him, the testator," Heb. ix. 16: for he was "the surety of this better testament," chap. vii. 22; which testament or "covenant he confirmed with many," by his being "cut off" for them, Dan. ix. 26, 27. Now, what are the promises that are thus confirmed unto us, and established by the blood of Christ? The sum of them you have, Jer. xxxi. 33, 34; whence they are repeated by the apostle, Heb. viii. 10–12, to set out the nature of that covenant which was ratified in the blood of Jesus, in which you have a summary description of all that free grace towards us, both in sanctification, verses 10, 11, and in justification, verse 12. Amongst these promises, also, is that most famous one of circumcising our hearts, and of giving new hearts and spirits unto us: as Deut. xxx. 6; Ezek. xxxvi. 26. So that our whole sanctification, holiness, with justification and reconciliation unto God, is procured by, and established unto us with, unchangeable promises in the death and blood-shedding of Christ, "the heavenly or spiritual things being purified with that sacrifice of his, Heb. ix. 23; "For we have redemption through his blood, even the forgiveness of sins," Col. i. 14; "By death he destroyed him that had the power of death, that is, the devil," that he might "deliver them who, through fear of death, were all their lifetime subject to bondage," Heb. ii. 14, 15.

Do but take notice of those two most clear places, Tit. ii. 14, Eph.

v. 25, 26: in both which our cleansing and sanctification is assigned to be the end and intendment of Christ the worker; and therefore the certain effect of his death and oblation, which was the work, as was before proved. And I shall add but one place more to prove that which I am sorry that I need produce any one to do,—to wit, that the blood of Christ purgeth us from all our sin, and it is, 1 Cor. i. 30, "Who of God is made unto us wisdom, and righteousness, and sanctification, and redemption." Of which, because it is clear enough, I need not spend time to prove that he was thus made unto us of God, inasmuch as he set him forth to be "a propitiation through faith in his blood;" as Rom. iii. 25. So that our sanctification, with all other effects of free grace, are the immediate procurement of the death of Christ. And of the things that have been spoken this is the sum:—Sanctification and holiness is the certain fruit and effect of the death of Christ in all them for whom he died; but all and every one are not partakers of this sanctification, this purging, cleansing, and working of holiness: therefore, Christ died not for all and every one, "quod erat demonstrandum."

It is altogether in vain to except, as some do, that the death of Christ is not the sole cause of these things, for they are not actually wrought in any without the intervention of the Spirit's working in them, and faith apprehending the death of Christ: for,—First, Though many total causes of the same kind cannot concur to the producing of the same effect, yet several causes of several kinds may concur to one effect, and be the sole causes in that kind wherein they are causes. The Spirit of God is the cause of sanctification and holiness; but what kind of cause, I pray? Even such an one as is immediately and really efficient of the effect. Faith is the cause of pardon of sin; but what cause? in what kind? Why, merely as an instrument, apprehending the righteousness of Christ. Now, do these causes, whereof one is efficient, the other instrumental, both natural and real, hinder that the blood of Christ may not only concur, but also be the sole cause, moral and meritorious, of these things? Doubtless, they do not. Nay, they do suppose it so to be, or else they would in this work be neither instrumental nor efficient, that being the sole foundation of the Spirit's operation and efficience, and the sole cause of faith's being and existence. A man is detained captive by his enemy, and one goes to him that detains him, and pays a ransom for his delivery; who thereupon grants a warrant to the keepers of the prison that they shall knock off his shackles, take away his rags, let him have new clothes, according to the agreement, saying, "Deliver him, for I have found a ransom." Because the jailer knocks off his shackles, and the warrant of the judge is brought for his discharge, shall he or we say that the price and ransom which was paid was not the cause, yea, the sole cause of his delivery?

Considering that none of these latter had been, had not the ransom been paid, they are no less the effect of that ransom than his own delivery. In our delivery from the bondage of sin, it is true, there are other things, in other kinds, which do concur besides the death of Christ, as the operation of the Spirit and the grace of God; but these being in one kind, and that in another, these also being no less the fruit and effect of the death of Christ than our deliverance wrought by them, it is most apparent that that is the only main cause of the whole. Secondly, To take off utterly this exception, with all of the like kind, we affirm that faith itself is a proper immediate fruit and procurement of the death of Christ in all them for whom he died; which (because, if it be true, it utterly overthrows the general ransom, or universal redemption; and if it be not true, I will very willingly lay down this whole controversy, and be very indifferent which way it be determined, for go it which way it will, free-will must be established), I will prove apart by itself in the next argument.

ARG. IX. Before I come to press the argument intended, I must premise some few things; as,—

1. Whatever is freely bestowed upon us, in and through Christ, that is all wholly the procurement and merit of the death of Christ. Nothing is bestowed through him on those that are his which he hath not purchased; the price whereby he made his purchase being his own blood, 1 Pet. i. 18, 19; for the covenant between his Father and him, of making out all spiritual blessings to them that were given unto him, was expressly founded on this condition, "That he should make his soul an offering for sin," Isa. liii. 10.

2. That confessedly, on all sides, faith is, in men of understanding, of such absolute indispensable necessity unto salvation,—there being no sacrifice to be admitted for the want of it under the new covenant,—that, whatever God hath done in his love, sending his Son, and whatever Christ hath done or doth, in his oblation and intercession for all or some, without this in us, is, in regard of the event, of no value, worth, or profit unto us, but serveth only to increase and aggravate condemnation; for, whatsoever is accomplished besides, that is most certainly true, "He that believeth not shall be damned," Mark xvi. 16. (So that if there is in ourselves a power of believing, and the act of it do proceed from that power, and is our own also, then certainly and undeniably it is in our power to make the love of God and death of Christ effectual towards us or not, and that by believing we actually do the one by an act of our own; which is so evident that the most ingenious and perspicacious of our adversaries have in terms confessed it, as I have declared elsewhere).[1] Such being, then, the absolute necessity of faith, it seems to me that the cause of that must needs be the prime and principal cause of salva-

[1] Display of Arminianism.

tion, as being the cause of that without which the whole would not be, and by which the whole is, and is effectual.

3. I shall give those that to us in this are contrary-minded their choice and option, so that they will answer directly, categorically, and without uncouth, insignificant, cloudy distinctions, whether our Saviour, by his death and intercession (which we proved to be conjoined), did merit or procure faith for us, or no? or, which is all one, whether faith be a fruit and effect of the death of Christ, or no? And according to their answer I will proceed.

First, If they answer affirmatively, that it is, or that Christ did procure it by his death (provided always that they do not wilfully equivocate, and when I speak of faith as it is a grace in a particular person, taking it subjectively, they understand faith as it is the doctrine of faith, or the way of salvation declared in the gospel, taking it objectively, which is another thing, and beside the present question; although, by the way, I must tell them that we deny the granting of that new way of salvation, in bringing life and immortality to light by the gospel in Christ, to be procured for us by Christ, himself being the chiefest part of this way, yea, the way itself: and that he should himself be procured by his own death and oblation is a very strange, contradictory assertion, beseeming them who have used it (More, p. 35.) It is true, indeed, a full and plenary carrying of his elect to life and glory by that way we ascribe to him, and maintain it against all; but the granting of that way was of the same free grace and unprocured love which was also the cause of granting himself unto us, Gen. iii. 15.);—if, I say, they answer thus affirmatively, then I demand whether Christ procured faith for all for whom he died absolutely, or upon some condition on their part to be fulfilled? If *absolutely*, then surely, if he died for all, they must all absolutely believe; for that which is absolutely procured for any is absolutely his, no doubt. He that hath absolutely procured an inheritance, by what means soever, who can hinder, that it should not be his? But this is contrary to that of the apostle, "All men have not faith," 2 Thess. iii. 2; and, "Faith is of the elect of God," Tit. i. 1. If they say that he procured it for them, that is, to be bestowed on them *conditionally*, I desire that they would answer *bona fide*, and roundly, in terms without equivocation or blind distinctions, assign that condition, that we may know what it is, seeing it is a thing of so infinite concernment to all our souls. Let me know this condition which ye will maintain, and *en herbam amici!*[1] the cause is yours. Is it, as some say, if they do not resist the grace of God? Now, what is it not to resist the grace of God? is it not to obey it? And what is it to obey the grace of God? is it not to believe? So the condition of faith is faith itself. *Christ procured that they should believe, upon condition that they do believe!* Are these things so? But they

[1] "I own myself conquered," Facciolati.—ED.

can assign a condition, on our part required, of faith, that is not faith itself. Can they do it? Let us hear it, then, and we will renew our inquiry concerning that condition, whether it be procured by Christ or no. If not, then is the cause of faith still resolved into ourselves; Christ is not the author and finisher of it. If it be, then are we just where we were before, and must follow with our queries whether that condition was procured absolutely or upon condition. *Depinge ubi sistam.*

But, secondly, if they will answer negatively, as, agreeably to their own principles, they ought to do, and deny that faith is procured by the death of Christ, then,—

1. They must maintain that it is an act of our own wills, so our own as not to be wrought in us by grace; and that it is wholly situated in our power to perform that spiritual act, nothing being bestowed upon us by free grace, in and through Christ (as was before declared), but what by him, in his death and oblation, was procured: which is contrary,—(1.) To express Scripture in exceeding many places, which I shall not recount: (2.) To the very nature of the being of the new covenant, which doth not prescribe and require the condition of it, but effectually work it in all the covenantees, Jer. xxxi. 33, 34; Ezek. xxxvi. 26; Heb. viii. 10, 11: (3.) To the advancement of the free grace of God, in setting up the power of free-will, in the state of corrupted nature, to the slighting and undervaluing thereof. (4.) To the received doctrine of our natural depravedness and disability to any thing that is good; yea, by evident unstrained consequence, overthrowing that fundamental article of original sin: yea, (5.) To right reason, which will never grant that the natural faculty is able of itself, without some spiritual elevation, to produce an act purely spiritual; as 1 Cor. ii. 14.

2. They must resolve almost the sole cause of our salvation into ourselves ultimately, it being in our own power to make all that God and Christ do unto that end effectual, or to frustrate their utmost endeavours for that purpose: for all that is done, whether in the Father's loving us and sending his Son to die for us, or in the Son's offering himself for an oblation in our stead, or for us (in our behalf), is confessedly, as before, of no value nor worth, in respect of any profitable issue, unless we believe; which that we shall do, Christ hath not effected nor procured by his death, neither can the Lord so work it in us but that the sole casting voice (if I may so say), whether we will believe or no, is left to ourselves. Now, whether this be not to assign unto ourselves the cause of our own happiness, and to make us the chief builders of our own glory, let all judge.

These things being thus premised, I shall briefly prove that which is denied, namely, that faith is procured for us by the death of Christ; and so, consequently, he died not for all and every one, for "all men have not faith:" and this we may do by these following reasons:—

1. The death of Jesus Christ purchased holiness and sanctification for us, as was at large proved, Arg. viii.; but faith, as it is a grace of the Spirit inherent in us, is formally a part of our sanctification and holiness: therefore he procured faith for us. The assumption is most certain, and not denied; the proposition was sufficiently confirmed in the foregoing argument; and I see not what may be excepted against the truth of the whole. If any shall except, and say that Christ might procure for us some part of holiness (for we speak of parts, and not of degrees and measure), but not all, as the sanctification of hope, love, meekness, and the like, I ask,—first, What warrant have we for any such distinction between the graces of the Spirit, that some of them should be of the purchasing of Christ, others of our own store? secondly, Whether we are more prone of ourselves to believe, and more able, than to love and hope? and where may we have a ground for that?

2. All the fruits of election are purchased for us by Jesus Christ; for "we are chosen in him," Eph. i. 4, as the only cause and fountain of all those good things which the Lord chooseth us to, for the praise of his glorious grace, that in all things he might have the pre-eminence. I hope I need not be solicitous about the proving of this, that the Lord Jesus is the only way and means by and for whom the Lord will certainly and actually collate upon his elect all the fruits and effects or intendments of that love whereby he chose them. But now faith is a fruit, a principal fruit, of our election; for saith the apostle, "We are chosen in him before the foundation of the world, that we should be holy," Eph. i. 4,—of which holiness, faith, purifying the heart, is a principal share. "Moreover, whom he did predestinate, them he also called," Rom. viii. 30; that is, with that calling which is according to his purpose, effectually working faith in them by the mighty operation of his Spirit, "according to the exceeding greatness of his power," Eph. i. 19. And so they "believe" (God making them differ from others, 1 Cor. iv. 7, in the enjoyment of the means) "who are ordained to eternal life," Acts xiii. 48. Their being ordained to eternal life was the fountain from whence their faith did flow; and so "the election hath obtained, and the rest were blinded," Rom. xi. 7.

3. All the blessings of the new covenant are procured and purchased by him in whom the promises thereof are ratified, and to whom they are made; for all the good things thereof are contained in and exhibited by those promises, through the working of the Spirit of God. Now, concerning the promises of the covenant, and their being confirmed in Christ, and made unto his, as Gal. iii. 16, with what is to be understood in those expressions, was before declared. Therefore, all the good things of the covenant are the effects, fruits, and purchase of the death of Christ, he and all things for

him being the substance and whole of it. Farther; that faith is of the good things of the new covenant is apparent from the description thereof, Jer. xxxi. 33, 34; Heb. viii. 10–12; Ezek. xxxvi. 25–27, with divers other places, as might clearly be manifested if we affected copiousness in *causa facili*.

4. That without which it is utterly impossible that we should be saved must of necessity be procured by him by whom we are fully and effectually saved. Let them that can, declare how he can be said to procure salvation fully and effectually for us, and not be the author and purchaser of that (for he is the author of our salvation by the way of purchase) without which it is utterly impossible we should attain salvation. Now, without faith it is utterly impossible that ever any should attain salvation, Heb. xi. 6, Mark xvi. 16; but Jesus Christ, according to his name, doth perfectly save us, Matt. i. 21, procuring for us " eternal redemption," Heb. ix. 12, being " able to save to the uttermost them that come unto God by him," chap. vii. 25: and therefore must faith also be within the compass of those things that are procured by him.

5. The Scripture is clear, in express terms, and such as are so equivalent that they are not liable to any evasion; as Phil. i. 29, " It is given unto us, ὑπὲρ Χριστοῦ, on the behalf of Christ, for Christ's sake, to believe on him." Faith, or belief, is the gift, and Christ the procurer of it: " God hath blessed us with all spiritual blessings in him in heavenly places," Eph. i. 3. If faith be a spiritual blessing, it is bestowed on us " in him," and so also for his sake; if it be not, it is not worth contending about in this sense and way: so that, let others look which way they will, I desire to look unto Jesus as the " author and finisher of our faith," Heb. xii. 2. Divers other reasons, arguments, and places of Scripture might be added for the confirmation of this truth; but I hope I have said enough, and do not desire to say all. The sum of the whole reason may be reduced to this head,—namely, if the fruit and effect procured and wrought by the death of Christ absolutely, not depending on any condition in man to be fulfilled, be not common to all, then did not Christ die for all; but the supposal is true, as is evident in the grace of faith, which being procured by the death of Christ, to be absolutely bestowed on them for whom he died, is not common to all: therefore, our Saviour did not die for all.

ARG. X. We argue from the type to the antitype, or the thing signified by it; which will evidently restrain the oblation of Christ to God's elect. The people of Israel were certainly, in all remarkable things that happened unto them, typical of the church of God; as the apostle at large [declares], 1 Cor. x. 11. Especially, their institutions and ordinances were all representative of the spiritual things of the gospel; their priests, altar, sacrifices, were but all shadows of the good things to come in Jesus Christ; their Canaan was a type of heaven, Heb. iv. 3, 9; as also Jerusalem or Sion, Gal. iv. 26, Heb. xii. 22. The whole people itself was a type of God's church, his elect, his chosen and called people: whence as they were called a "holy people, a royal priesthood;" so also, in allusion to them, are believers, 1 Pet. ii. 5, 9. Yea, God's people are in innumerable places called his "Israel," as it is farther expounded, Heb. viii. 8. A true Israelite is as much as a true believer, John i. 47; and he is a Jew who is so in the hidden man of the heart. I hope it need not be proved that that people, as delivered from bondage, preserved, taken nigh unto God, brought into Canaan, was typical of God's spiritual church, of elect believers. Whence we thus argue:—Those only are really and spiritually redeemed by Jesus Christ who were designed, signified, typified by the people of Israel in their carnal, typical redemption (for no reason in the world can be rendered why some should be typed out in the same condition, partakers of the same good, and not others); but by the people of the Jews, in their deliverance from Egypt, bringing into Canaan, with all their ordinances and institutions, only the elect, the church of God, was typed out, as was before proved. And, in truth, it is the most senseless thing in the world, to imagine that the Jews were under a type to all the whole world, or indeed to any but God's chosen ones, as is proved at large, Heb. ix. x. Were the Jews and their ordinances types to the seven nations whom they destroyed and supplanted in Canaan? were they so to Egyptians, infidels, and haters of God and his Christ? We conclude, then, assuredly, from that just proportion that ought to be observed between the types and the things typified, that only the elect of God, his church and chosen ones, are redeemed by Jesus Christ.

CHAPTER V.

Being a continuance of arguments from the nature and description of the thing in hand; and first, of redemption.

ARG. XI. That doctrine which will not by any means suit with nor be made conformable to the thing signified by it, and the expression, literal and deductive, whereby in Scripture it is held out unto us, but implies evident contradictions unto them, cannot possibly be sound and sincere, as is the milk of the word. But now such is this persuasion of universal redemption; it can never be suited nor fitted to the thing itself, or redemption, nor to those expressions whereby in the Scripture it is held out unto us. Universal redemption, and yet many to die in captivity, is a contradiction irreconcilable in itself.

To manifest this, let us consider some of the chiefest words and phrases whereby the matter concerning which we treat is delivered in the Scripture, such as are, *redemption, reconciliation, satisfaction, merit, dying for us,* bearing our sins, suretiship,—his being God, a common person, a Jesus, saving to the utmost, a sacrifice putting away sin, and the like; to which we may add the importance of some prepositions and other words used in the original about this business: and doubt not but we shall easily find that the general ransom, or rather universal redemption, will hardly suit to any of them; but it is too long for the bed, and must be cropped at the head or heels.

Begin we with the word REDEMPTION itself, which we will consider, name and thing. Redemption, which in the Scripture is λύτρωσις sometimes, but most frequently ἀπολύτρωσις, is the delivery of any one from captivity and misery by the intervention λύτρου, of a price or ransom. That this ransom, or price of our deliverance, was the blood of Christ is evident; he calls it λύτρον, Matt. xx. 28; and [it is called] ἀντίλυτρον, 1 Tim. ii. 6,—that is, the price of such a redemption, that which was received as a valuable consideration for our dismission. Now, that which is aimed at in the payment of this price is, the deliverance of those from the evil wherewith they were oppressed for whom the price is paid; it being in this spiritual redemption as it is in corporal and civil, only with the alteration of some circumstances, as the nature of the thing enforceth. This the Holy Spirit manifesteth by comparing the "blood of Christ" in this work of redemption with "silver and gold," and such other things as are the intervening ransom in civil redemption, 1 Pet. i. 18, 19. The evil wherewith we were oppressed was the punishment which we had deserved;—that is, the satisfaction required when the debt is sin; which also we are, by the payment of this price, delivered from; so Gal. iii. 13: for we are "justified freely by his grace, through the redemption that is in Christ Jesus," Rom. iii. 24; "in whom we have redemption through his blood, the forgiveness of sins," Eph. i. 7; Col. i. 14. Free justification from the guilt, and pardon of sin, in the deliverance from the punishment due unto it, is the effect of the redemption procured by the payment of the price we before mentioned: as if a man should have his friend in bondage, and he should go and lay out his estate to pay the price of his freedom that is set upon his head by him that detains him, and so set him at liberty. Only, as was before intimated, this spiritual redemption hath some supereminent things in it, that are not to be found in other deliverances; as,—

First, He that receives the ransom doth also give it. Christ is a propitiation to appease and atone the Lord, but the Lord himself set him forth so to be, Rom. iii. 24, 25; whence he himself is often said to redeem us. His love is the cause of the price in respect of its procurement, and his justice accepts of the price in respect of its merit; for Christ "came down from heaven to do the will of him that sent him," John vi. 38; Heb. x. 9, 10. It is otherwise in the redemption amongst men, where he that receives the ransom hath no hand in the providing of it.

Secondly, The captive or prisoner is not so much freed from his power who detains him as brought into his favour. When a captive amongst men is redeemed, by the payment of a ransom, he is instantly to be set free from the power and authority of him that did detain him; but in this spiritual redemption, upon the payment of the ransom for us, which is the blood of Jesus, we are not removed from God, but are "brought nigh" unto him, Eph. ii. 13,—not delivered from his power, but restored to his favour,—our misery being a punishment by the way of banishment as well as thraldom.

Thirdly, As the judge was to be satisfied, so the jailer was to be conquered; God, the judge, giving him leave to fight for his dominion, which was wrongfully usurped, though that whereby he had it was by the Lord justly inflicted, and his thraldom by us rightly deserved, Heb. ii. 14; Col. ii. 15. And he lost his power, as strong as he was, for striving to grasp more than he could hold; for the foundation of his kingdom being sin, assaulting Christ who did no sin, he lost his power over them that Christ came to redeem, having no part in him. So was the strong man bound, and his house spoiled.

In these and some few other circumstances is our spiritual redemption diversified from civil; but for the main it answers the word in the propriety thereof, according to the use that it hath amongst men. Now, there is a twofold way whereby this is in the Scripture expressed: for sometimes our Saviour is said to die for our redemption, and sometimes for the redemption of our transgressions; both tending to the same purpose,—yea, both expressions, as I conceive, signify the same thing. Of the latter you have an example, Heb. ix. 15. He died εἰς ἀπολύτρωσιν παραβάσεων· which, say some, is a metonymy, transgressions being put for transgressors; others, that it is a proper expression for the paying of a price whereby we may be delivered from the evil of our transgressions. The other expression you have, Eph. i. 7, and in divers other places, where the words λύτρον and ἀπολύτρωσις do concur; as also Matt. xx. 28, and Mark x. 45. Now, these words, especially that of ἀντίλυτρον, 1 Tim. ii. 6, do always denote, by the not-to-be-wrested, genuine signification of them, the payment of a price, or an equal compensation, in lieu of something to be done or grant made by him to whom that price is paid. Having given these few notions concerning redemption in general, let us now see how applicable it is unto general redemption.

Redemption is the freeing of a man from misery by the intervention of a ransom, as appeareth. Now, when a ransom is paid for the liberty of a prisoner, is it not all the justice in the world that he should have and enjoy the liberty so purchased for him by a valuable consideration? If I should pay a thousand pounds for a man's deliverance from bondage to him that detains him, who hath power to set him free, and is contented with the price I give, were it not injurious to me and the poor prisoner that his deliverance be not accomplished? Can it possibly be conceived that there should be a redemption of men, and those men not redeemed? that a price should be paid, and the purchase not consummated? Yet all this must be made true, and innumerable other absurdities, if universal redemption be asserted. A price is paid for all, yet few delivered; the redemption of all consummated, yet few of them redeemed; the judge satisfied, the jailer conquered, and yet the prisoners inthralled! Doubtless, "*universal*" and "*redemption*," where the greatest part of men perish, are as irreconcilable as "*Roman*" and "*Catholic*." If there be a universal redemption of all, then all men are redeemed. If they are redeemed, then are they delivered from all misery, virtually or actually, whereunto they were inthralled, and that by the intervention of a ransom. Why, then, are not all saved? In a word, the redemption wrought by Christ being the full deliverance of the persons redeemed from all misery, wherein they were inwrapped, by the price of his blood, it cannot possibly be conceived to be universal unless all be saved: so that the opinion of the Universalists is unsuitable to redemption.

CHAPTER VI.

Of the nature of reconciliation, and the argument taken from thence.

ARG. XII. Another thing ascribed to the death of Christ, and, by the consent of all, extending itself unto all for whom he died, is RECONCILIATION. This in the Scripture is clearly proposed under a double notion; first, of God to us; secondly, of us to God;—both usually ascribed to the death and blood-shedding of Jesus Christ: for those who were "enemies he reconciled in the body of his flesh through death," Col. i. 21, 22. And, doubtless, these things do exactly answer one another. All those to whom he hath reconciled God, he doth also reconcile unto God: for unless both be effected, it cannot be said to be a perfect reconciliation; for how can it be, if peace be made only on the one side? Yea, it is utterly impossible that a division of these two can be rationally apprehended: for if God be reconciled, not man, why doth not he reconcile him, seeing it is confessedly in his power; and if man should be reconciled, not God, how can he be ready to receive all that come unto him? Now, that God and all and every one in the world are actually reconciled, and made at peace in Jesus Christ, I hope will not be affirmed. But to clear this, we must a little consider the nature of *reconciliation* as it is proposed to us in the gospel; unto which, also, some light may be given from the nature of the thing itself, and the use of the word in civil things.

Reconciliation is the renewing of friendship between parties before at variance, both parties being properly said to be reconciled, even both he that offendeth and he that was offended. God and man were set at distance, at enmity and variance, by sin. Man was the party offending, God offended, and the alienation was mutual, on either side;—but yet with this difference, that man was alienated in respect of affections, the ground and cause of anger and enmity; God in respect of the effects and issue of anger and enmity. The word in the New Testament is καταλλαγή, and the verb καταλλάσσω, *reconciliation, to reconcile;* both from ἀλλάττω, *to change*, or to turn from one thing, one mind, to another: whence the first native signification of those words is *permutatio*, and *permutare*, (so Arist. Eth. 3, Τὸν βίον πρὸς μικρὰ κέρδη—καταλλάττονται,[1]) because most commonly those that are reconciled are changed in respect of their affections, always in respect of the distance and variance, and in respect of the effects; thence it signifieth reconciliation, and to reconcile. And the word may not be affirmed of any business, or of any men, until both parties are actually reconciled, and all differences removed in respect of any former grudge and ill-will. If one be well pleased with the other, and that other continue ἀκατάλλακτος, unappeased and implacable, there is no reconciliation. When our Saviour gives that command, that he that brought his gift to the altar, and there remembered that his brother had aught against him,—was offended with him for any cause,—he should go and be reconciled to him, [he] fully intendeth a mutual returning of minds one to another, especially respecting the appeasing and atoning of him that was offended. Neither are these words used among men in any other sense, but always denote, even in common speech, a full redintegration of friendship between dissenting parties, with reference most times to some compensation made to the offended party. The reconciling of the one party and the other may be distinguished, but both are required to make up an entire reconciliation.

As, then, the folly of Socinus and his sectaries is remarkable, who would have the reconciliation mentioned in the Scripture to be nothing but our conversion to God, without the appeasing of his anger and turning away his wrath from us,—which is a reconciliation hopping on one leg,—so that distinction of some between the reconciliation of God to man, making that to be universal towards all, and

[1] Aristotle is speaking of soldiers who "barter their life for small gains." The quotation is exceedingly apt and felicitous when the reference is understood.—ED.

the reconciliation of man to God, making that to be only of a small number of those to whom God is reconciled, is a no less monstrous figment. Mutual alienation must have mutual reconciliation, seeing they are *correlata*. The state between God and man, before the reconciliation made by Christ, was a state of enmity. Man was at enmity with God; we were his "enemies," Col. i. 21; Rom. v. 10; hating him and opposing ourselves to him, in the highest rebellion, to the utmost of our power. God also was thus far an enemy to us, that his "wrath" was on us, Eph. ii. 3; which remaineth on us until we do believe, John iii. 36. To make perfect reconciliation (which Christ is said in many places to do), it is required, first, That the wrath of God be turned away, his anger removed, and all the effects of enmity on his part towards us; secondly, That we be turned away from our opposition to him, and brought into voluntary obedience. Until both these be effected, reconciliation is not perfected. Now, both these are in the Scripture assigned to our Saviour, as the effects of his death and sacrifice.

1. He turned away the wrath of God from us, and so appeased him towards us; that was the reconciling of God by his death: for "when we were enemies, we were reconciled to God by the death of his Son," Rom. v. 10. That here is meant the reconciling of God, as that part of reconciliation which consisteth in turning away his wrath from us, is most apparent, it being that whereby God chiefly commendeth his love to us, which certainly is in the forgiveness of sin, by the aversion of his anger due to it; as also being opposed to our being saved from the wrath to come, in the latter end of the verse, which compriseth our conversion and whole reconciliation to God. Besides, verse 11, we are said to receive τὴν καταλλαγήν, this "reconciliation" (which, I know not by what means, we have translated "atonement"); which cannot be meant of our reconciliation to God, or conversion, which we cannot properly be said to accept or receive, but of him to us, which we receive when it is apprehended by faith.

2. He turneth us away from our enmity towards God, redeeming and reconciling us to God by "the blood of his cross," Col. i. 20;—to wit, then meritoriously, satisfactorily, by the way of acquisition and purchase; accomplishing it in due time actually and efficiently by his Spirit. Both these ye have jointly mentioned, 2 Cor. v. 18–20; where we may see, first, God being reconciled to us in Christ, which consisteth in a non-imputation of iniquities, and is the subject-matter of the ministry, verses 18, 19; secondly, the reconciling of us to God, by accepting the pardon of our sins, which is the end of the ministry, verse 20;—as the same is also at large declared, Eph. ii. 13–15. The actual, then, and effectual accomplishment of both these, "simul et semel," in respect of procurement, by continuance, and in process of time, in the ordinances of the gospel, in respect of final accomplish-

ment on the part of men, do make up that reconciliation which is the effect of the death of Christ; for so it is in many places assigned to be: "We are reconciled to God by the death of his Son," Rom. v. 10; "And you, that were sometime alienated, hath he reconciled in the body of his flesh through death," Col. i. 21, 22: which is in sundry places so evident in the Scripture, that none can possibly deny reconciliation to be the immediate effect and product of the death of Christ.

Now, how this reconciliation can possibly be reconciled with universal redemption, I am no way able to discern; for if reconciliation be the proper effect of the death of Christ, as is confessed by all, then if he died for all, I ask how cometh it to pass,—First, That God is not reconciled to all? as he is not, for his wrath abideth on some, John iii. 36, and reconciliation is the aversion of wrath. Secondly, That all are not reconciled to God? as they are not, for "by nature all are the children of wrath," Eph. ii. 3; and some all their lives do nothing but "treasure up wrath against the day of wrath," Rom. ii. 5. Thirdly, How, then, can it be that reconciliation should be wrought between God and all men, and yet neither God reconciled to all nor all reconciled to God? Fourthly, If God be reconciled to all, when doth he begin to be unreconciled towards them that perish? by what alteration is it? in his will or nature? Fifthly, If all be reconciled by the death of Christ, when do they begin to be unreconciled who perish, being born children of wrath? Sixthly, Seeing that reconciliation on the part of God consists in the turning away of his wrath and not imputing of iniquity, 2 Cor. v. 18, 19, which is justification, rendering us blessed, Rom. iv. 6–8, why, if God be reconciled to all, are not all justified and made blessed through a non-imputation of their sin? They who have found out a redemption where none are redeemed, and a reconciliation where none are reconciled, can easily answer these and such other questions; which to do I leave them to their leisure, and in the meantime conclude this part of our argument. That reconciliation which is the renewing of lost friendship, the slaying of enmity, the making up of peace, the appeasing of God, and turning away of his wrath, attended with a non-imputation of iniquities; and, on our part, conversion to God by faith and repentance;—this, I say, being that reconciliation which is the effect of the death and blood of Christ, it cannot be asserted in reference to any, nor Christ said to die for any other, but only those concerning whom all the properties of it, and acts wherein it doth consist, may be truly affirmed; which, whether they may be of all men or not, let all men judge.

CHAPTER VII.

Of the nature of the satisfaction of Christ, with arguments from thence.

ARG. XIII. A third way whereby the death of Christ for sinners is expressed is SATISFACTION,—namely, that by his death he made satisfaction to the justice of God for their sins for whom he died, that so they might go free. It is true, the word *satisfaction* is not found in the Latin or English Bible applied to the death of Christ. In the New Testament it is not at all, and in the Old but twice, Num. xxxv. 31, 32; but the thing itself intended by that word is everywhere ascribed to the death of our Saviour, there being also other words in the original languages equivalent to that whereby we express the thing in hand. Now, that Christ did thus make satisfaction for all them, or rather for their sins, for whom he died, is (as far as I know) confessed by all that are but outwardly called after his name, the wretched Socinians excepted, with whom at this time we have not to do. Let us, then, first see what this satisfaction is; then how inconsistent it is with universal redemption.

Satisfaction is a term borrowed from the law, applied properly to things, thence translated and accommodated unto persons; and it is *a full compensation of the creditor from the debtor.* To whom any thing is due from any man, he is in that regard that man's creditor; and the other is his debtor, upon whom there is an obligation to pay or restore what is so due from him, until he be freed by a lawful breaking of that obligation, by making it null and void; which must be done by yielding *satisfaction* to what his *creditor* can require by virtue of that obligation: as, if I owe a man a hundred pounds, I am his debtor, by virtue of the bond wherein I am bound, until some such thing be done as recompenseth him, and moveth him to cancel the bond; which is called *satisfaction.* Hence, from things *real,* it was and is translated to things *personal.* Personal debts are injuries and faults; which when a man hath committed, he is liable to punishment. He that is to inflict that punishment, or upon whom it lieth to see that it be done, is, or may be, the creditor; which he must do, unless satisfaction be made. Now, there may be a twofold satisfaction:—First, By a solution, or paying the *very thing* that is in the obligation, either by the party himself that is bound, or by some other in his stead: as, if I owe a man twenty pounds, and my friend goeth and payeth it, my creditor is fully satisfied. Secondly, By a solution, or paying of so much, although in another kind, not the same that is in the obligation, which, by the creditor's acceptation, stands in the lieu of it; upon which, also, freedom from the obligation followeth, not necessarily, but by virtue of an act of favour.

In the business in hand,—First, the *debtor* is *man;* he oweth the ten thousand talents, Matt. xviii. 24. Secondly, The *debt* is *sin:* "Forgive us our debts," Matt. vi. 12. Thirdly, That which is required in lieu thereof to make satisfaction for it, is *death:* "In the day that thou eatest thereof, thou shalt surely die," Gen. ii. 17; "The wages of sin is death," Rom. vi. 23. Fourthly, The *obligation* whereby the debtor is tied and bound is the *law,* "Cursed is every one," etc., Gal. iii. 10; Deut. xxvii. 26; the justice of God, Rom. i. 32; and the truth of God, Gen. iii. 3. Fifthly, The *creditor* that requireth this of us is *God,* considered as the party offended, severe Judge, and supreme Lord of all things. Sixthly, That which interveneth to the destruction of the obligation is the *ransom* paid by Christ: Rom. iii. 25, "God set him forth to be a propitiation through faith in his blood."

I shall not enter upon any long discourse of the satisfaction made by Christ, but only so far clear it as is necessary to give light to the matter in hand. To this end two things must be cleared:—First, That Christ did make such satisfaction as whereof we treat; as also wherein it doth consist. Secondly, What is that act of God towards man, the debtor, which doth and ought to follow the satisfaction made. For the FIRST, I told you the word itself doth not occur in this business in the Scripture, but the thing signified by it (being a compensation made to God by Christ for our debts) most frequently. For to make satisfaction to God for our sins, it is required only that he undergo the punishment due to them; for that is the satisfaction required where sin is the debt. Now, this Christ has certainly effected; for "his own self bare our sins in his own body on the tree," 1 Pet. ii. 24; "By his knowledge shall my righteous servant justify many, for he shall bear their iniquities," Isa. liii. 11. The word נָשָׂא (*nasa*), also, verse 12, arguing a taking of the punishment of sin from us and translating it to himself, signifieth as much, yea all that we do by the word *satisfaction.* So also doth that of ἀνήνεγκεν, used by Peter in the room thereof: for to bear iniquity, in the Scripture language, is to undergo the punishment due to it, Lev. v. 1; which we call to *make satisfaction* for it;—which is farther illustrated by a declaration how he bare our sins, even by being "wounded for our transgressions, and bruised for our iniquities," Isa. liii. 5; whereunto is added, in the close, that "the chastisement of our peace was upon him." Every chastisement is either νουθετική, for instruction, or παραδειγματική, for example, punishment and correction. The first can have no place in our Saviour; the Son of God had no need to be taught with such thorns and briers. It must, therefore, be for punishment and correction, and that for our sins then upon him; whereby our peace or freedom from punishment was procured.

Moreover, in the New Testament there be divers words and expressions concerning the death of our Saviour, holding out that thing which by *satisfaction* we do intend; as when, first, it is termed προσφορά· Eph. v. 2, Παρέδωκεν ἑαυτὸν προσφορὰν καὶ θυσίαν,—an oblation or sacrifice of expiation; as appeareth by that type of it with which it is compared, Heb. ix. 13, 14. Of the same force also is the word אָשָׁם (*ascham*), Isa. liii. 10; Lev. vii. 2. "He made his soul an offering for sin,"—a piacular sacrifice for the removing of it away; which the apostle abundantly cleareth, in saying that he was made ἁμαρτία, "sin" itself, 2 Cor. v. 21, sin being there put for the adjunct of it, or the punishment due unto it. So also is he termed ἱλασμός, 1 John ii. 2. Whereunto answers the Hebrew *chitte*, used Gen. xxxi. 39, אָנֹכִי אֲחַטֶּנָּה, "Ego illud expiabam," which is to undergo the debt, and to make compensation for it; which was the office of him who was to be Job's goël, chap. xix. 25. All which and divers other words, which in part shall be afterward considered, do declare the very same thing which we intend by *satisfaction;* even a taking upon him the whole punishment due to sin, and in the offering of himself doing that which God, who was offended, was more delighted and pleased withal, than he was displeased and offended with all the sins of all those that he suffered and offered himself for. And there can be no more complete satisfaction made to any than by doing that which he is more contented with, than discontented and troubled with that for which he must be satisfied. God was more pleased with the obedience, offering, and sacrifice of his Son, than displeased with the sins and rebellions of all the elect. As if a good king should have a company of his subjects stand out in rebellion against him, and he were thereby moved to destroy them, because they would not have him reign over them, and the only son of that king should put in for their pardon, making a tender to his father of some excellent conquest by him lately achieved, beseeching him to accept of it, and be pleased with his poor subjects, so as to receive them into favour again; or, which is nearer, should offer himself to undergo that punishment which his justice had allotted for the rebels, and should accordingly do it;—he should properly make satisfaction for their offence, and in strict justice they ought to be pardoned. This was Christ, as that one *hircus*, ἀποπομπαῖος, sent-away goat, that bare and carried away all the sins of the people of God, to fall himself under them, though with assurance to break all the bonds of death, and to live for ever. Now, whereas I said that there is a twofold satisfaction, whereby the debtor is freed from the obligation that is upon him,—the one being *solutio ejusdem*, payment of the same thing that was in the obligation; the other, *solutio tantidem*, of that which is not the same, nor equivalent unto it, but only in the gracious acceptation of the creditor,—it is worth our inquiry which of these it was that our Saviour did perform.

He[1] who is esteemed by many to have handled this argument with most exactness, denieth that the payment made by Christ for us (by the payment of the debt of sin understand, by analogy, the undergoing of the punishment due unto it) was *solutio ejusdem*, or of the same thing directly which was in the obligation: for which he giveth some reasons; as,—First, Because such a solution, satisfaction, or payment, is attended with actual freedom from the obligation. Secondly, Because, where such a solution is made, there is no room for remission or pardon. "It is true," saith he, "deliverance followeth upon it; but this deliverance cannot be by way of gracious pardon, for there needeth not the interceding of any such act of grace. But now," saith he, "that satisfaction whereby some other thing is offered than that which was in the obligation may be admitted or refused, according as the creditor pleaseth; and being admitted for any, it is by an act of grace; and such was the satisfaction made by Christ." Now, truly, none of these reasons seem of so much weight to me as to draw me into that persuasion.

For the first reason rests upon that, for the confirmation of it, which cannot be granted,—namely, that actual freedom from the obligation doth not follow the satisfaction made by Christ; for by death he did deliver us from death, and that actually, so far as that the elect are said to die and rise with him. He did actually, or *ipso facto*, deliver us from the curse, by being made a curse for us; and the hand-writing that was against us, even the whole obligation, was taken out of the way and nailed to his cross. It is true, all for whom he did this do not instantly actually apprehend and perceive it, which is impossible: but yet that hinders not but that they have all the fruits of his death in actual right, though not in actual possession, which last they cannot have until at least it be made known to them. As, if a man pay a ransom for a prisoner detained in a foreign country, the very day of the payment and acceptation of it the prisoner hath right to his liberty, although he cannot enjoy it until such time as tidings of it are brought unto him, and a warrant produced for his delivery. So that that reason is nothing but a begging τοῦ ἐν ἀρχῇ.

Secondly, The satisfaction of Christ, by the payment of the same thing that was required in the obligation, is no way prejudicial to that free, gracious condonation of sin so often mentioned. God's gracious pardoning of sin compriseth the whole dispensation of grace towards us in Christ, whereof there are two parts:—*First*, The laying of our sin on Christ, or making him to be sin for us; which was

[1] The allusion is to Grotius, among whose varied and elaborate theological works there is a treatise entitled, "Defensio Fidei Catholicæ de Satisfactione Christi, contra F. Socinum." The distinguished reputation of Grotius in legal science explains some references which Owen makes in discussing his views.—ED.

merely and purely an act of free grace, which he did for his own sake. *Secondly,* The gracious imputation of the righteousness of Christ to us, or making us the righteousness of God in him; which is no less of grace and mercy, and that because the very merit of Christ himself hath its foundation in a free compact and covenant. However, that remission, grace, and pardon, which is in God for sinners, is not opposed to Christ's merits, but ours. He pardoneth all to us; but he spared not his only Son, he bated him not one farthing. The freedom, then, of pardon hath not its foundation in any defect of the merit or satisfaction of Christ, but in three other things:—*First,* The will of God freely appointing this satisfaction of Christ, John iii. 16; Rom. v. 8; 1 John iv. 9. *Secondly,* In a gracious acceptation of that decreed satisfaction in our steads; for so many, no more. *Thirdly,* In a free application of the death of Christ unto us.

Remission, then, excludes not a full satisfaction by the solution of the very thing in the obligation, but only the solution or satisfaction by him to whom pardon and remission are granted. So that, notwithstanding any thing said to the contrary, the death of Christ made satisfaction in the very thing that was required in the obligation. He took away the curse, by "being made a curse," Gal. iii. 13. He delivered us from sin, being "made sin," 2 Cor. v. 21. He underwent death, that we might be delivered from death. All our debt was in the curse of the law, which he wholly underwent. Neither do we read of any relaxation of the punishment in the Scripture, but only a commutation of the person; which being done, "God condemned sin in the flesh of his Son," Rom. viii. 3, Christ standing in our stead: and so reparation was made unto God, and satisfaction given for all the detriment that might accrue to him by the sin and rebellion of them for whom this satisfaction was made. His justice was violated, and he "sets forth Christ to be a propitiation" for our sins, "that he might be just, and the justifier of him which believeth in Jesus," Rom. iii. 25, 26. And never, indeed, was his justice more clearly demonstrated than in causing "the iniquity of us all to meet upon him." His law was broken; therefore Christ comes to be "the end of the law for righteousness," Rom. x. 4. Our offence and disobedience was to him distasteful; in the obedience of Christ he took full pleasure, Rom. v. 17; Matt. iii. 16.

Now from all this, thus much (to clear up the nature of the satisfaction made by Christ) appeareth,—namely, It was a full, valuable compensation, made to the justice of God, for all the sins of all those for whom he made satisfaction, by undergoing that same punishment which, by reason of the obligation that was upon them, they themselves were bound to undergo. When I say *the same,* I mean essentially the same in weight and pressure, though not in all accidents of duration and the like; for it was impossible that he should be detained by death. Now, whether this will stand in the justice of God, that any of these should perish eternally for whom Jesus Christ made so full, perfect, and complete satisfaction, we shall presently inquire; and this is the first thing that we are to consider in this business.

SECONDLY, We must look what act of God it is that is exercised either towards us or our Saviour in this business. That God in the whole is the party offended by our sins is by all confessed. It is his law that is broken, his glory that is impaired, his honour that is abased by our sin: "If I be a father," saith he, "where is mine honour?" Mal. i. 6. Now, the law of nature and universal right requireth that the party offended be recompensed in whatsoever he is injured by the fault of another. Being thus offended, the Lord is to be considered under a twofold notion:—First, In respect of *us*, he is as a creditor, and all we miserable debtors; to him we owe the "ten thousand talents," Matt. xviii. 24. And our Saviour hath taught us to call our sins our "debts," Matt. vi. 12; and the payment of this debt the Lord requireth and exacteth of us. Secondly, In respect of *Christ*,—on whom he was pleased to lay the punishment of us all, to make our iniquity to meet upon him, not sparing him, but requiring the debt at his hands to the utmost farthing,—God is considered as the supreme Lord and Governor of all, the only Lawgiver, who alone had power so far to relax his own law as to have the name of a surety put into the obligation, which before was not there, and then to require the whole debt of that surety; for he alone hath power of life and death, James iv. 12. Now, these two acts are eminent in God in this business:—First, An act of severe justice, as a creditor exacting the payment of the debt at the hands of the debtor; which, where sin is the debt, is punishment, as was before declared: the justice of God being repaired thereby in whatsoever it was before violated. Secondly, An act of sovereignty or supreme dominion, in translating the punishment from the principal debtor to the surety, which of his free grace he himself had given and bestowed on the debtor: "He spared not his own Son, but delivered him up to death for us all." Hence, let these two things be observed:—

1. That God accepteth of the punishment of Christ as a creditor accepteth of his due debt, when he spares not the debtor, but requires the uttermost farthing. It is true of punishment, as punishment, there is no creditor properly; for, "Delicta puniri publicè interest." But this punishment being considered also as a price, as it is, 1 Cor. vi. 20, it must be paid to the hands of some creditor, as this was into the hands of God; whence Christ is said to come to do God's will, Heb. x. 9, and to satisfy him, as John vi. 38. Neither, indeed, do the arguments that some have used to prove that God, as a creditor,

cannot inflict punishment, nor yet by virtue of supreme dominion, seem to me of any great weight. Divers I find urged by him whose great skill in the law, and such terms as these, might well give him sanctuary from such weak examiners as myself; but he that hath so foully betrayed the truth of God in other things, and corrupted his word, deserves not our assent in any thing but what by evidence of reason is extorted. Let us, then, see what there is of that in this which we have now in hand:—

First, then, he tells us that "The right of punishing in the rector or lawgiver can neither be a right of absolute dominion nor a right of a creditor; because these things belong to him, and are exercised for his own sake, who hath them, but the right of punishing is for the good of community."

Ans. Refer this reason unto God, which is the aim of it, and it will appear to be of no value; for we deny that there is any thing in him or done by him primarily for the good of any but himself. His αὐτάρκεια, or self-sufficiency, will not allow that he should do any thing with an ultimate respect to any thing but himself. And whereas he saith that the right of punishing is for the good of community, we answer, that "bonum universi," the good of community, is the glory of God, and that only. So that these things in him cannot be distinguished.

Secondly, He addeth, "Punishment is not in and for itself desirable, but only for community's sake. Now, the right of dominion and the right of a creditor are things in themselves expetible and desirable, without the consideration of any public aim."

Ans. First, That the comparison ought not to be between punishment and the right of dominion, but between the right of punishment and the right of dominion; the fact of one is not to be compared with the right of the other.

Secondly, God desireth nothing, neither is there any thing desirable to him, but only for himself. To suppose a good desirable to God for its own sake is intolerable.

Thirdly, There be some acts of supreme dominion, in themselves and for their own sake, as little desirable as any act of punishment; as the annihilation of an innocent creature, which Grotius will not deny but that God may do.

Thirdly, He proceedeth, "Any one may, without any wrong, go off from the right of supreme dominion or creditorship; but the Lord cannot omit the act of punishment to some sins, as of the impenitent."

Ans. God may, by virtue of his supreme dominion, omit punishment without any wrong or prejudice to his justice. It is as great a thing to impute sin where it is not, and to inflict punishment upon that imputation, as not to impute sin where it is, and to remove or not to inflict punishment upon that non-imputation. Now, the first of these God did towards Christ; and, therefore, he may do the latter.

Secondly, The wrong or injustice of not punishing any sin or sins doth not arise from any natural obligation, but the consideration of an affirmative positive act of God's will, whereby he hath purposed that he will do it.

Fourthly, He adds, "None can be called just for using his own right or lordship; but God is called just for punishing or not remitting sin," Rev. xvi. 5.

Ans. First, However it be in other causes, yet in this God may certainly be said to be just in exacting his debt or using his dominion, because his own will is the only rule of justice.

Secondly, We do not say punishing is an act of dominion, but an act of exacting a due debt; the requiring this of Christ in our stead supposing the intervention of an act of supreme dominion.

Fifthly, His last reason is, "Because that virtue whereby one goeth off from his dominion or remitteth his debt, is liberality; but that virtue whereby a man abstaineth from punishing is clemency: so that punishment can be no act of exacting a debt or acting a dominion."

Ans. The virtue whereby a man goeth off from the exacting of that which is due, universally considered, is not always liberality; for, as Grotius himself confesseth, a debt may arise and accrue to any by the injury of his fame, credit, or name, by a lie, slander, or otherwise. Now, that virtue whereby a man is moved not to exact payment by way of reparation, is not in this case liberality, but either clemency, or that grace of the gospel for which moralists have no name; and so it is with every party offended, so often as he hath a right of requiring punishment from his offender, which yet he doth not. So that, notwithstanding these exceptions, this is eminently seen in this business of satisfaction,—that God, as a creditor, doth exactly require the payment of the debt by the way of punishment.

2. The second thing eminent in it is, an act of supreme sovereignty and dominion, requiring the punishment of Christ, for the full, complete answering of the obligation and fulfilling of the law, Rom. viii. 3, x. 4.

Now, these things being thus at large unfolded, we may see, in brief, some natural consequences following and attending them as they are laid down; as,—First, That the full and due debt of all those for whom Jesus Christ was responsible was fully paid in to God, according to the utmost extent of the obligation. Secondly, That the Lord, who is a just creditor, ought in all equity to cancel the bond, to surcease all suits, actions, and molestations against the debtors, full payment being made unto him for the debt. Thirdly, That the debt thus paid was not this or that sin, but all the sins of all those for whom and in whose name this payment was made, 1 John i. 7, as was before demonstrated. Fourthly, That a second payment of a debt once paid, or a requiring of it, is not answerable to the justice which God demonstrated in setting forth Christ to be a propitiation for our sins, Rom. iii. 25. Fifthly, That whereas to receive a discharge from farther trouble is equitably due to a debtor who hath been in obligation, his debt being paid, the Lord, having accepted of the payment from Christ in the stead of all them for whom he died, ought in justice, according to that obligation which, in free grace, he hath put upon himself, to grant them a discharge. Sixthly, That considering that relaxation of the law which, by the supreme power of the lawgiver, was effected, as to the persons suffering the punishment required, such actual satisfaction is made thereto, that it can lay no more to their charge for whom Christ died than if they had really fulfilled, in the way of obedience, whatsoever it did require, Rom. viii. 32–34.

Now, how consistent these things (in themselves evident, and clearly following the doctrine of Christ's satisfaction, before declared) are with universal redemption is easily discernible; for,—First, If the full debt of all be paid to the utmost extent of the obligation, how comes it to pass that so many are shut up in prison to eternity, never freed from their debts? Secondly, If the Lord, as a just creditor, ought to cancel all obligations and surcease all suits against such as have their debts so paid, whence is it that his wrath smokes against some to all eternity? Let none tell me that it is because they walk not worthy of the benefit bestowed; for that not walking worthy is part of the debt which is fully paid, for (as it is in the third inference) the debt so paid is all our sins. Thirdly, Is it probable that God calls any to a second payment, and requires satisfaction of them for whom, by his own acknowledgment, Christ hath made that which is full and sufficient? Hath he an after-reckoning that he thought not of? for, for what was before him he spared him not, Rom. viii. 32. Fourthly, How comes it that God never gives a discharge to innumerable souls, though their debts be paid? Fifthly, Whence is it that any one soul lives and dies under the condemning power of the law, never released, if that be fully satisfied in his behalf, so as it had been all one as if he had done whatsoever it could require? Let them that can, reconcile these things. I am no Œdipus for them. The poor beggarly distinctions whereby it is attempted, I have already discussed. And so much for satisfaction.

CHAPTER VIII.

A digression, containing the substance of an occasional conference concerning the satisfaction of Christ.

MUCH about the time that I was composing that part of the last argument which is taken from the satisfaction of Christ, there came one (whose name, and all things else concerning him, for the respect I bear to his parts and modesty, shall be concealed) to the place where I live, and, in a private exercise about the sufferings of Christ, seemed to those that heard him to enervate, yea overthrow, the satisfaction of Christ: which I apprehending to be of dangerous consequence, to prevent a farther inconvenience, set myself briefly and plainly to oppose; and also, a little after, willingly entertained a conference and debate (desired by the gentleman) about the point in question: which being carried along with that quietness and sobriety of spirit which beseemed lovers of and searchers after truth, I easily perceived not only what was his persuasion in the thing in hand, but also what was the ground and sole cause of his misapprehension; and it was briefly this:—That the eternal, unchangeable love of God to his elect did actually instate them in such a condition as wherein they were in an incapacity of having any satisfaction made for them: the end of that being to remove the wrath due unto them, and to make an atonement for their sins; which, by reason of the former love of God, they stood in no need of, but only wanted a clear manifestation of that love unto their souls, whereby they might be delivered from all that dread, darkness, guilt, and fear, which was in and upon their consciences, by reason of a not-understanding of this love, which came upon them through the fall of Adam. Now, to remove this, Jesus Christ was sent to manifest this love, and declare this eternal good-will of God towards them, so bearing and taking away their sins, by removing from their consciences that misapprehension of God and their own condition which, by reason of sin, they had before, and not to make any satisfaction to the justice of God for their sins, he being eternally well-pleased with them. The sum is, election is asserted to the overthrow of redemption. What followed in our conference, with what success by God's blessing it did obtain, shall, for my part, rest in the minds and judgments of those that heard it, for whose sake alone it was intended. The things themselves being, first, of great weight and importance, of singular concernment to all Christians; secondly, containing in them a mixture of undoubted truth and no less undoubted errors, true propositions and false inferences, assertions of necessary verities to the exclusion of others no less necessary; and, thirdly, directly belonging to the business in hand,—I shall briefly declare and confirm the whole truth in this business, so far as occasion was given by the exercise and debate before mentioned, beginning with the first part of it, concerning the eternal love of God to his elect, with the state and condition they are placed in thereby: concerning which you may observe,—

First, That which is now by some made to be a new doctrine of free grace is indeed an old objection against it. That a non-necessity of satisfaction by Christ, as a consequent of eternal election, was more than once, for the substance of it, objected to Austin by the old Pelagian heretics, upon his clearing and vindicating that doctrine, is most apparent. The same objection, renewed by others, is also answered by Calvin, Institut. lib. ii. cap. 16; as also divers schoolmen had before, in their way, proposed it to themselves, as Thom. iii. g. 49, a. 4. Yet, notwithstanding the apparent senselessness of the thing itself, together with the many solid answers whereby it was long before removed, the Arminians, at the Synod of Dort, greedily snatched it up again, and placed it in the very front of their arguments against the effectual redemption of the elect by Jesus Christ. Now, that which was in them only an objection is taken up by some amongst us as a truth, the absurd inconsequent consequence of it owned as just and good, and the conclusion deemed necessary, from the granting of election to the denial of satisfaction.

Secondly, Observe that there is the same reason of election and reprobation (in things so opposed, so it must be): "Jacob have I loved, but Esau have I hated," Rom. ix. 13. By the one, men are "ordained to eternal life," Acts xiii. 48; by the other, "before of old ordained unto condemnation," Jude 4. Now, if the elect are justified, and sanctified, and saved, because of God's decree that so they shall be, whereby they need nothing but the manifestation thereof, then likewise are the reprobates, as soon as they are finally impenitent, damned, burned, and want nothing but a manifestation thereof; which, whether it be true or no, consult the whole dispensation of God towards them.

Thirdly, Consider what is the eternal love of God. Is it an affection in his eternal nature, as love is in ours? It were no less than blasphemy once so to conceive. His pure and holy nature, wherein there is neither change nor shadow of turning, is not subject to any such passion; it must be, then, an eternal act of his will, and that alone. In the Scripture it is called, his "good pleasure," Matt. xi. 26; his "purpose according to election," Rom. ix. 11; the "foundation of God," 2 Tim. ii. 19. Now, every eternal act of God's will is immanent in himself, not really distinguished from himself; whatever is so in God is God. Hence, it puts nothing into the creature concerning whom it is, nor alteration of its condition at all; producing, indeed, no effect until some external act of God's power do make it out. For instance: God decreed from eternity that he would make the world, yet we know the world was not made until about five thousand five hundred years ago. But ye will say, "It was made in God's purpose." That is, say I, he purposed to make it. So he purposeth there shall be a day of judgment; is there therefore actually a universal day of judgment already? God purposeth that he will, in and through Christ, justify and save such and such certain persons; are they therefore justified because God purposeth it? It is true, they shall be so, because he hath purposed it; but that they are so is denied. The consequence is good from the divine purpose to the futurition of any thing, and the certainty of its event, not to its actual existence. As when the Lord, in the beginning, went actually to make the world, there was no world; so when he comes to bestow faith and actually to justify a man, until he hath so done he is not justified. The sum is,—

First, The eternal love of God towards his elect is nothing but his purpose, good pleasure, a pure act of his will, whereby he determines to do such and such things for them in his own time and way. *Secondly,* No purpose of God, no immanent eternal act of his will, doth produce any outward effect, or change any thing in nature and condition of that thing concerning which his purpose is; but only makes the event and success necessary in respect of that purpose. *Thirdly,* The wrath and anger of God that sinners lie under is not any passion in God, but only the outward effects of anger, as guilt, bondage, etc. *Fourthly,* An act of God's eternal love, which is immanent in himself, doth not exempt the creature from the condition wherein he is under anger and wrath, until some temporal act of free grace do really change its state and condition. For example: God holding the lump of mankind in his own power, as the clay in the hand of the potter, determining to make some vessels unto honour, for the praise of his glorious grace, and others to dishonour, for the manifestation of his revenging justice, and to this end suffer them all to fall into sin and the guilt of condemnation, whereby they became all liable to his wrath and curse; his purpose to save some of these doth not at all exempt or free them from the common condition of the rest, in respect of themselves and the truth of their estate, until some actual thing be accomplished for the bringing of them nigh unto himself: so that notwithstanding his eternal purpose, his wrath, in respect of the effects, abideth on them until that eternal purpose do make out itself in some distinguishing act of free grace; which may receive farther manifestation by these ensuing arguments:—

1. If the sinner want nothing to acceptation and peace but a manifestation of God's eternal love, then evangelical justification is nothing but an apprehension of God's eternal decree and purpose.

But this cannot be made out from the Scripture,—namely, that God's justifying of a person is his making known unto him his decree of election; or [that] man's justification [is] an apprehension of that decree, purpose, or love. Where is any such thing in the book of God? It is true, there is a discovery thereof made to justified believers, and therefore it is attainable by the saints, "God shedding abroad his love in their hearts by the Holy Ghost which is given unto them," Rom. v. 5; but it is after they are "justified by faith," and have "peace with God," verse 1. Believers are to give "all diligence to make their calling and election sure;" but that justification should consist herein is a strange notion. Justification, in the Scripture, is an act of God, pronouncing an ungodly person, upon his believing, to be absolved from the guilt of sin, and interested in the all-sufficient righteousness of Christ: so God "justifieth the ungodly," Rom. iv. 5, "by the righteousness of God which is by the faith of Jesus Christ unto them," chap. iii. 22; making Christ to become righteousness to them who were in themselves sin. But of this manifestation of eternal love there is not the least foundation, as to be the form of justification; which yet is not without sense and perception of the love of God, in the improvement thereof.

2. The Scripture is exceeding clear in making all men, before actual reconciliation, to be in the like state and condition, without any real difference at all, the Lord reserving to himself his distinguishing purpose of the alteration he will afterward by his free grace effect: "There is none that doeth good, no, not one," Rom. iii. 12; for "we have proved both Jews and Gentiles that they are all under sin," verse 9. All mankind are in the same condition, in respect of themselves and their own real state: which truth is not at all prejudiced by the relation they are in to the eternal decrees; for "every mouth is stopped, and all the world is become guilty before God," Rom. iii. 19,—ὑπόδικος, obnoxious to his judgment. "Who maketh thee to differ from another? and what hast thou that thou didst not receive?" 1 Cor. iv. 7. All distinguishment, in respect of state and condition, is by God's actual grace; for even believers are "by nature children of wrath, even as others," Eph. ii. 3. The condition, then, of all men, during their unregeneracy, is one and the same, the purpose of God concerning the difference that shall be being referred to himself. Now, I ask whether reprobates in that condition lie under the effects of God's wrath, or no? If ye say "No," who will believe you? If so, why not the elect also? The same condition hath the same qualifications; an actual distinguishment we have proved there is not. Produce some difference that hath a real existence, or the cause is lost.

3. Consider what it is to lie under the effects of God's wrath, according to the declaration of the Scripture, and then see how the elect are delivered therefrom, before their actual calling. Now, this

consists in divers things; as,—(1.) To be in such a state of alienation from God as that none of their services are acceptable to him: "The prayer of the wicked is an abomination to the LORD," Prov. xxviii. 9. (2.) To have no outward enjoyment sanctified, but to have all things unclean unto them, Tit. i. 15. (3.) To be under the power of Satan, who rules at his pleasure in the children of disobedience, Eph. ii. 2. (4.) To be in bondage unto death, Heb. ii. 15. (5.) To be under the curse and condemning power of the law, Gal. iii. 13. (6.) To be obnoxious to the judgment of God, and to be guilty of eternal death and damnation, Rom. iii. 19. (7.) To be under the power and dominion of sin, reigning in them, Rom. vi. 19. These and such like are those which we call the effects of God's anger.

Let now any one tell me what the reprobates, in this life, lie under more? And do not all the elect, until their actual reconciliation, in and by Christ, lie under the very same? for,—(1.) Are not their prayers an abomination to the Lord? can they without faith please God? Heb. xi. 6. And faith we suppose them not to have; for if they have, they are actually reconciled. (2.) Are their enjoyments sanctified unto them? hath any thing a sanctified relation without faith? See 1 Cor. vii. 14. (3.) Are they not under the power of Satan? If not, how comes Christ, in and for them, to destroy the works of the devil? Did not he come to deliver his from him that had the power of death, that is, the devil? Heb. ii. 14; Eph. ii. 2. (4.) Are they not under bondage unto death? The apostle affirms plainly that they are so all their lives, until they are actually freed by Jesus Christ, Heb. ii. 14, 15. (5.) Are they not under the curse of the law? How are they freed from it? By Christ being made a curse for them, Gal. iii. 13. (6.) Are they not obnoxious unto judgment, and guilty of eternal death? How is it, then, that Paul says that there is no difference, but that all are subject to the judgment of God, and are guilty before him? Rom. iii. 9; and that Christ saves them from this wrath, which, in respect of merit, was to come upon them? Rom v. 9; 1 Thess. i. 10. (7.) Are they not under the dominion of sin? "God be thanked," says Paul, "that ye were the servants of sin, but ye have obeyed," etc., Rom. vi. 17. In brief, the Scripture is in nothing more plentiful than in laying and charging all the misery and wrath of and due to an unreconciled condition upon the elect of God, until they actually partake in the deliverance by Christ.

But now some men think to wipe away all that hath been said in a word, and tell us that all this is so but only in their own apprehension; not that those things are so indeed and in themselves. But if these things be so to them only in their apprehension, why are they otherwise to the rest of the whole world? The Scripture gives us no difference nor distinction between them. And if it be so with all, then let all get this apprehension as fast as they can, and all shall be well with the whole world, now miserably captived under a misapprehension of their own condition; that is, let them say the Scripture is a fable, and the terror of the Almighty a scarecrow to fright children; that sin is only in conceit; and so square their conversation to their blasphemous fancies. Some men's words eat as a canker.

4. Of particular places of Scripture, which might abundantly be produced to our purpose, I shall content myself to name only one: John iii. 36, "He that believeth not the Son, the wrath of God abideth on him." It abideth: there it was, and there it shall remain, if unbelief be continued; but upon believing it is removed. "But is not God's love unchangeable, by which we shall be freed from his wrath?" Who denies it? But is an apprentice free because he shall be so at the end of seven years? Because God hath purposed to free his in his own time, and will do it, are they therefore free before he doth it? "But are we not in Christ from all eternity?" Yes, chosen in him we are; therefore, in some sense, in him. But how? Even as we are. Actually, a man cannot be in Christ until he be. Now, how are we from eternity? are we eternal? No; only God from eternity hath purposed that we shall be. Doth this give us an eternal being? Alas! we are of yesterday; our being in Christ respecteth only the like purpose, and therefore from thence can be made only the like inference.

This, then, being cleared, it is, I hope, apparent to all how miserable a strained consequence it is, to argue from God's decree of election to the overthrow of Christ's merit and satisfaction; the redemption wrought by Jesus Christ being, indeed, the chief means of carrying along that purpose unto execution, the pleasure of the Lord prospering in his hand. Yea, the argument may be retorted, κατὰ τὸ βίαιον, and will hold undeniable on the other side, the consequence being evident, from the purpose of God to save sinners, to the satisfaction of Christ for those sinners. The same act of God's will which sets us apart from eternity for the enjoyment of all spiritual blessings in heavenly places, sets also apart Jesus Christ to be the purchaser and procurer of all those spiritual blessings, as also to make satisfaction for all their sins; which that he did (being the main thing opposed) we prove by these ensuing arguments.

CHAPTER IX.

Being a second part of the former digression—Arguments to prove the satisfaction of Christ.

I. If Christ so took our sins, and had them by God so laid and imposed on him, as that he underwent the punishment due unto them in our stead, then he made satisfaction to the justice of God for them, that the sinners might go free; but Christ so took and bare our sins, and had them so laid upon him, as that he underwent the punishment due unto them, and that in our stead: therefore, he made satisfaction to the justice of God for them. The consequent of the proposition is apparent, and was before proved. Of the assumption there be three parts, severally to be confirmed:—First, That Christ took and bare our sins, God laying them on him. Secondly, That he so took them as to undergo the punishment due unto them. Thirdly, That he did this in our stead.

For the first, that he took and bare our sins, ye have it, John i. 29, Ὁ αἴρων,[1] etc.,—"Who taketh away the sin of the world;" 1 Pet. ii. 24, Ὃς ἀνήνεγκεν,—"Who his own self bare our sins in his own body;" Isa. liii. 11, הוּא יִסְבֹּל,—"He shall bear their iniquities;" and verse 12, נָשָׂא,—"He bare the sin of many." That God also laid or imposed our sins on him is no less apparent: Isa. liii. 6, "The LORD, הִפְגִּיעַ, made to meet on him the iniquity of us all;" 2 Cor. v. 21, Ἁμαρτίαν ἐποίησε,—"He hath made him to be sin for us."

The second branch is, that in thus doing our Saviour underwent the punishment due to the sins which he bare, which were laid upon him; which may be thus made manifest:—Death and the curse of the law contain the whole of the punishment due to sin, Gen. ii. 17, מוֹת תָּמוּת, "Dying thou shalt die," is that which was threatened. Death was that which entered by sin, Rom. v. 12: which word in these places is comprehensive of all misery due to our transgressions; which also is held out in the curse of the law, Deut. xxvii. 26, "Cursed be he that confirmeth not all the words of this law to do them." That all evils of punishment whatsoever are comprised in these is unquestionably evident. Now, Jesus Christ in bearing our sins underwent both these: for "by the grace of God he tasted death," Heb. ii. 9; by death delivering from death, verse 14. He was not "spared, but given up to death for us all," Rom. viii. 32. So also the curse of the law: Gal. iii. 13, Γενόμενος κατάρα,—he "was made a curse for us;" and ἐπικατάρατος, "cursed." And this by the way of undergoing the punishment that was in death and curse: for by these "it pleased the LORD to bruise him, and put him to grief," Isa. liii. 10; yea, οὐκ ἐφείσατο, "he spared him not," Rom. viii. 32, but "condemned sin in his flesh," verse 3. It remaineth only to show that he did this in our stead, and the whole argument is confirmed.

Now, this also our Saviour himself maketh apparent, Matt. xx. 28. He came δοῦναι τὴν ψυχὴν αὐτοῦ λύτρον ἀντὶ πολλῶν,—"to give himself a ransom for many." The word ἀντί always supposeth a commutation, and change of one person or thing instead of another, as

[1] Aufert, sustulit, tulit.

shall be afterward declared: so Matt. ii. 22; so 1 Tim. ii. 6; 1 Pet. iii. 18, "He suffered for us, the just for the unjust;" and Ps. lxix. 4, "I restored" (or paid) "that which I took not away,"—namely, our debt, so far as that thereby we are discharged, as Rom. viii. 34, where it is asserted, upon this very ground, that he died in our stead. And so the several parts of this first argument are confirmed.

II. If Jesus Christ paid into his Father's hands a valuable price and ransom for our sins, as our surety, so discharging the debt that we lay under, that we might go free, then did he bear the punishment due to our sins, and make satisfaction to the justice of God for them (for to pay such a ransom is to make such satisfaction); but Jesus Christ paid such a price and ransom, as our surety, into his Father's hands, etc.: *ergo*,—

There be four things to be proved in the assumption, or second proposition:—First, That Christ paid such a price and ransom. Secondly, That he paid it into the hands of his Father. Thirdly, That he did it as our surety. Fourthly, That we might go free. All which we shall prove in order:—

First, For the first, our Saviour himself affirms it, Matt. xx. 28. He "came to give his life λύτρον," a ransom or price of redemption "for many," Mark x. 45; which the apostle terms ἀντίλυτρον, 1 Tim. ii. 6, a ransom to be accepted in the stead of others: whence we are said to have deliverance διὰ τῆς ἀπολυτρώσεως, "by the ransom-paying of Christ Jesus," Rom. iii. 24. "He bought us with a price," 1 Cor. vi. 20; which price was his own blood, Acts xx. 28; compared to and exalted above silver and gold in this work of redemption, 1 Pet. i. 18. So that this first part is most clear and evident.

Secondly, He paid this price into the hands of his Father. A price must be paid to somebody in the case of deliverance from captivity by it; it must be paid to the judge or jailer,—that is, to God or the devil. To say the latter were the highest blasphemy; Satan was to be conquered, not satisfied. For the former, the Scripture is clear: It was his "wrath" that was on us, John iii. 36. It was he that had "shut us all up under sin," Gal. iii. 22. He is the great king to whom the debt is owing, Matt. xviii. 23–34. He is the only "law-giver, who is able to save and to destroy," James iv. 12. Nay, the ways whereby this ransom-paying is in the Scripture expressed abundantly enforce the payment of it into the hands of his Father; for his death and blood-shedding is said to be προσφορά and θυσία, "an oblation and sacrifice," Eph. v. 2; and his soul to be אָשָׁם, a sacrifice or "offering for sin," Isa. liii. 10. Now, certainly offerings and sacrifices are to be directed unto God alone.

Thirdly, That he did this as surety, we are assured, Heb. vii. 22. He was made ἔγγυος, a "surety of a better testament;" and, in performance of the duty which lay upon him as such, "he paid that which he took not away," Ps. lxix. 4. All which could not possibly have any other end but that we might go free.

III. To make an atonement for sin, and to reconcile God unto the sinners, is in effect to make satisfaction unto the justice of God for sin, and all that we understand thereby; but Jesus Christ, by his death and oblation, did make an atonement for sin, and reconcile God unto sinners: *ergo*,—

The first proposition is in itself evident; the assumption is confirmed, Rom. iii. 24, 25. We are justified freely by the ransom-paying that is in Christ, whom God hath set forth to be ἱλαστήριον, a propitiation, an atonement, a mercy-seat, a covering of iniquity; and that εἰς ἔνδειξιν τῆς δικαιοσύνης, for the manifestation of his justice, declared in the going forth and accomplishment thereof. So likewise Heb. ii. 17, he is said to be a "merciful high priest, εἰς τὸ ἱλάσκεσθαι τὰς ἁμαρτίας τοῦ λαοῦ,"—"to make reconciliation for the sins of the people," to reconcile God unto the people: the meaning of the words being, ἱλάσκεσθαι τὸν Θεὸν περὶ τῶν ἁμαρτιῶν τοῦ λαοῦ,—to reconcile God, who was offended with the sins of the people; which reconciliation we are said to "receive," Rom. v. 11 (the word καταλλαγή there, in our common translation rendered "atonement," is in other places in the same rendered "reconciliation," being, indeed, the only word used for it in the New Testament.) And all this is said to be accomplished δι' ἑνὸς δικαιώματος,—by one righteousness or satisfaction; that is of Christ, (the words will not bear that sense wherein they are usually rendered, "By the righteousness of one," for then must it have been διὰ δικαιώματος τοῦ ἑνός.) And hereby were we delivered from that from which it was impossible we should be otherwise delivered, Rom. viii. 3.

IV. That wherein the exercise of the priestly office of Jesus Christ whilst he was on earth doth consist, cannot be rejected nor denied without damnable error; but the exercise of the priestly office of Jesus Christ whilst he was upon the earth consisted in this, to bear the punishment due to our sins, to make atonement with God, by undergoing his wrath, and reconciling him to sinners upon the satisfaction made to his justice: therefore cannot these things be denied without damnable error.

That in the things before recounted the exercise of Christ's priestly office did consist is most apparent,—first, From all the types and sacrifices whereby it was prefigured, their chief end being propitiation and atonement; secondly, From the very nature of the sacerdotal office, appointed for sacrificing, Christ having nothing to offer but his own blood, through the eternal Spirit; and, thirdly, From divers, yea, innumerable texts of Scripture affirming the same. It would be too long a work to prosecute these things severally and at large, and therefore I will content myself with one or two places wherein all those testimonies are comprised; as Heb. ix. 13, 14, "If the blood of bulls and of goats," etc., "how much more shall the blood of Christ, who through the eternal Spirit offered himself without spot to God?" etc. Here the death of Christ is compared to, exalted above, and in the antitype answereth, the sacrifices of expiation which were made by the blood of bulls and goats; and so must, at least spiritually, effect what they did carnally accomplish and typically prefigure,—namely, deliverance from the guilt of sin by expiation and atonement: for as in them the life and blood of the sacrifice was accepted in the stead of the offerer, who was to die for the breach of the law, according to the rigour of it, so in this of Christ was his blood accepted as an atonement and propitiation for us, himself being priest, altar, and sacrifice. So, Heb. x. 10–12, he is said expressly, in the room of all the old, insufficient, carnal sacrifices, which could not make the comers thereunto perfect, to offer up his own body a sacrifice for sins, for the remission and pardon of sins through that offering of himself; as it is verse 19. And in the performance also do we affirm that our Saviour underwent the wrath of God which was due unto us. This, because it is by some questioned, I shall briefly confirm, and that with these following reasons:—

First, The punishment due to sin is the wrath of God: Rom. i. 18, "The wrath of God is revealed against all ungodliness;" chap. ii. 5, "The day of wrath and revelation of the righteous judgment of God;" Eph. ii. 3, "Children of wrath;" John iii. 36. But Jesus Christ underwent the punishment due to sin: 2 Cor. v. 21, "Made sin for us;" Isa. liii. 6, "Iniquity was laid upon him;" 1 Pet. ii. 24, "He bare our sins in his own body on the tree." Therefore he underwent the wrath of God.

Secondly, The curse of the law is the wrath of God taken passively, Deut. xxix. 20, 21. But Jesus Christ underwent the curse of the law: Gal. iii. 13, "Made a curse for us," the curse that they lie under who are out of Christ, who are "of the works of the law," verse 10. Therefore he underwent the wrath of God.

Thirdly, The death that sinners are to undergo is the wrath of God. Jesus Christ did taste of that death which sinners for themselves were to undergo; for he died as "our surety," Heb. vii. 22, and in our stead, Matt. xx. 28. Hence his fear, Heb. v. 7; agony, Luke xxii. 44; astonishment and amazement, Mark xiv. 33; dereliction, Matt. xxvii. 46; sorrow, heaviness, and inexpressible pressures, chap. xxvi. 37–39.

V. That doctrine cannot be true nor agreeable to the gospel which strikes at the root of gospel faith, and plucks away the foundation of all that strong consolation which God is so abundantly willing we should receive; but such is that of denying the satisfaction made by Christ, his answering the justice and undergoing the wrath of his Father. It makes the poor soul to be like Noah's dove in its distress, not knowing where to rest the soles of her feet. When a soul is turned out of its self-righteousness, and begins to look abroad, and view the heaven and earth for a resting-place, and perceives an ocean, a flood, an inundation of wrath, to cover all the world, the wrath of God revealing itself from heaven against all ungodliness, so that it can obtain no rest nor abiding,—heaven it cannot reach by its own flight, and to hell it is unwilling to fall;—if now the Lord Jesus Christ do not appear as an ark in the midst of the waters, upon whom the floods have fallen, and yet has got above them all for a refuge, alas! what shall it do? When the flood fell there were many mountains glorious in the eye, far higher than the ark; but yet those mountains were all drowned, whilst the ark still kept on the top of the waters. Many appearing hills and mountains of self-righteousness and general mercy, at the first view, seem to the soul much higher than Jesus Christ, but when the flood of wrath once comes and spreads itself, all those mountains are quickly covered; only the ark, the Lord Jesus Christ, though the flood fall on him also, yet he gets above it quite, and gives safety to them that rest upon him.

Let me now ask any of those poor souls who ever have been wandering and tossed with the fear of the wrath to come, whether ever they found a resting-place until they came to this:—God spared not his only Son, but gave him up to death for us all; that he made him to be sin for us; that he put all the sins of all the elect into that cup which he was to drink of; that the wrath and flood which they feared did fall upon Jesus Christ (though now, as the ark, he be above it, so that if they could get into him they should be safe). The storm hath been his, and the safety shall be theirs. As all the waters which would have fallen upon them that were in the ark fell upon the ark, they being dry and safe, so all the wrath that should have fallen upon them fell on Christ; which alone causeth their souls to dwell in safety? Hath not, I say, this been your bottom, your foundation, your resting-place? If not (for the substance of it), I fear you have but rotten bottoms. Now, what would you say if a man should come and pull this ark from under you, and give you an old rotten post to swim upon in the flood of wrath? It is too late to tell you no wrath is due unto you; the word of truth and your own consciences have given you other information. You know the "wages of sin is death," in whomsoever it be; he must die in whomsoever it is found. So that truly the soul may well say, "Bereave me of the satisfaction of Christ, and I am bereaved. If he fulfilled not justice, I must; if he underwent not wrath, I must to eternity. O rob me not of my only pearl!" Denying the satisfaction of Christ destroys the foundation of faith and comfort.

VI. Another argument we may take from some few particular places of Scripture, which, instead of many, I shall produce:—

As, first, 2 Cor. v. 21, "He made him to be sin for us, who knew no sin." "He made him to be sin for us;" how could that be? are not the next words, "He knew no sin?" was he not a Lamb without blemish, and without spot? Doubtless; "he did no sin, neither was guile found in his mouth." What then is this, "God made him to be sin?" It cannot be that God made him sinful, or a sinner by any inherent sin; that will not stand with the justice of God, nor with the holiness of the person of our Redeemer. What is it, then? "He made him to be sin who knew no sin?" Why, clearly, by dispensation and consent, he laid that to his charge whereof he was not guilty. He charged upon him and imputed unto him all the sins of all the elect, and proceeded against him accordingly. He stood as our surety, really charged with the whole debt, and was to pay the utmost farthing, as a surety is to do if it be required of him; though he borrow not the money, nor have one penny of that which is in the obligation, yet if he be sued to an execution, he must pay all. The Lord Christ (if I may so say) was sued by his Father's justice unto an execution, in answer whereunto he underwent all that was due to sin; which we proved before to be death, wrath, and curse.

If it be excepted (as it is) "That God was always well pleased with his Son,—he testified it again and again from heaven,—how, then, could he lay his wrath upon him?" *Ans.* It is true he was always well pleased with him; yet it "pleased him to bruise him and put him to grief." He was always well pleased with the holiness of his person, the excellency and perfectness of his righteousness, and the sweetness of his obedience; but he was displeased with the sins that were charged on him: and therefore it pleased him to bruise and put him to grief with whom he was always well pleased.

Nor is that other exception of any more value, "That Christ underwent no more than the elect lay under; but they lay not under wrath and the punishment due to sin." *Ans.* The proposition is most false, neither is there any more truth in the assumption; for,—First, Christ underwent not only that wrath (taking it passively) which the elect were under, but that also which they should have undergone had not he borne it for them: he "delivered them from the wrath to come." Secondly, The elect do, in their several generations, lie under all the wrath of God in respect of merit and procurement, though not in respect of actual endurance,—in respect of guilt, not present punishment. So that, notwithstanding these exceptions, it stands firm that "he was made sin for us, who knew no sin."

Isa. liii. 5, "He was wounded for our transgressions, he was bruised for our iniquities: the chastisement of our peace was upon him; and with his stripes we are healed." Of this place something was said before; I shall add some small enlargements that conduce to discover the meaning of the words. "The chastisement of our peace was upon him;" that is, he was chastised or punished that we might have peace, that we might go free, our sins being the cause of his wounding, and our iniquities of his being bruised, all our sins meeting upon him, as verse 6; that is, he "bare our sins," in Peter's interpretation. He bare our sins (not, as some think, by declaring that we were never truly sinful, but) by being wounded for them, bruised for them, undergoing the chastisement due unto them, consisting in death, wrath, and curse, so making his soul an offering for sin. "He bare our sins;" that is, say some, he declared that we have an eternal righteousness in God, because of his eternal purpose to do us good. But is this to interpret Scripture, or to corrupt the word of God? Ask the word what it means by Christ's bearing of sin; it will tell you, his being "stricken" for our transgressions, Isa. liii. 8,—his being "cut off" for our sins, Dan. ix. 26. Neither hath the expression of bearing sins any other signification in the word: Lev. v. 1, "If a soul hear the voice of swearing, if he do not utter it, then he shall bear his iniquity." What is that? he shall declare himself or others to be free from sin? No, doubtless; but, he shall undergo the punishment due to sin, as our Saviour did in bearing our iniquities. He must be a cunning gamester indeed that shall cheat a believer of this foundation.

More arguments or texts on this subject I shall not urge or produce, though the cause itself will enforce the most unskilful to abound. I have proceeded as far as the nature of a digression will well bear. Neither shall I undertake, at this time, the answering of objections to the contrary; a full discussion of the whole business of the satisfaction of Christ, which should cause me to search for, draw forth, and confute all objections to the contrary, being not by me intended. And for those which were made at that debate which gave occasion to this discourse, I dare not produce them, lest haply I should not be able to restrain the conjectures of men that I purposely framed such weak objections, that I might obtain an easy conquest over a man of straw of mine own erection, so weak were they, and of so little force to the shaking of so fundamental a truth as that is which we do maintain. So of this argument hitherto.

CHAPTER X.

Of the merit of Christ, with arguments from thence.

ARG. XIV. A fourth thing ascribed to the death of Christ is MERIT, or that worth and value of his death whereby he purchased and procured unto us, and for us, all those good things which we find in the Scripture for his death to be bestowed upon us. Of this, much I shall not speak, having considered the thing itself under the notion of impetration already; only, I shall add some few observations proper to that particular of the controversy which we have in hand. The word *merit* is not at all to be found in the New Testament, in no translation out of the original that I have seen. The vulgar Latin once reads *promeretur*, Heb. xiii. 16; and the Rheimists, to preserve the sound, have rendered it promerited. But these words in both languages are uncouth and barbarous, besides that they no way answer εὐαρεστεῖται, the word in the original, which gives no colour to merit, name or thing. Nay, I suppose it will prove a difficult thing to find out any one word, in either of the languages wherein the holy Scripture was written, that doth properly and immediately, in its first native importance, signify merit. So that about the name we shall not trouble ourselves, if the thing itself intended thereby be made apparent, which it is both in the Old and New Testament; as Isa. liii. 5, "The chastisement of our peace was upon him, and with his stripes we are healed." The procurement of our peace and healing was the merit of his chastisement and stripes. So Heb. ix. 12, Διὰ τοῦ ἰδίου αἵματος αἰωνίαν λύτρωσιν εὑράμενος, "Obtaining by his blood eternal redemption," is as much as we intend to signify by the merit of Christ. The word which comes nearest it in signification we have, Acts xx. 28, Περιεποιήσατο, "Purchased with his own blood;" purchase and impetration, merit and acquisition, being in this business terms equivalent: which latter word is used in divers other places, as 1 Thess. v. 9; Eph. i. 14; 1 Pet. ii. 9. Now, that which by this name we understand is, the performance of such an action as whereby the thing aimed at by the agent is due unto him, according to the equity and equality required in justice; as, "To him that worketh, is the reward not reckoned of grace, but of debt," Rom. iv. 4. That there is such a merit attending the death of Christ is apparent from what was said before; neither is the weight of any operose proving [of] it imposed on us, by our adversaries seeming to acknowledge it no less themselves; so that we may take it for granted (until our adversaries close with the Socinians in this also).

Christ then, by his death, did merit and purchase, for all those for whom he died, all those things which in the Scripture are assigned to be the fruits and effects of his death. These are the things purchased and merited by his blood-shedding and death; which may be referred unto two heads:—First, Such as are *privative;* as,—1. Deliverance from the hand of our enemies, Luke i. 74; from the wrath to come, 1 Thess. i. 10. 2. The destruction and abolition of death in his power, Heb. ii. 14; 3. Of the works of the devil, 1 John iii. 8. 4. Deliverance from the curse of the law, Gal. iii. 13; 5. From our vain conversation, 1 Pet. i. 18; 6. From the present evil world, Gal. i. 4; 7. From the earth, and from among men, Rev. xiv. 3, 4. 8. Purging of our sins, Heb. i. 3, Secondly, *Positive;* as,—1. Reconciliation with God, Rom. v. 10; Eph. ii. 16; Col. i. 20. 2. Appeasing or atoning of God by propitiation, Rom. iii. 25; 1 John ii. 2. 3. Peace-making, Eph. ii. 14. 4. Salvation, Matt. i. 21. All these hath our Saviour by his death merited and purchased for all them for whom he died; that is, so procured them of his Father that they ought, in respect of that merit, according to the equity of justice, to be bestowed on them for whom they were so purchased and procured. It was absolutely of free grace in God that he would send Jesus Christ to die for any; it was of free grace for whom he would send him to die; it is of free grace that the good things procured by his death be bestowed on any person, in respect of those persons on whom they are bestowed: but considering his own appointment and constitution, that Jesus Christ by his death should merit and procure grace and glory for those for whom he died, it is of debt in respect of Christ that they be communicated to them. Now, that which is thus merited, which is of debt to be bestowed, we do not say that it *may* be bestowed, but it *ought* so to be, and it is injustice if it be not.

Having said this little of the nature of merit, and of the merit of Christ, the procurement of his death for them in whose stead he died, it will quickly be apparent how irreconcilable the general ransom is therewith; for the demonstration whereof we need no more but the proposing of this one question,—namely, If Christ hath merited grace and glory for all those for whom he died, if he died for all, how comes it to pass that these things are not communicated to and bestowed upon all? Is the defect in the merit of Christ, or in the justice of God? How vain it is to except, that these things are not bestowed absolutely upon us, but upon condition, and therefore were so procured; seeing that the very condition itself is also merited and procured, as Eph. i. 3, 4, Phil. i. 29,—hath been already declared.

ARG. XV. Fifthly, The very phrases of "DYING FOR US," "bearing our sins," being our "surety," and the like, whereby the death of Christ for us is expressed, will not stand with the payment of a ransom for all. To die for another is, in Scripture, to die in that other's stead, that he might go free; as Judah besought his brother Joseph to accept of him for a bondman instead of Benjamin, that he might be set at liberty, Gen. xliv. 33, and that to make good the engagement wherein he stood bound to his father to be a surety for him. He that is surety for another (as Christ was for us, Heb. vii. 22), is to undergo the danger, that the other may be delivered. So David, wishing that he had died for his son Absalom, 2 Sam. xviii. 33, intended, doubtless, a commutation with him, and a substitution of his life for his, so that he might have lived. Paul also, Rom. v. 7, intimates the same, supposing that such a thing might be found among men that one should die for another; no doubt alluding to the Decii,

Menœceus, Euryalus, and such others, whom we find mentioned in the stories of the heathen, who voluntarily cast themselves into death for the deliverance of their country or friends, continuing their liberty and freedom from death who were to undergo it, by taking it upon themselves, to whom it was not directly due. And this plainly is the meaning of that phrase, "Christ died for us;" that is, in the undergoing of death there was a subrogation of his person in the room and stead of ours. Some, indeed, except that where the word ὑπέρ is used in this phrase, as Heb. ii. 9, "That he by the grace of God should taste death for every man," there only the good and profit of them for whom he died is intended, not enforcing the necessity of any commutation. But why this exception should prevail I see no reason, for the same preposition being used in the like kind in other cases doth confessedly intimate a commutation; as Rom. ix. 3, where Paul affirms that he "could wish himself accursed from Christ ὑπὲρ τῶν ἀδελφῶν,"—"for his brethren,"—that is, in their stead, that they might be united to him. So also, 2 Cor. v. 20, Ὑπὲρ Χριστοῦ πρεσβεύομεν, "We are ambassadors in Christ's stead." So the same apostle, 1 Cor. i. 13, asking, and strongly denying by way of interrogation, Μὴ Παῦλος ἐσταυρώθη ὑπὲρ ὑμῶν; "Was Paul crucified for you?" plainly showeth that the word ὑπέρ, used about the crucifying of Christ for his church, doth argue a commutation or change, and not only designs the good of them for whom he died: for, plainly, he might himself have been crucified for the good of the church; but in the stead thereof, he abhorreth the least thought of it. But concerning the word ἀντί, which also is used, there is no doubt, nor can any exception be made; it always signifieth a commutation and change, whether it be applied to things or persons: so Luke xi. 11, Ὄφις ἀντὶ ἰχθύος, "A serpent instead of a fish;" so Matt. v. 38, Ὀφθαλμὸς ἀντὶ ὀφθαλμοῦ, "An eye for an eye;" so Heb. xii. 16;—and for persons, Archelaus is said to reign ἀντὶ Ἡρώδου τοῦ πατρός, "instead of his father," Matt. ii. 22. Now, this word is used of the death of our Saviour, Matt. xx. 28, "The Son of man came δοῦναι τὴν ψυχὴν αὐτοῦ λύτρον ἀντὶ πολλῶν,"—which words are repeated again, Mark x. 45,—that is, to give his life a ransom in the stead of the lives of many. So that, plainly, Christ dying for us, as a surety, Heb. vii. 22, and thereby and therein "bearing our sins in his own body," 1 Pet. ii. 24, being made a curse for us, was an undergoing of death, punishment, curse, wrath, not only for our good, but directly in our stead; a commutation and subrogation of his person in the room and place of ours being allowed, and of God accepted. This being cleared, I demand,—First, Whether Christ died thus for all? that is, whether he died in the room and stead of all, so that his person was substituted in the room of theirs? as, whether he died in the stead of Cain and Pharaoh, and the rest, who long before his death were under the power of the second death, never to be delivered? Secondly, Whether it be justice that those, or any of them, in whose stead Christ died, bearing their iniquities, should themselves also die and bear their own sins to eternity? Thirdly, What rule of equity is there, or example for it, that when the surety hath answered and made satisfaction to the utmost of what was required in the obligation wherein he was a surety, they for whom he was a surety should afterwards be proceeded against? Fourthly, Whether Christ hung upon the cross in the room or stead of reprobates? Fifthly, Whether he underwent all that which was due unto them for whom he died? If not, how could he be said to die in their stead? If so, why are they not all delivered? I shall add no more but this, that to affirm Christ to die for all men is the readiest way to prove that he died for no man, in the sense Christians have hitherto believed, and to hurry poor souls into the bottom of Socinian blasphemies.

CHAPTER XI.

The last general argument.

ARG. XVI. Our next argument is taken from some particular places of Scripture, clearly and distinctly in themselves holding out the truth of what we do affirm. Out of the great number of them I shall take a few to insist upon, and therewith to close our arguments.

1. The first that I shall begin withal is the first mentioning of Jesus Christ, and the first revelation of the mind of God concerning a discrimination between the people of Christ and his enemies: Gen. iii. 15, "I will put enmity between thee" (the serpent) "and the woman, and between thy seed and her seed." By the seed of the woman is meant the whole body of the elect, Christ in the first place as the head, and all the rest as his members; by the seed of the serpent, the devil, with all the whole multitude of reprobates, making up the malignant state, in opposition to the kingdom and body of Jesus Christ.

That by the first part, or the seed of the woman, is meant Christ with all the elect, is most apparent; for they in whom all the things that are here foretold of the seed of the woman do concur, are the seed of the woman (for the properties of any thing do prove the thing itself.) But now in the elect, believers in and through Christ, are to be found all the properties of the seed of the woman; for, for them, in them, and by them, is the head of the serpent broken, and Satan trodden down under their feet, and the devil disappointed in his temptations, and the devil's agents frustrated in their undertakings. Principally and especially, this is spoken of

Christ himself, collectively of his whole body, which beareth a continual hatred to the serpent and his seed.

Secondly, By the seed of the serpent is meant all the reprobate, men of the world, impenitent, unbelievers. For,

First, The enmity of the serpent lives and exerciseth itself in them. They hate and oppose the seed of the woman; they have a perpetual enmity with it; and every thing that is said of the seed of the serpent belongs properly to them.

Secondly, They are often so called in the Scripture: Matt. iii. 7, "O generation of vipers," or seed of the serpent; so also chap. xxiii. 33. So Christ telleth the reprobate Pharisees, "Ye are of your father the devil, and the lusts of your father ye will do," John viii. 44. So again, "Child of the devil," Acts xiii. 10,—that is, the seed of the serpent; for "he that committeth sin is of the devil," 1 John iii. 8.

These things being undeniable, we thus proceed:—Christ died for no more than God promised unto him that he should die for. But God did not promise him to all, as that he should die for them; for he did not promise the seed of the woman to the seed of the serpent, Christ to reprobates, but in the first word of him he promiseth an enmity against them. In sum, the seed of the woman died not for the seed of the serpent.

2. Matt. vii. 23, "I will profess unto them, I never knew you." Christ at the last day professeth to some he never knew them. Christ saith directly that he knoweth his own, whom he layeth down his life for, John x. 14–17. And surely he knows whom and what he hath bought. Were it not strange that Christ should die for them, and buy them that he will not own, but profess he never knew them? If they are "bought with a price," surely they are his own? 1 Cor. vi. 20. If Christ did so buy them, and lay out the price of his precious blood for them, and then at last deny that he ever knew them, might they not well reply, "Ah, Lord! was not thy soul heavy unto death for our sakes? Didst thou not for us undergo that wrath that made thee sweat drops of blood? Didst thou not bathe thyself in thine own blood, that our blood might be spared? Didst thou not sanctify thyself to be an offering for us as well as for any of thy apostles? Was not thy precious blood, by stripes, by sweat, by nails, by thorns, by spear, poured out for us? Didst thou not remember us when thou hungest upon the cross? And now dost thou say, thou never knewest us? Good Lord, though we be unworthy sinners, yet thine own blood hath not deserved to be despised. Why is it that none can lay any thing to the charge of God's elect? Is it not because thou diedst for them? And didst thou not do the same for us? Why, then, are we thus charged, thus rejected? Could not thy blood satisfy thy Father, but we ourselves must be punished? Could not justice content itself with that sacrifice, but we must now hear, 'Depart, I

never knew you?'" What can be answered to this plea, upon the granting of the general ransom, I know not.

3. Matt. xi. 25, 26, "I thank thee, O Father, Lord of heaven and earth, because thou hast hid these things from the wise and prudent, and hast revealed them unto babes. Even so, Father: for so it seemed good in thy sight." Those men from whom God in his sovereignty, as Lord of heaven and earth, of his own good pleasure, hideth the gospel, either in respect of the outward preaching of it, or the inward revelation of the power of it in their hearts, those certainly Christ died not for; for to what end should the Father send his only Son to die for the redemption of those whom he, for his own good pleasure, had determined should be everlasting strangers from it, and never so much as hear of it in the power thereof revealed to them? Now, that such there are our Saviour here affirms; and he thanks his Father for that dispensation at which so many do at this day repine.

4. John x. 11, 15, 16, 27, 28. This clear place, which of itself is sufficient to evert the general ransom, hath been a little considered before, and, therefore, I shall pass it over the more briefly. First, That all men are not the sheep of Christ is most apparent; for,—*First*, He himself saith so, verse 26, "Ye are not of my sheep." *Secondly*, The distinction at the last day will make it evident, when the sheep and the goats shall be separated. *Thirdly*, The properties of the sheep are, that they hear the voice of Christ, that they know him; and the like are not in all. Secondly, That the sheep here mentioned are all his elect, as well those that were to be called as those that were then already called. Verse 16, Some were not as yet of his fold of called ones; so that they are sheep by election, and not believing. Thirdly, That Christ so says that he laid down his life for his sheep, that plainly he excludes all others; for,—*First*, He lays down his life for them as sheep. Now, that which belongs to them as such belongs only to such. If he lays down his life for sheep, as sheep, certainly he doth it not for goats, and wolves, and dogs. *Secondly*, He lays down his life as a shepherd, verse 11; therefore, for them as the sheep. What hath the shepherd to do with the wolves, unless it be to destroy them? *Thirdly*, Dividing all into sheep and others, verse 26, he saith he lays down his life for his sheep; which is all one as if he had said he did it for them only. *Fourthly*, He describes them for whom he died by this, "My Father gave them me," verse 29; as also chap. xvii. 6, "Thine they were, and thou gavest them me:" which are not all; for "all that the Father giveth him shall come to him," chap. vi. 37, and he "giveth unto them eternal life, and they shall never perish," chap. x. 28. Let but the sheep of Christ keep close to this evidence, and all the world shall never deprive them of their inheritance. Farther to confirm this place, add Matt. xx. 28; John xi. 52.

5. Rom. viii. 32–34. The intention of the apostle in this place is, to hold out consolation to believers in affliction or under any distress; which he doth, verse 31, in general, from the assurance of the presence of God with them, and his assistance at all times, enough to conquer all oppositions, and to make all difficulty indeed contemptible, by the assurance of his loving-kindness, which is better than life itself. "If God be for us, who can be against us?" To manifest this his presence and kindness, the apostle minds them of that most excellent, transcendent, and singular act of love towards them, in sending his Son to die for them, not sparing him, but requiring their debt at his hand; whereupon he argues from the greater to the less, —that if he have done that for us, surely he will do every thing else that shall be requisite. If he did the greater, will he not do the less? If he give his Son to death, will he not also freely give us all things? Whence we may observe,—First, That the greatest and most eximious expression of the love of God towards believers is in sending his Son to die for them, not sparing him for their sake; this is made the chief of all. Now, if God sent his Son to die for all, he had [done] as great an act of love, and hath made as great a manifestation of it, to them that perish as to those that are saved. Secondly, That for whomsoever he hath given and not spared his Son, unto them he will assuredly freely give all things; but now he doth not give all things that are good for them unto all, as faith, grace, and glory: from whence we conclude that Christ died not for all. Again, verse 33, he gives us a description of those that have a share in the consolation here intended, for whom God gave his Son, to whom he freely gives all things; and that is, that they are his "elect,"—not all, but only those whom he hath chosen before the foundation of the world, that they should be holy; which gives another confirmation of the restraint of the death of Christ to them alone: which he yet farther confirms, verse 34, by declaring that those of whom he speaks shall be freely justified and freed from condemnation; whereof he gives two reasons,— first, Because Christ died for them; secondly, Because he is risen, and makes intercession for them for whom he died: affording us two invincible arguments to the business in hand. The first, taken from the infallible effects of the death of Christ: Who shall lay any thing to their charge? who shall condemn them? Why, what reason is given? "It is Christ that died." So that his death doth infallibly free all them from condemnation for whom he died. The second, from the connection that the apostle here makes between the death and intercession of Jesus Christ: For whom he died, for them he makes intercession; but he saveth to the utmost them for whom he intercedeth, Heb. vii. 25. From all which it is undeniably apparent that the death of Christ, with the fruits and benefits thereof, belongeth only to the elect of God.

6. Eph. i. 7, "In whom we have redemption." If his blood was

shed for all, then all must have a share in those things that are to be had in his blood. Now, amongst these is that redemption that consists in the forgiveness of sins; which certainly all have not, for they that have are "blessed," Rom. iv. 7, and shall be blessed for evermore: which blessing comes not upon all, but upon the seed of righteous Abraham, verse 16.

7. 2 Cor. v. 21, "He hath made him to be sin for us, that we might be made the righteousness of God in him." It was in his death that Christ was made sin, or an offering for it. Now, for whomsoever he was made sin, they are made the righteousness of God in him: "By his stripes we are healed," Isa liii. 5; John xv. 13, "Greater love hath no man than this, that a man lay down his life for his friends." Then, to intercede is not of greater love than to die, nor any thing else that he doth for his elect. If, then, he laid down his life for all, which is the greatest, why doth he not also the rest for them, and save them to the uttermost?

8. John xvii. 9, "I pray for them: I pray not for the world, but for them which thou hast given me; for they are thine." And verse 19, "For their sakes I sanctify myself."

9. Eph. v. 25, "Husbands, love your wives, even as Christ also loved the church, and gave himself for it;" as [also] Acts xx. 28. The object of Christ's love and his death is here asserted to be his bride, his church; and that as properly as a man's own wife is the only allowed object of his conjugal affections. And if Christ had a love to others so as to die for them, then is there in the exhortation a latitude left unto men, in conjugal affections, for other women besides their wives.

I thought to have added other arguments, as intending a clear discussing of the whole controversy; but, upon a review of what hath been said, I do with confidence take up and conclude that those which have been already urged will be enough to satisfy them who will be satisfied with any thing, and those that are obstinate will not be satisfied with more. So of our arguments here shall be an end.

BOOK IV.

CHAPTER I.

Things previously to be considered, to the solution of objections.

THERE being sundry places in holy Scripture wherein the ransom and propitiation made by the blood of Christ is set forth in general and indefinite expressions; as also a fruitlessness or want of success in respect of some, through their own default, for whom he died, seemingly intimated; with general proffers, promises, and exhortations, made for the embracing of the fruits of the death of Christ, even to them who do never actually perform it,—whence some have taken occasion to maintain *a universality of redemption*, equally respecting all and every one, and that with great confidence, affirming that the contrary opinion cannot possibly be reconciled with those places of Scripture wherein the former things are proposed;—these three heads being the only fountains from whence are drawn (but with violence) all the arguments that are opposed to the peculiar effectual redemption of the elect only, I shall, before I come to the answering of objections arising from a wrested interpretation of particular places, lay down some such fundamental principles as are agreeable to the word, and largely held forth in it, and no way disagreeable to our judgment in this particular, which do and have given occasion to those general and indefinite affirmations as they are laid down in the word, and upon which they are founded, having their truth in them, and not in a universal ransom for all and every one; with some distinctions conducing to the farther clearing of the thing in question, and waiving of many false imputations of things and consequences, erroneously or maliciously imposed on us.

1. The first thing that we shall lay down is concerning the dignity, worth, preciousness, and infinite value of the blood and death of Jesus Christ. The maintaining and declaring of this is doubtless especially to be considered; and every opinion that doth but seemingly clash against it is exceedingly prejudiced, at least deservedly suspected, yea, presently to be rejected by Christians, if upon search it be found to do so really and indeed, as that which is injurious and derogatory to the merit and honour of Jesus Christ. The Scripture, also, to this purpose is exceeding full and frequent in setting forth the excellency and dignity of his death and sacrifice, calling his blood, by reason of the unity of his person, "God's own blood," Acts xx. 28; exalting it infinitely above all other sacrifices, as having for its principle "the eternal Spirit," and being itself "without spot," Heb. ix. 14; transcendently more precious than silver, or gold, or corruptible things, 1 Pet. i. 18; able to give justification from all things, from which by the law men could not be justified, Acts xiii. 28. Now, such as was the sacrifice and offering of Christ in itself, such was it intended by his Father it should be. It was, then, the purpose and intention of God that his Son should offer a sacrifice of infinite worth, value, and dignity, sufficient in itself for the redeeming of all and every man, if it had pleased the Lord to employ it to that purpose; yea, and of other worlds also, if the Lord should freely make them, and would redeem them. Sufficient we say, then, was the sacrifice of Christ for the redemption of the whole world, and for the expiation of all

the sins of all and every man in the world. This sufficiency of his sacrifice hath a twofold rise:—First, The dignity of the person that did offer and was offered. Secondly, The greatness of the pain he endured, by which he was able to bear, and did undergo, the whole curse of the law and wrath of God due to sin. *And this sets out the innate, real, true worth and value of the blood-shedding of Jesus Christ.* This is its own true internal perfection and sufficiency. That it should be applied unto any, made a price for them, and become beneficial to them, according to the worth that is in it, is external to it, doth not arise from it, but merely depends upon the intention and will of God. It was in itself of infinite value and sufficiency to *have been made a price* to have bought and purchased all and every man in the world. That it did formally become a price for any is solely to be ascribed to the purpose of God, intending their purchase and redemption by it. The intention of the offerer and accepter that it should be for *such, some,* or *any,* is that which gives the formality of a price unto it; this is external. But the value and fitness of it to be made a price ariseth from its own internal sufficiency. Hence may appear what is to be thought of that old distinction of the schoolmen, embraced and used by divers protestant divines, though by others again rejected,—namely, "That Christ died for all in respect of the sufficiency of the ransom he paid, but not in respect of the efficacy of its application;" or, "The blood of Christ was a sufficient price for the sins of all the world;"—which last expression is corrected by some, and thus asserted, "That the blood of Christ was sufficient to have been made a price for all;" which is most true, as was before declared: for its being a price for all or some doth not arise from its own sufficiency, worth, or dignity, but from the intention of God and Christ using it to that purpose, as was declared; and, therefore, it is denied that the blood of Christ was a sufficient price and ransom for all and every one, not because it was not sufficient, but because it was not a ransom. And so it easily appears what is to be owned in the distinction itself before expressed. If it intend no more but that the blood of our Saviour was of sufficient value for the redemption of all and every one, and that Christ intended to lay down a price which should be sufficient for their redemption, it is acknowledged as most true. But the truth is, that expression, "To die for them," holds out the intention of our Saviour, in the laying down of the price, to have been their redemption; which we deny, and affirm that then it could not be but that they must be made actual partakers of the eternal redemption purchased for them, unless God failed in his design, through the defect of the ransom paid by Christ, his justice refusing to give a dismission upon the delivery of the ransom.

Now, the infinite value and worth which we assert to be in the death of Christ we conceive to be exceedingly undervalued by the assertors of universal redemption; for that it should be extended to this or that object, fewer or more, we showed before to be extrinsical to it. But its true worth consists in the immediate effects, products, and issues of it, with what in its own nature it is fit and able to do; which they openly and apparently undervalue, yea, almost annihilate. Hence those expressions concerning it:—First, That by it a *door of grace was opened for sinners:* where, I suppose, they know not; but that any were [ever] effectually carried in at the door by it, that they deny. Secondly, *That God might, if he would, and upon what condition he pleased, save those for whom Christ died.* That a right of salvation was by him purchased for any, they deny. Hence they grant, that after the death of Christ,—first, *God might have dealt with man upon a legal condition again;* secondly, *That all and every man might have been damned, and yet the death of Christ have had its full effect;* as also, moreover, *That faith and sanctification are not purchased by his death,* yea, no more *for any* (as before) *than what he may go to hell withal.* And divers other ways do they express their low thoughts and slight imaginations concerning the innate value and sufficiency of the death and blood-shedding of Jesus Christ. To the honour, then, of Jesus Christ our Mediator, God and man, our all-sufficient Redeemer, we affirm, such and so great was the dignity and worth of his death and blood-shedding, of so precious a value, of such an infinite fulness and sufficiency was this oblation of himself, that it was every way able and perfectly sufficient to redeem, justify, and reconcile and save all the sinners in the world, and to satisfy the justice of God for all the sins of all mankind, and to bring them every one to everlasting glory. Now, this fulness and sufficiency of the merit of the death of Christ is a foundation unto two things:—

First, The general publishing of the gospel unto "all nations," with the right that it hath to be preached to "every creature," Matt. xxviii. 19; Mark xvi. 15; because the way of salvation which it declares is wide enough for all to walk in. There is enough in the remedy it brings to light to heal all their diseases, to deliver them from all their evils. If there were a thousand worlds, the gospel of Christ might, upon this ground, be preached to them all, there being enough in Christ for the salvation of them all, if so be they will derive virtue from him by touching him in faith; the only way to draw refreshment from this fountain of salvation. It is, then, altogether in vain which some object, that the preaching of the gospel to all is altogether needless and useless, if Christ died not for all; yea, that it is to make God call upon men to believe that which is not true,—namely, that Christ died for them: for, first, besides that amongst those nations whither the gospel is sent there are some to be saved ("I have much people,") which they cannot be, in the way that God hath appointed to do it, unless the gospel be preached to others as well as themselves; and besides, secondly, that in the economy and dispensation of the new covenant, by which all external differences and privileges of people, tongues, and nations being abolished and taken away, the word of grace was to be preached without distinction, and all men called everywhere to repent; and, thirdly, that when God calleth upon men to believe, he doth not, in the first place, call upon them to believe that Christ died for them, but that there is no name under heaven given unto men whereby they might be saved, but only of Jesus Christ, through whom salvation is preached;—I say, besides these certain truths, fully taking off that objection, this one thing of which we speak is a sufficient basis and ground for all those general precepts of preaching the gospel unto all men, even that sufficiency which we have described.

Secondly, That the preachers of the gospel, in their particular congregations, being utterly unacquainted with the purpose and secret counsel of God, being also forbidden to pry or search into it, Deut. xxix. 29, may from hence justifiably call upon every man to believe, with assurance of salvation to every one in particular upon his so doing, knowing, and being fully persuaded of this, that there is enough in the death of Christ to save every one that shall so do; leaving the purpose and counsel of God, on whom he will bestow faith, and for whom in particular Christ died (even as they are commanded), to himself.

And this is one principal thing, which, being well observed, will crush many of the vain flourishes of our adversaries; as will in particular hereafter appear.

2. A second thing to be considered is, the *economy or administration of the new covenant* in the times of the gospel, with the amplitude and enlargement of the kingdom and dominion of Christ after his appearance in the flesh; whereby, all external differences being taken away, the name of Gentiles removed, the partition-wall broken down, the promise to Abraham that he should be heir of the world, as he was father of the faithful, was now fully to be accomplished. Now, this administration is so opposite to that dispensation which was restrained to one people and family, who were God's peculiar, and all the rest of the world excluded, that it gives occasion to many general expressions in the Scripture; which are far enough from comprehending a universality of all individuals, but denote only a removal of all such restraining exceptions as were before in force. So that a consideration of the end whereunto these general expressions are used, and of what is aimed at by them, will clearly

manifest their nature, and how they are to be understood, with whom they are that are intended by them and comprehended in them. For it being only this enlargement of the visible kingdom of Christ to all nations in respect of right, and to many in respect of fact (God having elect in all those nations to be brought forth, in the several generations wherein the means of grace are in those places employed), that is intended, it is evident that they import only a *distribution* of men through all differences whatsoever, and not a *universal collection* of all and every one; the thing intended by them requiring the one and not the other. Hence, those objections which are made against the particularity of the ransom of Christ, and the restraining of it only to the elect, from the terms of *all, all men, all nations, the world, the whole world,* and the like, are all of them exceeding weak and invalid, as wresting the general expressions of the Scripture beyond their aim and intent, they being used by the Holy Ghost only to evidence the removal of all personal and national distinctions,—the breaking up of all the narrow bounds of the Old Testament, the enlarging the kingdom of Christ beyond the bounds of Jewry and Salem, abolishing all old restrictions, and opening a way for the elect amongst all people (called "The fulness of the Gentiles,") to come in; there being now "neither Greek nor Jew, circumcision nor uncircumcision, Barbarian, Scythian, bond nor free, but Christ is all, and in all," Col. iii. 11. Hence the Lord promiseth to "pour out his Spirit upon all flesh," Joel ii. 28; which Peter interpreteth to be accomplished by the filling of the apostles with the gifts of the Spirit, that they might be enabled to preach to several nations, Acts ii. 17, "having received grace and apostleship for obedience to the faith among all nations" Rom. i. 5;—not the Jews only, but some among all nations, "the gospel being the power of God unto salvation to every one that believeth, to the Jew first, and also to the Greek," verse 16; intending only, as to salvation, the peculiar bought by Christ, which he "redeemed out of every kindred, and tongue, and people, and nation," Rev. v. 9, where ye have an evident distribution of that which in other places is generally set down; the gospel being commanded to be preached to all these nations, Matt. xxviii. 19, that those bought and redeemed ones amongst them all might be brought home to God, John xi. 52. And this is that which the apostle so largely sets forth, Eph. ii. 14–17. Now, in this sense, which we have explained, and no other, are those many places to be taken which are usually urged for universal grace and redemption, as shall afterward be declared in particular.

3. We must exactly distinguish between man's duty and God's purpose, there being no connection between them. The purpose and decree of God is not the rule of our duty; neither is the perform-

ance of our duty in doing what we are commanded any declaration of what is Gód's purpose to do, or his decree that it should be done. Especially is this to be seen and considered in the duty of the ministers of the gospel, in the dispensing of the word, in exhortations, invitations, precepts, and threatenings, committed unto them; all which are perpetual declaratives of our duty, and do manifest the approbation of the thing exhorted and invited to, with the truth of the connection between one thing and another, but not of the counsel and purpose of God, in respect of individual persons, in the ministry of the word. A minister is not to make inquiry after, nor to trouble himself about, those secrets of the eternal mind of God, namely,—whom he purposeth to save, and whom he hath sent Christ to die for in particular. It is enough for them to search his revealed will, and thence take their *directions*, from whence they have their *commissions.* Wherefore, there is no sequel between the universal precepts from the word concerning the *things*, unto God's purpose in himself concerning *persons.* They command and invite all to repent and believe; but they know not in particular on whom God will bestow repentance unto salvation, nor in whom he will effect the work of faith with power. And when they make proffers and tenders in the name of God to all, they do not say to all, "It is the purpose and intention of God that ye should believe," (who gave them any such power?) but, that it is his command, which makes it their duty to do what is required of them; and they do not declare his mind, what himself in particular will do. The external offer is such as from which every man may conclude his own duty; none, God's purpose, which yet may be known upon performance of his duty. Their objection, then, is vain, who affirm that God hath given Christ for all to whom he offers Christ in the preaching of the gospel; for his offer in the preaching of the gospel is not declarative to any in particular, neither of what God hath done nor of what he will do in reference to him, but of what he ought to do, if he would be approved of God and obtain the good things promised. Whence it will follow,—

First, That God always intends to save some among them to whom he sends the gospel in its power. And the ministers of it being, *first*, unacquainted with his particular purpose; *secondly*, bound to seek the good of all and every one, as much as in them lies; *thirdly*, to hope and judge well of all, even as it is meet for them,—they may make a proffer of Jesus Christ, with life and salvation in him, notwithstanding that the Lord hath given his Son only to his elect.

Secondly, That this offer is neither vain nor fruitless, being declarative of their duty, and of what is acceptable to God if it be performed as it ought to be, even as it is required. And if any ask, What it is of the mind and will of God that is declared and made known when men are commanded to believe for whom Christ did not die? I answer, *first*, What they ought to do, if they will do that which is acceptable to God; *secondly*, The sufficiency of salvation that is in Jesus Christ to all that believe on him; *thirdly*, The certain, infallible, inviolable connection that is between faith and salvation, so that whosoever performs the one shall surely enjoy the other, for whoever comes to Christ he will in no wise cast out. Of which more afterward.

4. The ingraffed erroneous persuasion of the Jews, which for a while had a strong influence upon the apostles themselves, restraining salvation and deliverance by the Messiah, or promised seed, to themselves alone, who were the offspring of Abraham according to the flesh, must be considered as the ground of many general expressions and enlargements of the objects of redemption; which yet, being so occasioned, give no colour of any unlimited universality. That the Jews were generally infected with this proud opinion, that all the promises belonged only to them and theirs, towards whom they had a universality, exclusive of all others, whom they called "dogs, uncircumcised," and poured out curses on them, is most apparent. Hence, when they saw the multitudes of the Gentiles coming to the preaching of Paul, they were "filled with envy, contradicting, blaspheming, and raising up persecution against them," Acts xiii. 45–50; which the apostle again relates of them, 1 Thess. ii. 15, 16. "They please not God," saith he, "and are contrary to all men; forbidding us to speak to the Gentiles that they might be saved;" being not with any thing more enraged in the preaching of our Saviour than his prediction of letting out his vineyard to others.

That the apostles themselves, also, had deeply drunk in this opinion, learned by tradition from their fathers, appeareth, not only in their questioning about the restoration of the kingdom unto Israel, Acts i. 6, but also most evidently in this, that after they had received commission to teach and baptize all nations, Matt. xxviii. 19, or every creature, Mark xvi. 15, and were endued with power from above so to do, according to promise, Acts i. 8; yet they seem to have understood their commission to have extended only to the lost sheep of the house of Israel, for they went about and preached only to the Jews, chap. xi. 19: and when the contrary was evidenced and demonstrated to them, they glorified God, saying, "Then hath God also to the Gentiles granted repentance unto life," verse 18; admiring at it, as a thing which before they were not acquainted with. And no wonder that men were not easily nor soon persuaded to this, it being the great mystery that was not made known in former ages, as it was then revealed to God's holy apostles and prophets by the Spirit —namely, "That the Gentiles should be fellow-heirs, and of the same body, and partakers of his promise in Christ by the gospel," Eph. iii. 5, 6.

But now, this being so made known unto them by the Spirit, and that the time was come wherein the little sister was to be considered, the prodigal brought home, and Japheth persuaded to dwell in the tents of Shem, they laboured by all means to root it out of the minds of their brethren according to the flesh, of whom they had a special care;—as also, to leave no scruple in the mind of the eunuch, that he was a dry tree; or of the Gentile, that he was cut off from the people of God. To which end they use divers general expressions, carrying a direct opposition to that former error, which was absolutely destructive to the kingdom of Jesus Christ. Hence are those terms of the *world, all men, all nations, every creature,* and the like, used in the business of redemption and preaching of the gospel; these things being not restrained, according as they supposed, to one certain nation and family, but extended to the universality of God's people scattered abroad in every region under heaven. Especially are these expressions used by John, who, living to see the first coming of the Lord, in that fearful judgment and vengeance which he executed upon the Jewish nation some forty years after his death, is very frequent in the asserting of the benefit of the world by Christ, in opposition, as I said before, to the Jewish nation,—giving us a rule how to understand such phrases and locutions: John xi. 51, 52, "He signified that Jesus should die for that nation; and not for that nation only, but that also he should gather together in one the children of God that were scattered abroad;" conformably whereunto he tells the believing Jews that Christ is not a propitiation for them only, "but for the sins of the whole world," 1 John ii. 2, or the people of God scattered throughout the whole world, not tied to any one nation, as they sometime vainly imagined. And this may and doth give much light into the sense and meaning of those places where the words *world* and *all* are used in the business of redemption. They do not hold out a collective universality, but a general distribution into men of all sorts, in opposition to the before-recounted erroneous persuasion.

5. The extent, nature, and signification of those general terms which we have frequently used indefinitely in the Scripture, to set out the object of the redemption by Christ, must seriously be weighed. Upon these expressions hangs the whole weight of the opposite cause, the chief if not the only argument for the universality of redemption being taken from words which seem to be of a latitude in their signification equal to such an assertion, as the *world,* the

whole world, all, and the like; which terms, when they have once fastened upon, they run with, "Io triumphe," as though the victory were surely theirs. *The world, the whole world, all, all men!*—who can oppose it? Call them to the context in the several places where the words are; appeal to rules of interpretation; mind them of the circumstances and scope of the place, the sense of the same words in other places; with other fore-named helps and assistances which the Lord hath acquainted us with for the discovery of his mind and will in his word,—they presently cry out, the *bare word,* the letter is theirs: "Away with the gloss and interpretation; give us leave to believe what the word expressly saith;"—little (as I hope) imagining, being deluded with the love of their own darling, that if this assertion be general, and they will not allow us the gift of interpretation agreeable to the proportion of faith, that, at one clap, they confirm the cursed madness of the Anthropomorphites,—assigning a human body, form and shape, unto God, who hath none; and the alike cursed figment of transubstantiation, overthrowing the body of Christ, who hath one; with divers other most pernicious errors. Let them, then, as long as they please, continue such empty clamours, fit to terrify and shake weak and unstable men; for the truth's sake we will not be silent: and I hope we shall very easily make it appear that the general terms that are used in this business will indeed give no colour to any argument for universal redemption, whether absolute or conditionate.

Two words there are that are mightily stuck upon or stumbled at;—first, The *world;* secondly, *All.* The particular places wherein they are, and from which the arguments of our adversaries are urged, we shall afterward consider, and for the present only show that the words themselves, according to the Scripture use, do not necessarily hold out any collective universality of those concerning whom they are affirmed, but, being words of various significations, must be interpreted according to the scope of the place where they are used and the subject-matter of which the Scripture treateth in those places.

First, then, for the word *world,* which in the New Testament is called κόσμος (for there is another word sometimes translated world, namely, αἰών, that belongs not to this matter, noting rather the duration of time than the thing in that space continuing): he that doth not acknowledge it to be πολύσημον, need say no more to manifest his unacquaintedness in the book of God. I shall briefly give you so many various significations of it as shall make it apparent that from the bare usage of a word so exceedingly equivocal, no argument can be taken, until it be distinguished, and the meaning thereof in that particular place evinced from whence the argument is taken.

THE SCHEME.

Mundus sumitur,

- 1. Subjectivè,
  - 1. 'Ολικῶς.
  - 2. Μερικῶς, idque vel pro
    - 1. Cœlo aspectabili.
    - 2. Terra habitabili.
- 2. Adjunctivè, ratione
  - 1. Incolarum, idque
    - 1. Collectivè, seu κατὰ πάντας.
    - 2. Distributivè, pro
      - 1. Quibusvis.
      - 2. Multis.
    - 3. Signanter, pro
      - 1. Bonis, seu electis.
      - 2. Malis, seu reprobis.
    - 4. 'Αορίστως, seu communiter.
    - 5. Restrictivè, seu συνεκδοχικῶς, pro
      - 1. Præcipuis.
      - 2. Romanis.
  - 2. Accidentium
    - 1. Corruptionis, unde sumitur pro
      - 1. Ipsa corruptione.
      - 2. Sede corruptionis.
      - 3. Terrena conditione.
    - 2. Maledictionis.[1]

All these distinctions of the use of the word are made out in the following observations:—

The word *world* in the Scripture is in general taken five ways:—

First, *Pro mundo continente;* and that,—*First*, generally, ὅλως, for the whole fabric of heaven and earth, with all things in them contained, which in the beginning were created of God: so Job xxxiv. 13; Acts xvii. 24; Eph. i. 4, and in very many other places. *Secondly*, Distinctively, first, for the heavens, and all things belonging to them, distinguished from the earth, Ps. xc. 2; secondly, The habitable earth, and this very frequently, as Ps. xxiv. 1, xcviii. 7; Matt. xiii. 38; John i. 9, iii. 17, 19, vi. 14, xvii. 11; 1 Tim. i. 15, vi. 7.

Secondly, *For the world contained*, especially men in the world; and that either,—*First*, universally for all and every one, Rom. iii. 6, 19, v. 12. *Secondly*, Indefinitely for men, without restriction

[1] The following is a translation of the above scheme:—

The *World* is taken,

- I. Subjectively
  - 1. Universally.
  - 2. Partially; for
    - (1.) The visible heaven.
    - (2.) The habitable earth.
- II. Adjunctively, in respect of,
  - 1. The inhabitants, and that,—
    - (1.) Collectively for the whole.
    - (2.) Distributively; for,—
      - [1.] Any.
      - [2.] Many.
    - (3.) Signally,—
      - [1.] The good, or elect.
      - [2.] The wicked, or reprobate.
    - (4.) Indifferently, or in common.
    - (5.) Restrictively, or synecdochically; for,—
      - [1.] The chief.
      - [2.] The Romans.
  - 2. The accidents;
    - (1.) Of corruption.
      - [1.] Corruption itself.
      - [2.] The seat of corruption.
      - [3.] The earthly condition.
    - (2.) Of the curse.

—Ed.

or enlargement, John vii. 4; Isa. xiii. 11. *Thirdly,* Exegetically, for many, which is the most usual acceptation of the word, Matt. xviii. 7; John iv. 42, xii. 19, xvi. 8, xvii. 21; 1 Cor. iv. 9; Rev. xiii. 3. *Fourthly,* Comparatively, for a great part of the world, Rom. i. 8; Matt. xxiv. 14, xxvi. 13; Rom. x. 18. *Fifthly,* Restrictively, for the inhabitants of the Roman empire, Luke ii. 1. *Sixthly,* For men distinguished in their several qualifications, as,—1*st,* For the good, God's people, either in designation or possession, Ps. xxii. 27; John iii. 16, vi. 33, 51; Rom. iv. 13, xi. 12, 15; 2 Cor. v. 19; Col. i. 6; 1 John ii. 2. 2*dly,* For the evil, wicked, rejected men of the world, Isa. xiii. 11; John vii. 7, xiv. 17, 22, xv. 19, xvii. 25; 1 Cor. vi. 2, xi. 32; Heb. xi. 38; 2 Pet. ii. 5; 1 John v. 19; Rev. xiii. 3.

Thirdly, *For the world corrupted,* or that universal corruption which is in all things in it, as Gal. i. 4, vi. 14; Eph. ii. 2; James i. 27, iv. 4; 1 John ii. 15–17; 1 Cor. vii. 31, 33; Col. ii. 8; 2 Tim. iv. 10; Rom. xii. 2; 1 Cor. i. 20, 21, iii. 18, 19.

Fourthly, *For a terrene worldly estate or condition* of men or things, Ps. lxxiii. 12; Luke xvi. 8; John xviii. 36; 1 John iv. 5, and very many other places.

Fifthly, *For the world accursed,* as under the power of Satan, John vii. 7, xiv. 30, xvi. 11, 33; 1 Cor. ii. 12; 2 Cor. iv. 4; Eph. vi. 12. And divers other significations hath this word in holy writ, which are needless to recount.

These I have rehearsed to show the vanity of that clamour wherewith some men fill their mouths, and frighten unstable souls with the Scripture mentioning *world* so often in the business of redemption, as though some strength might be taken thence for the upholding of the general ransom. "Parvas habet spes Troja, si tales habet." If their greatest *strength be but sophistical craft, taken from the ambiguity of an equivocal word, their whole endeavour is like to prove fruitless.* Now, as I have declared that it hath divers other acceptations in the Scripture, so when I come to a consideration of their objections that use the word for this purpose, I hope, by God's assistance, to show that in no one place wherein it is used in this business of redemption, it is or can be taken for all and every man in the world, as, indeed, it is in very few places besides. So that, forasmuch as concerning this word our way will be clear, if to what hath been said ye add these observations,—

First, That as in other words, so in these, this is in the Scripture usually an ἀντανάκλασις, whereby the same word is ingeminated in a different sense and acceptation. So Matt. viii. 22, "Let the dead bury their dead;"—dead in the first place denoting them that are spiritually dead in sin; in the next, those that are naturally dead by a dissolution of soul and body. So John i. 11, He came εἰς τὰ ἴδια, "to his own," even all things that he had made; καὶ οἱ ἴδιοι, "his own," that is, the greatest part of the people, "received him not." So, again, John iii. 6, "That which is born of the Spirit is spirit." Spirit in the first place is the almighty Spirit of God; in the latter, a spiritual life of grace received from him. Now, in such places as these, to argue that as such is the signification of the word in one place, therefore in the other, were violently to pervert the mind of the Holy Ghost. Thus also is the word *world* usually changed in the meaning thereof. So John i. 10, "He was in the world, and the world was made by him, and the world knew him not." He that should force the same signification upon the *world* in that triple mention of it would be an egregious glosser: for in the first, it plainly signifieth some part of the habitable earth, and is taken *subjectivè* μερικῶς· in the second, the whole frame of heaven and earth, and is taken *subjectivè* ὁλικῶς· and, in the third, for some men living in the earth,—namely, unbelievers, who may be said to be the world *adjunctivè*. So, again, John iii. 17, "God sent not his Son into the world to condemn the world, but that the world through him might be saved;" where, by the *world* in the first, is necessarily to be understood that part of the habitable world wherein our Saviour conversed; in the second, all men in the world, as some suppose (so also there is a truth in it, for our Saviour came not to condemn all men in the world: for, *first*, condemnation of any was not the prime aim of his coming; *secondly*, he came to save his own people, and so not to condemn all); in the third, God's elect, or believers living in the world, in their several generations, who were they whom he intended to save, and none else, or he faileth of his purpose, and the endeavour of Christ is insufficient for the accomplishment of that whereunto it is designed.

Secondly, That no argument can be taken from a phrase of speech in the Scripture, in any particular place, if in other places thereof where it is used the signification pressed from that place is evidently denied, unless the scope of the place or subject-matter do enforce it. For instance: God is said to love the *world*, and send his Son; to be in Christ reconciling the *world* to himself; and Christ to be a propitiation for the sins of the *whole world*. If the scope of the places where these assertions are, or the subject-matter of which they treat, will enforce a universality of all persons to be meant by the word *world*, so let it be, without control. But if not, if there be no enforcement of any such interpretation from the places themselves, why should the *world* there signify all and every one, more than in John i. 10, "The world knew him not," which, if it be meant of all without exception, then no one did believe in Christ, which is contrary to verse 12; or in Luke ii. 1, "That all the world should be taxed," where none but the chief inhabitants of the Roman empire can be understood; or in John viii. 26, "I speak to the world those things which I have heard of him," understanding the Jews to whom he spake, who then lived in the world, and not every one, to whom he was not sent; or in John xii. 19, "Behold, the world is gone after him!" which world was nothing but a great multitude of one small nation; or in 1 John v. 19, "The whole world lieth in wickedness," from which, notwithstanding, all believers are to be understood as exempted; or in Rev. xiii. 3, "All the world wondered after the beast," which, whether it be affirmed of the whole universality of individuals in the world, let all judge? That *all nations*, an expression of equal extent with that of *the world*, is in like manner to be understood, is apparent, Rom. i. 5; Rev. xviii. 3, 23; Ps. cxviii. 10; 1 Chron. xiv. 17; Jer. xxvii. 7. It being evident that the words *world, all the world, the whole world*, do, where taken adjunctively for men in the world, usually and almost always denote only some or many men in the world, distinguished into good or bad, believers or unbelievers, elect or reprobate, by what is immediately in the several places affirmed of them, I see no reason in the world why they should be wrested to any other meaning or sense in the places that are in controversy between us and our opponents. The particular places we shall afterward consider.

Now, as we have said of the word *world*, so we may of the word *all*, wherein much strength is placed, and many causeless boastings are raised from it. That it is nowhere affirmed in the Scripture that Christ died for *all men*, or gave himself a ransom for all men, much less for all and every man, we have before declared. That he "gave himself a ransom for all" is expressly affirmed, 1 Tim. ii. 6. But now, who this *all* should be, whether all believers, or all the elect, or some of all sorts, or all of every sort, is in debate. Our adversaries affirm the last; and the main reason they bring to assert their interpretation is from the importance of the word itself: for, that the circumstances of the place, the analogy of faith, and other helps for exposition, do not at all favour their gloss, we shall show when we come to the particular places urged. For the present, let us look upon the word in its usual acceptation in the Scripture, and search whether it always necessarily requires such an interpretation.

That the word *all*, being spoken of among all sorts of men, speaking, writing, any way expressing themselves, but especially in holy writ, is to be taken either *collectively* for all in general, without exception, or *distributively* for some of all sorts, excluding none, is more apparent than that it can require any illustration. That it is sometimes taken in the first sense, for all collectively, is granted, and I need not prove it, they whom we oppose affirming that this is the only sense of the word,—though I dare boldly say it is not once in ten times so to be understood in the usage of it through the whole book of God; but that it is commonly, and indeed properly, used in the latter sense, for some of all sorts, concerning whatsoever it is affirmed, a few instances, for many that might be urged, will make it clear. Thus, then, ye have it, John xii. 32, "And I, if I be lifted up from the earth, will draw all unto me." That we translate it "all men," as in other places (for though I know the sense may be the same, yet the word *men* being not in the original, but only πάντας), I cannot approve. But who, I pray, are these *all?* Are they all and every one? Then are all and every one drawn to Christ, made believers, and truly converted, and shall be certainly saved; for those that come unto him by his and his Father's drawing, "he will in no wise cast out," John vi. 37. *All*, then, can here be no other than many, some of all sorts, no sort excluded, according as the word is interpreted in Rev. v. 9, "Thou hast redeemed us out of every kindred, and tongue, and people, and nation." These are the *all* he draws to him: which exposition of this phrase is with me of more value and esteem than a thousand glosses of the sons of men. So also, Luke xi. 42, where our translators have made the word to signify immediately and properly (for translators are to keep close to the propriety and native signification of every word) what we assert to be the right interpretation of it; for they render πᾶν λάχανον (which ῥητῶς is "every herb"), "all manner of herbs," taking the word (as it must be) *distributively*, for herbs of all sorts, and not for any individual herb, which the Pharisees did not, could not tithe. And in the very same sense is the word used again, Luke xviii. 12, "I give tithes of all that I possess;" where it cannot signify every individual thing, as is apparent. Most evident, also, is this restrained signification of the word, Acts ii. 17, "I will pour out of my Spirit, ἐπὶ πᾶσαν σάρκα·" which, whether it compriseth every man or no, let every man judge, and not rather men of several and sundry sorts. The same course of interpretation as formerly is followed by our translators, Acts x. 12, rendering πάντα τὰ τετράποδα, (literally, "all beasts or four-footed creatures,") "all manner of beasts," or beasts of sundry several sorts. In the same sense also must it be understood, Rom. xiv. 2, "One believeth that he may eat all things;" that is, what he pleaseth of things to be eaten of. See, moreover, 1 Cor. i. 5. Yea, in that very chapter where men so eagerly contend that the word *all* is to be taken for all and every one (though fruitlessly and falsely, as shall be demonstrated),—namely, 1 Tim. ii. 4, where it is said that "God will have all men to be saved,"—in that very chapter confessedly the word is to be expounded according to the sense we give, namely, verse 8, "I will, therefore, that men pray ἐν παντὶ τόπῳ·" which, that it cannot signify every individual place in heaven, earth, and hell, is of all confessed, and needeth no proof; no more than when our Saviour is said to cure πᾶσαν νόσον, as Matt. ix. 35, there is need to prove that he did not cure every disease of every man, but only all sorts of diseases.

Sundry other instances might be given to manifest that this is the most usual and frequent signification of the word *all* in the holy Scripture; and, therefore, from the bare word nothing can be inferred to enforce an absolute unlimited universality of all individuals to be intimated thereby. The particular places insisted on we shall afterward consider. I shall conclude all concerning these general expressions that are used in the Scripture about this business in these observations:—

First, The word *all* is certainly and unquestionably sometimes restrained, and to be restrained, to *all of some sorts,* although the qualification be not expressed which is the bond of the limitation: so for all believers, 1 Cor. xv. 22; Eph. iv. 6; Rom. v. 18, "The free gift came upon all men to justification of life:" which "all men," that are so actually justified, are no more nor less than those that are Christ's,—that is, believers; for certainly justification is not without faith.

Secondly, The word *all* is sometimes used for *some of all sorts,* Jer. xxxi. 34. The word כֻּלָּם is by Paul rendered πάντες, Heb. viii. 11; so John xii. 32; 1 Tim. ii. 1–3; which is made apparent by the mention of "kings," as one sort of people there intended. And I make no doubt but it will appear to all that the word must be taken in one of these senses in every place where it is used in the business of redemption; as shall be proved.

Thirdly, Let a diligent comparison be made between the general expressions of the New with the predictions of the Old Testament, and they will be found to be answerable to, and expository of, one another; the Lord affirming in the New that that was done which in the Old he foretold should be done. Now, in the predictions and prophecies of the Old Testament, that *all nations, all flesh, all people, all the ends, families,* or *kindreds of the earth, the world, the whole earth,* the *isles,* shall be converted, look up to Christ, come to the mountain of the Lord, and the like, none doubts but that the elect of God in all nations are only signified, knowing that in them alone those predictions have the truth of their accomplishment. And why should the same expressions used in the Gospel, and many of them aiming directly to declare the fulfilling of the other, be wire-drawn to a large extent, so contrary to the mind of the Holy Ghost? In fine, as when the Lord is said to wipe tears from all faces, it hinders not but that the reprobates shall be cast out to eternity where there is weeping and wailing, etc.; so when Christ is said to die for all, it hinders not but that those reprobates may perish to eternity for their sins, without any effectual remedy intended for them, though occasionally proposed to some of them.

6. Observe that the Scripture often speaketh of things and persons according to the appearance they have, and the account that is of

them amongst men, or that esteem that they have of them to whom it speaketh,—frequently speaking of men and unto men as in the condition wherein they are according to outward appearance, upon which human judgment must proceed, and not what they are indeed. Thus, many are called and said to be *wise*, *just*, and *righteous*, according as they are so esteemed, though the Lord knows them to be foolish sinners. So Jerusalem is called "The holy city," Matt. xxvii. 53, because it was so in esteem and appearance, when indeed it was a very "den of thieves." And 2 Chron. xxviii. 23, it is said of Ahaz, that wicked king of Judah, that "he sacrificed to the gods of Damascus that smote him." It was the Lord alone that smote him, and those idols to which he sacrificed were but stocks and stones, the work of men's hands, which could no way help themselves, much less smite their enemies; yet the Holy Ghost useth an expression answering his idolatrous persuasion, and saith, "They smote him." Nay, is it not said of Christ, John v. 18, that he had broken the Sabbath, which yet he only did in the corrupt opinion of the blinded Pharisees?

Add, moreover, to what hath been said, that which is of no less an undeniable truth,—namely, that many things which are proper and peculiar to the children of God are oft and frequently assigned to them who live in the same outward communion with them, and are partakers of the same external privileges, though indeed aliens in respect of the participation of the grace of the promise. Put, I say, these two things, which are most evident, together, and it will easily appear that those places which seem to express a possibility of perishing and eternal destruction to them who are said to be redeemed by the blood of Christ, are no ways advantageous to the adversaries of the effectual redemption of God's elect by the blood of Christ; because such may be said to be redeemed κατὰ τὴν δόξαν, not κατὰ τὴν ἀλήθειαν,—κατὰ τὸ φαίνεσθαι, not κατὰ τὸ εἶναι,—in respect of appearance, not reality, as is the use of the Scripture in divers other things.

7. That which is spoken according to the *judgment of charity* on our parts must not always be exactly squared and made answerable to *verity* in respect of them of whom any thing is affirmed. For the rectitude of our judgment, it sufficeth that we proceed according to the rules of judging that are given us; for what is out of our cognizance, whether that answer to our judgments or no, belongs not to us. Thus, oftentimes the apostles in the Scriptures write unto men, and term them "holy," "saints," yea, "elected;" but from thence positively to conclude that they were all so indeed, we have no warrant. So Peter, 1 Epist. i. 1, 2, calls all the strangers to whom he wrote, scattered throughout Pontus, Galatia, Cappadocia, Asia, and Bithynia, "elect according to the foreknowledge of God the Father," etc.; and yet that I have any warrant to conclude, *de fide*, that all were such, none

dare affirm. So Paul tells the Thessalonians, the whole church to whom he wrote, that he "knew their election of God," 1 Thess. i. 4; 2 Thess. ii. 13, he blesseth God "who had chosen them to salvation." Now, did not Paul make this judgment of them by the rule of charity? according as he affirms in another place, "It is meet for me to think so of you all," Phil. i. 7; and can it, ought it, hence to be infallibly concluded that they were all elected? If some of these should be found to fall away from the gospel and to have perished, would an argument from thence be valid that the elect might perish? would we not presently answer, that they were said to be elected according to the judgment of charity, not that they were so indeed? And why is not this answer as sufficient and satisfying when it is given to the objection taken from the perishing of some who were said to be redeemed merely in the judgment of charity, as when they were said to be elected?

8. The *infallible connection*, according to God's purpose and will, of faith and salvation, which is frequently the thing intended in gospel proposals, must be considered. The Lord hath in his counsel established it, and revealed in his word, that there is an indissoluble bond between these two things, so that "he that believeth shall be saved," Mark xvi. 16; which, indeed, is the substance of the gospel, in the outward promulgation thereof. This is the testimony of God, that eternal life is in his Son; which whoso believeth, he sets to his seal that God is true; he who believes not doing what in him lieth to make God a liar, 1 John v. 9–11. Now, this connection of the means and the end, faith and life, is the only thing which is signified and held out to innumerable to whom the gospel is preached, all the commands, proffers, and promises that are made unto them intimating no more than this will of God, that believers shall certainly be saved; which is an unquestionable divine verity and a sufficient object for supernatural faith to rest upon, and which being not closed with is a sufficient cause of damnation: John viii. 24, "If ye believe not that I am he" (that is, "the way, the truth, and the life"), "ye shall die in your sins."

It is a vain imagination of some, that when the command and promise of believing are made out to any man, though he be of the number of them that shall certainly perish, yet the Lord hath a conditional will of his salvation, and intends that he shall be saved, on condition that he will believe; when the condition lieth not at all in the will of God, which is always absolute, but is only between the things to them proposed, as was before declared. And those poor deluded things, who will be standing upon their own legs before they are well able to crawl, and might justly be persuaded to hold by men of more strength, do exceedingly betray their own conceited ignorance, when, with great pomp, they hold out the broken pieces of an old Arminian sophism with acclamations of grace to this *new* discovery (for so they think of all that is new to them),—namely, "As is God's proffer, so is his intention; but he calls to all to believe and be saved: therefore he intends it to all." For,—

First, God doth not proffer life to *all* upon the condition of faith, passing by a great part of mankind without any such proffer made to them at all.

Secondly, If by God's *proffer* they understand his command and promise, who told them that these things were declarative of his will and purpose or intention? He commands Pharaoh to let his people go; but did he intend he should so do according to his command? had he not foretold that he would so order things that he should not let them go? I thought always that God's commands and promises had revealed our duty, and not his purpose; what God would have us to do, and not what he will do. His promises, indeed, as *particularly* applied, hold out his mind to the *persons* to whom they are applied; but as *indefinitely* proposed, they reveal no other intention of God but what we before discovered, which concerns *things*, not *persons*, even his determinate purpose infallibly to connect faith and salvation.

Thirdly, If the proffer be (as they say) universal, and the intention of God be answerable thereunto,—that is, he intends the salvation of them to whom the tender of it upon faith is made, or may be so; then,—*First*, What becomes of election and reprobation? Neither of them, certainly, can consist with this universal purpose of saving us all. *Secondly*, If he intend it, why is it, then, not accomplished? doth he fail of his purpose? "Dum vitant stulti vitia, in contraria currunt." Is not this certain *Scylla* worse than the other feared *Charybdis?* But they say, "He intendeth it only upon condition; and the condition being not fulfilled, he fails not in his purpose, though the thing be not conferred." But did the Lord foreknow whether the condition would be fulfilled by them to whom the proposal was made, or not? If not, where is his prescience, his omniscience? If he did, how can he be said to intend salvation to them of whom he certainly knew that they would never fulfil the condition on which it was to be attained; and, moreover, knew it with this circumstance, that the condition was not to be attained without his bestowing, and that he had determined not to bestow it? Would they ascribe such a will and purpose to a wise man as they do ignorantly and presumptuously to the only wise God,—namely, that he should intend to have a thing done upon the performance of such a condition as he knew full well without him could never be performed, and he had fully resolved not to effect it: for instance, to give his daughter in marriage to such a one, upon condition he would give unto him such a jewel as he hath not, nor can have, unless he bestow it upon him, which he is resolved never to do? Oh, whither will blindness and ignorance, esteemed light and knowledge, carry poor deluded souls? This, then, is the main thing demonstrated and held out in the promulgation of the gospel, especially for what concerns unbelievers, even the strict connection between the duty of faith assigned and the benefit of life promised; which hath a truth of universal extent, grounded upon the plenary sufficiency of the death of Christ, towards all that shall believe. And I see no reason why this should be termed part of *the mystery of the Universalists*, though the lowest part (as it is by M—— S——, page 202), *that the gospel could not be preached to all unless Christ died for all;* which, with what is mentioned before concerning another and higher part of it, is an old, rotten, carnal, and long-since-confuted sophism, arising out of the ignorance of the word and right reason, which are no way contrary.

9. The mixed distribution of the elect and reprobates, believers and unbelievers, according to the purpose and mind of God, throughout the whole world, and in the several places thereof, in all or most of the single congregations, is another ground of holding out a tender of the blood of Jesus Christ to them for whom it was never shed, as is apparent in the event by the ineffectualness of its proposals. The ministers of the gospel, who are stewards of the mysteries of Christ, and to whom the word of reconciliation is committed, being acquainted only with revealed things (the Lord lodging his purposes and intentions towards particular persons in the secret ark of his own bosom, not to be pryed into), are bound to admonish all, and warn all men, to whom they are sent; giving the same commands, proposing the same promises, making tenders of Jesus Christ in the same manner, to all, that the elect, whom they know not but by the event, may obtain, whilst the rest are hardened. Now, these things being thus ordered by Him who hath the supreme disposal of all,—namely, First, That there should be such a mixture of elect and reprobate, of tares and wheat, to the end of the world; and, secondly, That Christ, and reconciliation through him, should be preached by men ignorant of his eternal discriminating purposes; there is an absolute necessity of two other things: First, That the promises must have a kind of unrestrained generality, to be suitable to this dispensation before recounted. Secondly, That they must be proposed to them towards whom the Lord never intended the good things of the promises, they having a share in this proposal by their mixture in this world with the elect of God. So that, from the general proposition of Christ in the promises, nothing can be concluded concerning his death for all to whom it is proposed, as having another rise and occasion. The sum is:—The word of reconciliation being committed to men unacquainted with God's distinguishing counsels, to be

preached to men of a various, mixed condition in respect of his purpose, and the way whereby he hath determined to bring his own home to himself being by exhortations, entreaties, promises, and the like means, accommodated to the reasonable nature whereof all are partakers to whom the word is sent, which are suited also to the accomplishment of other ends towards the rest, as conviction, restraint, hardening, inexcusableness, it cannot be but the proposal and offer must necessarily be made to some upon condition, who intentionally, and in respect of the purpose of God, have no right unto it in the just aim and intendment thereof. Only, for a close, observe these two things:—First, That the proffer itself neither is nor ever was absolutely universal to all, but only indefinite, without respect to outward differences. Secondly, That Christ being not to be received without faith, and God giving faith to whom he pleaseth, it is manifest that he never intendeth Christ to them on whom he will not bestow faith.

10. The faith which is enjoined and commanded in the gospel hath divers several acts and different degrees, in the exercise whereof it proceedeth orderly, according to the natural method of the proposal of the objects to be believed: the consideration whereof is of much use in the business in hand, our adversaries pretending that if Christ died not for all, then in vain are they exhorted to believe, there being, indeed, no proper object for the faith of innumerable, because Christ did not die for them; as though the gospel did hold out this doctrine in the very entrance of all, that Christ died for every one, elect and reprobate; or as though the first thing which any one living under the means of grace is exhorted to believe were, that Christ died for him in particular;—both which are notoriously false, as I hope, in the close of our undertaking, will be made manifest to all. For the present I shall only intimate something of what I said before, concerning the order of exercising the several acts of faith; whereby it will appear that no one in the world is commanded or invited to believe, but that he hath a sufficient object to fix the act of faith on, of truth enough for its foundation, and latitude enough for its utmost exercise, which is enjoined him.

First, then, The first thing which the gospel enjoineth sinners, and which it persuades and commands them to believe, is, that salvation is not to be had in themselves, inasmuch as all have sinned and come short of the glory of God; nor by the works of the law, by which no flesh living can be justified. Here is a saving gospel truth for sinners to believe, which the apostle dwells upon wholly, Rom. i. ii. iii., to prepare a way for justification by Christ. Now, what numberless numbers are they to whom the gospel is preached who never come so far as to believe so much as this! amongst whom you may reckon almost the whole nation of the Jews, as is apparent, Rom. ix.,

x. 3, 4. Now, not to go one step farther with any proposal, a contempt of this object of faith is the sin of infidelity.

Secondly, The gospel requires faith to this, that there is salvation to be had in the promised seed,—in Him who was before ordained to be a captain of salvation to them that do believe. And here also at this trial some millions of the great army of men, outwardly called, drop off, and do never believe, with true divine faith, that God hath provided a way for the saving of sinners.

Thirdly, That Jesus of Nazareth, who was crucified by the Jews, was this Saviour, promised before; and that there is no name under heaven given whereby they may be saved besides his. And this was the main point upon which the Jews broke off, refusing to accept of Christ as the Saviour of men, but rather prosecuted him as an enemy of God; and are thereupon so oft charged with infidelity and damnable unbelief. The question was not, between Christ and them, whether he died for them all or no? but, whether he was that Messiah promised? which they denied, and perished in their unbelief.

Now, before these three acts of faith be performed, in vain is the soul exhorted farther to climb the uppermost steps, and miss all the bottom foundation ones.

Fourthly, The gospel requires a resting upon this Christ, so discovered and believed on to be the promised Redeemer, as an all-sufficient Saviour, with whom is plenteous redemption, and who is able to save to the utmost them that come to God by him, and to bear the burden of all weary labouring souls that come by faith to him; in which proposal there is a certain infallible truth, grounded upon the superabundant sufficiency of the oblation of Christ in itself, for whomsoever (fewer or more) it be intended. Now, much self-knowledge, much conviction, much sense of sin, God's justice, and free grace, is required to the exercise of this act of faith. Good Lord! how many thousand poor souls within the pale of the church can never be brought unto it! The truth is, without the help of God's Spirit none of those three before, much less this last, can be performed; which worketh freely, when, how, and in whom he pleaseth.

Fifthly, These things being firmly seated in the soul (and not before), we are every one called in particular to believe the efficacy of the redemption that is in the blood of Jesus towards our own souls in particular: which every one may assuredly do in whom the free grace of God hath wrought the former acts of faith, and doth work this also, without either doubt or fear of want of a right object to believe if they should so do; for certainly Christ died for every one in whose heart the Lord, by his almighty power, works effectually faith to lay hold on him and assent unto him, according to that orderly proposal that is held forth in the gospel. Now, according to this order (as by some it is observed) are the articles of our faith disposed in the apostles' creed (that ancient summary of Christian religion commonly so called), the remission of our sins and life eternal being in the last place proposed to be believed; for before we attain so far the rest must be firmly rooted. So that it is a senseless vanity to cry out of the nullity of the object to be believed, if Christ died not for all, there being an absolute truth in every thing which any is called to assent unto, according to the order of the gospel.

And so I have proposed the general foundations of those answers which we shall give to the ensuing objections; whereunto to make particular application of them will be an easy task, as I hope will be made apparent unto all.

CHAPTER II.

An entrance to the answer unto particular arguments.

NOW we come to the consideration of the objections wherewith the doctrine we have, from the word of God, undeniably confirmed is usually, with great noise and clamour, assaulted; concerning which I must give you these three cautions, before I come to lay them down:—

The first whereof is this, that for mine own part I had rather they were all buried than once brought to light, in opposition to the truth of God, which they seem to deface; and therefore, were it left to my choice, I would not produce any one of them: not that there is any difficulty or weight in them, that the removal should be operose or burdensome, but only that I am not willing to be any way instrumental to give breath or light to that which opposeth the truth of God. But because, in these times of liberty and error, I suppose the most of them have been objected to the reader already by men lying in wait to deceive, or are likely to be, I shall therefore show you the poison, and withal furnish you with an antidote against the venom of such self-seekers as our days abound withal.

Secondly, I must desire you, that when ye hear an objection, ye would not be carried away with the sound of words, nor suffer it to take impression on your spirits, remembering with how many demonstrations and innumerable places of Scripture the truth opposed by them hath been confirmed, but rest yourselves until the places be well weighed, the arguments pondered, the answers set down; and then the Lord direct you to "prove all things, and hold fast that which is good."

Thirdly, That you would diligently observe what comes near the stress of the controversy, and the thing wherein the difference lieth, leaving all other flourishes and swelling words of vanity, as of no weight, of no importance.

Now, the objections laid against the truth maintained are of two sorts;—the first, taken from Scripture perverted; the other, from reason abused.

We begin with the first, the OBJECTIONS TAKEN FROM SCRIPTURE; all the places whereof that may any way seem to contradict our assertion are, by our [1]strongest adversaries, in their greatest strength, referred to three heads:—First, Those places that affirm that Christ died for the *world*, or that otherwise make mention of the word *world* in the business of redemption. Secondly, Those that mention *all* and *every man*, either in the work of Christ's dying for them, or where God is said to will their salvation. Thirdly, Those which affirm Christ *bought* or died for them that perish. Hence they draw out three principal arguments or sophisms, on which they much insist. All which we shall, by the Lord's assistance, consider in their several order, with the places of Scripture brought to confirm and strengthen them.

I. The first whereof is taken from the word "*world*," and is thus proposed by them, to whom our poor pretenders are indeed very children:—

"He that is given out of the love wherewith God loved the world, as John iii. 16; that gave himself for the life of the world, as John vi. 51; and was a propitiation for the sins of the whole world, as 1 John ii. 2" (to which add, John i. 29, iv. 42; 2 Cor. v. 19, cited by Armin. pp. 530, 531, and Corv. ad Molin. p. 442, chap. 29); "he was given and died for every man in the world;—but the first is true of Christ, as appears by the places before alleged: therefore he died for all and every one," Remon. Act. Synod. p. 300. And to this they say their adversaries have not any colour of answer.

But granting them the liberty of boasting, we flatly deny, without seeking for colours, the consequent of the first proposition, and will, by the Lord's help, at any time, put it to the trial whether we have not just cause so to do. There be two ways whereby they go about to prove this consequent from the *world* to *all* and *every one;*—first, By reason and the sense of the word; secondly, From the consideration of the particular places of Scripture urged. We will try them in both.

First, If they will make it out by the way of reasoning, I conceive they must argue thus:—

The whole world contains all and every man in the world; Christ died for the whole world: therefore, etc.

Ans. Here are manifestly four terms in this syllogism, arising from the ambiguity of the word "world," and so no true *medium* on which the weight of the conclusion should hang; the *world*, in the first proposition, being taken for the world containing; in the

[1] Remon. Scripta Synod.

second, for the world contained, or men in the world, as is too apparent to be made a thing to be proved. So that unless ye render the conclusion, *Therefore Christ died for that which contains all the men in the world*, and assert in the *assumption* that Christ died for the *world containing*, or the fabric of the habitable earth (which is a frenzy), this syllogism is most sophistically false. If, then, ye will take any proof from the word "world," it must not be from the thing itself, but from the signification of the word in the Scripture; as thus:—

This word "world" in the Scripture signifieth all and every man in the world; but Christ is said to die for the world: ergo, etc.

Ans. The first proposition, concerning the signification and meaning of the word *world* is either *universal*, comprehending all places where it is used, or particular, intending only some. If the first, the proposition is apparently false, as was manifested before; if in the second way, then the argument must be thus formed:—

In some places in Scripture the word "world" signifieth all and every man in the world, of all ages, times, and conditions; but Christ is said to die for the world: ergo, etc.

Ans. That this *syllogism* is no better than the former is most evident, a universal conclusion being inferred from a particular proposition. But now the first proposition being rightly formed, I have one question to demand concerning the second, or the assumption,—namely, whether in every place where there is mention made of the death of Christ, it is said he died for the world, or only in some? If ye say in every place, that is apparently false, as hath been already discovered by those many texts of Scripture before produced, restraining the death of Christ to his elect, his sheep, his church, in comparison whereof these are but few. If the second, then the argument must run thus:—

In some few places of Scripture the word "world" doth signify all and every man in the world; but in some few places Christ is said to die for the world (though not in express words, yet in terms equivalent): ergo, etc.

Ans. This argument is so weak, ridiculous, and sophistically false, that it cannot but be evident to any one; and yet clearly, from the word *world* itself, it will not be made any better, and none need desire that it should be worse. It concludes a universal upon particular affirmatives, and, besides, with four terms apparently in the syllogism; unless the *some places* in the *first* be proved to be the very *some places* in the *assumption*, which is the thing in question. So that if any strength be taken from this word, it must be an argument in this form:—

If the word "world" doth signify all and every man that ever were or shall be, in those places where Christ is said to die for the world, then Christ died for all and every man; but the word "world," in all those places where Christ is said to die for the world, doth signify all and every man in the world: therefore Christ died for them.

Ans. First, That it is but *in one place* said that Christ gave his life for the world, or died for it, which holds out the intention of our Saviour; all the other places seem only to hold out the sufficiency of his oblation for all, which we also maintain. Secondly, We absolutely deny the assumption, and appeal for trial to a consideration of all those particular places wherein such mention is made.

Thus have I called this argument to rule and measure, that it might be evident where the great strength of it lieth (which is indeed very weakness), and that for their sakes who, having caught hold of the word *world,* run presently away with the bait, as though all were clear for universal redemption; when yet, if ye desire them to lay out and manifest the strength of their reason, they know not what to say but *the world* and *the whole world,* understanding, indeed, neither what they say nor whereof they do affirm. And now, *quid dignum tanto?* what cause of the great boast mentioned in the entrance? A weaker argument, I dare say, was never by rational men produced in so weighty a cause; which will farther be manifested by the consideration of the several particular places produced to give it countenance, which we shall do in order:—

1. The first place we pitch upon is that which by our adversaries is first propounded, and not a little rested upon; and yet, notwithstanding their clamorous claim, there are not a few who think that very text as fit and ready to overthrow their whole opinion as Goliath's sword to cut off his own head, many unanswerable arguments against the universality of redemption being easily deduced from the words of that text. The great peaceable King of his church guide us to make good the interest of truth to the place in controversy which through him we shall attempt;—first, by opening the words; and, secondly, by balancing of reasonings and arguments from them. And this place is John iii. 16, "God so loved the world, that he gave his only-begotten Son, that whosoever believeth in him should not perish but have everlasting life."

This place, I say, the Universalists exceedingly boast in; for which we are persuaded they have so little cause, that we doubt not but, with the Lord's assistance, to demonstrate that it is destructive to their whole defence: to which end I will give you, in brief, a double paraphrase of the words, the first containing their sense, the latter ours. Thus, then, our adversaries explain these words:—"'*God so loved,*' had such a natural inclination, velleity, and propensity to the good of '*the world,*' Adam, with all and every one of his posterity, of all ages, times, and conditions (whereof some were in heaven, some in hell long before), '*that he gave his only-begotten Son*,' causing him to be incarnate in the fulness of time, to die, not with a purpose and resolution to save any, but '*that whosoever*,' what persons soever of those which he had propensity unto, '*believeth in him should not perish, but have everlasting life*,' should have this fruit and issue, that he should escape death and hell, and live eternally." In which explication of the sense of the place these things are to be observed:—

First, What is that *love* which was the cause of the sending or giving of Christ; which they make to be *a natural propensity to the good of all*. Secondly, Who are the objects of this love; *all and every man of all generations*. Thirdly, Wherein this giving consisteth; of which I cannot find whether they mean by it the appointment of Christ to be a recoverer, or his actual exhibition in the flesh for the accomplishment of his ministration. Fourthly, *Whosoever*, they make distributive of the persons in the world, and so not restrictive in the intention to some. Fifthly, That life eternal *is the fruit obtained by believers*, but not the end intended by God.

Now, look a little, in the second place, at what we conceive to be the mind of God in those words; whose aim we take to be the advancement and setting forth of the free love of God to lost sinners, in sending Christ to procure for them eternal redemption, as may appear in this following paraphrase:—

"'*God*' the Father '*so loved*,' had such a peculiar, transcendent love, being an unchangeable purpose and act of his will concerning their salvation, towards '*the world*,' miserable, sinful, lost men of all sorts, not only Jews but Gentiles also, which he peculiarly loved, '*that*,' intending their salvation, as in the last words, for the praise of his glorious grace, '*he gave*,' he prepared a way to prevent their everlasting destruction, by appointing and sending '*his only-begotten Son*' to be an all-sufficient Saviour to all that look up unto him, '*that whosoever believeth in him*,' all believers whatsoever, and only they, '*should not perish, but have everlasting life*,' and so effectually be brought to the obtaining of those glorious things through him which the Lord in his free love had designed for them."

In which enlargement of the words, for the setting forth of what we conceive to be the mind of the Holy Ghost in them, these things are to be observed:—

First, What we understand by the "*love*" of God, even that act of his will which was the cause of sending his Son Jesus Christ, being the most eminent act of love and favour to the creature; for love is *velle alicui bonum*, "to will good to any." And never did God will greater good to the creature than in appointing his Son for their redemption. Notwithstanding, I would have it observed that I do not make the purpose of sending or giving Christ to be absolutely subordinate to God's love to his elect, as though that were the end of the other absolutely, but rather that they are both co-ordinate to the same supreme end, or the manifestation of God's glory by the way of mercy tempered with justice; but in respect of our apprehension, that is the relation wherein they stand one to another. Now, this love we say to be that, greater than which there is none.

Secondly, By the "*world*," we understand the elect of God only, though not considered in this place as such, but under such a notion as, being true of them, serves for the farther exaltation of God's love towards them, which is the end here designed; and this is, as they are poor, miserable, lost creatures in the world, of the world, scattered abroad in all places of the world, not tied to Jews or Greeks, but dispersed in any nation, kindred, and language under heaven.

Thirdly, Ἵνα πᾶς ὁ πιστεύων, is to us, "*that every believer*," and is declarative of the intention of God in sending or giving his Son, containing no distribution of the world beloved, but a direction to the persons whose good was intended, that love being an unchangeable intention of the chiefest good.

Fourthly, "*Should not perish, but have life everlasting*," contains an expression of the particular aim and intention of God in this business; which is, the certain salvation of believers by Christ. And this, in general, is the interpretation of the words which we adhere unto, which will yield us sundry arguments, sufficient each of them to evert the general ransom; which, that they may be the better bottomed, and the more clearly convincing, we will lay down and compare the several words and expressions of this place, about whose interpretation we differ, with the reason of our rejecting the one sense and embracing the other:—

The first difference in the interpretation of this place is about the cause of sending Christ; called here *love*. The second, about the object of this love; called here the *world*. Thirdly, Concerning the intention of God in sending his Son; said to be that believers might be *saved*.

For the First, By "love" in this place, all our adversaries agree that *a natural affection and propensity in God to the good of the creature, lost under sin, in general, which moved him to take some way whereby it might possibly be remedied*, is intended. We, on the contrary, say that by *love* here is not meant an inclination or propensity of his nature, but an *act of his will* (where we conceive his love to be seated), *and eternal purpose to do good to man, being the most transcendent and eminent act of God's love to the creature.*

That both these may be weighed, to see which is most agreeable to the mind of the Holy Ghost, I shall give you, first, some of the reasons whereby we oppose the former interpretation; and, secondly, those whereby we confirm our own.

First, If *no natural affection*, whereby he should necessarily be carried to any thing without himself, can or ought to be ascribed unto God, then no such thing is here intended in the word *love;* for that cannot be here intended which is not in God at all. But now, that there neither is nor can be any such natural affection in God is most apparent, and may be evidenced by many demonstrations. I shall briefly recount a few of them:—

First, Nothing that includes any imperfection is to be assigned to Almighty God: he *is God all-sufficient;* he is our *rock, and his work is perfect.* But a natural affection in God to the good and salvation of all, being never completed nor perfected, carrieth along with it a great deal of imperfection and weakness; and not only so, but it must also needs be exceedingly prejudicial to the absolute blessedness and happiness of Almighty God. Look, how much any thing wants of the fulfilling of that whereunto it is carried out with any desire, natural or voluntary, so much it wanteth of blessedness and happiness. So that, without impairing of the infinite blessedness of the ever-blessed God, no natural affection unto any thing never to be accomplished can be ascribed unto him, such as this general love to all is supposed to be.

Secondly, If the Lord hath such a natural affection to all, as to love them so far as to send his Son to die for them, whence is it that this affection of his doth not receive accomplishment? whence is it that it is hindered, and doth not produce its effects? why doth not the Lord engage his power for the fulfilling of his desire? "It doth not seem good to his infinite wisdom," say they, "so to do." Then is there an affection in God to that which, in his wisdom, he cannot prosecute. This among the sons of men, the worms of the earth, would be called a brutish affection.

Thirdly, No affection or natural propensity to good is to be ascribed to God which the Scripture nowhere assigns to him, and is contrary to what the Scripture doth assign unto him. Now, the Scripture doth nowhere assign unto God any natural affection whereby he should be naturally inclined to the good of the creature; the place to prove it clearly is yet to be produced. And that it is contrary to what the Scripture assigns him is apparent; for it describes him to be free in showing mercy, every act of it being by him performed freely, even as he pleaseth, for "he hath mercy on whom he will have mercy." Now, if every act of mercy showed unto any do proceed from the free distinguishing will of God (as is apparent), certainly there can be in him no such natural affection. And the truth is, if the Lord should not show mercy, and be carried out towards the creature, merely upon his own distinguishing will, but should naturally be moved to show mercy to the miserable, he should, first, be no more merciful to men than to devils, nor, secondly, to those that are saved than to those that are damned: for that which is natural must be equal in all its operations; and that which is natural to God must be eternal. Many more effectual reasons are produced by our divines for the denial of this natural affection in God, in the resolution of the Arminian distinction (I call it so, as now by them abused) of God's antecedent and consequent will, to whom the learned reader may repair for satisfaction. So that the love mentioned in this place is not that natural affection to all in general, which is not. But,—

Secondly, It is the *special love of God to his elect*, as we affirm, and so, consequently, not any such thing as our adversaries suppose to be intended by it,—namely, a *velleity* or *natural inclination to the good of all.* For,—

First, The love here intimated is absolutely the most eminent and transcendent love that ever God showed or bare towards any miserable creature; yea, the intention of our Saviour is so to set it forth, as is apparent by the emphatical expression of it used in this place. The particles "so," "that," declare no less, pointing out an eximiousness peculiarly remarkable in the thing whereof the affirmation is [made], above any other thing in the same kind. Expositors usually lay weight upon almost every particular word of the verse, for the exaltation and demonstration of the love here mentioned. "*So*," that is, in such a degree, to such a remarkable, astonishable height: "*God*," the glorious, all-sufficient God, that could have manifested his justice to eternity in the condemnation of all sinners, and no way wanted them to be partakers of his blessedness: "*loved*," with such an earnest, intense affection, consisting in an eternal, unchangeable act and purpose of his will, for the bestowing of the chiefest good (the choicest effectual love): "*the world*," men in the world, of the world, subject to the iniquities and miseries of the world, lying in their blood, having nothing to render them commendable in his eyes, or before him: "*that he gave*," did not, as he made all the world at first, speak the word and it was done, but proceeded higher, to the performance of a great deal more and longer work, wherein he was to do more than exercise an act of his almighty power, as before; and therefore gave "*his Son;*" not any favourite or other well-pleasing creature; not sun, moon, or stars; not the rich treasure of his creation (all too mean, and coming short of expressing this love); but his Son: "*begotten Son*," and that not so called by reason of some near approaches to him, and *filial, obediential* reverence of him, as the angels are called the sons of God; for it was not an angel that he gave, which yet had been an expression of most intense love; nor yet any son by adoption, as believers are the sons of God; but his begotten Son, begotten of his own person from eternity; and that "*his only-begotten Son;*" not any one of his sons, but whereas he had or hath but one only-begotten Son, always in his bosom, his Isaac, he gave him:—than which how could the infinite wisdom of God make or give any higher testimony of his love? especially if ye will add what is here evidently included, though the time was not as yet come that it should be openly expressed, namely, whereunto he gave his Son, his only one; not to be a king, and worshipped in the first place,—but he "spared him not, but delivered him up" to death "for us all," Rom. viii. 32. Whereunto, for a close of all, cast your eyes upon his design and purpose in this whole business, and ye shall find that it was that believers, those whom he thus loved, "*might not perish,*"—that is, undergo the utmost misery and wrath to eternity, which they had deserved,—"*but have everlasting life,*" eternal glory with himself, which of themselves they could no way attain; and ye will easily grant that "greater love hath no man than this." Now, if the love here mentioned be the greatest, highest, and chiefest of all, certainly it cannot be that common affection towards all that we discussed before; for the love whereby men are actually and eternally saved is greater than that which may consist with the perishing of men to eternity.

Secondly, The Scripture positively asserts this very love as the chiefest act of the love of God, and that which he would have us take notice of in the first place: Rom. v. 8, "God commendeth his love toward us, in that, while we were yet sinners, Christ died for us;" and fully, 1 John iv. 9, 10, "In this was manifested the love of God toward us, because that God sent his only-begotten Son into the world, that we might live through him. Herein is love, not that we loved God, but that he loved us, and sent his Son to be the propitiation for our sins." In both which places the eminency of this love is set forth exceeding emphatically to believers, with such expressions as can no way be accommodated to a natural velleity to the good of all.

Thirdly, That seeing all love in God is but *velle alicui bonum,* to will good to them that are beloved, *they* certainly are the object of his love to whom he intends that good which is the issue and effect of that love; but now the issue of this love or good intended, being *not perishing,* and *obtaining eternal life* through Christ, happens alone to, and is bestowed on, only elect believers: therefore, they certainly are the object of this love, and they alone;—which was the thing we had to declare.

Fourthly, That love which is the cause of giving Christ is also always the cause of the bestowing of all other good things: Rom. viii. 32, "He that spared not his own Son, but delivered him up for us all, how shall he not with him also freely give us all things?"

Therefore, if the love there mentioned be the cause of sending Christ, as it is, it must also cause all other things to be given with him, and so can be towards none but those who have those things bestowed on them; which are only the elect, only believers. Who else have grace here, or glory hereafter?

Fifthly, The word here, which is ἠγάπησε, signifieth, in its native importance, *valde dilexit*,—to love so as to rest in that love; which how it can stand with hatred, and an eternal purpose of not bestowing effectual grace, which is in the Lord towards some, will not easily be made apparent. And now let the Christian reader judge, whether by the love of God, in this place mentioned, be to be understood a natural velleity or inclination in God to the good of all, both elect and reprobate, or the peculiar love of God to his elect, being the fountain of the chiefest good that ever was bestowed on the sons of men. This is the first difference about the interpretation of these words.

SECONDLY, The second thing controverted is the *object of this love*, pressed by the word "world;" which our adversaries would have to signify all and every man; we, the elect of God scattered abroad in the world, with a tacit opposition to the nation of the Jews, who alone, excluding all other nations (some few proselytes excepted), before the actual exhibition of Christ in the flesh, had all the benefits of the promises appropriated to them, Rom. ix. 4; in which privilege now all nations were to have an equal share. To confirm the exposition of the word as used by the Universalists, nothing of weight, that ever yet I could see, is brought forth, but only the word itself; for neither the love mentioned in the beginning, nor the design pointed at in the end of the verse, will possibly agree with the sense which they impose on that word in the middle. Besides, how weak and infirm an inference from the word *world*, by reason of its ambiguous and wonderful various acceptations, is, we have at large declared before.

Three poor shifts I find in the great champions of this course, to prove that the word *world* doth not signify the *elect*. Justly we might have expected some reasons to prove that it signified or implied *all* and *every man* in the world, which was their own assertion; but of this ye have a deep silence, being conscious, no doubt, of their disability for any such performance. Only, as I said, three pretended arguments they bring to disprove that which none went about to prove,—namely, that by the *world* is meant the *elect* as such; for though we conceive the persons here designed directly men in and of the world, to be all and only God's elect, yet we do not say that they are here so considered, but rather under another notion, as men scattered over all the world, in themselves subject to misery and sin. So that whosoever will oppose our exposition of this place must either, first, prove that by the *world* here must be necessarily understood all and every man in the world; or, secondly, that it cannot be taken indefinitely for men in the world which materially are elect, though not considered under that formality. So that all those vain flourishes which some men make with these words, by putting the word *elect* into the room of the word *world*, and then coining absurd consequences, are quite beside the business in hand. Yet, farther, we deny that by a supply of the word *elect* into the text any absurdity or untruth will justly follow. Yea, and that flourish which is usually so made is but a bugbear to frighten weak ones; for, suppose we should read it thus, "God so loved the elect, that he gave his only-begotten Son, that whosoever believeth in him should not perish," what inconvenience will now follow? "Why," say they, "that some of the elect, whom God so loved as to send his Son for, may perish." Why, I pray? Is it because he sent his Son that they might not perish? or what other cause? "No; but because it is said, that whosoever of them believeth on him should not perish; which intimates that some of them might not believe." Very good! But where is any such intimation? God designs the salvation of all them in express words for whom he sends his Son; and certainly all that shall be saved shall believe. But it is in the word *whosoever*, which is distributive of the world into those that believe and those that believe not. *Ans.* First, If this word *whosoever* be distributive, then it is restrictive of the love of God to some, and not to others,—to one part of the distribution, and not to the other. And if it do not restrain the love of God, intending the salvation of some, then it is not distributive of the fore-mentioned object of it; and if it do restrain it, then all are not intended in the love which moved God to give his Son. Secondly, I deny that the word here is distributive of the object of God's love, but only declarative of his end and aim in giving Christ in the pursuit of that love,—to wit, that all believers might be saved. So that the sense is, "God so loved his elect throughout the world, that he gave his Son with this intention, that by him believers might be saved." And this is all that is by any (besides a few worthless cavils) objected from this place to disprove our interpretation; which we shall now confirm both positively and negatively:—

First, Our first reason is taken from what was before proved concerning the nature of that love which is here said to have the world for its object, which cannot be extended to all and every one in the world, as will be confessed by all. Now, such is the world, here, as is beloved with that love which we have here described, and proved to be here intended;—even such a love as is, first, the most transcendent and remarkable; secondly, an eternal act of the will of God; thirdly, the cause of sending Christ; fourthly, of giving all good things in and with him; fifthly, an assured fountain and spring of salvation to all beloved with it. So that the world beloved with this love cannot possibly be all and every one in the world.

Secondly, The word *world* in the next verse, which carries along the sense of this, and is a continuation of the same matter, being a discovery of the intention of God in giving his Son, must needs signify the elect and believers, at least only those who in the event are saved; therefore so also in this. It is true, the word *world* is three times used in that verse in a dissonant sense, by an inversion not unusual in the Scripture, as was before declared. It is the latter place that this hath reference to, and is of the same signification with the *world* in verse 16, "That the world through him might be saved,"—ἵνα σωθῇ, "that it should be saved." It discovers the aim, purpose, and intention of God, what it was towards the world that he so loved, even its salvation. Now, if this be understood of any but believers, God fails of his aim and intention, which as yet we dare not grant.

Thirdly, It is not unusual with the Scripture to call God's chosen people by the name of the *world*, as also of *all flesh, all nations, all families of the earth*, and the like general expressions; and therefore no wonder if here they are so called, the intention of the place being to exalt and magnify the love of God towards them, which receives no small advancement from their being every way a world. So are they termed where Christ is said to be their Saviour, John iv. 42; which certainly he is only of them who are saved. A Saviour of men not saved is strange. Also John vi. 51, where he is said to give himself for their life. Clearly, verse 33 of the same chapter, he "giveth life unto the world:" which whether it be any but his elect let all men judge; for Christ himself affirms that he gives life only to his "sheep," and that those to whom he gives life "shall never perish," chap. x. 27, 28. So Rom. iv. 13, Abraham is said by faith to be "heir of the world;" who, verse 11, is called to be father of the faithful. And Rom. xi. 12, the fall of the Jews is said to be "the riches of the world;" which world compriseth only believers of all sorts in the world, as the apostle affirmed that the word bare fruit "in all the world," Col. i. 6. This is that "world" which "God reconcileth to himself, not imputing their trespasses unto them," 2 Cor. v. 19; which is attended with blessedness in all them to whom that non-imputation belongeth, Rom. iv. 8. And for divers evident reasons is it that they have this appellation; as,—First, to distinguish the object of this love of God from the nature angelical, which utterly perished in all the fallen individuals; which the Scripture also carefully doth in express terms, Heb. ii. 16, and by calling this love of God φιλανθρωπία, Tit. iii. 4. Secondly, To evert and reject the boasting of the Jews, as though all the means of grace and all the benefits intended were to them appropriated. Thirdly, To denote that great difference and distinction between the old administration of the covenant, when it was tied up to one people, family, and nation, and the new, when all boundaries being broken up, the fulness of the Gentiles and the corners of the world were to be made obedient to the sceptre of Christ. Fourthly, To manifest the condition of the elect themselves, who are thus beloved, for the declaration of the free grace of God towards them, they being divested of all qualifications but only those that bespeak them terrene, earthly, lost, miserable, corrupted. So that thus much at least may easily be obtained, that from the word itself nothing can be opposed justly to our exposition of this place, as hath been already declared, and shall be farther made manifest.

Fourthly, If every one in the world be intended, why doth not the Lord, in the pursuit of this love, reveal Jesus Christ to every one whom he so loved? Strange! that the Lord should so love men as to give his only-begotten Son for them, and yet not once by any means signify this his love to them, as to innumerable he doth not!—that he should love them, and yet order things so, in his wise dispensation, that this love should be altogether in vain and fruitless!—love them, and yet determine that they shall receive no good by his love, though his love indeed be a willing of the greatest good to them!

Fifthly, Unless ye will grant,—first, Some to be beloved and hated also from eternity; secondly, The love of God towards innumerable to be fruitless and vain; thirdly, The Son of God to be given to them who, *first*, never hear word of him; *secondly*, have no power granted to believe in him; fourthly, That God is mutable in his love, or else still loveth those that be in hell; fifthly, That he doth not give all things to them to whom he gives his Son, contrary to Rom. viii. 32; sixthly, That he knows not certainly beforehand who shall believe and be saved;—unless, I say, all these blasphemies and absurdities be granted, it cannot be maintained that by the *world* here is meant all and every one of mankind, but only men in common scattered throughout the world, which are the elect.

The THIRD difference about these words is, concerning the *means* whereby this love of the Father, whose object is said to be the *world* is made out unto them. Now, this is *by believing*, ἵνα πᾶς ὁ πιστεύων,—"that whosoever believeth," or "that every believer." The intention of these words we take to be, the designing or manifesting of the way whereby the elect of God come to be partakers of the fruits of the love here set forth,—namely, by faith in Christ, God having appointed that for the only way whereby he will communicate unto us the life that is in his Son. To this something was said before, having proved that the term *whosoever* is not distributive of the object of the love of God; to which, also, we may add these following reasons:—

First, If the object be here restrained, so that some only believe and are saved of them for whose sake Christ is sent, then this restriction and determination of the fruits of this love dependeth on the will of God, or on the persons themselves. If on the persons themselves, then make they themselves to differ from others; contrary to 1 Cor. iv. 7. If on the will of God, then you make the sense of the place, as to this particular, to be, "God so loved all as that but some of them should partake of the fruits of his love." To what end, then, I pray, did he love those other some? Is not this, "Out with the sword, and run the dragon through with the spear?"

Secondly, Seeing that these words, *that whosoever believeth,* do peculiarly point out the aim and intention of God in this business, if it do restrain the object beloved, then *the salvation of believers* is confessedly the aim of God in this business, and that distinguished from others; and if so, the general ransom is an empty sound, having no dependence on the purpose of God, his intention being carried out in the giving of his Son only to the salvation of believers, and that determinately, unless you will assign unto him a *nescience* of them that should believe.

These words, then, *whosoever believeth,* containing a designation of *the means* whereby the Lord will bring us to a participation of life through his Son, whom he gave for us; and the following words, of *having life everlasting,* making out the whole counsel of God in this matter, subordinate to his own glory; it followeth,—

That God gave not his Son,—1. For them who never do believe; 2. Much less for them who never hear of him, and so evidently want means of faith; 3. For them on whom he hath determined not to bestow effectual grace, that they might believe.

Let now the reader take up the several parts of these opposite expositions, weigh all, try all things, especially that which is especially to be considered, the *love of God,* and so inquire seriously whether it be only a general affection, and a natural velleity to the good of all, which may stand with the perishing of all and every one so beloved, or the peculiar, transcendent love of the Father to his elect, as before laid down; and then determine whether a general ransom, fruitless in respect of the most for whom it was paid, or the effectual redemption of the elect only, have the firmest and strongest foundation in these words of our Saviour; withal remembering that they are produced as the strongest supportment of the adverse cause, with which, it is most apparent, both the cause of sending Christ and the end intended by the Lord in so doing, as they are here expressed, are altogether inconsistent.

CHAPTER III.

An unfolding of the remaining texts of Scripture produced for the confirmation of the first general argument for universal redemption.

NEXT to the place before considered, that which is urged with most confidence and pressed with most importunity, for the defence of the general ransom, in the prosecution of the former argument, is,—

2. 1 John ii. 1, 2, "If any man sin, we have an advocate with the Father, Jesus Christ the righteous: and he is the propitiation for our sins: and not for ours only, but also for the sins of the whole world." Now, these words, and the deductions from thence, have been set out in various dresses, with great variety of observations, to make them appear advantageous to the cause in hand. The weight of the whole hangs upon this, that the apostle affirms Christ to be the "propitiation for the sins of the whole world;" "which," say they, "manifestly appears to be all and every one in the world," and that,—

First, "From the words themselves without any wresting; for what can be signified by *the whole world*, but all men in the world?"

Secondly, "From the opposition that is made between world and believers, all believers being comprised in the first part of the apostle's assertion, that Christ is a propitiation for our sins; and therefore by the world, opposed unto them, all others are understood." If there be any thing of moment farther excepted, we shall meet with it in our following opening of the place.

Before I come to the farther clearing of the mind of the Holy Ghost in these words, I must tell you that I might answer the objection from hence very briefly, and yet so solidly as quite to cut off all the cavilling exceptions of our adversaries,—namely, that as by *the world*, in other places, men living in the world are denoted, so by *the whole world* in this can nothing be understood but men living throughout the whole world, in all the parts and regions thereof (in opposition to the inhabitants of any one nation, place, or country, as such), as the redeemed of Christ are said to be, Rev. v. 9. But because they much boast of this place, I shall, by God's assistance, so open the sense and meaning of it, that it shall appear to all how little reason they have to place any confidence in their wrested interpretation thereof.

To make out the sense of this place, three things are to be considered:—(1.) To whom the apostle writes. (2.) What is his purpose and aim in this particular place. (3.) The meaning of these two expressions,—[1.] Christ being a "propitiation;" [2.] "The whole world." Which having done, according to the analogy of faith, the scope of this and other parallel places, with reference to the things and use of the words themselves, we shall easily manifest, by undeniable reasons, that the text cannot be so understood (as by right) as it is urged and wrested for universal redemption.

(1.) A discovery *of them to whom the epistle was peculiarly directed* will give some light into the meaning of the apostle. This is one of those things which, in the investigation of the right sense of any place, is exceeding considerable; for although this and all other parts of divine Scripture were given for the use, benefit, and direction of the whole church, yet that many parts of it were directed to peculiar *churches*, and particular persons, and some distinct sorts of persons, and so immediately aiming at some things to be taught, reproved, removed, or established, with direct reference to those peculiar persons and churches, needs no labour to prove. Now, though we have nothing written expressly denominating *them* to whom this epistle was primarily directed, to make an assertion thereof infallibly true and *de fide*, yet, by clear and evident deduction, it may be made more than probable that it was intended to the Jews, or believers of the circumcision; for,—

First, John was in a peculiar manner a minister and an apostle to the Jews, and therefore they were the most immediate and proper objects of his care: "James, Cephas, and John gave to Paul and Barnabas the right hand of fellowship, that they should go unto the heathen, and themselves unto the circumcision," Gal. ii. 9. Now, as Peter and James (for it was that James of whom Paul there speaks who wrote the epistle, the brother of John being slain before), in the prosecution of their apostleship towards them, wrote epistles unto them in their dispersion, James i. 1, 1 Pet. i. 1; as Paul did to all the chief churches among the Gentiles by him planted; so it is more than probable that John, writing the epistle, directed it, chiefly and in the first place, unto them who, chiefly and in the first place, were the objects of his care and apostleship.

Secondly, He frequently intimates that those to whom he wrote were of them who heard of and received the word from the beginning; so twice together in this chapter, verse 7, "I write an old commandment, which ye had from the beginning, ... which ye heard from the beginning." Now, that the promulgation of the gospel had its beginning among the Jews, and its first entrance with them, before the conversion of any of the Gentiles,—which was a mystery for a season,—is apparent from the story of the Acts of the Apostles, chap. i.–v., x., xi. "To the Jew first, and also to the Greek," was the order divinely appointed, Rom. i. 16.

Thirdly, The opposition that the apostle makes between *us* and the *world* in this very place is sufficient to manifest unto whom he wrote. As a Jew, he reckoneth himself with and among the believing Jews to whom he wrote, and sets himself with them in opposition to the residue of believers in the world; and this is usual with this apostle, wherein how he is to be understood, he declares in his Gospel, chap. xi. 51, 52.

Fourthly, The frequent mention and cautions that he makes and gives of *false teachers, seducers, antichrists* (which in those first days were, if not all of them, yet for the greatest part, of the Circumcision, as is manifest from Scripture and ecclesiastical story; of whom the apostle said that "they went out from them," 1 John ii. 19), evidently declare that to them in especial was this epistle directed, who lay more open, and were more obnoxious to, the seducements of their countrymen than others.

Now, this being thus cleared, if withal ye will remind what was said before concerning the inveterate hatred of that people towards the Gentiles, and the ingrafted opinion they had concerning their own sole interest in the redemption procured and purchased by their Messiah, it will be no difficult thing for any to discern the aim of the apostle in this place, in the expression so much stuck at. "He," saith he, "is the propitiation for our sins,"—that is, our sins who are believers of the Jews; and lest by this assertion they should take occasion to confirm themselves in their former error, he adds, "And not for ours only, but for the sins of the whole world," or, "The children of God scattered abroad," as John xi. 51, 52, of what nation, kindred, tongue, or language soever they were. So that we have not here an opposition between the effectual salvation of all believers and the ineffectual redemption of all others, but an extending of the same effectual redemption which belonged to the Jewish believers to all other believers, or children of God throughout the whole world.

(2.) For the aim and intention of the apostle in these words, it is *to give consolation to believers* against their sins and failings: "If any man sin, we have an advocate with the Father, Jesus Christ the righteous: and he is the propitiation for our sins." The very order and series of the words, without farther enlargement, proves this to be so. That they were believers only to whom he intended this consolation, that they should not despair nor utterly faint under their infirmities, because of a sufficient, yea, effectual remedy provided, is no less evident: for,—First, They only have an *advocate;* it is confessed that believers only have an interest in Christ's advocation. Secondly, Comfort, in such a case, belongs to none but them; unto others in a state and condition of alienation, wrath is to be denounced, John iii. 36. Thirdly, They are the "little children" to whom he writes, 1 John ii. 1; whom he describes, verses 12, 13, to have "their sins forgiven them for his name's sake," and to "know the Father." So that the aim of the apostle being to make out consolation to believers in their failings, he can speak of none but them only. And if he should extend that whereof he speaks, namely,—that Christ was a propitiation to all and every one,—I cannot conceive how this can possibly make any thing to the end proposed, or the consolation of believers; for what comfort can arise from hence to them, by telling them that Christ died for innumerable that shall be damned? Will that be any refreshment unto me which is common unto me with them that perish eternally? Is not this rather a pumice-stone than a breast of consolation? If you ask how comfort can be given to all and every one, unless Christ died for them? I say, If by all and every one you mean all believers, Christ is, as in the text asserted, a propitiation and an advocate for them all. If all others, reprobates and unbelievers, we say that there is neither in the death of Christ nor in the word of God any solid spiritual consolation prepared for them; the children's bread must not be cast to dogs.

(3.) The meaning and purport of the word "propitiation," which Christ is said to be for "us," and "the whole world," is next to be considered:—

First, The word in the original is ἱλασμός, twice only used in the New Testament,—here, and chap. iv. 10 of this same epistle. The verb also, ἱλάσκομαι, is as often used;—namely, Heb. ii. 17, translated there (and that properly, considering the construction it is in) "to make reconciliation;" and Luke xviii. 13, it is the word of the publican, Ἱλάσθητί μοι, "Be merciful to me." There is also another word of the same original and a like signification, namely, ἱλαστήριον, twice also used;—Rom. iii. 25, there translated "a propitiation;" and Heb. ix. 5, where it is used for, and also rendered, "the mercy-seat:" which will give some light into the meaning of the word. That which, Exod. xxv. 17, is called *capporeth*, from *caphar*, properly to cover, is here called ἱλαστήριον, that which Christ is said to be, Rom. iii. 25. Now, this mercy-seat was a plate of pure gold, two cubits and a half long, and a cubit and a half broad, like the uppermost plate or board of a table; that was laid upon the ark, shadowed over with the wings of the cherubim. Now, this word כַּפֹּרֶת comes, as was said, from כָּפַר, whose first native and genuine sense is "to cover," (though most commonly used [for] "to expiate.") This plate or mercy-seat was so called because it was placed upon the ark, and covered it, as the wings of the cherubim hovered over that; the mystical use hereof being to hide, as it were, the law or rigid tenor of the covenant of works which was in the ark, God thereby declaring himself to be pacified or reconciled, the cause of anger and enmity being hidden. Hence the word cometh to have its second acceptation, even that which is rendered by the apostle ἱλαστήριον, "placamen," or "placamentum,"—that whereby God is appeased. This that did plainly signify, being shadowed with the wings of the cherubim, denoting God's presence in power and goodness; which were made crouching over it, as the wings of a hen over her chickens. Hence that prayer of David, to be "hid under the shadow of God's wings," Ps. xxxvi. 7, lvii. 1, lxi. 4, lxiii. 7, xci. 4 (and perhaps that allusion of our Saviour, Matt. xxiii. 37), intimating the favourable protection of God in mercy, denoted by the wings of the cherubim covering the propitiatory, embracing that which covered the bill of accusation; which, typically, was that table, or golden plate or covering, before described; truly and really Jesus Christ, as is expressly affirmed, Rom. iii. 25.

Now, all this will give us some light into the meaning of the word, and so, consequently, into the sense of this place, with the mind of the Holy Ghost therein. Ἱλασμός and ἱλαστήριον, both translated "a propitiation," with the verb of the same original (the bottom of them all being ἱλάω, not used in the New Testament, which in Eustathius is from ἵεμαι λάειν, "intently and with care to look upon any thing," like the oracle on the mercy-seat), do signify that which was done or typically effected by the mercy-seat,—namely, to appease, pacify, and reconcile God in respect of aversation for sin. Hence that phrase, Heb. ii. 17, Ἱλάσκεσθαι τὰς ἁμαρτίας τοῦ λαοῦ, which the Latinists render "Expiare peccata populi," "To expiate the sins of the people." ("Expiare" is, in this business, to turn away anger by an atonement. So the historian, "Solere reges ostenta cœlestia cæde aliquâ illustri expiare, atque a semet in capita procerum depellere," Suet. in Neron. 36.) We render it, "To make reconciliation for the sins of the people." The word will bear both, the meaning being, to appease, or pacify, or satisfy God for sin, that it might not be imputed to them towards whom he was so appeased. Ἱλάσκεσθαι τὰς ἁμαρτίας τοῦ λαοῦ is as much as Ἱλάσκεσθαι τὸν Θεὸν περὶ τῶν ἁμαρτιῶν, "To pacify God concerning sin." Hence the word receiveth another signification, that wherein it is used by the publican, Luke xviii. 13, Ἱλάσθητί μοι, "Be merciful to me;" that is, "Let me enjoy that mercy from whence flows the pardon of sin, by thy being appeased towards me, and reconciled unto me." From all which it appeareth that the meaning of the word ἱλασμός, or "propitiation," which Christ is said to be, is that whereby the law is covered, God appeased and reconciled, sin expiated, and the sinner pardoned; whence pardon, and remission of sin is so often placed as the product and fruit of his blood-shedding, whereby he was a "propitiation," Matt. xxvi. 28; Eph. i. 7; Col. i. 14; Heb. ix. 22; Rom. iii. 25, v. 9; 1 John i. 7; 1 Pet. i. 2; Rev. i. 5.

From that which hath been said, the sense of the place is evident to be, that Christ hath so expiated sin, and reconciled to God, that the sinner is pardoned and received to mercy for his sake, and that the law shall never be produced or brought forth for his condemnation. Now, whether this can be tolerably applied to the *whole world* (taking it for all and every man in the world), let all the men in the world that are able judge. Are the sins of every one expiated? Is God reconciled to every one? Is every sinner pardoned? Shall no one have the transgression of the law charged on him? Why, then, is not every one saved? Doubtless, all these are true of every believer, and of no one else in the whole world. For them the apostle affirmed that Christ is a *propitiation;* that he might show from whence ariseth, and wherein chiefly, if not only, that advocation for them, which he promiseth as the fountain of their consolation, did consist,—even in a presentation of the atonement made by his blood. He is also a propitiation only by faith, Rom. iii. 25; and surely none have faith but believers: and, therefore, certainly it is they only throughout the world for whom alone Christ is a propitiation. Unto them alone God says, "Ἵλεως ἔσομαι, "I will be propitious,"—the great word of the new covenant, Heb. viii. 12, they alone being covenanters.

Secondly, Let us consider the phrase ὅλου τοῦ κόσμου,—"of the whole world." I shall not declare how the word *world* is in the Scripture πολύσημον, of divers significations; partly because I have in some measure already performed it; partly because it is not in itself so much here insisted on, but only with reference to its general adjunct, *whole,* "the whole world:" and, therefore, we must speak to the whole phrase together. Now, concerning this expression, I say,—

First, That whereas, with that which is equivalent unto it, *all the world,* it is used seven or eight times in the New Testament, it cannot be made appear, clearly and undeniably, that in any place (save perhaps one, where it is used in *re necessariâ*) it compriseth all and every man in the world; so that unless some circumstance in this place enforce that sense (which it doth not), it will be a plain wresting of the words to force that interpretation upon them. Let us, then, briefly look upon the places, beginning with the last, and so ascending. Now, that is, Rev. iii. 10, "I will keep thee from the hour of temptation, which shall come ἐπὶ τῆς οἰκουμένης ὅλης,"—"upon all the world," (the word *world* is other in the original here than in the place we have before us, there being divers words to express the same thing, considered under several notions); where that it cannot signify all and every one is evident, because some are promised to be preserved from that which is said to come upon it. Passing the place of which we treat, the next is, Col. i. 6, "Which is come unto you καθὼς καὶ ἐν παντὶ τῷ κόσμῳ,"—"as in all the world." Where,—1. All and every man cannot be understood; for they had not all then received the gospel. 2. Only believers are here signified, living abroad in the world; because the gospel is said to "bring forth fruit" in them to whom it comes, and there is no true gospel fruit without faith and repentance. Another place is Rom. i. 8, "Your faith is spoken of ἐν ὅλῳ τῷ κόσμῳ,"—"throughout the whole world." Did every one in the world hear and speak of the Roman faith? You have it also Luke ii. 1, "There went out a decree from Cæsar Augustus, ἀπογράφεσθαι πᾶσαν τὴν οἰκουμένην,"—"that all the world should be taxed;" which yet was but the Roman empire, short enough of comprising all singular persons in the world. It were needless to repeat the rest, being all of the same indefinite importance and signification. If, then, the expression itself doth not hold out any such universality as is pretended, unless the matter concerning which it is used and the circumstances of the place do require it (neither of which enforcements has any appearance in this place), there is no colour to fasten such an acceptation upon it; rather may we conclude that *all the world,* and *the whole world,* being in other places taken indefinitely for men of all sorts throughout the world, the same words are no otherwise here to be understood. So that ὅλος ὁ κόσμος is here no more than ἐκκλησία καθολική.

Secondly, The *whole world* can signify no more than *all nations, all the families of the earth, all flesh, all men, all the ends of the world.* These surely are expressions equivalent unto, and as comprehensive of particulars as the whole world; but now all these expressions we find frequently to bear out believers only, but as of all sorts, and throughout the world. And why should not this phrase also be affirmed to be, in the same matter, of the same and no other importance? We may instance in some places: "All the ends of the earth have seen the salvation of our God," Ps. xcviii. 3; "All the ends of the world shall remember and turn unto the LORD, and all the kindreds of the nations shall worship before thee," Ps. xxii. 27; "All nations shall serve thee," Ps. lxxii. 11;—which general expressions do yet denote no more but only the believers of all the several nations of the world, who alone see the salvation of God, remember and turn to him and serve him. So Joel ii. 28, "I will pour out of my Spirit upon all flesh;" as the words are again repeated on the accomplishment of the promise, Acts ii. 17;—Luke using the same expression, as part of a sermon of John Baptist, "All flesh shall see the salvation of God." What a conquest should we have had proclaimed, if it had been anywhere affirmed that Christ died for *all flesh, all nations, all kindreds,* etc.! which yet are but liveries of believers, though garments as wide and large as this expression, *the whole world.* Believers are called "all nations," Isa. ii. 2, lxvi. 18; yea, "all men," Tit. ii. 11: for to them alone the salvation-bringing grace of God is manifest. If they, then, the children of God, be, as is apparent in the Scripture phrase, *all flesh, all nations, all kindreds, all the ends of the world, all the ends of the earth, all men,* why not also *the whole world?*

Thirdly, The *whole world* doth sometimes signify the worser part of the world; and why may it not, by a like synecdoche, signify the better part thereof? Rev. xii. 9, "The Devil, and Satan, which deceiveth the whole world, is cast out;" that is, the wicked and reprobate in the whole world, others rejoicing in his overthrow, verse 10.

1 John v. 19, Ὁ κόσμος ὅλος, "The whole world lieth in wickedness;" where "the whole world" is opposed to them which are "of God," in the beginning of the verse. The contrary sense you have Col. i. 6.

This, then, being spoken, to clear the signification of the expression here insisted on, will make it evident that there is nothing at all in the words themselves that should enforce any to conceive that all and every man in the world are denoted by them, but rather believers, even all that did or should believe, throughout the whole world, in opposition only to believers of the Jewish nation: which, that it is the meaning of the place, besides what hath been clearly demonstrated, I prove by these reasons:—

First, This place treateth not of the ransom of Christ in respect of *impetration,* but of *application;* for it affirms Christ to be that by his death which he is only by faith, as was manifested from Rom. iii. 25. Also, from application only ariseth consolation; now, never any said that the application of the death of Christ was universal: therefore, this place cannot have regard to all and every one.

Secondly, Christ is here said to be a propitiation only for such as are intended in the place, which is apparent; but now believers only are here intended, for it is to give them consolation in their failings (in which case consolation belongeth to them alone): therefore, it is believers only, though of all sorts, times, places, and conditions, for whom Christ is said to be a propitiation.

Thirdly, This kind of phrase and expression in other places cannot possibly be tortured to such an extension as to comprehend all and every one, as was apparent from the places before alleged; to which add, Matt. iii. 5, "Then went out to him πᾶσα ἡ Ἰουδαία, καὶ πᾶσα ἡ περίχωρος τοῦ Ἰορδάνου,"—"all Judea, and all the region round about Jordan;" among whom, notwithstanding, the Pharisees rejected his baptism. Why, then, should it be so understood here, especially all circumstances (as hath been showed) being contrary to such an interpretation?

Fourthly, The most clear parallel places in the Scripture are opposite to such a sense as is imposed. See Col. i. 6; John xi. 51, 52.

Fifthly, If the words are to be understood to signify all and every one in the world, then is the whole assertion useless as to the chief end intended,—namely, to administer consolation to believers; for what consolation can arise from hence unto any believer, that Christ was a propitiation for them that perish? Yea, to say that he was *a sufficient propitiation* for them, though not effectual, will yield them no more comfort than it would have done Jacob and his sons to have heard from Joseph that he had corn enough, sufficient to sustain them, but that he would do so was altogether uncertain; for had he told them he would sustain them sufficiently, though not effectually, they might have starved notwithstanding his courtesy. "The whole world," then, in this place, is the whole people of God (opposed to the Jewish nation), scattered abroad throughout the *whole world,* of what nation, kindred, tongue, or family soever, who are some of all sorts, not all of every sort. So that *this place makes nothing for general redemption.*

Some few objections there are which are usually laid against our interpretation of *this* passage of the apostle, but they are all prevented or removed in the explication itself; so that it shall suffice us to name one or two of them:—

Obj. 1. "It is the intention of the apostle to comfort all in their fears and doubts; but every one in the world may be in fears and doubts: therefore, he proposeth this, that they all may be comforted."

Ans. The *all* that may be in fears and doubts, in the business of consolation, must of necessity be restrained to believers, as was before declared.

Obj. 2. "All believers are comprehended in the first branch, 'For our sins;' and, therefore in the increase and extension of the assertion, by adding, 'For the sins of the whole world,' all others are intended."

Ans. 1. In the first part, the believing *Jews* alone are intended, of whom John was one; and the addition is not an extending of the propitiation of Christ to *others than believers,* but only to *other believers.* 2. If it might be granted that in the first branch all believers then living were comprehended, who might presently be made partakers of this truth, yet the increase or accession must be, by analogy, only those who *were to be* in after ages and remoter places than the name of Christ had then reached unto,—even all those who, according to the prayer of our Saviour, John xvii. 20, should believe on his name to the end of the world. And thus the two main places produced for the confirmation of the first argument are vindicated from the false glosses and violent wrestings of our adversaries; the rest will be easily cleared.

3. The next place urged in the argument is John vi. 51, where our Saviour affirms that he will give his "flesh for the life of the world." This giving of himself was the sanctifying and offering up of himself an acceptable oblation for the sins of them for whom he suffered; his intention being, that they for whom in dying he so offered himself might have life eternal thereby: which, because it was not for the Jews only, but also for all the elect of God everywhere, he calleth them "the world." That the *world* here cannot signify all and every one that ever were or should be, is as manifest as if it were written with the beams of the sun; and that because it is made the object of Christ's intendment, to purchase for them, and bestow upon them, life and salvation. Now, I ask, Whether any man, not bereaved of all spiritual and natural sense, can imagine that Christ, in

his oblation, intended to purchase life and salvation for all them whom he knew to be damned many ages before, the irreversible decree of wrath being gone forth against them? Or who dares once affirm that Christ gave himself for the life of them who, notwithstanding that, by his appointment, do come short of it to eternity? So that if we had no other place to manifest that the word *world* doth not always signify *all*, but only some of all sorts, as the elect of God are, but this one produced by our adversaries to the contrary, I hope with all equitable readers our defence would receive no prejudice.

4. Divers other places I find produced by Thomas More, chap. xiv. of the "Universality of Free Grace," to the pretended end in hand; which, with that whole chapter, shall be briefly considered.

The first insisted on by him is 2 Cor v. 19, "God was in Christ reconciling the world unto himself, not imputing their trespasses unto them."

Ans. 1. Really he must have no small confidence of his own strength and his reader's weakness, who from this place shall undertake to conclude the universality of redemption, and that the *world* doth here signify all and every one therein. They who are called the "world," verse 19, are termed "us," verse 18, "He hath reconciled us to himself by Jesus Christ;" as also verse 21, where they are farther described by Christ's being "made sin for them," and their being "made the righteousness of God in him." Are these things true of all in the world? If this text may receive any light from what is antecedent and consequent unto it,—if the word any interpretation from those expressions which are directly expository of it,—by the *world* here can be meant none but elect believers. 2. God's reconciling the world unto himself is described evidently either to consist in, or necessarily to infer, a *non-imputation of sin* to them, or that *world;* which is farther interpreted to be an imputation of the righteousness of Christ, verse 21. Now, in these two things consisteth the blessedness of justification in Christ, Rom. iv. 6, 7; therefore this *whole world,* which God in Christ reconcileth to himself, is a blessed, justified world,—not all and every one of the sons of men that ever were, are, or shall be in the world, the greatest part of whom *lie in evil.* 3. This *God in Christ reconciling,* holdeth out an effectual work of reconciliation. Now, this must be either an absolute reconciliation or a conditionate. If *absolute,* why are not all actually and absolutely reconciled, pardoned, justified? If conditionate, then,—First, How can a *conditionate reconciliation* be reconciled with that which is actual? Secondly, Why is no condition here mentioned? Thirdly, What is that condition? Is it faith and believing? Then the sense of the words must be either,—first, "God was in Christ, reconciling a believing world unto himself," of which there is no need, for believers are reconciled; or, secondly, "God was in Christ reconciling an unbelieving world unto himself, upon condition that it do believe;" that is, upon condition that it be not unbelieving; that is, that it be reconciled. Is this the mind of the Holy Spirit? Fourthly, If this reconciliation of the world consist (as it doth) in a non-imputation of sin, then this is either of all their sins, or only of some sins. If of some only, then Christ saves only from some sins. If of all, then of unbelief also, or it is no sin; then all the men in the world must needs be saved, as whose unbelief is pardoned. The *world* here, then, is only the world of blessed, pardoned believers, who are "made the righteousness of God in Christ."

That which Thomas More bringeth to enforce the opposite signification of the word is, in many words, very little. Much time he spends, with many uncouth expressions, to prove a twofold reconciliation intimated in the text,—the first of God to us by Christ, the other of us to God by the Spirit; which we also grant, though we do not divide them, but make them several parts of the same reconciliation, the former being the rule of the latter: for look, to whomsoever God is reconciled in and by Christ, they shall certainly every one of them be reconciled to God by the Spirit;—God's reconciliation to them consisting in a non-imputation of their sins; their reconciliation unto him, in an acceptance of that non-imputation in Jesus Christ. And as it is the rule of, so is it the chief motive unto, the latter, being the subject or matter of the message in the gospel whereby it is effected. So that the assertion of this twofold reconciliation, or rather two branches of the same complete work of reconciliation, establisheth our persuasion that the *world* can be taken only for the elect therein.

But he brings farther light from the context to strengthen his interpretation. "For," saith he, "those of the world here are called 'men,' verse 11; men that must 'appear before the judgment-seat of Christ,' verse 10; that were 'dead,' verse 14; that ought to live unto Christ, verse 15: therefore, *all* men." Now, "homini homo quid interest?" How easy is it for some men to prove what they please! Only let me tell you, one thing more is to be done that the cause may be yours,—namely, a proving that the elect of God are not men; that they must not appear before the judgment-seat of Christ; that they were not dead; that they ought not to live to Christ. This do, or ye lose the reward.

But he adds,—First, "Of these, some are reconciled to God," verse 18. *Ans.* Most false, that there is any limitation or restriction of reconciliation to some of those concerning whom he treats; it is rather evidently extended to all of them. Secondly, "But some are not reconciled," verse 11. *Ans.* Not a word of any such thing in the text, nor can the least colour be possibly wrested thence for any such assertion. "Many corrupt the word of God."

A second place he urgeth is John i. 9, "That was the true Light, which lighteth every man that cometh into the world." "This *world*," saith he, "is the world of mankind, verse 4, made by Christ, verse 3; which was his own by creation, mercy, and purchase, yet 'received him not,' verses 5, 10, 11: therefore, it is manifest that there is life, and that Christ died for all."

Ans. That by the *world* here is meant, not men in the world, all or some, but the habitable part of the earth, is more apparent than can well admit of proof or illustration. The phrase of *coming into the world* cannot possibly be otherwise apprehended. It is as much as *born*, and coming to breathe the common air. Now, among the expositions of this place, that seems most consonant and agreeable to the discourse of the apostle, with other expressions here used, which refers the word ἐρχόμενον, "coming," unto φῶς, "light," and not to ἄνθρωπον, "man," with which it is vulgarly esteemed to agree; so that the words should be rendered, "That was the true Light, which, coming into the world, lighteth every man." So John iii 19, "Light is come into the world;" and chap. xii. 46, "I am come a light into the world;"—parallel expressions unto this. So that from the word *world* nothing can hence be extorted for the universality of grace or ransom. The whole weight must lie on the words "every man," which yet Thomas More doth not at all insist upon; and if any other should, the word, holding out actual illumination, can be extended in its subject to no more than indeed are illuminated.

Christ, then, coming into the world, is said to enlighten every man, partly because every one that hath any light hath it from him, partly because he is the only true light and fountain of illumination; so that he doth enlighten every one that is enlightened: which is all the text avers, and is by none denied. But whether all and every one in the world, before and after his incarnation, were, are, and shall be actually enlightened with the knowledge of Christ by his coming into the world, let Scripture, experience, reason, and sense determine. And this, in brief, may suffice to manifest the weakness of the argument for universal redemption from this place; waiving for the present, not denying or opposing, another interpretation of the words, rendering the enlightening here mentioned to be that of reason and understanding, communicated to all, Christ being proposed as, in his divine nature, the light of all, even the eternal wisdom of his Father.

A third place is John i. 29, "Behold the Lamb of God, which taketh away the sin of the world;" and this, saith he, is spoken of the world in general.

Ans. 1. If it should be spoken of the world in general, yet nothing could thence be inferred to a universality of individuals. 2. That Christ is he, ὁ αἴρων, that taketh away, beareth, purgeth, pardoneth, as the word is used, 2 Sam. xxiv. 10 (taketh away by justification that it should not condemn, by sanctification that it should not reign, by glorification that it should not be), τὴν ἁμαρτίαν, "the sin," great sin, original sin, τοῦ κόσμου, "of the world," common to all, is most certain; but that he taketh it away from, beareth it for, pardoneth it unto, purgeth it out of, all and every man in the world, is not in the least manner intimated in the text, and is in itself exceeding false.

John iii. 17 is by him in the next place urged, "God sent not his Son into the world to condemn the world, but that the world through him might be saved."

Ans. A notable ἀντανάκλασις, or eminent inversion of the word *world* in this place was before observed; like that of chap. i. 10, "He was in the world," or on the earth, a part of it, "and the world was made by him," the whole world, with all things therein contained, "and the world knew him not," or the most of men living in the world. So here, by the *world*, in the first place, that part of the world wherein our Saviour conversed hath the name of the whole assigned unto it. In the second, you may take it for all and every one in the world, if you please (though from the text it cannot be enforced); for the prime end of our Saviour's coming was not to condemn any, but to save his own, much less to condemn all and every one in the world, out of which he was to save his elect. In the third place, they only are designed whom God sent his Son on purpose to save, as the words eminently hold out. The saving of them who then are called the *world* was the very purpose and design of God in sending his Son. Now, that these are not all men, but only believers of Jews and Gentiles throughout the world, is evident:—1. Because all are not saved, and the Lord hath said "he will do all his pleasure, and his purpose shall stand." 2. Because the most of men were at the instant actually damned. Did he send his Son that they might be saved? 3. Because Christ was appointed for the fall of some, Luke ii. 34, and, therefore, not that all and every one might be saved. 4. The end of Christ's actual exhibition and sending in the flesh is not opposite to any of God's eternal decrees, which were eternally fixed concerning the condemnation of some for their sins. Did he send his Son to save such? Doth he act contrary to his own purposes, or fail in his undertakings? *The saved world is the people of God scattered abroad throughout the world.*

John iv. 42, and 1 John iv. 14, with John vi. 51 (which was before considered), are also produced by Thomas More; in all which places Christ is called the "Saviour of the world."

Ans. Christ is said to be the Saviour of the *world*, either, first, because there is no other Saviour for any in the world, and because he saves all that are saved, even the people of God (not the Jews only), all over the world; or, secondly, because he doth actually save all the world, and every one in it. If in this latter way, *vicisti*, Mr More; if in the former, μένομεν ὥσπερ ἐσμέν,—"we are still where we were."

The urging of John xii. 46, "I am come a light into the world," in this business, deserves to be noted, but not answered. The following places of John iii. 16, 17, 1 John ii. 1, 2, have been already considered. Some other texts are produced, but so exceedingly wrested, strangely perverted, and so extremely useless to the business in hand, that I dare not make so bold with the reader's patience as once to give him a repetition of them.

And this is our defence and answer to the first principal argument of our opposers, our explication of all those texts of Scripture which they have wrested to support it, the bottom of their strength being but the ambiguity of one word. Let the Christian reader "Prove all things, and hold fast that which is good."

CHAPTER IV.

Answer to the second general argument for the universality of redemption.

II. THE second argument, wherewith our adversaries make no less flourish than with the former, is raised from those places of Scripture where there is mention made of *all men* and *every man*, in the business of redemption. With these bare and naked words, attended with swelling, vain expressions of their own, they commonly rather proclaim a victory than study how to prevail. Their argument needs not to be drawn to any head or form, seeing they pretend to plead from express words of Scripture. Wherefore we shall only consider the several places by them in this kind usually produced, with such enforcements of their sense from them as by the ablest of that persuasion have been used. The chief places insisted on are, 1 Tim. ii. 4, 6; 2 Pet. iii. 9; Heb. ii. 9; 2 Cor. v. 14, 15; 1 Cor. xv. 22; Rom. v. 18.

For the use and signification of the word *all* in Scripture, so much hath been said already by many that it were needless for me to insist upon it. Something also to this purpose hath been spoken before, and that abundantly sufficient to manifest that no strength of argument can be taken from the word itself; wherefore I shall apply myself only to the examination of the particular places urged, and the objections from them raised:—

1. The first and chief place is, 1 Tim. ii. 4, 6, "God will have all men to be saved, and come to the knowledge of the truth...... Christ gave himself a ransom for all, to be testified in due time." Hence they draw this argument, Rem. Act. Synod:—"If God will have all men to be saved, then Christ died for all; but God will have all men to be saved, and come to the knowledge of the truth: therefore, Christ died for all men."

Ans. The whole strength of this argument lies in the ambiguity of the word *all*, which being of various significations, and to be interpreted suitably to the matter in hand and the things and persons whereof it is spoken, the whole may be granted, or several propositions denied, according as the acceptation of the word is enforced on us That *all* or *all men* do not always comprehend all and every man that were, are, or shall be, may be made apparent by near five hundred instances from the Scripture. Taking, then, *all* and *all men distributively*, for some of all sorts, we grant the whole; taking them *collectively*, for all of all sorts, we deny the minor,—namely, that God will have them all to be saved. To make our denial of this appear to be an evident truth, and agreeable to the mind of the Holy Ghost in this place, two things must be considered:—1. What is that will of God here mentioned, whereby he willeth all to be saved. 2. Who are the *all* of whom the apostle is in this place treating.

1. The will of God is usually distinguished into his *will intending* and his *will commanding;* or rather, that word is used in reference unto God in this twofold notion,—(1.) For his purpose, what he will do; (2.) For his approbation of what we do, with his command thereof. Let now our opposers take their option in whether signification the will of God shall be here understood, or how he willeth the salvation of all.

First, If they say he doth it "voluntate signi," with his will commanding, requiring, approving, then the sense of the words is this:—"God commandeth all men to use the means whereby they may obtain the end, or salvation, the performance whereof is acceptable to God in any or all;" and so it is the same with that of the apostle in another place, "God commandeth all men everywhere to repent." Now, if this be the way whereby God willeth the salvation of all here mentioned, then certainly those *all* can possibly be no more than to whom he granteth and revealeth the means of grace; which are indeed a great many, but yet not the one hundredth part of the posterity of Adam. Besides, taking God's *willing* the salvation of men in this sense, we deny the *sequel* of the first proposition, —namely, that Christ died for as many as God thus willeth should be saved. The foundation of God's command unto men to use the *means* granted them is not Christ's dying for them in particular, but the *connection* which himself, by his decree, hath fixed between these two things, faith and salvation; the death of Christ being abundantly sufficient for the holding out of that *connection* unto all, there being enough in it to save all believers.

Secondly, If the will of God be taken for his efficacious will, the will of his purpose and good pleasure (as truly to me it seems exceedingly evident that that is here intended, because the will of

God is made the ground and bottom of our supplications; as if in these our prayers we should say only, "Thy will be done,"—which is to have them all to be saved: now, we have a promise to receive of God "whatsoever we ask according to his will," 1 John iii. 22, v 14; and therefore this will of God, which is here proposed as the ground of our prayers, must needs be his effectual or rather efficacious will, which is always accomplished);—if it be, I say, thus taken, then certainly it must be fulfilled, and all those saved whom he would have saved; for whatsoever God can do and will do, that shall certainly come to pass and be effected. That God can save all (not considering his decree) none doubts; and that he will save all it is here affirmed: therefore, if these *all* here be all and every one, all and every one shall certainly be saved. "Let us eat and drink, for to-morrow we shall die." "Who hath resisted God's will?" Rom. ix. 19. "He hath done whatsoever he hath pleased," Ps. cxv. 3. "He doeth according to his will in the army of heaven, and among the inhabitants of the earth," Dan. iv. 35. If *all*, then, here be to be understood of all men universally, one of these two things must of necessity follow:—either that God faileth of his purpose and intention, or else that all men universally shall be saved; which puts us upon the second thing considerable in the words, namely, who are meant by *all men* in this place.

2. By *all men* the apostle here intendeth all sorts of men indefinitely living under the gospel, or in these latter times, under the enlarged dispensation of the means of grace. That men of these times only are intended is the acknowledgment of Arminius himself, treating with Perkins about this place. The scope of the apostle, treating of the amplitude, enlargement, and extent of grace, in the outward administration thereof, under the gospel, will not suffer it to be denied. This he lays down as a foundation of our praying for all,—because the means of grace and the habitation of the church is now no longer confined to the narrow bounds of one nation, but promiscuously and indefinitely extended unto all people, tongues, and languages; and to all sorts of men amongst them, high and low, rich and poor, one with another. We say, then, that by the words *all men* are here intended only of all sorts of men, suitable to the purpose of the apostle, which was to show that all external difference between the sons of men is now taken away; which *ex abundanti* we farther confirm by these following reasons:—

First, The word *all* being in the Scripture most commonly used in this sense (that is, for many of all sorts), and there being nothing in the subject-matter of which it is here affirmed that should in the least measure impel to another acceptation of the word, especially for a universal collection of every individual, we hold it safe to cleave to the most usual sense and meaning of it. Thus, our Saviour is said to cure all diseases, and the Pharisees to tithe πᾶν λάχανον, Luke xi. 42.

Secondly, Paul himself plainly leadeth us to this interpretation of it; for after he hath enjoined us to pray for all, because the Lord will have all to be saved, he expressly intimates that by *all men* he understandeth men of all sorts, ranks, conditions, and orders, by distributing those *all* into several kinds, expressly mentioning some of them, as "kings and all in authority." Not unlike that expression we have, Jer. xxix. 1, 2, "Nebuchadnezzar carried away all the people captive to Babylon, Jeconiah the king, and the queen, and the eunuchs, the princes of Judah and Jerusalem, the carpenters, and the smiths;" where *all the people* is interpreted to be some of all sorts, by a distribution of them into the several orders, classes, and conditions whereof they were. No otherwise doth the apostle interpret the *all men* by him mentioned, in giving us the names of some of those orders and conditions whom he intendeth. "Pray for all men," saith he; that is, all sorts of men, as magistrates, all that are in authority, the time being now come wherein, without such distinctions as formerly have been observed, the Lord will save some of all sorts and nations.

Thirdly, We are bound to pray for all whom God would have to be saved. Now, we ought not to pray for all and every one, as knowing that some are reprobates and sin unto death; concerning whom we have an express caution not to pray for them.

Fourthly, All shall be saved whom God will have to be saved; this we dare not deny, for "who hath resisted his will?" Seeing, then, it is most certain that all shall not be saved (for some shall stand on the left hand), it cannot be that the universality of men should be intended in this place.

Fifthly, God would have no more to be "saved" than he would have "come to the knowledge of the truth." These two things are of equal latitude, and conjoined in the text. But it is not the will of the Lord that all and every one, in all ages, should come to the knowledge of the truth. Of old, "he showed his word unto Jacob, his statutes and his judgments unto Israel. He hath not dealt so with any nation: and as for his judgments, they have not known them," Ps. cxlvii. 19, 20. If he would have had them all come to the knowledge of the truth, why did he show his word to some and not to others, without which they could not attain thereunto? "He suffered all nations" in former ages "to walk in their own ways," Acts xiv. 16, and "winked at the time of this ignorance," Acts xvii. 30, hiding the mystery of salvation from those former ages, Col. i. 26, continuing the same dispensation even until this day in respect of some; and that because "so it seemeth good in his sight," Matt. xi. 25, 26. It is, then, evident that God doth not will that all and every one in the world, of all ages and times, should come to the knowledge of the truth, but only all sorts of men without difference; and, therefore, they only are here intended.

These, and the like reasons, which compel us to understand by *all men*, verse 4, whom God would have to be saved, men of all sorts, do also prevail for the same acceptation of the word *all*, verse 6, where Christ is said to give himself "a ransom for all;" whereunto you may also add all those whereby we before declared that it was of absolute necessity and just equity that all they for whom a ransom was paid should have a part and portion in that ransom, and, if that be accepted as sufficient, be set at liberty. Paying and accepting of a ransom intimate a commutation and setting free of all them for whom the ransom is paid and accepted. By *all*, then, can none be understood but the redeemed, ransomed ones of Jesus Christ,—such as, for him and by virtue of the price of his blood, are vindicated into the glorious liberty of the children of God; which, as some of all sorts are expressly said to be, Rev. v. 9 (which place is interpretative of this), so that all in the world universally are so is confessedly false.

Having thus made evident the meaning of the words, our answer to the objection (whose strength is a mere fallacy, from the ambiguous sense of the word *all*) is easy and facile. For if by *all men*, you mean the *all* in the text, that is, all sorts of men, we grant the whole,—namely, that Christ died for *all;* but if by *all men*, you mean all universally, we absolutely deny the minor, or assumption, having sufficiently proved that there is no *such all* in the text.

The enforcing of an objection from this place, Thomas More, in his "Universality of Free Grace," makes the subject of one whole chapter. It is also *one* of the two places which he lays for the bottom and foundation of the whole building, and whereunto at a dead lift he always retires. Wherefore, I thought to have considered that chapter of his at large; but, upon second considerations, have laid aside that resolution, and that for three reasons:—

First, Because I desired not *actum agere*, to do that which hath already been done, especially the thing itself being such as scarce deserveth to be meddled with at all. Now, much about the time that I was proceeding in this particular, the learned work of Mr Rutherford,[1] about the death of Christ, and the drawing of sinners thereby, came to my hand; wherein he hath fully answered that chapter of Mr More's book; whither I remit the reader.

Secondly, I find that he hath not once attempted to meddle with any of those reasons and arguments whereby we confirm our answer

[1] He refers to the eminent Scotch divine, Samuel Rutherford, 1600–1661. The work mentioned above was published in 1647, and is entitled, "Christ Dying, and Drawing to Himself; or, a survey of our Saviour in his soul's suffering," etc. The opinions of More are discussed in it from page 375 to 410.—Ed.

to the objection from the place, and prove undeniably that by *all men* is meant only men of all sorts.

Thirdly, Because, setting aside those bare naked assertions of his own, whereby he seeks to strengthen his argument from and interpretation of this place, the residue wherewith he flourisheth is a poor fallacy running through the whole; the strength of all his argumentations consisting in this, that by the *all* we are to pray for are not meant only all who are at present believers; which as no man in his right wits will affirm, so he that will conclude from thence, that because they are not only all present believers, therefore they are all the individuals of mankind, is not to be esteemed very sober. Proceed we, then, to the next place urged for the general ransom, from the word *all*, which is,—

2. 2 Pet. iii. 9, "The Lord is long-suffering to us-ward, not willing that any should perish, but that all should come to repentance." "The will of God," say some, "for the salvation of *all*, is here set down both *negatively*, that he would not have any perish, and *positively*, that he would have all come to repentance; now, seeing there is no coming to repentance nor escaping destruction, but only by the blood of Christ, it is manifest that that blood was shed for *all*."

Ans. Many words need not be spent in answer to this objection, wrested from the misunderstanding and palpable corrupting of the sense of these words of the apostle. That indefinite and general expressions are to be interpreted in an answerable proportion to the things whereof they are affirmed, is a rule in the opening of the Scripture. See, then, of whom the apostle is here speaking. "The Lord," saith he, "is long-suffering to us-ward, not willing that any should perish." Will not common sense teach us that *us* is to be repeated in both the following clauses, to make them up complete and full,—namely, "Not willing that any of *us* should perish, but that all of *us* should come to repentance?" Now, who are these of whom the apostle speaks, to whom he writes? Such as had received "great and precious promises," chap. i. 4, whom he calls "beloved," chap. iii. 1; whom he opposeth to the "scoffers" of the "last days," verse 3; to whom the Lord hath respect in the disposal of these days; who are said to be "elect," Matt. xxiv. 22. Now, truly, to argue that because God would have none of those to perish, but all of them to come to repentance, therefore he hath the same will and mind towards all and every one in the world (even those to whom he never makes known his will, nor ever calls to repentance, if they never once hear of his way of salvation), comes not much short of extreme madness and folly. Neither is it of any weight to the contrary, that they were not all elect to whom Peter wrote: for in the judgment of charity he esteemed them so, desiring them "to give all diligence to make their calling and election sure," chap. i. 10; even as he expressly calleth those to whom he wrote his former epistle, "elect," chap. i. 2, and a "chosen generation," as well as a "purchased people," chap. ii. 9. I shall not need add any thing concerning the contradictions and inextricable difficulties wherewith the opposite interpretation is accompanied (as, that God should will such to come to repentance as he cuts off in their infancy out of the covenant, such as he hateth from eternity, from whom he hideth the means of grace, to whom he will not give repentance, and yet knoweth that it is utterly impossible they should have it without his bestowing). The text is clear, that it is all and only the elect whom he would not have to perish. A place supposed parallel to this we have in Ezek. xviii. 23, 32, which shall be afterward considered. The next is,—

3. Heb. ii. 9, "That he by the grace of God should taste death for every man."

Ans. That ὑπὲρ παντός, "for every one," is here used for ὑπὲρ πάντων, "for all," by an enallage of the number, is by all acknowledged. The whole question is, who these *all* are, whether all men universally, or only all those of whom the apostle there treateth. That this expression, *every man*, is commonly in the Scripture used to signify men under some restriction, cannot be denied. So in that of the apostle, "Warning every man, and teaching every man," Col. i. 28; that is, all those to whom he preached the gospel, of whom he is there speaking. "The manifestation of the Spirit is given to every man to profit withal," 1 Cor. xii. 7; namely, to all and every one of those who were endued with the gifts there mentioned, whether in the church at Corinth or elsewhere. The present place I have frequently met withal produced in the behalf of universal redemption, but never once had the happiness to find any endeavour to prove from the text, or any other way, that *all* here is to be taken for all and every one, although they cannot but know that the usual acceptation of the word is against their purpose. Mr More spends a whole chapter about this place; which I seriously considered, to see if I could pick out any thing which might seem in the least measure to tend that way,—namely, to the proving that all and every one are in that place by the apostle intended,—but concerning any such endeavour you have deep silence. So that, with abundance of smooth words, he doth nothing in that chapter but humbly and heartily beg the thing in question; unto which his petition, though he be exceeding earnest, we cannot consent, and that because of these following reasons:—

First, To *taste death*, being to *drink up the cup* due to sinners, certainly for whomsoever our Saviour did taste of it, he left not one drop for them to drink after him; he tasted or underwent death in their stead, that the cup might pass from them which passed not from him. Now, the cup of death passeth only from the elect, from believers; for whomsoever our Saviour tasted death, he swallowed it up into victory.

Secondly, We see an evident appearing cause that should move the apostle here to call those for whom Christ died *all*,—namely, because he wrote to the Hebrews, who were deeply tainted with an erroneous persuasion that all the benefits purchased by Messiah belonged alone to men of their nation, excluding all others; to root out which pernicious opinion, it behoved the apostle to mention the extent of free grace under the gospel, and to hold out a universality of God's elect throughout the world.

Thirdly, The present description of the *all* for whom Christ tasted death by the grace of God will not suit to all and every one, or any but only the elect of God. For, verse 10, they are called, "many sons to be brought to glory;" verse 11, those that are "sanctified," his "brethren;" verse 13, the "children that God gave him;" verse 15, those that are "delivered from the bondage of death;"—none of which can be affirmed of them who are born, live, and die the "children of the wicked one." Christ is not a captain of salvation, as he is here styled, to any but those that "obey him," Heb. v. 9; righteousness coming by him "unto all and upon all them that believe," Rom. iii. 22. For these and the like reasons we cannot be induced to hearken to our adversaries' petition, being fully persuaded that by *every one* here is meant all and only God's elect, in whose stead Christ, by the grace of God, tasted death.

4. Another place is 2 Cor. v. 14, 15, "For the love of Christ constraineth us; because we thus judge, that if one died for all, then were all dead: and that he died for all, that they which live should not henceforth live unto themselves, but unto him that died for them." "Here," say they, "verse 14, you have two *alls*, which must be both of an equal extent. If *all* were dead, then Christ died for *all*,—that is, for as many as were dead. Again; he died for all that must live unto him; but that is the duty of every one in the world: and therefore he died for them all. Farther; that *all* are all individuals is clear from verse 10, where they are affirmed to be all that must 'appear before the judgment-seat of Christ;' from which appearance not any shall be exempted."

Ans. 1. Taking the words, as to this particular, in the sense of some of our adversaries, yet it doth not appear from the texture of the apostle's arguing that the two *alls* of verse 14 are of equal extent. He doth not say that Christ died for all that were dead; but only, that all were dead which Christ died for: which proves no more than this, that all they for whom Christ died for were dead, with that kind of death of which he speaks. The extent of the words is to be taken from the first *all*, and not the latter. The apostle affirms so many to be dead as Christ died for; not that Christ died for so many as were dead. This the words plainly teach us: "If he died for all, then were all dead,"—that is, *all* he died for; so that the *all that were dead* can give no light to the extent of the *all that Christ died for*, being merely regulated by this. 2. That all and every one are *morally* bound to live unto Christ, *virtute præcepti*, we deny; only *they* are bound to live to him to whom he is revealed,—indeed only they who live by him, that have a spiritual life in and with him: all others are under previous obligations. 3. It is true, all and every one must appear before the judgment-seat of Christ,—he is ordained to be judge of the world; but that they are intended, verse 10 of this chapter, is not true. The apostle speaks of *us all, all believers*, especially all preachers of the gospel; neither of which all men are. Notwithstanding, then, any thing that hath been said, it no way appears that by *all* here is meant any but the elect of God, *all believers;* and that they only are intended I prove by these following reasons, drawn from the text:—

First, The resurrection of Christ is here conjoined with his death: "He died for them, and rose again." Now, for whomsoever Christ riseth, he riseth for their "justification," Rom. iv. 25; and they must be justified, chap. viii. 34. Yea, our adversaries themselves have always confessed that the fruits of the resurrection of Christ are peculiar to believers.

Secondly, He speaks only of those who, by virtue of the death of Christ, "live unto him," verse 15; who are "new creatures," verse 17; "to whom the Lord imputeth not their trespasses," verse 19; who "become the righteousness of God in Christ," verse 21;—which are only believers. All do not attain hereunto.

Thirdly, The article οἱ joined with πάντες evidently restraineth that *all* to all of some sort. "Then were they all" (or rather *all these*) "dead." These *all;*—what all? Even all those believers of whom he treats, as above.

Fourthly, All those of whom the apostle treats are proved to be dead, because Christ died for them: "If one died for all, then were all dead." What death is it which here is spoken of? Not a death natural, but spiritual; and of deaths which come under that name, not that which is *in sin*, but that which is *unto sin*. For,—*First*, The greatest champions of the Arminian cause, as Vorstius and Grotius (on the place), convinced by the evidence of truth, acknowledge that it is a death unto sin, by virtue of the death of Christ, that is here spoken of; and accordingly held out that for the sense of the place. *Secondly*, It is apparent from the text; the intention of the apostle being to prove that those for whom Christ died are so dead to sin, that henceforth they should live no more thereunto, but to him that died for them. The subject he hath in hand is the same with that he handleth more at large, Rom. vi. 5–8, where we are said to be "dead unto sin," by being "planted together in the likeness of the death of Christ;" from whence, *there* as *here*, he presseth them to "newness of life." These words, then, "If Christ died for all, then were all dead," are concerning the death of them unto sin for whom Christ died, at least of those concerning whom he there speaketh; and what is this to the general ransom?

Fifthly, The apostle speaks of the death of Christ in respect of application. The effectualness thereof towards those for whom he died, to cause them to live unto him, is insisted on. That Christ died for all in respect of application hath not yet by any been affirmed. Then must all live unto him, yea, live with him for evermore, if there be any virtue or efficacy in his applied oblation for that end. In sum, here is no mention of Christ's dying for any, but those that are dead to sin and live to him.

5. A fifth place urged to prove universal redemption from the word *all*, is 1 Cor. xv. 22, "For as in Adam all die, even so in Christ shall all be made alive."

Ans. There being another place, hereafter to be considered, wherein the whole strength of the argument usually drawn from these words is contained, I shall not need to speak much to this, neither will I at all turn from the common exposition of the place. Those concerning whom Paul speaketh in this chapter are in this verse called *all.* Those are they who are implanted into Christ, joined to him, as the members to the head, receiving a glorious resurrection by virtue of his; thus are they by the apostle described. That Paul, in this whole chapter, discourseth of the resurrection of believers is manifest from the arguments which he bringeth to confirm it, being such as are of force only with believers. Taken they are from the resurrection of Christ, the hope, faith, customs, and expected rewards of Christians; all which, as they are of unconquerable power to confirm and establish believers in the faith of the resurrection, so they would have been, all and every one of them, exceedingly ridiculous had they been held out to the men of the world to prove the resurrection of the dead in general. Farther; the very word ζωοποιηθήσονται denotes such a living again as is to a good life and glory, a blessed resurrection; and not the quickening of them who are raised to a second death. The Son is said ζωοποιεῖν, John v. 21, to "quicken" and make alive (not all, but) "whom he will." So he useth the word again, chap. vi. 63, "It is the Spirit, τὸ ζωοποιοῦν, that" (thus) "quickeneth;" in like manner, Rom. iv. 17. And not anywhere is it used to show forth that common resurrection which all shall have at the last day. *All*, then, who by virtue of the resurrection of Christ shall be made alive, are all those who are partakers of the nature of Christ; who, verse 23, are expressly called "they that are Christ's," and of whom, verse 20, Christ is said to be the "first-fruits;" and certainly

Christ is not the first-fruits of the damned. Yea, though it be true that all and every one died in Adam, yet that it is here asserted (the apostle speaking of none but believers) is not true; and yet, if it were so to be taken here, it could not prove the thing intended, because of the express limitation of the sense in the clause following. Lastly; granting all that can be desired,—namely, the universality of the word *all* in both places,—yet I am no way able to discern a medium that may serve for an argument to prove the general ransom.

6. Rom. v. 18 is the last place urged in this kind, and by some most insisted on: "As by the offence of one judgment came upon all men to condemnation; even so by the righteousness of one the free gift came upon all men unto justification of life." It might suffice us briefly to declare that by *all men* in the latter place can none be understood but those whom the free gift actually comes upon unto justification of life; who are said, verse 17, to "receive abundance of grace and of the gift of righteousness," and so to "reign in life by one, Jesus Christ;" and by his obedience to be "made righteous," verse 19; which certainly, if any thing be true and certain in the truth of God, all are not. Some believe not,—"all men have not faith;" on some "the wrath of God abideth," John iii. 36; upon whom, surely, grace doth not reign through righteousness to eternal life by Jesus Christ, as it doth upon all those on whom the free gift comes to justification, verse 17. We might, I say, thus answer only; but seeing some, contrary to the clear, manifest intention of the apostle, comparing Adam and Christ, in the efficacy of the sin of the one unto condemnation, and of the righteousness of the other unto justification and life, in respect of those who are the natural seed of the one by propagation, and the spiritual seed of the other by regeneration, have laboured to wrest this place to the maintenance of the error we oppose with more than ordinary endeavours and confidence of success, it may not be unnecessary to consider what is brought by them to this end and purpose:—

Verse 14. Adam is called τύπος, the type and "figure of him that was to come;" not that he was an *instituted type*, ordained for that only end and purpose, but only that in what he was, and what he did, with what followed thereupon, there was a *resemblance* between him and Jesus Christ. Hence by him and what he did, by reason of the resemblance, many things, by way of opposition, concerning the obedience of Christ and the efficacy of his death, may be well represented. That which the apostle here prosecuteth this resemblance in (with the showing of many diversities, in all which he exalteth Christ above his type) is this, that an alike though not an equal efficacy (for there is more merit and efficacy required to save one than to lose ten thousand) of the demerit, sin, disobedience, guilt, transgression of the one, to condemn, or bring the guilt of condemnation upon all them in whose room he was a public person (being the head and natural fountain of them all, they all being wrapped up in the same condition with him by divine institution), and the righteousness, obedience, and death of the other, for the absolution, justification, and salvation of all them to whom he was a spiritual head by divine institution, and in whose room he was a public person, is by him in divers particulars asserted. That these last were all and every one of the first, there is not the least mention. The comparison is solely to be considered intensively, in respect of efficacy, not extensively, in respect of object; though the *all* of Adam be called his *many*, and the *many* of Christ be called his *all*, as indeed they are, even all the seed which is given unto him.

Thomas More, in his "Universality of Free Grace," chap. viii. p. 41, lays down this comparison, instituted by the apostle, between Adam and Christ, as one of the main foundations of his universal redemption; and this (after some strange mixtures of truth and errors premised, which, to avoid tediousness, we let pass) he affirmeth to consist in four things:—

First, "That Adam, in his first sin and transgression, was a public person, in the room and place of all mankind, by virtue of the covenant between God and him; so that whatever he did therein, all were alike sharers with him. So also was Christ a public person in his obedience and death, in the room and place of all mankind, represented by him, even every one of the posterity of Adam."

Ans. To that which concerneth Adam, we grant he was a public person in respect of all his that were to proceed from him by natural propagation; that Christ also was a public person in the room of his, and herein prefigured by Adam. But that Christ, in his obedience, death, and sacrifice, was a public person, and stood in the room and stead of all and every one in the world, of all ages and times (that is, not only of his elect and those who were given unto him of God, but also of reprobate persons, hated of God from eternity; of those whom he never knew, concerning whom, in the days of his flesh, he thanked his Father that he had hid from them the mysteries of salvation; whom he refused to pray for; who were, the greatest part of them, already damned in hell, and irrevocably gone beyond the limits of redemption, before he actually yielded any obedience), is to us such a monstrous assertion as cannot once be apprehended or thought on without horror or detestation. That any should perish in whose room or stead the Son of God appeared before his Father with his perfect obedience; that any of those for whom he is a mediator and advocate, to whom he is a king, priest, and prophet (for all these he is, as he was a public person, a sponsor, a surety, and undertaker for them), should be taken from him, plucked out of his arms, his satisfaction and advocation in their behalf being refused;—I suppose is a doctrine that will scarce be owned among those who strive to preserve the witness and testimony of the Lord Jesus.

But let us a little consider the reasons whereby Mr More undertakes to maintain this strange assertion; which, as far as I can gather, are these, page 44:—First, He stood not in the room only of the elect, because Adam lost not election, being not intrusted with it. Secondly, If he stood not in the room of all, then he had come short of his figure. Thirdly, It is said he was to restore all men, lost by Adam, Heb. ii. 9. Fourthly, He took flesh, was subjected to mortality, became under the law, and bare the sins of mankind. Fifthly, He did it in the room of all mankind, once given unto him, Rom. xiv. 9; Phil. ii. 8–11. Sixthly, Because he is called the "last Adam;"—and, Seventhly, Is said to be a public person, in the room of all, ever since the "first Adam," 1 Cor. xv. 45, 47; 1 Tim. ii. 5; Rom. v.

Ans. Never, surely, was a rotten conclusion bottomed upon more loose and tottering principles, nor the word of God more boldly corrupted for the maintenance of any error, since the name of Christian was known. A man would think it quite lost, but that it is so very *easy* a labour to remove such hay and stubble. I answer, then, to the first, that though Adam lost not election, and the eternal decrees of the Almighty are not committed to the keeping of the sons of men, yet in him all the elect were lost, whom Christ came to seek, whom he found,—in whose room he was a public person. To the second, Christ is nowhere compared to Adam in respect of the *extent of the object* of his death, but only of the *efficacy of his obedience*. The third is a false assertion;—see our foregoing consideration of Heb. ii. 9. Fourthly, For his taking of flesh, etc., it was necessary he should do all this for the saving of his elect. He took flesh and blood because the children were partakers of the same. Fifthly, No such thing is once affirmed in the whole book of God, that all the sons of men were given unto Christ to redeem, so that he should be a public person in their room. Nay, himself plainly affirms the contrary, John xvii. 6, 9. Some only are given him out of the world, and those he saved; not one of them perisheth. The places urged hold out no such thing, nor any thing like it. They will also afterward come under farther consideration. Sixthly, He is called the "last Adam" in respect of the efficacy of his death unto the justification of the seed promised and given unto him, as the sin of the "first Adam" was effectual to bring the guilt of condemnation on the seed propagated from him; which proves not at all that he stood in the room of all those to whom his death was never known, nor any ways profitable. Seventhly, That he was a public person is confessed: that he was so in the room of all is not proved, neither by what hath been already said, nor by the texts, that there follow, alleged, all which have been considered. This being all that is produced by Mr More to justify his assertion, it may be an instance what weighty inferences he usually asserts from such weak, invalid premises. We cannot also but take notice, by the way, of one or two strange passages which he inserts into this discourse; whereof the first is, that Christ by his death brought all men out of that death whereinto they were fallen by Adam. Now, the death whereinto all fell in Adam being a death in sin, Eph. ii. 1–3, and the guilt of condemnation thereupon, if Christ freed all from this death, then must all and every one be made alive with life spiritual, which only is to be had and obtained by Jesus Christ; which, whether that be so or not, whether to live by Christ be not the peculiar privilege of believers, the gospel hath already declared, and God will one day determine. Another strange assertion is, his affirming the end of the death of Christ to be his presenting himself alive and just before his Father; as though it were the ultimate thing by him intended, the Holy Ghost expressly affirming that "he loved the church, and gave himself for it, that he might present it to himself a glorious church," Eph. v. 25–27.

The following parallels, which he instituted between Adam and Christ, have nothing of proof in them to the business in hand,—namely, that Christ was a public person, standing, in his obedience, in the room of all and every one that were concerned in the disobedience of Adam. There is, I say, nothing at all of proof in them, being a confused medley of some truths and divers unsavoury heresies. I shall only give the reader a taste of some of them, whereby he may judge of the rest, not troubling myself or others with the transcribing and reading of such empty vanities as no way relate to the business in hand.

First, then, In the second part of his parallel he affirms, "That when Christ finished his obedience, in dying and rising, and offering himself a sacrifice, and making satisfaction, it was, by virtue of the account of God in Christ, and for Christ with God (that is, accepted with God for Christ's sake), the death, resurrection, the sacrifice and satisfaction, and the redemption of all,—that is, all and every one;" and therein he compares Christ to Adam in the performance of the business by him undertaken. Now, but that I cannot but with trembling consider what the apostle affirms, 2 Thess. ii. 11, 12, I should be exceedingly amazed that any man in the world should be so far forsaken of sense, reason, faith, and all reverence of God and man, as to publish, maintain, and seek to propagate, such abominable, blasphemous, senseless, contradictious errors. That the death of Christ should be accepted of and accounted before God as the death of all, and yet the greatest part of these all be adjudged to eternal death in their own persons by the same righteous God; that all and every one should arise in and with Jesus Christ, and yet most of them continue dead in their sins, and die for sin eternally; that satisfaction should be made and accepted for them who are never spared, nor shall be, one farthing of their debt; that atonement should be made by sacrifice for such as ever lie undelivered under wrath; that all the reprobates, Cain, Pharaoh, Ahab, and the rest, who were actually damned in hell, and under death and torments, then when Christ died, suffered, made satisfaction, and rose again, should be esteemed with God to have died, suffered, made satisfaction, and risen again with Christ;—that, I say, such senseless contradictions, horrid errors, and abominable assertions, should be thus nakedly thrust upon Christians, without the least colour, pretence, or show of proof, but the naked authority of him who hath already embraced such things as these, were enough to make any man admire and be amazed, but that we know the judgments of God are oft-times hid, and far above out of our sights.

Secondly, In the third of his parallels he goeth one step higher, comparing Christ with Adam in respect of the efficacy, effect, and fruit of his obedience. He affirms, "That as by the sin of Adam all his posterity were deprived of life, and fell under sin and death, whence judgment and condemnation passed upon all, though this be done secretly and invisibly, and in some sort inexpressibly" (what he means by *secretly and invisibly*, well I know not,—surely he doth not suppose that these things might possibly be made the objects of our senses; and for *inexpressibly*, how that is, let Rom. v. 12, with other places, where all this and more is clearly, plainly, and fully expressed, be judge whether it be so or no); "so," saith he, "by the efficacy of the obedience of Christ, all men without exception are redeemed, restored, made righteous, justified freely by the grace of Christ, through the redemption that is in Jesus Christ, the 'righteousness that is by the faith of Jesus Christ' being 'unto all,' Rom. iii. 22," (where the impostor wickedly corrupteth the word of God, like the devil, Matt. iv., by cutting off the following words, "and upon all that believe," both *alls* answering to believers). "What remains now but that all also should be saved? the Holy Ghost expressly affirming that those 'whom God justifieth, he also glorifieth,'" Rom. viii. 30. "Solvite mortales animas, curisque levate." Such assertions as these, without any colour of proof, doth this author labour to obtrude upon us. Now, that men should be restored, and yet continue lost; that they should be made righteous, and yet remain detestably wicked, and wholly abominable; that they should be justified freely by the grace of God, and yet always lie under the condemning sentence of the law of God; that the righteousness of God by the faith of Jesus Christ should be upon all unbelievers,—are not only things exceedingly opposite to the gospel of Jesus Christ, but so absolutely at variance and distance one with another, that the poor salve of Mr More's following cautions will not serve to heal their mutual wounds. I cannot but fear that it would be tedious and offensive to rake any longer in such a dunghill. Let them that have a mind to be captivated to error and falsehood by corruption of Scripture and denial of common sense and reason, because they cannot receive the truth in the love thereof, delight themselves with such husks as these. What weaker arguments we have had, to maintain that Christ, in his obedience to the death, was a public person in the room of all and every one, hath been already demonstrated. I shall now, by the reader's leave, a little transgress the rule of disputation, and, taking up the opposite part of the arguments, produce some few reasons and testimonies to demonstrate that our Saviour Christ, in his obedience unto death, in the *redemption* which he wrought, and *satisfaction* which he made, and *sacrifice* which he offered, was not a public person in the room of *all and every man* in the world, elect and reprobate, believers and infidels, or unbelievers; which are briefly these:—

First, The *seed of the woman* was not to be a public person in the place, stead, and room of the *seed of the serpent.* Jesus Christ is the seed of the woman κατ' ἐξοχήν· all the reprobates, as was before proved, are the seed of the serpent: therefore, Jesus Christ was not, in his oblation and suffering, when he brake the head of the father of the seed, a public person in their room.

Secondly, Christ, as a public person, representeth only them for whose sake he set himself apart to that office and employment wherein he was such a *representative;* but upon his own testimony, which we have, John xvii. 19, he set himself apart to the service and employment wherein he was a public person for the sakes only of some that were given him out of the world, and not of all and every one: therefore, he was not a public person in the room of all.

Thirdly, Christ was a "surety," as he was a public person, Heb. vii. 22; but he was not a surety for all,—for, first, All are not taken into that covenant whereof he was a surety, whose conditions are effected in all the covenantees, as before; secondly, None can perish for whom Christ is a surety, unless he be not able to pay the debt:—therefore, he was not a public person in the room of all.

Fourthly, For whom he was a public person, in their rooms he suffered, and for them he made satisfaction, Isa. liii. 5, 6; but he suffered not in the stead of all, nor made satisfaction for all,—for, first, Some must suffer themselves, which makes it evident that Christ did not suffer for them, Rom. viii. 33, 34; and, secondly, The justice of God requireth satisfaction from themselves, to the payment of the utmost farthing.

Fifthly, Jesus Christ, as a public person, did nothing in vain in respect of any for whom he was a public person; but many things which Christ, as a public person, did perform were altogether in vain and fruitless, in respect of the greatest part of the sons of men being under an incapability of receiving any good by any thing he did,—to wit, all that then were actually damned, in respect of whom, redemption, reconciliation, satisfaction, and the like, could possibly be no other than empty names.

Sixthly, If God were well pleased with his Son in what he did, as a public person, in his representation of others (as he was, Eph. v. 2), then must he also be well pleased with them whom he did represent, either absolutely or conditionally; but with many of the sons of men God, in the representation of his Son, was not well pleased, neither absolutely nor conditionally,—to wit, with Cain, Pharaoh, Saul, Ahab, and others, dead and damned before: therefore, Christ did not, as a public person, represent all.

Seventhly, For testimonies, see John xvii. 9; Matt. xx. 28, xxvi. 26–28; Mark. x. 45; Heb. vi. 20; Isa. liii. 12; John x. 15; Heb. xiii. 20; Matt. i. 21; Heb. ii. 17; John xi. 51, 52; Acts xx. 28; Eph. v. 2,. 23–25; Rom. viii. 33, 34.

CHAPTER V.

The last argument from Scripture answered.

III. I COME, in the next place, to the third and last argument, drawn from the Scripture, wherewith the Arminians and their successors (as to this point) do strive to maintain their figment of universal redemption; and it is taken from such texts of Scripture as seem to hold out the perishing of some of them for whom Christ died, and the fruitlessness of his blood in respect of divers for whom it was shed. And on this theme their wits are wonderfully luxuriant, and they are full of rhetorical strains to set out the unsuccessfulness and fruitlessness of the blood of Christ in respect of the most for whom it was shed, with the perishing of bought, purged, reconciled sinners. Who can but believe that this persuasion tends to the consolation of poor souls, whose strongest defence lieth in making vile the precious blood of the Lamb, yea, trampling upon it, and esteeming it as a common thing? But, friends, let me tell you, I am persuaded it was not so unvaluable in the eyes of his Father as to cause it to be poured out in vain, in respect of any one soul. But seeing we must be put to this defence,—wherein we cannot but rejoice, it tending so evidently to the honour of our blessed Saviour,—let us consider what can be said by Christians (at least in name) to enervate the efficacy of the blood-shedding, of the death of him after whose name they desire to be called. Thus, then, they argue:—

"If Christ died for reprobates and those that perish, then he died for all and every one, for confessedly he died for the elect and those that are saved; but he died for reprobates, and them that perish: therefore," etc.

Ans. For the *assumption*, or second proposition of this argument, we shall do what we conceive was fit for all the elect of God to do,—positively deny it (taking the death of Christ, here said to be for them, to be considered not in respect of its own internal worth and sufficiency, but, as it was intended by the Father and Son, in respect of them for whom he died). We deny, then, I say, that Christ, by the command of his Father, and with intention to make satisfaction for sins, did lay down his life for reprobates and them that perish.

This, then, they prove from Rom. xiv. 15; 1 Cor. viii. 11; 2 Pet. ii. 1; Heb. x. 29. Now, that no such thing as is pretended is proved from any of the places alleged, we shall show by the consideration of them in the order they are laid down in.

1. The first is Rom. xiv. 15, "But if thy brother be grieved with thy meat, now walkest thou not charitably. Destroy not him with thy meat for whom Christ died."

Ans. Had we not experience of the nimbleness of our adversaries in framing arguments for their cause, I should despair to find their conclusion pressed out of this place; for what coherence or dependence, I beseech you, is here to be discerned? "The apostle exhorteth strong and sound believers to such a moderate use of Christian liberty that they do not grieve the spirit of the weak ones, that were believers also (professors, all called 'saints, elect, believers, redeemed,' and so in charity esteemed), and so give them occasion of stumbling and falling off from the gospel: therefore, Jesus Christ died for all reprobates, even all those that never heard word nor syllable of him or the doctrine of the gospel." Must he not be very quick-sighted that can see the dependence of this inference on that exhortation of the apostle? But ye will say, "Is it not affirmed that he may perish for whom Christ died?" *Ans.* In this place there is no such thing at all once mentioned or intimated; only others are commanded not to do that which goeth in a direct way to destroy him, by grieving him with their uncharitable walking. "But why should the apostle exhort him not to do that which he could no way do, if he that Christ died for could not perish?" *Ans.* Though the one could not perish in respect of the event, the other might sinfully give occasion of perishing in respect of a procuring cause. May not a man be exhorted from attempting of that which yet if he should attempt he could not effect? No thanks to the soldier who ran a spear into the side of our dead Redeemer, that therewith he brake none of his bones. Besides, is every one damned that one attempts to destroy, by grieving him with uncharitable walking? Such arguments as these are poor men of straw. And yet, notwithstanding, we do not deny but that many may perish, and that utterly, whom we, in our walking towards them and converse with them, are bound to conceive redeemed by Christ; even all being to be thought so who are to be esteemed "saints and brethren," as the language of the Scripture is concerning the professors of the gospel. And this is most certain, that no one place makes mention of such to be bought or redeemed by our Saviour, but those which had the qualification of being members of this visible church; which come infinitely short of all and every one.

2. But let us see a second place, which is 1 Cor. viii. 11, "And through thy knowledge shall thy weak brother perish, for whom Christ died." This seemeth to have more colour, but really yieldeth no more strength to the persuasion for whose confirmation it is produced, than the former. A brother is said to *perish for whom Christ died.* That by *perishing* here is understood eternal destruction and damnation, I cannot apprehend. That which the apostle intimates whereby it is done, is eating of things offered to an idol, with conscience or regard of an idol, by the example of others who pretended to know that an idol was nothing, and so to eat freely of the things offered to them. That so doing was a sin in its own nature damnable, none can doubt. All sin is so; every time we sin, for any thing that lieth in us, we perish, we are destroyed. So did the eater of things offered to idols. But that God always revengeth sin with damnation on all in whom it is, we deny; he hath otherwise revealed himself in the blood of Jesus Christ. That every such a one did actually perish eternally, as well as meritoriously, cannot be proved. Besides, he that is said to perish is called a *brother*,—that is, a believer; we are brethren only by faith, whereby we come to have one Father. As he is said to be a *brother*, so Christ is said to *die for him.* That a true believer cannot finally perish may easily be proved; therefore, he who doth perish is manifestly declared never to have been any: "They went out from us, because they were not of us." If any perish, then, he was never a true believer. How, then, is he said to be a brother? Because he is so in profession, so in our judgment and persuasion; it being meet for us to think so of them all. As he is said to be a brother, so Christ is said to die for him, even in that judgment which the Scripture allows to us of men. We cannot count a man a brother, and not esteem that Christ died for him; we have no brotherhood with reprobates. Christ died for all believers, John xvii. So we esteem all men walking in the due

profession of the gospel, not manifesting the contrary; yet of these, that many may perish none ever denied. Farther; this, *so shall he perish,* referreth to the sin of him that layeth the offence; for aught that lieth in him, he ruins him irrecoverably. Hence see their argument:—"The apostle telleth persons walking offensively, that by this abusing their liberty, others will follow them, to the wounding of their conscience and ruin, who are brethren, acknowledged so by you, and such as for whom Christ died: therefore, Christ died for all the reprobates in the world. 'Is it just and equal,' saith the apostle, 'that ye should do such things as will be stumbling-blocks in the way of the weak brother, at which he might stumble and fall?' therefore, Christ died for all." We do not deny but that some may perish, and that eternally, concerning whom we ought to judge that Christ died for them, whilst they live and converse with us according to the rule of the gospel.

3. The next place is much insisted on,—namely, 2 Pet. ii. 1, "There shall be false teachers, denying the Lord that bought them, and bringing upon themselves swift destruction." All things here, as to any proof of the business in hand, are exceedingly dark, uncertain, and doubtful. *Uncertain,* that by the *Lord* is meant *the Lord Christ,* the word in the original being Δεσπότης, seldom or never ascribed to him; *uncertain,* whether the purchase or buying of these false teachers refer to the eternal redemption by the blood of Christ, or a deliverance by God's goodness from the defilement of the world in idolatry, or the like, by the knowledge of the truth,—which last the text expressly affirms; *uncertain,* whether the apostle speaketh of this purchase according to the reality of the thing, or according to their apprehension and their profession.

On the other side, it is most *certain,*—First, That there are no spiritual distinguishing fruits of redemption ascribed to these false teachers, but only common gifts of light and knowledge, which Christ hath purchased for many for whom he did not make his soul a ransom. Secondly, That, according to our adversaries, the redemption of any by the blood of Christ cannot be a peculiar aggravation of the sins of any, because they say he died for all; and yet this buying of the false teachers is held out as an aggravation of their sin in particular.

Of the former *uncertainties,* whereon our adversaries build their inference of universal redemption (which yet can by no means be wire-drawn thence, were they most certain in their sense), I shall give a brief account, and then speak something as to the proper intendment of the place.

For the first, It is most *uncertain* whether Christ, as mediator, be here intended by *Lord* or no. There is not any thing in the text to enforce us so to conceive, nay, the contrary seems apparent,—

First, Because in the following verses, God only, as God, with his dealings towards such as these, is mentioned; of Christ not a word. *Secondly*, The name Δεσπότης, properly "Herus," attended by dominion and sovereignty, is not usually, if at all, given to our Saviour in the New Testament; he is everywhere called Κύριος, nowhere clearly Δεσπότης, as is the Father, Luke ii. 29, Acts iv. 24, and in divers other places. Besides, if it should appear that this name were given our Saviour in any one place, doth it therefore follow that it must be so here? nay, is the name proper for our Saviour, in the work of redemption? Δεσπότης is such a Lord or Master as refers to servants and subjection; the end of Christ's purchasing any by his blood being in the Scripture always and constantly expressed in other terms, of more endearment. It is, then, most uncertain that Christ should be here understood by the word *Lord*.

[Secondly], But suppose he should, it is most *uncertain* that by buying of these false teachers is meant his purchasing of them with the ransom of his blood; for,—*First*, The apostle insisteth on a comparison with the times of the Old Testament, and the false prophets that were then amongst the people, backing his assertion with divers examples out of the Old Testament in the whole chapter following. Now, the word ἀγοράζω, here used, signifieth primarily the buying of things; translatitiously, the redemption of persons;—and the word פָּדָה in the Old Testament, answering thereunto, signifieth any deliverance, as Deut. vii. 8, xv. 15, Jer. xv. 21, with innumerable other places: and, therefore, some such deliverance is here only intimated. *Secondly*, Because here is no mention of blood, death, price, or offering of Jesus Christ, as in other places, where proper redemption is treated on; especially, some such expression is added where the word ἀγοράζω is used to express it, as 1 Cor. vi. 20, Rev. v. 9, which otherwise holds out of itself deliverance in common from any trouble. *Thirdly*, The apostle setting forth at large the deliverance they had had, and the means thereof, verse 20, affirms it to consist in the "escaping of the pollutions of the world," as idolatry, false worship, and the like, "through the knowledge of the Lord and Saviour Jesus Christ;" plainly declaring that their buying was only in respect of this separation from the world, in respect of the enjoyment of the knowledge of the truth; but of washing in the blood of the Lamb, he is wholly silent. Plainly, there is no purchase mentioned of these false teachers, but a deliverance, by God's dispensations towards them, from the blindness of Judaism or Paganism, by the knowledge of the gospel; whereby the Lord bought them to be servants to him, as their supreme head. So that our adversaries' argument from this place is this:—"God the Lord, by imparting the knowledge of the gospel, and working them to a professed acknowledgment of it and subjection unto it, separated and delivered from the world divers that were saints in show,—really wolves and hypocrites, of old ordained to condemnation: therefore, Jesus Christ shed his blood for the redemption and salvation of all reprobates and damned persons in the whole world." Who would not admire our adversaries' chemistry?

Thirdly, Neither is it more certain that the apostle speaketh of the purchase of the wolves and hypocrites, in respect of the reality of the purchase, and not rather in respect of that estimation which others had of them,—and, by reason of their outward seeming profession, ought to have had,—and of the profession that themselves made to be purchased by him whom they pretended to preach to others; as the Scripture saith [of Ahaz], "The gods of Damascus smote him," because he himself so imagined and professed, 2 Chron. xxviii. 23. The latter hath this also to render it probable,—namely, that it is the perpetual course of the Scripture, to ascribe all those things to every one that is in the fellowship of the church which are proper to them only who are true spiritual members of the same; as to be *saints, elect, redeemed,* etc. Now, the truth is, from this their profession, that they were bought by Christ, might the apostle justly, and that according to the opinion of our adversaries, press these false teachers, by the way of aggravating their sin. For the thing itself, their being bought, it could be no more urged to them than to heathens and infidels that never heard of the name of the Lord Jesus.

Now, after all this, if our adversaries can prove universal redemption from this text, let them never despair of success in any thing they undertake, be it never so absurd, fond, or foolish. But when they have wrought up the work already cut out for them, and proved,—*first,* That by the *Lord* is meant Christ as mediator; *secondly,* That by *buying* is meant spiritual redemption by the blood of the Lamb; *thirdly,* That these *false teachers were really and effectually so redeemed,* and not only so accounted because of the church; *fourthly,* That those who are so redeemed may perish, contrary to the express Scripture, Rev. xiv. 4; *fifthly,* Manifest the strength of this inference, "Some in the church who have acknowledged Christ to be their purchaser, fall away to blaspheme him, and perish for ever; therefore, Christ bought and redeemed all that ever did or shall perish;" *sixthly,* That that which is common to all is a peculiar aggravation to the sin of any one more than others;—I will assure them they shall have more work provided for them, which themselves know for a good part already where to find.

4. The last place produced for the confirmation of the argument in hand is Heb. x. 29, "Of how much sorer punishment, suppose ye, shall he be thought worthy, who hath trodden under foot the Son of God, and hath counted the blood of the covenant, wherewith he was sanctified, an unholy thing, and hath done despite unto the Spirit of

grace?" "Nothing," say our adversaries, "could be affirmed of all this concerning apostates,—namely, 'That they have trodden under foot,' etc., unless the blood of Christ was in some sense shed for them."

Ans. The intention of the apostle in this place is the same with the general aim and scope of the whole epistle,—to persuade and urge the Jews, who had embraced the doctrine of the gospel, to perseverance and continuance therein. This, as he doth perform in other places, with divers and various arguments,—the most of them taken from a comparison at large instituted between the gospel in its administration, and those legal shadows which, before their profession, they lived under and were in bondage unto,—so here he urgeth a strong argument to the same purpose "ab incommodo, seu effectu pernicioso," from the miserable, dangerous effects and consequences of the sin of backsliding, and wilful renunciation of the truth known and professed, upon any motives and inducements whatsoever; which he assureth [them] to be no less than a total casting off and depriving themselves of all hopes and means of recovery, with dreadful horror of conscience in expectation of judgment to come, verses 26, 27. Now, this he confirms, as his manner is in this epistle, from some *thing*, *way*, and *practice* which was known to them, and wherewith they were all acquainted by that administration of the covenant under which they had before lived, in their Judaism; and so makes up his inference from a comparison of the less; taking his example from the punishment due, by God's own appointment, to all them who transgressed Moses' law in such a manner as apostates sin against the gospel,—that is, "with an high hand," or "presumptuously:" for such a one was to die without mercy, Num. xv. 30, 31. Whereupon, having abundantly proved that the gospel, and the manifestation of grace therein, is exceedingly preferred to and exalted above the old ceremonies of the law, he concludes that certainly a much sorer punishment (which he leaves to their judgment to determine) awaits for them who wilfully violate the holy gospel, and despise the declaration of grace therein contained and by it revealed; which farther also to manifest, he sets forth the nature and quality of this sin in all such as, professing redemption and deliverance by the blood of Christ, shall wilfully cast themselves thereinto. "It is," saith he, "no less than to tread under foot or contemn the Son of God; to esteem the blood of the covenant, by which he was set apart and sanctified in the profession of the gospel, to be as the blood of a vile man; and thereby to do despite to the Spirit of grace." This being (as is confessed) the plain meaning and aim of the apostle, we may observe sundry things, for the vindication of this place from the abuse of our adversaries; as,—

First, He speaketh here only of those that were professors of the faith of the gospel, separated from the world, brought into a church state and fellowship, professing themselves to be sanctified by the blood of Christ, receiving and owning Jesus Christ as the Son of God, and endued with the gifts of the Holy Spirit, as chap. vi. 4, 5. Now, it is most certain that these things are peculiar only to some, yea to a very few, in comparison of the universality of the sons of men; so that what is affirmed of such only can by no means be so extended as to be applied unto all. Now, if any one may be exempted, universal redemption falleth to the ground; from the condition of a very few, with such qualifications as the multitude have not, nothing can be concluded concerning all.

Secondly, The apostle doth neither declare what hath been nor assert what may be, but only adds a commination upon a supposition of a thing; his main aim being to deter from the thing rather than to signify that it may be, by showing the misery that must needs follow if it should so come to pass. When Paul told the soldiers, Acts xxvii. 31, that if the mariners fled away in the boat they could not be saved, he did not intend to signify to them that, in respect of the event, they should be drowned, for God had declared the contrary unto him the night before, and he to them; but only to exhort them to prevent that which of itself was a likely way for their ruin and perishing. Neither shall the Remonstrants, with all their rhetoric, ever persuade us that it is in vain and altogether fruitless to forewarn men of an evil, and to exhort them to take heed of those ways whereby it is naturally, and according to the order among the things themselves, to be incurred; although, in respect of the purpose of God, the thing itself have no futurition, nor shall ever come to pass. A commination of the judgment due to apostasy, being an appointed means for the preserving of the saints from that sin, may be held out to them, though it be impossible the elect should be seduced. Now, that Paul here deals only upon a supposition (not giving being to the thing, but only showing the connection between apostasy and condemnation, thereby to stir up all the saints to "take heed lest there should be in any of them an evil heart of unbelief in departing from the living God") is apparent from verse 26, where he makes an entrance upon this argument and motive to perseverance: "For *if* we sin wilfully." That *believers* may do so, he speaks not one word; but if they should do so, he shows what would be the event;—as, that the soldiers in the ship should perish, Paul told them not; but yet showed what must needs come to pass if the means of prevention were not used. Now, if this be the intention of the apostle, as it is most likely, by his speaking in the first person, "If *we* sin wilfully," then not any thing in the world can be hence concluded either for the universality of redemption or the apostasy of saints, to both which ends this place is usually urged; for "suppositio nil ponit in esse."

Thirdly, It is most certain that those of whom he speaks did make profession of all those things whereof here is mention,—namely, that Jesus Christ was the Son of God, that they were sanctified by the blood of the covenant, and enlightened by the Spirit of grace; yea, as is apparent from the parallel place, Heb. vi. 4, 5, had many gifts of illumination; besides their initiation by baptism, wherein open profession and demonstration was made of these things. So that a renunciation of all these, with open detestation of them, as was the manner of apostates, accursing the name of Christ, was a sin of so deep an abomination, attended with so many aggravations, as might well have annexed to it this remarkable commination, though the apostates never had themselves any true effectual interest in the blood of Jesus.

Fourthly, That it was the manner of the saints, and the apostles themselves, to esteem of all baptized, initiated persons, ingrafted into the church, as sanctified persons; so that, speaking of backsliders, he could not make mention of them any otherwise than as they were commonly esteemed to be, and at that time, in the judgment of charity, were to be considered. Whether they were true believers or no, but only temporary, to whom this argument against apostasy is proposed, according to the usual manner of speech used by the Holy Ghost, they could not be otherwise described.

Fifthly, If the text be interpreted positively, and according to the truth of the thing itself, in both parts thereof (namely, 1. That those of whom the apostle speaketh were truly sanctified; 2. That such may totally perish), then these two things will inevitably follow, —*first,* That faith and sanctification are not the fruit of election; *secondly,* That believers may fall finally from Christ;—neither of which I as yet find to be owned by our new Universalists, though both contended for by our old Arminians.

Sixthly, There is nothing in the text of force to persuade that the persons here spoken of must needs be truly justified and regenerated believers, much less that Christ died for them; which comes in only by strained consequences. One expression only seems to give any colour hereunto,—that they were said to be "sanctified by the blood of the covenant." Now, concerning this, if we do but consider,—*first,* The manner and custom of the apostles writing to the churches, calling them all "saints" that were called,—ascribing that to every one that belonged only to some; *secondly,* That these persons were baptized, (which ordinance among the ancients was sometimes called φωτισμός, "illumination," sometimes ἁγιασμός, "sanctification,") wherein, by a solemn aspersion of the symbol of the blood of Christ, they were externally sanctified, separated, and set apart, and were by all esteemed as saints and believers; *thirdly,* The various significations of the word ἁγιάζω (here used) in the Scripture, whereof one most frequent is, to consecrate and set apart to any holy use, as 2 Chron.

xxix. 33, Lev. xvi. 4;[1] *fourthly,* That Paul useth in this epistle many words and phrases in a temple sense, alluding, in the things and ways of the Christian church, unto the old legal observances; *fifthly,* That supposed and professed sanctity is often called so, and esteemed to be so indeed;—if, I say, we shall consider these things, it will be most apparent that here is indeed no true, real, internal, effectual sanctification, proper to God's elect, at all intimated, but only a common external setting apart (with repute and esteem of real holiness) from the ways of the world and customs of the old synagogue, to an enjoyment of the ordinance of Christ representing the blood of the covenant. So that this commination being made to all so externally and apparently sanctified, to them that were truly so it declared the certain connection between apostasy and condemnation; thereby warning them to avoid it, as Joseph [was] warned to flee into Egypt, lest Herod should slay the child; which yet, in respect of God's purpose, could not be effected. In respect of them that were only apparently so, it held out the odiousness of the sin, with their own certain inevitable destruction if they fell into it; which it was possible they might do.

And thus, by the Lord's assistance, have I given you, as I hope, a clear solution to all the arguments which heretofore the Arminians pretended to draw from the Scripture in the defence of their cause; some other sophisms shall hereafter be removed. But because of late we have had a multiplication of arguments on this subject, some whereof, at least in form, appear to be new, and may cause some trouble to the unskilful, I shall, in the next place, remove all those objections which Thomas More, in his book of the "Universality of Free Grace," hath gathered together against our main thesis, of Christ's dying only for the elect, which himself puts together in one bundle, chap. xxvi., and calleth them *reasons.*

CHAPTER VI.

An answer to the twentieth chapter of the book entitled, "The Universality of God's Free Grace," etc., being a collection of all the arguments used by the author throughout the whole book to prove the universality of redemption.

THE *title* pretends satisfaction to them who desire to have reason satisfied: which, that it is a great undertaking, I easily grant; but for the performance of it, "hic labor, hoc opus." That ever Christian reason, rightly informed by the word of God, should be satisfied with any doctrine *so discrepant* from the word, so full of contradiction in itself and to its own principles, as the doctrine of universal redemp-

[1] In these passages the LXX. has ἡγιασμένοι μόσχοι, and χιτῶνα ἡγιασμένον.—ED.

tion is, I should much marvel. Therefore, I am persuaded that the author of the arguments following (which, lest you should mistake them for others, he calleth *reasons*) will fail of his intention with all that have so much reason as to know how to make use of reason, and so much grace as not to love darkness more than light. The only reason, as far as I can conceive, why he calls this collection of all the arguments and texts of Scripture which he had before cited and produced at large so many *reasons*, being a supposal that he hath given them a logical, argumentative form in this place, I shall briefly consider them; and, by the way, take notice of his skill in a regular framing of arguments, to which here he evidently pretends. His first reason, then, is as followeth:—

I. "That which the Scripture oft and plainly affirmeth in plain words is certainly true and to be believed, Prov. xxii. 20, 21; Isa. viii. 20; 2 Pet. i. 19, 20;

"But that Jesus Christ gave himself a ransom, and by the grace of God tasted death for every man, is oft and plainly affirmed in Scripture, as is before shown, chap. vii. to xiii.:

"Therefore, the same is certainly a truth to be believed, John xx. 31, Acts xxvi. 27."

First, The proposition of this argument is clear, evident, and acknowledged by all professing the name of Christ; but yet universally with this caution and proviso, that by *the Scripture affirming any thing in plain words that is to be believed,* you understand the plain sense of those words, which is clear by rules of interpretation so to be. It is the thing signified that is to be believed, and not the words only, which are the sign thereof; and, therefore, the *plain sense and meaning* is that which we must inquire after, and is intended when we speak of believing plain words of the Scripture. But now if by *plain words* you understand the literal importance of the words, which may perhaps be *figurative,* or at least of *various signification,* and capable of extension or restriction in the interpretation, then there is nothing more false than this assertion; for how can you then avoid the blasphemous folly of the Anthropomorphites, assigning a body and human shape unto God, the *plain words of the Scripture* often mentioning his eyes, hands, ears, etc., it being apparent to every child that the true importance of those expressions answers not at all their gross carnal conception? Will not also transubstantiation, or its younger brother consubstantiation, be an article of our creed? With this limitation, then, we pass the proposition, with the places of Scripture brought to confirm it; only with this observation, that there is not one of them to the purpose in hand,—which, because they do not relate to the argument in consideration, we only leave to men's silent judgments.

Secondly, The assumption, or minor proposition, we absolutely deny as to some part of it; as that Christ should be said to give himself a ransom for every man, it being neither often, nor once, nor plainly, nor obscurely affirmed in the Scripture, nor at all proved in the place referred unto: so that this is but an empty flourishing. For the other expression, of "tasting death for every man," we grant that the words are found Heb. ii. 9; but we deny that *every man* doth always necessarily signify *all and every man in the world.* Νουθετοῦντες πάντα ἄνθρωπον, καὶ διδάσκοντες πάντα ἄνθρωπον, Col. i. 28,—"Warning every man, and teaching every man." *Every man* is not there every man in the world; neither are we to believe that Paul warned and taught every particular man, for it is false and impossible. So that *every man,* in the Scripture, is not universally collective of all of all sorts, but either distributive, for some of all sorts, or collective, with a restriction to all of some sort; as in that of Paul, *every man,* was only of those to whom he had preached the gospel. Secondly, In the original there is only ὑπὲρ παντός, *for every,* without the substantive *man,* which might be supplied by other words as well as *man,*—as elect, or believer.

Thirdly, That *every one* is there clearly restrained to all the members of Christ, and the children by him brought to glory, we have before declared. So that this place is no way useful for the confirmation of the assumption, which we deny in the sense intended; and are sure we shall never see a clear, or so much as a probable, testimony for the confirming of it.

To the conclusion of the syllogism, the author, to manifest his skill in disputing in such an argumentative way as he undertaketh, addeth some farther proofs. Conscious, it seems, he was to himself that it had little strength from the propositions from which it is enforced; and, therefore, thought to give some new supportments to it, although with very ill success, as will easily appear to any one that shall but consult the places quoted, and consider the business in hand. In the meantime, this new logic, of filing proofs to the conclusion which are suitable to neither proposition, and striving to give strength to that by new testimony which it hath not from the premises, deserves our notice in this age of learned writers. "Heu quantum est sapere." Such logic is fit to maintain such divinity. And so much for the first argument.

II. "Those whom Jesus Christ and his apostles, in plain terms, without any exception or restraint, affirm that Christ came to save, and to that end died, and gave himself a ransom for, and is a propitiation for their sin, he certainly did come to save, and gave himself a ransom for them, and is the propitiation for their sins, Matt. xxvi. 24; John vi. 38; 1 Cor. xv. 3, 4; Heb. x. 7; John viii. 38, 45; 2 Pet. i. 16; Heb. ii. 3, 4;

"But Jesus Christ and his apostles have, in plain terms, affirmed that 'Christ came to save sinners,' 1 Tim. i. 15; the 'world,' John iii. 17; that he died for the 'unjust,' 1 Pet. iii. 18; the 'ungodly,' Rom. v. 6;

for 'every man,' Heb. ii. 9; 'gave himself a ransom for all men,' 1 Tim. ii. 6; and is the 'propitiation for the sins of the whole world,' 1 John ii. 2; and every one of these affirmations without any exception or restraint, all being unjust, ungodly, sinners, and men, and of the world, Rom. iii. 10, 19, 20, 23; Eph. ii. 1–3; Tit. iii. 3; John iii. 4, 6:

"Therefore, Jesus Christ came to save, died, and gave himself a ransom for all men, and is the propitiation for their sins, John i. 29."

To the proposition of this argument I desire only to observe, that we do not affirm that the Scripture doth, in any place, lay an exception or restraint upon those persons for whom Christ is said to die, as though in one place it should be affirmed he died for all men, and in another some exception against it, as though some of those *all men* were excluded,—which were to feign a repugnancy and contradiction in the word of God; only, we say, one place of Scripture interprets another, and declares that sense which before in one place was ambiguous and doubtful. For instance: when the Scripture showeth that Christ died or gave himself a ransom for *all*, we believe it; and when, in another place, he declares that *all* to be his *church*, his *elect*, his *sheep*, all *believers*,—some of all sorts, *out of all kindreds, and nations, and tongues, under heaven;* this is not to lay an exception or restraint upon what was said of *all* before, but only to declare that the *all* for which he gave himself for a ransom were all his church, all his elect, all his sheep, some of all sorts: and so we believe that he died for all. With this observation we let pass the proposition, taking out its meaning as well as the phrase whereby it is expressed will afford it, together with the vain flourish and pompous show of many texts of Scripture brought to confirm it, whereof not one is any thing to the purpose; so that I am persuaded he put down names and figures at a venture, without once consulting the texts, having no small cause to be confident that none would trace him in his flourish, and yet that some eyes might dazzle at his supernumerary quotations. Let me desire the reader to turn to those places, and if any one of them be any thing to the purpose or business in hand, let the author's credit be of weight with him another time. O let us not be as many, who corrupt the word of God! But perhaps it is a mistake in the impression, and for Matt. xxvi. 24, he intends verse 28, where Christ is said to shed his blood for many. In John vi., he mistook verse 38 for 39, where our Saviour affirms that he came to save that which his Father gave him,—that none should be lost; which certainly are the elect. In 1 Cor. xv. 3, 4, he was not much amiss, the apostle conjoining in those verses the death and resurrection of Christ, which he saith was for us; and how far this advantageth his cause in hand, we have before declared. By Heb. x. 7, I suppose he meant verse 10 of the chapter, affirming that by the will of God, which Christ came to do, we are sanctified, even through the offering of the body of Jesus,—ascribing our sanctification to his death, which is not effected in all and every one; though perhaps he may suppose the last clause of the verse, "once for all," to make for him. But some charitable man, I hope, will undeceive him, by letting him know the meaning of the word ἐφάπαξ. The like may be observed of the other places,—that in them is nothing at all to the proposition in hand, and nigh them at least is enough to evert it. And so his proposition in sum is:—"All those for whom the Scripture affirms that Christ did die, for them he died;" which is true, and doubtless granted.

The assumption affirms that Christ and his apostles in the Scriptures say that he died to save *sinners, unjust, ungodly*, the *world, all;* whereupon the conclusion ought barely to be, "Therefore Christ died for sinners, unjust, ungodly, the world, and the like." To which we say,—First, That this is the very same argument, for substance, with that which went before, as also are some of those that follow; only some words are varied, to change the outward appearance, and so to make show of a number. Secondly, That the whole strength of this argument lies in turning indefinite propositions into universals, concluding that because Christ died for sinners, therefore he died for all sinners; because he died for the unjust, ungodly, and the world, that therefore he died for every one that is unjust, or ungodly, and for every one in the world; because he died for all, therefore for all and every one of all sorts of men. Now, if this be good arguing, I will furnish you with some more such arguments against you have occasion to use them:—*First*, God "justifieth the ungodly," Rom. iv. 5; therefore, he justifieth every one that is ungodly. Now, "whom he justifieth, them he also glorifieth;" and therefore every ungodly person shall be glorified. *Secondly*, When Christ came, "men loved darkness rather than light," John iii. 19; therefore, all men did so, and so none believed. *Thirdly*, "The world knew not Christ," John i. 10; therefore, no man in the world knew him. *Fourthly*, "The whole world lieth in wickedness," 1 John v. 19; therefore, every one in the world doth so. Such arguments as these, by turning indefinite propositions into universals, I could easily furnish you withal, for any purpose that you will use them to. Thirdly, If you extend the words in the conclusion no farther than the intention of them in the places of Scripture recited in the assumption, we may safely grant the whole,—namely, that Christ died for sinners and the world, for sinful men in their several generations living therein; but if you intend a universality collective of all in the conclusion, then the syllogism is sophistical and false, no place of Scripture affirming so much that is produced, the assignation of the object of the death of Christ in them being in terms indefinite, receiving light and clearness for a more restrained sense in those places where they are expounded to be meant of all his own people, and the children of God scattered throughout the world. Fourthly, For particular places of Scripture urged, 1 Tim. i. 15; 1 Pet. iii. 18; Rom. v. 6, in the beginning of the assumption, are not at all to the purpose in hand. John iii. 17; Heb. ii. 9; 1 John ii. 2, have been already considered. Rom. iii. 10, 19, 20, 23; Eph. ii. 1–3; Tit. iii. 3; John iii. 4, 6, added in the close of the same proposition, prove that all are sinners and children of wrath; but of Christ's dying for all sinners, or for all those children of wrath, there is not the least intimation. And this may suffice in answer to the first two arguments, which might easily be retorted upon the author of them, the Scripture being full and plain to the confirmation of the position which he intends to oppose.

III. "That which the Scripture layeth forth as one end of the death of Christ, and one ground and cause of God's exalting Christ to be the Lord and Judge of all, and of the equity of his judging, that is certainly to be believed, Ps. xii. 6, xviii. 130, cxix. 4;

"But the Scripture layeth forth this for one end of the death and resurrection of Christ, that he might be the Lord of all, Rom. xiv. 9; 2 Cor. v. 14, 15. And for that cause (even his death and resurrection) hath God exalted him to be the Lord and Judge of all men, and his judgments shall be just, Rom. xiv. 9, 11, 12; 2 Cor. v. 10; Phil. ii. 7–11; Acts xvii. 31; Rom. ii. 16:

"Therefore, that Christ so died, and rose again for all, is a truth to be believed, 1 Tim. ii. 6."

First, The unlearned framing of this argument, the uncouth expressions of the thing intended, and failing in particulars, by the by, being to be ascribed to the person and not the cause, I shall not much trouble myself withal; as,—*First*, To his artificial regularity in bring his minor proposition, namely, Christ being made Lord and Judge of all, into the major; so continuing one term in all three propositions, and making the whole almost unintelligible. *Secondly*, His interpreting, "For this cause God exalted Christ," to be his death and resurrection, when his resurrection, wherein he was "declared to be the Son of God with power," Rom. i. 4, was a glorious part of his exaltation. To examine and lay open the weakness and folly of innumerable such things as these, which everywhere occur, were to be lavish of precious moments. Those that have the least taste of learning or the way of reasoning do easily see their vanity; and for the rest, especially the poor admirers of these foggy sophisms, I shall not say, "Quoniam hic populus vult decipi, decipiatur," but, "God give them understanding and repentance, to the acknowledgment of the truth."

Secondly, To this whole argument, as it lies before us, I have nothing to say but only to entreat Mr More, that if the misery of our times should be calling upon him to be writing again, he would cease expressing his mind by syllogisms, and speak in his own manner; which, by its confusion in innumerable tautologies, may a little puzzle his reader. For, truly, this kind of arguing here used,—for want of logic, whereby he is himself deceived, and delight in sophistry, whereby he deceiveth others,—is exceedingly ridiculous; for none can be so blind but that, at first reading of the argument, he will see that he asserts and infers that in the conclusion, strengthening it with a new testimony, which was not once dreamed of in either of the premises; they speaking of the exaltation of Christ to be judge of all, which refers to his own glory; the conclusion, of his dying for all, which necessarily aims at and intends their good. Were it not a noble design to banish all human learning, and to establish such a way of arguing in the room thereof? "Hoc Ithacus velit et magno mercentur Atridæ."

Thirdly, The force and sum of the argument is this:—"Christ died and rose again that he might be Lord and Judge of all; therefore, Christ died for all." Now, ask what he means by dying for all, and the whole treatise answers that it is a paying a ransom for them all, that they might be saved. Now, how this can be extorted out of Christ's dominion over all, with his power of judging all committed to him, which also is extended to the angels for whom he died not, let them that can understand it rejoice in their quick apprehension; I confess it flies my thoughts.

Fourthly, The manner of arguing being so vain, let us see a little whether there be any more weight in the matter of the argument. Many texts of Scripture are heaped up and distributed to the several propositions. In those out of Ps. xii. 6, xviii. 30 (as I suppose it should be, not 130, as it is printed), cxix. 4, there is some mention of the precepts of God, with the purity of his word and perfection of his word; which that they are any thing to the business in hand I cannot perceive. That of 2 Tim. ii. 6, added to the conclusion, is one of those places which are brought forth upon every occasion, as being the supposed foundation of the whole assertion, but causelessly, as hath been showed oft. [Among] those which are annexed to the minor proposition, [is] 2 Cor. v. 14, 15: as I have already cleared the mind of the Holy Ghost in it, and made it manifest that no such thing as universal redemption can be wrested from it, so unto this present argument it hath no reference at all, not containing any one syllable concerning the judging of Christ and his power over all, which was the medium insisted on. Phil. ii. 7–11; Acts. xvii. 31; Rom. ii. 16, mention, indeed, Christ's exaltation, and his judging all at the last day; but because he shall judge all at the last day, therefore he died for all, will ask more pains to prove than our adversary intends to take in this cause.

The weight, on the whole, must depend on Rom. xiv. 9, 11, 12; which being the only place that gives any colour to this kind of arguing, shall a little be considered. It is the lordship and dominion of Christ over all which the apostle, in that place, at large insists on and evidenceth to believers, that they might thereby be provoked to walk blameless, and without offence one towards another, knowing the terror of the Lord, and how that all men, even themselves and others, must come to appear before his judgment-seat, when it will be but a sad thing to have an account to make of scandals and offences. Farther to ingraft and fasten this upon them, he declares unto them the way whereby the Lord Christ attained and came to this dominion and power of judging, all things being put under his feet, together with what design he had, as to this particular, in undertaking the office of mediation, there expressed by "dying, rising, and reviving,"—to wit, that he might have the execution of judging over all committed to him, that being part of the "glory set before him," which caused him to "endure the cross and despise the shame," Heb. xii. 2.

So that all which here is intimated concerning the death of Christ is about the end, effects, and issue that it had towards himself, not any thing of what was his intention towards them for whom he died. To die for others does at least denote to die for their good, and in the Scripture always to die in their stead. Now, that any such thing can be hence deducted as that Christ died for all, because by his death himself made way for the enjoyment of that power whereby he is Lord over all, and will judge them all, casting the greatest part of men into hell by the sentence of his righteous judgment, I profess sincerely that I am no way able to perceive. If men will contend and have it so, that Christ must be said to die for all, because by his death and resurrection he attained the power of judging all, then I shall only leave with them these three things:—*First*, That innumerable souls shall be judged by him for not walking according to the light of nature left unto them, directing them to seek after the eternal power and Godhead of their Creator, without the least rumour of the gospel to direct them to a Redeemer once arriving at their ears, Rom. ii. 12; and what good will it be for such that Christ so died for them? *Secondly*, That he also died for the devils, because he hath, by his death and resurrection, attained a power of judging them also. *Thirdly*, That the whole assertion is nothing to the business in hand; our inquiry being about them whom our Saviour intended to redeem and save by his blood; this return, about those he will one day judge: "quæstio est de alliis, responsio de cepis."

IV. "That which the Scripture so sets forth in general for the world of mankind, as a truth for them all, that whosoever of the particulars so believe as to come to Christ and receive the same shall not perish, but have everlasting life, is certainly a truth to be believed, Acts v. 20;

"But that God sent forth his Son to be the Saviour of the world is in Scripture so set forth in general for all men, that whosoever of the particulars so believe as they come to Christ and receive the same, they shall not perish, but have everlasting life, John iii. 16–18, 36, i. 4, 11, 12:

"Therefore, that God sent his Son to be the Saviour of the world is a certain truth, 1 John iv. 14."

I hope no ingenuous man, that knows any thing of the controversy in hand, and to what head it is driven between us and our adversary, or is in any measure acquainted with the way of arguing, will expect that we should spend many words about such poor flourishes, vain repetitions, confused expressions, and illogical deductions and argumentations, as this pretended new argument (indeed the same with the first two, and with almost all that follow), will expect that I should cast away much time or pains about them. For my own part, I were no way able to undergo the tediousness of the review of such things as these, but that "eundum est quo trahunt fata ecclesiæ." Not, then, any more to trouble the reader with a declaration of that in particulars which he cannot but be sufficiently convinced of by a bare overlooking of these reasons,—namely, that this author is utterly ignorant of the way of reasoning, and knows not how tolerably to express his own conceptions, nor to infer one thing from another in any regular way, I answer,—First, That whatsoever the Scripture holds forth as a truth to be believed is certainly so, and to be embraced. Secondly, That the Scripture sets forth the death of Christ, to all whom the gospel is preached [unto], as an all-sufficient means for the bringing of sinners unto God, so as that whosoever believe it and come in unto him shall certainly be saved. Thirdly, What can be concluded hence, but that the death of Christ is of such infinite value as that it is able to save to the utmost every one to whom it is made known, if by true faith they obtain an interest therein and a right thereunto, we cannot perceive. This truth we have formerly confirmed by many testimonies of Scripture, and do conceive that this innate sufficiency of the death of Christ is the foundation of its promiscuous proposal to elect and reprobate. Fourthly, That the conclusion, if he would have the reason to have any colour or show of an argument, should at least include and express the whole and entire assertion contained in the proposition,—namely, "That Christ is so set forth to be the Saviour of the world, that whosoever of the particulars believe," etc. And then it is by us fully granted, as making nothing at all for the universality of redemption, but only for the fulness and sufficiency of his satisfaction. Of the word *world* enough hath been said before.

V. "That which God will one day cause every man confess to the glory of God is certainly a truth, for God will own no lie for his glory, John iii. 33; Rom. iii. 3, 4;

"But God will one day cause every man to confess Jesus (by virtue of his death and ransom given) to be the Lord, even to the glory of God, Phil. ii. 7–11; Isa. xlv. 22, 23; Rom. xiv. 9, 11, 12; Ps. lxxxvi. 9:

"Therefore, it is certainly a truth that Jesus Christ hath given himself a ransom for all men, and hath thereby the right of lordship over them; and if any will not believe and come into this government, yet he abideth faithful, and cannot deny himself, but will one day bring them before him, and cause them to confess him Lord, to the glory of God; when they shall be denied by him, for denying him in the days of his patience, 2 Tim. ii. 12–14; Matt. x. 32, 33; 2 Cor. v. 10."

Ans. The conclusion of this argument ought to be thus, and no otherwise, if you intend it should receive any strength from the premises: "Therefore, that Jesus Christ is the Lord, and to be confessed to the glory of God, is certainly a truth." This, I say, is all the conclusion that this argument ought to have had, unless, instead of a syllogism, you intend three independent propositions, every one standing upon its own strength. That which is inserted concerning his giving himself a ransom for all, and that which follows of the conviction and condemnation of them who believe not nor obey the gospel, confirmed from 2 Cor. v. 10, 2 Tim. ii. 12–14, is altogether heterogeneous to the business in hand. Now, this being the conclusion intended, if our author suppose that the deniers of universal redemption do question the truth of it, I wonder not at all why he left all other employment to fall a-writing controversies, having such apparent advantages against his adversaries as such small mistakes as this are able to furnish his conceit withal. But it may be an act of charity to part him and his own shadow,—so terribly at variance as here and in other places; wherefore, I beseech him to hear a word in his heat, and to take notice,—[First,] That though we do not ascribe a fruitless, ineffectual redemption to Jesus Christ, nor say that he loved any with that entire love which moved him to lay down his life, but his own church, and that all his elect are effectually redeemed by him, yet we deny not but that he shall also judge the reprobates,—namely, even all them that know not, that deny, that disobey and corrupt the truth of his gospel,—and that all shall be convinced that he is Lord of all at the last day: so that he may spare his pains of proving such unquestionable things. Something else is extremely desirous to follow, but indignation must be bridled. Secondly, For that cause in the second proposition, "By virtue of his death and ransom given," we deny that it is anywhere in the Scripture once intimated that the ransom paid by Christ in his death for us was the cause of his exaltation to be Lord of all: it was his obedience to his Father in his death, and not his satisfaction for us, that is proposed as the antecedent of this exaltation; as is apparent, Phil. ii. 7–11.

VI. "That which may be proved in and by the Scripture, both by plain sentences therein and necessary consequences imported thereby, without wresting, wrangling, adding to, taking from, or altering the sentences and words of Scripture, is a truth to be believed, Matt. xxii. 29, 32; Rom. xi. 2, 5, 6;

"But that Jesus Christ gave himself a ransom for all men, and by the grace of God tasted death for every man, may be proved in and by the Scripture, both by plain sentences therein and necessary consequences imported thereby, without wresting, wrangling, adding, or taking away, or altering the words and sentences, as is already showed, chap. vii., xiii., which will be now ordered into several proofs:

"Therefore, that Jesus Christ gave himself for all men, and by the grace of God tasted death for every man, is a truth to be believed, Mark i. 15, xvi. 15, 18; 1 John iv. 14."

Ans. First, The meaning of this argument is, that universal redemption may be proved by the Scripture; which, being the very thing in question, and the thesis undertaken to be proved, there is no reason why itself should make an argument, but only to make up a number: and, for my part, they should pass without any other answer, namely, that they are a number, but that those *who are the number* are to be considered.

Secondly, Concerning the argument itself (seeing it must go for one), we say,—*First,* To the first proposition, that laying aside the unnecessary expressions, the meaning of it I take to be this: "That which is affirmed in the Scripture, or may be deduced from thence by just consequence, following such ways of interpretation, of affirmation, and consequences, as by which the Spirit of God leadeth us into the knowledge of the truth, is certainly to be believed;" which is granted of all, though not proved by the places he quoteth, Matt. xxii. 29, 32, Rom. xi. 2, 5, 6, and is the only foundation of that article of faith which you seek to oppose. *Secondly,* To the second, that Christ gave himself a ransom ὑπὲρ πάντων, for all, and tasted death ὑπὲρ παντός, for all, is the very word of Scripture, and was never denied by any. The making of *all* to be all men and every man, in both the places aimed at, is your addition, and not the Scripture's assertion. If you intend, then, to prove that Christ gave himself a ransom for all, and tasted death for all, you may save your labours; it is confessed on all hands, none ever denied it. But if you intend to prove those *all* to be all and every man, of all ages and kinds, elect and reprobate, and not all his children, all his elect, all his sheep, all his people, all the children given him of God,—some of all sorts, nations, tongues, and languages only, I will, by the Lord's assistance, willingly join issue with you, or any man breathing, to search out the meaning of the word and mind of God in it; holding ourselves to the proportion of faith, essentiality of the doctrine of redemption, scope of the places where such assertions are, comparing them with other places, and the like ways,—labouring in all humility to find the mind of the Lord, according to his own appointment. And of the success of such a trial, laying aside such failings as will adhere to my personal weakness, I am, by the grace of God, exceedingly confident; having, by his goodness, received some strength and opportunity to search into and seriously to weigh whatever the most famous assertors of universal redemption, whether Lutherans or Arminians, have been able to say in this cause. For the present, I address myself to what is before me; only desiring the reader to observe, that the assertion to be proved is, "That Jesus Christ, according to the counsel and will of his Father, suitable to his purpose of salvation in his own mind and intention, did, by his death and oblation, pay a ransom for all and every man, elect and reprobate,—both those that are saved and those that perish,—to redeem them from sin, death, and hell, [and] to recover salvation, life, and immortality for them; and not only for his elect, or church, chosen to an inheritance before the foundation of the world." To confirm this we have divers places produced; which, by the Lord's assistance, we shall consider in order.

Proof 1 *of argument* 6. "God so loved the world, that he gave his Son to be the Saviour of the world, 1 John iv. 14; and sends his servant to bear witness of his Son, that all men through him might believe, John i. 4, 7; that whosoever believes on him might have everlasting life, John iii. 16, 17. And he is willing that all should come to the knowledge of the truth, 1 Tim. ii. 4, and be saved, 1 Tim. i. 15. Nor will he be wanting in the sufficiency of helpfulness to them, if, as light comes, they will suffer themselves to be wrought on and to receive it, Prov. i. 23, viii. 4, 5. And is not this plain in Scripture?"

Ans. First, The main, yea, indeed, only thing to be proved, as we before observed, is, that those indefinite propositions which we find in the Scripture concerning the death of Christ are to be understood universally,—that the terms *all* and *world* do signify in this business, when they denote the object of the death of Christ, all and every man in the world. Unless this be done, all other labour is altogether useless and fruitless. Now, to this there is nothing at all urged in this pretended proof, but only a few ambiguous places barely recited, with a false collection from them or observation upon them, which they give no colour to.

Secondly, 1 John iv 14, God's sending his Son to be the "Saviour of the world," and his servant to testify it, is nothing but to be the Saviour of men living in the world; which his elect are. A hundred such places as these, so clearly interpreted as they are in other places, would make nought at all to the purpose. The next thing is from John i. 4, 7. Verse 4 is, that Christ was the "life of men;" which is most true, no life being to be had for any man but only in and through him. This not being at all to the question, the next words of verse 7 [are], "That all men through him might believe;" which words being thrust in, to piece-up a sense with another fraction of Scripture, seem to have some weight, as though Christ were sent that all men through him might believe. A goodly show! seeming no less to make for universal redemption than the Scripture cited by the devil, after he had cut off part of it, did for our Saviour's casting himself from the pinnacle of the temple. But if you cast aside the sophistry of the old serpent, the expression of this place is not a little available to invalidate the thesis sought to be maintained by it. The words are, "There was a man sent from God, whose name was John. The same came for a witness, to bear witness of the light, that all men through him might believe." Now, who do you think is there meant by δι' αὐτοῦ, "through him?" Is it Christ, think you, the light? or John, the witness of the light? Certainly John, as almost all expositors do agree, except certain among the Papists, and Grotius,—that Ishmael. So the Syriac interpreter, reading, "By his hand or ministry." So the word infers; for we are not said to believe διὰ Χρίστου, "by Christ," or, as it should be here, διὰ τοῦ φωτός, "by the light;" but εἰς τὸ φῶς, John xii. 36, "*in* the light," not *by* it. And ἐπι τὸν Κύριον, Acts ix. 42, "believed in the Lord;" so also, Rom. ix. 33, Καὶ πᾶς ὁ πιστεύων ἐπ' αὐτῷ, "Every one that believeth on him." So ἐν Χριστῷ, in divers places, *in him;* but no mention of believing *by him*, which rather denotes the instrument of believing, as is the ministry of the word, than the object of faith, as Christ is. This being apparent, let us see what is affirmed of John, why he was sent "that all through him might believe." Now, this word *all* here hath all the qualifications which our author requireth for it, to be always esteemed a certain expression of a collective universality, that it is spoken of God, etc. And who, I pray you, were these *all*, that were intended to be brought to the faith by the ministry of John? Were they not only all those that lived throughout the world in his days, who preached (a few years) in Judea only, but also all those that were dead before his nativity, and that were born after his death, and shall be to the end of the world in any place under heaven? Let them that can believe it enjoy their persuasion, with this assurance that I will never be their rival; being fully persuaded that by *all men* here is meant only some of all sorts, to whom his word did come. So that the necessary sense of the word *all* here is wholly destructive to the proposition.

For what, thirdly, is urged from John iii. 16, 17, that God so sent his Son, that "whosoever believeth on him might have everlasting life," as far as I know is not under debate, as to the sense of it, among Christians.

Fourthly, For God's willingness that all should be saved, from 1 Tim. ii. 4 (to which a word is needlessly added to make a show, the text being quite to another purpose, from 1 Tim. i. 15), taking *all men* there for the universality of individuals, then I ask,—*First*, What act it is of God wherein this his willingness doth consist? Is it in the eternal purpose of his will that all should be saved? Why is it not accomplished? "Who hath resisted his will?" Is it in an antecedent desire that it should be so, though he fail in the end? Then is the blessed God most miserable, it being not in him to accomplish his just and holy desires. Is it some temporary act of his, whereby he hath declared himself unto them? Then, I say, Grant that salvation is only to be had in a Redeemer, in Jesus Christ, and give me an instance how God, in any act whatsoever, hath declared his mind and revealed himself to all men, of all times and places, concerning his willingness of their salvation by Jesus Christ, a Redeemer, and I will never more trouble you in this cause. *Secondly*, Doth this will equally respect the *all* intended, or doth it not? If it doth, why hath it not equal effects towards all? what reason can be assigned? If it doth not, whence shall that appear? There is nothing in the text to intimate any such diversity. For our parts, by *all men* we understand some of all sorts throughout the world, not doubting but that, to the equal reader, we have made it so appear from the context and circumstances of the place, the will of God there being that mentioned by our Saviour, John vi. 40. That which follows in the close of this proof, of God's "not being wanting in the sufficiency of helpfulness to them who, as light comes, suffer themselves to be wrought upon and receive it," is a poisonous sting in the tail of the serpent, wherein is couched the whole Pelagian poison of free-will and Popish merit of congruity, with Arminian sufficient grace, in its whole extent and universality; to neither of which there is the least witness given in the place produced.

The sum and meaning of the whole assertion is, that there is a universality of sufficient grace granted to all, even of grace subjective, enabling them to obedience, which receives addition, increase, degrees, and augmentation, according as they who have it do make use of what they presently enjoy; which is a position so contradictory to innumerable places of Scripture, so derogatory to the free grace of God, so destructive to the efficacy of it, such a clear exaltation of the old idol free-will into the throne of God, as any thing that the decaying estate of Christianity hath invented and broached. So far is it from being "plain and clear in Scripture," that it is universally repugnant to the whole dispensation of the new covenant revealed to us therein; which, if ever the Lord call me to, I hope very clearly to demonstrate: for the present, it belongs not immediately to the business in hand, and therefore I leave it, coming to—

Proof 2. "Jesus Christ, the Son of God, came into the world to save the world, John xii. 47; to save sinners, 1 Tim. i. 15; to take away our sins, and destroy the works of the devil, 1 John iii. 5, 8; to take away the sins of the world, John i. 29: and therefore died for all, 2 Cor. v. 14, 15; and gave himself a ransom for all, 1 Tim. ii. 6; to save that which was lost, Matt. xviii. 11. And so his propitiation was made for the world, 2 Cor. v. 19; the whole world, 1 John ii. 2. And all this is full and plain in Scripture."

Ans. Those places of this proof where there is mention of *all* or *world,* as John xii. 47, i. 29; 2 Cor. v. 14, 15; 1 Tim. ii. 6; 2 Cor. v. 19; 1 John ii. 2, have been all already considered, and I am unwilling to trouble the reader with repetitions. See the places, and I doubt not but you will find that they are so far from giving any strength to the thing intended to be proved by him, that they much rather evert it. For the rest, 1 Tim. i. 15; Matt. xviii. 11; 1 John iii. 5, 8, how any thing can be extracted from them to give colour to the universality of redemption I cannot see; what they make against it hath been declared. Pass we then to—

Proof 3. "God in Christ doth, in some means or other of his appointment, give some witness to all men of his mercy and goodness procured by Christ, Ps. xix. 4; Rom. x. 18; Acts xiv. 17; and therethrough, at one time or other, sendeth forth some stirrings of his Spirit, to move in and knock at the hearts of men, to invite them to repentance and seeking God, and so to lay hold on the grace and salvation offered: and this not in a show or pretence, but in truth and good-will, ready to bestow it on them. And this is all fully testified in Scripture, Gen. vi. 3; Isa. xlv. 22; Acts xvii. 30, 31; John i. 19."

Ans. First, "Parvas habet spes Troja, si tales habet." If the universality of redemption have need of such proofs as these, it hath indeed great need and little hope of supportment. *Universal vocation* is here asserted, to maintain *universal redemption.* "Manus manum fricat," or rather, "Muli se mutuo scabiunt;" this being called in oftentimes to support the other; and they are both the two legs of that idol free-will, which is set up for men to worship, and when one stumbles the other steps forward to uphold the Babel. Of *universal vocation* (a gross figment) I shall not now treat; but only say, for the present, that it is true that God at all times, ever since the creation, hath called men to the knowledge of himself as the great Creator, in those things which of him, by the means of the visible creation, might be known, "even his eternal power and Godhead," Rom. i. 19, 20; Ps. xix. 1, 2; Acts xiv. 17. Secondly, That after the death of Christ, he did, by preaching of the gospel extended far and wide, call home to himself the children of God, scattered abroad in the world, whereas his elect were before confined almost to one nation; giving a right to the gopsel to be preached to "every creature," Mark xvi. 15; Rom. x. 18; Isa. xlv. 22; Acts xvii. 30, 31. But, thirdly, That God should at all times, in all places, in all ages, grant means of grace or call to Christ as a redeemer, or to a participation of his mercy and goodness in him manifested, with strivings and motions of his Spirit for men to close with those invitations, is so gross and groundless an imagination, so opposite to God's distinguishing mercy, so contradictory to express places of Scripture and the experience of all ages, as I wonder how any man hath the boldness to assert it, much more to produce it as a proof of an untruth more gross than itself. Were I not resolved to tie myself to the present controversy, I should not hold from producing some reasons to evert this fancy; something may be done hereafter, if the Lord prevent not. In the meantime, let the reader consult Ps. cxlvii. 19, 20; Matt. xi. 25, xxii. 14; Acts xiv. 16, xvi. 7; Rom. x. 14, 15. We pass to—

Proof 4. "The Holy Ghost, that cometh from the Father and the Son, shall reprove the world of sin (even that part of the world that refuseth now to believe that they are under sin), because they believe not on Christ, and that it is their sin that they have not believed on him. And how could it be their sin not to believe in Christ, and they for that cause under sin, if there were neither enough in the atonement made by Christ for them, nor truth in God's offer of mercy to them, nor will nor power in the Spirit's moving in any sort sufficient to have brought them to believe, at one time or other? And yet is this evident in Scripture, and shall be by the Holy Spirit, to be their great sin, that fastens all other sins on them, John iii. 18, 19, viii. 24, xii. 48, xv. 22, 24, xvi. 7–11."

Ans. The intention of this proof is, to show that men shall be condemned for their unbelief, for not believing in Christ; which, saith the author, cannot be unless three things be granted,—First, That there be enough in the atonement made by Christ for them. Secondly, That there be truth in God's offer of mercy to them. Thirdly, That there be sufficient will and power given them by the Spirit, at some time or other, to believe. Now, though I believe no man can perceive what may be concluded hence for the universality of redemption, yet I shall observe some few things: and to the first thing required do say, That if, by "Enough in the atonement for them," you understand that the atonement, which was made for them, hath enough in it, we deny it; not because the atonement hath not enough in it for them, but because the atonement was not for them. If you mean that there is a sufficiency in the merit of Christ to save them if they should believe, we grant it, and affirm that this sufficiency is the chief ground of the proposing it unto them (understanding those to whom it is proposed, that is those to whom the gospel is preached). To the second, That there is truth, as in all the ways and words of God, so in his offer of mercy to whomsoever it is offered. If we take the command to believe, with the promise of life upon so doing, for an offer of mercy, there is an eternal truth in it; which is, that God will assuredly bestow life and salvation upon all believers, the proffers being immediately declarative of our duty; secondly, of the concatenation of faith and life, and not at all of God's intention towards the particular soul to whom the proffer is made: "For who hath known the mind of the Lord, and who hath been his counsellor?" To the third, the Spirit's giving will or power, I say,—*First,* That ye set the cart before the horse, placing will before power. *Secondly,* I deny that any internal assistance is required to render a man inexcusable for not believing, if he have the object of faith propounded to him, though of himself he have neither power nor will so to do, having lost both in Adam. *Thirdly,* How a man may have given him a will to believe, and yet not believe, I pray, declare the next controversy ye undertake. This being observed, I shall take leave to put this proof into such form as alone it is capable of, that the strength thereof may appear, and it is this: "If the Spirit shall convince all those of sin to whom the gospel is preached, that do not believe, then Christ died for all men, both those that have the gospel preached unto them and those that have not; but the first is true, for their unbelief is their great sin: ergo, Jesus Christ died for all." Which, if any, is an argument "a baculo ad angulum, "from the beam to the shuttle." The places of Scripture, John iii. 18, 19, viii. 24, xii. 48, xv. 22, 24, prove that unbelief is a soul-condemning sin, and that for which they shall be condemned in whom it is privative, by their having the gospel preached to them. But *quid ad nos?*

One place is more urged, and consequently more abused, than the rest, and therefore must be a little cleared; it is John xvi. 7–11. The words are, "I will send the Comforter to you. And when he is come, he will reprove the world of sin, and of righteousness, and of judgment: of sin, because they believe not in me; of righteousness, because I go to my Father, and ye see me no more; of judgment, because the prince of this world is judged." First, It is uncertain whether our author understands the words of the Spirit in and with Christ at the last day, or in and with the ministry of the word now in the days of the gospel. If the first, he is foully mistaken; if the latter, then the conviction here meant intends only those to whom the gospel is preached,—and what that will advantage universal redemption, which compriseth all as well before as after the death of Christ, I know not. But, secondly, It is uncertain whether he supposeth this conviction of the Spirit to attend the preaching of the gospel only, or else to consist in strivings and motions even in them who never hear the word of the gospel; if he mean the latter, we wait for a proof. Thirdly, It is uncertain whether he supposeth those thus convinced to be converted and brought to the faith by that conviction and that attending effectualness of grace, or no.

But omitting those things, that text being brought forth and insisted on, farther to manifest how little reason there was for its producing, I shall briefly open the meaning of the words. Our Saviour Christ intending, in this his last sermon, to comfort his apostles in their present sad condition, whereto they were brought by his telling them that he must leave them and go to his Father,—which sorrow and sadness he knew full well would be much increased when they should behold the vile, ignominious way whereby their Lord and Master should be taken from them, with all those reproaches and persecutions which would attend them so deprived of him,—bids them not be troubled, nor filled with sorrow and fear, for all this; assuring them that all this loss, shame, and reproach should be abundantly made up by what he would do for them and bestow upon them when his bodily presence should be removed from them. And as to that particular, which was the head of all, that he should be so vilely rejected and taken out of the world as a false teacher and seducer, he telleth them he will send them ἄλλον παράκλητον, John xiv. 16, "another Comforter," one that shall "vicariam navare operam," as Tertul.,—be unto them in his stead, to fill them with all that consolation whereof by his absence they might be deprived; and not only so, but also to be present with them in other greater things than any he had as yet employed them about. This again he puts them in mind of, chap. xvi. 7. Now, ὁ παράκλητος, who is there promised, is properly "an advocate,"—that is, one that pleadeth the cause of a person that is guilty or accused before any tribunal,—and is opposed τῷ κατηγόρῳ, Rev. xii. 10; and so is this word by us translated, 1 John ii. 1. Christ, then, here telleth them, that as he will be their advocate with the Father, so he will send them an advocate to plead his cause, which they professed, with the world; that is, those men in the world, which had so vilely traduced and condemned him as a seducer, laying it as a reproach upon all his followers. This, doubtless, though in some respect it be continued to all ages in the ministry of the word, yet it principally intended the plentiful effusion of the Spirit upon the apostles at Pentecost, after the ascension of our Saviour; which also is made more apparent by the consideration of what he affirmeth that the advocate so sent shall do, namely,—1. "He shall reprove," or rather, evidently, "convince, the world of sin, because they believed not on him;" which, surely, he abundantly did in that sermon of Peter, Acts ii., when the enemies themselves and haters of Christ were so reproved and convinced of their sin, that, upon the pressing urgency of that conviction, they cried out, "Men and brethren, what shall we do to be saved?" Then was the world brought to a voluntary confession of the sin of murdering Jesus Christ. 2. He shall do the same of "righteousness, because he went to his Father;"—not of its own righteousness, to reprove it for that, because it is not; but he shall convince the men of the world, who condemned Christ as a seducer, of his righteousness,—that he was not a blasphemer, as they pretended, but the Son of God, as himself witnessed: which they shall be forced to acknowledge when, by the effusion and pouring out of the Spirit upon his apostles, it shall be made evident that he is gone to and received of his Father, and owned by him, as the centurion did presently upon his death. 3. He shall "convince the world of judgment, because the prince of this world is judged;" manifesting to all those of whom he speaketh, that he whom they despised as the carpenter's son, and bade come down from the cross if he could, is exalted to the right hand of God, having all judgment committed to him, having beforehand, in his death, judged, sentenced, and overcome Satan, the prince of this world, the chief instigator of his crucifiers, who had the power of death. And this I take to be the clear, genuine meaning of this place, not excluding the efficacy of the Spirit, working in the same manner, though not to the same degree, for the same end, in the majesty of the word, to the end of the world. But what this is to universal redemption, let them that can understand it keep it to themselves, for I am confident they will never be able to make it out to others.

Proof 5. "God hath testified, both by his word and his oath, that he would that his Son should so far save as to work a redemption for all men, and likewise that he should bring all to the knowledge of the truth, that there-through redemption might be wrought in and upon them, 1 Tim. ii. 4, with John iii. 17. So he willeth not, nor hath any pleasure in, the death of him (even the wicked) that dieth, but rather that he turn and live, Ezek. xviii. 23, 32, xxxiii. 11. And dare any of us say, the God of truth saith and sweareth that of which he hath no inward and serious meaning? O far be such blasphemy from us!"

Ans. First, This assertion, "That God testifieth, by his word and oath, that he would that Christ should so far save us," etc., is a bold calling of God to witness that which he never affirmed, nor did it ever enter into his heart; for he hath revealed his will that Christ should save to the utmost them that come to him, and not save so far or so far, as is boldly, ignorantly, and falsely intimated. Let men beware of provoking God to their own confusion; he will not be a witness to the lie of false hearts. Secondly, "That Christ should so bring all to the knowledge of the truth, that there-through redemption might be wrought in and upon them," is another bold corruption of the word, and false-witness-bearing in the name of God. Is it a small thing for you to weary and seduce men? will you weary our God also? Thirdly, For places of Scripture corrupted to the sense imposed: In John iii. 17, God is said to "send his Son, that the world through him might be saved;" not be saved so far or so far, but saved "from their sins," Matt. i. 21, and "to the uttermost," Heb. vii. 25: so that the world of God's elect, who only are so saved, is only there to be understood, as hath been proved. In 1 Tim. ii. 4, there is something of the will of God for the saving of all sorts of men, as hath been declared; nothing conducing to the bold assertion used in this place. Fourthly, To those are added that of Ezek. xviii. 23, that God hath no "pleasure at all that the wicked should die;" and, verse 32, "no pleasure in the death of him that dieth." Now, though these texts are exceeding useless to the business in hand, and might probably have some colour of universal vocation, but none possibly of universal redemption, there being no mention of Christ or his death in the place from whence they are cited; yet because our adversaries are frequently knitting knots from this place to inveigle and hamper the simple, I shall add some few observations upon it to clear the meaning of the text, and demonstrate how it belongs nothing at all to the business in hand.

First, then, let us consider to whom and of whom these words are spoken. Is it to and of all men, or only to the house of Israel? Doubtless these last; they are only intended, they only are spoken to: "Hear now, O house of Israel," verse 25. Now, will it follow that because God saith he delights not in the death of the house of Israel, to whom he revealed his mind, and required their repentance and conversion, that therefore he saith so of all, even those to whom he never revealed his will by such ways as to them, nor called to repentance, Ps. cxlvii. 19, 20? So that the very ground-work of the whole conclusion is removed by this first observation. Secondly, "God willeth not the death of a sinner," is either, "God purposeth and determineth he shall not die," or, "God commandeth that he shall do those things wherein he may live." If the first, why are they not all saved? why do sinners die? for there is an immutability in the counsel of God, Heb. vi. 17; "His counsel shall stand, and he will do all his pleasure," Isa. xlvi. 10. If the latter way, by commanding, then the sense is, that the Lord commandeth that those whom he calleth should do their duty, that they may not die (although he knows that this they cannot do without his assistance); now, what this makes to general redemption, I know not. Thirdly, To add no more, this whole place, with the scope, aim, and intention of the prophet in it, is miserably mistaken by our adversaries, and wrested to that whereof there is not the least thought in the text. The words are a part of the answer which the Lord gives to the repining Jews, concerning their proverb, "The fathers have eaten sour grapes, and the children's teeth are set on edge." Now, about what did they use this proverb? Why, "concerning the land of Israel," verse 2, the land of their habitation, which was laid waste by the sword (as they affirmed) for the sins of their fathers, themselves being innocent. So that it is about God's temporal judgments in overturning their land and nation that this dispute is; wherein the Lord justifieth himself by declaring the equity of these judgments by reason of their sins, even those sins for which the land devoured them and spewed them out; telling them that his justice is, that for such things they should surely die, their blood should be upon them, verse 13,—they shall be slain with the sword, and cut off by those judgments which they had deserved: not that the shedding of their blood and casting out of their carcases was a thing in itself so pleasurable or desirable to him as that he did it only for his own will, for let them leave their abominations, and try whether their lives were not prolonged in peace. This being the plain, genuine scope and meaning of this place, at the first view presenting itself to every unprejudiced man, I have often admired how so many strange conclusions for a general purpose of showing mercy to all, universal vocation and redemption, have been wrested from it; as also, how it came to be produced to give colour to that heap of blasphemy which our author calleth his fifth proof.

Proof 6. "The very words and phrases used by the Holy Ghost in Scripture, speaking of the death of Christ, and the ransom and propitiation, to whom it belongs, and who may seek it, and in believing find life, implies no less than all men. As to instance: "All nations," Matt. xxviii. 19, 20; "the ends of the earth," Isa. xlv. 22, xlix. 6; "every creature," Mark xvi. 15; "all," 2 Cor. v. 14, 15, 1 Tim. ii. 6; "every man," Heb. ii. 9; "the world," John iii. 16, 17, 2 Cor. v. 19; "the whole world," 1 John ii. 2; "that which was lost," Luke xix. 10; "sinners," Matt. ix. 13; "unjust," 1 Pet. iii. 18; "ungodly," Rom. v. 6; and that whosoever of these repent and believe in Christ shall receive his grace, John iii. 16, 18, Acts x. 43. Now, all these so often and indifferently used, were it not pride and error to devise glosses to restrain the sense the Scripture holdeth forth, so full and large for all men?"

Ans. First, This argument, taken from the words and phrases whereby the object of the death of Christ is in the Scripture expressed, is that which filleth up both pages of this book, being repeated, and most of the places here cited urged, a hundred times over; and yet it is so far from being any pressing argument, as that indeed it is nothing but a bare naked repetition of the thing in debate, concluding according to his own persuasion; for the main *quære* between us is, whether the words *all* and *the world* be to be taken universally? He saith so, and he saith so; which is all the proof we have, repeating over the thing to be proved instead of a proof. Secondly, For those places which affirm Christ to die for "sinners," "ungodly," "that which was lost," etc.,—as Luke xix. 10; Matt. ix. 13; 1 Pet. iii. 18; Rom. v. 6,—I have before declared how exceedingly unserviceable they are to universal redemption. Thirdly, For those places where the words "all," "every man," "the world," "the whole world," are used, we have had them over and over; and they likewise have been considered. Fourthly, For those expressions of "all nations," Matt. xxviii. 19, 20, "every creature," Mark xvi. 15, used concerning them to whom the gospel is preached, I say,—*First*, That they do not comprise all individuals, nay, not all nations at all times, much less all singular persons of all nations if we look upon the accomplishment and fulfilling of that command; neither, *de facto*, was the gospel ever so preached to all, although there be a fitness and a suitableness in the dispensation thereof to be so preached to all, as was declared. *Secondly*, The command of preaching the gospel to all doth not in the least manner prove that Christ died with an intention to redeem all; but it hath other grounds and other ends, as hath been manifested. *Thirdly*, That the ransom belongs to all to whom it is proposed we deny; there be other ends of that proposal; and Christ will say to some of them that he never knew them: therefore, certainly, he did not lay down his life for them. *Fourthly*, "The ends of the earth," Isa. xlv. 22, are those that look up to God from all parts, and are saved; which surely are not all and every one. And Christ being given to be a "salvation unto the end of the earth," chap. xlix. 6, is to do no more among the Gentiles than God promiseth in the same place that he shall do for his own people,—even "gather the preserved of Israel;" so shall he bear forth the salvation of God, and gather the preserved remnant of his elect to the ends of the earth.

And now, I hope, I need not mind the intelligent reader that the author of these collections could not have invented a more ready way for the ruin of the thesis which he seeks to maintain than by producing those places of Scripture last recounted for the confirmation of it, granting that *all* and *the world* are no more than "all the ends of the earth," mentioned in Isa. xlv. 22, xlix. 6; it being evident beyond denial that by these expressions, in both these places, only the elect of God and believers are clearly intimated: so that, interpreting the one by the other, in those places where *all* and *the world* are spoken of, those only are intended. "If pride and error" had not taken full possession of the minds of men, they could not so far deny their own sense and reason as to contradict themselves and the plain texts of Scripture for the maintenance of their false and corrupt opinions.

Proof 7. "That whereas there are certain high and peculiar privileges of the Spirit contained in the New Testament, sealed by the blood of Christ, which belong not to all men, but only to the saints, the called and chosen of the Lord, and when they are alone distinctly mentioned, they are even so spoken of as belonging to them only, Matt. xiii. 11; John xiv. 17, 21–23, xvi. 13–15, xvii. 19, 20; Acts ii. 38, 39; 1 Cor. ii. 9, 14; Heb. ix. 15, viii.; 1 Pet. ii. 3, 9; yet many of these peculiar privileges are so spoken of as joined together with the ransom and propitiation, which belongs to all. Then are they not spoken of in such a restraining and exclusive manner, or with such appropriating words, but so, and with such words, as room is left to apply the ransom to all men, in speech; and withal, so hold out the privileges to them that believe that are proper to them, that they may both have their comfort and especial hope, and also hold forth the ransom and keep open the door for others, in belief and receipt of the propitiation, to come in and partake with them. And so it is said for his "sheep," and for "many;" but nowhere but only for his sheep, or but only for many: which is a strong proof of the ransom for all men, as is shown, chap. iii. x."

Ans. The strength of this proof, as to the business in hand, is wholly hid from me; neither do I perceive how it may receive any such tolerable application as to deserve the name of a proof, as to the main thesis intended to be maintained. The force which it hath is in an observation which, if it hath any sense, is neither true nor once attempted to be made good; for,—First, That there are peculiar high privileges belonging to the saints and called of God is a thing which needs no proof. Amongst these is the death of Christ for them, not as saints, but as elect, which, by the benefit of that death and blood-shedding, are to be made saints, and accounted to be the holy ones of God: for "he redeemed his church with his own blood," Acts xx. 28; he "loved and gave himself for it," Eph. v. 25; even "us," Tit. ii. 14;—even as divers of those [privileges] here intimated are expressly assigned unto them, as elect, such as those, John xvii. 19, 20; amongst which also, as in the same rank with them, is reckoned Jesus' "sanctifying himself for their sakes," that is to be an oblation, verse 19. In a word, all peculiar saving privileges belong only to God's elect, purchased for them, and them alone, by the blood of Jesus Christ, Eph. i. 3, 4. Secondly, For the other part of the observation, that where mention is made of these together with the ransom, there is room left to extend the ransom to all, I answer,—*First,* This is said, indeed, but not once attempted to be proved. We have but small cause to believe the author, in any thing of this importance, upon his bare word. *Secondly,* For the "leaving of room for the application," I perceive that if it be not left, ye will make it, though ye justle the true sense of the Scripture quite out of its place. *Thirdly*, I have already showed that where "many" are mentioned, the ransom only (as ye use to speak) is expressed, as also where "sheep" are spoken of; the like is said where the word "all" is used;—so that there is not the least difference. *Fourthly*, In divers places the ransom of Christ and those other peculiar privileges (which indeed are fruits of it) are so united together, as it is impossible to apply the latter to *some* and the other to *all*, being all of them restrained to his saved ones only, Rev. v. 9, 10. The redemption of his people by the ransom of his blood, and their making kings and priests, are united, and no room left for the extending of the ransom to all, it being punctually assigned to those saved crowned ones, distinguished from the rest of the nations and languages from among whom they were taken, who were passed by in the payment of the ransom; which is directly opposite to all the sense which I can observe in this observation. *Fifthly*, Of "sheep, and sheep only," enough before.

Proof 8. "The restoration wrought by Christ in his own body for mankind is set forth in Scripture to be as large and full for all men, and of as much force, as the fall of the first Adam, by and in himself, for all men; in which respect the first Adam is said to have been a figure of Christ, the second Adam, Rom. iii. 22–25, v. 12, 14, 18; 1 Cor. xv. 21, 22, 45–47: as is before shown, chap. viii."

Ans. First, It is most true that Christ and Adam are compared together (in respect of the righteousness of the one, communicated to them that are his, and the disobedience and transgression of the other, in like manner communicated to all them that are of him) in some of the places here mentioned, as Rom. v. 12, 18. But evidently the comparison is not instituted between the righteousness of Christ and the disobedience of Adam *extensively*, in respect of the *object*, but *intensively*, in respect of the *efficacy* of the one and the other; the apostle asserting the effectualness of the righteousness of Christ unto justification, to answer the prevalency of the sin of Adam unto condemnation,—that even as the transgression of Adam brought a guilt of condemnation upon all them that are his natural seed, so the righteousness of Christ procured the free gift of grace unto justification towards all them that are his, his spiritual seed, that were the children given unto him of his Father.

Secondly, 1 Cor. xv. 21, 22, speaketh of the resurrection from the dead, and that only of believers; for though he mentions them all, verse 22, "In Christ shall all be made alive," yet, verse 23, he plainly interprets those *all* to be all that are "Christ's:" not but that the other dead shall rise also, but that it is a resurrection to glory, by virtue of the resurrection of Christ, which the apostle here treats of; which certainly all shall not have.

Thirdly, The comparison between Christ and Adam, verse 45 (to speak nothing of the various reading of that place), is only in respect of the principles which they had, and were intrusted withal to communicate to others: "Adam a living soul," or a "living creature;" there was in him a principle of life natural, to be communicated to his posterity;—"Christ a quickening Spirit," giving life, grace, and spirit to his. And here I would desire that it may be observed, that all the comparison that is anywhere instituted between Christ and Adam still comes to one head, and aims at one thing,—namely, that they were as two common stocks or roots, communicating to them that are ingrafted into them (that is, into Adam *naturally*, by generation; into Christ *spiritually*, by regeneration) that wherewith they were replenished;—Adam, sin, guilt, and disobedience; Christ, righteousness, peace, and justification. [As] for the number of those that do thus receive these things from one and the other, the consideration of it is exceedingly alien from the scope, aim, and end of the apostle in the places where the comparison is instituted.

Fourthly, It is true, Rom. iii. 23, it is said, "All have sinned, and come short of the glory of God," which the apostle had at large proved before, thereby to manifest that there was no salvation to be attained but only by Jesus Christ; but if ye will ask to whom this righteousness of Christ is extended, and that redemption which is in his blood, he telleth you plainly, it is "unto all and upon all them that believe," verse 22, whether they be Jews or Gentiles, "for there is no difference."

Proof 9. "The Lord Jesus Christ hath sent and commanded his servants to preach the gospel to all nations, to every creature, and to tell them withal that whoever believeth and is baptized shall be saved, Matt. xxviii. 19, 20; Mark xvi. 15, 16: and his servants have so preached to all, 2 Cor. v. 19; Rom. x. 13, 18. And our Lord Jesus Christ will make it to appear one day that he hath not sent his servants upon a false errand, nor put a lie in their mouths, nor wished them to dissemble, in offering that to all which they knew belonged but to some, even to fewest of all, but to speak truth, Isa. xliv. 26, lxi. 8; 1 Tim. i. 12."

Ans. The strength of this proof is not easily apparent, nor manifest wherein it lieth, in what part or words of it: for,—First, It is true, Christ commanded his apostles to "preach the gospel to all nations and every creature,"—to tell them "that whosoever believeth shall be saved," Matt. xxviii. 19, 20, Mark xvi. 15, 16; that is, without distinction of persons or nations, to call all men to whom the providence of God should direct them, and from whom the Spirit of God should not withhold them (as from them, Acts xvi. 6, 7), warning them to repent and believe the gospel. Secondly, It is also true, that, in obedience unto this command, his servants did beseech men so to do, and to be reconciled unto God, even all over the nations, without distinction of any, but where they were forbidden, as above, labouring to spread the gospel to the ends of the earth, and not to tie it up to the confines of Jewry, 2 Cor. v. 19, 20; Rom. x. 18. Most certain also it is, that the Lord Jesus Christ sent not his servants with a lie, to offer that to all which belonged only to some, but to speak the truth; of which there needs no proof. But now, what can be concluded from hence for universal redemption is not easily discernible.

Perhaps some will say it is in this, that if Christ did not die for all to whom the word is preached, then how can they that preach it offer Christ to all? A poor proof, God wot! For,—First, The gospel was never preached to all and every one, nor is there any such thing affirmed in the places cited; and ye are to prove that Christ died for all, as well those that never hear of the gospel as those that do. Secondly, What do the preachers of the gospel offer to them to whom the word is preached? Is it not life and salvation through Christ, upon the condition of faith and repentance? And doth not the truth of this offer consist in this, that every one that believeth shall be saved? And doth not that truth stand firm and inviolable, so long as there is an all-sufficiency in Christ to save all that come unto him? Hath God intrusted the ministers of the gospel with his intentions, purposes, and counsels, or with his commands and promises? Is it a lie, to tell men that he that believeth shall be saved, though Christ did not die for some of them? Such proofs as these had need be well proved themselves, or they will conclude the thing intended very weakly.

Proof 10. "The Lord willeth believers to pray even for the unjust and their persecutors, Matt. v. 44, 48; Luke vi. 28; yea, even 'for all men;' yea, even 'for kings and all in authority,' when few in authority loved Christianity. Yet he said not, some of that sort, but, 'For all in authority;' and that on this ground,—it is good in the sight of God, 'who will have all men saved, and come to the knowledge of the truth,' Luke x. 5; 1 Tim. ii. 1–4. Surely there is a door of life opened for all men, 2 Tim. i. 10; for God hath not said to the seed of Israel, 'Seek ye me in vain,' Isa. xliv. 19. He will not have his children pray for vain things."

Ans. The strength of this proof lieth in supposing,—First, That *indefinite* assertions are to be interpreted as equivalent to *universal;* which is false, Rom. iv., v. Secondly, That by "all," 1 Tim. ii. 1, is not meant all sorts of men, and the word *all* is not to be taken distributively, when the apostle, by an enumeration of divers sorts, gives an evident demonstration of the distribution intended. Thirdly, That we are bound to pray for every singular man that he may be saved; which,—1. We have no warrant, rule, precept, or example for; 2. It is contrary to the apostolical precept, 1 John v. 16; 3. To our Saviour's example, John xvii. 9; 4. To the counsel and purpose of God, in the general made known to us, Rom. ix. 11, 12, 15, xi. 7, where evidently our praying for all is but for all sorts of men, excluding none, and that those may believe who are ordained to eternal life. Fourthly, It supposeth that there is nothing else that we are to pray for men but that they may be saved by Christ; which is apparently false, Jer. xxix. 7. Fifthly, That our ground of praying for any is an assurance that Christ died for them in particular; which is not true, Acts viii. 22, 24. Sixthly, It most splendidly takes for granted that our duty is to be conformed to God's secret mind, his purpose and counsel. Until every one of these supposals be made good, (which never a one of them will be very suddenly), there is no help in this proof nor strength in this argument, "We must pray for all; therefore God intends by the death of Christ to save all and every one," its sophistry and weakness being apparent. From our duty to God's purpose is no good conclusion, though from his command to our duty be most certain.

Proof 11. "The Lord hath given forth his word and promise to be with his servants so preaching the gospel to all, and with his people so praying for all where they come, that they may go on with confidence in both, Matt. xxviii. 20; 1 Tim. ii. 3, 8; Luke x. 5; Isa. liv. 17.

Ans. That God will be with his people, whether preaching or praying, according to his will and their own duty, is as apparent as it is that this makes nothing for universal redemption; than which what can be more evident.

Proof 12. "The Lord hath already performed and made good his word to his servants and people, upon some of all sorts of men and all sorts of sinners, showing them mercy to the very end, that none might exclude themselves, but all be encouraged to repent, believe, and hope thereby, Acts ii., iii., viii.–xi., xvi., xix., xxviii.; 1 Cor. vi. 10, 11; 1 Tim. i. 13–16."

Ans. If ye had told us that God had already made good his word to his servants, in saving all and every man, and proved it clearly, ye had evidently and undeniably confirmed the main opinion; but now, affirming only that he hath showed mercy to some of all sorts, and all sorts of sinners, that others of the like sort (as are the remainder of his elect, yet uncalled) might be induced to believe, ye have evidently betrayed your own cause, and established that of your adversaries, showing how the Lord in the event declareth on their side, saving in the blood of Jesus only some of all sorts, as they affirm, not all and every one, which your tenet leads you to.

Proof 13. "The blessing of life hath streamed in this doctrine of the love of God to mankind; yea, in the tender and spiritual discovery of the grace of God to mankind (in the ransom given and atonement made by Christ for all men, with the fruits thereof) hath God, in the first place, overcome his chosen ones to believe and turn to God, Acts xiii. 48; Titus ii. 11, 13, iii. 4, 5."

Ans. First, That the freedom of God's grace, and the transcendency of his eternal love towards men, with the sending of his Son to die for them, to recover them to himself from sin and Satan, is a most effectual motive, and (when set on by the Spirit of grace) a most certain operative principle of the conversion of God's elect, we most willingly acknowledge. It is that wherein our hearts rejoice, whereby they were endeared, and for which we desire to return thankful obedience every moment. But that ever this was effectual, extending this love to all, or at least that any effectualness is in that aggravation of it, we utterly deny; and that,—1. Because it is false, and a corrupting of the word of God, as hath been showed; and of a lie there can be no good consequence. 2. It quite enervates and plucks out the efficacy of this heavenly motive, by turning the most intense and incomparable love of God towards his elect into a common desire, wishing, and affection of his nature (which, indeed, is opposite to his nature), failing of its end and purpose; which might consist with the eternal destruction of all mankind, as I shall abundantly demonstrate, if Providence call me to the other part of this controversy, concerning the cause of sending Jesus Christ. Secondly, There is nothing of this common love to all in the places urged; for,—1. The "grace" mentioned, Tit. ii. 11, 13, is the grace that certainly brings salvation, which that common love doth not, and was the cause of sending Christ, "that he might redeem us from all iniquity, and purify to himself a peculiar people, zealous of good works;" where our redemption and sanctification are asserted to be the immediate end of the oblation of Jesus Christ; which how destructive it is to universal redemption hath been formerly declared. 2. So also is that "love and kindness" mentioned, chap. iii. 4, 5, such as by which we receive the "washing of regeneration and renewing of the Holy Ghost," verse 5; and justification, and adoption to heirship of eternal life, verse 7;—which, whether it be a common or a peculiar love, let all men judge. 3. Acts xiii. 47 (for verse 48, there cited, contains as clear a restriction of this love of God to his elect, as can be desired) sets out the extent of the mercy of God in Christ, through the preaching of the gospel to the Gentiles also, and not only to the Jews, as was foretold by Isaiah, chap. xlix. 6; which is far enough from giving any colour to the universality of grace, it being nothing but the same affirmation which ye have John xi. 52, of "gathering together in one the children of God that were scattered abroad."

Proof 14. "Those that, when the gospel comes, and any spiritual light therein, to them, when they refuse to believe, and suffer themselves to be withdrawn by other things, they are affirmed to love or choose "darkness rather than light," John iii. 19, (which how could it be, if no light in truth were for them?) in following lying vanities; to forsake their own mercies, Jonah ii. 8; to harden their own hearts, Rom. ii. 5; to lose their souls, Matt. xvi. 26; and to destroy themselves, Hos. xiii. 9. And they being from Adam fallen into darkness, hardness, and their souls [lost], and death passed on them, how could these things be if by Jesus Christ no life had been attained, no atonement made, no restoration of their souls, nor means procured and used, that they might be saved? God is no hard master, to gather where he hath not strown."

Ans. The sum of this argument is, That those who do not believe upon the preaching of the gospel are the cause of their own ruin and destruction; therefore, Jesus Christ died for all and every man in the world. Now, though it cannot but be apprehended that it is time cast away and labour lost, to answer such consequences as these, yet I must add a few observations, lest any scruple should remain with the weakest reader; as,—First, All have not the gospel preached to them, nay, from the beginning of the world, the greatest part of men have been passed by in the dispensation of the means of grace, Rom. ii. 14; Acts xiv. 16, xvii. 30,—"winked at." All these, then, must be left out in this conclusion, which renders it altogether useless to the business in hand; for the universality of redemption falls to the ground if any one soul be not intended in the payment of the ransom. Secondly, It is not the disbelieving the death of Christ for every individual soul that ever was or shall be (which to believe is nowhere in Scripture required) that is the cause of man's destruction, but a not-believing in the all-sufficiency of the passion and oblation of Jesus Christ for sinners, so as to accept of the mercy procured thereby, upon those terms and conditions that it is held forth in the gospel; which doth not attend the purpose and intention of God for whom Christ should die, but the sufficiency and efficacy of his death for all that receive him in a due manner, he being the only true way, life, and light, no other name being given under heaven whereby men may be saved. It is a "loving darkness rather than light," as in John iii. 19, the place urged in the proof; which word μᾶλλον, "rather," there, doth not institute a comparison between their love of darkness and light, as though they loved both, but darkness chiefly; but plainly intimates an opposition unto the love of light by a full love of darkness. And this "men" are said to do; which being spoken indefinitely, according to the rules of interpreting Scripture followed by this author, should be taken universally, for all men: but we are contented that it be the most of those men to whom Christ preached; for some also of them "received him," to whom he "gave this privilege, that they should become the sons of God," John i. 12.

Why ye should interpret "love" here by "choose," as though either the words were equivalent, or the word in the original would signify either, I can see no reason, for both these are exceeding false. There is a difference between loving and choosing; and as for ἠγάπησαν, he would be as bad a translator as ye are an interpreter that should render it "they choose." Now, what is this loving of darkness more than light, but a following and cleaving in affection and practice to the ways wherein they were, being alienated from the life of God, labouring in the unfruitful works of darkness, and refusing to embrace the heavenly doctrine of the gospel, holding forth peace and reconciliation with God through Christ, with life and immortality thereby. To conclude from hence, [that] therefore Christ died for all and every man in the world, because the greatest part of them to whom he preached the gospel did not believe, is a wild kind of reasoning; much better may we infer, that therefore he died not for all men, because it is not "given unto them, for his sake, to believe on him," Phil. i. 29.

Neither will that parenthesis—"Which how could it be, if no light in truth were for them?"—give any light to the former inference; for if the word "for" should denote the intention and purpose of God, the truth is, we dare not say that God intends and purposeth that they should receive light who do not, lest by so saying we should make the Strength of Israel to be like to ourselves, and contradict him who hath said, "My counsel shall stand, and I will do all my pleasure," Isa. xlvi. 10. "The counsel of the LORD standeth for ever," Ps. xxxiii. 11; he being "the LORD, and changing not," Mal. iii. 6; James i. 17; 2 Tim. ii. 19; Rom. ix. 11. If by "for them," ye mean such a stock and fulness of light and grace as there is of light in the sun for all the men in the world, though some be blind and cannot see it, then we say that such a light there is for all in the gospel to whom it is preached, and their own blindness is the sole cause of their not receiving it: so that this hath not got the stone a step forward, which still rolls back upon him.

Thirdly, The other scriptures urged have not so much as any colour that should give advantage to consider them, as with any reference to the business in hand. That of Jonah ii. 8 is concerning such as forsake the true God to follow idols, so forfeiting the mercies, temporal and spiritual, which from the true God they had before received. Rom. ii. 5 speaks of the Gentiles who had the works of God to teach them, and the patience of God to wait upon them, yet made no other use of them both than, by vile rebellions, to add new degrees of farther hardness upon their own hearts. That of men's losing their souls, Matt. xvi. 26, and destroying themselves (Hos. xiii. 9) by sin, is of equal force with what went before.

But, fourthly, The close of this reason seems to intimate a farther view of the author, which at the first view doth not appear,—namely, that all men are in a restored condition by Christ; not a door of mercy opened for them all, but that they are all actually restored into grace and favour, from which if they do not fall, they shall surely be saved. And the argument whereby he proves this is, because, being lost in Adam, they could not be said to lose themselves unless they were restored by Christ; being darkness and hardness in him, unless all were enlightened and mollified by Christ, they could not be said to love darkness nor to harden themselves. Now, if this be his intention (as it is too apparent that so it is), I must say something,—first, To the argument; secondly, To the thing itself. And,—

First, For the argument, it is this:—Because by original sin men are guilty of death and damnation, therefore they cannot by actual sins make sure of and aggravate that condemnation, and so bring upon themselves a death unto death: or, Because there is a native, inbred hardness of heart in man, therefore, none can add farther degrees of contracted hardness and induration by actual rebellions; that because men are blind, therefore they cannot undervalue light (when indeed the reason why they do so is because they are blind); that men who have time, and opportunity, and means, to save their souls, cannot be said to lose them, that is, to be condemned, unless their souls were in a saved condition before. Now, this is one of the proofs which, in the close, is called "plain, and according to Scripture;" when, indeed, nothing can be more contrary to reason, Scripture, and the principles of the oracles of God, than this and some other of them are. I shall add no more, knowing that no reader can be so weak as to conceive that the refusing of a proposed remedy, accompanied with infinite other despites done to the Lord, is not sufficient to make men guilty of their own condemnation. I speak of those that enjoy the preaching of the gospel.

Secondly, For the thing itself, or an actual restoration of all men by Christ into such a state (as is intimated) as they had at the first in Adam (I mean in respect of covenant, not innocency), which I take to be the meaning of the author, and that because in another place he positively affirms that it is so, and that all are justified by Christ, though how it should be so he is not able to declare. To this, then, I say,—1. That there is nothing in the Scripture that should give the least colour to this gross error, nor can any thing be produced so much as probably sounding that way. 2. It is contrary,—(1.) To very many places, affirming that we are "dead in trespasses and sins," Eph. ii. 1; that "except we be born again, we cannot see the kingdom of God," John iii. 3; that until we come by faith to Christ, "the wrath of God abideth on us," chap. iii. 36; with those innumerable places which discover the universal alienation of all men from God, until actual peace and reconciliation be made through Christ. (2.) To the very nature and essence of the new covenant of grace, proceeding from the free mercy of God to his elect, carried along with distinguishing promises from the first to the last of them, putting a difference between the seed of the woman and the seed of the serpent, as well in the members as in the Head; being effective and really working every good thing it promised in and towards all to whom it doth belong (which certainly it doth not in all), and being everywhere said to be made with the people of God, or those whom he will own, in opposition to the world;—of all which, and divers other things, so plentifully affirmed of it in the Scripture, not one can be true if all men receive a restoration by Christ into covenant. (3.) To the eternal purpose of God in election and reprobation; of which the latter is a resolution to leave men in their fallen condition, without any reparation by Christ. (4.) It is attended with very many strange, absurd, groundless consequences; as,—

[1.] That all infants dying before they come to the use of reason and the committing of actual sin must necessarily be saved (although our Saviour hath said, that "except a man be born again, he cannot see the kingdom of God," John iii. 3; and Paul from him, that the children of infidels are "unclean," 1 Cor. vii. 14;—now no unclean thing shall enter the new Jerusalem, Rev. xxi. 27), whereby the infants of Turks, Pagans, infidels, persecutors, are placed in a far more happy condition than the apostles of Christ, if they depart in their infancy,—than the best of believers, who are not, according to the authors of this doctrine, out of danger of eternal perishing. [2.] That there is no more required of any to be saved than a continuance in the estate wherein he was born (that is, in covenant, actually restored by Christ thereunto), when the whole word of God crieth out that all such as so abide shall certainly perish everlastingly. [3.] That every one that perisheth in the whole world falls away from the grace of the new covenant, though the promises thereof are, that there shall never be any total falling away of them that are in covenant. [4.] That none can come unto Christ but such as have in their own persons fallen from him, for all others abide in him.

Innumerable other such consequences as these do necessarily attend this false, heretical assertion, that is so absolutely destructive to the free grace of God. I doubt not but that such proofs as these will make considering men farther search into the matter intended to be proved, and yield them good advantages to discover the wretched lie of the whole.

Fifthly, To the last words of the proof I answer, that God sowed that seed in Adam, and watered it with innumerable temporal blessings towards all, and spiritual in some, whose fruit he will come to require from the world of unbelievers, and not in the blood of Jesus

Christ, any farther than as it hath been certainly proposed to some of them and despised.

Proof 15. "God's earnest expostulations, contendings, charges, and protestations, even to such as whereof many perished, Rom. ix. 27; Isa. x. 22. As, to instance:—'O that there were such an heart in them, that they would fear me,' etc., 'that it might be well with them!' Deut. v. 29. 'What could have been done more to my vineyard, that I have not done in it?' etc., Isa. v. 4, 5. 'What iniquity have your fathers found in me, that they are gone far from me?' Jer. ii. 5. 'Have I been a wilderness unto Israel? a land of darkness? wherefore say my people, We are lords; we will come no more unto thee?' verse 31. 'O my people, what have I done unto thee? wherein have I wearied thee? testify against me,' Mic. vi. 3. 'How often would I have gathered,' etc., 'and ye would not!' Matt. xxiii. 37. 'O that my people had hearkened unto me!' etc., 'I should soon have subdued their enemies,' etc., Ps. lxxxi. 13, 14. 'Because I have called, and ye refused; I have stretched out my hand, and no man regarded,' etc., Prov. i. 24–31. 'Because, when they knew God, they glorified him not as God,' etc., Rom. i. 21, 28. 'Therefore thou art inexcusable, O man,' etc. 'Thou, after thy hardness and impenitent heart, treasurest up unto thyself wrath,' etc., Rom. ii. 1, 5. No Christian, I hope, will reply against God, and say, 'Thou never meantest us good; there was no ransom given for us, no atonement made for us, no good done us, no mercy shown us,—nothing, in truth, whereby we might have been saved, nothing but an empty show, a bare pretence.' But if any should reason so evilly, yet shall not such answers stand."

Ans. To this collection of expostulations I shall very briefly answer with some few observations, manifesting of how little use it is to the business in hand; as,—First, That in all these expostulations there is no mention of any ransom given or atonement made for them that perish (which is the thing pretended in the close), but they are all about temporal mercies, with the outward means of grace. To which [add] what we observed in the argument last foregoing,—namely, that as God doth not expostulate with them about it, no more shall they with God about it at the last day. Not that I deny that there is sufficient matter of expostulation with sinners about the blood of Christ and the ransom paid thereby, that so the elect may be drawn and wrought upon to faith and repentance, and believers more and more endeared to forsake all ungodliness and worldly lusts, to live unto him who died for them, and that others may be left more inexcusable; only for the present there are no such expostulations here expressed, nor can any be found holding out the purpose and intention of God in Christ towards them that perish. Secondly, That all these places urged (excepting only those of Rom. i. 28, ii. 5, which apparently and evidently lay the inexcusableness of sin upon that knowledge which they might have had, by the works of creation and providence, of God, as eternal, almighty, and powerful, without the least intimation of any ransom, atonement, and redemption),—that all the rest, I say, are spoken to and of those that enjoyed the means of grace, who, in the days wherein those expostulations were used towards them, were a very small portion of all men; so that from what is said to them nothing can be concluded of the mind and purpose of God towards all others, Ps. cxlvii. 19, 20,—which is destructive to the general ransom. Thirdly, That there are no men, especially none of those that enjoy the means of grace, but do receive so many mercies from God, as that he may justly plead with them about their unthankfulness and not returning of obedience proportionable to the mercies and light which they received. Fourthly, It is confessed, I hope by all, that there are none of those things for the want whereof God expostulateth with the sons of men, but that he could, if it so seemed good before him, effectually work them in their hearts, at least, by the exceeding greatness of his power: so that these things cannot be declarative of his purpose, which he might, if he pleased, fulfil; "for who hath resisted his will," Rom. ix. 19. Fifthly, That desires and wishings should properly be ascribed unto God is exceedingly opposite to his all-sufficiency and the perfection of his nature; they are no more in him than he hath eyes, ears, and hands. These things are to be understood θεοπρεπῶς. Sixthly, It is evident that all these are nothing but pathetical declarations of our duty in the enjoyment of the means of grace, strong convictions of the stubborn and disobedient, with a full justification of the excellency of God's ways to draw us to the performance of our duties; *ergo*, Christ died for all men, ὅπερ ἔδει δεῖξαι. Seventhly, Some particular places, that seem to be of more weight than the rest, have been already examined.

Proof 16. "The Scripture's manner of setting forth the sin of such as despise and refuse this grace, and their estate, and the persons perishing; as to say they 'turn the grace of God into wantonness,' Jude 4; 'tread under foot the Son of God, profane the blood of the covenant, with which they were sanctified, offer despite to the Spirit of grace,' Heb. x. 29; 'deny the Lord that bought them,' 2 Pet. ii. 1; 'they perish for whom Christ died,' 1 Cor. viii. 11; 'trees twice dead, plucked up by the roots,' Jude 12, 13; 'and bring upon themselves swift destruction,' 2 Pet. ii. 1. And how could all this be if God had given his Son in no sort for them? if Christ had shed no blood to procure remission for them? if he had not bought them, nor had any grace or life by his Spirit to bestow on them?"

Ans. First, There are in this proof three places of Scripture which are frequently urged in this cause,—namely, Heb. x. 29; 2 Pet. ii. 1; 1 Cor. viii. 11: and, therefore, they have been considered already apart at large; where it was evidenced that they no way incline to the assertion of that whereunto they are violently wrested, and their sense for that end perverted. Secondly, For those other places out of Jude 4, 12, 13, I cannot perceive how they can be hooked into the business in hand. Some are said, verse 4, to "turn the grace of God into wantonness,"—that is, to abuse the doctrine of the gospel and the mercy of God revealed thereby, to encourage themselves in sin; whence to conclude that therefore Jesus Christ died for all men is an uncouth inference, especially the apostle intimating that he died not for these abusers of his grace, affirming that they were "before of old ordained to condemnation;" which ordination standeth in direct opposition to that love which moved the Lord to send his Son Christ to procure the salvation of any. The strength of the proof lieth in the other places, which have been already considered.

Proof 17. "Jesus Christ, by virtue of his death, shall be their judge, and by the gospel, in which they might have been saved, will he judge them to a second death; and how can that be, if he never died the first death for them, and if there were not truth in his gospel preached to them? Rom. xiv. 9–12; Phil. ii. 7–11; Rom. ii. 16; John xii. 47, 48, 50."

Ans. First, That Jesus Christ shall be judge of all, and that all judgment is already committed to him, is confessed: that it doth not hence follow that he died for all hath been already declared, unless ye will affirm that he died for the devils also, because they also must be judged by him. Secondly, That all shall be judged by the gospel, even such as never heard word of it, is directly contrary to the gospel: "For as many as have sinned without law shall also perish without law: and as many as have sinned in the law shall be judged by the law," Rom. ii. 12. Every man, doubtless, shall be judged according to the light and rule which he did or might have enjoyed, and not according to that whereof he was invincibly deprived. Thirdly, That Christ should be said to die only the first death is neither an expression of the word, nor can be collected from thence; he died the death which was in the curse of the law: but of this only by the way. Fourthly, Ye intimate as though there were no truth in the gospel preached unless Christ died for all, when indeed there is no assertion more opposite to the truth of the gospel. The places urged mention Christ being Lord of all, exalted above all, being Judge of all, judging men according to the gospel,—that is, those men who enjoy it; but how they may be wrested to the end proposed I know not.

Proof 18. "Believers are exhorted to contend for the faith of this common salvation, which was once delivered to the saints; which some having heard oppose, and others turn the offers of it into wantonness, and, through not heeding and not walking in the faith of this salvation, already wrought by Christ for men, they deprive themselves of, and wind out themselves from, that salvation, which Christ by his Spirit, in application of the former, hath wrought in them, and so deprive themselves of the salvation to come, Jude 3–5.

"And every [one] of these proofs be plain and according to Scripture, and each of force, how much more altogether!—still justifying the sense that 1 Tim. ii. 6 and Heb. ii. 9 importeth, and the truth of the proposition in the beginning."

Ans. I can see nothing in this proof, but only that the salvation purchased by Christ is called "common salvation;" which if ye conclude from thence to be common to all, ye may as well conclude so of faith that it belongs to all, because it is called the "common faith," Tit. i. 4, though termed the "faith of God's elect," verse 1. Doubtless there is a community of believers, and that is common amongst them which is extended to the whole church of God; there is *totus mundus ex toto mundo;* and that common salvation is that whereby they are all saved, without any colour of that strange common salvation whereby no one is saved, maintained by this disputer. The remainder of this proof is a fulness of words, suitable to the persuasion of the author, but in no small part of them exceedingly unsuitable to the word of God and derogatory to the merits of Christ, making the salvation purchased by him to be in itself of no effect, but left to the will of sinful, corrupted, accursed men, to make available or to reject.

And these are the proofs which this author calls "*plain* and according to Scripture," being a recapitulation of almost all that he hath said in his whole book; at least, for the argumentative part thereof, there is not any thing of weight omitted: and therefore this chapter I fixed on to return a full and punctual answer unto. Now, whether the thing intended to be proved, namely, *The paying of a ransom by Christ for all and every man, be plainly, clearly, and evidently* from the Scripture *confirmed,* as he would bear us in hand; or whether all this heap of words, called arguments, reasons, and proofs, be not, for their manner of expression, obscure, uncouth, and ofttimes unintelligible,—for their way of inference, childish, weak, and ridiculous,—in their allegations and interpretations of Scripture, perverse, violent, mistaken, through ignorance, heedlessness, and corruption of judgment, in direct opposition to the mind and will of God revealed therein,—is left to the judgment of the Christian reader that shall peruse them, with the answers annexed.

CHAPTER VII.

The removal of other remaining objections.

THE removal of some usual sophisms and captious arguments of the Arminians, of late made common and vulgar, shall be the close of our treatise, and wind up the whole controversy, which hath drawn us with violence thus far. And in this performance I shall labour to be as brief as possible; partly because these things have been handled at large by others; partly because all colour of opposition to the truth by us maintained from the Scriptures being removed, all other objections will indeed naturally sink of themselves. Yet, because great boastings and swelling words of vanity have been used concerning some that follow, it is necessary that something be said to show the emptiness of such flourishes, that the weakest may not be entangled by them.

OBJECTION I. That which we shall begin withal is an argument of as great fame and as little merit as any that, in this cause, or indeed in any other controversy, hath been used of late days; and it is this:—"That which every one is bound to believe is true; but every one is bound to believe that Jesus Christ died for him: therefore it is true, namely, that Jesus Christ died for every one."

This is an argument which, to discover their conviction of the weakness of the rest of their arguments, the Arminians and their friends never use, but withal they add some notable encomium of it, with some terms of affront and threatening to their adversaries; insomuch as, by consent on both sides, it hath obtained the name of the Remonstrants' Achilles. Now, truly, for my part, as I shall not transcribe any thing hither out of the many full answers given to it by our divines, by which this Achilles, or rather Goliath, hath been often cast to the ground, so I heartily wish that the many operose, prolix answers which the boasting of our adversaries hath drawn forth had not got, [for] this poor nothing, more repute a thousand times than its own strength, or any addition of force from the managers of it could have procured unto it. Supposing then, first, That the term "believe," be used in the same sense in both propositions (for if otherwise the syllogism is false in the form of it); secondly, That by *believing* is understood *a saving application of Christ to the soul, as held out in the promise*, for to believe that Christ died for me in particular, as is asserted to be the duty of every one, can be nothing else but such a saving application; thirdly, That believing that Christ died for any, according to the business in question, must be with reference to the purpose of the Father and intention of Jesus Christ himself, for that is it which, with regard to any *universality*, is by us opposed; fourthly, For the term "every one," it must relate unto all men as considered in an *alike condition*, for several respects and conditions of the same persons may cause them to come under several obligations unto duties: now, there is no one condition common unto all but only the state of wrath and death, Eph. ii. 3, and therefore every man must be considered as in that condition; so that, in sum, the sense of the minor proposition is, "All men in the world, as considered in a state of wrath and unregeneracy, are bound to believe, as before described, that it was the intention of God that Christ should die for every one of them in particular."

Now, not to say any thing to the major proposition, which yet is false, that which men are bound to believe in this sense being, as hath been observed by many, neither *true* nor *false*, but *good*, the assumption is absolutely false, and hath not the least colour of reason or Scripture to support it; and (taking "every one" for every individual in the world) when our adversaries prove it, I engage myself to be their proselyte: for,—First, Then must some be bound to believe that which is false; which cannot be, every obligation to believe being from the God of truth. Now, it is false that Christ died for all and every individual of human kind, as hath been before proved at large. Secondly, Then should men be bound immediately to believe that which is not revealed, though *divine revelation* be the object of all faith; for the Scriptures do not hold out anywhere that Christ died for this or that particular man as *such*, but only for sinners indefinitely, specified ofttimes antecedently by God's purpose, and *consequently* by their own purchased obedience. Thirdly, Neither, indeed, is the *intention* and *purpose* of God, concerning which we now inquire, proposed as the object of the faith of any; but only his commands, promises, and threatenings,—the other being left to be collected and assured to the soul by an experience and sense of some sweet infallible issue and effect thereof in the heart actually enjoyed. Nor, fourthly, can any command in the Scripture to believe be interpreted by the purpose and intention of God, as though the meaning of it should be, "God intended that Christ should die for thee in particular;" nor doth any promise contain that sense. Besides, fifthly, which of itself is enough to break the neck of this argument, all have not any such object of faith as Christ's death at all proposed to them. How can they believe unless they hear? Can they be bound to believe that of which they never heard the least rumour? How many millions of infants and others, in barbarous nations, go to their "own place" without hearing the least report of Jesus Christ, or his sufferings for them or others, even in these days of the gospel! how much more, then, before the coming of Christ in the flesh, when the means of grace were restrained to one small nation, with some few proselytes! Were all these, are they that remain, all and every one, bound to believe that Christ died for them, all and every one in particular? Those that think so are, doubtless, bound to go tell all of them so; I mean those that are yet in the land of the living. Is not *unbelief* the great damning sin, where faith is required? John iii. 36? and yet doth not Paul prove that many shall be condemned for sinning against the light of nature, Rom. ii. 12? an evident demonstration that faith is not required of all,—all are not bound to believe.

But perhaps our adversaries will except, as they must except if they intend to have any colour or show of strength left unto this argument, that they mean it only in respect of them who are called by the word, and so it is of force; to which end let it be thus proposed:—

"That which every one called by the word, to whom the gospel is preached, is bound to believe, is true; but that Christ died for him in particular, every one so called is bound to believe: *ergo*," etc.

Ans. 1. Only the last exception foregoing is taken off by this *reformed argument;* all the rest stand in their full force, which are sufficient to evert it. 2. Who seeth not that this very reforming of the argument hath made it altogether useless to the cause in whose defence it was produced? for if any one, much more the greatest part of men, be excepted, which are now excluded from the verge of this argument, the *general ransom* falls to the ground. From the *innumerable multitudes of all*, we are come to the *many that are called*, and doubt not but that we shall instantly descend to the *few that are chosen.* Unto the exception, that that which is true in respect of them to whom it is proposed would also be true in respect of all if it should be proposed to them, I answer, by the way,—First, That the argument is to be taken from the scriptural obligation to believe, and can be extended no farther than it is actually extended. Secondly, That it is no safe disputing of what would be or should be, if things were not as God hath appointed and ordained them. We see the will of God for the present; neither are we to suppose so as to make our supposal a bottom for any argument that they could have been otherwise disposed. Thirdly, That if the gospel should be preached to all the world, or all in the world, this is all the mind and will of God that would or can in general be signified to them by it, "He that believeth and is baptized shall be saved, but he that believeth not shall be damned;" or, that God hath concatenated and knit these two things together, *faith* and *salvation*, so that whosoever will enjoy the latter must perform the former. If the gospel should now be preached to the Turks and the Indians, and they should reject it, certainly they should be damned for not believing that which they were, upon the preaching of it, bound to believe. Now, what is this? that Christ died for every one of them in particular? No, doubtless; but this, "There is none other name under heaven given among men, whereby we must be saved," but only by the name of Christ, made known to us in the gospel, Acts iv. 12. [They would be damned] for rejecting the counsel and wisdom of God to save sinners by the blood of Jesus; for not believing the necessity of a Redeemer, and that Jesus of Nazareth was that Redeemer,—according to his own word to the Jews, "If ye believe not that I am he, ye shall die in your sins;" as, indeed, the peculiar infidelity of that people was their not believing him to be their Messiah, whom they saw to be declared to be the Son of God with power. The not believing these things would be the soul-damning infidelity of such obstinate refusers to come in upon the call of the gospel, and not a refusing to believe that Christ died for every one of them in particular; which could not, by the rule of the gospel, be proposed unto them, and which they never come so far as to question or esteem.

Still, then, we deny the minor proposition of the reduced syllogism; and that partly for the reasons before produced, partly for these subjoined:—

1. They to whom the gospel is preached are bound to believe with that faith which is required to justification only. Now, this is not a full persuasion that Christ died for any one in particular, in the intention and purpose of God, which revealeth not the object of justification, nor the way whereby a sinner may be justified.[1]

2. Because there is an order, natural in itself, and established by God's appointment, in the things that are to be believed; so that until some of them are believed the rest are not required (a man is not commanded, nor can he reasonably, to get to the top of a ladder by skipping all the lower rounds),—namely, (1.) Repent, and believe the gospel to be the word of God, to contain his will, and that Jesus Christ, therein revealed, is the wisdom and power of God unto salvation. (2.) That there is an inseparable connection, by God's appointment, between faith and salvation, gospel faith carrying a sinner quite out of himself and from off his own righteousness. (3.) That there be a particular conviction, by the Spirit, of the necessity of a Redeemer to their souls in particular; whereby they become weary, heavy laden, and burdened. (4.) A serious full recumbency and rolling of the soul upon Christ in the promise of the gospel, as an all-sufficient Saviour, able to deliver and save to the utmost them that come to God by him; ready, able, and willing, through the preciousness of his blood and sufficiency of his ransom, to save every soul that shall

[1] The last clauses of this sentence are obscure. In the edition by the Rev. Adam Gib, 1755, it is proposed to render them,—"which is not revealed to the object of justification, or in the way whereby a sinner may be justified." If we were at liberty to change the "nor" into "but," a meaning sufficiently intelligible would be obtained, without any violent alteration of the text, and quite in harmony with the scope of the reasoning.—Ed.

freely give up themselves unto him for that end, amongst whom he is resolved to be. And in doing of all this, there is none called on by the gospel once to inquire after the purpose and intention of God concerning the particular object of the death of Christ, every one being fully assured that his death shall be profitable to them that believe in him and obey him.

Now, fourthly, after all this, and not before, it lies upon a believer to assure his soul, according as he finds the fruit of the death of Christ in him and towards him, of the good-will and eternal love of God to him in sending his Son to die for him in particular. What a preposterous course, and how opposite to the rule of the gospel, were it, to call upon a man to believe that it was the intention and purpose of God that Christ should die for him in particular, and desire him to assure his soul thereof, before he be convinced either,—1. Of the truth of the gospel in general; or, 2. That faith is the only way of salvation; or, 3. That himself standeth in need of a Saviour; or, 4. That there is enough in Christ to save and recover him if he give up himself unto him in his own way! Now, it is most apparent that it is only such as these that are bound to believe that whereof we discourse.

The argument, then, must be once again reformed, and thus proposed:—

"That which every one, convinced of the necessity of a Saviour, and of the right way of salvation, hungering, thirsting, and panting after Jesus Christ, as able alone to give him refreshment, is bound to believe, is true; but every such a one is bound to believe that Christ died for him in particular: *ergo*, it is true." And some grant the whole without any prejudice to the cause we have undertaken to defend. It is most apparent, then,—1. That all that are called by the word are not, in what state or condition soever they continue, bound to believe that Christ died for them; but only such as are so qualified as before described. 2. That the precept of believing, with fiduciary confidence, that Christ died for any in particular is not proposed nor is obligatory to all that are called; nor is the non-performance of it any otherwise a sin, but as it is in the root and habit of unbelief, or not turning to God in Christ for mercy. 3. That no reprobate, for whom Christ died not, shall be condemned for not believing that Christ died for him in particular, which is not true; but for not believing those things whereunto he was called, before related, which are all most true, and that in reference to him. 4. That the command of believing in Christ, which is especially urged as given unto all, is not, in that particular contended about, obligatory unto any but upon fulfilling of the conditions thereto required. 5. To "believe on the name of Jesus Christ," which is the command, 1 John iii. 23, is not to believe that it was the intention of God that Christ should die for us in particular, but to rest upon him for salvation, as Isa. l. 11. Neither,—6. Is the testimony of God, to which we ought to set our seal that it is true, any other but this, "He that hath the Son hath life, but he that hath not the Son of God hath not life," 1 John v. 12; which reprobates disbelieving, do what in them lies to make God a liar, and are justly condemned for it. He that desireth to see more of this argument, let him consult, if he please, Piscator, Perkins, Twisse, Synod of Dort, Du Moulin, Baronius, Rutherford, Spanheim, Amesius, others, etc.

OBJ. II. "That doctrine which fills the minds and souls of poor miserable sinners with doubts and scruples whether they ought to believe or no, when God calls them thereunto, cannot be agreeable to the gospel. But this doth the doctrine of the particularity of redemption. It fills the minds of sinners with scruples and fears whether they may believe or no, and that because they are uncertain whether it was the intention of God that Christ should die for them in particular or no, seeing it is supposed that he died not for all, but only for his elect; whereupon the soul, when it is called upon to believe, may justly fall a-questioning whether it will be available or no for him so to do, and whether it be his duty or no, seeing he knoweth not whether Christ died for him or no."

Ans. 1. That scruples, doubts, and fears, the proper issue of unconquered remaining unbelief, will often arise in the hearts of sinners, sometimes against, sometimes taking occasion from, the truth of the gospel, is too evident upon experience. All the question is, whether the doctrine itself scrupled or stumbled at do of itself, in its own nature, give cause thereto unto those who rightly perform their duty? or whether all those fears and scruples be the natural product and issue of corruption and unbelief, setting up themselves against the truth as it is in Jesus? The first we deny, concerning the doctrine of the particularity of effectual redemption; the latter God alone can remedy.

2. This objection supposeth that a man is bound to know and be persuaded (that is, to believe) that Jesus Christ died by the appointment of God for him in particular, before he believe in Jesus Christ. Nay, this they make the bottom of their argument, that men, according to our persuasion, may scruple whether they ought to believe or no, because they are not assured before that Christ died for them in particular, by the designation and appointment of God. Now, if this be not to involve themselves in a plain contradiction, I know not what is; for what, I pray, is it, according to Scripture, for a man to be assured that Christ died for him in particular? Is it not the very highest improvement of faith? doth it not include a sense of the spiritual love of God shed abroad in our hearts? Is it not the top of the apostle's consolation, Rom. viii. 34, and the bottom of all his joyful assurance, Gal. ii. 20? So that they evidently require that a man must believe before

he do believe,—that he cannot believe, and shall exceedingly fear whether he ought to do so or no, unless he believe before he believe! Methinks such removing of scruples were the ready way to entangle doubting consciences in farther inextricable perplexities.

3. We deny that a persuasion that it was the will of God that Christ should die for him in particular either is or can be any way necessary that a sinner be drawn to believe. For, considering sinners as such whose duty it is to believe the call of Christ, Matt. xi. 28, Isa. lv. 1; that command of God, 1 John iii. 23; that promise of life upon believing, John iii. 36; that threat of unbelief, *ibid;* the all-sufficiency of the blood of Christ to save all believers, Acts xx. 21, Eph. v. 2; the assured salvation of all believers without exception, Mark xvi. 16, and the like, are enough to remove all doubts and fears, and are all that the Scripture holds out for that purpose.

4. That persuasion which (1.) asserts the certainty of salvation by the death of Christ unto all believers whatsoever; (2.) that affirms the command of God and the call of Christ to be infallibly declarative of that duty which is required of the person commanded and called,—which, if it be performed, will be assuredly acceptable to God; (3.) that holds out purchased free grace to all distressed, burdened, consciences in general; (4.) that discovers a fountain of blood, all-sufficient to purge all the sin of every one in the world that will use the appointed means for coming unto it;—that doctrine, I say, cannot possibly be the cause of any doubt or scruple in the minds of convinced, burdened sinners, whether they ought to believe or no. Now, all this is held forth by the doctrine of particular effectual redemption, in the dispensation of the gospel suitable thereto.

I shall, then, let go this objection without farther pursuit, only attended with this query, What it is that, according to the authors of universal redemption, men are bound to believe, when they know beforehand that Christ died for them in particular? A persuasion of the love of God and good-will of Christ it cannot be; that they have beforehand, John iii. 16; Rom. v. 8: nor a coming to God by Christ for an enjoyment of the fruits of his death; for what is that, I pray? No fruits of the death of Christ, according to them, but what are common to all; which may be damnation as well as salvation, for more are damned than saved,—infidelity as well as faith, for the most are unbelievers. The immediate fruits of the death of Christ can be nothing but that which is common to them with those that perish. Plainly, their faith in Christ will at length appear to be Socinian obedience.

There be two[1] things that remain, about which there is no small contention, both things in themselves excelling and valuable, both laid claim to by the several persuasions concerning which we treat;

[1] From the particulars enumerated in the following sentence, and the three objections that are considered, "two" seems to have been written, by an oversight, for "three."—ED.

but with such an unequal plea, that an easy judgment might serve to decide the controversy. Now, these are, first, the exaltation of God's free grace, the merit of Christ, and the consolation of our souls. Let us consider them in order, and let each persuasion take its due.

OBJ. III. For the first, or the *exaltation of God's free grace.* I know not how it comes to pass, but so it is, men have entertained a persuasion that the opinion of *universal redemption* serveth exceedingly to set forth the *love and free grace of God,* yea, they make free grace, that glorious expression, to be nothing but that which is held forth in this their opinion,—namely, that God loveth *all*, and gave Christ to die for *all*, and is ready to save *all*, if *they will come to him.* "Herein," say they, "is *free grace* and love magnified indeed; this is the universality of free grace,"—and such other flourishing expressions; "whereas the contrary opinion chains up the love and grace of God to a few."

But stay a little. What, I pray, is this your grace, free grace, that is universal? Is it the grace of election? Truly no; God hath not chosen all to salvation, Rom. ix. 11, 12; Eph. i. 4; Rom. viii. 28. Is it the grace of effectual vocation? No, neither. Doubtless that it cannot be; for "whom God calls he also justifies," and "glorifies," Rom. viii. 30, xi. 25, 26, 29. Nay, all have not been, are not, outwardly called, chap. x. 14. Is it the grace of cleansing and sanctification? Why, are all purged? are all washed in the blood of Jesus? Or is it the church only, Eph. v. 25–27. Some, sure, are also defiled still, Tit. i. 15. Faith is the principle of the heart's purification, and "all men have not faith." Is it the grace of justification, —the free love and mercy of God in pardoning and accepting sinners? But, friends, is this universal? Are all pardoned? are all accepted? see Rom i. 17, iii. 22, v. 1. Is it the grace of redemption in the blood of Christ? see, I pray, Rev. v. 9. What then, I pray, is this your universal free grace? Is it not universally a figment of your own brains? or is it not a new name for that old idol free-will? Is it not destructive to free grace in every branch of it? Doth it not tend to the eversion of the whole covenant of distinguishing grace, evidently denying that the conditions thereof are wrought in any of the federates by virtue of the promise of the covenant? Are not the two great aims of their free grace to mock God and exalt themselves? Do not they propose the Lord as making a pretence of love, good-will, free grace, and pardon unto all, yet never once acquainting incomparably the greatest number of them with any such love or good-will at all, although he know that without his effecting of it they can never come to any such knowledge? For those that are outwardly called to the knowledge of these things, do they not, by their universal grace, feign the Lord to pretend that he loves them all, has sent his Son to die for them all, and to desire that they all may be saved, yet upon such a condition as, without him, they can no more effect than to climb to heaven by a ladder, which yet he will not do? Do not they openly make God to say, "Such is this my love, my universal grace, that by it I will freely love them, I dare joyfully embrace them, in all things but only that which will do them good?" Would not they affirm him to be a grossly counterfeiting hypocrite that should go to a poor blind man, and tell him, "Alas, poor man, I pity thy case, I see thy want, I love thee exceedingly; open thine eyes, and I will give thee a hundred pounds?" And dare they assign such a deportment to the most holy God of truth? Is their universal grace any thing but a mock? Did that ever do good to any, as to salvation, which is common to all? Are they not the two properties of the grace of God in the Scripture, that it is discriminating and effectual? And is not their grace any thing else but these? Let it be granted that all is true which they say concerning the extent of grace; is it such grace as that ever any soul was saved by? Why, I pray, then, are not all? "Why," they will say, "because they do not believe." So, then, the bestowing of faith is no part of this free grace. See your second aim, even to exalt yourselves and your free-will into the room of grace; or, at least, leaving it room to come in, to have the best share in the work of salvation,—namely, believing itself, that makes all the rest profitable. See, now, what your universality of free grace leads and tends to. Are not the very terms opposite to one another? In a word, to bring in reprobates to be objects of free grace, you deny the free grace of God to the elect; and to make it universal, you deny it to be effectual. That all may have a share of it, they deny any to be saved by it; for saving grace must be restrained.

On the other side; in what one tittle, I pray you, doth the doctrine of the effectual redemption of God's elect only, in the blood of Jesus, impair the free grace of God? Is it in its *freedom?* Why, we say it is so free, that if it be not altogether free it is no grace at all. Is it in its *efficacy?* Why, we say that by grace we are saved, ascribing the whole work of our recovery and bringing to God, in "solidum," thereto. Is it in its *extent?* We affirm it to be extended to every one that is, was, or ever shall be delivered from the pit. It is true, we do not call grace that goeth into hell free grace, in a gospel notion; for we deem the free grace of God so powerful, that wherever it hath designed and chosen out itself a subject, that it brings God, and Christ, and salvation with it, to eternity.

"But you do not extend it unto all; you tie it up to a few." *De te largitor, puer.* Is the extending of the love and favour of God in our power? Hath he not mercy on whom he will have mercy, and doth he not harden whom he will? Yet, do not we affirm that it is extended to the universality of the saved ones? Should we throw the children's bread to dogs? Friends, we believe that the grace of God in Christ worketh faith in every one to whom it is extended; that the conditions of that covenant which is ratified in his blood are all effectually wrought in the heart of every covenantee; that there is no love of God that is not effectual; that the blood of Christ was not shed in vain; that of ourselves we are dead in trespasses and sins, and can do nothing but what the free grace of God worketh in us: and, therefore, we cannot conceive that it can be extended to all. [As] for you, who affirm that millions of those that are taken into a new covenant of grace do perish eternally, that it is left to men to believe that the will of God may be frustrate and his love ineffectual, that we distinguish ourselves one from another,—you may extend it whither you please, for it is indifferent to you whether the objects of it go to heaven or to hell.

But in the meanwhile, I beseech you, friends, give me leave to question whether this you talk of be God's free grace, or your fond figment? his love, or your wills? for truly, for the present, it seems to me the latter only. But yet our prayers shall be that God would give you infinitely more of his love than is contained in that ineffectual universal grace wherewith you so flourish. Only, we shall labour that poor souls be not seduced by you with the specious pretences of free grace to all,—not knowing that this your free grace is a mere painted cloth, that will give them no assistance at all to deliver them from that condition wherein they are, but only give them leave to be saved if they can; whereas they are ready, by the name you have given to the brat of your own brain, to suppose you intend an effectual, almighty, saving grace, that will certainly bring all to God to whom it is extended, of which they have heard in the Scripture; whilst you laugh in your sleeves, to think how simply these poor souls are deluded with that empty show, the substance whereof is this, "Go your ways; be saved if you can, in the way revealed; God will not hinder you."

Obj. IV. Each party contests about the *exaltation of the merit of Christ;* for so are their mutual pretences. Something hath been said to this before, so that now I shall be brief. Take, then, only a short view of the difference that is between them, where each pretends to exalt the merit of Christ in that which is by the other denied, and this plea will suddenly be at an end.

There is but one only thing that concerns the death of Christ in which the authors of the *general ransom* are upon the affirmative, and whereby they pretend to set forth the excellency of his death and oblation, namely, that the benefits thereof are extended unto all and every one, whereas their adversaries straiten it unto a few, a very few,—none but the elect; which, they say, is derogatory to the honour of the Lord Jesus Christ. And this is that wherein they pretend so exceedingly to advance his name and merit above the pitch that they aim at who assert the effectual redemption of the elect only. The truth is, the measure of the honour of Jesus Christ is not to be assigned by us, poor worms of the dust; that he takes to be honour which he gives and ascribes unto himself, and nothing else. He hath no need of our lie for his glory: so that if *this* did, in our eyes, seem for the exaltation of the glory of Christ, yet, arising from a lie of our own hearts, it would be an abomination unto him. Secondly, We deny that this doth any way serve to set out the nature and dignity of the death of Christ; because the extent of its efficacy to all (if any such thing should be) doth not arise from its own innate sufficiency, but from the free pleasure and determination of God: which how it is enervated by a pretended universality was before declared. Thirdly, The value of a thing ariseth from its own native sufficiency and worth unto any purpose whereunto it is to be employed; which the maintainers of effectual redemption do assert, in the death of Christ, to be much above what any of their adversaries ascribe unto it.

Should I now go about to declare in how many things the honour of Christ, and the excellency of his death and passion, with the fruits of it, is held forth in that doctrine which we have sought to open from the Scriptures, above all that can be assigned to it agreeable to their own principal maxims who maintain universal redemption (and that according to truth itself), I should be forced to repeat much that hath already been spoken, so that it shall suffice me to present the reader with this following antithesis:—

Universalists.	Scriptural Redemption.
1. Christ died for all and every one, elect and reprobate.	1. Christ died for the elect only.
2. Most of them for whom Christ died are damned.	2. All those for whom Christ died are certainly saved.
3 Christ, by his death, purchased not any saving grace for them for whom he died.	3. Christ by his death purchased all saving grace for them for whom he died.
4. Christ took no care for the greatest part of them for whom he died, that ever they should hear one word of his death.	4. Christ sends the means and reveals the way of life to all them for whom he died.
5. Christ, in his death, did not ratify nor confirm a covenant of grace with any federates, but only procured by his death that God might, if he would, enter into a new covenant with whom he would, and upon what condition he pleased.	5. The new covenant of grace was confirmed to all the elect in the blood of Jesus.

Universalists.	Scriptural Redemption.
6. Christ might have died, and yet no one be saved.	6. Christ, by his death, purchased, upon covenant and compact, an assured peculiar people, the pleasure of the Lord prospering to the end in his hand.
7. Christ had no intention to redeem his church, any more than the wicked seed of the serpent.	7. Christ loved his church, and gave himself for it.
8. Christ died not for the infidelity of any.	8. Christ died for the infidelity of the elect.

Divers other instances of the like nature might be easily collected, upon the first view whereof the present difference in hand would quickly be determined. These few, I doubt not, are sufficient, in the eyes of all experienced Christians, to evince how little the *general ransom* conduceth to the honour and glory of Jesus Christ, or to the setting forth of the worth and dignity of his death and passion.

OBJ. V. The next and last thing which comes under debate in this contest is *gospel consolation,* which God in Christ is abundantly willing we should receive. A short disquisition whether of the two opinions treated on doth give the firmest basis and soundest foundation hereunto, will, by the Lord's assistance, lead us to an end of this long debate. THE GOD OF TRUTH AND COMFORT GRANT THAT ALL OUR UNDERTAKINGS, OR RATHER HIS WORKINGS IN US, FOR TRUTH, MAY END IN PEACE AND CONSOLATION!

To clear this, some things are to be premised; as,—

1. All true evangelical consolation belongeth only to believers, Heb. vi. 17, 18,—God's people, Isa. xl. 1, 2; upon unbelievers the "wrath of God abideth," John iii. 36.

2. To make out consolation unto them to whom it is not due is no less a crime than to hide it from them to whom it doth belong, Isa. v. 20; Jer. xxiii. 14; Ezek. xiii. 10.

3. T. M[ore]'s attempt to set forth the death of Christ so that all might be comforted, meaning all and every one in the world, as appeareth, is a proud attempt to make that straight which God hath made crooked, and most opposite to the gospel.

4. That doctrine which holds out consolation from the death of Christ to unbelievers, cries, "Peace, peace," when God says, "There is no peace."

These things being premised, I shall briefly demonstrate these four following positions:—1. That the extending of the death of Christ unto a universality, in respect of the object, cannot give the least ground of consolation to them whom God would have to be comforted by the gospel. 2. That the denying of the efficacy of the death of Christ towards them for whom he died cuts the nerves and sinews of all strong consolation, even such as is proper to believers to receive, and peculiar to the gospel to give. 3. That there is nothing in the doctrine of redemption of the elect only that is yet in the least measure to debar them from consolation to whom comfort is due. 4. That the doctrine of the effectual redemption of the sheep of Christ, by the blood of the covenant, is the true solid foundation of all durable consolation.

1. Begin we with the first,—that the extending of the death of Christ unto a *universality*, in respect of the object, hath nothing in it, as peculiar unto it, that can give the least ground of consolation unto them whom God would have to be comforted. That gospel consolation, properly so called, being a fruit of actual reconciliation with God, is proper and peculiar only to believers, I laid down before, and suppose it to be a truth out of all question and debate. Now, that no consolation can be made out to them as such, from any thing which is peculiar to the persuasion of a general ransom, is easily proved by these following reasons:—

(1.) No consolation can arise unto believers from that which is nowhere in the Scripture proposed as a ground, cause, or matter of consolation, as the general ransom is not: for,—first, That which hath no being can have no affection nor operation; secondly, All the foundations and materials of consolation are things particular, and peculiar only to some, as shall be declared.

(2.) No consolation can accrue unto believers from that which is common unto them with those whom,—first, God would not have comforted; secondly, that shall assuredly perish to eternity; thirdly, that stand in open rebellion against Christ; fourthly, that never hear one word of gospel or consolation. Now, to all these, and such as these, doth the foundation of *consolation*, as proposed with and arising from the *general ransom*, equally appertain with the choicest of believers.

(3.) Let a man try in the time, not of disputation, but of desertion and temptation, what consolation or peace to his soul he can obtain from such a collection as this, "Christ died for all men; I am a man: therefore, Christ died for me." Will not his own heart tell him, that notwithstanding all that he is assured of in that conclusion, the wrath of God may abide on him for evermore? Doth he not see that, notwithstanding this, the Lord showeth so little love unto millions of millions of the sons of men, of whom the former collection (according to the present opinion) is true as well as of himself, as that he doth not once reveal himself or his Son unto them? What good will it do me to know that Christ died for me, if notwithstanding that I may perish for ever? If you intend me any consolation from that which is common unto all, you must tell me what it is which all enjoy which will satisfy my desires, which are carried out after assurance of the love of God in Christ. If you give me no more to comfort me than what you give, or might have given, to Judas, can you expect I should receive settlement and consolation? Truly, miserable comforters are ye all, physicians of no value, Job's visitors,—skilful only to add affliction unto the afflicted.

"But be of good comfort," will Arminians say; "Christ is a propitiation for all sinners, and now thou knowest thyself so to be." *Ans.* True; but is Christ a propitiation for all the sins of those sinners? If so, how can any of them perish? If not, what good will this do me, whose sins perhaps (as unbelief) are such as for which Christ was not a propitiation? "But exclude not thyself; God excludeth none; the love which caused him to send his Son was general towards all." Tell not me of God's excluding; I have sufficiently excluded myself. Will he powerfully take me in? Hath Christ not only purchased that I shall be admitted, but procured me ability to enter into his Father's arms? "Why, he hath opened a door of salvation to all." Alas! is it not a vain endeavour, to open a grave for a dead man to come out? Who lights a candle for a blind man to see by? To open a door for him to come out of prison who is blind, and lame, and bound, yea dead, is rather to deride his misery than to procure him liberty. Never tell me that will yield me strong consolation, under the enjoyment whereof the greatest portion of men perish everlastingly.

2. The opinion concerning a general ransom is so far from yielding firm consolation unto believers from the death of Christ, that it quite overthrows all the choice ingredients of strong consolation which flow therehence; and that,—first, By strange divisions and divulsions of one thing from another, which ought to be conjoined to make up one certain foundation of confidence; secondly, By denying the efficacy of his death towards them for whom he died: both which are necessary attendants of that persuasion.

First, They so divide the *impetration* of redemption and the *application* thereof,—the first being in their judgments the only proper immediate fruit and effect of the death of Christ,—that the one may belong to millions who have no share in the other; yea, that redemption may be obtained for all, and yet no one have it so applied unto them as to be saved thereby. Now, the first of these, such as it is, is an ineffectual possible redemption, notwithstanding which all the sons of men might perish everlastingly, being the whole object of the death of Christ (as is asserted), separated and divided from all such application of redemption unto any as might make it profitable and useful in the least measure (for they deny this application to be a fruit of the death of Christ; if it were, why is it not common to all for whom he died?) What comfort this can in the least degree afford to any poor soul will not dive into my apprehension. "What shall I do?" saith the sinner; "the iniquity of my heels compasseth me about. I have no rest in my bones by reason of my sin: and now, whither shall I cause my sorrow to go?" Be of good cheer; Christ died for sinners. "Yea, but shall the fruits of his death be certainly applied unto all them for whom he died? If not, I may perish for ever." Here let them that can, answer him, according to the principles of Universalists, without sending him to his own strength in believing, or that which, in the close, will be resolved into it, "et erit mihi magnus Apollo:" and if they send him thither, they acknowledge the consolation concerning which they boast properly to proceed from ourselves, and not from the death of Christ.

Secondly, Their separating between the oblation and intercession of Jesus Christ makes little for the consolation of believers, yea, indeed, quite everts it.

There are, amongst others, two eminent places of Scripture wherein the Holy Ghost holdeth forth consolation to believers, against these two general causes of all their troubles and sorrows,—namely, their afflictions and their sins. The first is Rom. viii. 32–34, the other 1 John ii. 1, 2; in both which places the apostles make the bottom of the consolation which they hold out to believers in their afflictions and failings to be that strait bond and inseparable connection that is between these two, with the identity of their objects,—namely, the oblation and intercession of Jesus Christ. Let the reader consult both the texts, and he shall find that on this lies the stress, and herein consists the strength, of the several proposals for the consolation of believers; which, in both places, is principally intended. A more direct undertaking for this end and purpose cannot be produced. Now, the authors of universal redemption do all of them divide and separate these two; they allow of no connection between them, nor dependence of one upon another, farther than is effected by the will of man. His oblation they stretch to all; his intercession to a few only. Now, the death of Christ, separated from his resurrection and intercession, being nowhere proposed as a ground of consolation, yea, positively declared to be unsuitable to any such purpose, 1 Cor. xv. 14, certainly they who hold it out as so done are no friends to Christian consolation.

Thirdly, Their denial of the procurement of faith, grace, holiness,—the whole intendment of the new covenant,—and perseverance therein, by the death and blood-shedding of Jesus Christ, unto all them, or any of them, for whom he died, doth not appear to be so suitable an assertion for to raise consolation from his cross as is vainly pretended. I pray, what solid consolation can be drawn from such dry breasts as from whence none of these things do flow? That they have not immediate dependence on the death of Christ, according to the persuasion of the assertors of universal grace, hath been before declared, and is by themselves not only confessed, but undertaken to be proved. Now, where should a soul look for these things, but in the purchase of Christ? Whence should they flow, but from his side? Or is there any consolation to be had without them? Is not the strongest plea for these things, at the throne of grace, the procurement of the Lord Jesus? What promise is there of any thing without him? Are not all the promises of God yea and amen in him? Is there any attainment of these things in our own strength? Is this the consolation you afford us, to send us from free grace to free will? Whither, I pray, according to this persuasion, should a poor soul go that finds himself in want of these things? "To God, who gives all freely." But doth God bless us with any spiritual blessings but only in Jesus Christ? Doth he bless us with any thing in him but what he hath procured for us? Is not all grace as well procured by as dispensed in a Mediator? Is this a way to comfort a soul, and that from the death of Christ, to let him know that Christ did not procure those things for him without which he cannot be comforted? "Credat Apella."

It is, then, most apparent, that the general ransom (which is pretended) is so far from being the bottom of any solid consolation unto them whose due it is, that it is directly destructive of, and diametrically opposed unto, all those ways whereby the Lord hath declared himself willing that we should receive comfort from the death of his Son, drying up the breast from whence, and poisoning the streams whereby, it should be conveyed unto our souls.

3. The next thing we have to do is, to manifest that the doctrine of the effectual redemption of the elect only by the blood of Jesus is not liable to any just exception as to this particular, nor doth any way abridge believers of any part or portion of that consolation which God is willing they should receive. That alone which, by the opposers of it, with any colour of reason, is objected (for as for the exclamation of shutting out innumerable souls from any share in the blood of Christ, seeing confessedly they are reprobate unbelievers and persons finally impenitent, we are not at all moved at it), comes to this head:—"That there is nothing in the Scripture whereby any man can assure himself that Christ died for him in particular, unless we grant that he died for all."

First, That this is notoriously false, the experience of all believers who, by the grace of God, have assured their hearts of their share and interest in Christ as held out unto them in the promise, without the least thought of universal redemption, is a sufficient testimony. Secondly, That the assurance arising from a practical syllogism, whereof one proposition is true in the word, and the second by the witness of the Spirit in the heart, is infallible, hath hitherto been acknowledged by all. Now, such assurance may all believers have that Christ died for them, with an intention and purpose to save their souls. For instance: all believers may draw out the truth of the word and the faith created in their hearts into this conclusion:—[*First*,] "Christ died for all believers,"—that is, all who choose him and rest upon him as an all-sufficient Saviour; not that he died for them as such, but that all such are of those for whom he died. He died not for believers as believers, though he died for all believers; but for all the elect as elect, who, by the benefit of his death, do become believers, and so obtain assurance that he died for them. [As] for such of those that are elected who are not yet believers, though Christ died for them, yet we deny that they can have any assurance of it whilst they continue such. You suppose it a foul contradiction, if a man should be said to have assurance that Christ died for him in particular, and yet continue an unbeliever. This first proposition, as in the beginning laid down, is true in the word, in innumerable places. *Secondly*, The heart of a believer, in the witness of the Spirit, assumes, "But I believe in Christ;" that is, "I choose him for my Saviour, cast and roll myself on him alone for salvation, and give up myself unto him, to be disposed of unto mercy in his own way." Of the truth of this proposition in the heart of a believer, and the infallibility of it, there are also many testimonies in the word, as is known to all; from whence the conclusion is, "Therefore the Lord Jesus Christ died for me in particular, with an intention and purpose to save me."

This is such a collection as all believers, and none but believers, can justly make, so that it is peculiar to them alone; and unto those only is this treasure of consolation to be imparted. The sufficiency of the death of Christ for the saving of every one, without exception, that comes unto him, is enough to fill all the invitations and entreaties of the gospel unto sinners, to induce them to believe; which when, by the grace of Christ, they do, closing with the promise, the fore-mentioned infallible assurance of the intention and purpose of Christ to redeem them by his death, Matt. i. 21, is made known unto them. Now, whether this be not a better bottom and foundation for a man to assure his soul unto rest and peace upon, than that reasoning which our opposers in this business must, suitably to their own principles, lay as a common stone,—namely, "Christ died for all men; I am a man: therefore Christ died for me,"—let any man judge; especially considering that indeed the first proposition is absolutely false, and the conclusion, if it could be true, yet, according to their persuasion, can be no more ground of consolation than Adam's fall. All this is spoken not as though either one opinion or other were able of itself to give consolation, which God alone, in the sovereignty of his free grace, can and doth create; but only to show what principles are suitable to the means whereby he worketh on and towards his elect.

4. The drawing of gospel consolation from the death of Christ, as held out to be effectual towards the elect only, for whom alone he died, should close up our discourse; but considering, first, how abundantly this hath been done by divers eminent and faithful labourers in the vineyard of the Lord already; secondly, how it is the daily task of the preachers of the gospel to make it out to the people of God; thirdly, how it would carry me out, besides my purpose, to speak of things in a *practical*, so *atheological* way, having designed this discourse to be purely *polemical;* and, fourthly, that such things are no more expected nor welcome to wise and learned men, in controversies of this nature, than knotty, crabbed, scholastic objections in popular sermons and doctrinal discourses, intended merely for edification,—I shall not proceed therein. Only, for a close, I desire the reader to peruse that one place, Rom. viii. 32–34; and I make no doubt but that he will, if not infected with the leaven of the error opposed, conclude with me, that if there be any comfort, any consolation, any assurance, any rest, any peace, any joy, any refreshment, any exultation of spirit, to be obtained here below, it is all to be had in the blood of Jesus long since shed, and his intercession still continued; as both are united and appropriated to the elect of God, by the precious effects and fruits of them both drawn to believe and preserved in believing, to the obtaining of an immortal crown of glory, that shall not fade away.

Μόνῳ σοφῷ Θεῷ, διὰ Ἰησοῦ Χριστοῦ ἡ δόξα εἰς τοὺς αἰῶνας. Ἀμήν.

SOME FEW TESTIMONIES OF THE ANCIENTS.

I. THE confession of the holy CHURCH of SMYRNA, a little after the commendation given it by the Holy Ghost, Rev. ii. 9, upon the martyrdom of Polycarpus:—"Οτι οὔτε τὸν Χριστόν ποτε καταλείπειν δυνησόμεθα τὸν ὑπὲρ τῆς τοῦ κόσμου τῶν σωζωμένων σωτηρίας παθόντα, οὔτε ἕτερον τιμῇ σέβειν.—Euseb. Hist. Eccles., lib. iv. cap. 15.—"Neither can we ever forsake Christ, him who suffered for the salvation of *the world of them that are saved*, nor worship any other."

[It is an extract from a letter of the church of Smyrna to the churches of Pontus, giving an account of the martyrdom of Polycarp.]

II. The witness of holy IGNATIUS, as he was carrying to Rome from Antioch, to be cast to beasts for the testimony of Jesus, Epist. ad Philad. [cap. ix., A.D. 107]:—Οὗτός ἐστιν ἡ πρὸς τὸν Πατέρα ἄγουσα ὁδός, ἡ πέτρα, ὁ φραγμός, ἡ κλείς, ὁ ποιμήν, τὸ ἱερεῖον, ἡ θύρα τῆς γνώσεως δι' ἧς εἰσῆλθον Ἀβραὰμ καὶ Ἰσαὰκ καὶ Ἰακώβ, Μωσῆς, καὶ ὁ σύμπας τῶν προφητῶν χορός, καὶ οἱ στύλοι τοῦ κόσμου οἱ ἀπόστολοι καὶ ἡ νύμφη τοῦ Χριστοῦ, ὑπὲρ ἧς, φερνῆς λόγῳ, ἐξέχεε τὸ οἰκεῖον αἷμα ἵνα αὐτὴν ἐξαγοράσῃ.—"This is the way leading to the Father, this the rock, the fold, the key; he is the shepherd, the sacrifice; the door of knowledge, by which entered Abraham, Isaac, Jacob, Moses, and the whole company of prophets, and the pillars of the world, the apostles, and the spouse of Christ; for whom, instead of a dowry, he poured out his own blood, that he might redeem her."

Surely Jesus Christ gives not a dowry for any but his own spouse.

III. CLEMENS, "whose name is in the book of life," Phil. iv. 3, with the whole church at Rome in his days, in the epistle to the church of Corinth:—Διὰ τὴν ἀγάπην ἣν ἔσχεν πρὸς ἡμᾶς τὸ αἷμα αὐτοῦ ἔδωκεν ὑπὲρ ἡμῶν ἐν θελήματι αὐτοῦ καὶ τὴν σάρκα ὑπὲρ τῆς σαρκὸς ἡμῶν καὶ τὴν ψυχὴν ὑπὲρ ψυχῶν ἡμῶν.—"For the love which he had unto us, he gave his blood for us, according to his purpose, and his flesh for our flesh, and his life for our lives."

Where you have assigned, 1. The cause of Christ's death,—his love to us; 2. The object of it,—us, or believers; 3. The manner how he redeemed us, even by commutation.

This triple testimony is taken from the very prime of undoubted antiquity.

IV. CYPRIAN, Epist. lxii. to Cæcilius, a holy, learned, and famous martyr, A.D. 250:—"Nos omnes portabat Christus, qui et peccata nostra portabat."—"He bare all us, who bare our sins;" that is, he sustained their persons on the cross for whom he died.

The same to Demetrian:—"Hanc gratiam Christus impertit, subigendo mortem trophæo crucis, redimendo *credentem* pretio sanguinis sui."—"This grace hath Christ communicated, subduing death in the trophy of his cross, redeeming believers with the price of his blood."

The same, or some other ancient and pious writer of the cardinal works of Christ, Serm. 7, secund. Rivet. Crit. Sac. in Cyp. [lib. ii. cap. 15] Scultet. Medul. Pat. Erasm. præfat. ad lib.[1]

[1] These seven sermons on the cardinal works of Christ are the production of Arnoldus Carnotensis, abbot of the Benedictine monastery of Bonneval, in the diocese of Chartres. He flourished about the middle of the twelfth century. Several of his practical treatises were for a time ascribed to Cyprian.—ED.

The same author also, in express terms, mentions the sufficiency of the ransom paid by Christ, arising from the dignity of his person:—"Tantæ dignitatis illa una Redemptoris nostri fuit oblatio, ut una ad tollenda mundi peccatum sufficeret."—"Of so great dignity was the oblation of our Redeemer, that it alone was sufficient to take away the sins of the world."

V. CYRIL of Jerusalem, Cataches. xiii. [A.D. 350]:—*Καὶ μὴ θαυμάσῃς εἰ κόσμος ὅλος ἐλυτρώθη, οὐ γὰρ ἦν ἄνθρωπος ψιλὸς ἀλλὰ υἱὸς Θεοῦ μονογενὴς ὁ ὑπεραποθνήσκων—καὶ εἰ τότε διὰ τὸ ξύλον τῆς βρώσεως ἐξεβλήθησαν ἐκ παραδείσου, ἆρα διὰ τὸ ξύλον Ἰησοῦ νῦν εὐκοπώτερον οἱ πιστεύοντες εἰς παράδεισον οὐκ εἰσελεύσονται;*—"Wonder not if the whole world be redeemed; for he was not a mere man, but the only-begotten Son of God that died. If, then, through the eating of the tree" (forbidden) "they were cast out of paradise, certainly now by the tree" (or cross) "of Jesus shall not believers more easily enter into paradise?"

So also doth another of them make it manifest in what sense they use the word *all*.

VI. ATHANASIUS, of the incarnation of the Word of God [A.D. 350]:—*Οὗτός ἐστιν ἡ πάντων ζωή, καὶ ὡς πρόβατον ὑπὲρ τῆς πάντων σωτηρίας ἀντίψυχον τὸ ἑαυτοῦ σῶμα εἰς θάνατον παραδούς.*—"He is the life of *all*, and as a sheep he delivered his body a price for the souls of *all*, that they might be saved."

All in both places can be none but the *elect;* as,—

VII. AMBROSE de Vocat. Gen., lib. i. cap. 3; or rather, PROSPER, lib. i. cap. 9, edit. Olivar. [A.D. 370]:—"Si non credis, non descendit tibi Christus, non tibi passus est."—"If thou believe not, Christ did not descend for thee, he did not suffer for thee."

Ambr. de Fide ad Gratianum:—"Habet populus Dei plenitudinem suam. In electis enim et præscitis, atque ab omnium generalitate discretis, specialis quædam censetur universitas, ut de toto mundo totus mundus liberatus, et de omnibus hominibus omnes homines videantur assumpti."—"The people of God hath its own fulness. In the elect and foreknown, distinguished from the *generality of all*, there is accounted a certain *special universality;* so that the whole world seems to be delivered from the whole world, and all men to be taken out of all men."

In which place he proceedeth at large to declare the reasons why, in this business, "all" and "the world" are so often used for "some of all sorts."

These that follow wrote after the rising of the Pelagian heresy, which gave occasion to more diligence of search and wariness of expression than had formerly been used by some.

VIII. AUGUSTINE, de Cor. et Grat. cap. xi. [A.D. 420]:—"Per hunc Mediatorem Deus ostendit eos, quos ejus sanguine redemit, facere se ex malis in æternum bonos."—"By him the Mediator, the Lord declareth himself to make those whom he hath redeemed with his blood, of evil, good to eternity." "Vult possidere Christus quod emit; tanti emit ut possideat."—"Christ will possess what he bought; he bought it with such a price that he might possess it."

Idem, Serm. xliv. de Verbis Apost.:—"Qui nos tanto pretio emit non vult perire quos emit."—"He that bought us with such a price will have none perish whom he hath bought."

Idem, Tract. lxxxvii. in Johan.:—"Ecclesiam plerumque etiam ipsam mundi nomine appellat; sicut est illud, 'Deus erat in Christo mundum reconcilians sibi;' itemque illud, 'Non venit Filius hominis ut judicet mundum, sed ut salvetur mundus per ipsum;' et in epistola sua Johannes ait, 'Advocatum habemus ad Patrem, Jesum

Christum justum, et ipse propitiator est peccatorum nostrorum, non tantum nostrorum sed etiam totius mundi.' Totus ergo mundus est ecclesia, et totus mundus odit ecclesiam. Mundus igitur odit mundum; inimicus reconciliatum, damnatus salvatum, inquinatus mundatum. Sed iste mundus quem Deus in Christo reconciliat sibi, et qui per Christum salvatur, de mundo electus est inimico, damnato, contaminato."—"He often calleth the *church* itself by the name of *the world;* as in that, 'God was in Christ reconciling the world unto himself;' and that, 'The Son of man came not to condemn the world, but that the world through him might be saved.' And John in his epistle saith, 'We have an Advocate, and he is the propitiation for [our sins, and not for ours only, but also for] the sins of the whole world.' The whole world, therefore, is the church, and the world hateth the church. The world, then, hateth the world; that which is at enmity, the reconciled; the condemned, the saved; the polluted, the cleansed world. And that world which God in Christ reconcileth to himself, and which is saved by Christ, is chosen out of the opposite, condemned, defiled world."

Much more to this purpose might be easily cited out of Augustine, but his judgment in these things is known to all.

IX. PROSPER [A.D. 440], Respon. ad Capit. Gall. cap. ix.:—"Non est crucifixus in Christo qui non est membrum corporis Christi. Cum itaque dicatur Salvator pro totius mundi redemptione crucifixus, propter veram humanæ naturæ susceptionem, potest tamen dici pro his tantum crucifixus quibus mors ipsius profuit. Diversa ab istis sors eorum est qui inter illos censentur de quibus dicitur, 'Mundus enim non cognovit.'"—"He is not crucified with Christ who is not a member of the body of Christ. When, therefore, our Saviour is said to be crucified for the redemption of the whole world, because of his true assumption of the human nature, yet may he be said to be crucified only for them unto whom his death was profitable. Diverse from these is their lot who are reckoned amongst them of whom it is said, 'The world knew him not.'"

Idem, Resp. Object. Vincen. Res. i.:—"Redemptionis proprietas, haud dubie penes illos est, de quibus princeps mundi missus est foras. Mors Christi non ita impensa est humano generi, ut ad redemptionem ejus etiam qui regenerandi non erant pertinerent."—"Doubtless the propriety of redemption is theirs from whom the prince of this world is cast out. The death of Christ is not to be so laid out for human-kind, that they also should belong unto his redemption who were not to be regenerated."

Idem, de Ingrat., cap. ix.:—

"Sed tamen hæc aliqua sivis ratione tueri
Et credi tam stulta cupis; jam pande quid hoc sit,
Quod bonus omnipotensque Deus, non omnia subdit
Corda sibi, pariterque omnes jubet esse fideles?
Nam si nemo usquam est quem non velit esse redemptum,
Haud dubie impletur quicquid vult summa potestas.
Non omnes autem salvantur" ——

"If there be none whom God would not have redeemed, why are not all saved?"

X. CONCIL. VALEN.,[1] can. iv.—"Pretium mortis Christi datum est pro illis tantum quibus Dominus ipse dixit, 'Sicut Moses exaltavit serpentem in deserto, ita exaltari oportet Filius hominis, ut omnis qui credit in ipso non pereat, sed habeat vitam eternam.'"—"The price of the death of Christ is given for them alone of whom the Lord himself said, 'As Moses lifted up the serpent in the wilderness, so must the Son of man be lifted up, that whosoever believeth on him should not perish.'"

[1] This was a council held at Valence in A.D. 855, and convened from the three provinces of Lyons, Vienne, and Arles. Remigius presided, five canons by a council in A.D. 853, at Chiersey, were condemned, and the cause of Godeschalcus, who had raised the controversy, was warmly supported. The canon quoted above is designed to contradict the fourth canon of the council at Chiersey, according to which "there never was, is, or will be a man for whom Christ has not died."—ED.

AN APPENDIX

UPON OCCASION OF

A LATE BOOK PUBLISHED BY MR JOSHUA SPRIGGE,[1]

CONTAINING ERRONEOUS DOCTRINE.

Reader,

I do earnestly entreat thy serious perusal of this short appendix. The total finishing and printing, not only of the body of the discourse, but also the preface, before occasion was given to those thoughts which I now desire to communicate, is the rise of this ataxy. This, being irrecoverable, will admit of no farther apology. In the third division of this treatise there are sundry chapters, namely, vii.–ix., etc., about the satisfaction of Christ, in which the doctrine is cleared and vindicated from the objections of some. The first aim I had therein was, to show the inconsistency of that with the general ransom, principally now opposed. In handling of it my eye was chiefly on the Socinians, the noted known opposers of the person, grace, and merit of Christ, the most wretched prevaricators in Christian religion which any age ever yet produced. In the manner of asserting it, I looked not beside the scriptural proposal of it, nor turned to any controversials, but only for the remarking some παρορᾶματα and (I fear wilful) failings and mistakes of Grotius,[2] in stating this business. His wretched apostasy into the very dregs of the error by himself (in the judgment of some) strongly opposed, sufficiently authorizeth any to lay open his treacherous dealing in his first undertaking. If any doubt of this, let him but compare the exposition of sundry texts of Scripture in that book against Socinus with those which the same person hath since given in his so much admired (indeed, in very many things, so much to be abhorred) Annotations on the Bible; and, by their inconsistency he will quickly perceive the steadfastness of that man to his first principles. *Great* as he was, he was not big enough to contend with truth. Moreover, I had it in my thoughts to endeavour the removal of (as I then thought) a scruple from the minds of some well-meaning persons, who weakly apprehend that the eternal love of God to his elect was inconsistent with the satisfaction of Christ, and therefore began to apprehend, and instantly to divulge abroad (for that is the manner of our days, for every one to cast upon others the crudities of their own stomach, and scatter abroad undigested conceptions, waiting for some to lick their deformed issues, and to see what other

[1] Mr Sprigge, after having been educated at Oxford, took the degree of M.A. at Edinburgh. He became a preacher at St Mary, Aldermanbury, and subsequently at St Pancras, London. After the Restoration he purchased an estate, Crayford, in Kent, and lived there in retirement. He married in 1673, Frances, the daughter of Lord Wimbledon, and widow of Lord Say. He returned to London and died at Highgate. He was the author of some political works, "Anglia Rediviva," a folio volume, containing the history of the army under Fairfax, and published in 1647; and "Certain Considerations tendered to the Consideration of the High Court of Justice for Trial of the King," 1648. His theological works are chiefly sermons. It is rather strange that Owen never indicates the title of the work by Sprigge on which he is animadverting; and Mr Orme mentions that he had not ascertained to which of Sprigge's works our author refers. It was, however, a collection of five sermons which Sprigge had delivered at St Pancras, and which were published under the title of, "A Testimony to Approaching Glory." Anthony Wood affirms that they contained "several blasphemies;" and they drew forth some pamphlets, besides this Appendix of Owen, in exposure of their errors. Two of these pamphlets, published in 1652, bore the titles, "The Beacons Quenched," and "The Beacons Flaming."—Ed.

[2] Lib. de Satisfac. Christi. Vos. Def. Grot. alii.

capricious brains can make of that which themselves know not how to improve) that Christ came only to declare the love of the Father, and to make it manifest to us, that we, in the apprehension thereof, might be drawn to him; so that as for satisfaction and merit, they are but empty names, obscuring the gospel, which holds out no such things. Now, concerning this I know,—

1. That this new-named *free grace*, this glorious height and attainment, this varnished deity, was at first in its original "truncus ficulnus,"—an old, rotten, overworn, Arminian objection, raised out of the *obs.* and *sols.* of the old schoolmen, to oppose the doctrine of effectual redemption by Christ, or else to overthrow the doctrine of eternal election; for they framed it to look both ways (either we are not so chosen, or not so redeemed), not caring which part of their work it did, so it were in any measure useful. This was the birth and rise of this glorious discovery.

2. That of its own accord it tends to the very bottom of Socinian folly, yea, indeed, is the very same opinion, for substance, with that whereby they have so long vexed the churches of God, and are themselves deservedly by them all esteemed accursed, for preaching another gospel. Doth not the sum of this discovery come hither, that there is no vindicative justice in God, no wrath or anger against sin, nothing requiring satisfaction for it; that Christ came to declare this, and to make known the way of going to the Father? And is not this that very Helena for which the Socinians have, with so much fraud and subtlety, with so many Sinonian arts, so long contended?

3. That it is extremely to the dishonour of Jesus Christ, destructive to the gospel faith and all solid consolation, and forces men either to a familistical contempt or sophistical corrupting of the word of God in its defence.

Upon these and the like considerations and apprehensions, I deemed it might not be in vain to disprove the main assertion, as also to manifest the miserable inconsequence, from the asserting of God's eternal love to the denial of satisfaction; which in what manner the Lord enabled me to perform, you must know, reader, in the place above mentioned. At that time I had only had one conference with one about it; and for books I had only seen some few, and those so exceedingly inconsiderable, and so fully familistical, forced with so much contempt of the word, that I was not willing to cast away the least moment on them.

But now, some few days ago (to come to the occasion of this appendix), there came to my hands a book written by Mr Sprigge who, both in his preface to the reader and in divers passages in the treatise itself, labours to commend to the world this glorious discovery, that Christ did not purchase, but only preach, peace unto us; that he came only to reveal and declare the love of God, not to procure it; that we only are reconciled to God by him, which he proves from Rom. v. 11; that no reconciliation with God is procured; that this discovery, and the like, are that which we have prayed for all this while.—Preface to the Reader. So also in many places of the treatise itself, pp. 65, 101. Indeed, everywhere it is his main scope. He bids us not think the heart of God was set upon the having a little blood (see Eph. v. 2) for the sins of his people, p. 59. These things are but pleasant tales and childish things to allure us withal, p. 46. In short, one main aim of the book is to make the whole ministration of Christ to be the discovery of a mystery nowhere revealed in the word.

It is not my purpose here to view the whole, or to separate the chaff from the wheat in it, to distinguish between the spiritual truths and smoky vapours that are interwoven in it, but only to cautionate the reader a little about that one thing I before intimated, with some brief expostulations about it.

Only let me inform thee a little, also, that my motive hereunto is not only from the book itself, but also from the pretended "imprimatur" annexed to it. The truth itself, in opposition to this dangerous notion (with a discovery of the whole fallacy), thou wilt find sufficiently confirmed from the Scripture in the foregoing treatise; and Christians will not easily, I hope, be shaken from the truth of the word by any pretended revelations whatsoever. Only, whereas [1]*tantum nomen* (as is that of the reverend and learned licenser) is (I know not whether duly) affixed to the treatise I speak of, until he shall have vindicated himself, lest it should insinuate itself by the help of his name into others (as upon that score, without farther view, it was left with commendation by myself in the hand wherein I first saw it), I desire to give thee these few observations here as a foretaste, reserving thee for full satisfaction unto what is held out from the word herein in the foregoing treatise.

First, then, observe that that absurd consequence, deduced from this position, that Christ is not the cause but the effect of love,—namely, *ergo*, he did not purchase life, peace, and salvation for us,—flows merely from ignorance of the love of God, and confounding those things which ought to be distinguished. Some look upon love in God as an unchangeable affection, when the truth is, as an affection or passion, it hath no place in God at all. All agree that love in spirits, yea partly in men, is *in appetitu intellectivo*, in the will, the intellectual appetite; and there defined to be θέλειν τινὶ τὸ ἀγαθόν, "to will good to any one." Certainly, then, in God his love is but a pure act of his will. That love which was the cause of sending his Son is, I say, an act of his will, his good pleasure,—not a natural affection to the creature. No such affection is there in God, as I have abundantly proved in this treatise. Now, this love, this act of God's will, was not purchased, not procured by Christ. Very true; who ever was so mad as to affirm it? Can a temporal thing be the cause of that which is eternal? This is not at all the sense of them who affirm that Christ procured the love of his Father for us. No; but the effects of this purpose, the fruits of this love, commonly called in the Scripture *love*, as affections are ascribed to God in respect of their effects. Now, that Christ purchased these for us, see afterward. This eternal act of God's will, this love, which was the rise of sending Jesus Christ, tended to his glory in these two acts:—*first*, The removing of wrath, death, curse, guilt, from them for whom he was sent, by satisfaction to his vindicative justice; *secondly*, The actual procuring of grace and glory for them, by merit and impetration. These things, though they are not the love of God, which is immanent in himself, yet they are those alone whereby we enjoy his love, and are purchased by Christ; which here I must not prove, lest I should *actum agere*.

Secondly, An eternal act of God's will, immanent in himself, puts no change of condition into the creature. See what the Scripture says of the elect notwithstanding this, Eph. ii. 3; John iii. 36. Let not the word be despised nor corrupted. Be not wise above what is written. "Though an angel," etc., Gal. i. 8. Until he draws us, the fruit of his death is kept for us in the justice and fidelity of God.

Thirdly, These things being premised, to clear the truth in this point, I desire a fair and candid answer to these queries:—

First, What is the meaning of that phrase, Heb. ii. 17, Εἰς τὸ ἱλάσκεσθαι τὰς ἁμαρτίας τοῦ λαοῦ, "To make reconciliation for the sins of the people," and this being done as a priest towards God, Heb. v. 1,—whether the meaning of it be declared love from God to man?

Secondly, Is not the end of sundry typical sacrifices to make an atonement with God on their behalf for whom they were sacrifices? Exod. xxix. 33, 36, xxx. 10, 15, 16; Lev. vi. 7; Num. xvi. 46, and very many other places;—and whether this were to turn away the wrath of God, or to reconcile men to him?

Thirdly, Is not the death of Christ a proper sacrifice? Eph. v. 2; Heb. ix. 26, 28; John i. 29; the antitype of all sacrifices, in which they have their ac-

[1] The reverend licenser being informed of this book of Mr Sprigge, disclaimeth the licensing of any more thereof than that Serm. on Cant. i. 1.

complishment? And did it not really effect what they carnally and typically figured? Heb. ix. 11–14, etc., x. 1–7, etc. And was it not offered to God?

Fourthly, Was not Jesus Christ a priest for his people, in their behalf to deal with God, Heb. ii. 17, v. 1, 2, vii. 26, 27; as well as a prophet, to deal with them in the behalf of God? and whether the acts of his priestly office do not all of them immediately tend towards God for the procuring good things for those in whose behalf he is a priest?

Fifthly, Whether Christ by his intercession doth appear before God to declare the love of God to his? or whether it be to procure farther fruits of love for his? Rom. viii. 34; Heb. vii. 25, ix. 24.

Sixthly, Did not Christ, by and in the oblation of himself, through the eternal Spirit, pay a ransom, or valuable price of redemption, into the hand of his Father for the sins of the people? Matt. xxvi. 28; Mark x. 45; 1 Tim. ii. 6; Eph. v. 2; Job xxxiii. 24. And whether a ransom be a price of deliverance, arguing a commutation? Exod. xxi. 30, xxx. 12. Or whether Christ paid a ransom to his Father for the souls and sins of his people, thereby to declare to his people that there was no need of any such thing? And what think you of the old saying of Tertullian, "Omnia in imagines vertunt, imaginarii ipsi Christiani?"

Seventhly, Did not Christ in his death bear our sins? John i. 29; 1 Pet. ii. 24; Isa. liii. 6, 11; 2 Cor. v. 21. And whether to bear sin in the Scripture be not to bear the punishment due to sin? Lev. v. 1, etc. And is not to undergo the punishment due to sin, to make satisfaction for sin?

Eighthly, Did not Christ, as our surety, undergo all that is anywhere threatened against sin, and by the justice of God is due unto it? Heb. vii. 22, iv. 15; Gal. iii. 13; 2 Cor. v. 21; Heb. v. 7; Luke xxii. 44, etc.

Ninthly, Is there not a purchase and procurement of good things assigned to the death of Christ? Isa. liii. 5; Heb. ix. 12; Acts xx. 28; 1 Thess. v. 9; Luke i. 74; Rom. v. 10; Eph. ii. 16, etc.

Tenthly, Seeing that place of Rom. v. 11, "By whom we have now received the atonement," is urged to disprove the purchase of peace and reconciliation with God for us, whether by "the atonement" there be meant our reconciliation to God? and whether it be proper to say we have received or accepted of our conversion or reconciliation?

Eleventhly, Whether to affirm that all that was done in and by Christ was but a sign and representation of what is done spiritually in us, be not to overthrow the first promise, Gen. iii. 15, yea, the whole gospel, and to make it, as it is called, a "childish thing?"

Twelfthly, Whether it be fair and allowable, for men professing the name of Christ, in the trial of truth, to decline the word of God? And whether such declension be not an invincible demonstration of a guilt of falsehood? Deut. iv. 2, xii. 32; Josh. i. 7; Ps. xix. 7; Prov. xxx. 6; Isa. viii. 20; Luke i. 4, xvi. 29; John v. 39, xx. 30, 31; Gal. i. 8, 9; 2 Thess. ii. 2; 1 Tim. vi. 20; 2 Tim. iii. 16, 17; 2 Pet. i. 19, etc.

Thus much, courteous reader, I thought good to premise unto thee, though something out of order, upon the discovery of a new opposition made to a precious truth of God, which thou wilt find explained and asserted in the foregoing treatise; and this liberty I hope I have assumed without the offence of any. It is not about trifles that I contend (I abhor such ways), but for the faith once delivered to the saints. Now, "Peace be to the brethren, and love with faith, from God the Father and the Lord Jesus Christ. Grace be with all them that love our Lord Jesus Christ in sincerity. Amen."

COGGESHALL, *April* 25, 1648.

OF

THE DEATH OF CHRIST,

THE PRICE HE PAID, AND THE PURCHASE HE MADE;

OR,

THE SATISFACTION AND MERIT OF THE DEATH OF CHRIST CLEARED;
THE UNIVERSALITY OF REDEMPTION THEREBY OPPUGNED;

AND

THE DOCTRINE CONCERNING THESE THINGS, FORMERLY DELIVERED IN A TREATISE AGAINST UNIVERSAL REDEMPTION, VINDICATED FROM THE EXCEPTIONS AND OBJECTIONS OF MR R[ICHARD] B[AXTER.]

PREFATORY NOTE.

This reply to the animadversions of Baxter on the preceding treatise was prepared by Owen while he was busily occupied in Dublin with arranging the affairs of Trinity College,—the work for which he had been taken to Ireland by Cromwell. It may be viewed simply as an appendix to the important treatise which it vindicates; and it discusses several points, such as the nature of the payment made by Christ, the penalty undergone by him, the condition of believers antecedent to the death of Christ and to their own faith in Christ, etc.,—questions on which momentous issues hang, if treated in relation to Socinianism, or even to certain equivocal views of Grotius, but which savour much of a logomachy, as the subject of dispute between Owen and Baxter.

The animadversions of Baxter, to which the following treatise is an answer, appeared at the close of his "Aphorisms on Justification;" to which some interest attaches, as the first of the voluminous publications of Baxter, which have been computed to amount to more than double all the manifold and lengthened productions of his antagonist, Owen! Baxter's second appearance in this controversy was in his "Confession of Faith," 1655. In this work he accuses our author most unjustly of Antinomianism; and it is remarkable that while he persists in condemning Owen's work against universal redemption, he declares, nevertheless, "In the article of the extent of redemption, wherein I am most suspected and accused, I do subscribe to the Synod of Dort, without any exception, limitation, or exposition of any word as doubtful and obscure." It may seem difficult to reconcile this statement with his opposition to the sentiments of Owen. The latter replied in an appendix to his "Vindiciæ Evangelicæ;" and the dispute closed with a final reply from Baxter, appended to a work which he published against Mr Blacke, entitled, "Certain Disputations of Right to the Sacraments, and the True Nature of Visible Christianity," 1656.

There is a feeling of pain in perusing the record of such disputes between men who held so much of precious truth in common,—who had both higher work on hand against common enemies,—men at one, doubtless, in all the sympathies of genuine faith and spiritual brotherhood, and now for ever at one in the songs and services of heaven. Good will spring from all the evil of these keen debates, if we can hold with a firmer grasp the truth which they may have been overruled to elicit and establish; and though a spirit of pugnacity appears in the conduct of Baxter, how few share his candour and modesty in the subsequent acknowledgment which he made, that he had been imprudent and incautious in meddling on this occasion with Owen!—Ed.

TO THE READER.

Of all the controversies wherewith the disciples of Christ, through the craft of Satan, and their own knowing but in part, have in several ages been exercised, there have been none of so great weight and importance, upon all considerations whatever, as those which immediately concern the person and grace of Him by whose name they are called. As his person was almost the sole subject of contest (of any moment) for the space of many ages succeeding his converse in the flesh with the sons of men; so in these latter days, through the darkness of their own spirits and the seducements of the spirit of darkness, many in an especial manner do draw forth a variety of uncouth thoughts concerning his grace, and the dispensation of the love of God towards mankind in him. Yet have not these things been so distinctly managed, but that as they of old, with their oppositions to his person, did also labour to decry and disannul the work of his grace; so many of those who, of latter days, have been led away into dangerous misapprehensions of his grace, both as to the foundation and efficacy of it, have also wrested the things concerning his person to their own destruction.

Of those that have entangled the spirits of the men of this generation, turning aside many from the simplicity of the gospel and the truth as it is in Jesus, none have been obtruded upon the saints of God with greater confidence, nor carried out to a more unhappy issue, than such as, assisting corrupted nature to unbend itself from under the sovereignty of God, and loosening the thoughts of men's hearts from their captivity to the obedience of the gospel, do suit the mystery of God in Christ reconciling sinners unto himself to the fleshly wisdom and reasonings of a man. It was in our hopes and expectations, not many years ago, that the Lord would graciously have turned back all those bitter streams which, issuing from the pride, unthankfulness, and wisdom of the carnal mind, had many ways attempted to overflow the doctrine of the grace of God, that bringeth salvation; but finding now, by experience, that the day of the church's rest from persecution is the day of Satan's main work for seducing and temptation, and that not a few are attempting once more to renew the contest of sinful, guilty, defiled nature, against the sovereign distinguishing love and effectual grace of God, it cannot but be convenient, yea necessary, that the faith once delivered to the saints be contended for and asserted from the word of truth in the like public way wherein it is opposed.

It hath been the constant practice of all persons, in all ages, who have made it their design to beget and propagate a belief of any doctrine contrary to the form of wholesome words, to begin with, and insist mainly upon, those parts of their beloved conception and offspring which seem to be most beautiful and taking, for the turning aside of poor, weak, unlearned, and unstable souls; knowing full well that their judgments and attention being once engaged, such is the frame of men's spirits under delusion, they will choose rather to swallow down all that follows than to discharge themselves of what they have already received. Upon this account, those who of late days have themselves drunk large draughts of the very dregs of Pelagianism, do hold out at first only a desire to be pledged in a taste of the universality of the merit of Christ for the redemption (or rather something else, well I wot not what) of all and every man. Finding this rendered plausible from some general expressions in the word seeming to cast an eye of favour that way, in the light wherein they stand, as also to be a fit subject for them to varnish over and deck up, with loose, ambiguous, rhetorical expressions, they attempt with all their might to get entertainment for it, knowing that those who shall receive it may well call it Gad, being sent before only to take up quarters for the troop that follows.

To obviate this evil, which, being thus planted and watered through other subtleties and advantages, hath received no small increase, I have once and again[1] cast in my mite into the treasury of that rich provision which the Lord hath enabled many men of eminent learning and piety to draw forth from the inexhaustible storehouse of divine truth, and to prepare it for the use of the saints.

In one[2] of those treatises, having at large handled the several concernments of the death of Christ, as to the satisfaction and merit thereof, in their nature and tendency, as well as their object and extent, and finding some opposition made to sundry truths therein delivered, I have attempted, through the assistance of grace, to vindicate them from that opposition in this ensuing discourse, as also taken occasion to hold forth sundry other things of weight and importance; of all which you have an account given in the first chapters thereof, whither I remit the reader.

For the present, there are some few things which, Christian reader, I desire to acquaint thee withal in particular, which something nearly concern the business we have in hand.

Since not only the complete finishing of this treatise under my hand, which is now about five months ago, but also the printing of some part of it, the two dissertations of Dr Davenant, of the Death of Christ, and of Predestination and Reprobation, were set forth; in both which, especially the former, there are sundry assertions, positions, and theses, differing from what is delivered in the ensuing treatise, and, as I suppose, repugnant unto truth itself. The whole of those persuasions, I confess, which he endeavoureth in them to maintain, is suited to the expressions of sundry learned men, as Austin, Hilary, Fulgentius, Prosper, who in their generations deserved exceeding well of the church of God; but that it is free from opposition to the Scripture, or indeed self-contradiction, is not so apparent. Yea, through the patience and goodness of God, I undertake to demonstrate that the main foundation of his whole dissertation about the death of Christ, with many inferences from thence, are neither found in, nor founded on the word; but that the several parts thereof are mutually conflicting and destructive of each other, to the great prejudice of the truth therein contained.

It is a thing of the saddest consideration possible, that wise and learned men should once suppose, by tempering the truths of God so that they may be suited to the self-indulgency of unsubdued carnal affections, to give any lustre to them, or in the least to remove that scandal and offence which the fleshly-minded[3] doth take continually at those ways of God which are far above out of his sight. That this is the grand design of such undertakings as that of the learned bishop now mentioned, even to force the mysteries of the gospel to a condescension and suitableness unto the unpurged relics of the wisdom of nature, when all other thoughts ought to be captivated to the obedience thereof, is to me most apparent. Whence else should it proceed that so many unscriptural distinctions of the various intentions of God in the business of redemption, with the holding out, for the confirmation of one part of their opinion,—namely, "That Christ died for all and every

[1] Display of Arminianism; Salus Electorum, Sanguis Jesu. [2] Salus Elect. [3] Rom. viii. 7.

one in such a sense,"—those very arguments which the most that own the truth of their inferences do employ merely against the latter part of their opinion,—namely, "In some sense he died only for the elect,"—with sundry inextricable entanglements, should fill up both the pages of their discourses?

It is no way clear to me what glory redoundeth to the grace of God, what exaltation is given to the death of Christ,[1] what encouragement to sinners in the things of God, by maintaining that our Saviour, in the intention and the designment of his Father, died for the redemption of millions for whom he purchased not one dram of saving grace, and concerning whom it was the purpose of God from eternity not to make out unto them effectually any of those means for a participation in the fruits of his death, without which it is impossible but it should be useless and unprofitable unto them; and yet this is the main design of that Dissertation concerning the Death of Christ. What in that and the ensuing discourse is argued and contended for according to the mind of God we thankfully accept; and had it not been condited with the unsavoury salt of human wisdom, it had been exceeding acceptable, especially at this time: for that there are some more than ordinary endeavours for the supportment and re-enforcing of the almost conclamated cause of Arminianism[2] ready to be handed unto public view is commonly reported and believed; concerning which, also, many swelling words (of which there lies great abundance on every side) are daily vented, as of some unparalleled product of truth and industry, as though "Nil oriturum alias, nil ortum tale," for the most part by such as are utterly ignorant how far these controversies have been sifted, and to what issue they have been driven long ago.

For my part, as I have not as yet of late heard or read any thing of this kind, either from public disputes or in printed sheets, but only long-since-exploded sophisms, inconsequent consequences, weak objections, fully, soundly answered many a day since; nor, by the taste which I have already received, have I any reason to expect, from the great endeavours which are entering the city of God with "Io triumphe," any thing beyond fruitless attempts to varnish over with plausible appearances formerly-decried invectives and reasonings, whose deformity and nakedness have been often discovered, to the loathing of them by the saints of God: so I no way doubt but that the Lord, whose truth is precious to him, will continue to pour out, from the rich provision which he hath made for the use of his church, and laid up in the Lord Jesus, suitable gifts and abilities[3] against all opposition whereunto, by the craft of Satan, it is exposed. I shall say no more, though occasion be administered to deplore that success which the spirit of seduction, that is gone out in this hour of temptation, hath had in prevailing upon them that live in the earth to turn away their minds from sound doctrine and the form of wholesome words. Only, I desire to commend the reader unto those two apostolical cautions,—one, 1 Tim. i. 18, 19; the other, 1 Tim. vi. 20,—and so commit him to the grace of God.

J. O.

May 15th, [1650.]

1 ——— ἡ νύμφη τοῦ Χριστοῦ ὑπὲρ ἧς φερνῆς λόγῳ ἐξέχεε τὸ οἰκεῖον αἷμα, ἵνα αὐτὴν ἐξαγοράσῃ.—Ignat. ad Philad.

2 Ἐπέων δὲ πολὺς νομὸς ἔνθα καὶ ἔνθα.—Homer, Iliad, ῥαψ. υ, 249.

3 Eph. iv. 11-13. "Hæreses, de quorundam infirmitatibus habent, quod valent, nihil valentes, si in bene valentem fidem incurrant."—Tertul. de Præsc. ad Hær., Matt. xxiv. 24.

OF THE DEATH OF CHRIST.

CHAPTER I.

The occasion of this discourse, with the intendment of the whole.

A FEW words will briefly acquaint the reader with the occasion of this discourse ensuing. It is now about two years since I published a treatise about the redemption and satisfaction that is in the blood of Christ. My aim was, to hold out the whole work of redemption, as flowing from the love of the Father, dispensed in the blood of the Son, and made effectual by the application of the Spirit of grace: and because in this whole dispensation, and in all the method of God's proceedings to make us nigh to himself in the blood of Jesus, there is no one thing so commonly controverted as the object of that redemption in respect of the extent of it, that in the whole I did specially intend.

What, by the grace of Him who supplieth seed to the sower, was attained in that undertaking, is left unto the judgment of men, upon the issue of his blessing thereunto. Altogether, I am not out of hopes that that labour in the Lord was not in vain. The universality of redemption, one thing in that treatise mainly opposed, having of old and of late got room in the minds of some men otherwise furnished with many precious truths and eminent gifts, I was not without expectation of some opposition to be made thereunto. Something also, I have been informed, hath been attempted that way; but I am yet at so much quiet in that regard as an utter nescience of them can afford. Only, whereas many other questions are incidentally and by the way handled therein,—as about the satisfaction and merit of Christ, etc.,—it pleased Mr Baxter, a learned divine, in an appendix to a treatise of justification,[1] by him lately published, to turn aside in the censure of some of them, and opposition to them. Indeed, most of his exceptions do lie rather against words than things, expressions than opinions, ways of delivering things than the doctrines themselves, as the reader will perceive; so that of this labour I might ease myself with this just apology,—that I was desired and pressed to handle the things of that discourse in the most popular way they were capable of, and in the best accommodation to vulgar capacities, so that it is no wonder if some expressions therein may be found to want some grains of accurateness (though they have not one dram the less of truth) in a scholastical balance.

Notwithstanding, because I am not as yet convinced, by any thing in Mr Baxter's censure and opposition, that there was any such blamable deviation as is pretended, but rather the words of truth and sobriety, clothing a doctrine of wholesomeness; and especially, because the things pointed at are in themselves weighty, and needing some exactness in the delivery to give a right apprehension of them; I was willing once more to attempt whether the grace of God with me, who am less than the least of all saints, might give any farther light into the right understanding of them, according to the truth, to the advantage of any that love the Lord Jesus in sincerity.

[1] "The Aphorisms of Justification." See Prefatory Note to this treatise.—ED.

The true nature of the satisfaction of Christ, with the kind of payment of our debt by him made and accomplished, is doubtless worthy of our most serious inquiry. The right constitution of the immediate effects of the death of Christ, the relation of men to the election of God and the redemption of Christ, with their several states and conditions in reference unto those works of grace, ought to be of no less esteem; and that not only for the nature and excellency of the things themselves, but also because a right disposal of them gives more light into the stating and settling many other controverted truths about faith, justification, vocation, and the like. These are the subjects about which I am called forth in my own, or rather truth's defence. For the treatise and subject thereof, whose latter part gives rise to this, I shall say no more, but as there are in it many footsteps of commendable learning, industry, and diligence, so, to my present apprehension, the chief intendments of it, with very many occasional expressions of the author's judgment in sundry particulars, are obnoxious to just opposition from truth itself.

It is not at all in my thoughts to engage myself into the chief controversy there agitated, though I could desire that some, to whom Providence hath given more leisure and opportunities for such employments, would candidly examine those "Aphorisms," for the farther advantage of the truth and light. But whereas the learned author hath, to make straight the work he had in hand, endeavoured to cast some part of the doctrine of the satisfaction and redemption of Christ, as by me delivered, into a crooked frame, and that with some such passages of censure as might have been omitted without losing the least grace of his book or style, I shall, with the Lord's assistance, endeavour to re-enforce what of truth hath been thereby assaulted in vain; and more especially, take occasion from thence farther to unfold those mysteries which, to our apprehension, are wrapped up in no small darkness, there being in them some things difficult and hard to be understood.

The first thing, then, which that learned divine chose to stand in distance from me in, is concerning the nature of the payment made for sin by the blood of Christ,—whether it be *ejusdem* or *tantidem;* and of the sense of these expressions is our first debate: in handling whereof, I hope I shall not only satisfy the reader as to the truth of what I had before written, but also farther clear the whole doctrine of satisfaction, with special reference to the kind of the payment that Christ made, and punishment which he underwent.

The other head wrappeth in itself many particulars concerning the immediate fruit or effects of the death of Christ, the state of the elect redeemed ones before actual believing, the nature of redemption, reconciliation, the differencing of persons in God's eternal purposes: to the consideration of all which, and sundry other particulars, I have occasion offered, in defence of the truth impugned.

These now, and the like, being things in themselves weighty, and the difference about them being, for the most part, rather as to the way of the delivery than as to the things themselves, in the handling of them, I could not attend merely to the advantage offered by Mr Baxter's discourse, but chose rather to cast them into another method, which might be distinct, clear, and accommodate to the things themselves; so that I hope the reader may, with some profit, see the whole dispensation of the love of God to his elect through Christ, with the relation of the elect, in several conditions, unto the several actings of God in that dispensation, succinctly laid down. The accommodation, also, of all delivered, to many weighty controversies, I have added.

If the way of handling these things here used be blamed by any, I hope the judicious will see that it is such as the matter itself will bear.

There have not been many things, in my whole inquiry after the mind of God in his word, which have more exercised my thoughts than the right ordering and distinct disposal of those whereof we treat. If the Lord hath discovered any thing unto me, or made out any thing by me, that may be for the benefit of any of his, I shall rejoice; it being always in my desire that all things might fall out to the advantage of the gospel: and so I address myself to the matter before me.

CHAPTER II.

An entrance into the whole—Of the nature of the payment made by Christ, with the right stating of the things in difference.

MR BAXTER having composed his Aphorisms of Justification, with their explications, before the publishing of them in print, he communicated them (as should appear) to some of his near acquaintance. Unto some things in them contained one of his said friends gives in some exceptions. Amongst other things he opposed unto those aphorisms, he also points at my contrary judgment in one or two particulars, with my reasons produced for the confirmation thereof. This provoketh their learned author (though unwilling) to turn aside to the consideration of those reasons. Now, the first of those particulars being about the payment made for sin in the blood of Christ, of what sort and kind it is, I shall willingly carry on the inquiry to this farther issue, whereunto I am drawn out.

1. He looks upon the stating of the question as I professedly laid it down at my entrance into that disputation, and declares that it is nothing at all to the question he hath in hand, nor looking that way.

"He distinguisheth," saith Mr Baxter, "betwixt paying the very thing that is in the obligation and paying so much in another kind; now, this is not our question, nor any thing to it," Append. p. 137.

If it be so, I know no reason why I was plucked into the following dispute, nor why Mr Baxter should cast away so many pages of his book upon that which is nothing at all to the business he had in hand. But though there be nothing to this purpose, p. 137 [265][1] of my book, the place he was sent to, yet, p. 140 [267], there is, as also something contrary to what is expressed in the former place, which he intimates in these words:—

"In p. 140 [267] he states the question far otherwise, and yet supposeth it the same, namely,—Whether Christ paid the *idem* or the *tantundem?* which he interpreteth thus, 'That which is not the same, nor equivalent unto it, but only in the gracious acceptation of the creditor.' Now, what he means by 'not equivalent' I cannot tell.

"If he mean, not of equal value, then he fights with a shadow. He wrongeth Grotius, for aught I can find in him, who teacheth no such doctrine. However, I do not so use to English *solutio tantidem*. But if he mean, that it is not equivalent in procuring its end *ipso facto*, delivering the debtor, without the intervention of a new concession or contract of the creditor, as *solutio ejusdem* doth, then I confess Grotius is against him, and so am I.

"So, also, God's gracious acceptance is either in accepting less in value than was due, and so remitting the rest without payment (this I plead not for); or else it is his accepting a refusable payment, which, though equal in value, yet he may choose to accept according to the tenor of the obligation. This is gracious acceptance, which Grotius maintaineth, and so do I; and so distinguish betwixt *solutio* and *satisfactio*, 'payment' and 'satisfaction.'" Thus far he.

Sundry things are here imagined and asserted:—First, Several passages are pointed at in my treatise, and a contradiction between them intimated. Secondly, Various conjectures given at my plain, very plain meaning, and divers things objected answerable to those conjectures, etc.

1 The figures in brackets indicate where the passages are to be found in the present volume.—ED.

Wherefore, to clear the whole, I shall,—1. Give you in the passages opposed; and, 2. Vindicate them from mutual opposition, with what is besides charged on them.

The first place mentioned in my treatise is in p. 137 [265], where, after I had discoursed of the nature of satisfaction, in reference both unto things real and personal, I laid down a distinction in these words:—

"There may be a twofold satisfaction,—First, By a solution or payment of the very thing that is in the obligation, either by the party himself who is bound, or by some other in his stead; as, if I owe a man twenty pounds, and my friend goeth and payeth it, my creditor is fully satisfied. Secondly, By a solution or paying of so much, although in another kind, not the same that is in the obligation, which by the creditor's acceptation stands in lieu of it; upon which also freedom followeth from the obligation, by virtue of an act of favour."

What now says Mr B. to this? Why, "it is nothing to the business he hath in hand."

Let then this pass, and look to the next passage which is opposed, and supposed to stand in opposition to the other.

Having laid down the former distinction, passing on to some other things concerning the nature of satisfaction, and the establishment of that of Christ from the Scripture, in p. 140 [267], I apply that distinction laid down before in general to the kind of satisfaction made by Christ, in these words:—

"Whereas I said that there is a twofold satisfaction whereby the debtor is freed from the obligation that is upon him,—the one being *solutio ejusdem*, payment of the same thing that was in the obligation; the other *solutio tantidem*, of that which is not the same, nor equivalent unto it, but only in the gracious acceptation of the creditor,—it is worth our inquiry which of these it was that our Saviour did perform."

And accordingly I refer it to the first.

"This," saith Mr B., "is a stating of the question far otherwise than before, yet supposing it the same."

But this I was so far from once mistrusting before, as that, being informed of it, I cannot as yet apprehend it to be so.

In p. 137 [265] I lay down a distinction in general about the several kinds of satisfaction, which, p. 140 [267], I plainly apply to the satisfaction of Christ, without any new, much less changed stating of the question. My whole aim, in that inquiry, was to search out that kind of punishment which Christ underwent in making satisfaction for sin,—namely, "Whether it were the same that was threatened to the transgressors themselves, or whether something else which God accepted in lieu thereof, relaxing the law not only as to the person suffering, but also as to the penalty to be undergone?"

The first of these, and that with the concurrent suffrage of far the greatest number of protestant divines, I assert with sundry arguments, pp. 141, 142, etc., 154–156 [268, etc., 280–282]. Unto which assertion he neither opposeth himself nor once attempteth to answer any of the arguments whereby I proved it.

This being my intendment, p. 137 [285], I intimate that Christ paid the same thing that was in the obligation; as if, in things real, a friend should pay twenty pounds for him that owed so much, and not any thing in another kind. And p. 140 [267], I affirm that he paid *idem*, that is, the *same thing* that was in the obligation, and not *tantundem*, *something equivalent* thereunto, in another kind.

"The first of these is nothing to our purpose," saith Mr B., "but the latter crossing the former."

But truly, such is my dulness, I cannot as yet be won to his mind herein. But I agree with myself; perhaps I do not with the truth. That description of *solutio tantidem*, namely, that it is a payment of that which is not the same, nor equivalent unto it, but only in the gracious acceptation of the creditor, is peculiarly opposed.

To make this expression obnoxious to an exception, Mr B. divides it, that so it may be entangled with a fallacy, παρὰ τῶν πλείων ἐρωτημάτων. And, first, he asks as before what I mean by *not equivalent;* and hereunto supposing two answers, to the first he opposeth a shadow, to the latter himself.

First, "If," saith he, "by *not equivalent*, you mean not of equal value, you fight with a shadow, and wrong Grotius. However, I do not use so to English *solutio tantidem.*"

By *not equivalent*, I mean that which is *not of equal value*, or certainly I mistook the word; and if so, had need enough to have gone to Mr B., or some other learned man, to have learned to English *solutio tantidem*. But do I not, then, fight with a shadow? Truly, cut my words thus off in the middle of their sense, and they will be found fit to cope with no other adversary; but take them as they lie, and as intended, and there is scarce any shadow of opposition to them cast by Mr B. passing by. My words are, "It is not equivalent, but only in the gracious acceptation of the creditor." Is not this the plain meaning of these words, that *tantundem* in satisfaction is not equivalent to *idem* ἁπλῶς, but only κατά τί? What is denied of it absolutely is affirmed in some respect. He that says it is not equivalent but only in gracious acceptation, in that sense affirms it to be equivalent, and that it is in respect of that sense that the thing so called is said to be *tantundem*, that is, *equivalent.*

Now, what excepts Mr B. hereunto? Doth he assert *tantundem* to be in this matter equivalent unto *idem* ἁπλῶς? It is the very thing he opposeth all along, maintaining that *solutio tantidem* stands in need of gracious acceptance, *ejusdem* of none; and, therefore, they are not as to their end ἁπλῶς, *equivalent*. Or will he deny it to be equivalent in God's gracious acceptance? This he also contendeth for himself: "Though *refusable*, yet equivalent." What, then, is my crime? I wrong Grotius! Wherein? In imposing on him that he should say, "It was not of equal value to the *idem* that Christ paid." Not one such word in any of the places mentioned. I say, Grotius maintains that the satisfaction of Christ was *solutio tantidem.* Will you deny it? Is it not his main endeavour to prove it so? Again; *tantundem*, I say, is not in this case equivalent to *idem* ἁπλῶς, but only κατά τί. Doth not Mr B. labour to prove the same? Where, then, is the difference? Were it not for *Ignoratio elenchi* in the bottom, and *Fallacia plurium interrogationum* at the top, this discourse would have been very empty.

Secondly, But he casts my words into another frame, to give their sense another appearance, and saith,—

"If you mean that it is not equivalent in procuring its end *ipso facto*, delivering the debtor without the intervention of a new concession or contract of the creditor, as *solutio ejusdem* doth, then I confess Grotius is against you, and so am I."

Of Grotius I shall speak afterward; for the present I apply myself to Mr B., and say,—

1. If he intend to oppose himself to any thing I handle and assert in the place he considereth, he doth, by this query, plainly μεταβαίνειν εἰς τὸ ἄλλο γένος, and that from a second inadvertency of the argument in hand. It is of the nature of the penalty undergone, and not of the efficacy of the satisfaction made thereby, that I there dispute.

2. I conceive that in this interrogation and answer he wholly gives up the cause that he pretends to plead, and joins with me, as he conceives my sense to be, against Grotius and himself. "If," saith he, "he mean that it is not equivalent in procuring its end *ipso facto*, without the intervention of a new concession or contract, as *solutio ejusdem* doth, then I am against him." Well, then, Mr B. maintains that

solutio tantidem is equivalent with *solutio ejusdem* in obtaining its end *ipso facto;* for, saith he, if I say it is not equivalent, he is against me. Τὸ σὸν ὄναρ σοὶ διηγοῦμαι. But is this his mind indeed? Will his words bear any other sense?

3. Whether *tantundem* and *idem,* in the way of satisfaction, be equivalent to the obtaining the end *ipso facto* aimed at, which he here asserts, though elsewhere constantly denies,—couching in this distinction the πρῶτον ψεῦδος of a great part of his discourse,—certainly it is nothing at all to the question I there agitated, maintaining that it was *idem,* and not *tantundem,* that Christ paid, and so the end of it obtained *ipso facto* answerable to the kind of the efficacy and procurement thereof.

But perhaps I do not conceive his mind aright; peradventure his mind is, that if I do maintain the satisfaction of Christ to procure the end aimed at, *ipso facto,* as *solutio ejusdem* would have done, then to profess himself my adversary. But,—

1. This is not here expressed nor intimated.

2. It is nothing at all to me who place the matter of the satisfaction of Christ *in solutione ejusdem.*

3. About the end of satisfaction in the place opposed I speak not, but only of the nature of the penalty undergone, whereby it was made.

4. To the thing itself, I desire to inquire,—

(1.) What Mr B. intends by *solutio ejusdem* in the business in hand? Doth he not maintain it to be the offender's own undergoing the penalty of the law? What end, I pray, doth this obtain *ipso facto?* Can it be any other but the glory of God's justice in the everlasting destruction of the creature? How, then, can it possibly be supposed to attain the end spoken of *ipso facto?* If this be the only meaning of *solutio ejusdem,* in this sense, the end of it is distant from the end of satisfaction ὡς οὐρανός ἐστ' ἀπὸ γαίας. By the laying the penalty on Christ, that God intended the freedom of those for whom he underwent that penalty, I suppose cannot be doubted; but in inflicting it on the offenders themselves, that he hath any such aim, wants an Origen to assert.

(2.) Whether the penalty due to one may not be undergone by another? and if so, whether it be not the same penalty, the *idem,* or no? In things real I gave an instance before. If a man pay twenty pounds for another who owed it, doth not he pay the *idem* in the obligation? And may not this hold in things personal also?

Of the satisfaction of Christ procuring its end *ipso facto,* I mean in its own kind,—for the death of Christ must be considered as meritorious as well as satisfactory, if the deliverance be attended as the end of it,—I shall speak afterward in its proper place. The present controversy is no more but this:—

Whether Christ underwent the penalty threatened unto us, or some other thing accepted instead thereof, by a new constitution? or, which is all one, whether, in laying our iniquities upon Christ, the law of God was relaxed only as to the persons suffering, or also as to the penalty suffered? that is, whether Christ paid the *idem* in the obligation, or *tantundem?*

To suppose that the *idem* of the obligation is not only the penalty itself, but also the offender's own suffering that penalty, and then to inquire whether Christ underwent the *idem,* is to cause an easy enemy to triumph in his dejection.

That the law was relaxed as to the person suffering, I positively assert; but as to the penalty itself, that is not mentioned. Of these two things alone, then, must be our inquiry:—

1. Whether Christ, in making satisfaction, underwent that penalty that was threatened to the offenders themselves?

2. Whether the penalty, though undergone by another, be not the *idem* of the obligation?

Of both these, after the clearing of the residue of Mr Baxter's exceptions.

Nextly, he requireth what I intend by "gracious acceptance," or rather giveth in his own sense of it in these words, pp. 138, 139 [266, 267]:—"So also God's gracious acceptance is either his accepting less in value than was due, and so remitting the rest without payment. This I plead not for. Or else it is his accepting of a refusable payment, which, though equal in value, yet he may choose to accept according to the tenor of the obligation. This is gracious acceptance, which Grotius maintaineth, and so do I." Thus far he.

Now, neither is this any more to the business I have in hand; for,—

1. The value of any satisfaction in this business ariseth not from the innate worth of the things whereby it is made, but purely from God's free constitution of them to such an end. A distinction cannot be allowed of more or less value in the things appointed of God for the same end; all their value ariseth merely from that appointment; they have so much as he ascribeth to them, and no more. Now, neither *idem* nor *tantundem* is here satisfactory, but by virtue of divine constitution. Only, in *tantundem* I require a peculiar acceptance, to make it equivalent to *idem* in this business,—that is, as to satisfaction; or, if you please, an acceptance of that which is not *idem*, to make it *tantundem*. So that this gracious acceptance is not an accepting of that which is less in value than what is in the obligation, but a free constitution appointing another thing to the end, which before was not appointed.

2. He supposeth me (if in so many mistakes of his I mistake him not) to deny all gracious acceptance where the *idem* is paid; [which], in the present case, is to assert it necessary, because not paid *per eundem;* yea, and that other person not procured by the debtor, but graciously assigned by the creditor.

3. To make up his gracious acceptance in this latter sense, he distinguisheth of payments refusable and not refusable: in the application of which distinction unto the payment made by Christ I cannot close with him; for a payment is refusable either absolutely and in itself, or upon supposal. The death of Christ, considered absolutely and in itself, may be said to be refusable as to be made a payment,—not a refusable payment; and that not because not refusable, but because not a payment. Nothing can possibly tend to the procurement and compassing of any end, by the way of payment, with the Lord, but what is built upon some free compact, promise, or obligation of his own. But now consider it as an issue flowing from divine constitution making it a payment, and so it was no way refusable as to the compassing of the end appointed. Thus, also, as to the obligation of the law for the fulfilling thereof, it was refusable in respect of the person paying, not in respect of the payment made. That former respect being also taken off by divine constitution, and relaxation of the law as to that, it becometh wholly unrefusable,—that is, as it was paid, it was so; for satisfaction was made thereby, upon the former supposals of constitution and relaxation.

4. Doth not Mr B. suppose that in the very tenor of the obligation there is required a solution, tending to the same end as satisfaction doth? Nay, is not that ἀβλεψία the πρῶτον ψεῦδος of this discourse? Deliverance is the aim of satisfaction, which receives its spring and being from the constitution thereof; but is there any such thing as deliverance once aimed at or intended in the tenor of the obligation? I suppose no.

5. Neither is the distinction of *solutio* and *satisfactio*, which Mr B. closeth withal, of any weight in this business, unless it would hold ὅλως καὶ πάντως, which it will not, and so is of no use here; for,—

(1.) There is *solutio tantidem* as well as *ejusdem*, and therein consists satisfaction, according to Mr B.

(2.) Whether satisfaction be inconsistent with *solutio ejusdem*, but not *per eundem*, is the τὸ κρινόμενον. After all this Mr B. adds,—

"Yet here Mr Owen enters the list with Grotius."

Where, I pray? I might very justly make inquiry, from the beginning to the ending of this discourse, to find out what it is that this word "here" particularly answereth unto. But to avoid as much as possible all strife of words, I desire the reader to view the controversy agitated between Grotius and myself, not as here represented by Mr Baxter, so changed by a new dress that I might justly refuse to take any acquaintance with it, but as by myself laid down in the places excepted against, and he will quickly find it to be,—

1. Not whether the law were at all relaxed, but whether it were relaxed as well in respect of the penalty to be suffered as of the person suffering; that is, whether God be only a rector, or a rector and creditor also, in this business. Which controversy, by the way, is so confusedly proposed, or rather strangely handled by Mr B., p. 145, where he adjudges me in a successless assault of Grotius, as makes it evident he never once perused it.

2. Nor, secondly, whether there be any need of God's gracious acceptance in this business or no; for I assert it necessary, as before described, in reference to *solutio ejusdem, sed non per eundem.*

3. Neither, thirdly, whether the satisfaction of Christ, considered absolutely, and in *statu diviso*, and materially, be refusable, which I considered not; or be unrefusable, supposing the divine constitution which Grotius, as I take it, delivered not himself in. Nor,—

4. About the value of the payment of Christ in reference to acceptance; but merely, as I said before, whether the Lord, appointing an end of deliverance neither intimated nor couched in the obligation nor any of its attendancies, constituting a way for the attainment of that end by receiving satisfaction to the obligation, did appoint that the thing in the obligation should be paid, though by another, or else some new thing, that of itself and by itself never was in the obligation, either before or after its solution; as the payment made by Christ must be granted such, unless it were for substance the same which the law required. And here, with most divines, I maintain the first,—namely, That the law was relaxed in respect of the person suffering, but executed in respect of the penalty suffered. Relaxation and execution are not in this business opposed ἁπλῶς, but only κατά τί.

He that would see this farther affirmed may consult what I wrote of it in the place opposed; which is not once moved by any thing here spoken to the contrary.

By the way observe, I speak only of the penalty of the law, and the passive righteousness of Christ, strictly so called. For his active righteousness, or obedience to the law (though he did many things we were not obliged unto, for the manifestation of himself, and confirmation of the doctrine of the gospel), that it was the very *idem* of us required, I suppose none can doubt. What place that active righteousness of Christ hath, or what is its use in our justification, I do not now inquire, being unwilling to immix myself unnecessarily in any controversy; though I cannot but suppose that Mr B.'s discourse hereabouts gives advantage enough even *minorum gentium theologis*, "to ordinary divines," as he calls them, to deal with him in it.

CHAPTER III.

The arguments of Grotius, and their defence by Mr Baxter, about the penalty undergone by Christ in making satisfaction, considered.

THE state of the question in hand being as above laid down, let us now see what Mr Baxter's judgment is of my success in that undertaking, concerning which he thus delivereth himself: "Yet here Mr Owen enters the list with Grotius." And,—

First, "He overlooketh his greatest arguments."

Secondly, "He slightly answereth only two."

Thirdly, "And when he hath done, he saith as Grotius doth, and yieldeth the whole cause. These three things I will make appear in order," Appendix, p. 139.

A most unhappy issue as can possibly be imagined, made up of deceit, weakness, and self-contradiction! But how is all this proved? To make the first thing appear, he produceth the argument overlooked.

"The chief argument of Grotius and Vossius," saith he, "is drawn from the tenor of the obligation and from the event. The obligation chargeth punishment on the offender himself. It saith, 'In the day thou eatest, thou shalt die;' and, 'Cursed is every one that continueth not in all things,' etc. Now, if the same in the obligation be paid, then the law is executed, and not relaxed, and then every sinner must die himself; for that is the *idem* and very thing threatened: so that here *dum alius solvit, simul aliud solvitur*. The law threatened not Christ, but us (besides that Christ suffered not the loss of God's love, nor his image and graces, nor eternity of torment; of which I have spoken in the treatise.) What saith Mr Owen to any of this?"

Let the reader observe what it is we have in hand. It is not the main of the controversy debated by Grotius wherein I do oppose him, neither yet all in that particular whereabout the opposition is. Now suppose, as he doth, that the punishing of the person offending is in the obligation, yet I cannot but conceive that there be two distinct things here,—first, The constitution of the penalty itself to be undergone; secondly, The terminating of this penalty upon the person offending. For this latter I assert a relaxation of the law; which might be done and yet the penalty itself in reference to its constitution be established. In those places, then, 'In the day thou eatest,' etc., there is death and the curse appointed for the penalty, and the person offending appointed for the sufferer. That the law is relaxed in the latter I grant. That the former was executed on Christ I prove. Now, what says this argument to the contrary?

"If the same in the obligation be paid, then the law is executed, not relaxed, and then every sinner must die himself; for that is the *idem* and very thing threatened: so that here *dum alias solvit, aliud solvitur*."

1. The matter of the obligation having a double consideration, as before, it may be both executed and relaxed in sundry respects.

2. The *idem* and very thing threatened in the constitution of the law is death. The terminating of that penalty to the person offending was in the commination, and had it not been relaxed, must have been in the execution; but in the constitution of the obligation, which respects purely the kind of penalty, primarily it was not. "Death is the reward of sin," is all that is there.

3. We inquire not about payment, but suffering. To make that suffering a payment supposeth another constitution, by virtue whereof Christ suffering the same that was threatened, it became another thing in payment than it would have been if the person offending had suffered himself.

4. That the law threatened not Christ but us is most true; but the question is, whether Christ underwent not the threatening of the law, not we? A commutation of persons is allowed, Christ undergoing the penalty of the offence; though he were not the person offending, I cannot but still suppose that he paid the *idem* of the obligation.

5. For the parenthesis about Christ's not suffering the loss of God's love, etc., and the like objections, they have been answered near a thousand times already, and that by "no ordinary divines" neither; so that I shall not farther trouble any therewith.

Now, this is the argument, the great, chief argument, of Grotius and Vossius, which Mr Baxter affirms I overlooked.

That I did not express it I easily grant, neither will I so wrong the ingenuous reader as to make any long apology for my omission of it, considering the state of the matter in difference as before proposed. When Mr B. or any man else shall be able to draw out any conclusion from thence, "That, granting the relaxation of the law as to the persons suffering, the Lord Christ did not undergo the penalty constituted therein;" or that, "Undergoing the very penalty appointed, he did not pay the *idem* in the obligation" (supposing a new constitution for the converting of suffering into a satisfactory payment), I shall then give a reason why I considered it not.

In the next place, Mr B. giveth in the two arguments wherein I deal.

And for the first, about an acquitment *ipso facto* upon the payment of the *idem* in the obligation, with my answer, [he] refers it, to be considered in another place; which, though I receive no small injury by, as shall be there declared, yet, that I may not transgress the order of discourse set me, I pass it by also until then.

The second argument of Grotius, with my answer, he thus expresseth:—

"To the second argument, that the payment of the same thing in the obligation leaveth no room for pardon, he answereth thus:—

"'God's pardoning compriseth the whole dispensation of grace in Christ; as,— 1. The laying of our sin on Christ; 2. The imputation of his righteousness to us, which is no less of grace and mercy. However, God pardoneth all to us, but nothing to Christ; so that the freedom of pardon hath its foundation,—1. In God's will freely appointing this satisfaction of Christ; 2. In a gracious acceptation of the decreed satisfaction in our stead; 3. In a free application of the death of Christ to us.' To which I answer," etc. So far he.

Though this may appear to be a distinct expression of my answer, yet because it seems to me that the very strength of it as laid down is omitted, I shall desire the reader to peruse it as it is there proposed, and it will give him some light into the thing in hand. I apply myself to what is here expressed, and answer:—

To the objection proposed from Grotius, as above, I gave a threefold answer:—

1. "That gracious condonation of sin, which I conceive to be the sum of the glad tidings of the gospel, seemeth to comprise those two acts before recounted, both which I there prove to be free, because the very merit and satisfaction of Christ himself was founded on a free compact and covenant or constitution."

Now, I had three reasons (among others) that prevailed with me to make gracious condonation of so large extent, which I shall express, and leave them to the thoughts of every judicious reader whether they are enforcing thereunto or no, being exceedingly indifferent what his determination is; for the weight of my answer depends not on it at all. And they are these:—

(1.) Because that single act of remission of sins to particular persons (which is nothing but a dissolution of the obligation of the law as unto them, whereby they are bound over to punishment), as it is commonly restrained, is affirmed by them whom Grotius in that book opposed (into whose tents he was afterward a renegado) to be inconsistent with any satisfaction at all; yea, that which Grotius maintains *per tantundem*. But now, if you extend that gospel phrase to the compass I have mentioned, they have not the least colour so to do.

(2.) Whereas the Scripture mentioneth that "through Christ is preached the forgiveness of sins," Acts xiii. 38, I do suppose that phrase to be comprehensive of the whole manifestation of God in the covenant of grace.

(3.) God expressly saith that this is his covenant, "That he will be merciful to our unrighteousness," Heb. viii. 12.

By the way, I cannot close with Mr B. that this place to the Hebrews, and the other of Jeremiah xxxi. 31–34, do comprise but part of the covenant, not the whole, God saying expressly, "This is my covenant." To say it is not, is not to interpret the word, but to deny it. It is true, it is not said that is the whole covenant; no more is it that Christ is the way, the truth, and the life only. As the want of that term of restriction doth not enlarge in that, no more doth the want of the note of universality restrain in this. To say thus because here is no condition expressed is προσκόπτειν εἰς χεῖρον. If you mean such a condition as God requireth of us, and yet worketh in us, it is there punctually expressed with reference to the nature of the covenant whereof it is a condition, which is to effect all the conditions thereof in the covenanters. This by the way, having resolvedly tied up myself from a debate of those positions which Mr B. dogmatizeth; though a large field, and easy to be walked in, lies open on every hand for the scattering of many magisterial dictates, which, with confidence enough, are crudely asserted.

This is (to return) my first answer to the fore-mentioned objection, with the reasons of it; whereunto Mr B. excepteth as followeth:—

1. "Pardon implieth Christ's death as a cause; but I would he had showed the Scripture that makes pardon so large a thing as to comprise the whole dispensation of grace, or that maketh Christ's death to be a part of it, or comprised in it.

2. "If such a word were in the Scripture, will he not confess it to be figurative and not proper, and so not fit for this dispute.

3. "Else when he saith, that Christ's death procured our pardon, he meaneth that it procured itself." So he.

To all which I say,—

1. The death of Christ, as it is a cause of pardon, is not once mentioned in any of my answers. There is a wide difference (in consideration) between God's imputation of sin to Christ, and the death of Christ as the meritorious cause of pardon. So that this is *pura ignoratio elenchi*.

2. Take pardon in the large sense I intimated, and so the death of Christ is not the meritorious cause of the whole, but only of that particular in it wherein it is commonly supposed solely to consist; of which before.

But in what sense, and upon what grounds, I extended gracious condonation of sin unto that compass here mentioned, I have now expressed. Let it stand or fall as it suits the judgment of the reader; the weight of my answer depends not on it at all.

My second answer to that objection I gave in these words:—

2. "That remission, grace, and pardon, which is in God for sinners, is not opposed to Christ's merits and satisfaction, but ours. He pardoneth all to us, but he spared not his only Son; he bated him not one farthing."

To this Mr B., thus expressing it, "But it is of grace to us, though not to Christ," answereth, "Doth not that clearly intimate that Christ was not in the obligation, that the law doth threaten every man personally, or else it had been no favour to accept it of another?"

(1.) It is marvellous to me, that a learned man should voluntarily choose an adversary to himself, and yet consider the very leaves which he undertakes to confute with so much contempt or oscitancy as to labour to prove against him what he positively asserts *terminis terminantibus*. That Christ was not in the obligation, that he was put in as a surety by his own consent, God by his sovereignty dispensing with the law as to that, yet as a creditor exacting of him the due debt of the law, is the main intendment of the place Mr Baxter here considereth.

(2.) Grant all that here is said, how doth it prove that Christ underwent not the very penalty of the law? Is it because he was not primarily in the obligation? He was put in as a surety, to be the object of its execution. Is it because the law doth threaten every man personally? Christ underwent really what was threatened to others, as shall be proved. But it is not then of favour to accept it. But this is the τὸ κρινόμενον. And thus to set it down is but a petition τοῦ ἐν ἀρχῇ.

(3.) How doth this elude the force of my answer? I see it not at all.

After this I gave a third answer to the former objection, manifesting how the freedom of pardon may consist with Christ's satisfaction, in these words:—

3. "The freedom, then, of pardon hath not its foundation in any defect of the merit or satisfaction of Christ, but in three other things:—

(1.) "The will of God freely appointing the satisfaction of Christ, John iii. 16; Rom. v. 8; 1 John iv. 9.

(2.) "In a gracious acceptation of that decreed satisfaction in our steads; so many, no more.

(3.) "In a free application of the death of Christ unto us. Remission, then, excludes not a full satisfaction by the solution of the very thing in the obligation, but only the solution or satisfaction of him to whom pardon and remission is granted."

It being the freedom of pardon that is denied, upon the supposals of such a satisfaction as I assert, I demonstrate from whence that freedom doth accrue unto it, notwithstanding a supposal of such a satisfaction: not that pardon consisteth in the three things there recounted, but that it hath its freedom from them; that is, supposing those three things, notwithstanding the intervention of payment made by Christ, it cannot be but remission of sin unto us be a free and gracious act.

To all this Mr B. opposeth divers things; for,—

1. "Imputation of righteousness," saith he, "is not any part of pardon, but a necessary antecedent.

2. "The same may be said of God's acceptation.

3. "Its application is a large phrase, and may be meant of several acts, but of which here I know not."

In a word, this mistake is very great. I affirm the freedom of a pardon to depend on those things. He answereth that pardon doth not consist in these things. It is the freedom of pardon, whence it is,—not the nature of pardon, wherein it is, that we have under consideration.

"But," saith he, "how can he call it a 'gracious acceptation,' a 'gracious imputation,' a 'free application,' if it were the same thing the law requireth that was paid?

"To pay all, according to the full exaction of the obligation, needeth no favour to procure acceptance, imputation, or application. Can justice refuse to accept of such a payment? or can it require any more?"

1. Though I know not directly what it is he means by saying, "I call it," yet I pass it over.

2. If all this were done by the persons themselves, or any one in their stead procured and appointed by themselves, then were there some difficulty in these questions; but this being otherwise, there is none at all, as hath been declared.

3. How the payment made by Christ was of grace, yet in respect of the obligation of the law needed no favour, nor was refusable by justice, supposing its free constitution, shall be afterward declared. To me the author seems not to have his wonted clearness in this whole section, which might administer occasion of farther inquiry and exceptions, but I forbear.

And thus much be spoken for the clearing and vindicating my answer to the arguments of Grotius against Christ's paying the *idem* of the obligation. The next shall farther confirm the truth.

CHAPTER IV.

Farther of the matter of the satisfaction of Christ; wherein is proved that it was the same that was in the obligation.

It being supposed not to be sufficient to have showed the weakness of my endeavour to assert and vindicate from opposition what I had undertaken, Mr Baxter addeth that I give up the cause about which I contend, as having indeed not understood him whom I undertook to oppose, in these words:—"Mr Owen giveth up the cause at last, and saith as Grotius, having not understood Grotius' meaning, as appeareth, pp. 141, 143" [268, 270].

Whether I understand Grotius or no will by-and-by appear. Whether Mr B. understandeth me, or the controversy by me handled, you shall have now a trial.

The assertion which alone I seek to maintain is this:—

"That the punishment which our Saviour underwent was the same that the law required of us, God relaxing his law as to the person suffering, but not as to the penalty suffered."

Now, if from this I draw back in any of the concessions following, collected from pp. 141, 143 [268, 270], I deprecate not the censure of giving up the cause I contended for. If otherwise, there is a great mistake in somebody of the whole business.

Of the things, then, observe, according to Mr B.'s order, I shall take a brief account:—

1. "He acknowledgeth," saith he, "that the payment is not made by the party to whom remission is granted; and so saith every man that is a Christian."

This is a part of the position itself I maintain, and so no going back from it; so that as to this I may pass as a "Christian."

2. "He saith," adds he, "'it was a full, valuable compensation;' therefore not of the same."

First, This inference would trouble Mr B. to prove.

Secondly, Therefore not made by the same, nor by any of the debtor's appointment, will follow, perhaps, but no more.

3. "That by reason of the obligation upon us, we ourselves were bound to undergo the punishment. Therefore, Christ's punishment was not in the obligation, but only ours; and so the law was not fully executed, but relaxed."

First, This is my thesis fully: The law was executed as to its penalty, relaxed as to the person suffering.

Secondly, The punishment that Christ underwent was in the obligation, though threatened to us.

4. "He saith, he meaneth not that Christ bore the same punishment due to us in all accidents of duration, and the like, but the same in weight and measure; therefore, not the same in the obligation, because not fully the same act."

The accidents I mention follow and attend the person suffering, and not the penalty itself. All evils in any suffering, as far as they are sinful, attend the condition of the parties that suffer. Every thing usually recounted by those who make this and the like exceptions, as far as they are purely penal, were on Christ.

5. "He saith God had power so far to relax his own law as to have the name of a surety put into the obligation, which before was not there, and then to require the whole debt of that surety. And what saith Grotius more than this? If the same things in the obligation be paid, then the law is executed; and if executed, then not relaxed. Here he confesseth that the surety's name was not in the obligation, and that God relaxed the law to put it in. Now, the main business that Grotius drives at there is, to prove this relaxation of the law, and the non-execution of it on the offenders threatened." Thus far Mr Baxter.

First, All this proves not at all the things intended, neither doth any concession here mentioned in the least take off from the main assertion I maintain, as is apparent to any at first view. Secondly, Grotius is so far from saying more than I do, that he says not so much. Thirdly, This paralogism, "If the law be executed, then not relaxed," and on the contrary, ariseth merely from a non-consideration of the nature of contradictories. The opposition fancied here is not πρὸς τὸ αὐτό, κατὰ τὸ αὐτό, ὡσαύτως καὶ ἐν τῷ αὐτῷ χρόνῳ, as is required of contradictions. Fourthly,

The observation, that Grotius' main business is otherwise discovereth the bottom of Mr B.'s mistake, even a supposal that I should oppose Grotius in his main intendment in the place considered; which was not once in my thoughts. It was merely about the nature of the penalty that Christ underwent that I discoursed. How the relaxation of the law as to the commutation of persons may be established, whether we affirm Christ to have paid the *idem* or *tantundem*, and that Mr B. affirms the same with me, I can prove by twenty instances. The reader, if he please, may consult p. 18, and pp. 25, 33–35, 42, 48; and, in plain terms, p. 81, "In respect of punishment abstracting from persons, the law was not dispensed withal as to Christ." And what said I more?

And so much, if not too much, to Mr Baxter's exceptions; which of what weight and force they are, I leave to others to judge.

That which I maintain as to this point in difference I have also made apparent. It is wholly comprised under these two heads,—first, Christ suffered the same penalty which was in the obligation; secondly, To do so is to make payment *ejusdem*, and not *tantidem*.

The reasons of both I shall briefly subjoin. And first, as to the first, they are these following:—1. The Scripture hath expressly revealed the translation of punishment in respect of the subjects suffering it, but hath not spoken one word of the change of the kind of punishment, but rather the contrary is affirmed: Rom. viii. 32, "He spared not his own Son, but delivered him up for us all."

2. All the punishment due to us was contained in the curse and sanction of the law; that is, the penalty of the obligation whereof we spake. But this was undergone by the Lord Christ; for "he hath redeemed us from the curse of the law, being made a curse for us," Gal. iii. 13.

3. Where God condemneth sin, there he condemns it in that very punishment which is due unto it in the sinner, or rather to the sinner for it. He hath revealed but one rule of his proceeding in this case. Now, he condemned sin in the flesh of Christ, or in him sent in the likeness of sinful flesh: Rom. viii. 3, "God sending his own Son in the likeness of sinful flesh, and for sin, condemned sin in the flesh." The condemning of sin is the infliction of punishment due to sin.

4. The whole penalty of sin is death, Gen. ii. 17. This Christ underwent for us: Heb. ii. 9, "He tasted death." And to die for another is to undergo that death which that other should have undergone, 2 Sam. xviii. 33. It is true, this death may be considered either in respect of its essence (if I may be allowed so to speak), which is called the "pains of hell," which Christ underwent, Ps. cxvi. 3, xxii. 1, Luke xxii. 44; or of its attendancies, as duration and the like, which he could not undergo, Ps. xvi. 8–11, Acts ii. 24–28. So that whereas eternal death may be considered two ways, either as such *in potentia*, and in its own nature, or as actually, so our Saviour underwent it not in the latter, but first sense, Heb. ii. 9, 14, which, by the dignity of his person, 1 Pet. iii. 18, Heb. ix. 26, 28, Rom. v. 10, which raises the estimation of punishment, is *æquipotent* to the other. There is a sameness in Christ's sufferings with that in the obligation in respect of essence, and equivalency in respect of attendancies.

5. In the meeting of our iniquities upon Christ, Isa. liii. 6, and his being thereby made sin for us, 2 Cor. v. 21, lay the very punishment of our sin, as to us threatened, upon him.

6. Consider the scriptural descriptions you have of his perpessions, and see if they do not plainly hold out the utmost that ever was threatened to sin. There is the חַבּוּרָה, Isa. liii. 5; Peter's *μώλωψ*, 1 Pet. ii. 24; the "livor, vibex," "wound, stripe," that in our stead was so on him,—that whereby we are healed. Those expressions of the condition of his soul in his sufferings, whereby he is said *λυπεῖσθαι*, Matt. xxvi. 37; *ἐκθαμβεῖσθαι*, *ἀδημονεῖν*, Mark xiv. 33; *θρόμβοι αἵματος ἐν τῇ ἀγωνίᾳ*, Luke xxii. 44; sadness unto death, Matt. xxvi. 38; that dreadful cry, "Why hast

thou forsaken me?"—those cries out of the deep, and mighty supplications under his fear, Heb. v. 7, that was upon him, do all make out that the bitterness of the death due to sin was fully upon his soul. Sum all his outward appearing pressures, mocks, scoffs, scorns, cross, wounds, death, etc., and what do some of their afflictions who have suffered for his name come short of it? And yet how far were they above those dreadful expressions of anguish which we find upon the "Fellow of the Lord of hosts," the "Lion of the tribe of Judah," who received not the Spirit by measure, but was anointed with the oil of gladness above his fellows! Certainly his inconceivable sufferings were in another kind, and such as set no example to any of his to suffer in after him. It was no less than the weight of the wrath of God and the whole punishment due to sin that he wrestled under.

Secondly, The second part of my position is to me confirmed by these and the like arguments.

That there is a distinction to be allowed between the penalty and the person suffering is a common apprehension, especially when the nature of the penalty is only inquired after. If a man that had but one eye were censured to have an eye put out, and a dear friend, pitying his deplorable condition, knowing that by undergoing the punishing decreed he must be left to utter blindness, should, upon the allowance of commutation, as in Zaleucus' case, submit to have one of his own eyes put out, and so satisfy the sentence given, though, by having two eyes, he avoid himself the misery that would have attended the other's suffering, who had but one;—if, I say, in this case, any should ask whether he underwent the *idém* the other should have done, or *tantundem,* I suppose the answer would be easy. In things real, it is unquestionable; and in things personal I shall pursue it no farther, lest it should prove a strife of words. And thus far of the sufferings of Christ in a way of controversy. What follows will be more positive.

CHAPTER V.

The second head; about justification before believing.

THE next thing I am called into question about, is concerning actual and absolute justification before believing. This Mr Baxter speaks to, page 146, and so forward; and first answers the arguments of Maccovius for such justification, and then, page 151, applies himself to remove such farther arguments and places of Scripture as are by me produced for the confirmation of that assertion.

Here, perhaps, I could have desired a little more candour. To have an opinion fastened on me which I never once received nor intimated the least thought of in that whole treatise, or any other of mine, and then my arguments answered as to such an end and purpose as I not once intended to promote by them, is a little too harsh dealing. It is a facile thing to render any man's reasonings exceedingly weak and ridiculous, if we may impose upon them such and such things to be proved by them, which their author never once intended. For pactional justification, evangelical justification, whereby a sinner is completely justified, that it should precede believing, I have not only not asserted but positively denied, and disproved by many arguments. To be now traduced as a patron of that opinion, and my reasons for it publicly answered, seems to me something uncouth; however, I am resolved not to interpose in other men's disputes and differences. Yet, lest I should be again and farther mistaken in this, I shall briefly give in my thoughts to the whole difficulty, after I have discovered and discussed the ground and occasion of this mistake.

In an answer to an argument of Grotius about the satisfaction of Christ, denying that by it we are *ipso facto* delivered from the penalty due to sin, I affirmed that by his death Christ did actually, or *ipso facto*, deliver us from the curse, by being made a curse for us: and this is that which gave occasion to that imputation before mentioned.

To clear my mind in this, I must desire the reader to consider that my answer is but a denial of Grotius' assertions In what kind and respect Grotius doth there deny that we are *ipso facto* delivered by the satisfaction of Christ, in that sense, and that only, do I affirm that we are so; otherwise, there were no contradictions between his assertion and mine, not speaking *ad idem* and *eodem respectu*. The truth is, Grotius doth not, in that place whence this argument is taken, fully or clearly manifest what he intends by deliverance which is not actual or *ipso facto;* and, therefore, I made bold to interpret his mind by the analogy of that opinion wherewith he was thoroughly infected about the death of Christ. According to that, Christ delivering us by his satisfaction, not actually nor *ipso facto*, is so to make satisfaction for us as that we shall have no benefit by his death but upon the performance of a condition, which himself by that death of his did not absolutely procure. This was that which I opposed; and therefore affirmed that Christ by his death did actually, or *ipso facto*, deliver us.

Let the reader, then, here observe,—

1. That our deliverance is to be referred to the death of Christ, according to its own causality,—that is, as a cause meritorious. Now, such causes do actually and *ipso facto* produce all those effects which immediately flow from them; not in an immediation of time but causality. Look, then, what effects do follow, or what things soever are procured by them, without the interposition of any other cause in the same kind, they are said to be procured by them actually, or *ipso facto*.

2. That I have abundantly proved, in the treatise mentioned, that if the fruits of the death of Christ be to be communicated unto us upon a condition, and that condition to be among those fruits, and be itself to be absolutely communicated upon no condition, then all the fruits of the death of Christ are as absolutely procured for them for whom he died as if no condition had been prescribed; for these things come all to one.

3. I have proved in the same place that faith, which is this condition, is itself procured by the death of Christ for them for whom he died, to be freely bestowed on them, without the prescription of any such condition as on whose fulfilling the collation of it should depend.

These things being considered, as I hoped they would have been by every one that should undertake to censure any thing, as to this business, in that treatise (they being there all handled at large), it is apparent what I intended by this actual deliverance,—namely, That the Lord Jesus, by the satisfaction and merit of his death and oblation, made for all and only his elect, hath actually and absolutely purchased and procured for them all spiritual blessings of grace and glory; to be made out unto them, and bestowed upon them, in God's way and time, without dependence on any condition to be by them performed, not absolutely procured for them thereby; whereby they become to have a right unto the good things by him purchased, to be in due time possessed, according to God's way, method, and appointment.

From a faithful adherence unto this persuasion, I see nothing as yet of the least efficacy or force to dissuade me; and am bold to tell those concerned therein, that their conditional satisfaction, or their suspending the fruits of the death of Christ upon conditions, as though the Lord should give him to die for us upon condition of such and such things, is a vain figment, contrary to the Scriptures, inconsistent in itself, and destructive of the true value and virtue of the death of Christ: which, by the Lord's assistance, I shall be ready at any time to demonstrate.

My intention in the place excepted against being cleared, I shall now tender my thoughts to these two things:—

1. The distinct consideration of the acts of the will of God, before and after the satisfaction of Christ, as also before and after our believing, towards us, as unto justification.

2. The distinct estate of the sinner upon that consideration, with what is the right to the fruits of the death of Christ which the elect of God have before believing.

CHAPTER VI.

Of the acts of God's will towards sinners, antecedent and consequent to the satisfaction of Christ—Of Grotius' judgment herein.

THE distinct consideration of the acts of God's will in reference to the satisfaction of Christ and our believing, according to the former proposal, is the first thing to be considered.

Grotius, who with many, and in an especial manner with Mr Baxter, is of very great account, and that in theology, distinguisheth (as himself calls them with a school term) "three moments" or instances of the divine will:—

1. "Before [1] the death of Christ, either actually accomplished, or in the purpose and foreknowledge of God. In this instance," he saith, "God is angry with the sinner, but so as that he is not averse from all ways of laying down his anger."

2. "Upon [2] the death of Christ, or that being supposed; wherein God not only purposeth but also promiseth to lay aside his anger."

3. "When [3] a man by true faith believeth in Christ, and Christ, according to the tenor of the covenant, commendeth him to God. Here now God lays aside his anger, and receiveth man into favour." Thus far he.

Amongst all the attempts of distinguishing the acts of God's will in reference unto Christ and sinners, whatever I considered, I never found any more slight, atheological, and discrepant from the truth than this of Grotius.

To [4] measure the Almighty by the standard of a man, and to frame in the mind a mutable idol, instead of the eternal, unchangeable God, is a thing that the fleshly reasonings of dark understandings are prone unto;—to feign the Lord in one instant angry, afterward promising to cease to be so, then in another instant laying down his anger, and taking up a contrary affection: and you seem to me to do no less.

What it may be esteemed in law, which was that author's faculty, I know not; but suppose in divinity that (notwithstanding the manifold attempts of some ἀκίνητα κινεῖν in most heads of religion) [5] the ascribing unto the Most Holy things alien and opposite unto his glorious nature, is, by common consent, accounted no less than blasphemy.[6] Whether this be here done or no, may easily appear. I hope, then, without the offence of any, I may be allowed to call those dictates of Grotius to the rule and measure of truth.

I. "Before the foresight of the death of Christ," saith he, "God is angry with sinners, but not wholly averse from all ways of laying aside that anger." To which I answer,—

1. That God should be conceived angry after the manner of men, or with any

[1] "Distinguenda sunt tria momenta divinæ voluntatis. Primum est, ante Christi mortem positam aut re ipsa, aut in decreto Dei et præscientia. In hoc momento iratus peccatori est Deus, sed ita, ut non aversetur omnes iræ deponendæ vias, ac rationes."

[2] "Secundum momentum est, positâ jam Christi morte, in quo Deus jam non constituit tantum, sed et promittit iram se depositurum."

[3] "Tertium est, cum homo verâ fide in Christum credit, et Christus ex fœderis formula credentem Deo commendat. Hic jam Deus deponit iram, hominemque id gratiam recipit."—De Satisfact. Christi, cap. vii.

[4] Ps. l. 21; Exod. iii. 14; 1 Sam. xv. 29: Job xxiii. 13; Ps. cii. 26, 27; Isa. xiv. 27.

[5] 2 Kings xix. 6; Isa. xxxvii. 3; 1 Tim. i. 13.

[6] "Quicunque negat aliquid de Deo, quod ei convenit, vel asserit de eo, quod ei non convenit, derogat divinæ bonitati, et est blasphemus."—Thom. 22, æ. q. 13, a. 1. c.

such kind of passion, is gross Anthropomorphism,[1]—as bad, if not worse than the assigning of him a bodily shape. [2] The anger of God is a pure act of his will, whereby he will effect and inflict the effects of anger. Now, what is before the foresight of the death of Christ is certainly from eternity. God's anger must respect either the purpose of God or the effects of it. The latter it cannot be, for they are undoubtedly all temporal. It must be, then, his purpose from eternity to inflict punishment that is the effect of anger. This, then, is the first thing in the business of redemption assigned by Grotius unto the Lord,—namely, he purposed from eternity to inflict punishment on sinners. And on what sinners? Even on those for whom he gives Christ to die, and afterward receives into favour, as he expresseth himself. Behold here a mystery of Vorstian theology; God changing his eternal purposes! [3] This Arminius at first could not down withal; inferring from hence that the will of God differed not from his essence;—that every act thereof is, first, most simple; secondly, infinite; thirdly, eternal; fourthly, immutable; fifthly, holy. Reason itself would fain speak in this cause, but that the scriptures do so abound. Many places are noted in the margin.[4] James i. 17; 2 Tim. ii. 19; Ps. xxxiii. 9-11; Acts xv. 18, etc., may be added. A mutable god is of the dunghill.

2. That the death of Christ is not comprised in the first consideration of God's mind and act of his will towards sinners to be saved, is assumed gratis.

3. "He is not," saith he, "averse from all ways of laying down this anger." This scheme Grotius placeth, as is evident, in God, as the foundation and bottom of sending Christ for our redemption. This he immediately subjoins, without the least intimation of any farther inclination in God towards sinners, for whom he gives his Son. But,—

(1.) This is a mere negation of inflicting anger for the present, or a suspension of that affection from working according to its quality; which how it can be ascribed to the pure and active will of God I know not.[5] Yea, it is above disproved.

(2.) Such a kind of frame, as it is injurious to God so to be held out as the fountain of his sending Christ to die for us, is, I am persuaded, an abhorrency to Christians. And,—

(3.) Whether this answer that which the Scripture holds out as the most intense distinguishing love, John iii. 16; Rom. v. 8, viii. 32; 1 John iv. 9, 10, is easily discernible. A natural velleity to the good of the creature is the thing here couched, but was never proved.

II. "In the second instance, God," saith he, "the death of Christ being supposed, not only determineth, but also promiseth to lay aside his anger."

1. What terms can be invented to hold out more expressly a change and alteration in the unchangeable God than these here used, I know not.

2. That the will or mind of God is altered, from one respect towards us to another, by the consideration of the death of Christ, is a low, carnal conception. The will of God is not moved by any thing without itself.[6] Alterations are in the things altered, not in the will of God concerning them.

3. To make this the whole effect of the death of Christ, that God should determine and promise to lay aside his wrath, is no Scripture discovery,[7] either as to name or thing.

4. The purposes of God, which are all eternal, and the promises of God, which are all made in time, are very inconveniently ranged in the same series.

1 Quæ dicuntur ἀνθρωποπαθῶς intelligenda sunt θεοπρεπῶς. Amor et gaudium, et alia ejusmodi, cum attribuuntur Deo, significant simplicem actum voluntatis, cum similitudine effectus, absque passione.—Aquin. 12. q. 22. a. 3.

2 Libera voluntas ulciscendæ injuriæ.—Eph. i. 11.

3 Arm. Disp. Pub. de Natur. Dei, thes. 51.

4 What has become of the references alluded to, it is difficult to say.—Ed.

5 Eph. i. 13.

6 Aliud est mutare voluntatem, aliud velle aliquarum rerum mutationem.

7 Matt. xviii. 11; 1 Tim. i. 15; Eph. v. 25-27, ii. 15, 16; Col. i. 13; 1 John i. 7, etc.

5. That by the death of Christ atonement is made, everlasting redemption purchased, that God is reconciled, a right unto freedom obtained, for those for whom he died, shall be afterward declared.

6. If God doth only purpose and promise to lay aside his anger upon the death of Christ, but doth it not until our actual believing,—then, first, our faith is the proper procuring cause of reconciliation, the death of Christ but a requisite antecedent; which is not the Scripture phrase, Rom. v. 10; 2 Cor. v. 18; Eph. ii. 16; Col. i. 20, 21; Dan. ix. 24; Heb. ii. 17; Eph. i. 7; Heb. ix. 12. Secondly, how comes the sinner by faith, if it is the gift of God?[1] It must be an issue of anger and enmity; for that scheme only is actually ascribed to him before our enjoyment of it. Strange! that God should be so far reconciled as to give us faith, that we may be reconciled to him, that thereupon he may be reconciled to us.

III. For the third instance,—of God's receiving the sinner into love and favour upon his believing, quite laying aside his anger,—I answer, to waive the Anthropomorphism wherewith this assertion is tainted as the former, if by receiving into favour he intend absolute, complete, pactional justification, being an act of favour quitting the sinner from the guilt of sin, charged by the accusation of the law, terminated in the conscience of a sinner, I confess it, in order of nature, to follow our believing.

I might consider farther the attempts of others for the right stating of this business, but it would draw me beyond my intention. His failings herein who is so often mentioned and so much used by him who gives occasion to this rescript, I could not but remark. What are my own thoughts and apprehensions of the whole, I shall in the next place briefly impart.

Now, to make way hereunto, some things I must suppose; which, though some of them otherwhere controverted, yet not at all in reference to the present business: and they are these:—

That Christ died only for the elect; or, God gave his Son to die only for those whom he chooseth for life and salvation, for the praise of his glorious grace.

This is granted by Mr Baxter, where he affirms, "That Christ bare not punishment for them who must bear punishment themselves in eternal fire," thes. 33, p. 162; and again, "Christ died not for final unbelief," thes. 33, p. 159: therefore, not for them who are finally unbelievers, as all non-elected are and shall be. For what sinners he died, he died for all their sins, Rom. v. 6–8; 2 Cor. v. 21; 1 John i. 7.

If any shall say, that as he died not for the final unbelief of others, so not for the final unbelief of the elect, and so not for final unbelief at all, I answer,—

First, If by final unbelief you mean that which is actually so, Christ satisfied not for it. His satisfaction cannot be extended to those things whose existence is prevented by his merit. The omission of this, in the consideration of the death of Christ, lies at the bottom of many mistakes. Merit and satisfaction are of equal extent as to their objects; both also tend to the same end, but in sundry respects.

Secondly, If by final unbelief you understand that which would be so, notwithstanding all means and remedies, were it not for the death of Christ, so he did satisfy for it, its existence being prevented by his merit. So, then, if Christ died not for final unbelief, he died not for the finally unbelieving. Though the satisfaction of his death hath not paid for it, the merit of his death would remove it.

Thirdly, I suppose that the means as well as the ends, grace as glory, are the purchase and procurement of Jesus Christ. See this proved in my treatise of Redemption, lib. iii. cap. 4, etc.

Fourthly, That God is absolutely immutable and unchangeable in all his attributes; neither doth his will admit of any alteration. This proved above.

[1] Eph. ii. 8; Phil. i. 29.

Fifthly, That the will of God is not moved, properly, by any external cause whatsoever, unto any of its acts, whether immanent or transient; for,—

1. By [1]a moving cause we understand a cause morally efficient; and if any thing were so properly in respect of any act of God's will, then the act, which is the will of God acting, must in some respect,—namely, as it is an effect,—be less worthy, and inferior to the cause; for so is every effect in respect to its cause. And,—

2. Every effect produced proceedeth from a passive possibility unto the effect; which can no way be assigned unto God. Besides, it must be temporary; for nothing that is eternal can have dependence upon that whose rise is in time. And such are all things external to the will of God, even the merit of Christ himself.

3. I cannot imagine how there can be any other cause why God willeth any thing than why he not willeth or willeth not other things; which for any to assign will be found difficult, Matt. xi. 25, 26, xx. 15. So, then, when God willeth one thing for another, as our salvation for the death of Christ, the one is the cause of the other; neither moveth the will of God. Hence,—

Sixthly, All alterations are in the things concerning which the acts of the will of God are; none in the will of God itself.

These things being premised, what was before proposed I shall now in order make out, beginning with the eternal acts of the will of God towards us, antecedent to all or any consideration of the death of Christ.

CHAPTER VII.

In particular of the will of God towards them for whom Christ died, and their state and condition as considered antecedaneous to the death of Christ and all efficiency thereof.

First, then, the habitude of God towards man, antecedent to all foresight of the death of Christ, is an act of supreme sovereignty and dominion, appointing them, by means suited to the manifestation of his glorious properties, according to his infinitely wise and free disposal, to eternal life and salvation, for the praise of his glorious grace.

That this salvation was never but one, or of one kind, consisting in the same kind of happiness, in reference unto God's appointment, needs not much proving. To think that God appointed one kind of condition for man if he had continued in innocency, and another upon his recovery from the fall, is to think that his prescience is but conjectural and his will alterable.

In this instance, then, we suppose no kind of affection in God, properly so called, no changeable resolution, no inclinableness and propensity of nature to the good of the creature in general, no frame of being angry, with only a non-averseness to the laying down of his anger, etc.; all which, and the like, are derogatory to the infinite perfection of God;—nor yet any act of pitying and pardoning mercy, much less any quitting or clearing of sinners, whereby they should be justified from eternity; the permission of sin itself in the purpose of it being not presupposed, but included in this habitude of God's will towards man, to make it complete;—neither any absolute intention of doing good unto man, without respect unto Christ and his merits, they referring to the good to be done, not to his appointment; for by them is this purpose of his to be accomplished. Nor, lastly, doth it contain any actual relaxation, suspension, or abrogation of that law and its penalties by which it is his will the creature shall be regulated, in reference to the person concerning whom this act of his will is; they standing, indeed, in that relation thereunto, as, in

[1] Cum voluntas sit ejus essentia, non movetur ab alio a se, sed a se tantum, eo modo loquendi, quo intelligere, et velle, dicitur motus, et secundum hoc Plato dixit, primum movens movet seipsum.—Aq. p. 1, q. 19, a. 2, a. 3.

the season of their existence, their several conditions expose them to, by virtue of the first constitution of that law.

But it is such an act of his will as in the Scripture is termed πρόγνωσις, Acts ii. 23; Rom. viii. 29; 1 Pet. i. 20;—πρόθεσις, Rom. viii. 28, ix 11; Eph iii. 11;—εὐδοκία, Matt. xi. 26; Eph. i. 5; 2 Thess. i. 11; Luke xii. 32;—βουλὴ θελήματος, Eph. i. 11;—θεμέλιος τοῦ Θεοῦ, 2 Tim. ii. 19;—προορισμός, Eph. i. 5, 11; Rom. viii. 29;—ordination or appointment unto life, Acts xiii. 48; 1 Thess. v. 5, 9. All which, and divers other expressions, point at the same thing.

Divines commonly, in one word, call it his "decree of election," and sometimes, according to Scripture, "election" itself, Eph. i. 4. Neither doth the word hold out any habitude of God towards man, antecedaneous to all efficiency of the death of Christ, but only this. I speak of them only, in this whole discourse, for whom he died.

That this is an act of sovereignty or supreme dominion, and not of mercy, properly so called, hath been by others abundantly proved. And this I place as the *causa*, προηγουμένη, of the satisfaction of Christ, and the whole dispensation of making out love unto us, through various acts of mercy.

This in the Scripture is called the "love" of God, Rom. ix. 13, and is set out as the most intense love that ever he beareth to any of his creatures, John iii. 16; Rom. v. 8; 1 John iv. 9, 10; being, indeed, as properly love as love can be assigned unto God. His love is but an act of his will, whereby θέλει τινὶ τ' ἀγαθόν· and in respect of effects (in which respect chiefly affections are ascribed unto God), it hath the most eminent possible. Now, this being discriminating, can no way be reconciled with the common affection before disproved.

For the order and series of the purposes of God, as most natural for our apprehension of God, and agreeable to his own infinite wisdom, tending to the completing of this love in all its issues and fruits, as it is more curious perhaps in the framing than necessary to be known, so certainly it would be too long and intricate a work for me to discuss at present, in reference to this intendment. Only, in general, this must be granted, that all the thoughts of God concerning the way of accomplishing this act of his will must be subordinate hereunto, as comprising the end, and co-ordinate among themselves, as being concerning the means.

In particular, the constitution or appointment of the covenant of free grace, for the recovery and bringing home unto God of fallen man, hath immediate dependence thereon; I mean in that way of dependence which their order gives unto them. I cannot assent to what Mr Baxter hath asserted in this matter, thes. 14, expl. p. 90. "The satisfaction of Christ," saith he, "to the law goes before the new covenant, though not in regard of its payment, which was in the fulness of time, yet in undertaking, acceptance, and efficacy: there could be no treating on new terms until the old obligation was satisfied and suspended."

Had he attempted the proof of this assertion, perhaps he would have found it a more difficult undertaking than barely to affirm it. Some few reasons to the contrary that present themselves I shall briefly set down:—

1. Christ himself, with his whole satisfaction and merit, is included in the covenant; therefore, his satisfaction is not antecedent to the covenant. The first appeareth, in that all promises of pardoning mercy are in and of this new covenant, Heb. viii. 10–12; but now, in them, as the foundation of that mercy, is Christ himself, with his satisfaction, comprised, Gen. iii. 15; Isa. ix. 6, 7.

2. He who in all that he is, as made unto us, was the Mediator of the new covenant, and whose merit and satisfaction, in all that they are, are appointed for the procuring the mercies of the new covenant, his satisfaction is not antecedent to the covenant, Heb. vii. 22, viii. 6, etc

3. The constitution of the new covenant, as it is in the purpose of God, is the rise and fountain of giving Christ with his satisfaction for us. It is in the purpose of

God to save us, through faith, by pardoning mercy: in the pursuit of that design, and for the praise of that glorious grace, is Christ given, John iii. 16; Rom. viii. 32. Or thus:—

4. If the designation of that way of life and salvation which is administered by the gospel be antecedent to the satisfaction of Christ, then the satisfaction of Christ is not antecedent to the new covenant; for nothing can be before and after the same thing. Understand the designation of the way of life, and the satisfaction of Christ, in the same order of decree or execution; now the supposal is manifest,—the satisfaction of Christ being appointed as the means of accomplishing that way of life.

If Mr Baxter intendeth those latter words, "There could be no treating on new terms before the old obligation was satisfied or suspended," as a proof of his former assertion, he will fail in his intendment, as I suppose; for,—

1. Treating on new terms denoteth either *consilium ineundi fœderis*, or *exequendi*. If the first, it is nothing but the purpose of God to save his elect by pardoning mercy, for the praise of his glorious grace. This is wholly antecedent to any efficiency of the death and satisfaction of Christ, as being of mere and absolute grace, Jer. xxxi. 3; Heb. viii. 7, 8. If the latter be intended, or the actual taking of sinners into covenant, by working an acceptance of it upon their spirits, and obedience to the condition of it in their hearts, then, though the satisfaction of Christ be an antecedent hereunto, yet it is not thence antecedent to the new covenant; for the new covenant, and taking into covenant, are distinct.

This, then, being assigned unto God, after our manner of apprehension, the next inquiry is into the state and condition of those persons who are the peculiar object of the act of God's will before described, in reference thereunto, antecedaneous to all consideration of the death of Christ, and all efficacy thereof.

The Scripture, speaking of them in this condition, saith that they are "beloved," Rom. ix. 13, xi. 28; "elected," Eph. i. 4; "ordained to eternal life," Acts xiii. 48; 2 Thess. ii. 13. Whether only the eternal actings of the will of God towards them [be intended], or also their own change, either actual, in respect of real state and condition, or relative, in reference to the purpose of God, is not certainly evident. Hereunto, then, I propose these two things:—

1. By the eternal love, purpose, and act of God's will towards them that shall be saved (who are so from thence), they are not actually changed from that condition which is common to them with all the sons of men after the fall.

2. By virtue of that love alone, they have not so much as personal right unto any of those things which are the proper effects of that love, and which it produceth in due season, beseemingly to the wisdom and justice of God.

Either of these assertions shall be briefly proved.

1. For the first, it is manifest,—

(1.) From the act of God's will, which to this love is contradistinct. What change is wrought in the loved or elected by the purpose of God according to election, an answerable change must be wrought in the hated and appointed to condemnation by the decree of reprobation. Now, that this should really alter the condition of men, and actually dispose them under the consequences of that purpose, cannot be granted.

(2.) Analogy from other eternal purposes of God gives a demonstration hereof. The eternal purposes of the divine will for the creation of the world out of nothing left that nothing as very nothing as ever, until an act of almighty power gave, in the beginning, existence and being to the things that are seen. Things have their certain futurition, not instant actual existence, from the eternal purposes of God concerning them.

(3.) The Scripture plainly placeth all men in the same state and condition before conversion and reconciliation. "We have proved both Jews and Gentiles, that they are all under sin," Rom. iii. 9. So "every mouth is stopped, and all the world is become guilty before God," verse 19; all being "by nature children of wrath," Eph. ii. 3. The condition of all in unregeneracy is really one and the same. Those who think it is a mistaken apprehension in the elect to think so, are certainly too much mistaken in that apprehension. "He that believeth not the Son, the wrath of God abideth on him," John iii. 36. If the misapprehension be, as they say it is, unbelief, it leaves them in whom it is under the wrath of God. He that would see this farther cleared and confirmed may consult my treatise of Redemption, lib. iii. cap. 8, where it is purposely and expressly handled at large.

Hence Mr Baxter may have some directions how to dispose of that censure concerning me, which yet he is pleased to say that he suspendeth, p. 158,—namely, That I should affirm justification to be nothing but the manifestation of eternal love; which I have more than in one place or two expressly opposed. That any one should but here and there consult a few lines or leaves of my treatise, I no way blame,—in such things we all use our liberty,—but upon so slight a view as cannot possibly represent the frame, structure, and coherence of my judgment in any particular, to undertake a confutation and censure of it, cannot well be done without some regret to candid ingenuity.

2. For the second assertion laid down, which goeth something farther than the former, it is easily deduced from the same principles therewithal. I shall therefore add only one argument for the confirmation thereof.

God having appointed that his eternal love, in the fruits thereof, should be no otherwise communicated but only in and by Christ, all right thereunto must of necessity be of his procurement and purchasing. Yea, the end of the mediation of the Lord Jesus is to give right, title, and possession, in their several order and seasons, unto and in all the fruits, issues, and tendencies of that love unto them whose mediator he is appointed to be.

Thus far, then, all is seated in the bosom of the Almighty, all differencing acts of grace flowing from hence being to be made out as seems good unto him in his infinite wise sovereignty; from whence alone is the disposal of all these things, as to that order which may most conduce to his glory. And this also writes vanity upon the objection insisted on by Mr Baxter, p. 157, that when we have a right we must presently have a possession; all these things being to be moderated according to his free, sovereign disposal.

And this concerneth the first instant proposed.

CHAPTER VIII.

Of the will of God in reference to them for whom Christ died, immediately upon the consideration of his death; and their state and condition before actual believing in relation thereunto.

THE second instance proposed to be considered is in the immediate issue of the death of Christ, as proposed and accomplished. Purpose and accomplishment are, indeed, different, but their effects in respect of God are the same. In reference to us, also, the death of Christ hath the same efficacy as promised and as performed. What acts the Scripture ascribes unto God, antecedent unto any consideration of the death of Christ, or at least such as are absolutely free and of sovereignty, without any influence of causality from thence, we saw before; for as for the order of God's decrees compared among themselves, I will not with any one contend. Here we inquire what it holdeth out of him, *that* being in all its efficacy supposed. And we affirm,—

1. That the will of God is not moved to any thing thereby, nor changed into any other respect towards those for whom Christ died than what it had before. This was formerly proved, and must again be touched on. But,—

2. The death of Christ [being] proposed and accounted effectual, as before, God can, agreeable to his infinite justice, wisdom, truth, and appointment, make out unto sinners for whom Christ died, or was to die, all those good things which he before purposed and willed by such means to them; those things being purchased and procured, and all hinderances of bestowing them being removed, by that satisfaction and merit which, by free compact, he agreed and consented should be in that death of Christ.

3. That as [to] the making out of all spiritual blessings, first proposed by the Father, then purchased by the Son, that they might be bestowed condecently to divine justice, God hath reserved it to his own sovereign disposal. That it be done so that they for whom this whole dispensation is appointed may really enjoy the fruits of it, is all that necessarily is included either in the purpose or purchase.

Hence it is that the discharge of the debtor doth not immediately follow the payment of the debt by Christ; not because that payment is refusable, but because in that very covenant and compact from whence it is that the death of Christ is a payment, God reserveth to himself this right and liberty to discharge the debtor when and how he pleaseth,—I mean as to times and seasons: for otherwise the means of actual freedom are procured by that payment, though not considered merely as a payment, which denotes only satisfaction, but as it had adjoined merit also.

Therefore, that principle much used and rested on by Mr Baxter in the business of satisfaction, to obviate this very difficulty of a not immediate discharge, if Christ paid the debt,—namely, That the satisfaction of Christ is a refusable payment,—which he presseth, pp. 149, 150, is neither true in itself nor accommodate to this difficulty. Not true; for,

The suffering of Christ may be considered either,—

(1.) Absolutely, as in itself, abstracting from the consideration of any covenant or compact thereabout; and so it cannot be said to be a refusable payment; not because not refusable, but because no payment. That any thing should have any such reference unto God as a payment or satisfaction, whether refusable or otherwise, is not from itself and its own nature, but from the constitution of God alone. Between God and the creature there is no equality,—not so much as of proportion. Christ, in respect of his human nature, though united to the Deity, is a creature, and so could not absolutely satisfy or merit any thing at the hand of God; I mean, with that kind of merit which ariseth from an absolute proportion of things. This merit can be found only among creatures, and the advancement of Christ's humanity takes it not out of that number. Neither, in this sense, can any satisfaction be made to God for sin. The sinner's own undergoing the penalty neither is satisfaction in the sense whereof we speak, neither can it properly be said to be so at all; no more than a thing [can be said] to be done which is endlessly in doing.

(2.) It may be considered with reference unto God's constitution and determination, predestinating Christ unto that work, and appointing the work by him to be accomplished to be satisfactory; equalling, by that constitution, the end and the means. And thus the satisfaction of Christ, in the justice of God, was not refusable, the wisdom, truth, justice, and suitable purpose of God being engaged to the contrary.

This distinction is not accommodate to this difficulty; the sole reason thereof being what was held out before,—of the interest of God's sovereign right to the bestowing of purposed, purchased, promised blessings, as to times and seasons, according to the free counsel of his own will.

Hence, then, it is that God, in the Scripture, upon the death of Christ is said to be reconciled, to be returned unto peace with them for whom he so died, the enmity being slain and peace actually made, Eph. ii. 14–16, Col. i, 20; because he now will and may, suitably to his justice, wisdom, and appointment, make out unto them for whom the atonement was made all the fruits of love, peace, and amity, Heb. ii. 17; Rom. v. 10, 11; 2 Cor. v. 19.

The objection unto this, "How, then, can God deny us the present possession of heaven?" used by Mr Baxter, p. 157, is not of any force, the whole disposal of these things being left to his own pleasure.

And this is the scheme which, upon the death of Christ, we assign unto God: He is atoned, appeased, actually reconciled, at peace, with those for whom Christ died; and in due time, for his sake, will bestow upon them all the fruits and issues of love and renewed friendship.

This, possibly, may give some light into the immediate effect of the death of Christ; which though I shall not purposely now handle, yet Mr Baxter, with much diligence, having employed himself in the investigation thereof, I shall turn aside a little to consider his assertions in this particular.

CHAPTER IX.

A digression concerning the immediate effect of the death of Christ.

"It is one of the greatest and noblest questions in our controverted divinity, What are the immediate effects of Christ's death? He that can rightly answer this, is a divine indeed, and, by help of this, may expedite most other controversies about redemption and justification. In a word, the effects of redemption undertaken could not be upon a subject not yet existent, and so no subject, though it might be for them. None but Adam and Eve were then existent; yet as soon as we do exist, we receive benefit from it. The suspending of the rigorous execution of the sentence of the law is the most observable immediate effect of the death of Christ; which suspension is some kind of deliverance from it." Thus far Mr Baxter, thes. 9, explicat. p. 67.

There are scarce more lines than mistakes in this discourse; some of them may be touched on:—

1. Effects are to be considered with respect to their causes. Causes are real or moral. Real or physical causes produce their effects immediately, either *immediatione suppositi* or *virtutis*. Unto them the subject must be existent. I speak not of creating power, where the act produceth its object.

Moral causes do never immediately actuate their own effects, nor have any immediate influence into them. There is between such causes and their effects the intervention of some third thing previous to them both,—namely, proportion, constitution, law, covenant,—which takes in the cause and lets out the effect; and this for all circumstances of where, how, when, suitable to the limitations in them expressed or implied, with the nature of the things themselves.

The death of Christ is a moral cause in respect of all its effects. Whether those subjects on which it is to have its effects be existent or not existent, at the time of its performance, is nothing at all considerable. If it wrought physically and efficiently, the existence of the subjects on which it were to work were requisite. It is altogether in vain to inquire of the immediate effects of Christ's death upon an existent subject. By the way, That Adam and Eve only were existent when Christ undertook the work of redemption, to me is not clear; no, nor yet the following assertion, That as soon as we do exist we receive benefit by it, —taking benefit for a benefit actually collated, as Mr Baxter doth not for a right to a benefit, or the purpose of bestowing one, which will operate in its due time. This is easily affirmed, and therefore *eâdem facilitate* is denied.

I have no fancy to strive to carry the bell, and to be accounted "a divine indeed," by attempting at this time a right stating of and answer to this question proposed. I am not altogether ignorant of the endeavour of others even as to this particular, and have formerly spoken something that way myself.

Mr Baxter seems here to understand by this question,—namely, What is the immediate effect of the death of Christ?—What is the first benefit which, from the death of Christ, accrueth unto them for whom he died? not what is the first thing that every particular person is actually, in his own person, in his own time, made partaker of; but a benefit generally established and in being upon the designment of the work of redemption, which every one for whom Christ died hath a share of. And of this he positively affirms that the suspending of the rigorous execution of the sentence of the law is the most observable immediate effect of the death of Christ; and so deserves the title of "a divine indeed."

Now, truly, though not to contend for the bell with Mr Baxter,—whereof I confess myself utterly unworthy, and willingly, for many commendable parts, ascribe it unto him,—I cannot close with him, nor assent unto that assertion. Very gladly would I see Mr Baxter's arguments for this; but those, as in most other controverted things in this book, he is pleased to conceal: and, therefore, though it might suffice me to give in my dissent, and so wait for farther proof, yet, that it may be apparent that I do not deny this merely because it is said, not proved (which, in things not clear in themselves, is a provocation so to do), I shall oppose one or two arguments unto it:—

1. All the effects of the death of Christ are peculiar only to the elect; to some, the suspension of the rigorous execution of the law is not so: *ergo*, etc.

The *minor* is apparent, the *major* proved by all the arguments against universal redemption used in my former treatise.

2. All the effects of the death of Christ are spiritual, distinguishing, and saving, to the praise of God's free grace; the suspending of the rigorous execution of the law is not so: *ergo*, etc.

The assumption is manifest. It is only a not immediate casting into hell, which is not a spiritual, distinguishing mercy, but, in respect to many, tends to the manifestation of God's justice, Rom. ix. 22.

The proposition is evident. The promises made unto Christ upon his undertaking this work doubtless do hold out all that he effected by his death. Of what nature they are, and what is the main tendence of them, I have elsewhere discovered. From the first to the last, they are restrained to distinguishing mercies. See Isa. xlix. 6–12, liii. 10–12, lxi. 1–3; and no less is positively affirmed, Eph. i. 4; Rev. i. 5, 6.

If Mr Baxter say that the meaning in this is, that if Christ had not undertaken the work of redemption and satisfaction, then the law must have had rigorous execution upon all, and therefore, this being suspended upon his undertaking of it, is the first fruit of the death of Christ, I answer,—

Notwithstanding this, yet that suspension, which in respect of the different persons towards whom it is actually exercised hath different ends, is not a fruit nor effect of the death of Christ, but a free issue of the same eternally wise providence, sovereignty, and grace, as the death of Christ himself is. If, then, by the rigorous execution of the law, you intend the immediate execution of the law in all its rigour and punishment, this, if it had been effected, could, in your own judgment, have reached Adam and Eve, and no more; and would have so reached them as to cut off the generation of mankind in that root. If so, and this be the fruit of Christ's death, why do you not reckon the procreation of the human race among those fruits also? for had it not been for this suspension, that also had failed; which is as good a causative connection as that between the death of Christ and this suspension. Had not he undertaken the work of redemption, it had not been. If by a rigorous execution you intend the penalty of the law, inflicted in that way which hath pleased the will of the Law-giver,—by several parts and degrees, from conception, through birth, life, death, to eternity, the curse of it being wholly incumbent in respect of desert, and making out itself according to God's appointment,—then the suspension thereof is not the immediate effect of the death of Christ; which (supposing the first arguments to the former acceptation) I farther prove: If those for whom Christ died do lie under this rigorous execution of the law (that is, the curse of it) until some other effect of Christ's death be wrought upon them, then that is not the first effect of the death of Christ; but that supposal is true, John iii. 36, Eph. ii. 3: therefore, so also the inference.

In a word: Take the suspending of the rigorous execution of the law for the purpose of God, and his acting accordingly, not to leave his elect under the actual curse of it; so it is no fruit of the death of Christ, but an issue of the same grace from whence also the death of Christ proceeds.

Take it for an actual freeing of their persons from the breach of it and its curse, and so it differs not from justification, and is not the immediate effect of Christ's death, in Mr Baxter's judgment.

Take it for the not immediate executing of the law upon the first offence, and I can as well say, Christ died because the law was suspended, as you, that the law was suspended because Christ died; had not either been, the other had not been.

Take it for the actual forbearance of God towards all the world, and so it falls under my first two arguments.

Take it thus, That God, for the death of Christ, will deal with all men upon a new law, freeing all from the guilt of the first broken law and covenant; so it is *non ens.*

If you mean by it God's entering into a new way of salvation with those for whom Christ died, this, on the part of God, is antecedaneous to the consideration of the death of Christ, and of the same free grace with itself.

For the question itself, as I said before, I shall not here in terms take it up; the following discourse will give light into it. I have also spoken largely to it in another place, and that distinctly.

The sum is: I conceive that all the intermediate effects of the death of Christ, tending to its ultimate procurement of the glory of God, are all, in respect of his death, immediate; that is, with such an immediation as attends moral causes. Now, these concerning them for whom he died, as they are not immediately bestowed on them, the ultimate attingency of the cause and the first rise of the effect lying in an intervening compact, so not *simul,* at once neither, though *simul* and alike procured; the cause of this being that relation, coherence, and causality which the Lord hath appointed between the several effects, or rather parts of the same effect, of the death of Christ, in reference to the main and ultimate end to be thereby attained, as at large I have discussed, lib. ii. cap. 1, pp. 52, 53, etc.;—in one word, the first effect of the death of Christ, in this sense, is the first fruit of election; for, for the procuring and purchasing of the fruits thereof, and them alone, did Christ die.

If I mistake not, Mr Baxter himself is not settled fully in this persuasion, that the suspension of the rigorous execution of the law is the most immediate effect of the death of Christ; for, p. 52, these words which he useth, "God the Father doth accept the suffering and merits of his Son as a full satisfaction to his violated law, and as a valuable consideration, upon which he will wholly acquit and forgive the offenders themselves, and receive them again into favour, so that they will but receive his Son upon the terms expressed in the gospel," seem to place the ultimate efficacy of the death of Christ in God's acceptation of it, as to our good, on the condition of faith and obedience.

Which, first, makes the suspension of the law to be so far from being the first effect of the death of Christ, that the last reacheth not so far; and, secondly, the fond absurdity of this conditional acceptation I have before declared.

Neither am I clear to which of those assertions, that of p. 92, where he affirms that some benefit by Christ the condemned did receive, is most accommodate. Neither can I easily receive what is here asserted, if by "benefit" you understand that which, in respect of them, is intentionally so; for,—

1. Condemned persons, as condemned persons, surely receive no benefit by Christ, for they are condemned.

2. The delay of the condemnation of reprobates is no part of the purchase of Christ. The Scripture says nor more nor less of any such thing, but peculiarly assigns it to another cause, Rom. ix. 22.

CHAPTER X.

Of the merit of Christ, and its immediate efficacy—What it effecteth—In what it resteth—With the state of those for whom Christ died in reference to his death, and of their rights to the fruits of his death before believing.

THAT they for whom Christ died have a right to the things which he purchased thereby,—that is, an actual right, for so men may have to what they have not in actual possession,—is no singular conception of mine. Our divines freely express themselves to this purpose.

Even the commender and publisher of Grotius' book of "Satisfaction," the learned Vossius, himself affirmeth that Christ by his death purchased for us a double right,—first, a right of escaping punishment, and then a right of obtaining the reward. By the way, I cannot close with his distinction in that place, of some things that Christ by his life and death purchased for us, and others that he daily bestoweth; for the things he daily bestoweth are of them which by his death he purchased.

My expressions then, alone, are not subject to the consequences charged on them, for asserting a right to life and salvation in them for whom Christ died, even before believing. Yea, some have gone farther, and affirmed [1] that those for whom Christ died are in some manner restored into saving favour; not to mention some of them, to whose judgment Mr Baxter seems to accede, who assert universal justification and restoration into grace upon the death of Christ. But I lay no weight upon these things.

To clear my thoughts in this particular, two things must necessarily be inquired into and made out:—

1. Seeing the satisfaction and merit of Christ do tend directly for the good of them for whom he died, and that there is a distance and space of time between that death and their participation of the good things purchased thereby, wherein lieth or in what resteth the efficacy of that his death, with the principle of the certain futurition of the spiritual things so procured, which those for whom he died shall assuredly in due time enjoy?

2. Wherein lies the obligation unto death, hell, and wrath, which, before believing, the Scripture affirms to be upon the elect, seeing Christ hath actually purchased for them freedom from these things? And this, without more ado, will be cleared in the former.

[1] "Omnes illi, pro quibus Christus ex intentione Dei satisfecit, sunt Deo reconciliati, *i. e.*, in favorem salutiferum aliquo modo restituti."—Ames. Antisynod., p. 104.

For the first, then, upon the issue of the death of Christ, something being supposed in God beyond his mere purpose (of which before), some things being actually procured and purchased by it, which yet they for whom they are so purchased neither do nor possibly can, upon the purchase, immediately possess and enjoy, it is inquired wherein resteth the efficacy of his death which in due time causeth the making out of all those spiritual blessings which by it are so procured?

Now, this must be either in those for whom he died, or in himself as mediator, or in his Father who sent him.

1. That it is not in them for whom he died is apparent. Upon the death of Christ, in purpose and promise, when first its efficacy took place, they were not; I mean, actually existent. True, they were potentially in the purpose of God; but will that make them a meet subject for the residence of this right and merit whereof we speak? As is the thing, such are all its affections and adjuncts;—but possible, if it be no more. This is something actual whereof we speak.

2. That it is not in Christ as mediator is no less evident. He that makes satisfaction and he to whom it is made, he who meriteth any thing and he at whose hands he meriteth it, must be distinguished. The second person, under the notion of performing the work of mediation, receiveth not satisfaction. The power Christ receiveth of the Father, because he is the Son of man, to give eternal life to those given him of his Father, is of later consideration to that we have in hand, being a result and consequence thereof.

3. It must, therefore, be in the Father, or God, as receiving satisfaction.

Of all the attributes of God, where this may be placed, to speak after the manner of men, one of these four must needs be the proper seat of it, power, will, justice, truth:—

(1.) His power. And then it must be, not that God hath any addition of power, for that cannot be to him who is omnipotent, but that a way is made for the exercise of his power, which before, by somewhat from himself, was shut up.

And, as some suppose, it is no otherwise; that whereas the Lord could not make out grace and favour unto sinners, because of his justice necessarily inclining him to their punishment and destruction, now, that justice being satisfied in Christ, he can collate any spiritual blessings upon them, as he seeth good.

But this I have disproved elsewhere, and manifested,—

[1.] That the foundation of this apprehension (being an impossibility in God to forgive sin without satisfaction, because of the contrariety of it to the properties of his nature) is a groundless assertion; and,—

[2.] The foundation of God in sending his Son to die for his elect is oppugned hereby; and,—

[3.] It is destructive to all the proper fruits and effects of the death of Christ, etc., lib. ii. cap. 2.

(2.) In the will of God it seems that the merit and fruits of the death of Christ, whereof we treat, seem better to be treasured; and from hence it is that he can will, or willeth, to us the good things purchased by it. But,—

[1.] That the will of God should, by the death of Christ, be changed into any other habitude than what it was in before, was before disproved.

[2.] That now God can will good things to us, holds out the enlargement of his power as to the acting thereof, mentioned above, rather than any thing properly belonging to the will of God.

[3.] God's willing good things to us it cannot consist in. His willing of a thing is operative of it. It is his efficacious, energetical will whereof we speak. When he actually willeth grace, we have grace; and when he willeth glory, we have glory. But that concerning which we speak is antecedent to the actual making out of grace and glory to us, being the procuring cause of them, though not of that act of the will of God whereby they are bestowed.

(3.) His justice and truth only remain. For justice, that which is commutative properly, with one consent, is removed from God. "Who hath given first unto him, and it shall be rendered unto him again?" Neither [1]is distributive justice to be supposed in him antecedent to some free engagement of his own. Where no obligation is, there cannot be so much as distributive justice properly. All obligation from God to the creature is from his own free engagement; otherwise he stands in no relation to it but of absolute dominion and sovereignty. All the justice of God, then (we consider not the universal rectitude of his nature, but) in reference to the creature, is "justitia regiminis," Ps. xxxiii. 4, 5, 1 John i. 5; and therefore must suppose some free constitution of his will.

This, then, rightly considered, [2]do I affirm to be effected with the merit of Christ; there I place the procuring efficacy thereof, whence it is that all the fruits of it are made out unto us. But this in due order.

The first thing of immediate concernment hereunto is the covenant of the Father with the Son, the free engagement of God to do such and such things for Christ, upon the performance of such other things to him appointed. This is the foundation of the merit of Christ, as was before declared. Hence his distributive justice ascribed to God as to this thing. It is righteous with him, being engaged by his own free purpose and promise, to make out those things which he appointed to be the fruit and procurement of the death of Christ. And from thence it is that all the things purchased by the death of Christ become due to those for whom he died, even from the equity attending this justice of God.

(4.) Herein, also, his truth hath a share. By his truth I understand his fidelity and veracity in the performance of all his engagements. This immediately attends every obligation that, by any free act of his will, God is pleased in his wisdom to put upon himself, and is naturally under consideration before that distributive justice whereby he is inclined to the performance itself of them

This, then, is that I say:—

God, by free purpose and compact, making way for the merit of Christ, which absolutely could be none, is obliged, from the veracity and justice which attend all his engagements, to make out, as in his infinite wisdom shall seem meet, all those things which he hath set, appointed, and proposed as the fruit and purchase of his death, unto all them for whom he died. And in this rests the merit of Christ.

Here two things may be observed:—

1. What we ascribe to the merit of Christ,—namely, the accomplishment of that condition which God required to make way, that the obligation which he had freely put upon himself might be in actual force. And so much (how rightly I leave to himself to consider) doth Mr Baxter assign to our own works, thes. 26, p. 140.

2. The mistake of those who wind up the merit of Christ, as affecting God, if I may so speak, unto a conditional engagement,—namely, that we shall be made partakers of the fruits of it upon such and such conditions, to be by us fulfilled; for,—

(1.) All such conditions (if spiritual blessings) are part of the purchase of the death of Christ; and if not, are no way fit to be conditions of such an attainment.

(2.) It cannot be made apparent how any such conditional stipulation can be ascribed unto God; that God should engage upon the death of Christ to make

[1] "Si de debito quæratur, respectu creaturæ in Deum cadere non potest; nisi ex aliqua suppositione ipsi Deo voluntaria et libera: quæ non potest esse nisi promissio aut pactio aliqua, ex quibus fidelitatis aut justitiæ debitum oriri solet."—Suares. Relect. de Lib. Div. Volu. Disp. L. Di. sec. ii. n. 5.

[2] "Nulla justitia proprie esse potest, ubi nulla intercedit obligatio; Deus autem nulla obligatione tenetur, antequam ipse fidem suam astringat; ergo ante promissionem nulla justitia etiam distributiva in Deo reperitur."—Vas. n. 1, q. 21, a. 1, disp. 86.

out grace and glory, liberty and beauty, unto those for whom he died, upon condition they do so or so,—

[1.] Leaves no proper place for the merit of Christ.

[2.] Is very improperly ascribed unto God. Lawyers tell us that all stipulations about things future are either *sub conditione* or *sub termino*. Stipulations or engagements upon condition, that are properly so, do suppose him that makes the engagement to be altogether uncertain of the event thereof. Stipulations *sub termino* are absolute, to make out the things engaged about at such a season. Upon the very instant of such a stipulation as this, an obligation follows as to the thing, though no action be allowed to him to whom it is made, until the term and time appointed be come.

In those stipulations that are under condition, no obligation ariseth at all from them, it being wholly uncertain whether the condition will be fulfilled or no. Only in two cases doth such an engagement bring on an immediate obligation:—

1*st*, If the condition required be in things necessary and unalterable; as if Caius should engage himself unto Tilius to give him a hundred pounds for his house on the morrow if the sun shine. Here ariseth an immediate obligation, and it is the same as if it had been conceived only *sub termino*, without condition at all.

2*dly*, If by any means he that makes the stipulation knows infallibly that the condition will be fulfilled, though he to whom it is made knows it not, in this respect, also, the stipulation *sub conditione* introduceth an immediate obligation, and in that regard is coincident with that which is only *sub termino*.

Whether an engagement upon condition properly, without the former respects,—that is, a stipulation to an event dubious and uncertain,—can be ascribed unto God, is easy to determine. To assert it oppugns the whole nature of the Deity, and overthrows the properties thereof, immediately and directly. All other stipulations under condition are coincident, as I said before, with that which is *sub termino* only, from whence ariseth an immediate obligation for the performance of the thing stipulated about, though there be not an immediate action granted him unto whom it is made.

Surely they are wide, if not very wild, who affirm that all the stipulations on the part of God, upon the death of Christ, are upon a condition which he himself knows to be impossible for them to perform to whom they are made; which amongst wise men are always accounted nugatory and null.

This being, then, so vain, I say that the merit of Christ, flowing from the free purpose and compact of God, resteth on his justice thence also arising, fixing thereon an obligation to make out all the fruits of it unto them for whom he died *sub termino* only; whereby a present right is granted them thereunto, though they cannot plead for present enjoyment.

CHAPTER XI.

More particularly of the state and right of them for whom Christ died, before believing.

THE former assertions about the death of Christ being in some measure cleared, we may hence have light into the state and condition of those for whom Christ died, in their several generations, before believing.

To make this the more fully appear, we must distinguish between their present state or possession, and their present right. Their state is not changed because all the procurements of the death of Christ are to be made out unto them by virtue of a stipulation *sub termino*, that term or season being not come. So that still, in present actual state, I leave them as before, not justified, not sanctified, not entered into covenant.

Right also is twofold:—

1. *In re;*—as the father hath a right to his estate. And this *jus in re* holds, though the estate be unjustly or forcibly detained from him.

2. *Ad rem;*—so the son hath a right to the estate of his father, being to enjoy it at his death.

The first right is presently actionable upon any detainment; the latter not so. The first we do not ascribe to the elect in this condition,—namely, that which is *in re,* and instantly actionable; but that which is *ad rem* and *sub termino.*

This being that which I aimed at, and being by Mr Baxter opposed, I will farther consider it, that it may appear whether any thing in this assertion be justly blamable.

I said that by the death of Christ we have actual right to the good things purchased by that death. That right which is not actual (to speak a word to that term) is not. The contradistinct affection hereunto is potential; and this is totally destructive to the nature of a right. All right is actual, or not at all.

To evince the main assertion, I shall,—1. Show the nature and quality of this right; 2. The bottom or foundation of it; and, 3. Prove the thesis.

1. By right I understand *jus* in general. Now, "Jus est quod justum est," Aug. in Ps. cxliv. sub. fin;—"That is right which it is just should be." And, "Quidquid rectum est, justum est," Ansel. de Verit. cap. 13;—"It is just all that should be, which hath a rectitude in itself." Farther; what this *justum* is, Aquinas tells you, 22 æ. q. 57, a. 1, c.: "Justum est quod respondet secundum aliquam æqualitatem alteri;"—"Then a thing is just, when it stands in some equality unto those things whereunto it relates." And this equality or adequation of things is twofold:—

First, That which ariseth from the nature of the things themselves; as an eye for an eye, a tooth for a tooth, etc.

Secondly, That which ariseth from a proportion condescended unto, by condict, agreement, covenant, or common consent. "Dupliciter est aliquid adæquatum; uno modo ex natura ipsius rei; alio modo cum est commensuratum ex condicto sive ex communi placito," Aquin.

In the first sense, as to a right that should accrue unto the creatures in respect of God, from the commensuration of the things themselves, we showed before that it cannot be. It must be from some grant, compact, covenant, or the like, from whence a right in reference to the faithfulness or righteousness of God may arise. The right, then, whereof we speak, which they for whom Christ died have to the things which by his death are procured, consists in that equity, proportion, and equality, which, upon the free compact, constitution, and consent of God the Father, is between the death of Christ and their enjoyment of the fruits of that death. It is just and equal that they should enjoy the fruits of his death in due time. Neither is the right of any man to any thing any more but such a frame and order of things as is just, either from the nature of the things themselves, or from common consent and agreement that he should enjoy that thing. This is the right whereof we speak; which, in their sense, the very Socinians grant. "Christus jus quoddam ad obtinendam remissionem peccatorum et salutem (morte sua) nobis dedit," Crellius adv. Groti. cap. i.

2. For the foundation of this right, seeing that before the consideration of the death of Christ (as was declared) it is not, from thence it must needs be, nothing of any likelihood to be such a foundation being coincident therewithal.

Now, whereas in the death of Christ two things are considered,—(1.) The satisfaction; and (2.) The merit thereof,—it may be inquired after, under whether respect this right relates thereunto.

(1.) The satisfaction of Christ tends, in all that it is, to the honour and reparation of the justice of God. This, then, in its utmost extent and efficacy, cannot give ground to build such a right upon. The ultimate effect of satisfaction may be accomplished, and yet not the least right to any good thing communicated to them for whom this satisfaction is made. The good things attending the death of Christ may be referred unto two heads,—the amotion of evil, and the collation of good. For the first,—the amotion of evil, the taking that from us that it may not grieve us, and subducting us from the power and presence thereof,—it is immediately aimed at by satisfaction. That the curse of the law be not executed, that the wrath to come be not poured out, is the utmost reach of the death of Christ, considered as satisfactory. Yea, in itself, as only such, it proceedeth not so far as to give us a right to escape these things, but only presents that to the justice of God whereby it may be preserved in all its glory, severity, and exact purity, though these things be not inflicted on us. This, I say, I conceive to be the utmost tendency of the death of Christ, as satisfactory. That condemnation cannot possibly *de facto* follow, when such satisfaction hath been made, is immediately from the equity of justice so repaired as above. For positive good things in grace and glory, by satisfaction alone, they are not at all respected.

(2.) There is the merit of the death of Christ; and that principally intendeth the glory of God in our enjoying those good things whereof it is the merit or desert. And this is the foundation of that right whereof we treat. What Christ hath merited for us, it is just and equal we should have,—that is, we have a right unto it,—and this before believing. Faith gives us actual possession as to some part, and a new pactional right as to the whole; but this right or that equalling of things upon divine constitution,[1] whereby it becomes just and right that we should obtain the things purchased by it, is from the merit of Christ alone. What Christ hath merited is so far granted as that they for whom it is so merited have a right unto it.

The sum, then, of what we have to prove is,—

That the merit of the death of the Lord Jesus hath, according to the constitution of the Father, so procured of him the good things aimed at and intended thereby, that it is just, right, and equal that they for whom they are so procured should certainly and infallibly enjoy them at the appointed season; and, therefore, unto them they have an actual right even before believing, faith itself being of the number of those things so procured.

3. All which I prove as followeth:—

(1.) The very terms before mentioned enforce no less. If it be *justum* before their believing that those for whom Christ died should enjoy the fruits of his death, then have they, even before believing, *jus*, or a right thereunto; for "jus est quod justum est." That it is right and equal that they should enjoy those fruits is manifest; for,—

[1.] It was the engagement of the Father to the Son, upon his undertaking to die for them, that they should so do, Isa. liii. 10–12.

[2.] In that undertaking he accomplished all that was of him required, John xvii. 4.

(2.) That which is merited and procured for any one, thereunto he for whom it is procured certainly hath a right. That which is obtained for me is mine in actual right, though not perhaps in actual possession. The thing that is obtained is granted by him of whom it is obtained, and that unto them for whom it is obtained. In some sense or other, that is a man's which is procured for him. In saying it is procured for him, we say no less. If this, then, be not in respect of possession, it must be in respect of right. Now, all the fruits of the death of Christ are obtained and procured by his merit for them for whom he died. He obtains for them eternal redemption, Heb. ix. 12; purchasing them with his own blood, Acts xx. 28; Heb. ii. 14, 15; 1 Pet. i. 18, 19; Gal. i. 4; Rev. xiv. 3, 4. The very

1 "Jus est operatio illa qua sit æqualitas."—Pesant. in Thom. 22, æ. q. 57.

nature of merit described by the apostle, Rom. iv. 4, infers no less. Where merit intercedes, the effect is reckoned as of debt; that which is my due debt I have right unto. The fruits of the death of Christ are the issues of merit, bottomed on God's gracious acceptation, and reckoned as of debt. He for whom a ransom is paid hath a right unto his liberty by virtue of that payment.

(3.) 2 Pet. i. 1, the saints are said to obtain "precious faith, through the righteousness of God." It is a righteous thing with God to give faith to them for whom Christ died, because thereby they have a right unto it. Faith being amongst the most precious fruits of the death of Christ, by virtue thereof becometh their due for whom he died.

(4.) The condition of persons under merit and demerit, in respect of good or evil, is alike; the proportion of things requires it. Now, men under demerit are under an obligation unto punishment, and "it is a righteous thing with God to recompense tribulation to them," 2 Thess. i. 6; it being "the judgment of God, that they which commit such things are worthy of death," Rom. i. 32. They, then, who are under merit have also a right unto that whereof it is the merit. It is not of any force to say that they are not under that merit but only upon condition (for this is, first, false; secondly, with God this is all one as if there were no condition, at the season and term appointed for the making out the fruit of that merit, as hath been declared);—neither yet to object that it is not their own merit, but of another which respects them; that other being their surety, doing that whereby he merited only on their behalf, yea, in their stead, they dying with him, though the same in them could not have been meritorious, they being at best mere men, and at worst very sinful men.

(5.) A compact or covenant being made of giving life and salvation, upon the condition of obedience, to certain persons, that condition being completely fulfilled (as it was in the death of Christ), claim being made of the promise, according to the tenor of the compact, and the persons presented for the enjoyment of it, surely those persons have an actual right unto it. That all this is so, see Isa. xlix. 1-6, etc.; Ps. ii. 2-8; Isa. liii. 10-12; John xvii. 2, 4, 11, 21; Heb. ii.

And so much for this, also, concerning the issue of the death of Christ, and the right of the elect to the fruits of it before believing.

CHAPTER XII.

Of the way whereby they actually attain and enjoy faith and grace who have a right thereunto by the death of Christ.

THE way and causes of bestowing faith on them who are under the condition before described is the next thing to be inquired after.

What are the thoughts of God from eternity concerning those for whom Christ was to die, with the state they are left in, in relation to those thoughts, as also what is the will of God towards them immediately upon the consideration of the death of Christ, with the right which to them accrues thereby, being considered, it remaineth, I say, that we declare the way and method whereby they obtain faith through the righteousness of God.

And here we must lay down certain positions; as,—

1. Notwithstanding the right granted them for whom Christ died, upon his death, to a better state and condition in due time,—that is, in the season suiting the infinitely wise sovereignty of God,—yet as to the present condition, in point of enjoyment, they are not actually differenced from others. Their prayers are an abomination to the Lord, Prov. xxviii. 9; all things are to them unclean, Tit.

i. 15; they are under the power of Satan, Eph. ii. 2; in bondage unto death, Heb. ii. 15; obnoxious to the curse and condemning power of the law in the conscience, Gal. iii. 13; having sin reigning in them, Rom. vi. 17, etc.

2. What spiritual blessings soever are bestowed on any soul, I mean peculiarly distinguishing mercies and graces, they are all bestowed and collated for Christ's sake; that is, they are purchased by his merit, and procured by his intercession thereupon.

That supernatural graces cannot be traduced from any natural faculty, or attained by the utmost endeavour of nature, howsoever affected with outward advantages, I now take for granted. These things I looked upon as the free gifts of love: so the Scripture, John xv. 5; 2 Cor. iii. 5; Eph. ii. 8; 1 Cor. iv. 7; Eph. ii. 10; Matt. xi. 25, 26; Acts xvi. 14, etc.

Now, the dispensation of all these, as it is *through* Christ, so they are *for* Christ. On whomsoever they are bestowed, it is for Christ's sake. For instance, Peter and Judas are unbelievers. Faith is given to Peter, not to Judas. Whence is this difference? Presupposing God's sovereign discriminating purpose, the immediate procuring cause of faith for Peter is the merit of Christ: "To us it is given on the behalf of Christ to believe on him," Phil. i. 29. We are "blessed with all spiritual blessings in him," Eph. i. 3. Whatsoever is in the promise of the covenant is certainly of his procurement; for therefore he is the surety, Heb. vii. 22. And his blood, the ransom he paid, is the blood of the covenant, Matt. xxvi. 28; whereby "all the promises" thereof become "in him yea, and in him Amen," 2 Cor. i. 20. And whether faith be of the blessings of the covenant, and included in the promise thereof, or no, let the Scripture be judge, Jer. xxxi. 31–34; Ezek. xxxvi. 26, 27; Heb. viii. 8–12.

Furthermore; what we have through him, we have for him; all these things being made out on this condition, that "he should make his soul an offering for sin," Isa. liii. 10.

3. That all the procurements of the death of Christ, in the behalf of his, are to be made out by virtue of a stipulation *sub termino;* or, in respect of their actual collation and bestowing, they are to be made out in the season limited and appointed by the will of the Father. Of this before.

4. No blessing can be given us for Christ's sake, unless, in order of nature, Christ be first reckoned unto us.

Here I must do two things:—(1.) Declare what I mean by reckoning Christ unto us; and then, (2.) Prove the assertion as laid down.

(1.) God's reckoning Christ, in our present sense, is the imputing of Christ unto ungodly, unbelieving sinners for whom he died, so far as to account him theirs, and to bestow faith and grace upon them for his sake.

This, then, I say, at the accomplishment of the appointed time, the Lord reckons, and accounts, and makes out his Son Christ, to such and such sinners, and for his sake gives them faith, etc. Exercising of love actually, in the bestowing of grace upon any particular soul, in a distinguishing manner, for Christ's sake, doth suppose this accounting of Christ to be his; and from thence he is so indeed,—which is the present thesis. And,—

(2.) This may be proved; for,—

[1.] Why doth the Lord bestow faith on Peter, not on Judas? Because Christ dying for Peter, and purchasing for him the grace of the covenant, he had a right unto it, and God according to his promise bestowed it; with Judas, it was not so. But then, why doth the Lord bestow faith on Peter at the fortieth year of his age, and not before or after? Because then the term was expired which, upon the purchase, was by the counsel of God's will prefixed to the giving in the beginning of the thing purchased unto him. What, then, doth the Lord do when he thus bestoweth faith on him? For Christ's sake,—his death procuring the gift, not moving the will of the giver,—he creates faith in him by the way and means suited to such a work, Eph. i. 18, 19, ii. 1, etc. If, then, this be done for Christ's sake, then is Christ made ours before we believe. Else, why is faith given him at this instant for Christ's sake, and not to another, for whom also he died? That it is done then, is because the appointed time is come; that it is done then for Christ, is because Christ is first given to him. I cannot conceive how any thing should be made out to me for Christ, and Christ himself not be given to me, he being "made unto us of God, righteousness," 1 Cor. i. 30.

[2.] The apostle holds out this very method of the dispensation of grace: Rom. viii. 32, "He that spared not his own Son, but delivered him up for us all, how shall he not with him also freely give us all things?"

First, Christ is given *for* us, then *to* us, then *with him* (he having the pre-eminence in all things) all things; and this being, also, for him, Phil. i. 29, he is certainly in the order of nature given in the first place. He being made ours, "we receive the atonement by him," Rom. v. 11.

How Christ is said to be received by faith, if he be ours before believing, is easily resolved. Christ is ours before and after believing in a different sense. He who is made ours in an act of God's love, that for him we may have faith, may be found and made ours in a promise of reconciliation by believing.

I offer [suggest], also, whether absolution from the guilt of sin and obligation unto death, though not as terminated in the conscience for complete justification, do not precede our actual believing; for what is that love of God which through Christ is effectual to bestow faith upon the unbelieving? and how can so great love, in the actual exercise of it, producing the most distinguishing mercies, consist with any such act of God's will as at the same instant should bind that person under the guilt of sin?

Perhaps, also, this may be the justification of the ungodly, mentioned Rom. iv. 5, God's absolving a sinner in heaven, by accounting Christ unto him, and then bestowing him upon him, and for his sake enduing him with faith to believe.

That we should be blessed with all spiritual blessings in Christ, and yet Christ not be ours in a peculiar manner before the bestowing of those blessings on us, is somewhat strange. Yea, he must be our Christ before it is given to us for him to believe; why else is it not given to all others so to do? I speak not of the supreme distinguishing cause, Matt. xi. 25, 26, but of the proximate procuring cause, which is the blood of Christ. Neither yet do I hence assert complete justification to be before believing. Absolution in heaven, and justification, differ as part and whole.

Again: absolution may be considered either as a pure act of the will of God in itself, or as it is received, believed, apprehended, in and by the soul of the guilty. For absolution in the first sense, it is evident it must precede believing; as a discharge from the effects of anger naturally precedes all collation of any fruits of love, such as is faith.

But if God account Christ unto, and bestow him upon, a sinner before believing, and upon that account absolve him from the obligation unto death and hell, which for sin he lies under, what wants this of complete justification?

Much every way.

1. It wants that act of pardoning mercy on the part of God which is to be terminated and completed in the conscience of the sinner; this lies in the promise.

2. It wants the heart's persuasion concerning the truth and goodness of the promise, and the mercy held out in the promise.

3. It wants the soul's rolling itself upon Christ, and receiving of Christ as the author and finisher of that mercy, an all-sufficient Saviour to them that believe.

So that by faith alone we obtain and receive the forgiveness of sin; for notwithstanding any antecedent act of God concerning us, in and for Christ, we do not actually receive a complete soul-freeing discharge until we believe.

And thus the Lord Christ hath the pre-eminence in all things. He is "the author and finisher of our faith."

This, then, is that which here we assign unto the Lord: Upon the accomplishment of the appointed season for the making out the fruits of the death of Christ unto them for whom he died, he loves them freely, says to them, "Live;" gives them his Son, and with and for him all things; bringing forth the choicest issue of his being reconciled in the blood of Jesus whilst we are enemies, and totally alienated from him.

It will not be requisite at all, as to our purpose in hand, to make particular inquiry into the state and condition of them towards whom such are the actings of God, as we before described. What it is that gives them the first real alteration of condition and distinguishment from others I have now no occasion to handle.

So far as advantage hath been offered, I have laboured to distinguish aright those things whose confusion and misapprehension lie at the bottom of very many dangerous mistakes: how the foregoing discourse may be accommodated and improved for the removal of those mistakes, I shall leave to the consideration of others.

CHAPTER XIII.

The removal of sundry objections to some things formerly taught about the death of Christ, upon the principles now delivered.

HAVING fully declared, not only what was my intendment in the expressions so exceedingly mistaken by Mr Baxter, as hath in part already been made manifest, and will instantly more fully appear, I shall now take a view of what is imposed on me as my judgment, and the opposition made thereunto, so far as may be needful for the clearing of the one and removing of the other, at least in what they may really concern what I did deliver in the treatise impugned.

In p. 146 of his Appendix, Mr Baxter endeavours to vindicate a thesis of his from some exceptions that he was by his friend pointed to, unto which it seemed liable and obnoxious.

The thesis he lays down is, "That no man is actually and absolutely justified upon the mere payment of the debt by Christ, till they become believers."

Against this "article," as he calls it, he produceth some objections of Maccovius,[1] censuring his assertions to be "senseless," his positions "strange and abhorred," his arguments "weak and ineffectual;" with some other expressions to the same purpose.

1. I am now, by the providence of God, in a condition of separation from my own small library, neither can here attain the sight of Maccovius' disputations, so that I shall not at all interpose myself in this contest; only I must needs say,—

(1.) I did not formerly account Maccovius to be so senseless and weak a disputant as here he is represented to be.

(2.) That for Mr Baxter's answer to that argument, "Where the debt is paid, there discharge must follow," by asserting the payment made by Christ to be refusable, and the interest of sinners in that payment to be purely upon the performance of a condition, I have fully before, in both parts of it, demonstrated it to be weak and inconsistent with itself and truth. That the interesting of sinners in the payment

[1] Several works by this author were published, partly during his lifetime and partly posthumous, at Franeker and Amsterdam, from 1623 to 1680, such as his "Quæstiones Theologicæ," "Collegia Theologica," etc. Maccovius, or Makowski, is said to have been the first among the Reformed that restored the scholastic treatment of theology.—ED.

made by Christ, at such and such a season, is from the sovereignty of God, and his free engagement *sub termino* for this end, hath been also fully manifested.

2. But Mr Baxter affirms that to these arguments of Maccovius, Mr Owen adds some in the place against Grotius whereunto he was referred.

"To what end," you will say, "doth Mr Owen add these arguments?" Why, to prove that men are actually and absolutely justified upon the mere payment of the debt by Christ, before believing!

But, *fidem tuam!* Is there any one argument in my whole book used to any such purpose? Do I labour to prove that which I never affirmed, never thought, never believed? In what sense I affirmed that by the death of Christ we are actually and *ipso facto* delivered from death,—that is, ὡς ἔπος εἰπεῖν, we have in due time, the time appointed, free and full deliverance thereby, without the intervention of any condition on our part not absolutely procured for us by his death,—I have before declared. How much this comes short of actual and absolute justification I need not now mention; I shall therefore only so far consider the answers given by Mr Baxter as they may seem to impair or intrench upon the main truth I assert, and that in the order by him laid down.

"These," saith he, "Mr Owen layeth down."

1. "By death he delivereth us from death." To which he answers: "Not immediately nor absolutely, nor by his death alone, but by that as a price, supposing other causes on his part and conditions on ours to concur before the actual deliverance."

(1.) To what end I mention that place of the apostle was before declared.

(2.) By the death of Christ we are immediately delivered from death with that immediation which is proper to the efficiency of causes which produce their effects by the way of moral procurement; that is, certainly, without the intervention of any other cause of the like kind. And,—

(3.) Absolutely, no condition being interposed between the cause and the effect, Christ's death and our total deliverance, but such as is part of our deliverance, and solely procured by that death, though that death of Christ be not considered as alone, that is, separated from his obedience, resurrection, and intercession, when the work of redemption is assigned to it in the Scripture.

(4.) By the death of Christ as a price, I suppose you understand his purchase as well as his payment, his merit as well as his satisfaction; or else this is a false notion of the death of Christ as the cause of our deliverance.

(5.) All other causes concurring on the part of Christ for our deliverance are, first, either not of the same kind with his death; or, secondly, bottomed on his death and flowing from thence: so that, summarily, all may be resolved thereinto.

(6.) The conditions on our part, in the sense intended, are often mentioned, never proved; nor, I am persuaded, will ever be. But he adds:—

2. "He saith the elect are said to die and rise with Christ." Saith he,—

"(1.) Not in respect of time, as if we died and rose at the same time, either really or in God's esteem.

"(2.) Not that we died in his dying, and rose in his rising. But,—

"(3.) It is spoken of the distant mediate effects of his death, and the immediate effects of his Spirit on us, rising by regeneration to union and communion with Christ." So he.

(1.) I pass the first and second exceptions, notwithstanding that of God's not esteeming of us as in Christ, upon his performance of the acts of his mediation for us, might admit of some consideration.

(2.) The inference here couched, that these things are the immediate effects of Christ's Spirit on us, therefore the distant and mediate effects of his death for us, is very weak and unconcluding. The death of Christ procureth these things as a cause moral and impelling, the Spirit worketh as an efficient; and therefore the same thing may be the immediate effect of them both, according to their several kinds of efficacy; and so, indeed, they are. Our actual conversion, the efficient whereof is the Spirit, is the immediate procurement of the merit of Christ. See this at large in my treatise opposed. I know not any man that hath run out into more wide mistakes about the immediate effects of the death of Christ than Mr Baxter, who pretends to so much accurateness in this particular.

3. "He saith," adds Mr Baxter, "Christ hath redeemed us from the curse, being made a curse for us."

"I explained," saith he, "before how far we are freed by redemption. He hath restored us, that is, paid the price, but with no intent that we should by that redemption be immediately or absolutely freed. Yet when we are freed, it is to be ascribed to his death as the meritorious cause, but not as the only cause."

(1.) A being freed so far or so far by redemption, and not wholly, fully, or completely, whatever men may explain, the Scripture is wholly silent of.

(2.) That Christ, in paying a price, had no intent that those he paid it for should be immediately or absolutely freed, is crudely enough asserted. Of the immediateness of their delivery I have spoken already. It hath as strict an immediation as the nature of such causes and effects will bear.

If he intended not that those for whom he died should be absolutely freed, then either he intended not their freedom at all, and so the negation is upon the term *freed;* or the negation of his intention is only as to the qualification *absolutely,* and so his intention to free them is asserted, and the affection of absoluteness in that intention only denied.

If the first he meant,—first, It is contrary to innumerable express testimonies of Scripture; secondly, It renders the Son of God dying with no determinate end or designed purpose at all, in reference to them for whom he died,—a thing we would not ascribe to a wise man in a far more easy undertaking.

If the second,—

[1.] I desire to know what is this intention here assigned to our Saviour? He paid a price or ransom for us; he bought and purchased us by his blood to be a peculiar people to himself; he redeemed us from the curse and wrath due to us, that we may be conditionally freed! All things intended under condition are, as to their accomplishment, uncertain. The condition may be fulfilled, or it may not be fulfilled; and therefore the thing intended thereon can have no certainty, as to its accomplishment, in the mind of the intender. This, then, is that which is ascribed to the Lord Jesus: "Making his soul an offering for sin; laying down his life a ransom for many; and tasting death, to free the children given him from death; praying that those for whom he died might together be partakers of his glory;" yet was he altogether uncertain whether ever any one of them should at all partake of the good things which, in his whole undertaking of mediation, he aimed at. Thus is he made a surety of an uncertain covenant, a purchaser of an inheritance perhaps never to be enjoyed, a priest sanctifying none by his sacrifice, etc.

[2.] Is the accomplishment of this condition, upon which freedom depends in the intention of Christ, certain in his mind under that intention? I ask, then, whence that assurance doth accrue? Is it from his foresight of their good using of their abilities to fulfil the condition to them prescribed? See, then, whither you have rolled this stone! The folly and absurdity of this hath been long since sufficiently discovered.

But is it from hence, because by his death he purchaseth for them the completing the condition in them? Thus he pays a price, with intention that those for whom he pays it shall be freed, by enjoying that freedom under such a condition as he procures for them, and thereupon knows that at the appointed time it shall be wrought in them. What differs this, in the close, from absolute freedom?

Farther; feign some of them for whom Christ died to fulfil this condition, others not, and it will be more evident that the greatest uncertainty possible, as to the issues of his death, must be assigned to him in his dying. The pretence of an effectual discriminating purpose of free grace, following the purpose of giving Christ promiscuously for all, will not salve the contradictions of this assertion. But the truth is, this whole figment of conditional freedom is every way unsavoury, that very thing which is assigned for the condition of our freedom being itself the chiefest part of it. The whole, indeed, as here begun, potential, conditional, not actual, not absolute issues and effects of the death of Christ, have been abundantly disproved already.

That which follows in Mr Baxter, from p. 152 unto p. 155, chap. xix., belongs not to me, being only a declaration of his own judgment about the things in hand; wherein, although many things are not only incommodiously expressed, to suit the unscriptural method of these mysteries which he hath framed in his mind, but also directly opposite to the truth, yet I shall not here meddle with it, referring them who desire satisfaction in this business to a serious consideration of what I have written to this purpose.

Page 155, chap. xx., he returns to the consideration of my assertion concerning our deliverance *ipso facto* by the blood of Christ, and tells you,

"I do not understand Mr Owen's meaning; for he saith that Christ did actually and *ipso facto* deliver us from the curse and obligation, yet we do not instantly apprehend and perceive it, nor yet possess it, but only we have actual right to all the fruits of his death," etc. So he.

The things of that treatise were written with the pen of a vulgar scribe, that every one might run and read; whence, then, it should be that so learned a man should not understand my meaning, unless from his own prejudice, I know not. However, I have now so fully delivered my sense and meaning as to these things, that I hope no place remaineth for disceptation thereabout. But let us look a little into Mr Baxter's inquiry after that which he professeth not well to understand:—

1. "Whether," saith he, "a man may fitly be said actually and *ipso facto* to be delivered and discharged who is not at all delivered, but only hath a right to deliverance, I doubt."

To unriddle this, with most of the following exceptions, and to resolve his doubt so far as I am concerned, as having administered occasion thereunto, I shall transcribe the place from whence these difficulties are pretended to arise.

The passage is in lib. iii. cap. 7 of that treatise, pp. 140, 141 [268, 269], as followeth:—1. "That actual freedom from the obligation doth not follow the satisfaction made by Christ cannot be granted; for by death he did deliver us from death, and that actually, so far as that the elect are said to die and rise with him. He did actually, or *ipso facto*, deliver us from the curse, by being made a curse for us; and the hand-writing that was against us, even the whole obligation, was taken out of the way, and nailed to his cross. It is true, all for whom he did this do not instantly actually apprehend and perceive it, which is impossible; but yet that hinders not but that they have all the fruits of his death in actual right, though not in actual possession,—which last they cannot have until at least it be made known to them. As, if a man pay a ransom for a prisoner detained in a foreign country, the very day of the payment and acceptation of it the prisoner hath right to his liberty, although he cannot enjoy it until such time as tidings of it are brought unto him, and a warrant produced for his delivery. So that that reason is nothing but a begging τοῦ ἐν ἀρχῇ. 2. The satisfaction of Christ, by the payment of the same thing that was required in the obligation, is no way prejudicial to that free, gracious condonation of sin so often mentioned. God's gracious pardoning of sin compriseth the whole dispensation of grace towards us in Christ, whereof there are two parts:—First, The laying of our sin on Christ, or making him to be sin for us; which was merely and purely an act of free grace, which he did for his own sake. Secondly, The gracious imputation of the righteousness of Christ to us, or making us the righteousness of God in him; which is no less of grace and mercy, and that because the very merit of Christ himself hath its foundation in a free compact and covenant. However, that remission, grace, and pardon which is in God for sinners, is not opposed to Christ's merits, but ours. He pardoneth all to us, but he spared not his only Son, he bated him not one farthing. The freedom, then, of pardon hath not its foundation in any defect of the merit or satisfaction of Christ, but in three other things:—First, The will of God freely appointing this satisfaction of Christ, John iii. 16; Rom. v. 8; 1 John iv. 9. Secondly, In a gracious acceptation of that decreed satisfaction in our steads; for so many, no more. Thirdly, In a free application of the death of Christ unto us. Remission, then, excludes not a full satisfaction by the solution of the very thing in the obligation, but only the solution or satisfaction by him to whom pardon and remission are granted," etc.

All that is here affirmed may be reduced to these heads:—

(1.) Actual freedom from the obligation is the immediate fruit of the death of Christ. Understand such an immediation as I have often described.

(2.) Hence Christ is said actually, or *ipso facto,* to deliver us, because our deliverance, which is to be accomplished *sub termino,* is the infallible, absolute, immediate issue and product of what he did for us. *Actual* and *ipso facto* are opposed to the intervention of any such thing as should make our deliverance to be only potential or conditional.

(3.) Those for whom Christ doth work this deliverance are not as to a simulty of time actually delivered; they neither enjoy nor are acquainted with any such deliverance until the appointed time be come, but have actual right thereunto, to possess it in due season.

This being the sum and plain intendment of that place, I suppose there will not need any operose endeavour to remove the objections that are laid against it. And therefore, to that before expressed, I say, Christ hath actually and *ipso facto* procured our deliverance. Hence we have actual right unto it, but not actual possession of it; and where the difficulty of this should rest I know not. Men may, as oft as they please, create contradictions in their own minds, and entangle themselves with doubts in the knots which themselves have tied. But,—

2. "Knowledge," saith he, "and possession of a deliverance, are far different things."

(1.) He maketh them so, who plainly intimates that the reason why it is not apprehended is because it is not possessed, and always speaks disjunctively of them.

(2.) Besides, this proposition of the distance of these two is not universally true, as I could easily demonstrate.

3. "Our knowledge, therefore," he adds, "doth not give us possession, so that the similitude fails: for it is the creditor's knowledge and satisfaction that are requisite to deliverance; and our creditor was not in a far and strange country, but knew immediately, and could either have made us quickly know, or turned us free before we had known the cause."

(1.) Whether or no, or how far, knowledge gives us possession, I shall not now dispute; only, considering in what sense knowledge is here used, and often in the Scripture, the deliverance also spoken of being such as no small part thereof consists in this knowledge, and without it (in the seed at least) is not, I cannot but say that such kind of affirmations in things of this weight are very slender proofs. Yea, farther, whereas the enjoyment of this deliverance is either as to the being of it or to the comfort of it, the latter is given us by this knowledge merely; the former consists therein mainly, John xvii. 3.

(2.) Similitudes are allowed their grains to make them current; but yet, as our creditor's knowledge and satisfaction are required to our deliverance, so not that only but ours also, as to our actual enjoyment of it. It is true, he could have made us quickly know it; but who hath been his counsellor? This is left to his sovereign and free disposal, our deliverance being purchased, to be made out in the season thereby appointed. But that God could have made us free before we knew the cause, supposing his constitution of the way of salvation, revealed in the blood of Jesus, which lies at the bottom of all these disputes, is a most anti-evangelical assertion, and diametrically opposed to the whole way of God's dealing with sinners. But he adds,—

4. "Neither can it be understood how God can so long deny us the possession of heaven, if we had such actual, absolute right so long ago; which seems to me to express a *jus ad rem* and *in re*."

(1.) I love not to inquire into the reason of God's actings, which are [1]"after the counsel of his own will;" and yet think it not very difficult to conceive how a son is for a season kept as "a servant, though he be lord of all."

(2.) He speaks as though this deliverance lay all in heaven, whereas it is here [2]fully enjoyed on the earth, though not in all the degrees of the fruits thereof.

(3.) If the right whereof we speak were *jus in re*, I see not well, indeed, how God could keep us from the possession of it, as Mr Baxter says; a man cannot be kept long from what he hath. But, saith he,—

5. "If he mean a right to future possession, I do not see how right and possession should stand at so many years' distance. To have right to God's favour and possession of that favour seem to me of nearer kin, except he should think that possession of favour is nothing but the knowledge or feeling of it, and that faith justifieth only in *foro conscientiæ*. But I will not censure so hardly until I know."

(1.) If at so many years' distance it may not be allowed, he had done well to express at how many it might. For my part, placing this right upon the purchase of Christ, as before, and possession in the actual enjoyment of the fruits of that purchase, then referring the distance between them to the good pleasure of God, who had granted and established that right to an enjoyment *sub termino*, I see no difficulty, no perplexity in this at all.

(2.) That no small portion of favour consists in a [3]sense and knowledge of the kindness of God, in its actings terminated upon the conscience, I must believe, whatever Mr Baxter be pleased to censure. It is far more facile to give the hardest censures than to answer the easiest arguments.

(3.) The place where faith justifieth I am not so solicitous about, as the manner how; which, of all other ways commonly insisted on, I conceive not to be as it is our new obedience: yet that in this work it looks farther than the conscience I easily grant.

The most of what is subjoined to these exceptions is fully answered in what went before.

As much as possible I shall avoid all repetitions of the same things; only, whereas he affirmeth that to have right to justification and to have possession of it is all one, I must needs enter my dissent thereunto; which may suffice until it be attempted to be put upon the proof. If he shall say, that a right to a future justification at the day of judgment is the same with the possession of present actual justification, it is neither true nor any thing to the business in hand.

In the close he shuts up this discourse, and enters into another, giving in his thoughts about the immediate effects of the death of Christ; a matter wherein he pretends to great accurateness, censuring others for not being able to distinguish aright of them, and so to spend abundance of labour in vain in their discourse

[1] Eph. i. 11; Gal. iv. 1. [2] John i. 12; Rom. v. 11; Eph. i. 11; Col. i. 12–14.
[3] Ps. iv. 6, 7; 2 Cor. iv. 6.

thereabout.[1] Particularly, here he denies, and calls it a dangerous error to suppose, that actual remission and justification are immediate effects of his death, or any right thereunto; which he attempteth to prove by sundry arguments.

Of the effects of the death of Christ, and what relation they all stand in thereunto, I have spoken at large before. Now, because actual remission is denied to be an immediate effect of the death of Christ, and so potential remission, not once mentioned in the book of God, is tacitly substituted in the room thereof, and this also in opposition to what I had delivered, I shall briefly consider his arguments, and so give an end to this debate:—

1. "What right soever God giveth unto men in things supernatural, such as justification, remission, and adoption, he giveth it by his written laws; but by these laws he hath given no such thing to any unbelievers, such as are the elect before conversion: therefore, etc.

"The major is evident; God's decree giveth no man a personal right to the mercy intended him. And for the minor, no man can produce the Scripture giving to unbelievers such a right."

(1.) Taking the laws of God in the strict and proper sense, it is so far from being a truth, that what right God gives to any he gives it by his written laws, that indeed the laws of God give no right to any one concerning any thing, whether supernatural or otherwise. The end of the law is not to give right, but to [2]exact obedience, and that chiefly, if not, upon the sum, solely. The usual, proper, genuine signification of God's laws being his revealed will for our obedience, I know not why Mr Baxter should bring them in, in the latitude of his single apprehension, to be a medium in an argument. Hence,—

(2.) Here is not a sufficient enumeration of causes; the promises of God are to be added, and those either made to us, or to any other for our good. But,—

(3.) That the decree of God gives to no man a right to the thing concerning which the decree is, is so far from being a sufficient proof of the major that it is in itself very questionable, if not unquestionably false. That the decree gives not being and existence to the things concerning which it is, is an old rule. That no right should from it arise unto that thing by virtue thereof, is not yet so clear. Right is but "jus:" "Jus est quod justum est." If it be just or right that any one should have such a thing, he is said to have a right thereunto. Now, supposing the [3]decree of God, that a man shall by such means have such a thing, is it not just, equitable, and condecent unto righteousness that he should have it? But yet farther,—

(4.) We are not at all speaking of a right founded on God's decrees (which considering what was proposed to be proved by this argument, I wonder how it found any mention here),[4] but upon two other things:—

[1.] The covenant of God with Christ about the pardoning, justifying, and saving of those for whose sin he should make his soul an offering; which covenant, respecting Christ as mediator, God and man, is not to be reckoned among the mere decrees and purposes of God, containing in itself all those promises and engagements whereon the Lord Jesus in the work of redemption rolled himself. Now, in this covenant God engaged himself, as I said before, to make out to those for whom Christ undertook whatsoever was the fruit of his purchase; and that was [5]what in his good pleasure was assigned thereunto. And this is the first bottom of this right.

[2.] The purchase of Christ being completed, by the performance of all things by divine constitution thereunto allotted,[6] and himself acquitted and exonerated of

[1] Ῥᾷον τὸ μωμεῖσθαι, ἢ μιμεῖσθαι.

[2] "Lex aut punit, aut vetat, aut permittit, aut consulit, aut hortatur."—F. de Leg. 1 John iii. 4. "Decretum nil ponit in esse, prædestinatio in prædestinato."—Aquin.

[3] Eph. i. 4; 2 Pet. i. 1.

[4] "Cur urceus exit?"

[5] Isa. l. 5-9.

[6] John xvii. 4; 1 Tim. iii. 16; John xvii.; Heb. ix. 14.

the whole debt of their sin for whom he suffered, which was charged on him, he makes demand of the accomplishment of the fore-mentioned engagement made to him, concerning the freedom and deliverance of the persons whose sins were laid on him, and whose bringing unto glory he undertook.

On these two, I say, it is that our right to the fruits of the death of Christ, even before believing, doth depend; from hence, at least, it is right and equal that we do, in the time appointed, enjoy these things. Yea, to say that we have right, upon believing, to the fruits of the death of Christ, affirmed universally, can only be affirmed of a *jus in re*, such a right as hath, at least in part, conjoined actual possession, believing itself being no small portion of these fruits.

This argument, then, being fallacious, omitting the chief causes in enumeration, includes not the thing proposed. Besides, it is in no small measure faulty, in that the first thing proposed to be confirmed was, that remission of sin and justification are not the immediate effects of Christ's death, whereof in this argument there is οὐδὲ γρῦ.

2. "If God 'hate all workers of iniquity,' and we are all 'by nature the children of wrath,' and 'without faith it is impossible to please God,' and 'he that believeth not is condemned already,' then certainly the elect, while they are unbelievers, are not actually *de facto*, no, nor in personal right, delivered from this hatred, wrath, displeasure, and condemnation; but, etc.: *ergo*."

(1.) This argument, for what indeed it will prove, is handled at large in my treatise of Redemption, as also re-urged in the pages foregoing. Against actual justification from eternity it hath its efficacy.

(2.) It doth also conclude that the elect, whilst unbelievers, are not actually and *de facto* put in possession of the issues of love, faith being with the first of them. But,—

(3.) That they have not, upon the grounds fore-mentioned, a right to these things; or,—

(4.) That justification is not the immediate effect of the death of Christ (being the sole things in question), it hath the same unhappiness with the former, not once to mention.

3. "If we are justified only by faith, then certainly not before faith; but we are justified only by faith: *ergo*."

(1.) If I mistake not, it is not justification before faith, but a right to the fruits of the death of Christ before faith, that is to be proved.

(2.) That justification is not the immediate effect of the death of Christ; to which ends for this argument, "valeat quantum valere potest;" to me it comes not within many miles of the thing in question: so that, with the absurd answers supposed thereunto, we pass it by.

The like also I am enforced to say of the two others that follow, being of the same length and breadth with those foregoing,—too short and narrow to cover the things in question; so that though they may have their strength to their own proper end, yet as to the things proposed to be proved, there is nothing in their genuine conclusions looking that way.

If I might take the liberty of guessing, I should suppose the mistake which led this author to all this labour in vain is, that the immediate effects of the death of Christ must be immediately enjoyed by them for whom he died; which assertion hath not indeed the least colour of truth. The effects of the death of Christ are not said to be immediate in reference to others' enjoyment of them, but unto their causality by that death. Whatever it be that in the first place is made out to sinners for the death of Christ, whenever it be done, that is the immediate effect thereof as to them; as to them, I say, for in its first tendency, it hath a more immediate object.

If Mr Baxter go on with his intentions about a tract concerning universal redemption, perhaps we may have these things cleared; and yet, we must tell him beforehand, that if he draw forth nothing on that subject but what is done by Amyraldus, and like things to them, he will give little satisfaction to learned and stable men upon the issue of his undertaking. I shall not presume to take another man's task out of his hand, especially one's who is so every way able to go through with it; else I durst undertake to demonstrate that treatise of Amyraldus, mentioned by Mr Baxter, to be full of weak and sophistical argumentations, absurd contradictions, vain strife of words, and, in sum, to be as birthless a tympanous endeavour as ever so learned a man was engaged in.

For the present, being by God's providence removed for a season from my native soil, attended with more than ordinary weaknesses and infirmities, separated from my library, burdened with manifold employments, with constant preaching to a numerous multitude of as thirsting a people after the gospel as ever yet I conversed withal, it sufficeth me that I have obtained this mercy, briefly and plainly to vindicate the truth from mistakes, and something farther to unfold the mystery of our redemption in Christ, all with so facile and placid an endeavour as is usually upon the spirits of men in the familiar writings of one friend to another. That it hath been my aim to seek after truth, and to keep close to the form of wholesome words delivered to us, will, I hope, appear to them that love truth and peace.

Τῷ Θεῷ ἀριστομεγίστῳ δόξα.

DUBLIN CASTLE, *December* 20, 1649.

A

DISSERTATION ON DIVINE JUSTICE:

OR,

THE CLAIMS OF VINDICATORY JUSTICE VINDICATED;

WHEREIN THAT ESSENTIAL PROPERTY OF THE DIVINE NATURE IS DEMONSTRATED FROM THE SACRED WRITINGS, AND DEFENDED AGAINST SOCINIANS, PARTICULARLY THE AUTHORS OF THE RACOVIAN CATECHISM, JOHN CRELLIUS, AND F. SOCINUS HIMSELF;

LIKEWISE THE NECESSARY EXERCISE THEREOF;

TOGETHER WITH THE INDISPENSABLE NECESSITY OF THE SATISFACTION OF CHRIST FOR THE SALVATION OF SINNERS IS ESTABLISHED AGAINST THE OBJECTIONS OF CERTAIN VERY LEARNED MEN, G. TWISSE, G. VOSSIUS, SAMUEL RUTHERFORD, AND OTHERS.

BY JOHN OWEN,

DEAN OF CHRIST CHURCH COLLEGE, OXFORD.

"Is God unrighteous who taketh vengeance? God forbid: for then how shall God judge the world?"—ROM. iii. 5, 6.

OXFORD: THOMAS ROBINSON.

1653.

PREFATORY NOTE.

This work is devoted to a refutation of the doctrine that sin could be pardoned by a mere volition on the part of God, without any satisfaction to his justice; or, to state the question in the abstract form which it chiefly assumes in the reasonings of Owen, that justice is not a natural attribute of the divine nature, but so much an act of the divine will, that God is free to punish or to refrain from punishing sin. Owen clearly saw that if such a doctrine were entertained, there could be no evidence for the necessity of the atonement, and a stronghold would be surrendered to the Socinian heresy. He was the more induced to engage in the refutation of it, as it was maintained by some divines of eminent worth and ability. Calvin has been cited in its favour; and Owen, without naming him, refers to the only passage in his writings which, so far as we are aware, conveys the obnoxious sentiment, when in the second chapter he speaks of the learned men who, along with Augustine, and amongst orthodox divines, held the view in question. The passage occurs in his commentary on John xv. 13:—"Poterat nos Deus verbo aut nutu redimere, nisi aliter nostrâ causâ visum esset, ut proprio et unigenito Filio non parcens, testatum faceret in ejus personâ quantam habeat salutis nostræ curam." An isolated phrase, however, when the question was not specially under his review, is scarcely sufficient basis from which to infer that Calvin held the possibility of sin being forgiven without an atonement; and other parts of his works might be quoted, in which he speaks of the death of Christ as a satisfaction to divine justice, in such terms as almost to preclude the theory for which the sanction of his name has been pleaded. Dr William Twisse, the learned prolocutor of the Westminster Assembly, published in 1632 a large work, now almost fallen into oblivion, but which passed through several editions, and was justly held in high esteem, "Vindiciæ Gratiæ. Potestatis, ac Providentiæ Divinæ." In the midst of his discussions he inserts several digressions on special topics; and the eighth digression contains an argument to prove that God punishes sin, not by any necessity of nature, or under the promptings of justice, as essential to the perfection of his character, but simply in virtue of a decree, originating in a free act of his will, and regulating, in this subordinate sense, all his procedure towards our race. He was followed by Rutherford in his "Disputatio Scholastica de Divinâ Providentiâ," 1649; and in his work on "Christ Dying, and Drawing Sinners," etc. One extract from the latter gives a plausible and condensed statement of the whole theory:—"If we speak of God's absolute power without respect to his free decree, he could have pardoned sin without a ransom, and gifted all mankind and fallen angels with heaven without any satisfaction of either the sinner or his surety; for he neither punisheth sin, nor tenders heaven to men or angels, by necessity of nature,—as the fire casteth out heat, and the sun light,—but freely."

Owen, in one of the public disputations at Oxford, had asserted that the exercise of divine justice was necessary and absolute in the punishment of sin. Though his arguments were directed against Socinians, some divines in the university, it was found, held a different opinion from our author on this particular point, and, in full explanation of his views, in 1653 he published his Diatriba. "It is almost entirely," says Mr Orme, "of a scholastic nature, discovering, indeed, much acuteness, and a profound acquaintance with the subject, but not likely now to be read with much interest." We concur in this criticism, but must take exception to the last remark. The work, in our judgment, at least deserves to be read with interest, as the conclusive settlement of a question of vital moment, one of the most vigorous productions of Owen's intellect, a specimen of controversy conducted in the best spirit, and displaying powers of thought which remind us of the massive theology of Edwards, while rich in the stores of a learning to which the great American could not lay claim. In the first part of it, Owen proves that "sin-punishing justice is natural, and its exercise necessary to God," by four leading arguments,—1. The statements of Holy Writ; 2. The consent of mankind; 3. The course of Providence; and, lastly, The attributes of God as revealed in the cross of Christ. Various subsidiary arguments of considerable importance follow. The second part refutes in succession the opposing arguments of the Socinians, Twisse, and Rutherford.

Thomas Gilbert, so great an admirer of Owen that he was employed to write his epitaph, nevertheless combated the views maintained in the Diatriba, in a work entitled, "Vindiciæ Supremi Dei Domini (cum Deo) Initæ," etc., 1665. Baxter, in a brief premonition to his treatise against infidelity, dissented from the doctrine of Owen on this subject.

The Diatriba was published in Latin. We have compared Mr Hamilton's translation of it, which appeared in 1794, with the original, and have been constrained to make some serious changes on it, which we cannot but deem improvements. The title-page is more exactly and fully rendered; a translation of the dedication to Cromwell is now, for the first time, inserted; passages which had been placed at the foot of the page are restored to their proper place in the body of the text; several passages altogether omitted are now supplied; minor errors have been corrected; and where the change was so extensive as to interfere with the translator's responsibilities, we have appended a different rendering in a note.—Ed.

TO THE PUBLIC.

THE numerous and valuable writings of Dr Owen have long ago secured his praise in all the churches as a first-rate writer upon theological subjects. Any recommendation, therefore, of the present work seems unnecessary. As the treatise, however, now offered to the public, has long been locked up in a dead language, it may not be improper to say, what will be granted by all competent judges, that the author discovers an uncommon acquaintance with his subject; that he has clearly explained the nature of divine justice, and demonstrated it to be, not merely an arbitrary thing, depending upon the sovereign pleasure of the supreme Lawgiver, but essential to the divine nature. In doing this, he has overthrown the arguments of the Socinians and others against the atonement of Christ, and proved that a complete satisfaction to the law and justice of God was necessary, in order that sinners might be pardoned, justified, sanctified, and eternally saved, consistently with the honour of all the divine perfections.

Whoever makes himself master of the Doctor's reasoning in the following treatise will be able to answer all the objections and cavils of the enemies of the truth therein contended for. It is, therefore, earnestly recommended to the attention and careful perusal of all who wish to obtain right ideas of God, the nature and extent of the divine law, the horrid nature and demerit of sin, etc., but especially to the attention of young divines. The translation, upon the whole, is faithful. If it have any fault, it is perhaps its being too literal.

That it may meet with that reception which it justly merits from the public, and which the importance of the subject demands, is the earnest prayer of the servants in the gospel of Christ,

S. STAFFORD, D.D.
J. RYLAND, sen., M.A.
ROB. SIMPSON.

TO HIS ILLUSTRIOUS HIGHNESS

LORD OLIVER CROMWELL,

COMMANDER-IN-CHIEF OF THE PARLIAMENTARY FORCES OF THE COMMONWEALTH OF ENGLAND,

THE RIGHT HONOURABLE CHANCELLOR OF THE VERY CELEBRATED UNIVERSITY OF OXFORD.

HAD it not been almost a crime for me, holding my present place in this most celebrated university, under your appointment and auspices, to have inscribed any literary production with a dedication to any other name, I would not have held in such poor account the weight of business you sustain as to make an endeavour to divert your thoughts and attention, so constantly directed to the welfare of the commonwealth, to a little by-work of this kind. But since, according to the nature of my office, I am under frequent necessity to address your Highness in the name of literature and of learned men, the affability of your nature will not suffer me to remain under any anxiety but that you will condescend to examine even this humble production of ours. Perhaps the dedication of books to you (amid prevailing "wars and rumours of wars," and the fury and commotion of parties bent with eagerness on mutual destruction) will seem unseasonable, and not unlike the celebrated abstraction of him who, amid the destruction of his country and the sack of the city to which he belonged, neglecting all concern about his personal safety, was so obstinately bent on learned trifles as to be slain by a soldier while persisting in those pursuits on account of his skill in which the commander had resolved to spare his life. But even Christian authors have their *polemics;* and these, alas! too much fitted to excite, increase, and promote bloody strife ;—such is the blindness, nay, the madness of most men. Even this small piece of ours is polemical, I confess; but it fights by means of weapons not offensive to peace, not imbued with hostility, but appropriate to truth,—namely, by the word of God and reason. In this arena, in this fortress, within this list and limit, if all controversies on divine things took place, no longer, on account of seditions and wars, would religion herself, over all Christendom, be so evil spoken of. The cause I maintain will not be esteemed by many of such consequence that I should contend for it so earnestly. But of how much importance it is in war (for it is a war in which we are engaged, and that a sacred one, with the enemies of truth) to secure a citadel or breast-work, your Excellency knows right well; that it is so to the army of the living God, redeemed and purified by the blood of Christ, whose truth we have undertaken, according to our ability, to defend, any man on serious reflection will easily perceive. Surely we may be permitted to contend for the truth. Some there are who, under pretence of zeal for the gospel, delight to mingle of their own accord in wars, tumults, strifes, and commotion, sufficiently skilled

"Ære ciere viros, Martemque accendere cantu."

We pretend, however, to no such eloquence, nor have we so learned Christ. My hope is, that the Lord and Judge of all will find me intently occupied in preaching Christ and him crucified, in season and out of season, and wrestling in prayer with God our gracious Father, for the salvation of the little flock of his well-beloved Son. Not as if it were in our power to keep free from controversies, for He who declared himself to have been sent, according to his own and the Father's counsel, not to destroy but to save the lives of men (that is, spiritually and eternally), predicted, however, that from the innate malice of men perversely opposing themselves to heavenly truth, not love, not tranquillity and peace, but strife, hatred, war, and the sword, would ensue upon the promulgation of that truth. Peace, indeed, he bequeathed to his own; but it was that divine peace which dwells in the bosom of the Father, and in the inmost recesses of their own souls. In truth, while his disciples live mingled with other men, and are exposed to national disturbances, how can they but share, like a small boat attached to a ship, in the same tempest and agitation with the rest? But since we have it in command, "if it be possible, and as much as lieth in us, to live peaceably with all men," that contention is alone pleasing which is in defence of truth; and it is pleasing only because for the truth we are bound to contend. Therefore, we address ourselves to this work, however humble it may be, in the service of our beloved Saviour, to whom we know that a work of this kind, although feeble and imperfect, is pleasing and acceptable; in whom alone, also, we would find both an encouragement and an aim in the prosecution of our studies, not unwilling to undergo any risk or danger under the guidance of such a Leader. But seeing what is acceptable to him cannot displease your Highness, I dedicate with pleasure to your Excellency, in testimony of my gratitude, what I have accomplished in fulfilment of my duty to him. For what remains (since a reason must elsewhere be rendered to the reader for undertaking this work, and

"—— in publica commoda peccem,
Si longo sermone morer tua tempora"),

I bow before God, the best and greatest, beseeching him in Jesus Christ that he would continually direct, by his own Spirit, all the counsels, undertakings, and actions of your Highness; that he would turn all these to his own glory, and to the peace, honour, and advantage of the church, commonwealth, and university; and that he would preserve your spirit, in the midst of a crooked and perverse generation, blameless unto the coming of our Lord Jesus Christ, to whom be honour and glory for ever. This I write under ill health at Oxford, the last day of the year 1652.

The devoted Servant of your Illustrious Highness, and your Vice-Chancellor in this famous University,

John Owen.

THE PREFACE TO THE READER.

As perhaps, learned reader, you will think it strange that I, who have such abundance of various and laborious employment of another kind, should think of publishing such a work as this, it may not be improper to lay before you a summary account of the reasons that induced me to this undertaking; and I do it the rather that this little production may escape free from the injurious suspicions which the manners of the times are but too apt to affix to works of this kind. It is now four months and upwards since, in the usual course of duty, in defending certain theological theses in our university, it fell to my lot to discourse and dispute on the vindicatory justice of God, and the necessity of its exercise, on the supposition of the existence of sin. Although these observations were directed, to the best of my abilities, immediately against the Socinians, yet it was understood that many very respectable theologians entertained sentiments on this subject very different from mine; and although the warmest opposers of what we then maintained were obliged to acknowledge that our arguments are quite decisive against the adversaries, yet there were not wanting some, who, not altogether agreeing with us, employed themselves in strictures upon our opinion, and accused it of error, while others continued wavering, and, in the diversity of opinions, knew not on which to fix. Much controversy ensuing in consequence of this, I agreed with some learned men to enter, both in writings and conversation, upon an orderly and deliberate investigation of the subject. And after the scruples of several had been removed by a more full consideration of our opinion (to effect which the following considerations chiefly contributed, namely, that they clearly saw this doctrine conduced to the establishment of the necessity of the satisfaction of Jesus Christ, a precious truth, which these worthy and good men, partakers of the grace and gift of righteousness through means of the blood of Christ, not only warmly favoured, but dearly venerated, as the most honourable[1] treasure of the church, the seed of a blessed immortality, and the darling jewel of our religion), I was greatly encouraged in the conferences with these gentlemen to take a deeper view of the subject, and to examine it more closely, for the future benefit of mankind.

Besides; several of those who had before examined and were acquainted with our sentiments, or to whom, in consequence of our short discourse in the university on the subject, they began to be more acceptable,—and these, too, considerable both for their number and rank,—ceased not to urge me to a more close consideration and accurate review of the controversy; for in that public dissertation, it being confined, according to the general custom of such exercises in universities, within the narrow limits of an hour, I could only slightly touch on the nature of vindicatory justice, whereas the rules and limits of such exercises would not permit me to enter on the chief point, the great hinge of the controversy,—namely, concerning the necessary exercise of that justice. This is the difficulty that requires the abilities of the most judicious and acute to investigate and solve. In this situation of matters, not only a more full view of the whole state of the controversy, but likewise of the weight of those arguments on which the truth of that side of the question which we have espoused depends, as also an explanation and confutation of certain subtilties whereby the opponents had embarrassed the minds of some inquirers after truth, became objects of general request. And, indeed, such

[1] Ὑπερτίμιον, invaluable, unspeakably precious.—ED.

were the circumstances of this controversy, that any one might easily perceive that a scholastic dissertation on the subject must take a very different turn, and could bear no farther resemblance, and owe nothing more to the former exercise, than the having furnished an opportunity or occasion for its appearance in public.

Although, then, I was more than sufficiently full of employment already, yet, being excited by the encouragement of good men, and fully persuaded in my own mind that the truth which we embrace is so far from being of trivial consequence in our religion, that it is intimately connected with many, the most important articles of the Christian doctrine, concerning the attributes of God, the satisfaction of Christ, and the nature of sin, and of our obedience, and that it strikes its roots deep through almost the whole of theology, or the acknowledging of the truth which is according to godliness;—fully persuaded, I say, of these facts, I prevailed with myself, rather than this doctrine should remain any longer neglected or buried, and hardly even known by name, or be held captive by the reasonings of some enslaving the minds of mankind, "through philosophy and vain deceit," to exert my best abilities in its declaration and defence.

Several things, however, which, with your good leave, reader, I shall now mention, almost deterred me from the task when begun. The first and chief was, the great *difficulty of the subject* itself, which, among the more abstruse points of truth, is by no means the least abstruse: for as every divine truth has a peculiar majesty and reverence belonging to it, which debars from the spiritual knowledge of it (as it is in Christ) the ignorant and unstable,—that is, those who are not taught of God, or become subject to the truth,—so those points which dwell in more intimate recesses, and approach nearer its immense fountain, the "Father of lights," darting brighter rays, by their excess of light present a confounding darkness to the minds of the greatest men (and are as darkness to the eyes, breaking forth amidst so great light):—

"Suntque oculis tenebræ per tantum lumen obortæ."

For what we call darkness in divine subjects is nothing else than their celestial glory and splendour striking on the weak ball of our eyes, the rays of which we are not able in this life, which "is but a vapour" (and that not very clear), "which appeareth but for a little," to bear. Hence God himself, who is "light, and in whom there is no darkness at all," who "dwelleth in light inaccessible," and who "clotheth himself with light as with a garment," in respect of us, is said to have made "darkness his pavilion."

Not, as the Roman Catholics say, that there is any reason that we should blasphemously accuse the holy Scriptures of obscurity; for "the law of the LORD is *perfect*, converting the soul; the testimony of the LORD is *sure*, making wise the simple: the statutes of the LORD are *right*, rejoicing the heart; the commandment of the LORD is *pure*, enlightening the eyes." Nor is there reason to complain that any one part of the truth hath been too sparingly or obscurely revealed: for even the smallest portion of the divine word is, by the grace of the Holy Spirit, assisting to dispose and frame either the subject or our hearts, so as to view the bright object of divine truth in its proper and spiritual light, sufficient to communicate the knowledge of truths of the last importance; for it is owing to the nature of the doctrines themselves and their exceeding splendour that there are some things hard to be conceived and interpreted, and which surpass our capacity and comprehension. Whether this article of divine truth which we are now inquiring into be not akin to those which we have now mentioned, let the learned judge and determine, especially those who shall reflect what a close connection there is between it and the whole doctrine concerning the nature of God, the satisfaction of Christ, the desert of sin, and every one of the dark and more abstruse heads of our religion. I have, therefore, determined to place my chief dependence on His aid "who giveth to all liberally, and upbraideth not." For those unhappy gentlemen only lose their labour, and may not improperly be compared to the artists who used more than common exertions in building Noah's ark,[1] and who, like bees, work for others and not for themselves in the search of truth, who, relying on their own abilities and industry, use every effort to ascertain and comprehend divine truths, while, at the same time, they continue utterly regardless whether "He who commanded the light to shine out of darkness hath hitherto shone in their hearts, to give them the light of the knowledge of his glory in the face of Jesus Christ;" for, after all, they can accomplish nothing more, by their utmost efforts, but to discover their technical or artificial ignorance.[2]

Setting aside, then, the consideration of some phrases, and even of some arguments, as to what relates to the principal point of the controversy, I hold myself bound, in conscience and in honour, not even to imagine that I have attained a proper knowledge of any one article of truth, much less to publish it, unless through the Holy Spirit I have had such a taste of it, in its spiritual sense, as that I may be able from the heart to say with the psalmist, "I have believed, and therefore have I spoken." He who, in the investigation of truth, makes it his chief care to have his mind and will rendered subject to the faith, and obedient to the "Father of lights," and who with attention waits upon Him whose throne is in the heavens; he alone (since the things of God knoweth no man, but the Spirit of God) attains to true wisdom,—the others walk in a "vain show." It has, then, been my principal object, in tracing the depths and secret nature of the subject in question,—while I, a poor worm, contemplated the majesty and glory of Him concerning whose perfections I was treating,—to attend and obey, with all humility and reverence, what the great God the Lord hath spoken in his word; not at all doubting but that, whatever way he should incline my heart, by the power of his Spirit and truth, I should be enabled, in a dependence on his aid, to bear the contradictions of a false knowledge, and all human and philosophical arguments.

And, to say the truth, as I have adopted the opinion which I defend in this dissertation from no regard to the arguments of either one or another learned man, and much less from any slavish attachment to authority, example, or traditionary prejudices, and from no confidence in the opinion or abilities of others, but, as I hope, from a most humble contemplation of the holiness, purity, justice, right, dominion, wisdom, and mercy of God; so by the guidance of his Spirit alone, and power of his heart-changing grace, filling my mind with all the fulness of truth, and striking me with a deep awe and admiration of it, I have been enabled to surmount the difficulty of the research. Theology is the "wisdom that is from above," a habit of grace and spiritual gifts, the manifestation of the Spirit, reporting what is conducive to happiness. It is not a science to be learned from the precepts of man, or from the rules of arts, or method of other sciences, as those represent it who also maintain that a "natural man" may attain all that artificial and methodical theology, even though, in the matters of God and mysteries of the gospel, he be blinder than a mole. What a distinguished theologian must he be "who receiveth not the things of the Spirit of God!"

But again · having sailed through this sea of troubles,[3] and being ready to launch out upon the subject, that gigantic spectre, "It is everywhere spoken against," should have occasioned me no delay, had it not come forth inscribed with the mighty names of Augustine, Calvin, Musculus, Twisse, and Vossius. And although I could not but entertain for these divines that honour and respect which is due to such great names, yet, partly by considering myself as entitled to that "freedom wherewith CHRIST hath made us free," and partly by opposing to these the names of other very learned theologians,—namely, Paræus, Piscator, Molinæus, Lubbertus, Rivetus, Cameron, Maccovius, Junius, the professors at Saumur, and others,—who, after the spreading of the poison of Socinianism, have with great ac-

1 Thereby hastening their own destruction.—TR.
2 The meaning is, "But to make a most elaborate display of their ignorance."—ED.
3 Vado isto enavigato, "Having cleared these shallows."—ED.

curacy and caution investigated and cleared up this truth, I easily got rid of any uneasiness from that quarter.

Having thus surmounted these difficulties, and begun the undertaking by devoting to it a few leisure hours stolen from other engagements, the work prospered beyond all expectation; and, by the favour of the "Father of lights," who "worketh in us both to will and to do of his good pleasure," in a few days it was brought to a conclusion.

And now that the labour of composing was ended, I again entertained doubts, and continued for some time in suspense, whether, considering the manners of the times in which we live, it would not be more prudent to throw the papers, with some other kindred compositions on other subjects of divinity, into some secret coffers, there to be buried in eternal oblivion, than bring them forth to public discussion.

For even all know with what vain arrogance, malice, party spirit, and eager lust of attacking the labours of others, the minds of many are corrupted and infected. Not only, then, was it necessary that I should anticipate and digest in my mind the contempt and scoffings which these bantering, saucy, dull-witted, self-sufficient despisers of others, or any of such a contemptible race, whose greatest pleasure it is to disparage all kinds of exertions, however praiseworthy, might pour out against me; but I likewise foresaw that I should have to contend with the soured tempers and prejudiced opinions of others, who, being carried away by party zeal, and roused by the unexpected state and condition of public affairs,[1] and who thinking themselves to be the men, and that wisdom was born and will die with them, look down with contempt upon all who differ from them; and not with these only, but I likewise knew that I had a more severe scrutiny to undergo from some learned men, to whom, it was easy to conjecture, this work, for many reasons, would not be acceptable,—for there are some by whom all labour employed in the search of any more obscure or difficult truth is accounted as misemployed, nor do these want the ingenuity of assigning honourable pretences for their indolence. I should, however, be ashamed to enter into any serious argument with such, nor is it worth while to enter upon a review of their long declamations. And although these, and many other things of such a kind, may appear grievous and hard to be borne to your dainty gentlemen, who eagerly court splendour and fame, yet, ingenuously to say the truth, I am very fully persuaded that no man can either think or speak of me and my works with so much disregard and contempt as I myself, from my soul, both think and speak. And having in no respect any other expectation than that of contempt to myself and name, provided divine truth be promoted, all these considerations had long ago become not only of small consequence to me, but appeared as the merest trifles; for why should we be anxious about what shall become either of ourselves or our names, if only we "commit our souls to God in well-doing, as unto a faithful Creator," and by continuing in well-doing, stop the mouths of ignorant babblers? "God careth for us;" let us "cast our burdens upon him, and he will sustain us." Let but the truth triumph, vanquish, rout, and put to flight its enemies; let the word of the cross have "free course and be glorified;" let wretched sinners learn daily more and more of fellowship with Christ in his sufferings, of the necessity of satisfaction for sins by the blood of the Son of God, so that he who is "white and ruddy, and the chiefest among ten thousand," may appear so to them, "yea, altogether lovely," till, being admitted into the chambers of the church's husband, they drink "love that is better than wine," and "become a willing people in the day of his power, and in the beauty of holiness;" and I shall very little regard being "judged of man's judgment."

Since, then, I not only have believed what I have spoken, but as both my own heart and God, who is greater than my heart, are witnesses that I have engaged in this labour for the truth under the influence of the most sacred regard and

1 This treatise was written in the time of the Commonwealth.—TR.

reverence for the majesty, purity, holiness, justice, grace, and mercy of God, from a detestation of that abominable thing which his soul hateth, and with a heart inflamed with zeal for the honour and glory of our dearest Saviour Jesus Christ, who is fairer than the sons of men and altogether lovely, whom with my soul and all that is within me I worship, love, and adore, whose glorious coming I wish and long for ("Come, Lord Jesus, come quickly"), for "whose sake I count all things but as loss and dung;"—since, I say, I have engaged in this labour from these motives alone, I am under no anxiety or doubt but it will meet with a favourable reception from impartial judges, from those acquainted with the terror of the Lord, the curse of the law, the virtue of the cross, the power of the gospel, and the riches of the glory of divine grace.

There are, no doubt, many other portions and subjects of our religion, of that blessed trust committed to us for our instruction, on which we might dwell with greater pleasure and satisfaction of mind. Such, I mean, as afford a more free and wider scope of ranging through the most pleasant meads of the holy Scripture, and contemplating in these the transparent fountains of life and rivers of consolation; subjects which, unencumbered by the thickets of scholastic terms and distinctions, unembarrassed by the impediments and sophisms of an enslaving philosophy or false knowledge, sweetly and pleasantly lead into a pure, unmixed, and delightful fellowship with the Father and with his Son, shedding abroad in the heart the inmost loves of our Beloved, with the odour of his sweet ointment poured forth. This truth, [however, which is under our consideration], likewise has its uses, and such as are of the greatest importance to those who are walking in the way of holiness and evangelical obedience. A brief specimen and abstract[1] of them is added, for the benefit of the pious reader, in the end of the dissertation, in order to excite his love towards our beloved High Priest and Chief Shepherd, and true fear towards God, who is a "consuming fire," and whom we cannot serve "acceptably" unless with "reverence and godly fear."

There can be no doubt but that many points of doctrine still remain, on which the labours of the godly and learned may be usefully employed: for although many reverend and learned divines, both of the present and former age, [from the time, at least, when God vouchsafed to our fathers that glorious regeneration, or time of reformation, of a purer religion and of sound learning, after a long reign of darkness,] have composed from the sacred writings a synopsis, or methodical body, of doctrine or heavenly truth, and published their compositions under various titles; and although other theological writings, catechetical, dogmatical, exegetical, casuistical, and polemical, have increased to such a mass that the "world can hardly contain the books that have been written;" yet such is the nature of divine truth, so deep and inexhaustible the fountain of the sacred Scriptures, whence we draw it, so innumerable the salutary remedies and antidotes proposed in these to dispel all the poisons and temptations wherewith the adversary can ever attack either the minds of the pious or the peace of the church and the true doctrine, that serious and thinking men can entertain no doubt but that we perform a service praise-worthy and profitable to the church of Christ, when, under the direction of "the Spirit of wisdom and revelation," we bring forward, explain, and defend the most important and necessary articles of evangelical truth.

But to be more particular: how sparingly, for instance, yea, how obscurely, how confusedly, is the whole economy of the Spirit towards believers (one of the greatest mysteries of our religion,—a most invaluable portion of the salvation brought about for us by Christ) described by divines in general! or rather, by the most, is it not altogether neglected? In their catechisms, common-place books, public and private theses, systems, compends, etc.; even in their commentaries, harmonies, and

1 [A few crumbs of these, by way of specimen are] added, etc. "Abstract" conveys a widely different idea from ἀποσπασμάτα.—Ed.

expositions, concerning the indwelling, sealing testimony, unction, and consolation of the Spirit,—Good God! concerning this inestimable fruit of the death and resurrection of Jesus Christ, this invaluable treasure of the godly, though copiously revealed and explained in the Scriptures, there is almost a total silence; and with regard to union and communion with Christ, and with his Father and our Father, and some other doctrines respecting his person, as the husband and head of the church, the same observation holds good.

For almost from the very period in which they were capable of judging even of the first principles of religion,[1] the orthodox have applied themselves to clear up and explain those articles of the truth which Satan, by his various artifices, hath endeavoured to darken, pervert, or undermine. But as there is no part of divine truth which, since the eternal and sworn enmity took place between him and the seed of the woman, he hath not opposed with all his might, fury, and cunning; so he hath not thought proper wholly to intrust the success of his interest to instruments delegated from among mankind,—though many of them seem to have discovered such a wonderful promptitude, alacrity, and zeal in transacting his business, that one would think they had been formed and fashioned for the purpose,—but he hath reserved, according to that power which he hath over darkness and all kind of wickedness, a certain portion of his work, to be administered in a peculiar manner by himself. And as he has, in all ages, reaped an abundant crop of tares from that part of his [domain] which he hired out to be improved by man, though, from the nature of human affairs, not without much noise, tumult, blood, and slaughter; so from that which he thought proper to manage himself, without any delegated assistance, he has received a more abundant and richer crop of infernal fruit.

The exertions of Satan against the truth of the gospel may be distinguished into two divisions. In the first, as the god of this world, he endeavours to darken the minds of unbelievers, "that the light of the glorious gospel of Christ may not shine unto them." With what success he exercises this soul-destroying employment we cannot pretend to say; but there is reason to lament that he hath succeeded, and still succeeds, beyond his utmost hope. In the other, he carries on an implacable war, an unremitting strife; not, as formerly, with Michael about the body of Moses, but about the Spirit of Christ, about some of the more distinguished articles of the truth, and the application of each of them in order to cultivate communion with God the Father, and with his Son, our Lord Jesus Christ,—against the hearts of the godly and the new creature formed within them.

In this situation of affairs, most Christian writers have made it their study to oppose that first effort of the devil, whereby, through means of his instruments, he openly endeavours to suppress the light, both natural and revealed; but they have not been equally solicitous to succour the minds of believers when wrestling, "not against flesh and blood, but against principalities and powers, against the rulers of the darkness of this world, against spiritual wickedness in high places," and almost ready to sink under the contest. Hence, I say, a very minute investigation hath been set on foot by many of those articles of religion which he has openly, through the instrumentality of the slaves of error and darkness, attacked, and the vindication of them made clear and plain. But those which, both from their relation to practice and a holy communion, full of spiritual joy, to be cultivated with God, the old serpent hath reserved for his own attack in the hearts of believers, most writers, (partly either because they were ignorant of his wiles, or because they saw not much evil publicly arising thence, and partly because the arguments of the adversary were not founded on any general principle, but only to be deduced from the private and particular state and case of individuals,) have either passed over or very slightly touched upon.

[1] "Ab ipsis ferè religionis nostræ cunis et primordiis." Surely the rendering above is a wide deviation from Owen's meaning,—"From the infancy and origin of *our* religion," that is, the Christian religion.—ED.

As to what pertains to theology itself, or that "knowledge of the truth which is according to godliness," wherewith being filled "we ourselves become perfect, and throughly furnished to every good work," and "able ministers of the new testament, not of the letter, but of the spirit,"—"apt to teach, rightly dividing the word of truth;" that subject, I say, though a common and chief topic in the writings both of the schoolmen and others on religion, many have acknowledged, to their fatal experience, when too late, is treated in too perplexed and intricate a manner to be of any real and general service.

For while they are warmly employed in disputing whether theology be an art or a science, and whether it be a speculative or practical art or science; and while they attempt to measure it exactly by those rules, laws, and methods which human reason has devised for other sciences, thus endeavouring to render it more plain and clear,—they find themselves, to the grief and sorrow of many candidates for the truth, entangled in inextricable difficulties, and left in possession only of a human system of doctrines, having little or no connection at all with true theology.[1] I hope, therefore,—"if the Lord will, and I live,"—to publish (but from no desire of gainsaying any one) some specimens of evangelical truth on the points before mentioned, as well as on other subjects.[2]

As to the work that I have now in hand, the first part of the dissertation is concerning *the cause of the death of Christ;* and in the execution of which I have the greatest pleasure and satisfaction (though proudly defied by the adversaries, so conceited with themselves and their productions are they), because "I have determined to know nothing but Jesus Christ and him crucified,"—at least, nothing that could divert my attention from that subject.[3]

But now, learned reader, lest, as the saying is, "the gate should become wider than the city," if you will bear with me while I say a few things of myself, however little worthy of your notice, I shall immediately conclude the preface.

About two years ago, the parliament of the commonwealth promoted me, while diligently employed, according to the measure of the gift of grace bestowed on me, in preaching the gospel, by their authority and influence, though with reluctance on my part, to a chair in the very celebrated university of Oxford. I mean not to relate what various employments fell to my lot from that period; what frequent journeys I became engaged in; not, indeed, expeditions of pleasure, or on my own or private account, but such as the unavoidable necessities of the university, and the commands of superiors, whose authority was not be gainsaid, imposed upon me. And now I clearly found that I, who dreaded almost every academical employment, as being unequal to the task (for what could be expected from a man not far advanced in years, who had for several years been very full of employment, and accustomed only to the popular mode of speaking; who, being altogether devoted to the investigation and explanation of the saving grace of God through Jesus Christ, had for some time taken leave of all scholastic studies; whose genius is by no means quick, and who had even forgot, in some measure, the portion of polite learning that he might have formerly acquired, and at a time, too, when I had

1 The full sentence in the original runs in the following terms:—"Not a few wooers of truth having followed their guidance, grieve and lament how they have strayed in their whole course, after finding themselves pushed into inextricable difficulties, (like that old man in Terence, who was directed by a villain of a slave backward and forward, by steeps, and precipices, and obscure corners, to land at length in a narrow alley with no thoroughfare,) and left in possession only of a *human system* of doctrine, having scarcely any thing in common with true theology."—Ed.

2 See Owen on the Holy Spirit. [This note is by the translator. We apprehend that Owen alludes to his work on "Communion with God." See vol. ii. of his works.—Ed.]

3 This paragraph is neither correctly rendered nor consistent with fact. The whole paragraph stands thus in the original:—"As to the work now in hand, it is the first part of *a dissertation* concerning *the causes of the death of Christ;* to which I willingly apply, because I have determined to know nothing but Jesus Christ, and him crucified: though sadly provoked to turn my thoughts in another direction by the insolent haughtiness of adversaries, who cannot think highly enough of themselves and their productions;—a sort of persons than whom none are more silly, or held more cheap by wise and thoughtful men." Owen does not seem to have ever fulfilled his intention to complete this work on the causes of our Lord's agony. The subject is fully considered in the Exercitations xxix. and xxx., prefixed to his Exposition of the Epistle to the Hebrews.—Ed.

entertained hope that, through the goodness of God, in giving me leisure, and retirement, and strength for study, the deficiency of genius and penetration might be made up by industry and diligence), was now so circumstanced that the career of my studies must be interrupted by more and greater impediments than ever before.

For, to mention first what certainly is most weighty and important, the task of lecturing in public was put upon me; which would, strictly and properly, require the whole time and attention even of the most grave and experienced divine; and in the discharge of which, unless I had been greatly assisted and encouraged by the candour, piety, submission, and self-denial of the auditors, and by their respect for the divine institution and their love of the truth, with every kind of indulgence and kind attention towards the earthen vessel, which distinguish most academicians, of every rank, age, and description, beyond mankind in general, I should have long ago lost all hope of discharging that province, either to the public advantage or my own private satisfaction and comfort.

And as most of them are endowed with a pious disposition and Christian temper, and well furnished with superior gifts, and instructed in learning of every kind,—which, in the present imperfect and depraved state of human nature, is apt to fill the minds of men with prejudices against "the foolishness of preaching," and to disapprove "the simplicity that is in Christ,"—I should be the most ungrateful of mankind were I not to acknowledge that the humility, diligence, and alacrity with which they attended to and obeyed the words of the cross, indulging neither pride of heart, nor animosity of mind, nor itching of ears, though dispensed by a most unworthy servant of God in the gospel of his Son, have given, and still give me, great courage in the discharge of the different duties of my office.

The most merciful Father of all things shall, in his infinite wisdom and goodness, dispose of the affairs of our university. Reports, however, are everywhere spread abroad concerning the abolition and destruction of the colleges, and efforts for that purpose made by some who, being entire strangers to every kind of literature, or at least ignorant of every thing of greater antiquity than what their own memory or that of their fathers can reach, and regardless of the future, imagine the whole globe and bounds of human knowledge to be contained within the limits of their own little cabins, ignorant whether the sun ever shone beyond their own little island or not,—"neither knowing what they say nor whereof they affirm;" and by others who are deeply sunk in the basest of crimes, and who would, therefore, wish all light distinguishing between good and evil entirely extinguished (for "evil doers hate the light, nor do they come to the light, lest their deeds should be reproved"), that they (mean lurchers hitherto) may "fill up the measure of their iniquity" with some kind of eclat. With this faction are combined those who, never having become candidates for literature themselves, yet, by pushing themselves forward, have unseasonably thrust themselves into such services and offices as necessarily require knowledge and learning. These, I say, like the fox which had lost his tail, would wish all the world deprived of the means of knowledge, lest their own shameful ignorance, despicable indolence, and total unfitness for the offices which they solicit or hold, should appear to all who have the least degree of understanding and sense. And lastly, too, [the same reports are spread] by a despicable herd of prodigal, idle fellows, eagerly gaping for the revenues of the university. I could not, therefore, but give such a public testimony, as a regard to truth and duty required from me, to these very respectable and learned men (however much these treacherous calumniators and falsifying sycophants may rail and show their teeth upon the occasion), the heads of the colleges, who have merited so highly of the church [and of the commonwealth], for their distinguished candour, great diligence, uncommon erudition, blameless politeness;[1] many of whom are zealously studious of every kind of literature; and many, by

1 "Inculpatæ πολιτείας,"—rather, "Blameless administration."—ED.

their conduct in the early period of their youth, gave the most promising hopes of future merit: so that I would venture to affirm, that no impartial and unprejudiced judge will believe that our university hath either been, for ages past, surpassed, or is now surpassed, either in point of a proper respect and esteem for piety, for the saving knowledge of our Lord and Saviour Jesus Christ, manners orderly and worthy of the Christian vocation, or for a due regard to doctrines, arts, languages, and all sciences that can be ornamental to wise, worthy, and good men, appointed for the public good, by any society of men in the world.

Relying, then, on the humanity, piety, and candour of such men (who may be "afflicted, but not straitened; persecuted, but not forsaken; cast down, but not destroyed;" who carry about with them the life and death of the Lord Jesus Christ), though destitute of all strength of my own, and devoting myself entirely to Him "who furnisheth seed to the sower," and who "from the mouths of babes and sucklings ordaineth strength," who hath appointed Christ a perpetual source of help, and who furnishes a seasonable aid to every pious effort,—I have, in conjunction with my very learned colleague[1] (a very eminent man, and whose equal in the work of the gospel if the parliament of the commonwealth had conjoined with him, they would have attended to the best interests of the university), continued in the discharge of the duties of this laborious and difficult province.

But not on this account alone would I have been reluctant to return, after so long an interval of time, to this darling university; but another care, another office, and that by far the most weighty, was, by the concurring voice of the senate of the university, and notwithstanding my most earnest requests to the contrary, intrusted and assigned to me, and by the undertaking of which I have knowingly and wittingly compounded with the loss of my peace and all my studious pursuits.[2]

Such, candid reader, is the account of the author of the following little treatise, and of his situation when composing it; a man not wise in the estimation of others,—in his own, very foolish; first called from rural retirement and the noise of arms to this university, and very lately again returned to it from excursions in the cause of the gospel, not only to the extremities of this island, but to coasts beyond the seas, and now again deeply engaged in the various and weighty duties of his station. Whether any thing exalted or refined can be expected from such a person is easy for any one to determine.

With regard to our manner of writing, or Latin diction, as some are wont to acquire great praise from their sublimity of expression, allow me but a word or two. Know, then, reader, that you have to do with a person who, provided his words but clearly express the sentiments of his mind, entertains a fixed and absolute disregard for all elegance and ornaments of speech; for,—

> "Dicite, pontifices, in sacris quid facit aurum?"
> "Say, bishops, of what avail is glitter to sacred subjects?"

In my opinion, indeed, he who, in a theological contest, should please himself with the idea of displaying rhetorical flourishes, would derive no other advantage therefrom but that his head, adorned with magnificent verbose garlands and pellets, would fall a richer victim to the criticisms of the learned.

But whatever shall be the decision of the serious and judicious with respect to this treatise, if I shall any how stir up an emulation in others, on whom the grace of God may have bestowed more excellent gifts, to bring forward to public utility their pious, solid, and learned labours, and shall excite them, from their light, to confer light on the splendour of this university, I shall be abundantly gratified. Farewell, pious reader, and think not lightly of him who hath used his most zealous endeavours to serve thy interest in the cause of the gospel.

JOHN OWEN.

1 Mr T. Goodwin, president of Magdalen College.

2 In the year 1651 Dr Owen was settled in the deanery of Christ Church, and in 1652 chosen vice-chancellor of that university.

A

DISSERTATION ON DIVINE JUSTICE

CHAPTER I.

The introduction—The design of the work—Atheists—The prolepsis[1] of divine justice in general—The divisions of justice, according to Aristotle—The sentiments of the schoolmen respecting these—Another division—Justice considered absolutely; then in various respects.

In this treatise we are to discourse of God and of his justice, the most illustrious of all the divine perfections, but especially of his vindicatory justice;[2] of the certainty of which I most firmly believe that all mankind will, one time or other, be made fully sensible, either by faith in it here, as revealed in the word, or by feeling its effects, to their extreme misery, in the world hereafter, Rom. ii. 8, 9, 12; 2 Thess. i. 7–9. But as the human mind is blind to divine light, and as both our understandings and tongues are inadequate to conceive of God aright and to declare him (hence that common and just observation, that it is an arduous thing to speak of God aright), [and much darkness rests upon divine things],[3] that we may handle so important a subject with that reverence and perspicuity wherewith it becomes it to be treated, we must chiefly depend on His aid who was "made the righteousness[4] of God for us," himself "God blessed for ever," 1 Cor. i. 30; 2 Cor. v. 21; Rom. ix. 5. But whatever I have written, and whatever I have asserted, on this subject, whether I have written and asserted it with modesty, sobriety, judgment, and humility, must be left to the decision of such as are competent judges.

[1] This word commonly means a previous and concise view of a subject, or an anticipation of objections. In this treatise it means a natural or innate conception of divine justice.—Tr. [See note on page 517.—Ed.]

[2] The word in the original means either to claim and assert a right, or to punish the violation of it. By "vindicatory justice," then, we are to understand that perfection of the Deity which disposes him to vindicate his right by punishing its violators. It ought never to be translated vindictive, or understood as meaning revengeful.—Tr. [Though Dr Owen uses the expression, "My book of the Vindictive Justice of God," see vol. xii., "Vindiciæ Evangelicæ," chap. xxx., he explains his meaning in different parts of his works: see vol. xi., "Saints' Perseverance," chap. vii.; vol. xii., chap. xxiii.; and vol. ii., "On Communion with God," chap. iii., digression ii., p. 84.—Ed.]

[3] Πολὺς ταραγμὸς ἔν τε τοῖς θεοῖς ἔνι.—Eurip. Iphig. in Taur. 572.

[4] Or justice.—Tr.

We think proper to divide this dissertation into two parts. In the FIRST PART, which contains the body of our opinion, after having premised some general descriptions of divine justice, I maintain sin-punishing justice to be natural, and in its exercise necessary, to God. The truth of this assertion forms a very distinguished part of natural theology. The defence of it, to the best of my abilities, both against Socinians, who bitterly oppose it, as well as against certain of our own countrymen, who, in defiance of all truth, under a specious pretext, support the same pernicious scheme with them, shall be the subject of the LATTER PART.

In almost all ages there have existed some who have denied the *being* of a God, although but very few, and these the most abandoned.[1] And as mankind, for the most part, have submitted to the evidence of a divine existence, so there never has existed one who has ever preferred an indictment of injustice against God, or who hath not declared him to be infinitely just.[2] The despairing complaints of some in deep calamities, the unhallowed expostulations of others at the point of death, do not bespeak the real sentiments of the man, but the misery of his situation: as, for instance, that expostulation of Job, chap. x. 3, "Is it good unto thee that thou shouldest oppress?" and among the Gentiles, that of Brutus, "O wretched virtue! how mere a nothing art thou, but a name!" and that furious exclamation of Titus when dying, related by Suetonius,[3] "who, pulling aside his curtains, and looking up to the heavens, complained that his life was taken from him undeservedly and unjustly." Of the same kind was that late dreadful epiphonema[4] of a despairing Italian, related by Mersennus,[5] who, speaking of God and the devil, in dread contempt of divine justice, exclaimed, "Let the strongest take me."

But as "the judgments of God are unsearchable, and his ways past finding out," Rom. xi. 33, those who have refused to submit to his absolute dominion and supreme jurisdiction (some monstrous human characters) have been hardy enough to assert that there is no God, rather than venture to call him unjust. Hence that common couplet:—

> "Marmoreo tumulo Licinus jacet, at Cato parvo,
> Pompeius nullo; credimus esse deos?"

> "Licinus lies buried in a marble tomb, Cato in a mean one,
> Pompey has none;—can we believe that there are gods?"

[1] "Nullos unquam fuisse aut esse posse ἀθέους proprie dictos et speculative, seu plene persuasos, agnoscunt pene omnes."—Vid. Voet. Disp. de Atheismo. Ps. xiv. 1. "Non est potestas Dei in terris."—Chal. Par. "Eorum qui antiquitus horrendi criminis rei existimabantur vindicias instituerunt inulti."—Vid. Vos. de Idol. li. cap. 1. Ὡς τοῦ πιεῖν γε, καὶ φαγεῖν τοὐφ' ἡμέραν, Ζεὺς οὗτος ἀνθρώποισι τοῖσι σώφροσι.—Eurip. in Cyclop. 335.

[2] "Veritatis argumentum est omnibus aliquid videri tanquam deos esse, quod omnibus de diis opinio insita sit, neque ulla gens usquam est, adeo extra leges moresque posita ut non aliquos Deos credat."—Seneca, Epist. iii.

[3] Sueton. in Vitâ Titi, cap. x.

[4] A sudden, unconnected exclamation.—TR.

[5] Mersen. ad Deistas Gall.

And hence Ulysses is introduced by Euripides, expressing his horror of the gormandizing of the man-devouring Cyclops, in these verses:—[1]

> "O Jupiter, behold such violations of hospitality; for if thou regardest them not,
> Thou art in vain accounted Jupiter, for thou canst be no god."

Beyond any doubt, the audacity of those abandoned triflers, who would wish to seem to act the mad part with a show of reason, is more akin to the madness of atheism than to the folly of ascribing[2] to the God whom they worship and acknowledge such attributes as would not only be unworthy but disgraceful to him. Protagoras,[3] therefore, not comprehending the justice of God in respect of his government, hath written, "With regard to the gods, I do not know whether they exist or do not exist." Yet, even among the Gentiles themselves, and those who were destitute of the true knowledge of the true God (for they, in some sense, were without God in the world), writers, of whom Seneca[4] and Plutarch were the most distinguished, have not been wanting who have endeavoured, by serious and forcible arguments, to unravel the difficulty respecting the contrary lots of good and bad men in this life. Our first idea, therefore, of the Divine Being, and the natural conceptions of all men, demand and enforce the necessity of justice being ascribed to God.[5] To be eloquent, then, in so easy a cause, or to triumph with arguments on a matter so universally acknowledged, we have neither leisure nor inclination. What, and of what kind, the peculiar quality and nature of sin-punishing justice is, shall now be briefly explained. And that we may do this with the greater perspicuity and force of evidence, a few observations seem necessary to be premised concerning justice in general, and its more commonly received divisions.

The philosopher Aristotle, long ago, as is well known, hath divided justice into *universal* and *particular*. Concerning the former, he says that he might compare it to the celebrated saying, "In justice every virtue is summarily comprehended," Ethic. ad Nicom., lib. v. cap. 1, 2; and he affirms that it in no wise differs from virtue in general, unless in respect of its relation to another being.

But he says that particular justice is a part thereof under the same

[1] Eurip. in Cyclop., verse 350.

[2] A slight alteration seems needed to elicit the real meaning,—"than to folly, in ascribing," etc. Owen is speaking of "the audacity of these triflers" "in ascribing" unworthy attributes to God.—Ed.

[3] Diogen. Laert. in Protag., Ep. iii. 12.

[4] "Cur bonis mala fiant, cum sit providentia."—Sen.

[5] "Illos qui nullum esse Deum dixerunt non modo philosophos, sed ne homines quidem esse dixerim, qui brutis simillimi solo corpore constiterunt, nihil omnino cernentes animo, sed ad sensum corporis cuncta referentes, qui nihil putabunt esse, nisi quod oculis tuebuntur."—Lactan. de plur., lib. i., etc. cap. 8. "Quia rationem mali non intellexerunt, et natura ejus abscondita fuit, duo principia bonum et malum finxit tota ethnicorum (ante natum Marcionem) antiquitas."—Vid. Vos. de Idol., lib. i. cap. 5.

name, which he again distinguishes into *distributive* and *commutative*.[1] The schoolmen,[2] too, agreeing with him (which is rather surprising), divide the divine justice into universal and particular; for that excellence, say they, is spoken of God and man by way of analogy.[3] Nor is it like that bird mentioned by Homer, which goes by a double name, by one among mortals, by another among the immortals,—

"The gods call it Chalcis, but men Cumindis," Hom.;—

but is understood as existing in God principally, as in the first analogised[4] being. Nor do later divines dissent from them; nay, all of them who have made the divine attributes the subject of their contemplations have, by their unanimous voice, approved of this distinction, and given their suffrages in its favour.[5]

But, farther, they assert that particular justice, in respect of its exercise, consists either in *what is said* or in *what is done.* That which is displayed in things said, in commands, is equity; in declarations, truth;—both which the holy Scriptures[6] do sometimes point out under the title of Divine Justice. But the justice which respects things done is either that of *government,* or *jurisdiction* or judgment; and this, again, they affirm to be either *remunerative* or *corrective,* but that corrective is either *castigatory* or *vindicatory.* With the last member of this last distinction I begin this work; and yet, indeed, although the most learned of our divines, in later ages, have assented to this distribution of divine justice into these various significations, it seems proper to me to proceed in a manner somewhat different, and more suited to our purpose.

I say, then, that the justice of God may be considered in a twofold manner:—First, *Absolutely,* and in itself. Secondly, In respect of its *egress and exercise.*

First, The justice of God, *absolutely* considered, is the universal *rectitude and perfection* of the divine nature; for such is the divine nature antecedent to all acts of his will and suppositions of objects towards which it might operate. This excellence is most universal; nor, from its own nature, as an excellence, can it belong[7] to any other being.

Secondly, It is to be viewed with respect to its *egress and exercise.* And thus, in the order of nature, it is considered as conse-

[1] That which relates to fair exchange.—TR.

[2] Lombard., lib. iv. dist. 46; Thom. ii. 2, ti. 51; Pesant. in Thom., 2. a. ti. 58, ar. 4; Suarez. Relec. de Just. Div.; Hom. Iliad, ξ. 291.

[3] Analogy means a resemblance between things with regard to some qualities or circumstances, properties or effects, though not in all.—TR.

[4] That is, the first being whose perfections have been explained by analogy, or by tracing a resemblance between these perfections and something like them in ourselves, in kind or sort, though differing infinitely with respect to manner and degree.—TR.

[5] Zanch. de Nat. Dei., lib. i.; Ames. Cas. Consc., lib. v. cap. 2; Armin. Disput., part iv. thes. 15; Voet. Dis. de Jure et Just. Mares; Hyd. Socin., lib. i. c. 25, etc.

[6] Rom. i. 17, iii. 21; Ezra ix. 15; Neh. ix. 8; Deut. iv. 8; Ps. cxix. 7; Heb. vi. 10; 2 Tim. iv. 8; 2 Thess. i. 5.

[7] Or, have a respect to any other being.—TR.

quent, or at least as concomitant, to some acts of the divine will, assigning or appointing to it a proper object. Hence, that rectitude, which in itself is an absolute property of the divine nature, is considered as a relative and hypothetical[1] attribute, and has a certain habitude to its proper objects.

That is to say, this rectitude, or universal justice, has certain egresses towards objects out of itself, in consequence of the divine will, and in a manner agreeable to the rule of his supreme right and wisdom,—namely, when some object of justice is supposed and appointed (which object must necessarily depend on the mere good pleasure of God, because it was possible it might never have existed at all, God, notwithstanding, continuing just and righteous to all eternity). And these egresses are twofold:—

1. They are *absolute* and perfectly free,—namely, in *words.*

2. They are *necessary,*—namely, in *actions.*

For the justice of God is neither altogether one of that kind of perfections which create and constitute an object to themselves, as power and wisdom do, nor of that kind which not only require an object for their exercise, but one peculiarly affected and circumstanced, as mercy, patience, and forbearance do; but may be considered in both points of view, as shall be more fully demonstrated hereafter.

1. For the first, it has *absolute egresses in words* (constituting, and, as it were, creating an object to itself); as, for instance, in words of legislation, and is then called *equity;* or in words of declaration and narration, and is then called *truth.* Both these[2] I suppose for the present to take place absolutely and freely. Whether God hath necessarily prescribed a law to his rational creatures, at least one accompanied with threats and promises, is another consideration.

2. There are respective egresses of this justice in *deeds,* and according to the distinctions above mentioned;—that is to say, it is exercised either in the government of all things according to what is due to them by the counsel and will of God, or in judgments rewarding or punishing, according to the rule of his right and wisdom; which also is the rule of equity in legislation, and of truth in the declarations annexed. In respect of these,[3] I call the egresses of the divine justice *necessary,* and such that they could not possibly be otherwise; which, by divine help, I shall prove hereafter: and this is the same as saying that vindicatory justice is so *natural* to God, that, sin being supposed, he cannot, according to the rule of his right, wisdom,

[1] Conditional.—Tr.

[2] Namely, the egresses in words of legislation and in words of declaration and narration.—Tr.

[3] Namely, the egresses in the government of things according to what is due to them by the counsel of his will; or in judgments rewarding or punishing, according to the rule of his right and wisdom.—Tr.

and truth, but punish it. But antecedent to this whole exercise of the divine justice, I suppose a *natural right*, which indispensably requires the dependence and moral subjection of the rational creature, in God, all the egresses of whose justice, in words, contain an arrest of judgment till farther trial, in respect of the object.

It now, then, appears that all these distinctions of divine justice respect it not as considered in itself, but its egresses and exercise only; to make which clear was the reason that I departed from the beaten track. Nay, perhaps it would be a difficult matter to assign any virtue to God but in the general, and not as having any specific ratio[1] of any virtue. But that which answers to the ratio of any particular virtue in God consists in the exercise of the same. For instance: mercy is properly attributed to God, so far as it denotes the highest perfection in the will of God, the particular ratio or quality of which,—namely, a disposition of assisting the miserable, with a compassion of their misery,—is found not altogether as to some, as to others altogether and only, in the exercise of the above-mentioned perfection;[2] but it is called a proper attribute of God, because by means of it some operation is performed agreeable to the nature of God, which, in respect of his other attributes, his will would not produce. This kind, therefore, of the divine attributes, because they have proper and formal *objects*, thence only derive their formal and specific ratios. But all these observations upon justice must be briefly examined and explained, that we may arrive at the point intended.

CHAPTER II.

The universal justice of God—The idle fancies of the schoolmen—The arguments of Durandus against commutative justice—Suarez's censure of the scholastic reasonings—His opinion of divine justice—The examination of it—A description of universal justice from the sacred writings—A division of it in respect of its egress—Rectitude of government in God, what, and of what kind—Definitions of the philosophers and lawyers—Divisions of the justice of government—A caution respecting these—Vindicatory justice—The opinions of the partisans—An explication of the true opinion—Who the adversaries are—The state of the controversy farther considered.

WE are first, then, briefly to treat of the universal justice of God, or of his justice considered in itself and absolutely, which contains in it all the divine excellencies. The schoolmen, treading in the steps of the philosophers, who have acknowledged no kind of justice

[1] That is, any distinguishing sort or quality.—TR.

[2] In the general sparing mercy of God, the particular quality of mercy,—namely, a disposition of assisting the miserable, with a compassion of their misery,—is not wholly found, because there are many of mankind towards whom this disposition of assisting is never effectually exerted; but, in the pardoning mercy of God to his people, it is fully and gloriously displayed.—TR.

which has not naturally some respect to another object, are for the most part silent concerning this justice. And once, by the way, to take notice of these [hair-splitters], on this, as almost on every other subject, they are strangely divided. Duns Scotus, Durandus, and Paludamus deny that there is commutative justice in God.[1]

For the Master of the Sentences himself calls God an impartial and just distributer, but says not a word of commutation. Thomas Aquinas[2] and Cajetan do the same; though the latter says "that some degree of commutative justice is discernible." So also Ferorariensis, on the same place; and Sotus, in the third book of his treatise, "Of Nature and Grace," chap. vii. Durandus, in particular, contends, with many arguments, that this kind of justice ought not to be assigned to God;—first, Because that this justice observes an equality between the thing given and received, which cannot be the case between us and God;—and, secondly, Because that we cannot be of any service to him (which he proves from Rom. xi. 35; Job xxii. 3, xxxv. 7; Luke xvii. 10), whereby he can be bound to make an equality with us by virtue of commutation;—and, thirdly, Because that we cannot make an equal return to God for benefits received;—and, finally, That as there is no proper commutative justice between a father and his children, according to Aristotle's[3] opinion, much less can it subsist between God and us.

But the same Durandus likewise denies to God distributive justice,[4] because he is not indebted to any one. He, however, acknowledges some mode of distributive justice, and Pesantius[5] follows his opinion.

But Gabriel, on the same[6] distinction, asserts commutative justice to be inherent in God; for there is a certain equality, as he says, between God and man, from the acceptation of God the receiver. Proudly enough said, indeed!

But what shall we say of these triflers? They resemble those advocates in Terence, whose opinion, after Demipho, embarrassed by the cheats of Phormio the sycophant, had asked, he exclaims, "Well done, gentlemen; I am now in a greater uncertainty than before!" so intricate were their answers, and resembling the practices of the Andabatæ.[7]

Hence, Francis Suarez himself, after he had reviewed the opinions of the schoolmen concerning the justice of God, bids adieu to them all, declaring, "That the expressions of Scripture had greater weight with him than their philosophic human arguments," Opusc. vi. de Just. Div. sec. 1. But with much labour and prolixity he insists that both distributive and commutative justice are to be ascribed to God,

1 Palud. on the Sent., book iv. dist. 46.
2 Thomas, first page of quest. 21, and Cajetan, ii. 2, q. 61, a. 4.
3 Ethics, book viii. chap. 8.
4 On dist. 46.
5 In ii. 2, Thomas.
6 A work to which he alludes.—Tr.
7 A kind of fencers who fought on horseback hood-winked.—Tr.

that so he might pave the way for that rotten fiction concerning the merits of Roman Catholics with God,—a doctrine which, were even all his suppositions granted, appears not to follow, much less to be confirmed.[1] This opinion of Suarez concerning vindicatory justice, as it is deservedly famous in scholastic theology, we think proper to lay before you in few words.

In his discourses concerning the justice of God,[2] he contends that the affection[3] of punishing, which he calls "a perfection elicitive[4] of the act of punishing," is properly and formally inherent in God; and it is so because it hath a proper object, namely, to punish the guilt of sin, which is honourable; nor does it include any imperfection; and, therefore, that some formal and proper divine attribute ought to correspond to that effect.

He farther maintains that this affection of punishing is neither commutative nor distributive justice. His conclusions here I do not oppose, though I cannot approve of many of his reasonings and arguments. In fine, he contends that vindicatory justice in God is the same with universal, or legal, or providential justice, which we call the justice of government. But he makes a dishonourable and base conclusion from a distinction about the persons punished, namely, into such as are merely passive sufferers, and such as spontaneously submit themselves to punishment, that they may satisfy the punitory justice of God; reasoning in such a manner, that after he has forced the whole doctrine concerning the commutative and distributive justice of God to become subservient to that sacrilegious and proud error concerning the merits of man with God, and even of one from the supererogation of another,[5] he strenuously endeavours to establish a consistency between this doctrine of vindicatory justice and a fiction not less impious and disgraceful to the blood of Christ, which "cleanseth us from all sin," about penal satisfaction, to be performed by such ways and means as God hath never prescribed, or even thought of.

—— "Ut turpiter atrum
Desinat in piscem mulier formosa superne."—*Hor.*

Dismissing these bunglers (who know not the righteousness of God), then, from our dissertation, let us attend to the more sure word of prophecy. That word everywhere asserts God to be just, and possessed of such justice as denotes the universal rectitude and perfection of his divine nature. His essence is most wise, most perfect, most excellent, most merciful, most blessed; that, in fine, is the justice of God, according to the Scriptures, namely, considered absolutely and in itself. Nor would the holy Scriptures have us to un-

[1] Suarez's Lectures of the Justice of God. [2] Sect. 5. [3] Or quality.—TR.
[4] That is, inducing to, or drawing forth, the act of punishing.—TR.
[5] In the original, "Immo etiam ex condigno," "And that, too, of condignity."—ED.

derstand any thing else by divine justice than the power and readiness of God to do all things rightly and becomingly, according to the rule of his wisdom, goodness, truth, mercy, and clemency. Hence the above-mentioned sophists agree that justice, taken precisely and in itself, and abstracting it from all human imperfections, simply means perfection without intrinsic imperfection; for it is not a virtue that rules the *passions*, but directs their *operations*.

Hence it presides, as it were, in all the divine decrees, actions, works, and words, of whatsoever kind they be. There is no egress of the divine will, no work or exercise of providence, though immediately and distinctly breathing clemency, mercy, anger, truth, or wisdom, but in respect thereof God is eminently said to be just, and to execute justice. Hence, Isa. li. 6, he is said to be just in bringing salvation; Rom. iii. 25, 26, just in pardoning sin; Rev. xvi. 5, 6, just in avenging and punishing sin; Rom. iii. 5, 6, just in all the exercises of his supreme right and dominion, Job xxxiv. 12–14; Rom. ix. 14, 15, 18, he is just in sparing according to his mercy; just in punishing according to his anger and wrath. In a word, whatsoever, by reason of his right, he doeth or worketh "according to the counsel of his will," whatever proceeds from his faithfulness, mercy, grace, love, clemency, anger, and even from his fury, is said to be done by, through, and because of his justice, as the perfection inducing to, or the cause effecting and procuring, such operations. It is evident, then, that justice, universally taken, denotes the highest rectitude of the divine nature, and a power and promptitude of doing all things in a manner becoming and agreeable to his wisdom, goodness, and right.

The more solemn egresses of this justice, to which all particular acts may be easily reduced, have been already pointed out; but equity in legislation, fidelity and truth in threatenings and promises annexed to it, in which God is often said to be just, and to execute justice, I think may be passed over, as being too remote from our purpose. But as it appears that some light may be thrown on this subject which we are now treating of, from the consideration of the relation of rectitude and divine wisdom, that is, of universal justice, to government and judgment, we must say a few words on that head.

But rectitude of government, to which that justice analogically corresponds, is that which philosophers and civilians unanimously agree to be the highest excellence, though they have variously described it. Aristotle calls it "a habit by which men are capable of doing just things, and by which they both will and do just things;"[1] attributing to it aptitude, will, and action. Cicero calls it "an affection of the mind, giving to every one his due;"[2] understanding by

[1] Ethics, book v. chap. 1.

[2] De Finibus.

"affection" not any passion of the mind, but a habit. The civilians understand by it "a constant and perpetual will, assigning to every one his due." The propriety of their definition we leave to themselves. That "constant and perpetual will" of theirs is the same as the "habit" of the philosophers; which, whether it be the proper genus[1] of this virtue, let logicians determine. Again; as they constantly attribute three acts to right, which is the object of justice,—namely, "to live honestly, to hurt nobody, and to give every one his due,"—how comes it to pass that they define justice by one act, when doubtless it respects all right? therefore it is, they say, that to give every one his due is not of the same extent in the definition of justice and in the description of the acts of right.

But let them both unite in their sentiments as they please, neither the "habit" or "affection" of the philosophers, nor the "living honestly and hurting nobody" of the civilians, can be assigned to God; for in ascribing the perfection of excellencies to him, we exclude the ratio of habit or quality, properly so called, and every material and imperfect mode of operation. He must be a mortal man, and subject to a law, to whom these things apply.

Moreover, those (I speak of our own countrymen) who divide this justice of government into *commutative* and *distributive* rob God entirely of the *commutative*, which consists in a mutual giving and receiving. For, "Who hath first given to him?" "Who maketh thee to differ from another?" "He giveth not account of any of his matters." But *distributive*, which belongs to him as the supreme governor of all things, who renders to every one his due, is proper to himself alone. This we have above asserted to be the justice of government or judgment. Of this justice of government frequent mention is made in the sacred writings. *It is that perfection of the Divine Being whereby he directs all his actions in governing and administering created things, according to the rule of his rectitude and wisdom.* But this excellence, or habitude for action, in no wise differs from universal justice, unless in respect of its relation to another being. But what is a *law* to us, in the administration of things, in God is his *right*, in conjunction with his most wise and just will; for God, as it is said, is a law unto himself. To this justice are these passages to be referred, Zeph. iii. 5; 2 Chron. xii. 6; Ps. vii. 9; Jer. xii. 1; 2 Tim. iv. 8, with almost innumerable others. But in all the effects and egresses of this justice God is justified, not from the reason of things, but from his dominion and supreme right. Thus, Job xiv. 14, xxxiii. 12, xxxiv. 12–15. And this is the first egress of the divine rectitude in *works.*

The other egress of this justice is in *judgment*, the last member of the divisions of which, above mentioned,—namely, that by which

[1] Or class.—TR.

God punishes the crimes of rational beings, to whom a law hath been given, according to the rule of his right,—is the vindicatory justice of which we are treating.

Here again, reader, I would wish to put you in mind that I by no means assert many species of universal justice, or, so to speak, particular or special justices, as distinct perfections in God, which others seem to do, but one only,—namely, the universal and essential rectitude of the divine nature variously exercised; and therefore I maintain that this vindicatory justice is the very rectitude and perfection of the Deity.

Some of the schoolmen, however, agree with me in opinion; for Cajetan[1] upon Thomas grants that vindicatory justice in a public person differs nothing from legal and universal justice; although he maintains that there is a peculiar species of justice in a private person,—a position which, I confess, I do not understand, since punishment, considered as punishment, is not the right of a private person. God certainly does not punish us as being injured, but as a ruler and judge. But again, concerning this justice, another question arises, Whether it be natural to God, or an *essential attribute of the divine nature*,—that is to say, such that, the existence of sin being admitted, God must necessarily exercise it, because it supposes in him a constant and immutable will to punish sin, so that while he acts consistently with his nature he cannot do otherwise than punish and avenge it,—or whether it be a free act of the divine will, which he may exercise at pleasure? On this point theologians are divided. We shall consider what has been determined on the matter by the most notorious enemies of divine truth, and especially by those of our own times.

1. Then, they own, "That such a kind of justice is applicable[2] to God, which were he always inclined to exercise, he might, consistently with right, destroy all sinners without waiting for their repentance, and so let no sin pass unpunished."

2. "That he will not pardon any sins but those of the penitent." Nor do they deny, so far as I know,—

3. "That God hath determined the punishment of sin by the rule of his right and wisdom." But they deny,—

1. That perfection by which God punishes sins either to be his justice or to be so called in Scripture, but only anger, fury, or fierce indignation,—expressions denoting in the clearest manner the freedom of the divine will in the act of punishing; although some of Socinus' followers, among whom is Crellius, have declared openly against him on this point. Again, they deny,—

2. That there is any such attribute in God as requires a satisfaction for sins, which he is willing to forgive, but maintain that he is

[1] Quest. 2, 2, quest. 108, a. 2.

[2] Competere, "belongs."—ED.

entirely free to "yield up his claim of right," as they phrase it, at pleasure; that, therefore, divine justice ought, by no means, to be reckoned among the causes of Christ's death. Nay more, say they, "Such a kind of justice may be found in the epistles of Iscariot to the Pharisees" (they are the words of Gitichius ad Luc.), "but is not to be found in the holy Scriptures."

Such are the opinions of those concerning whom we are disputing at this present day, whether they be *heretics* because they are not *Christians.* Between their sentiments and ours on this point there is the widest difference; for we affirm the justice by which God punishes sin to be the very essential rectitude of Deity itself, exercised in the punishment of sins, according to the rule of his wisdom, and which is in itself no more free than the divine essence.

This kind of justice Faustus Socinus opposes with all his might in almost all his writings, but especially in his Theological Lectures of the Saviour, book i. chap. 1, etc.; Moscorovius, also, on the Racovian Catechism, chap. viii. quest. 19; Ostorodius, a most absurd heretic, in his Institutions, chap. xxxi., and in his Disputations to Tradelius; Volkelius, of the True Religion, book v. chap. 21; also Crellius, the most acute and learned of all the adversaries, in that book which he wished to have prefixed to the Dissertations of Volkelius, chap. xxviii., and in his Vindications against Grotius, chap. i.; in a little work, also, entitled, "Of the Causes of the Death of Christ," chap. xvi. He pursued the same object in almost all his other writings, both polemical and dogmatical, and likewise in his commentaries;—a very artful man, and one that employed very great diligence and learning in the worst of causes. Michael Gitichius has the same thing in view in his writings against Paræus, and in his dispute with Ludovicus Lucius in defence of his first argument;—a most trifling sophist, a mere copyist of Socinus, and a servile follower of his master. Of mightier powers, too, rise up against us Valentinus Smalcius against Franzius; and (who is said to be still alive) the learned Jonas Schlichtingius. All these, with the rest of that herd, place all their hopes of overturning the doctrine of the satisfaction of Christ in opposing this justice.

But these are not the only adversaries we have to do with: there are others, pious, worthy, and very learned divines, who, respecting the point of Christ's satisfaction, are most strictly orthodox, and who, though they cannot find in their hearts directly to deny that such an attribute or power is essential to God, yet maintain all its egresses and its whole exercise respecting sin to be so free and dependent on the mere free motion and good pleasure of the divine will, that should not that oppose, God might by his nod, by his word, without any trouble, by other modes and ways besides the satisfaction of Christ, if it only seemed proper to his wisdom, take away, pardon, and make an end of sin, without inflicting any penalty for the transgression of his law; and this, it is said, was the opinion of Augustine. By which, I will say, rash and daring assertion,—be it spoken without offence, for they are truly great men,—by their nod and breath, they suspend and disperse the very strongest arguments by which the adversaries feel themselves most hardly pushed, and by which the belief of Christ's satisfaction is strongly supported, and deliver up our most holy cause, I had almost said defenceless, to be the sport of the Philistines. Nay, not very long ago, it has been discovered and lamented by the orthodox, that very considerable assistance has been imprudently given by a learned countryman of our own to these aliens, who defy the armies of the living God. "For if we could but get rid of this justice, even if we had no other proof," says Socinus, "that human fiction of Christ's satisfaction would be thoroughly exposed, and would vanish," Soc. of the Saviour, book iii. chap. 1, etc.

Of our own countrymen, the only one I know is Rutherford, a Scotch divine, who roundly and boldly asserts "*punitive justice to be a free act of the divine will.*" Nor is he content with the bare assertion, but, supported chiefly by his arguments to whom the schoolmen are so much indebted, he defends the fallacy against both Cameron and Voetius, those two thunderbolts of theological war; though, in my opinion, neither with a force of argument nor felicity of issue equal to his opponents. But both the one and the others grant that *God hath decreed to let no sin pass unpunished without a satisfaction; but that decree being supposed, with a law given, and a sanction of the same by threatenings, that a satisfaction was necessary.* But that punitive justice necessarily requires the punishment of all sins, according to the rule of God's right and wisdom, this is what they deny, and endeavour to overturn.

But to me these arguments are altogether astonishing,—namely, "That sin-punishing justice should be natural to God, and yet that God, sin being supposed to exist, *may either exercise it or not exercise it.*" They may also say, and with as much propriety, that truth is natural to God, but, upon a supposition that he were to converse with man, *he might either use it or not;* or, that omnipotence is natural to God, but upon a supposition that he were inclined to do any work without himself, that it were free to him to act *omnipotently or not;* or, finally, that sin-punishing justice is among the primary causes of the death of Christ, and that Christ was set forth as a propitiation to declare his righteousness, and yet that that justice required not the punishment of sin, for if it should require it, how is it possible that it should not necessarily require it, since God would be unjust if he should not inflict punishment? Or farther, they might as well assert that God willed that justice should be satisfied by so many and such great sufferings of his Son Christ, when that justice required no such thing; nay more, that setting aside the free act of the divine will, *sin and no sin* are the same with God, and that man's mortality hath not followed chiefly as the consequence of sin, but of the will of God. These and such like difficulties I leave to the authors of this opinion (for they are very learned men) to unravel; as to myself, they fill me with confusion and astonishment.

But this I cannot forbear to mention, that those very divines who oppose our opinion, when hard pushed by their adversaries, perpetually have recourse in their disputations to this justice as to their sacred anchor,[1] and assert that without satisfaction God could not pardon sin consistently with his nature, justice and truth. But as these are very great absurdities, it would have seemed strange to me that any men of judgment and orthodoxy should have been so entangled in some of these sophisms as to renounce the truth on their account, unless I had happened at one time myself to fall into the same snare; which, to the praise and glory of that truth, of which I am now a servant, I freely confess to have been my case.

But to avoid mistakes as much as possible in discussing the nature of this justice, we will make the following observations:—

1. There are some attributes of Deity which, in order to their exercise, require no determined object antecedent to their egress; of this kind are *wisdom* and *power*. These attributes, at least as to their first exercise, must be entirely free, and dependent on the mere good pleasure of God only; so that antecedent to their acting, the divine will is so indifferent as to every exercise of them, on objects without himself, that he might even will the opposite. But if we suppose that God wills to do any work without himself, he must act omnipotently and wisely.

There are, again, some attributes which can in no wise have an egress or be exercised without an object predetermined, and, as it were, by some circumstances prepared for them. Among these is punitive justice, for the exercise of which there would be no ground but upon the supposition of the existence of a rational being and its having sinned; but these being supposed, this justice must necessarily act according to its own rule.

2. But that rule is not any free act of the divine will, but a *supreme, intrinsic, natural* right of Deity, conjoined with wisdom, to which the entire exercise of this justice ought to be reduced. Those men entirely trifle, then, who, devising certain absurd conclusions of their own, annex them to a supposition of the necessity of punitive justice, as to its exercise: as, for instance, that God ought to

[1] The largest anchor in a vessel, used only in extreme danger, was so called.—ED.

punish sin to the full extent of his power, and that he ought to punish every sin with eternal punishment; and that, therefore, he must preserve every creature that sins to eternity, and that he cannot do otherwise. I say they trifle, for God does not punish to the *utmost extent of his power*, but so far as is *just;* and all modes and degrees of punishment are determined by the standard of the divine right and wisdom.

Whether that necessarily require that every sin should be punished with eternal punishment, let those inquire who choose. "Nobis non licet esse tam disertis."

3. But the existence of a rational creature, and the moral dependence which it has, and must have, upon God, being supposed, the first egress of this justice is in the constitution of a penal law; not as a law which, as was before observed, originates from the justice of government, but as a penal law.

For if such a law were not made necessarily, it might be possible that God should lose his natural right and dominion over his creatures, and thus he would not be God; or, that right being established, that the creature might not be subject to him, which implies a contradiction not less than if you were to say that Abraham is the father of Isaac, but that Isaac is not the son of Abraham: for in case of a failure in point of obedience (a circumstance which might happen, and really hath happened), that dependence could be continued in no way but through means of a vicarious punishment, and there must have been a penal law constituted necessarily requiring that punishment. Hence arises a *secondary right of punishing*, which extends to every amplification of that penal law, in whatever manner made. But it has a second egress, in the infliction of punishment.

4. And here it is to be remarked, that this justice necessarily respects *punishment in general*, as including in it the nature of punishment, and ordaining such a vindication of the divine honour as God can acquiesce in: not the *time* or *degrees*, or such like circumstances of punishment, yea, not this or that species of punishment; for it respects only the preservation of God's natural right and the vindication of his glory, both which may be done by punishment in general, however circumstanced. A dispensation, therefore, with punishment (especially temporary punishment), by a delay of time, an increase or diminution of the degree, by no means prejudiceth the necessity of the exercise of this justice, which only intends an infliction of punishment in general.

5. But, again, though we determine *the egresses of this justice* to be necessary, we do not deny that God exercises it freely; for that necessity doth not exclude a *concomitant liberty*, but only an *antecedent indifference*. This only we deny,—namely, that supposing a

sinful creature, the will of God can be indifferent (by virtue of the punitive justice inherent in it) to inflict or not inflict punishment upon that creature, or to the volition of punishment or its opposite. The whole of Scripture, indeed, loudly testifies against any such indifference, nor is it consistent with God's supreme right over his creatures; neither do they who espouse a different side contend with a single word brought from the Scriptures. But that God punishes sins with a concomitant liberty, because he is of all agents the most free, we have not a doubt. Thus, his intellectual will is carried towards happiness by an essential inclination antecedent to liberty, and notwithstanding it wills happiness with a concomitant liberty: for to act freely is the very nature of the will; yea, it must necessarily act freely.

Let our adversaries, therefore, dream as they please, that we determine God to be an absolutely necessary agent when he is a most free one, and that his will is so circumscribed, by some kind of justice which we maintain, that he cannot will those things which, setting the consideration of that justice aside, would be free to him; for we acknowledge the Deity to be both a *necessary* and *free agent,*—*necessary* in respect of all his actions *internally,* or in respect of the persons in the Godhead towards one another. The Father necessarily begets the Son, and loves himself. As to these and such like actions, he is of all necessary agents the most necessary. But in respect of the acts of the divine will which have their operations and effects upon external objects, he is an agent absolutely free, being one "who worketh all things according to the counsel of his own will." But of these acts there are two kinds; for some are absolute, and admit no respect to any antecedent condition.

Of this kind is his purpose of creating the world, and in it rational creatures, properly adapted to know and obey the Creator, Benefactor, and Lord of all. In works of this kind God hath exercised the greatest liberty. His infinitely wise and infinitely free will is the fountain and origin of all things; neither is there in God any kind of justice, or any other essential attribute, which could prescribe any limits or measure to the divine will. But this decree of creating being supposed, the divine will undergoes a double necessity, so to speak, both in respect of the event and in respect of its manner of acting: for in respect of the event, it is necessary, from the immutability of God, that the world should be created; and in respect of the manner of doing it, that it should be done omnipotently, because God is essentially omnipotent, and it being once supposed that he wills to do any work without himself, he must do it omnipotently. Yet, notwithstanding these considerations, in the creation of the world God was entirely a free agent; he exercised will and understanding in acting, although the choice of acting or not acting, and of acting in one particular way or another, is taken away by his immutability and omnipotence.

There is another kind of the acts of the divine will which could have no possible existence but upon a condition supposed.

This kind contains the egresses and exercise of those attributes which could not be exercised but upon a supposition of other antecedent acts, of which we have treated before. Of this kind are all the acts of the divine will in which justice, mercy, etc., exert their energy. But these attributes of the divine nature are either for the purpose of preserving or continuing to God what belongs to him of right, supposing that state of things which he hath freely appointed, or for bestowing on his creatures some farther good. Of the former kind is *vindicatory justice;* which, as it cannot be exercised but upon the supposition of the existence of a rational being and of its sin, so, these being supposed, the supreme right and dominion of the Deity could not be preserved entire unless it were exercised. Of the latter kind is *sparing mercy*, by which God bestows an undeserved good on miserable creatures; for, setting aside the consideration of their misery, this attribute cannot be exercised, but that being supposed, if he be inclined to bestow any undeserved good on creatures wretched through their own transgression, he may exercise this mercy if he will. But again; in the exercise of that justice, although, if it were not to be exercised, according to our former hypothesis, God would cease from his right and dominion, and so would not be God, still he is a free and also an absolutely necessary agent; for he acts from will and understanding, and not from an impetus of nature only, as fire burns. And he freely willed that state and condition of things; which being supposed, that justice must necessarily be exercised. Therefore, in the exercise of it he is not less free than in speaking; for supposing, as I said before, that his will were to speak any thing, it is necessary that he speak the *truth.* Those loud outcries, therefore, which the adversaries so unseasonably make against our opinion, as if it determined God to be an absolutely necessary agent, in his operations *ad extra*, entirely vanish and come to nought. But we will treat more fully of these things when we come to answer objections.

Finally, let it be observed that the nature of mercy and justice are different in respect of their exercise: for between the act of mercy and its object no natural obligation intervenes; for God is not bound to any one to exercise any act of mercy, neither is he bound to reward obedience, for this is a debt due from his natural right, and from the moral dependence of the rational creature, and indispensably thence arising. But between the act of justice and its object a natural obligation intervenes, arising from the indispensable subordination of the creature to God; which, supposing disobedience or sin, could not otherwise be secured than by punishment. Nor is the liberty of the divine will diminished in any respect more by the necessary egresses of divine justice than by the exercise of other attributes; for these necessary egresses are the consequence, not of an absolute but of a conditional necessity,—namely, a rational creature and its sin being supposed, and both existing freely in respect of God, but the necessary suppositions being made, the exercise of other perfections is also necessary; for it being supposed that God were disposed to speak with man, he must necessarily speak according to truth.

CHAPTER III.

A series of arguments in support of vindicatory justice—First, from the *Scriptures*—Three divisions of the passages of Scripture—The first contains those which respect the purity and holiness of God—The second, those which respect God as the judge—What it is to judge with justice—The third, those which respect the divine supreme right.

A second argument is taken from the *general consent* of mankind—A threefold testimony of that consent—The first from the Scriptures—Some testimonies of the heathens—The second from the power of conscience—Testimonies concerning that power—The mark set upon Cain—The expression of the Emperor Adrian when at the point of death—The consternation of mankind at prodigies—The horror of the wicked, whom even fictions terrify—Two conclusions—The third testimony, from the confession of all nations—A vindication of the argument against Rutherford—The regard paid to sacrifices among the nations—Different kinds of the same—Propitiatory sacrifices—Some instances of them.

THESE preliminaries being thus laid down, to facilitate our entrance on the subject, I proceed to demonstrate, by a variety of arguments, both against enemies and against friends from whom I dissent, that this *punitive justice is natural to God, and necessary as to its egresses respecting sin.* But because, since the entrance of sin into the world, God hath either continued or increased the knowledge of himself, or accommodated it to our capacities by four ways,—namely, by the written word, by a rational conscience, by his works of providence, and, lastly, by the person of Jesus Christ, his only-begotten Son, and by the mystery of godliness manifested in him,—we will show that by each of these modes of communication he hath revealed and made known to us this his justice.

I. Our first argument, then, is taken from the testimony of the sacred writings, which, in almost numberless places, ascribe this vindicatory justice to God.

The passages of holy Scripture which ascribe this justice to God may be classed under three divisions. The first contains those which certify that the purity and holiness of God hostilely oppose and detest sin. Whether holiness or purity be an attribute natural to God, and immutably residing in him, has not yet been called in question by our adversaries. They have not yet arrived at such a pitch of madness. But this is that universal perfection of God, which, when he exercises [it] in punishing the transgressions of his creatures, is called vindicatory justice; for whatever there be in God perpetually inherent, whatever excellence there be essential to his nature, which occasions his displeasure with sin, and which necessarily occasions this displeasure, this is that justice of which we are speaking.

But here, first, occurs to us that celebrated passage of the prophet Habakkuk, chap. i. 13, "Thou art of purer eyes than to behold evil, and canst not look on iniquity." The prophet here ascribes to God the greatest detestation, and such an immortal hatred of sin that he cannot look upon it, but, with a wrathful aversion of his countenance, abominates and dooms it to punishment. But perhaps God thus hates sin because he wills to do so, and by an act of his will entirely free, though the state of things might be changed without any injury to him or diminution of his essential glory. But the Holy Spirit gives us a reason very different from this, namely,—the purity of God's eyes: "Thou art of purer eyes than to behold evil." But there is no one who can doubt that the prophet here intended the holiness of God. The incomprehensible, infinite, and most perfect holiness or purity of God is the cause why he hates and detests all sin; and that justice and holiness are the same, as to the common and general notion of them, we have shown before.

Of the same import is the admonition of Joshua in his address to the people of Israel, chap. xxiv. 19, "Ye cannot serve the LORD" (that is, he will not accept of a false and hypocritical worship from you): "for he is an holy God; he is a jealous God; he will not forgive your transgressions nor your sins." God, then, will not forgive transgressions,—that is, he will most certainly punish them,—because he is most holy. But this holiness is the universal perfection of God, which, when exercised in punishing the sins of the creatures, is called vindicatory justice; that is, in relation to its exercise and effects, for in reality the holiness and justice of God are the same, neither of which, considered in itself and absolutely, differs from the divine nature, whence they are frequently used the one for the other.

Moreover, it is manifest that God meant this holiness in that promulgation of his glorious name, or of the essential properties of his divine nature, made face to face to Moses, Exod. xxxiv. 5–7; which name he had also before declared, chap. xxiii. 7. That non-absolution or punishment denotes an external effect of the divine will is granted; but when God proclaims this to be his name, "The LORD, The LORD God," etc., "that will by no means clear the guilty," he manifestly leads us to the contemplation of that excellence essentially inherent in his nature, which induces him to such an act. But that, by whatever name it be distinguished, in condescension to our capacities, is the justice that we mean.

That eulogium of divine justice by the psalmist, Ps. v. 4–6, favours this opinion: "For thou art not a God that hath pleasure in wickedness: neither shall evil dwell with thee. The foolish shall not stand in thy sight: thou hatest all workers of iniquity. Thou shalt destroy them that speak leasing: the LORD will abhor the bloody and deceitful man." But those who deny this hatred of sin and sinners, and the disposition to punish them, to be perpetually, immutably, and habitually inherent in God, I am afraid have never strictly weighed in their thoughts the divine purity and holiness.

To the second class may be referred those passages of Scripture which ascribe to God the office of a judge, and which affirm that he judges, and will judge, all things with justice. The first which occurs is that celebrated expression of Abraham, Gen. xviii. 25, "Shall not the Judge of all the earth do right?" These are not the words of one who doubts, but of one enforcing a truth acknowledged and confessed among all; a truth upon which the intercession of this faithful friend of God for the pious and just inhabitants of Sodom is founded: for Abraham here ascribes to God the power and office of a just judge; in consequence of which character he must necessarily exercise judgment according to the different merits of mankind. This the words in the preceding clause of the verse, accompanied with a vehement rejection and detestation of every suspicion that might arise to the contrary, sufficiently demonstrate: "That be far from thee to do,"—namely, "to slay the righteous with the wicked." God, then, is a judge, and a just one; and it is impossible for him not to exercise right or judgment. But that justice wherewith he is now endowed, and by which he exerciseth right, is not a free act of his will, (for who would entertain such contemptible thoughts even of an earthly judge?) but a habit or excellence at all times inherent in his nature.

But this supreme excellence and general idea which Abraham made mention of and enforced, the apostle again afterward supports and recommends: Rom. iii. 5, 6, "Is God unrighteous who taketh vengeance? God forbid: for then how shall God judge the world?" Unless he were just, how shall he judge the world? Therefore, this most righteous of all judges exerciseth justice in judging the world "because he is just."

For why should God so often be said to judge the world justly, and in justice, unless his justice were that perfection whence this righteous and just judgment flows and is derived? Acts xvii. 31, "He hath appointed a day, in the which he will judge the world in righteousness by that man whom he hath ordained;" and in Rom. ii. 5, the day of the last judgment is called "the day of wrath and revelation of the righteous judgment of God."

But, again, on this very account the justice of God is celebrated, and he himself, in an especial manner, is said to be just, because he inflicts punishment and exercises his judgments according to the demerits of sinners: Rev. xvi. 5, 6, "Thou art righteous, O Lord, which art, and wast, and shalt be, because thou hast judged thus. For they have shed the blood of saints and prophets, and thou hast given them blood to drink; for they are worthy."

But all retaliation[1] for a crime proceeds from vindicatory justice; but that God exercises that justice, and is thence denominated just, is evident. The Holy Spirit establishes this truth in the plainest words, Ps. ix. 4, 5, where he gloriously vindicates this justice of God: "Thou hast maintained my right and my cause," says the psalmist; "thou satest in the throne judging right. Thou hast rebuked the heathen, thou hast destroyed the wicked, thou hast put out their name for ever and ever." God exerciseth justice and determines causes as he sits upon his throne,—that is, as being endowed with supreme judiciary power,—and that as he is a judge of righteousness, or most righteous judge: Ps. cxix. 137, "Righteous art thou, O LORD, and upright are thy judgments."

Thirdly, It now remains that we take a view of one or two of those passages of Scripture which, in consideration of this divine justice, assert the infliction of punishment for sin in itself, and as far as relates to the thing itself, to be just. To this purpose is that of the apostle to the Romans, chap. i. 32, "Who knowing the judgment," or justice, "of God, that they which commit such things are worthy of death." Whatever, or of what kind soever, that justice or right of God may be of which the apostle is speaking, it seems evident that the three following properties belong to it:—

1. That it is *universally* acknowledged; nay, it is not unknown even to the most abandoned of mankind, and to those schools of every kind of wickedness which the apostle is there describing. Whence they derive this knowledge of the divine law and justice shall be made to appear hereafter.

2. That it is the *cause, source,* and *rule* of all punishments to be inflicted; for this is the right of God, "that those who commit sin are worthy of death." From this right of God it follows that "the wages of" every "sin is death."

3. That it is *natural* and *essential* to God: for although, in respect of its *exercise,* it may have a handle or occasion from some things external to the Deity, and in respect of its *effects* may have a meritorious cause, yet in respect of its source and root, it respects

[1] "*Compensatio*" is the word in the original, and as "retaliation" is frequently used in a particular sense as connected with evil feeling, perhaps "retribution" would better express the meaning of Owen.—ED.

himself as its subject, if God be absolutely perfect. If belonging to any other being, it cannot agree to him.[1]

You will say that this right of God is free; but I deny that any right of God which respects his creatures can, as a habit inherent in his nature, be free, though in the exercise of every right God be absolutely free. Neither can any free act of the divine will towards creatures be called any right of Deity; it is only the exercise of some right. But an act is distinguished from its habit or root.

And now it appears evident that this right is not that supreme right or absolute dominion of God, which, under the primary notion of a Creator, must be necessarily ascribed to him; for it belongs not to the supreme Lord, as such, to inflict punishment, but as ruler or judge.

The supreme dominion and right of God over his creatures, no doubt, so far as it supposes dependence and obedience, necessarily requires that a vicarious punishment should be appointed in case of transgression or disobedience: but the very appointment of punishment, as well as the infliction of it, flows from his right as the governor; which right, considered with respect to transgressors, is nothing else than vindicatory justice. The apostle, therefore, signifies that that is the justice always resident in God, as a legislator, ruler, and judge of all things; which, by common presumption, even the most abandoned of mankind acknowledge.

To these may be added two other passages which occur in the writings of the same apostle: 2 Thess. i. 6, "Seeing it is a righteous thing with God to recompense tribulation to them that trouble you." A recompense of tribulation is a real peculiar act of vindicatory justice; but that belongs to God as he is just. Thence the punishment of sin is called in Heb. ii. 2, "A just recompense of reward;" and by Jude, verse 7, "The vengeance," or justice, "of eternal fire;" because, namely, it follows from that justice of God that such crimes are justly recompensed by such a punishment.

But we will not be farther troublesome in reciting particular proofs; from those already mentioned, and from others equally strong, we thus briefly argue:—That to that Being whose property it is to "render unto every man according to his deeds," not to clear the guilty, to condemn sinners as worthy of death and to inflict the same upon them, to hate sin, and who will in no wise let sin pass unpunished, and all this because he is just, and because his justice so requires, sin-punishing justice naturally belongs, and that he cannot act contrary to that justice; but the passages of Scripture just now mentioned, with many others, assert that all these properties above recounted belong to

[1] Here it is necessary to supply another translation: "Yet in respect of its *source* and *root*, so far as pertains to its subject, if God be absolutely perfect, it cannot be derived to him from any other source."—ED.

and are proper to God, because he is just: therefore, this justice belongs to God, and is natural to him.

It matters not what we affirm of vindicatory justice, whether that it be meant of God essentially, and not only denominatively, that it has an absolute name (for it is called "holiness" and "purity"), that we have it expressed both in the abstract and concrete; for, what is more than that, it is affirmed expressly, directly, and particularly, ofttimes, in the passages above mentioned, that it requires the punishment of sinners, that it implies a constant and immutable will of punishing every sin according to the rule of divine wisdom and right.[1] Impudent to a high degree indeed, then, must Socinus have been, who hath maintained that that perfection of Deity by which he punisheth sin is not called justice, but always anger or fury. Anger, indeed, and fury, analogically and effectively, belong to justice.

So much for our first argument.

II. The *universal consent of mankind* furnishes us with a second, from which we may reason in this manner: "What common opinion and the innate conceptions of all assign to God, that is natural to God; but this corrective justice is so assigned to God: therefore, this justice is natural to God."

The major proposition is evident; for what is not natural to God neither exists in him by any mode of habit or mode of affection, but is only a free act of the divine will, and the knowledge of that can by no means be naturally implanted in creatures; for whence should there be a universal previous conception of an act which might either take place or never take place? No such thing was at the first engraven on the hearts of men, and the fabric of the world teaches us no such thing.

But the minor proposition is established by a threefold proof:—1. By the testimony of the Scripture; 2. By the testimony of every sinner's conscience; and 3. By that of the public consent of all nations.

First, The holy Scriptures testify that such an innate conception[2] is

[1] The sentence might be more intelligibly rendered: "There is nothing which we affirm of vindicatory justice,—whether that it is meant of God essentially, and not only denominatively, that it has an absolute name (for it is called "holiness" and "purity"), that we have it expressed both in the abstract and concrete, that it requires the punishment of sinners, that it implies a constant and immutable will of punishing every sin, according to the rule of divine wisdom and right,—but what is ofttimes affirmed expressly, directly, and particularly, in the passages above mentioned."—Ed.

[2] The Greek word *πρόληψις* is employed in the original, for which perhaps it was difficult to find a precise rendering in one English word. It was a word employed in the *canonics* or psychology of Epicurus to denote the second of his conditions or criteria of truth, which related to *ideas* as distinguished from *sensations* or *emotions*, though, like them, derived from sensuous perception. It implied such a primary and absolute *idea* of a thing as existed in the mind antecedently to any objective presentation of it, and without which no mental act can take place regarding it, whether of naming, thinking, doubting, or inquiring. It is used by Owen to describe a principle in the human mind which is not created by the evidence of testimony or any course of training, which is naturally and essentially interwoven with our mental constitu-

implanted by God in the minds of men. Thus the apostle to the Romans, chap. i. 32, "Who knowing the judgment of God, that they which commit such things are worthy of death." He is here speaking of those nations that were the most forsaken by God, and delivered over to a reprobate mind; yet even to these he ascribes some remaining knowledge of this immutable right of God, which renders it necessary that "every transgression should receive its just recompense of reward," and that sinners should be deserving of death in such a manner that it would be unworthy of God not to inflict it. That is to say, although the operations of this observing and acknowledging principle should often become very languid, and be even almost entirely overwhelmed by abounding wickedness,—for "what they know naturally, as brute beasts, in those things they corrupt themselves,"—yet that mankind must cease to exist before they can altogether lose this innate sense of divine right and judgment. Hence the barbarians concluded against Paul, then a prisoner and in bonds, seeing the viper hanging on one of his hands, that "no doubt he was a murderer, whom, though he had escaped the sea, yet vengeance suffered not to live." Here they argue from the effect to the cause; which, in matters relating to moral good or evil, they could not, unless convinced in their consciences that there is an inviolable connection between sin and punishment, which they here ascribe to Justice.[1]

Justice among them, according to their fabulous theology, which was particularly favoured by the bulk of the people, was the daughter of Jupiter, whom he set over the affairs of mortals, to *avenge the injuries* which they should do to one another, and to inflict condign punishment on all those who should impiously offend against the gods. Hence Hesiod, speaking of Jupiter, says,—

> "He married a second wife, the fair Themis, who brought forth the Hours,
> And Eunomia, and Justice, etc.,
> Who should watch o'er the actions of mortal men."—Hesiod in Theog. 901.

Again, the same author says,—

> "Justice is a virgin, descended from Jupiter,
> Chaste, and honour'd by the heavenly deities;
> And when any one hath injured her with impious indignity,
> [Instantly she, seated beside her father, Saturnian Jupiter,
> Complains of the iniquity of men," etc.]—Hesiod in Oper. 256.

Also, Orpheus in the hymns,—

> "I sing the eye of Justice, who looketh behind her, and is fair,
> Who likewise sits upon the sacred throne of sovereign Jupiter
> As the avenger of the unjust."

tion, and is ready beforehand, by *anticipation*, as the word πρόληψις simply means, to respond to the abstract idea of equity, or to confirm the concrete application of it in the common awards of good or evil.—ED.

[1] Ὤιμωξα κἀγὼ πρὸς τέκνων χειρουμένης.
Νέμει τοι δίκαν θεὸς ὅταν τύχῃ.
Σχέτλια μὲν ἔπαθες, ἀνόσια δ' εἰργάσω
Τάλαιν' εὐνέταν.—Eurip. Elec., 1168.

Hence, these common sayings,—

"God hath an avenging eye;
God hath found the transgressor."

In all which, and in numberless other such passages, the wisest men in those times of ignorance have announced their sense of this vindicatory justice.

And among the Latins, the following passages prove their sense of the same:—

"Aspiciunt oculis superi mortalia justis."
"The gods above behold the affairs of mortals with impartial eyes."

"Raro antecedentem scelestum,
Deseruit pede Poena claudo."

"Seldom hath Punishment, through lameness of foot, left off pursuit of the wicked man, though he hath had the start of her."—Horace.

Also, that celebrated response of the Delphic oracle, recorded by Ælian:—

"But divine Justice pursues those who are guilty of crimes,
Nor can it be avoided even by the descendants of Jupiter;
But it hangs over the heads of the wicked themselves, and over the heads of their
Children; and one disaster to their race is followed by another."

All which assert this vindicatory justice.

This, then, as Plutarch says, is the "ancient faith of mankind;" or, in the words of Aristotle, "opinion concerning God," which Dion Prusæensis calls "a very strong and eternal persuasion, from time immemorial received, and still remaining among all nations."

Secondly, The consciences of all mankind concur to corroborate this truth; but the cause which has numberless witnesses to support it cannot fail. Hence, not only the flight, hiding-place, and fig-leaf aprons of our primogenitors, but every word of dire meaning and evil omen, as *terror*, *horror*, *tremor*, and whatever else harasses guilty mortals, have derived their origin. Conscious to themselves of their wickedness, and convinced of the divine dominion over them, this idea above all dwells in their minds, that he with whom they have to do is supremely just, and the avenger of all sin. From this consideration even the people of God have been induced to believe that death must inevitably be their portion should they be but for once sisted in his presence. Not that the mass of the body is to us an obscure and dark prison, as the Platonists dream, whence, when we obtain a view of divine things, being formerly enveloped by that mass, it is immediately suggested to the mind that the bond of union between mind and body must be instantly dissolved.

It must, indeed, be acknowledged, that through sin we have been transformed into worms, moles, bats, and owls; but the cause of this general fear and dismay is not to be derived from this source.

The justice and purity of God, on account of which he can bear nothing impure or filthy to come into his presence, occurs to sinners' minds; wherefore, they think of nothing else but of a present God, of punishment prepared, and of deserved penalties to be immediately inflicted. The thought of the Deity bursting in upon the mind, immediately every sinner stands confessed a debtor,—a guilty and self-condemned criminal. Fetters, prisons, rods, axes, and fire, without delay and without end, rise to his view. Whence some have judged the mark set upon Cain to have been some horrible tremor, by which, being continually shaken and agitated, he was known to all. Hence, too, these following verses:—

> "Whither fliest thou, Enceladus? Whatever coasts thou shalt arrive on,
> Thou wilt always be under the eye of Jupiter."

And these:—

> "As every one's conscience is, so in his heart he conceives hope or fear, according to his actions.
>
> "This is the first[1] punishment, that even in his own judgment no guilty person is acquitted.
>
> "Do you think that those have escaped whom a guilty conscience holds abashed, and lashes with its inexorable scourge, the mind, the executioner, shaking the secret lash?"
> —See Voss. on Idol. book i. chap. 2.

It is the saying of a certain author, that punishment is coeval with injustice, and that the horror of natural conscience is not terminated by the limits of human life:—

> "Sunt aliquid manes: lethum non omnia finit,
> Lucidaque evictos effugit umbra rogos."
>
> "The soul is something: death ends not at all,
> And the light spirit escapes the vanquished funeral pile."

Hence the famous verses of Adrian, the Roman emperor, spoken on his death-bed:—

> "Animula vagula, blandula,
> Hospes comesque corporis,
> Quæ nunc abibis in loca?
> Pallidula, rigida, nudula,
> Nec, ut soles, dabis joca."

"Alas! my soul, thou pleasing companion of this body, thou fleeting thing, that art now deserting it! whither art thou flying? to what unknown scene? All trembling, fearful, and pensive! What now is become of thy former wit and humour? Thou shalt jest and be gay no more."[2]

[1] Or, chief.—Tr.

[2] Translated thus by Pope:—

> "Ah! fleeting spirit! wandering fire,
> That long hast warm'd my tender breast,
> Must thou no more this frame inspire?
> No more a pleasing, cheerful guest?
>
> Whither, ah! whither art thou flying?
> To what dark undiscover'd shore?
> Thou seem'st all trembling, shiv'ring, dying,
> And wit and humour are no more." Tr.

"That which is truly evil," says Tertullian, "not even those who are under its influence dare defend as good. All evil fills nature with fear or shame. Evil doers are glad to lie concealed; they avoid making their appearance; they tremble when apprehended." Hence the heathens have represented Jove himself, when conscious of any crime, as not free from fear. We find Mercury thus speaking of him in Plautus:—

> "Etenim ille," etc.
>
> "Even that Jupiter, by whose order I come hither,
> Dreads evil no less than any of us:
> Being himself descended from a human father and mother,
> There is no reason to wonder that he should fear for himself."

Hence, too, mankind have a dread awe of every thing in nature that is grand, unusual, and strange, as thunders, lightnings, or eclipses of the heavenly bodies, and tremble at every prodigy, spectre, or comet, nay, even at the hobgoblins of the night, exclaiming, like the woman of Zarephath upon the death of her son, "What have I to do with thee? art thou come unto me to call my sin to remembrance?" Hence, even the most abandoned of men, when vengeance for their sins hangs over their heads, have confessed their sins and acknowledged the divine justice.

It is related by Suetonius, that Nero, that disgrace of human nature, just before his death, exclaimed, "My wife, my mother, and my father, are forcing me to my end."[1] Most deservedly celebrated, too, is that expression of Mauricius the Cappadocian, when slain by Phocas, "Just art thou, O Lord, and thy judgments are righteous!"

But, moreover, while guilty man dreads the consequences of evil, which he knows he has really committed, he torments and vexes himself even with fictitious fears and bugbears. Hence these verses of Horace:—

> "Somnia, terrores magicos, miracula, sagas,
> Nocturnos lemures, portentaque Thessala finxit," [rides ?][2]

—ideas for the most part ridiculous, but, as the old proverb says, "'Tis but reasonable that they should wear the fetters which themselves have forged." Hence the guilty trembling mob is imposed upon and cheated by impostors, by vagrant fortune-tellers and astrologers. If any illiterate juggler shall have foretold a year of darkness, alluding, namely, to the night-season of the year, the consternation is as great as if Hannibal were at the gates of the city. The stings of conscience vex and goad them, and their minds have such presentiments of divine justice that they look upon every

[1] His mother, Agrippina, had poisoned her last husband, the Emperor Claudius, to make way for his succession, and Nero rewarded her by causing her to be murdered. He likewise caused his wife, Octavia, and his tutor, Seneca, to lose their lives; and was in every respect, perhaps, one of the greatest monsters of wickedness that ever disgraced human nature.—Tr.

[2] Hor. Epis. ii. 2., 208.

new prodigy as final, or portentous of the final consummation. I pass over observing at present that if once a conviction of the guilt of any sin be carried home to the mind, this solemn tribunal cannot thoroughly be dislodged from any man's bosom either by dismal solitude or by frequent company, by affluence of delicacies or by habits of wickedness and impiety, nor, in fine, by any endeavours after the practice of innocence. The apostle in his epistle to the Romans, chap. ii., enters more fully into this subject. Two things, then, are to be concluded from what has been said, that mankind are guilty, and that they acknowledge,—

1. *That God hates sin, as contrary to himself*, and that therefore it is impossible for a sinner with safety to appear before him. But if God hate sin, he does it either from his *nature* or because he so *wills* it. But it cannot be because he wills it, for in that case he might not will it; a supposition most absurd. And, indeed, that assertion of Socinus is every way barbarous, abominable, and most unworthy of God, wherein he says, " I maintain that our damnation derives its origin, not from any justice of God, but from the free-will of God," Socinus de Serv. p. 3. cap. 8. But if God hate sin by nature, then by nature he is just, and vindicatory justice is natural to him.

2. *That our sins are debts*, and therefore we shun the sight of our creditor. But I mean such a debt as, with relation to God's supreme dominion, implies in it a perpetual right of punishment.

And such is the second proof of the minor proposition of the second argument; the third remains.

Thirdly, The *public consent of all nations* furnishes the third proof of this truth. There are writers, indeed, who have affirmed (a thing by no means credible) that some nations have been so given up to a reprobate mind that they acknowledge no deity. Socinus hath written[1] that a certain Dominican friar, a worthy honest man, had related this much to himself of the Brazilians and other natives of America. But who can assure us that this friar has not falsified, according to the usual custom of travellers, or that Socinus himself has not invented this story (for he had a genius fertile in falsehoods) to answer his own ends? But let this matter rest on the credit of Socinus, who was but little better than an infidel. But nobody, even by report, hath heard that there exist any who have acknowledged the being of a God, and who have not, at the same time, declared him to be just, to be displeased with sinners and sin, and that it is the duty of mankind to propitiate him if they would enjoy his favour.

But a respectable writer objects,—namely, Rutherford on Providence, chap. xxii. p. 355,—that this argument, that that which men know of God by the natural power of conscience must be naturally

[1] Socin., de Authoritate Scripturæ; lib. edit. sub nomine Dominici Lopez, Soc. Jes.

inherent in God, is of no weight. "For," says he, "by the natural power of conscience, men know that God does many good things freely, without himself; as, for instance, that he has created the world, that the sun rises and gives light;—and yet in these operations God does not act from any necessity of nature."

But this learned man blunders miserably here, as often elsewhere, in his apprehension of the design and meaning of his opponents; for they do not use this argument to prove that the egresses of divine justice are necessary, but that justice itself is necessary to God; which Socinians deny. What is his answer to these arguments? "Mankind acknowledge many things," says he, "which God does freely." To be sure they do, when he exhibits them before their eyes; but what follows from that? So, too, they acknowledge that God punishes sin, when he punishes it. But because all mankind, from the works of God and from the natural power of conscience, acknowledge God to be good and bountiful, we may, without hesitation, conclude goodness and bounty to be essential attributes of God: so likewise, because, from the natural power of conscience and the consideration of God's works of providence, they conclude and agree that God is just, we contend that justice is natural to God.

But as mankind have testified this consent by other methods, so they have especially done it by *sacrifices;* concerning which Pliny says, "That all the world have agreed in them, although enemies or strangers to one another." But since these are plainly of a divine origin, and instituted to prefigure, so to speak, the true atonement by the blood of Christ, in which he hath been the Lamb slain from the foundation of the world,—that is, from the promise made of the seed of the woman, and from the sacrifice of Abel which followed,—the use of them descended to all the posterity of Adam: therefore, though afterward the whole plan and purpose of the institution was lost among by far the greatest part of mankind, and even the true God himself, to whom alone they were due, was unknown, and though no traces of the thing signified,—namely, the promised seed,—remained, yet still the thing itself, and the general notion of appeasing the Deity by sacrifices, hath survived all the darkness, impieties, dreadful wickedness, punishments, migrations of nations, downfalls and destructions of cities, states, and people, in which the world for these many ages hath been involved; for a consciousness of sin, and a sense of divine and avenging justice, have taken deeper root in the heart of man than that they can by any means be eradicated.

There were four kinds of sacrifices among the Gentiles:—First, the *propitiatory* or peace-making sacrifices; for by those they thought they could render the gods propitious or appease them, or avert the anger of the gods, and obtain peace with them. Hence these verses on that undertaking of the Greeks, in the exordium of Homer:—

"But let some prophet or some sacred sage
Explore the cause of great Apollo's rage:
Or learn the wasteful vengeance to remove
By mystic dreams; for dreams descend from Jove.
If broken vows this heavy curse have laid,
Let altars smoke and hecatombs be paid:
So Heaven atoned shall dying Greece restore,
And Phœbus dart his burning shafts no more."—Pope's Homer.

They were desirous of appeasing Apollo by sacrifices, who had inflicted on them a lamentable mortality. To the same purpose is that passage of Virgil,—

"The prophet[1] first with sacrifice adores
The greater gods; their pardon then implores."—Dryden's Virgil.

Hence, too, that lamentation of the person in the Pœnulus of Plautus, who could not make satisfaction to his gods:—

"Unhappy man that I am," says he, "to-day I have sacrificed six lambs to my much-incensed gods, and yet I have not been able to render Venus propitious to me; and as I could not appease her, I came instantly off."

And Suetonius, speaking of Otho, says, "He endeavours, by all kinds of piacular sacrifices, to propitiate the manes of Galba, by whom he had seen himself thrust down and expelled." And the same author affirms of Nero, "That he had been instructed that kings were wont to expiate the heavenly prodigies by the slaughter of some illustrious victim, and to turn them from themselves upon the heads of their nobles;" though this, perhaps, rather belongs to the second kind. But innumerable expressions to this purpose are extant, both among the Greek and Latin authors.

The second kind were the *expiatory* or purifying sacrifices, by which sins were said to be atoned, expiated, and cleansed, and sinners purified, purged, and reconciled, and the anger of the gods turned aside and averted. It would be tedious, and perhaps superfluous, to produce examples; the learned can easily trace them in great abundance. The other kinds were the *eucharistical* and *prophetical*, which have no relation to our present purpose.

In this way of appeasing the Deity, mankind, I say, formerly agreed; whence it is evident that an innate conception[2] of this sin-avenging justice is natural to all, and, therefore, that that justice is to be reckoned among the essential attributes of the divine nature; concerning which only, and not concerning the free acts of his will, mankind universally agree.

[1] Namely, Helenus, Æneid, book iii.—TR.

[2] See note, p. 517.

CHAPTER IV.

The origin of human sacrifices—Their use among the Jews, Assyrians, Germans, Goths, the inhabitants of Marseilles, the Normans, the Francs, the Tyrians, the Egyptians, and the ancient Gauls—Testimonies of Cicero and Cæsar that they were used among the Britons and Romans by the Druids—A fiction of Apion concerning the worship in the temple of Jerusalem—The names of some persons sacrificed—The use of human sacrifices among the Gentiles proved from Clemens of Alexandria, Dionysius of Halicarnassus, Porphyry, Philo, Eusebius, Tertullian, Euripides—Instances of human sacrifices in the sacred Scriptures—The remarkable obedience of Abraham—What the neighbouring nations might have gathered from that event—Why human sacrifices were not instituted by God—The story of Iphigenia—The history of Jephthah—Whether he put his daughter to death—The cause of the difficulty—The impious sacrifice of the king of Moab—The abominable superstition of the Rugiani—The craftiness of the devil—Vindications of the argument—The same concluded.

BUT it is strange to think what a stir was made by the ancient enemy of mankind to prevent any ray of light respecting the true sacrifice, that was to be made in the fulness of time, from being communicated to the minds of men through means of this universal ceremony and custom of sacrificing. Hence he influenced the most of the nations to the heinous, horrible, and detestable crime of offering human sacrifices, in order to make atonement for themselves, and render God propitious by such an abominable wickedness.

But as it seems probable that some light may be borrowed from the consideration of these sacrifices, in which mankind, from the presumption of a future judgment, have so closely agreed, perhaps the learned reader will think it not foreign to our purpose to dwell a little on the subject, and to reckon up some examples. This abomination, prohibited by God under the penalty of a total extermination, was divers times committed by the Jews, running headlong into forbidden wickedness, while urged on by the stings of conscience to this infernal remedy. They offered their children as burnt-sacrifices to Moloch,—that is, to the Saturn of the Tyrians; not to the planet of that name, not to the father of the Cretan Jupiter, but to the Saturn of the Tyrians,—that is, to Baal or to the sun; and not by making them to pass between two fires for purification, as some think, but by burning them in the manner of a whole burnt-offering. Ps. cvi. 36–38, "And they served their idols: which were a snare unto them. Yea, they sacrificed their sons and their daughters unto devils, and shed innocent blood, even the blood of their sons and of their daughters, whom they sacrificed unto the idols of Canaan: and the land was polluted with blood." Almost the whole world, during the times of that ignorance which God winked at, were indebted to the devil.[1] Since, then, it is abundantly evident from these sacri-

[1] "Were initiated by the devil in the same abomination."—ED.

fices by what a sense of vindicatory justice, horror of punishment, and consciousness of sin, mankind are constrained, we must enlarge a little on the consideration of them.

Tacitus, speaking of the Germans, says, "Of the gods, they chiefly worship Mercury; to whom, on certain days, they hold it as an article of religion and piety to sacrifice human victims. Mars they have always been accustomed to appease by a most cruel worship; for his victims were the deaths of the captives." Jornandes affirms the same of the Goths. And thus Lucan writes in his siege of Marseilles:—"Here the sacred rites of the gods are barbarous in their manner; altars are built for deadly ceremonies, and every tree is purified by human blood."

And the same author, in the sixth book, from his Precepts of Magic, has these verses:—

"Vulnere si ventris," etc.

"If, contrary to nature, the child be extracted through a wound in the belly, to be served up on the hot altars."

Virgil bears witness that such sacrifices were offered to Phœbus or the Sun, Æneid x.:—

> "Next Lycas fell; who, not like others born,
> Was from his wretched mother ripp'd and torn:
> Sacred, O Phœbus! from his birth to thee."—Dryden's Virgil.

But Acosta asserts that infants are sacrificed even at this very time to the Sun, in Cuscum, the capital of Peru.

And thus the Scriptures testify, 2 Kings xvii. 29–31, "Howbeit every nation made gods of their own, and put them in the houses of the high places which the Samaritans had made, every nation in their cities wherein they dwelt. And the men of Babylon made Succoth-benoth, and the men of Cuth made Nergal, and the men of Hamath made Ashima, and the Avites made Nibhaz and Tartak, and the Sepharvites burnt their children in fire to Adrammelech and Anammelech, the gods of Sepharvaim."

Ditmarus, in his first book, testifies "That the Normans and Danes sacrificed yearly, in the month of January, to their gods, ninety-nine human creatures, as many horses, besides dogs and cocks." But what Procopius, on the Gothic war, writes, is truly astonishing,—namely, "That the Francs made use of human victims in his time, even though they then worshipped Christ." Alas! for such a kind of Christianity. The practices of the Tyrians,[1] Carthaginians, and Egyptians, in this respect are known to every one. And Theodoret says, "That in Rhodes, some person was sacrificed to Saturn on the sixteenth of the calends of November, which, after

[1] Concerning the Tyrians, see Curtius, book iv.; and concerning the Carthaginians, see Diodorus, book xx.—Tr.

having been for a long time observed, became a custom; and they used to reserve one of those who had been capitally condemned till the feast of Saturn."

Porphyry, on "Abstinence from Animals," relates the customs of the Phœnicians concerning this matter. "The Phœnicians," says he, "in great disasters, either by wars, or commotions, or droughts, used to sacrifice one of their dearest friends or relations to Saturn, devoted to this fate by the common suffrages." They were called Phœnicians from the word *φοίνιξ*, which signifies a red colour. *Φοίνιξ*, according to Eustathius, is from *φόνος*, which signifies blood; thence the colour called *φοινίκεος*, or the purple colour. Hence the learned conjecture that the Phœnicians were the descendants of Esau or Edom, whose name also signifies red; and from whom, also, the Red Sea was named. Edom, then, *φοίνιξ*, and *ἐρυθραῖος*, mean the same,—namely, red. Why may we not, then, conjecture that the Phœnicians, or Idumæans, were first led to this custom from some corrupt tradition concerning the sacrificing of Isaac, the father of Esau, the leader and head of their nation? This, at least, makes for the conjecture, that while other nations sacrificed enemies or strangers, Porphyry bears witness that they sacrificed one of their dearest friends or relations. But Isaac was not to Abraham one of the dearest, but the only dear one. From such corrupt traditions as these, it is not to be wondered that the consciences of men, struck with a fear of punishment, should have been encouraged to persevere in so cruel and superstitious a worship.

Concerning the ancient Gauls, we have the most credible evidences,—Cicero and Julius Cæsar; the former of whom charges them with the practice of offering human sacrifices, as a horrid crime, and certain evidence of their contempt of Deity. The other, however, commends them on this very account, on the score of a more severe religion. "If at any time, induced by fear, they think it necessary that the gods should be appeased, they defile their altars and temples with human victims,—as if they could not practise religion without first violating it by their wickedness; for who does not know that, even at this day, they retain that savage and barbarous custom of sacrificing human beings, thinking that the immortal gods can be appeased by the blood and wickedness of man?" Cicero pro Fonteio. But Cæsar, the conqueror of the Gauls, gives us a very different account of these kind of sacrifices. "This nation," says he, "of the Gauls, is most of all devoted to religious observances; and for that reason, those who labour under any grievous distemper, or who are conversant in dangers and battles, either sacrifice human victims, or vow that they will sacrifice them, and they employ the Druids as the conductors of such sacrifices; for they have an opinion that unless a human life be given for a human life, the heavenly deities cannot be appeased." These last words seem to me to acknowledge a persuasion, that must have arisen from some ancient tradition, about the substitution of the Son of Man in the stead of sinners as a propitiation for sin.

No doubt can be entertained concerning the inhabitants of Britain but that they were guilty of the same practices; for from them came the Druids, the first promoters of that superstition, not only among the Gauls, but even in Italy and in the city of Rome itself. "The doctrine of the Druids," says Cæsar, "is thought to have been found in Britain, and brought thence into Gaul; and now such as are desirous to examine more particularly into that matter generally go thither for the sake of information," book vi. of the Wars in Gaul. But Tacitus informs us with what kind of sacrifices they performed their divine services there, in the fourteenth book of his Annals. "When the island of Anglesey was conquered by Paulinus, a guard," says he, "was placed over the vanquished, and the groves devoted to cruel superstitions were hewn down" (the same was done by Cæsar in the siege of Marseilles, Lucan, book iii.); "for it was an article of their religion to sacrifice their captives on the altars, and to consult their gods by human entrails."

Hence that verse in Horace:—

> "Visam Britannos, hospitibus feros."
>
> "I will visit the Britons, cruel to strangers."

At which remote place[1] the Britons used to sacrifice their guests for victims; yea, even in Rome itself, as Plutarch, in his Life of Marcellus, testifies, they buried, by order of the high priests, "a man and woman of Gaul, and a man and woman of Greece," alive in the cattle market, to avert some calamity by such a fatal sacrifice. Whether this was done yearly, as some think, I am rather inclined to doubt.

Of the same kind was the religion of the Decii, devoting themselves for the safety of the city. Hence a suspicion arose, and was everywhere rumoured, among the Gentiles, concerning the sacred rites of the Jews, with which they were unacquainted,—namely, that they were wont to be solemnized with human sacrifices: for although, after the destruction of the temple, it was manifest that they worshipped the God of heaven only, yet so long as they celebrated the secret mysteries appointed them by God, Josephus against Apion bears witness that they laboured under the infamy of that horrible crime,—namely, of sacrificing human victims, among those who were unacquainted with the Jewish polity; where he also recites, from the same Apion, a most ridiculous fiction about a young Greek captive being delivered by Antiochus, when he impiously spoiled the

[1] Namely, Anglesey.—TR.

temple, after having been fed there on a sumptuous diet for the space of a year, that he might make the fatter a victim.

A custom that prevailed with some, not-unlike this untruth about the young Greek kept in the temple, seems to have given rise to it; for thus Diodorus, in book v., writes of the Druids, "They fix up their malefactors upon poles, after having kept them five years" (it seems they fattened much slower than at Jerusalem), "and sacrifice them to their gods, and, with other first-fruits of the year, offer them on large funeral piles." Theodoret also mentions something of that kind concerning the Rhodians, in the first book of the "Greek Affections;" the words have been mentioned before.

But that young Greek, destined for sacrifice, in Apion, has no name; that is, there never was any such person.

> "But, friend, discover faithful what I crave,—
> Artful concealment ill becomes the brave;
> Say what thy birth, and what the name you bore,
> Imposed by parents in the natal hour."
>
> Pope's[1] Homer's Odyssey, book viii.

But, after having prepared the plot, he ought not to have shunned the task of giving names to the actors. We have the name of a Persian sacrificed even among the Thracians, in Herodotus, book ix. "The Thracians of Apsinthium," says he, "having seized Œobazus flying into Thrace, sacrificed him, after their custom, to Pleistorus, the god of the country."

There is still remaining, if I rightly remember, the name of a Spanish soldier, a captive, with other of his companions, among the Mexicans, well-known inhabitants of America, who being sacrificed, on a very high altar, to the gods of the country, when his heart was pulled out (if we can credit Peter Martyr, author of the History of the West Indies), tumbling down upon the sand, exclaimed, "O companions, they have murdered me!" Clemens of Alexandria makes mention of Theopompus, a king of the Lacedæmonians, being sacrificed by Aristomenes the Messenian. His words, which elegantly set forth this custom of all the nations, we shall beg leave to trouble the reader with: "But now, when they had invaded all states and nations as plagues (he is speaking of demons), they demanded cruel sacrifices; and one Aristomenes, a Messenian, slew three hundred in honour of Ithometan Jupiter, thinking that he sacrificed so many hecatombs in due form, and of such a kind. Among these, too, was Theopompus, king of the Lacedemonians, an illustrious victim. But the inhabitants of Mount Taurus, who dwell about the Tauric Chersonese, instantly sacrifice whatever shipwrecked strangers they find

1 The words in the original apply much better to our author's meaning. See them, Odyss., lib. viii. v. 550.—Tr.

upon their coasts to Diana of Taurus. Thence, ye inhospitable shores! Euripides again and again bewails in his scenes these your sacrifices," Clemens' Exhortations to the Greeks.

But what he says concerning Euripides has a reference to the story of "Iphigenia in Tauris;" where, however, the poet signifies that she detested such kinds of sacrifices, for he introduces Iphigenia, the priestess of Diana, thus bewailing her lot: "They have appointed me priestess in these temples, where Diana, the goddess of the festival, is delighted with such laws, whose name alone is honourable; but I say no more, dreading the goddess. For I sacrifice (and it long hath been a custom of the state) every Grecian that arrives in this country," Eur. Iph. in Tauris, v. 34.

Thus far Clemens, who also demonstrates the same thing of the Thessalians, Lycians, Lesbians, Phocensians, and Romans, from Monimus, Antoclides, Pythocles, and Demaratus. That deed, too, of Agamemnon, alluded to by Virgil, furnishes another proof:—

> "Sanguine placastis ventos, et virgine cæsâ."

> "O Grecians, when the Trojan shores you sought,
> Your passage with a virgin's blood was bought."
> Dryden's Virg.

Tertullian also bears witness to this wickedness: "In Africa they openly sacrificed infants to Saturn, even down to the time of the proconsulate of Tiberius; and what is surprising, even in that most religious city of the pious descendants of Æneas, there is a certain Jupiter, whom, at his games, they drench with human blood."

It is notoriously known, that in the sanguinary games of the Romans, they made atonement to the gods with human blood,—namely, that of captives. But Eusebius Pamphilus (Praep. Evang. lib. iv. cap. 16) enters the most fully of any into this matter; for he shows from Porphyry, Philo, Clemens, Dionysius of Halicarnassus, and Diodorus Siculus, that this ceremony of offering human sacrifices was practised all over the world. Porphyry, indeed, shows at large who instituted this kind of worship in different places, and who put an end to it. Another very ingenious poet brings an accusation of extreme folly and madness against this rite in these verses. It is a Plebeian addressing Agamemnon:—

> "Tu quum pro vitula, statuis dulcem Aulide natam,
> Ante aras, spargisque mola caput, improbe, salsa,
> Rectum animi servas?"—Hor., lib. ii. sat. iii. v. 199.

> "When your own child you to the altar led,
> And pour'd the salted meal upon her head;
> When you beheld the lovely victim slain,
> Unnatural father! were you sound of brain?"

Agamemnon is introduced thus, apologizing for himself on account of the utility and necessity of the sacrifice :—

> "Verum ego, ut hærentes adverso littore naves
> Eriperem, prudens placavi sanguine divos."

> "But I, while adverse winds tempestuous roar,
> To loose our fated navy from the shore,
> Wisely with blood the powers divine adore."
> Francis' Horace.

The Plebeian again charges him with madness :—

> "Nempe tuo furiose?"

> "What! your own blood, you madman?"

But Philo, in his first book, relates that one Saturn (there were many illustrious persons of that name, as well as of the name of Hercules), when the enemies of his country were oppressing it, sacrificed at the altars his own daughter, named Leüdem; which among them, namely, the Tyrians, means only-begotten.

I have little or no doubt but that this Saturn was Jephthah the Israelite; that their Hercules was Joshua, the celebrated Vossius has clearly proved, book i. of Idol.

But as we have made mention of Jephthah, it will not be foreign to our purpose briefly to treat of those three famous examples of human sacrifices recorded in the sacred writings. The first is contained in that celebrated history concerning the trial of Abraham; an undertaking so wonderful and astonishing that no age hath ever produced or will produce its like. It even exceeds every thing that fabulous Greece hath presumed in story. A most indulgent and affectionate father, weighed down with age,[1] is ordered to offer his only son, the pillar of his house and family, the trust of Heaven, a son solemnly promised him by God, the foundation of the future church, in whom, according to the oracles of God, all the nations of the earth were to be blessed; this most innocent and most obedient son he is ordered to offer as a burnt-offering,—a dreadful kind of sacrifice indeed! which required that the victim should be first slain, afterward cut in pieces, and lastly burnt, by the hands of a father! What though the purpose was not accomplished, God having graciously so ordained it, this obedience of the holy man is, notwithstanding, to be had in everlasting remembrance! And forasmuch as he began the task with a sincere heart and unfeigned faith, the Holy Spirit bears testimony to him as if he had really offered his son: Heb. xi. 17, "By faith Abraham, when he was tried, offered

1 Abraham is said to have been now a hundred and thirty-three years of age; for some are of opinion that Isaac, at the time he was to have been sacrificed, was thirty-three years old. Josephus says twenty-five; the Jews in Seder Olam, thirty-six. Nor is it any objection that he is called naar, for so Benjamin, the father of many children, is called, Gen. xliii.—Tr.

up Isaac; and he that had received the promises offered up his only-begotten." The fame of this transaction, no doubt, was spread in ancient times over many of the eastern nations. But that those who were altogether ignorant of the communion and friendship which Abraham cultivated with the Lord, and yet were convinced in their consciences that a more noble sacrifice than all cattle, and a more precious victim, was necessary to be offered to God (for if this persuasion had not been deeply impressed on their minds, the devil could not have induced them to that dreadful worship), assumed the courage of practising the same thing from that event, there is not any room to doubt. And, farther, if any report were spread abroad concerning the divine command and oracle which Abraham received, the eyes of all would be turned upon him as the wisest and holiest of men, and they would be led, perhaps, to conclude, falsely, that God might be propitiated by such kind of victims: for they did not this from any rivalship of Abraham, whom they respected as a wise and just man; but, being deceived by that action of his, and endeavouring at an expiation of their own crimes, they did the same thing that he did, but with a very different end, for the offering up of Isaac was a type of the sacrifice of Jesus Christ.

But from that right and dominion which God naturally hath over all the creatures, or from that superior excellence and eminence wherewith he is endowed and constituted, he might, without any degree or suspicion of injustice or cruelty, exact victims as a tribute from man. But he hath declared his will to the contrary: Exod. xxxiv. 19, 20, "But the firstling of an ass thou shalt redeem with a lamb; and the first-born of thy sons thou shalt redeem;"—partly, lest human blood, of which he has the highest care, should become of little account; but especially because all mankind in general being polluted with iniquities, a type of his immaculate Son could not be taken from among them.

But this history the falsifying poets of the Greeks have corrupted by that fable of theirs concerning the sacrifice of Iphigenia, begun by her father Agamemnon, but who was liberated by the substitution of a doe.[1] Hence, in Euripides, these words are falsely applied to the virgin destined to be sacrificed, which (the proper changes being made) might with more propriety be spoken of Isaac, when acting in obedience to the command of God and of his father.

—— *ὦ πάτερ πάρειμί σοι*, etc.

"O, father, I am here present; and I cheerfully deliver up my body for my country and for all Greece, to be sacrificed at the altar

[1] Agamemnon, as the story runs, had killed one of Diana's stags, and the goddess would be appeased on no other terms than by the sacrifice of his daughter; but after she was laid on the pile, Diana, pitying the virgin, put a doe in her room, and made Iphigenia her priestess.—TR.

of the goddess, by those who now conduct me thither, if the oracle so require," Euripid. Iphigenia in Aulis, near the end, v. 1552.

It is worth while to notice, by the way, the use of the word ὑπέρ. The virgin to be sacrificed declared that she was willing to appease the anger of the gods, and suffer punishment in behalf of, or instead of, her country and all Greece; and but a little before she is introduced exulting in these words,—

Ἑλίσσετ' ἀμφὶ ναόν, etc.

"Invoke to her temple, to her altar, Diana, queen Diana, the blessed Diana; for if it shall be necessary, by my blood and sacrifice I will obliterate the oracle," Ib. v. 1480.

Justly celebrated, too, in the second place, is the history of Jephthah's sacrificing his only daughter, related by the Holy Spirit in these words: Judges xi. 30, 31, 34, 39, "And Jephthah vowed a vow unto the LORD, and said, If thou shalt without fail deliver the children of Ammon into mine hands, then it shall be that whatsoever cometh forth of the doors of my house to meet me, when I return in peace from the children of Ammon, shall surely be the LORD'S, and I will offer it up for a burnt-offering." But when he returned, "his daughter came out to meet him;" and "at the end of two months, he did with her according to his vow." If any passage ever puzzled both Jewish and Christian interpreters, ancient and modern, as well as all your disputants upon and patchers up of common-place difficulties, this one has. For, on the one hand, here it is supposed that all offering of human sacrifices is detested and abhorred by God; and to ascribe such a thing to a man of piety, and one celebrated by the Holy Spirit for his faith, many will not venture. But again, on the other hand, the words of the history, the circumstances, the grief and lamentation of the father, seem hardly capable of admitting any other meaning. But to me these things are ambiguous.[1]

First, It is evident that a *gross ignorance* of the law, either in making the vow or in executing it, is by no means to be ascribed to Jephthah, who was, though a military man, a man of piety, a fearer of God, and well acquainted with the sacred writings. Now, then, if he simply made a vow, that a compensation and redemption, according to the valuation of the priests, ought to have been made, could not have escaped him; and therefore there was no reason why he should so much bewail the event of a vow by which he had engaged himself to the Lord, and to which he was bound, for he might

[1] That is, the expressions relating to this subject are capable of more meanings than one, and to ascertain the right one is attended with difficulties.—TR. [This seems a mistake. It is a Greek word in the original, ἀναμφισβήτητα, and signifies "indisputable," or "beyond controversy." Had the word been ἀμφισβήτητα, it might have borne the meaning attached to it by the translator.—ED.]

both keep his faith and free his daughter, according to the words of the law, Lev. xxvii. 1–8.

Or if we should conjecture that he was so grossly mistaken, and entirely unacquainted with divine matters, was there no priest or scribe among all the people, who, during that time which he granted to his daughter, at her own request, to bewail her virginity, could instruct this illustrious leader, who had lately merited so highly of the commonwealth, in the meaning of the law, so that he should neither vex himself, render his family extinct, nor worship God to no purpose, by a vain superstition? I have no doubt, then, but that Jephthah performed his duty in executing his vow, according to the precept of the law, however much he might have erred in his original conception of it.

Nor is it less doubtful, in the second place, that Jephthah did not offer his daughter as a burnt-offering, as the words of the vow imply, according to the ceremony and institution of that kind of sacrifice; for as these sacrifices could be performed by the priest only by killing the victim, cutting it in pieces, and consuming it by fire upon the altar,—offices in which no priest would have ministered or assisted,—so also, such kind of sacrifices are enumerated among the abominations to the Lord, which he hateth: Deut. xii. 31, "Thou shalt not do so unto the LORD thy God; for every abomination to the LORD, which he hateth, have they done unto their gods; for even their sons and their daughters have they burnt in the fire to their gods."

Thirdly, Nor does it seem probable that Jephthah had dedicated his daughter to God, that she should perpetually remain a virgin; for neither hath God instituted any such kind of worship, nor could the forced virginity of the daughter by any means ever be reckoned to the account of the father, as any valuable consideration, in place of a victim.

As, then, there were two kinds of things devoted to God, the first of which was of the class of those which, as God did not order that they should be offered in sacrifice, it was made a statute that they should be valued by the priest at a fair valuation, and be redeemed, and so return again to common use. The law of these is delivered, Lev. xxvii. 1, 2, etc.: "And the LORD spake unto Moses, saying, Speak unto the children of Israel, and say unto them, When a man shall make a singular vow, the persons shall be for the LORD by thy estimation. And thy estimation shall be of the male from twenty years old even unto sixty years old, even thy estimation shall be fifty shekels of silver, after the shekel of the sanctuary. And if it be a female, then thy estimation shall be thirty shekels," etc. And verse 8: "But if he be poorer than thy estimation, then he shall present himself before the priest, and the priest shall value him; according to his ability that vowed shall the priest value him."

But the second kind of these were called *Cherem*,[1] concerning which it was not a simple vow נֶדֶר, of which there was no redemption or estimation to be made by the priest. The law respecting these is given in the 28th and 29th verses of the same chapter: "Notwithstanding no devoted thing, that a man shall devote unto the LORD of all that he hath, both of man and beast, and of the field of his possession, shall be sold or redeemed: every devoted thing is most holy unto the LORD. None devoted, which shall be devoted of men, shall be redeemed; but shall surely be put to death."

The question, to which of these two kinds the vow of Jephthah belonged, creates, if I mistake not, the whole difficulty of the passage.

That it belonged not to the first is as clear as the day; because if we suppose that it did, he might easily have extricated himself and family from all grief on that account by paying the estimation made by the priest. It was, then, a *cherem* which by his vow Jephthah had vowed to the Lord, by no means to be redeemed, but accounted "most holy unto the LORD," as in verses 28, 29, before mentioned.

But it is doubted whether a rational creature could be made a *cherem;* but, in fact, there can hardly remain any room for doubt. To the person who considers the text itself it will easily appear. The words are, "Every devoted thing is most holy unto the LORD. None devoted, which shall be devoted of men, shall be redeemed; but shall surely be put to death." It is evident from the foregoing verse that the words, "of men," point not at the *efficient cause* but the *matter*[2] of the vow; where the same words, in the original, cannot be otherwise rendered than by "of," or "touching man," or by "out of," or "from among mankind or men," or "of the class of men." And all those writers interpret the words in this sense (and there are not a few of them, both among Jews and Christians), who are of opinion that the passage ought to be explained as relating to the enemies of God, devoted to universal slaughter and destruction.

As Jephthah, then, had devoted his daughter as a *cherem*, it seems hardly to admit of a doubt that the cause of his consternation and sorrow at meeting her was because that, according to the law, he had slain her, having devoted her to God in such a manner as not to be redeemed.

It would be foreign to our purpose to agitate this question any farther. We shall only say, then, that after having maturely weighed all the circumstances of the text and of the thing itself, according to the measure of our abilities, we have gone into the opinion of those who maintain that Jephthah gave up his daughter to death, she being devoted to God in such a manner as, according to the law, not

[1] A thing or person so devoted as not to be redeemed.—TR.

[2] That is, pointing not at the persons vowing, but at the object of their vow, or at the thing vowed or devoted by them.—TR.

to be redeemed, that Supreme Being, who has the absolute right and power of life and death, so requiring[1] it. The theologians of both nations[2] who espouse this side of the question are both numerous and renowned. Peter Martyr testifies that almost all the more ancient rabbins agreed in this opinion. Josephus in his Antiquities follows them, although he hath not determined Jephthah to be free of blame. Of the fathers, it is sufficient (for the matter is not to be determined by votes) that Jerome in his epistle to Julian, Ambrose on Virginity, book iii., Augustine on the book of Judges; and of those in later times, Peter Martyr in his commentary on the 11th of Judges, and Ludovicus Cappellus in that excellent treatise of his concerning Jephthah's vow, have either approved, or at least have not dissented from, this opinion. What Epiphanius[3] relates concerning the deification of Jephthah's daughter favours this opinion. "In Sebaste," says he, "which was formerly called Samaria, having deified the daughter of Jephthah, they yearly celebrate a solemn festival in honour of her." Yea, more, the most learned agree that the fame of this transaction was so spread among the Gentile nations, that thence Homer, Euripides, and others, seized the occasion of raising that fable about Agamemnon's sacrificing his daughter, and that there never was any other Iphigenia than Jephthegenia, nor Iphianassa[4] than Ιφθιαγασσα[5] or Jephtheanassa.

But this was a kind of human sacrifice by which, as God intended to shadow forth the true sacrifice of his Son, so the enemy of the human race, aping the Almighty, and taking advantage of and insulting the blindness of mankind and the horror of their troubled consciences, arising from a sense of the guilt of sin, influenced and compelled them to the performance of ceremonies of a similar kind.

There is no need that we should dwell on the third instance of this kind of sacrifices that occurs in the sacred writings,—namely, that of the king of Moab, during the siege of his city, offering up either his own son or the king of Edom's upon the wall, as he was a heathen and a worshipper of Saturn, according to the custom of the Phœnicians. Despairing of his situation, when it seemed to him that the city could no longer be defended, and when he had no hope of breaking through or of escaping, he offered his own son, in my

[1] The author here uses the words, "at least interpretatively," before "so requiring it;" meaning thereby, as I understand him, that the just and proper interpretation of the passage wherein this history is recorded, and of the others quoted, relating to vows, had clearly determined him to adopt this opinion.—Tr.

[2] That is, both of the Jewish and Christian persuasion.—Tr.

[3] Patriarch of Constantinople in the year 520.—Tr.

[4] Iphianassa, as the story says, was daughter of Prœtus, king of the Argives, who preferring herself in beauty to Juno, was struck with such a madness as to believe herself to be a cow, but was afterwards cured by Melampus, a famous physician, to whom she was given in marriage.—Tr.

[5] Or, than the daughter of Jephthah. For Iphigenia, see note on p. 532.

opinion (for the king of Edom had no first-born to succeed him in the government, being himself only a deputy king), as a sacrifice to the gods of his country, to procure a deliverance. The three kings then departed from the city which they were besieging, God so directing it, either having entered into an agreement to that purpose, or because of the war not being successfully ended (for the conjectures on this point are by no means satisfactory), some indignation having broke out among the troops of the Israelites, who also themselves were idolaters.[1] See 2 Kings iii. 26, 27.

We shall conclude this train of testimonies with that noted account of the Rugiani, certain inhabitants of an island of Sclavonia, related by Albertus Crantzius, from which we may learn the dreadful judgment of God against a late superstition of Christians.

"Some preachers of the gospel of Christ" (who and what they were the historian shows) "converted the whole island of the Rugiani to the faith. Then they built an oratory in honour of our Lord and Saviour Jesus Christ, and in memory of St Vitus, patron of Corveia. But after, by divine permission, matters were changed, and the Rugiani fell off from the faith, having instantly expelled the priests and Christians, they converted their religion into superstition;[2] for they worship St Vitus, whom we acknowledge as a martyr and servant of Christ, as God. Nor is there any barbarous people under heaven that more dread Christians and priests; whence also, in peculiar honour of St Vitus, they have been accustomed to sacrifice yearly any Christian that may accidentally fall into their hands." A more horrible issue of Christianity sinking into superstition would, perhaps, be difficult to be found. But we are now tired of dwelling on such horrid rites and abominable sacrifices. Forasmuch, then, as we ourselves are the offspring of those who were wholly polluted with such sacrifices, and by nature not better or wiser than they, but only, through the rich, free, and unspeakable mercy of God, have been

[1] Dr Gill agrees with our author that the king of Moab sacrificed his own son, and thinks that he might be induced to offer him thus publicly on the wall, that it might be seen by the camp of Israel, and move their compassion; but rather that he did it as a religious action, to appease the Deity by a human sacrifice; and that it was offered either to the true God, in imitation of Abraham, or to his idol Chemosh, the sun. It was usual with the heathens, particularly the Phœnicians, when in calamity and distress, to offer up what was most dear and valuable to them. See p. 527. Dr Gill seems of opinion that the cause why the three kings broke up the siege was, that after this barbarous and shocking sacrifice the Moabites became quite desperate, and that the kings, seeing them resolved to sell their lives so dear, and to hold out to the last man, thought fit to raise the siege; a very natural explication of these words, "And there was great indignation against Israel," if the indignation be understood as applicable only to the Moabites. But the concluding sentence of our author on this subject seems to imply it to be his opinion, that there were also dissensions and indignation in the allied army; perhaps between the Edomites, the idolatrous Israelites, and the worshippers of the true God, arising from the horrid spectacle they had witnessed. This is only ventured as a conjecture, that may better account for the sudden departure of the kings.—Tr.

[2] Their religion at best had been contaminated with the superstitions of the church of Rome.—Tr.

translated from the power of darkness, and the kingdom of Satan, into his marvellous light, it is most evident that, by every tie, we are bound to offer and devote ourselves wholly to Christ, our Deliverer and most glorious Saviour, "who hath loved us, and who gave himself for us, that he might redeem us from all iniquity, and purify to himself a peculiar people, zealous of good works."

Thus the prophecies concerning the oblation of Christ being but badly understood, mankind were seduced, through the instigation of the devil, to pollute themselves with these inhuman and accursed sacrifices. Perhaps, too, that most artful seducer had it in view, by such sacrifices, to prejudice the more acute and intelligent part of mankind against that life-giving sacrifice that was to be destructive of his kingdom; for such now hold these atrocious sacrifices and detestable rites in abhorrence. However, to keep the minds of men in suspense and in subjection to himself, he did not fail, from another quarter, by words dubious, to spread abroad and send forth ambiguous oracles, as if such rites and sacrifices were of no avail for the expiation of sins. Thence these verses in Cato's Distichs:—

> "Cum sis ipse nocens, moritur cur victima pro te?
> Stultitia est morte alterius sperare salutem."

"Since it is thyself that art guilty, why need any victim die for thee? It is madness to expect salvation from the death of another."

I have no doubt but that this last verse is a diabolical oracle.

By such deceitful practices, the old serpent, inflamed with envy, and being himself for ever lost, because he could not eradicate every sense of avenging justice (which is as a curb to restrain the fury of the wicked) from the minds of men, wished to lead them into mazes, that he might still keep them the slaves of sin, and subject to his own dominion.

There have been, and still are, some of mankind, I confess it, who, from indulging their vices, are seared in their consciences, and whose minds are become callous by the practice of iniquity; who, flattering themselves to their own destruction, have falsely conceived either that God does not trouble himself about such things, or that he can be easily appeased, and without any trouble. Hence that profane wretch introduced by Erasmus, after having settled matters with the Dominican commissaries, to a jolly companion of his own, when he asked him, "Whether God would ratify the bargain?" answers, "I fear rather lest the devil should not ratify it, for God by nature is easy to be appeased." It is from the same idea that many of the barbarous natives of America, idly fancying that there are two gods, one good and another evil, say that there is no need to offer sacrifices to the good one, because, being naturally good, he is not disposed to hurt or injure any one. But they use all possible care, both by words, and actions, and every kind of horrible sacrifice, to please the evil one. Likewise those who are called by Mersennus

Deists, exclaim "That the bigots, or superstitiously religious, who believe in infernal punishments, are worse than Atheists, who deny that there is a God." So, too, some new masters among our own countrymen talk of nothing in their discourses but of the *goodness* of God. His supreme right, dominion, and vindicatory justice are of no account with them. But he himself knows how to preserve his glory and his truth pure and entire, in spite of the abilities, and without regard to the delicacy, of these fashionable and dainty gentlemen.

But Rutherford on Providence answers, "That the Gentiles formerly borrowed their purgations and lustrations[1] from the Jews, and not from the light of nature." But he must be a mere novice in the knowledge of these matters into whose mind even the slightest thought of that kind could enter; for I believe there is no one who doubts the custom and ceremony of sacrificing among the Gentile nations to be much more ancient than the Mosaic institutions. Nor can any one imagine that this universal custom among all nations, tribes, and people, civilized and barbarous, unknown to one another, differently situated and scattered all over the world, could have first arisen and proceeded from the institutions of the Jews.

"But," says he, "the light is dark, that a sinful creature could dream of being able to perform a satisfaction, and make propitiatory expiation, to an infinite God incensed, and such, too, as would be satisfactory for sin." Yea, I say, that a sinful creature could perform this is false, and a presumption only, arising from that darkness which we are in by nature. But, notwithstanding, it is true that God must be appeased by a propitiatory sacrifice, if we would that our sins should be forgiven us; and this much he hath pointed out to all mankind by that light of nature, obscure indeed, but not dark. Nor is it necessary, in order to prove this, that we should have recourse to the fabulous antiquities of the Egyptians, the very modest writer of which, Manetho, the high priest of Heliopolis, who lived in the time of Ptolemy Philadelphus, and took his history from the Seriadic hieroglyphical[2] obelisks, writes, that the Egyptian empire had endured to the time of Alexander the Great, through thirty-one dynasties,[3] containing a period of five thousand three hundred and fifty-

[1] That is, their acts or ceremonies of cleansing or purifying themselves from guilt by sacrifice, or otherwise; the latter word more particularly means the operation of cleansing by water.—Tr.

[2] Hieroglyphics are emblems or pictures that were used in the first method of writing; but after characters were introduced, they became generally unintelligible, and contributed much to promote idolatry. They were used by the Egyptian priests to conceal the mysteries of their religion from the vulgar, and were thence called hieroglyphics; that is, sacred engravings or carvings. They were originally engraven or carved on walls and obelisks.—Tr. [It is hardly needful to advert to modern discoveries, from Champollion to Wilkinson, according to which it appears that, instead of being subservient merely to the purpose of concealment, these mystic characters, now that the key to them has been discovered, contain a rich treasury of information in regard both to the history and customs of ancient Egypt.—Ed.]

[3] A dynasty in history means a succession of kings in the same line.—Tr.

three years. This is the sum of the years according to that writer, as Scaliger collects it, to which Vossius has added two years. But other Egyptians have been by no means satisfied with this period of time; for "from Osiris and Isis, to the reign of Alexander, who built a city of his own name in Egypt, they reckon more than ten thousand years, and, as some write, little less than twenty-three thousand years," says Diodorus: during which period of time they say that the sun had four times changed his course, for that he had twice risen in the west and set in the east; which things, though they may seem the dreams of madmen, strictly and properly understood, yet some very learned men entertain a hope, by means of the distinction of the years which the Egyptians used, and the description of their festivals, of reconciling them with the truth of the holy Scriptures.

But passing over these things, it can hardly be doubted that Jupiter-ammon, among the Egyptians, was no other than Ham, the son of Noah, and Bacchus Noah himself; and that Vulcan, among other nations, was Tubal-cain: to all whom, and to others, sacrifices were offered before the birth of Moses. What, too, do they say to this, that Job, among the Gentiles, offered burnt-offerings before the institution of the Mosaic ceremonies? See chap. i. 5, xlii. 8. And Jethro, the priest of Midian, offered a burnt-offering and sacrifices to God even in the very camp of the Israelites in the wilderness, Exod. xviii. 12. Either, then, the sacrifice of Cain and Abel, or that of Adam himself and Eve, consisting of those beasts of whose skins coats were made to them by God,[1] and by whose blood the covenant was ratified, which could not have been made with them after their fall without shedding of blood, gave the first occasion to mankind of discharging that persuasion concerning the necessity of appeasing the offended Deity, which hath arisen from the light of nature, through this channel of sacrificing. Yea, it is evident that this innate notion concerning vindicatory justice, and the observation of its exercise and egress, have given rise to all divine worship. Hence that expression, "Primus in orbe deos fecit timor," "Fear first created gods." And hence these verses in Virgil, spoken by king Evander:—

"—— Non hæc solennia nobis," etc.—Æn. viii. 185.

"These rites, these altars, and this feast, O king!
From no vain fears or superstition spring,
Or blind devotion, or from blinder chance,
Or heady zeal, or brutal ignorance;
But saved from danger, with a grateful sense,
The labours of a god we recompense."

But I do not mention these things as if it were my opinion that sacrifices are prescribed by the law of nature. The most of the Romish clergy maintain this opinion, that so they may pave the

[1] Gen. iii. 21, "Unto Adam also and to his wife did the LORD God make coats of skins, and clothed them."—TR.

way for establishing the blasphemous sacrifice of the mass. Thus Lessius on "Justice and Right," book ii. Suarez, however, is of a different opinion; "for," says he, "there is no natural precept from which it can be sufficiently gathered that a determination to that particular mode of worship is at all necessary to good morals," in p. 3 of his Theol. on quest. 8, distinct. 71, sect. 8. But from the agreement of mankind in the ceremony of sacrificing, I maintain that they have possessed a constant sense of sin and vindicatory justice, discovering to them more and more of this rite, from its first commencement, by means of tradition.

But to return from this digression: it appears that such a presumption of corrective justice is implanted in all by nature, that it cannot by any means be eradicated. But since these universal conceptions by no means relate to what may belong or not belong to God at his free pleasure, it follows that sin-avenging justice is natural to God; the point that was to be proved.

I shall only add, in one word, that an argument from the consent of all is by consent of all allowed to be very strong: for thus says the philosopher, "What is admitted by all, we also admit; but he who would destroy such faith can himself advance nothing more credible," Aristotle, Nicom. iii.

And Hesiod says, "That sentiment cannot be altogether groundless which many people agree in publishing." And, "When we discourse of the eternity of the soul," says Seneca, "the consent of mankind is considered as a weighty argument; I content myself with this public persuasion," Seneca, Ep. 117.

And again, Aristotle says, "It is a very strong proof, if all shall agree in what we shall say." And in that observation another author concurs: "The things that are commonly agreed on are worthy of credit." And here endeth the second argument.

CHAPTER V.

The third argument—This divine attribute demonstrated in the works of providence—That passage of the apostle to the Romans, chap. i. 18, considered—Anger, what it is—The definitions of the philosophers—The opinion of Lactantius concerning the anger of God—Anger often ascribed to God in the holy Scriptures—In what sense this is done—The divine anger denotes, 1. The effect of anger; 2. The will of punishing—What that will is in God—Why the justice of God is expressed by anger—The manifestation of the divine anger, what it is—How it is "revealed from heaven"—The sum of the argument—The fourth argument—Vindicatory justice revealed in the cross of Christ—The attributes of God, how displayed in Christ—Heads of other arguments—The conclusion.

III. [1]It remains, then, that we should now consider, in the third

[1] See division, page 512.

place, what testimony God has given, and is still giving, to this essential attribute of his in the works of providence. This Paul takes notice of, Rom. i. 18. "The wrath of God," says he, "is revealed from heaven against all ungodliness and unrighteousness of men, who hold the truth in unrighteousness."

The philosopher Aristotle says that "anger is a desire of punishing on account of an apparent neglect;"[1] a definition, perhaps, not altogether accurate. Seneca says that Aristotle's definition of anger, that it is "a desire of requiting pain," differs but little from his own, namely, that "anger is a desire of inflicting punishment," book i. "Of Anger," chap. 3, where he discusses it with great elegance, according to the maxims of the Stoics. But Aristotle reckons ἀοργησίαν[2] among vices or extremes, Ethic. Nicom. lib. ii. cap. 7. But Phavorinus says that "anger is a desire to punish the person appearing to have injured you, contrary to what is fit and proper." But in whatever manner it be defined, it is beyond a doubt that it cannot, properly speaking, belong to God. Lactantius Firmianus, therefore, is lashed by the learned, who, in his book "Of the Anger of God," chap. iv., in refuting the Stoics, who contend that anger ought not in any manner whatever to be ascribed to God, has ventured to ascribe to the Deity commotions and affections of mind, but such as are just and good. Suarez, however, excuses him, in his disputation "On Divine Justice," sect. 5, and contends that the nature of anger is very specially preserved in the disposition of punishing offences.

But however this matter be, certain it is that God assumes no affection of our nature so often to himself in Scripture as this; and that, too, in words which for the most part, in the Old Testament, denote the greatest commotion of mind. Wrath, fury, the heat of great anger, indignation, hot anger, smoking anger, wrathful anger, anger appearing in the countenance, inflaming the nostrils, rousing the heart, flaming and consuming, are often assigned to him, and in words, too, which among the Hebrews express the parts of the body affected by such commotions.[3]

In fine, there is no *perturbation* of the mind, no *commotion* of the spirits, no *change* of the bodily parts, by which either the materiality or formality[4] (as they phrase it) of anger is expressed, when we are most deeply affected thereby, which he has not assumed to himself.

But since with God, beyond all doubt, "there is no variableness,

[1] Book viii. chap. 5, of his Topics.

[2] A deprivation of irascibility.

[3] Numb. xxv. 4; Deut. xiii. 17; Josh. vii. 26; Ps. lxxviii. 49; Isa. xiii. 9; Deut. xxix. 24; Judges ii. 14; Ps. lxxiv. 1, lxix. 24; Isa. xxx. 30; Lam. ii. 6; Ezek. v. 15; Ps. lxxviii. 49; Isa. xxxiv. 2; 2 Chron. xxviii. 11; Ezra x. 14; Hab. iii. 8, 12.

[4] The materiality of anger is what is essentially necessary to constitute anger; the formality means its external marks and characters.—Tr.

neither shadow of turning," it will be worth while strictly to examine what he means by this description of his most holy and unchangeable nature, so well accommodated to our weak capacities. Every material circumstance, such as in us is the commotion of the blood and gall about the heart, and likewise those troublesome affections of sorrow and pain with which it is accompanied, being entirely excluded, we shall consider what this anger of God means.

First, then, it is manifest that, by the anger of God, the *effects of anger* are denoted: "Is God unrighteous who taketh vengeance? God forbid," Rom. iii. 5. And it is said, Eph. v. 6, "Because of these things cometh the wrath of God upon the children of disobedience;" that is, God will most assuredly punish them. Hence the frequent mention of "the wrath to come;" that is, the last and everlasting punishment. Thus, that great and terrible day, "in which God will judge the world by that man whom he hath ordained," is called "The day of his wrath," because it is the day of "the revelation of the righteous judgment of God," Rom. ii. 5. And he is said to be "slow to wrath" because he oftentimes proceeds slowly, as it seems to us, to inflict punishment or recompense evil. But, perhaps, this difficulty is better obviated by Peter, who removes every idea of slowness from God, but ascribes to him patience and long-suffering in Christ towards the faithful. And of this dispensation even the whole world, in a secondary sense, are made partakers. "The Lord is not slack," says he, "concerning his promise" (the promise, namely, of a future judgment), "as some men count slackness; but is long-suffering to us-ward, not willing that any should perish, but that all should come to repentance," 2 Pet. iii. 9.

Nay, the threatening of punishment is sometimes described by the words "anger, fury, wrath," and "fierce wrath." Thus, Jonah iii. 9, "Who can tell if God will turn and repent, and turn away from his fierce anger, that we perish not?" that is, "whether he may not, upon our humiliation and repentance, avert from us the grievous punishment denounced by the prophet."

But, secondly, It denotes *a constant and immutable will in God of avenging and punishing, by a just punishment, every injury, transgression, and sin.* And hence that expression, Rom. ix. 22, "What if God, willing to show his wrath,"—that is, his justice, or constant will of punishing sinners; for when any external operations of the Deity are described by a word denoting a human affection that is wont to produce such effects, the holy Scripture means to point out to us some perfection perpetually resident in God, whence these operations flow, and which is their proper and next principle.[1]

And what is that perfection but this justice of which we are discoursing? For we must remove far from God every idea of anger,

[1] That is, the principle from which they immediately flow.—TR.

properly so called, which, in respect of its causes and effects, and of its own nature, supposes even the greatest perturbation, change, and inquietude of all the affections in its subject; and yet we are under the necessity of ascribing to him a nature adapted to effect those operations which are reckoned to belong to anger. But since the Scriptures testify that God works these works as he is just, and because he is just (and we have proved it above), it plainly appears that that perfection of the divine nature is nothing else but this vindicatory justice; whence Thomas Aquinas asserts[1] that anger is not said to be in God in allusion to any passion of the mind, but to the judgment or decision of his justice. Nay, that "anger" may not only be reduced to "justice," but that the words themselves are synonymous, and that they are taken so in Scripture, is certain: Ps. vii. 6, 9, "Arise, O LORD, in thine anger, lift up thyself because of the rage of mine enemies: and awake for me to the judgment that thou hast commanded. Oh let the wickedness of the wicked come to an end; but establish the just: for the righteous God trieth the hearts and reins." To "judge in anger," or with "justice," are phrases of the same import: Ps. lvi. 7, "Shall they escape by iniquity? in thine anger cast down the people, O God;" or, "In justice cast them down, because of their iniquity." Thus, when he justly destroyed the people of Israel by the king of Babylon, he says it came to pass through his anger: 2 Kings xxiv. 20, "For through the anger of the LORD it came to pass in Jerusalem and Judah, until he had cast them out from his presence, that Zedekiah rebelled against the king of Babylon."

But the apostle says that this anger or punitory justice is "revealed from heaven." The apostle uses the same word here that is translated "revealed" in the preceding verse, when speaking of the manifestation or revelation of the righteousness of faith in the gospel. Therefore, some have been of opinion that the apostle here asserts that this very anger of God is again and again made known and manifested, or openly declared, in the gospel against unbelievers. But to what purpose, then, is there any mention made of "heaven," whence that manifestation or revelation is said to have been made? The apostle, therefore, uses the word in a different sense in Rom. i. 18, from that which it is used in in the preceding. There it means a manifestation by the preaching of the word, here it signifies a declaration by examples; and therefore one might not improperly translate the word "is laid open," or "clearly appears,"—that is, is proved by numberless instances. Moreover, this verse is the principal of the arguments by which the apostle proves the necessity of justification by faith in the remission of sins through the blood of Christ, because that all have sinned, and thereby rendered God their open and avowed enemy.

[1] Quest. 47, art. 1.

The apostle, then, affirms that God hath taken care that his anger against sin, or that his justice, should appear by innumerable examples of punishments inflicted on mankind for their sins, in his providential government of the world, and that it should appear in so clear a manner that there should be no room left for conjectures about the matter. Not that punishment is always inflicted on the wicked and impious while in this world, or, at least, that it appears to be so, for very many of them enjoy all the pleasures of a rich and flourishing outward estate; but besides that he exercises his anger on their consciences, as we proved before, and that the external good things of fortune, as they call them, are only a fattening of them for the day of slaughter, even in this life he ofttimes, in the middle of their career, exercises his severe judgments against the public enemies of Heaven, the monsters of the earth, the architects of wickedness, sunk in the mire and filth of their vices; and that, too, even to the entire ruin and desolation both of whole nations and of particular individuals, whom, by a remarkable punishment, he thinks proper to make an example and spectacle of to the world, both to angels and to men.

Therefore, although "God, willing to show his wrath, and to make his power known," not in that way only,—namely, by exercising public punishments in this life,—of which we are now speaking, "endure with much long-suffering the vessels of wrath fitted to destruction," and though he should not instantly dart his lightnings against all and every individual of the abandoned and profane, yet mankind will easily discern[1] what the mind and thoughts of God are, what his right and pleasure, and of what kind his anger and justice are, with regard to every sin whatever. Therefore, the apostle affirms that the anger of God, of which he gives only some instances, is by these judgments openly declared against all unrighteousness and ungodliness of men whatever, whether they fail in the worship and duty which they owe to God, or in the duties which it is incumbent on them to perform to one another; moreover, that the solemn revelation of this divine justice consists, not only in those judgments which, sooner or later, he hath exercised upon particular persons, but also in the whole series of his divine dispensations towards men: in which, as he gives testimony both to his goodness and patience, inasmuch as "he maketh his sun to rise on the evil and on the good, and sendeth rain on the just and on the unjust," and "leaveth not himself without witness, in that he doeth good, and giveth us rain from heaven, and fruitful seasons, filling our hearts with food and gladness," Matt. v. 45; Acts xiv. 17; so also he gives equally clear signs and testimonies of his anger, severity, and indignation, or of his

[1] Namely, from those instances of punishment which he is pleased in his wisdom sometimes openly and awfully to inflict upon the wicked.—TR.

punitory justice. Hence, on account of the efficacy of the divine anger exercising its power and influence far and near, this visible world, as if the very fuel of the curse, is appointed as the seat and abode of all kinds of misery, grief, lamentation, cares, wrath, vanity, and inquietude. Why need I mention tempests, thunders, lightnings, deluges, pestilences, with many things more, by means of which, on account of the wickedness of man, universal nature is struck with horror? All these, beyond a doubt, have a respect to the revelation of God's anger or justice against the unrighteousness and the ungodliness of men.

Moreover, the apostle testifies this revelation to be *made from heaven.* Even the most abandoned cannot but observe punishments of various kinds making havoc everywhere in the world, and innumerable evils brooding, as it were, over the very texture of the universe. But because they wish for and desire nothing more ardently than either that there were no God, or that he paid no regard to human affairs, they either really ascribe, or pretend to ascribe, all these things to chance, fortune, the revolutions of the stars and their influence, or, finally, to natural causes. In order to free the minds of men from this pernicious deceit of atheism, the apostle affirms that all these things come to pass "from heaven;" that is, under the direction of God, or by a divine power and providence punishing the sins and wickedness of men, and manifesting the justice of God. Thus, "The LORD rained upon Sodom and upon Gomorrah brimstone and fire from the LORD out of heaven," Gen. xix. 24: which cities, by that punishment inflicted on them from heaven, he hath set up as an example, in every future age, to all those who should afterward persevere in the like impieties. To these considerations add, that the apostle, from this demonstration of the divine anger from heaven against the sins of men, argues the necessity of appointing an atonement through the blood of Christ, Rom. iii. 18–26; which would by no means follow but upon the supposition that that anger of God was such that it could not be averted without the intervention of an atonement.

But not to be tedious, it is evident that God, by the works of his providence, in the government of this world, gives a most copious testimony to his vindicatory justice, not inferior to that given to his goodness, or any other of his attributes; which testimony concerning himself and his nature he makes known, and openly exhibits to all, by innumerable examples, constantly provided and appointed for that purpose. He, then, who shall deny this justice to be essential to God, may, for the same reason, reject his goodness and long-suffering patience.

IV. The fourth argument shall be taken from the revelation of that *name,* glory, and nature, which God hath exhibited to us in and through Christ: John i. 18, "No man hath seen God at any time; the only-begotten Son, which is in the bosom of the Father, he hath declared him;"—him who, though he be light itself, and dwelling in light inaccessible, yet in respect of us, who without Christ are naturally blinder than moles, is covered with darkness. In creation, in legislation, and in the works of providence, God, indeed, hath plainly marked out and discovered to us certain traces of his power, wisdom, goodness, justice, and long-sufferance. But, besides that there are some attributes of his nature the knowledge of which could not reach the ears of sinners but by Christ,—such as his love to his peculiar people, his sparing mercy, his free and saving grace,—even the others, which he hath made known to us in some measure by the ways and means above mentioned, we could have no clear or saving knowledge of unless in and through this same Christ; for "in him are hid all the treasures of wisdom and knowledge." In him God hath fully and clearly exhibited himself to us, to be loved, adored, and known; and that not only in regard of his heavenly doctrine, in which he hath "brought life and immortality to light through the gospel,"[1] God finishing the revelation of himself to mankind by the mission and ministry of his Son, but also, exhibiting, both in the person of Christ and in his mediatorial office, the brightness of his own glory and the express image of his person, he glorified his own name and manifested his nature, to all those at least who, being ingrafted into Christ and baptized into his Spirit, enjoy both the Father and Son. But in the whole matter of salvation by the Mediator, God-man, there is no excellence of God, no essential property, no attribute of his nature, the glory of which is the chief end of all his works, that he hath more clearly and eminently displayed than this punitory justice.

It was for the display of his justice that he set forth Christ as a propitiation, through faith in his blood. He spared him not, but laid the punishment of us all upon him. It was for this that he was pleased to bruise him, to put him to grief, and to make his soul an offering for sin.

The infinite wisdom of God, his inexpressible grace, free love, boundless mercy, goodness, and benevolence to men, in the constitution of such a Mediator,—namely, a God-man,—are not more illustriously displayed, to the astonishment of men and angels, in bringing sinful man from death, condemnation, and a state of enmity, into a state of life, of salvation, of glory, and of union and communion with himself, than is this punitory justice, for the satisfaction, manifestation, and glory of which this whole scheme, pregnant with innumerable mysteries, was instituted. But that attribute whose glory and manifestation God intended and accomplished, both in the ap-

[1] 2 Tim. i. 10.

pointment of his only-begotten Son to the office of mediator, and in his mission, must be natural to him; and there is no need of arguments to prove that this was his vindicatory justice. Yea, supposing this justice and all regard to it entirely set aside, the glory of God's love in sending his Son, and delivering him up to the death for us all, which the Scriptures so much extol, is manifestly much obscured, if it do not rather totally disappear; for what kind of love can that be which God hath shown, in doing what there was no occasion for him to do?

We will not at present enter fully into the consideration of other arguments by which the knowledge of this truth is supported; among which that of the necessity of assigning to God (observing a just analogy) whatever perfections or excellencies are found among the creatures, is not of the least importance. These we pass, partly that we may not be tedious to the learned reader, partly because the truth flows in a channel already sufficiently replenished with proofs. It would be easy, however, to show that this justice denotes the highest perfection, and by no means includes any imperfection, on account of which it should be excluded from the divine nature. Neither, in the definition of it, does one iota occur that can imply any imperfection; but all perfection, simple or formal, simply and formally, is found in God. But when this perfection is employed in any operation respecting another being, and having for its object the common good, it necessarily acquires the nature of justice.

I shall not be farther troublesome to my readers; if what has been already said amount not to proof sufficient, I know not what is sufficient. I urge only one testimony more from Scripture and conclude. It is found in Heb. x. 26, 27: "For if we sin wilfully after that we have received the knowledge of the truth, there remaineth no more sacrifice for sins, but a certain fearful looking for of judgment and fiery indignation." "But perhaps God will pardon without any sacrifice." The apostle is of a contrary opinion. Where there is "no sacrifice for sin," he argues that, from the very nature of the thing, there must be "a looking for of judgment and fiery indignation;"—the very point that was to be proved.

I could heartily wish that some sinner whose conscience the hand of the omnipotent God hath lately touched, whose "sore ran in the night and ceased not," and whose "soul refused to be comforted," whose "grief is heavier than the sand of the sea," in whom "the arrows of the Almighty" stick fast, "the poison whereof drinketh up the spirit,"[1] were to estimate and determine this difficult and doubtful dispute. Let us, I say, have recourse to a person, who, being convinced by the Spirit of his debts to God, is weighed down by their burden, while the sharp arrows of Christ are piercing the heart, Ps. xlv. 5,

[1] Job vi. 2–4.

and let us inform him that God, with the greatest ease, by his nod, or by the light touch of his finger, so to speak, can blot out, hide, and forgive all sins. Will he rest satisfied in such a thought? will he immediately subscribe to it? Will he not rather exclaim, "I have heard many such things; 'miserable comforters are ye all;'[1] nay, 'ye are forgers of lies, physicians of no value.' The terrors of the Lord, which surround me, and beset me day and night, ye feel not. I have to do with the most just, the most holy, the supreme Judge of all, who 'will do right, and will by no means clear the guilty.' Therefore, 'my days are consumed like smoke, and my bones are burned as an hearth. My heart is smitten, and withered like grass; so that I forget to eat my bread. By reason of the voice of my groaning, my bones cleave to my skin.'[2] 'I am afflicted and ready to die from my youth up: while I suffer thy terrors I am distracted. Thy fierce wrath goeth over me; thy terrors have cut me off.'[3] I wish I were hid in the grave, yea, even in the pit, unless the Judge himself say to me, 'Deliver him from going down to the pit, I have found a ransom.'[4] Indeed, when the recollection of that very melancholy period comes into mind, when first God was pleased by his Spirit effectually to convince the heart of me, a poor sinner, of sin, and when the whole of God's controversy with me for sin is again presented to my view, I cannot sufficiently wonder what thoughts could possess those men who have treated of the remission of sins in so very slight, I had almost said contemptuous, a manner." But these reflections are rather foreign to our present business.

CHAPTER VI.

Another head of the first part of the dissertation—Arguments for the necessary egress of vindicatory justice from the supposition of sin—The first argument —God's hatred of sin; what—Whether God by nature hates sin, or because he wills so to do—Testimonies from holy Scripture—Dr Twisse's answer—The sum of it—The same obviated—The relation of obedience to reward and of sin to punishment not the same—Justice and mercy, in respect of their exercise, different—The second argument—The description of God in the Scriptures in respect of sin—In what sense he is called a "consuming fire"—Twisse's answer refuted—The fallacies of the answer.

We have sufficiently proved, if I be not mistaken, that sin-punishing justice is *natural* to God. The opposite arguments, more numerous than weighty, shall be considered hereafter. We are now to prove the second part of the question,—namely, that the existence and sin of a rational creature being supposed, the exercise of this justice is necessary. And, granting what appears from what we have

[1] Job xiii. 4, xvi. 2. [2] Ps. cii. 3–5. [3] Ps. lxxxviii. 15, 16. [4] Job xxxiii. 24.

already said concerning the nature of justice, especially from the first argument, our proofs must necessarily be conclusive. The first is this:—

I. He who cannot but hate all sin cannot but punish sin; for to hate sin is, as to the affection, to will to punish it, and as to the effect, the punishment itself. And to be unable not to will the punishment of sin is the same with the necessity of punishing it; for he who cannot but will to punish sin cannot but punish it: for "our God is in the heavens; he hath done whatsoever he hath pleased," Ps. cxv. 3. Now, when we say that God necessarily punishes sin, we mean, that on account of the rectitude and perfection of his nature, he cannot possess an indifference of will to punish; for it being supposed that God hates sin, he must hate it either by *nature* or by *choice*. If it be by nature, then we have gained our point. If by choice, or because he wills it, then it is possible for him not to hate it. Nay, he may even justly will the contrary, or exercise a contrary act about the same object; for those acts of the divine will are most free, namely, which have their foundation in the will only: that is to say, it is even possible for him to love sin; for the divine will is not so inclined to any object, but that, if it should be inclined to its contrary, *that* might, consistent with justice, be done. This reasoning Durandus agrees to, and this Twisse urges as an argument. The conclusion, then, must be, that God may love sin, considered as sin.

"Credat Apella."

"The sons of circumcision may receive
The wondrous tale, which I shall ne'er believe."
Francis' Horace.

For "God hates all workers of iniquity," Ps. v. 5. He calls it "The abominable thing that he hateth," Jer. xliv. 4. Besides these, other passages of Scripture testify that God hates sin, and that he cannot but hate it: "Thou art of purer eyes than to behold evil, and canst not look on iniquity," Hab. i. 13. On account of the purity of God's eyes,—that is, of his holiness, an attribute which none hath ever ventured to deny,—he "cannot look on iniquity;" that is, he cannot but hate it. "Thou art not a God that hath pleasure in wickedness," says the psalmist, Ps. v. 4, 5,—that is, "Thou art a God who hatest all wickedness;"—for "evil shall not dwell with thee, and the foolish shall not stand in thy sight; thou hatest all workers of iniquity." Is it a free act of the divine will that he here describes, which might or might not be executed without any injury to the holiness, purity, and justice of God; or the divine nature itself, as averse to, hating and punishing every sin? Why shall not the foolish stand in God's sight? Is it because he freely wills to punish them, or because our God to all workers of iniquity is a consuming fire? Not that the nature of God can wax hot at the sight of sin, in a natural manner, as fire doth after the combustible materials have been applied to it; but that punishment as naturally follows sin as its consequence, on account of the pressing demand of justice, as fire consumes the fuel that is applied to it.

But it is not without good reason that God, who is love, so often testifies in the holy Scriptures his hatred and abomination of sin: "The wicked, and him that loveth violence, his soul hateth," Ps. xi. 5. Speaking of sinners, Lev. xxvi. 30, he says, "My soul shall abhor you." He calls sin "That abominable thing," 1 Kings xxi. 26; Ps. xiv. 1; Deut. xvi. 22. There is nothing that God hates but sin; and because of sin only other things are liable to his hatred. In what sense passions and affections are ascribed to God, and what he would have us to understand by such a description of his nature and attributes, is known to everybody. But of all the affections of human nature, hatred is the most restless and turbulent, and to the person who is under its influence, and who can neither divest himself of it nor give a satisfactory vent to its motions, the most tormenting and vexatious; for as it takes its rise from a disagreement with and dislike of its object, so that its object is always viewed as repugnant and offensive, no wonder that it should rouse the most vehement commotions and bitterest sensations. But God, who enjoys eternal and infinite happiness and glory, as he is far removed from any such perturbations, and placed far beyond all variableness or shadow of change, would not assume this affection so often, for our instruction, unless he meant clearly to point out to us this supreme, immutable, and constant purpose of punishing sin,—as that monster whose property it is to be the object of God's hatred, that is, of the hatred of infinite goodness,—to be natural and essential to him.

The learned Twisse answers, "I cannot agree that God by nature equally punishes and hates sin, unless you mean that hatred in the Deity to respect his will as appointing a punishment for sin; in which sense I acknowledge it to be true that God equally, from nature and necessity, punishes and hates sin. But I deny it to be necessary that he should either so hate sin or punish it. If hatred be understood to mean God's displeasure, I maintain that it is not equally natural to God to punish sin and to hate it; for we maintain it to be necessary that every sin should displease God, but it is not necessary that God should punish every sin." The sum of the answer is this: God's hatred of sin is taken either for his will of punishing it, and so is not natural to God; or for his displeasure on account of sin, and so is natural to him: but it does not thence follow that God necessarily punishes every sin, and that he can let no sin pass unpunished.

But, first, this learned gentleman denies what has been proved; nor does he deign to advance a word to invalidate the proof. He denies that God naturally hates sin, hatred being taken for the will of punishing: but this we have before demonstrated, both from Scripture and sound reason. It would be easy indeed to elude the force of any argument in this manner. Afterward, he acknowledges that every sin must necessarily be displeasing to God. This, then, depends not on the free will of God, but on his nature. It belongs, then, immutably to God, and it is altogether impossible that it should not displease him. This, then, is supposed, that sin is always displeasing to God, but that God may or may not punish it, but pardon the sin and cherish the sinner, though his sin eternally displease him; for that depends upon his nature, which is eternally immutable. Nor is it possible that what hath been sin should ever be any thing but sin. From this natural displeasure, then, with sin, we may with propriety argue to its necessary punishment; otherwise, what meaneth that despairing exclamation of alarmed hypocrites, "Who among us shall dwell with the devouring fire? who among us shall dwell with everlasting burnings?"[1]

The learned doctor retorts, "Obedience must necessarily please God; but God is not bound by his justice necessarily to reward it." But the learned gentleman will hardly maintain that the relation of obedience to reward, and disobedience to punishment, is the same; for God is bound to reward no man for obedience performed, for that is due to him by natural right: Luke xvii. 10, "So likewise ye, when ye shall have done all those things which are commanded you, say, We are unprofitable servants; we have done that which was our duty to do." Ps. xvi. 2, "My goodness extendeth not unto thee." But every man owes to God obedience, or is obnoxious to a vicarious punishment; nor can the moral dependence of a rational creature on its Creator be otherwise preserved: "The wages of sin is death; but the gift of God is eternal life," Rom. vi. 23.

Away, then, with all proud thoughts of equalling the relation of obedience to reward and sin to punishment. "Who hath first given to him, and it shall be recompensed unto him again? For of him, and through him, and to him, are all things: to whom be glory for ever. Amen," Rom. xi. 35, 36. "What hast thou," O man, "that thou didst not receive? Now if thou didst receive it, why dost thou glory, as if thou hadst not received it?" 1 Cor. iv. 7. God requireth nothing of us but what he hath formerly given us; and, therefore, he has every right to require it, although he were to bestow no rewards. What! doth not God observe a just proportion in the infliction of punishments, so that the degrees of punishment, according to the rule of his justice, should not exceed the demerit of the transgression. "Shall not the Judge of all the earth do right?" But beware, Dr Twisse, of asserting that there is any proportion between the eternal fruition of God and the inexpressible participation of his

[1] Isa. xxxiii. 14.

glory, in which he hath been graciously pleased that the reward of our obedience should consist, and the obedience of an insignificant reptile, almost less than nothing. Whatever dignity or happiness we arrive at, we are still God's creatures.

It is impossible that he who is blessed for ever and ever, and is so infinitely happy in his own essential glory that he stands in no need of us or of our services, and who, in requiring all that we are and all that we can do, only requires his own, can, by the receipt of it, become bound in any debt or obligation. For God, I say, from the beginning, stood in no need of our praise; nor did he create us merely that he might have creatures to honour him, but that, agreeably to his goodness, he might conduct us to happiness.

But he again retorts, and maintains, "That God can punish where he does not hate; and, therefore, he may hate and not punish: for he punished his most holy Son, whom God forbid that we should say he ever hated." But, besides that this mode of arguing from opposites hardly holds good in theology, though God hated not his Son when he punished him, personally considered, he however hated the sins on account of which he punished him (and even himself, substitutively considered, with respect to the effect of sin), no less than if they had been laid to any sinner. Yea, and from this argument it follows that God cannot hate sin and not punish it; for when he laid sins, which he hates, to the charge of his most holy Son, whom he loved with the highest love, yet he could not but punish him.

II. The representation or description of God, and of the divine nature in respect of its habitude[1] to sin, which the Scriptures furnish us with, and the description of sin with relation to God and his justice, supply us with a second argument. They call God a "consuming fire;" "everlasting burnings,"[2] a God who "will by no means clear the guilty."[3]

They represent sin as "that abominable thing which he hateth," which he will destroy "as the fire devoureth the stubble, and the flame consumeth the chaff."[4] As, then, consuming fire cannot but burn and consume stubble, when applied to it, so neither can God do otherwise than punish sin, that abominable thing, which is consuming or destroying it, whenever presented before him and his justice.

But the very learned Twisse replies, "That God is a consuming fire, but an intelligent and rational one, not a natural and insensible one. And this," says he, "is manifest from this, that this fire once burnt something not consumable,[5] namely, his own Son, in whom there

[1] Habitude means the state of a person or a thing with relation to something else. The habitude of the divine nature with respect to sin is a disposition to punish it.—Tr.

[2] Heb. xii. 29; Deut. iv. 24; Isa. xxxiii. 14.

[3] Exod. xxxiv. 7.

[4] Jer. xliv. 4; Isa. v. 24.

[5] The word in the original is "combustible," meaning something that is susceptible of and consumable by fire. It must be evident to every one that the phrase is used

was no sin; which," says he, "may serve as a proof that this fire may not burn what is consumable, when applied to it."

But, in my opinion, this very learned man was never more unhappy in extricating himself; for, first, he acknowledges God to be "a consuming fire," though "a rational and intelligent one, not a natural and insensible one." But the comparison was made between the events of the operations, not the modes of operating. Nobody ever said that God acts without sense, or from absolute necessity and principles of nature, without any concomitant liberty. But although he acts by will and understanding, we have said that his nature as necessarily requires him to punish any sin committed, as natural and insensible fire burns the combustible matter that is applied to it. But the learned gentleman does not deny this; nay, he even confirms it, granting that with respect to sin God "is a consuming fire," though only "an intelligent and rational one."

I am sorry that this very learned author should have used the expression, that "this fire burnt something not consumable," when he punished his most holy and well-beloved Son; for God did not punish Christ as his most holy Son, but as our mediator and the surety of the covenant, "whom he made sin for us, though he knew no sin." Surely, "he laid upon him our sins," before "the chastisement of our peace was upon him." But in this sense he was very susceptible of the effects of this fire,—namely, when considered as bearing the guilt of all our sins; and therefore it was that by fire the Lord did plead with him.[1] Therefore, what this very learned man asserts in the third place falls to the ground; for the conclusion from such a very false supposition must necessarily be false. We go on to the third argument.

CHAPTER VII.

The third argument—The non-punishment of sin is contrary to the glory of God's justice—Likewise of his holiness and dominion—A fourth argument—The necessity of a satisfaction being made by the death of Christ—No necessary cause or cogent reason for the death of Christ, according to the adversaries—The objection refuted—The use of sacrifices—The end of the first part of the dissertation.

III. OUR third argument is this: It is absolutely necessary that God should preserve *his glory* entire to all eternity; but sin being sup-

in allusion to the metaphor which represents God as a consuming fire. The Son of God, then, was not, strictly and properly speaking, consumable, or susceptible of this fire,—that is, he was by no means the object of divine anger or punishment, considered as the Son of God, and without any relation to mankind,—but, on the contrary, was the beloved of his Father, with whom he was always well pleased. But he was liable to the effect of this fire,—that is, of God's vindicatory justice,—as our representative and federal head. And every sinner is consumable by this fire; that is, is properly and naturally the object of divine wrath and punishment.—TR.

[1] Isa. lxvi. 16.

posed, without the infliction of the punishment due to it he cannot preserve his glory free from violation: therefore, it is necessary that he should punish it. Concerning the major proposition[1] there is no dispute; for all acknowledge, not only that it is necessary to God that he should preserve his glory, but that this is incumbent on him by *a necessity of nature*, for he cannot but love himself. He is Jehovah, and will not give his glory to another.[2] The truth of the assumption is no less clear; for the very nature of the thing itself proclaims that the glory of justice or of holiness, and dominion, could not otherwise be preserved and secured than by the punishment of sin. For,—

First, The glory of God is displayed in doing the things that are *just;* but in omitting these it is impaired, not less than in doing the things that are contrary. "He that justifieth the wicked, and he that condemneth the just, even they both are abomination to the LORD."[3] "Shall not the Judge of all the earth do right?"[4] or what is just? But "it is a righteous" or just "thing with God to recompense tribulation" to the disobedient, and to punish those who, on account of sin, are "worthy of death."[5] Suppose, then, that God should let the disobedient, whom it is a just thing for him to punish, go unpunished, and that those who are worthy of death should never be required to die, but that he should clear the guilty and the wicked, although he hath declared them to be an abomination to him, where is the glory of his justice? That it is most evident that God thus punishes because he is just, we have proved before. "Is God unrighteous," or unjust, "who taketh vengeance? God forbid: for then how shall God judge the world?" And he is "righteous," or just, "because he hath given them blood to drink, who were worthy of it,"[6] and would be so far unjust were he not to inflict punishment on those deserving it.

Secondly, A proper regard is not shown to divine *holiness*, nor is its glory manifested, unless the punishment due to sin be inflicted. Holiness is opposed to sin; for "God is of purer eyes than to behold evil, and cannot look on iniquity,"[7] and is the cause why he cannot let sin pass unpunished. "Ye cannot serve the LORD; for he is an holy God: he will not forgive your transgressions nor your sins,"[8]

[1] Our author here speaks in the language, and reasons in the manner, of logicians; the prevalent mode of reasoning at the time when he wrote. For the sake of those unacquainted with that art, it may not be improper to observe that the above argument is what they call a syllogism, and that a syllogism consists of three propositions. The first is called the major, the second the minor, and the third the conclusion. In the above argument the major proposition is, "It is absolutely necessary that God should preserve his glory entire to all eternity." The minor is, "But sin being supposed, without any punishment due to it he cannot preserve his glory free from violation." The conclusion is, "Therefore, it is necessary that he should punish it." The minor is sometimes called the assumption, and sometimes the conclusion is so named. They are both included under this title by our author in the following sentence.—TR.

[2] Isa. xlii. 8. [3] Prov. xvii. 15. [4] Gen. xviii. 25. [5] 2 Thess. i. 6; Rom. i. 32.
[6] Rom. iii. 5, 6, Rev. xvi. 5–7. [7] Hab. i. 13. [8] Josh. xxiv. 19.

said Joshua to the Israelites. For why? Can any thing impure and polluted stand before his holy Majesty? He himself declares the contrary;—that he is "not a God that hath pleasure in wickedness;" that "evil shall not dwell with him;" that "the foolish shall not stand in his sight;" that "he hateth all workers of iniquity;" and that "there shall in no wise enter into the new Jerusalem any thing that defileth, neither whatsoever worketh abomination, or maketh a lie."[1] Nor can Jesus Christ present his church to his Father till it be "sanctified and cleansed with the washing of water by the word," and made "a glorious church, not having spot, or wrinkle, or any such thing, but holy and without blemish."[2] And we are enjoined to be holy, because he is holy. But all things are to be "purged with blood; and without shedding of blood is no remission."[3]

Thirdly, We have sufficiently shown above that the *natural dominion* which God hath over rational creatures, and which they by sin renounce, could not otherwise be preserved or continued than by means of a *vicarious punishment.* And now let impartial judges decide whether it be necessary to God that he should preserve entire the glory of his justice, holiness, and supreme dominion, or not.

IV. And which is a principal point to be considered on this subject, Were the opinions of the adversaries to be admitted, and were we to suppose that God might will the salvation of any sinner, it will be difficult, if not impossible, to assign any sufficient and *necessary* cause of the death of Christ. For let us suppose that God hath imposed on mankind a law, ratified by a threatening of eternal death, and that they, by a violation of that law, have deserved the punishment threatened, and consequently are become liable to eternal death; again, let us suppose that God in that threatening did not expressly intend the death of the sinner, but afterward declared what and of what kind he willed that the guilt of sin should be, and what punishment he might justly inflict on the sinner, and what the sinner himself ought to expect (all which things flow from the free determination of God), but that he might by his nod or word, without any trouble, though no satisfaction were either made or received, without the least diminution of his glory, and without any affront or dishonour to any attribute, or any injury or disgrace to himself, consistently with the preservation of his right, dominion, and justice, freely pardon the sins of those whom he might will to save;—what sufficient reason could be given, pray, then, why he should lay those sins, so easily remissible, to the charge of his most holy Son, and on their account subject him to such dreadful sufferings?

While Socinians do not acknowledge other ends of the whole of this dispensation and mystery than those which they assign, they will be unable, to all eternity, to give any probable reason why a

[1] Ps. v. 4-6; Rev. xxi. 27. [2] Eph. v. 26, 27. [3] Heb. ix. 22.

most merciful and just God should expose a most innocent and holy man,—who was his own Son by way of eminence, and who was introduced by himself into the world in a preternatural manner, as they themselves acknowledge,—to afflictions and sufferings of every kind, while among the living he pointed out to them the way of life, and at last to a cruel, ignominious, and accursed death.

I very well know that I cannot pretend to be either ingenious or quick-sighted; but respecting this matter I am not ashamed to confess my dulness to be such, that I cannot see that God,[1] consistently with the preservation of his right and glory entire, could, without the intervention of a ransom, pardon sins, as if justice did not require their punishment, or that Christ had died in vain. For why? Hath not God set him forth to be a propitiation for the demonstration or declaration of his sin-punishing justice? But how could that justice be demonstrated by an action which it did not require, or if the action might be omitted without any diminution of it,—if God would have been infinitely just to eternity, nor would have done any thing contrary and offensive to justice, though he had never inflicted punishment upon any sin? Could any ruler become highly famed and celebrated on account of his justice, by doing those things which, from the right of his dominion, he can do *without injustice*, but to the performance of which he is no way obligated by *the virtue of justice?* But if the adversaries suppose that when God freely made a law for his rational creatures, he freely appointed a punishment for transgression, freely substituted Christ in the room of transgressors; in fine, that God did all these things, and the like, because so it pleased him, and that therefore we are to acquiesce in that most wise and free will of his disposing all things at his pleasure; —they should not find me opposing them. Unless God himself had taught us in his word that sin is "that abominable thing which his soul hateth," which is affrontive to him, which entirely casteth off all regard to that glory, honour, and reverence, which are due to him; and that to the sinner himself it is something evil and bitter, for "he shall eat of the fruit of his way, and be filled with his own devices;" and that God, with respect to sinners, is a "consuming fire," an "everlasting burning," in which they shall "dwell;" that "he will by no means clear the guilty;" that "he judgeth those who are worthy of death, and by his just judgment taketh vengeance on them; and that, therefore, "without the shedding of blood, there can be no remission," and that without a victim for sin, there remaineth to sinners nothing but "a fearful looking for of judgment and fiery indig-

[1] The misprint of *quia* for *quin* has occasioned some confusion in the translation. It should run thus: "I cannot see but that Christ has died in vain, on the supposition that God could pardon sins without the intervention of a ransom, consistently with the preservation of his right and glory entire, justice not demanding their punishment." —ED.

nation, that shall consume the adversaries;" and that he had appointed from the beginning his only-begotten Son, for the declaration and satisfaction of his justice, and the recovery of his glory, to open the way to heaven, otherwise shut, and to remain shut for ever;—if, I say, God had not instructed us in these and such-like truths from his word, I should not oppose them; but these being clearly laid down in the word, we solemnly declare our belief that no sinner could obtain the remission of his sins, provided that we are disposed to acknowledge God to be just, without a price of redemption.[1]

Perhaps some one will say, "It doth not follow from the death of Christ that God necessarily punisheth sin; for Christ himself, in his agony, placeth the passing away of the cup among things possible. 'All things,' saith he, 'Father, are possible with thee. Let this cup pass from me.'"

I answer, It is well known that the word "impossibility" may be considered in a twofold point of view. The first is in itself *absolute*, which respects the absolute power of God, antecedent to any free act of the divine will: in this respect, it was not impossible that that cup should pass from Christ. The second is *conditional*, which respects the power of God, as directed in a certain order, that is determined, and (if I might so phrase it) circumscribed by some act of the divine will: and in this sense it was impossible; that is to say, it being supposed that God willed to pardon any sins to sinners, it could not be done without laying their punishment upon the surety. But we do not pursue this argument farther at present, because we intend to resume it again in the consideration of the doctrine of Christ's satisfaction.

There are yet many arguments very proper for establishing the truth on our side of the question, which we choose not to enter on largely and on set purpose, lest we should be tiresome to the reader. Perhaps, however, it will be judged worth while briefly to sketch out some heads of them, and annex them to the former arguments concerning justice and the exercise thereof. The first is to this purport:—

1. A *second* act presupposes a *first*, and a constant manner of operating proves a habit; a sign also expresses the thing signified. Because God doeth good to all, we believe him to be good, and endowed with supreme goodness; for how could he so constantly and uniformly do good, unless he himself were good? Yea, from second acts the holy Scriptures sometimes teach the first; as, for instance, that God is the *living* God, because he giveth *life* to all,—that he is *good*, because he *doeth good*. Why may we not also say that he is just, endowed with that justice of which we are treating, because "God perverteth not judgment, neither doth the Almighty pervert justice," but "the LORD is righteous, and upright are his judgments?"[2] A constant, then, and uniform course of just operation in punishing

[1] Or ransom.—TR. [2] Job viii. 3; Ps. cxix. 137.

sin proves punitory justice to be essentially inherent in God. From his law, which is the sign[1] of the divine will, the same is evident; for the nature of the thing signified is, that it resembles the sign appointed for the purpose of expressing it. That the same thing may be said of the anger, fury, and severity of God hath been shown above, Rom. i. 18.

2. It is not the part of a *just judge*, of his mere good pleasure, to let the wicked pass unpunished: "He that justifieth the wicked is an abomination to the LORD," and, "Woe to them that call evil good!" But God is a just judge. "But one who is not liable to render a reason," you will say, "and who is by no means subject to a law." But the nature of God is a law to itself. He cannot lie, because he himself is truth; nor act unjustly, because he is just. Such as God is by nature, such is he in the acts of his will.

3. The argument, from the *immutable difference* of things in themselves is of very considerable weight; for that which is sin, because it destroys that subjection of the creature which is due to the Creator, cannot, even by the omnipotence of God, be made to be not sin. To hate the supreme good implies a contradiction. But if, from the nature of the thing, sin be sin, in relation to the supreme perfection of God, from the nature of the thing, too, is its punishment. Yea, God hath ordered children to obey their parents, because this is right.[2]

4. The adversaries acknowledge "That God cannot save the impenitent and obstinately wicked without injury to the glory, and holiness, and perfection of his nature." Why so? "The justice of God," say they, "will not suffer it." But what kind of justice is that, I ask, which can regard certain modes and relations of transgression or sin, and will not regard the transgression or sin itself?

5. God punishes sin either because he simply wills it, or because it is just that sin should be punished. If because he simply wills it, then the will of God is the alone cause of the perdition of a sinful creature. But he himself testifies to the contrary,—namely, that man's ruin is of himself: "O Israel, thou hast destroyed thyself; but in me is thine help."[3] Again; justice does not require that the things which God doeth of his mere good pleasure should come to pass, more than that they should not come to pass. But if it be not more just that sins should be punished than that they should not be punished, it is certain that the non-punishment or free pardon of sin is more agreeable to the goodness, grace, love, and compassion of God than the infliction of punishment; how, then, comes it to pass that, disregarding these attributes, he should freely will that which no essential property of his nature requires? If, then, sin be

[1] That is, which showeth what the divine will is.—TR.

[2] In the original, "just."—TR.

[3] Hos. xiii. 9.

sin because God wills it, if the transgression of the law deserve punishment because God wills it, and the punishment be at length inflicted because God wills it, the order of things, or the condition which they are in by virtue of their respect and relation to the dominion and perfection of God, requiring no such thing, why, pray, should we either hate or abhor sin, when the bare will of God alone is to be considered, both in respect of the decree, which supposes that there is nothing in sin, and which implies no change of the state of things, and also in respect of its execution? But if God punish sin because, by virtue of his natural justice, it is just that it should be punished, then it is unjust not to punish it. But is God unjust? God forbid!

I am truly ashamed of those divines who have nothing more commonly in their mouths, both in their disputations and discourses to the people, than "that God might by other means have provided for the safety and honour of his justice, but that that way by the blood of his Son was more proper and becoming." So said Augustine of old. But what then? Of that absolute power which they dream of, by which he might, without any intervening sacrifice, forgive sins, not the least syllable is mentioned in the whole sacred writings; nor am I afraid to affirm that a more convenient device to weaken our faith, love, and gratitude, cannot be invented. Away, then, with such speculations, which teach that the mystery of the love of God the Father, of the blood of Jesus Christ, of the grace of the Holy Spirit, are either indifferent, or at least were not necessary, for procuring and bestowing salvation and eternal glory on miserable sinners. But it is manifest that by such artifices Socinians endeavour to overthrow the whole healing and heavenly doctrine of the gospel. "My soul, come not thou into their secret!" But that God should institute so many typical expiatory sacrifices, and attended with so great labour and cost, with a sanction of severe punishments upon delinquents, with this view only, to communicate instruction, and to serve to lead us to Christ, though they could in no wise take away the guilt of sin;[1] that he should appoint his own Son, not only to death, but to a bloody, ignominious, accursed death, to be inflicted with such shame and disgrace as hath not been purged away through so many generations that have passed since that death, even to the present time; that Jehovah himself should have been pleased to bruise him, to put him to grief; that he made his own sword to awake against him, and forsook him;[2]—that God, I say, should have done these and such like things, without being induced to it by any *necessary cause*, let those who can, comprehend and explain.

[1] Heb. x. 1. There the apostle argues for the necessity of the satisfaction of Christ, which he could not if the guilt of sin could have been taken away by any other way whatever.—TR.

[2] See Isa. liii. 10.

PART II.

CHAPTER VIII.

Objections of the adversaries answered—The Racovian catechism particularly considered—The force of the argument for the satisfaction of Christ from punitory justice—The catechists deny that justice to be inherent in God; and also sparing mercy—Their first argument weighed and refuted—Justice and mercy are not opposite—Two kinds of the divine attributes—Their second and third arguments, with the answers annexed.

It is now time to meet the objections of the adversaries, and so at length put an end to this dispute, as far as regards the subject-matter of it, already drawn out to such a length, and yet farther to be continued. We must first, then, encounter the Socinians themselves, on whose account we first engaged in this undertaking; and afterward we shall compare notes with a few learned friends. But as very lately the Racovian Catechism[1] of these heretics hath been repeatedly printed among us, we shall first consider what is to be met with there in opposition to the truth which we assert.

The Socinians grant, in that catechism of theirs, the argument for the satisfaction of Christ, drawn from the nature of this punitory justice, to be "plausible in appearance;" yea, they must necessarily acknowledge it to be such as that they cannot, even in appearance, oppose it, without being guilty of the dreadful sacrilege of robbing God of his essential attributes, and, therefore, they deny either this justice or sparing mercy to be naturally inherent in God. And they endeavour to defend the robbery by a threefold argument. Their first is this:—"As to mercy, that it is not inherent in God, in the manner that they think,[2] is evident from this consideration, that if it were naturally inherent in God, God would not wholly punish any sin; as, in like manner, if that justice were naturally inherent in God, as they think, God could forgive no sin: for God can never do any thing against what is naturally inherent in him. As, for instance, as wisdom is naturally inherent in God, God never doeth any thing contrary to it, but whatsoever he doeth, he doeth all things wisely. But as it is manifest that God forgives and punishes sins when he

[1] The Racovian Catechism is generally said to have been compiled by Smalcius, from the writings which Faustus Socinus left behind him at his death. Other authorities, who seem to have investigated this point with particular care, hold that a catechism under this name was in existence before Socinus repaired to Poland. The catechism of Smalcius is now, however, commonly regarded as the Racovian Catechism. An English translation of it was published by Biddle in 1652. It is fully reviewed and discussed in Owen's "Vindiciæ Evangelicæ," vol. xii. of his works.—Ed.

[2] Let the reader remember that the compilers of the Racovian Catechism are now speaking, and that the words "they think" allude to the sentiments of the orthodox. —Tr.

will, it appears that such a kind of mercy and justice as they think of is not naturally inherent in God, but is the effect of his own will." I answer, first, that we have laid it down as a fixed principle that mercy is essential to God; and that the nature of it in God is the same with justice we willingly grant. Rutherford alone[1] hath asserted that mercy is essential to God, but that this justice is a free act of the divine will. The falsity and folly of his assertion let himself be answerable for; the thing speaks for itself. To speak the truth, justice is attributed to God *properly* and by way of habit, mercy only *analogically* and by way of affection; and in the first covenant God paved no way for the display of his mercy, but proceeded in that which led straight to the glory of his justice: nevertheless, we maintain the one to be no less naturally inherent in God than the other. "But if it were naturally inherent in God," say the catechists, "God would not punish any sin." Why? I say; mention some plea. "Because," say they, "God cannot do any thing contrary to what is naturally inherent in him; but it is manifest that God punishes sin." But whose sins doth God punish? The sins of the impenitent, the unbelieving, the rebellious, for whose offences the justice of God hath never been satisfied. But is not this contrary to mercy? Let every just judge, then, be called cruel. The punishment of sin, then, is contrary to mercy, either in respect of the infliction of the punishment itself, or because it supposes in God a quality opposite to mercy. The contrariety is not in respect of the infliction of punishment, for between an external act of divine power and eternal attributes of Deity, no opposition can be supposed;—nor can it be because punishment supposes some quality in God opposite to mercy, for that which is opposite to mercy is cruelty; but God is free from every suspicion of cruelty, yet he punishes the sins of the impenitent, as the Socinians themselves acknowledge.

But, "That punitory justice," say they, "which you assign as the source of punishment, is opposite to mercy." How, I say, can that be? Punitory justice, essentially considered, is the very perfection and rectitude of God itself, essentially considered; and the essence of mercy, so to speak, is the same. But the essence of God, which is most simple, is not opposed to itself. Moreover, both have their actual egresses by means of the acts of the divine will, which is always one alone and self-consistent. Objectively considered, I acknowledge they have different but not contrary effects; for to punish the impenitent guilty, for whom no satisfaction hath been made, is not contrary to the pardoning of those who believe and are penitent, through the blood of the Mediator, which was shed for the remission of sins. In one word, it is not necessary that, though actions be contrary, the essential principles should also be contrary.

[1] De Provid., cap. xxii. assert. 6, p. 345.

But they again urge, "Wisdom is naturally inherent in God, and he never doeth any thing contrary to it; for whatsoever he doeth, he doeth all things wisely." We answer, It hath been proved before that the punishment of sin is not contrary to mercy. But they urge something farther, and insinuate that God not only cannot act contrary to his wisdom, but that in every work he exerciseth it: "Whatsoever he doeth," say they, "he doeth wisely." But the nature of all the divine attributes, in respect of their exercise, is not the same: for some create and constitute an object to themselves, as power and wisdom, which God must necessarily exercise in all his works; some require an object constituted for their egress, and for these it is sufficient that no work be done that is opposite or derogatory to their honour; of this kind are mercy and justice, as was said before.

Thus far concerning mercy.

The objections that they bring against justice are easily answered. "If justice be naturally inherent in God," say they, "then he could let no sin pass unpunished." We readily grant that God passes by no sin unpunished, nor can do it. He forgives our sins, but he doth not absolutely let them pass unpunished. Every sin hath its just recompense of reward, either in the sinner or the surety; but to pardon sin for which justice hath been satisfied is no wise contrary to justice. That the nature of justice and mercy, in respect of their relation to their object, is different, hath been shown before. Such is their first argument; the second follows, which is this:—

"That justice which the adversaries oppose to mercy," say they, "whereby God punisheth sins, the sacred Scriptures nowhere point out by the name of 'justice,' but call it the 'anger and fury of God.'"

We answer, in the first place, that it is a very gross mistake that we oppose justice to mercy. These catechists have need themselves to be catechised. In the second place, let those who shall please to consult the passages formerly mentioned and explained on this head, determine whether the sacred Scriptures call this justice[1] by its own proper name or not? In the third place, anger and fury are, in reality, as to their effects, reducible to justice; hence that which is called "wrath," or "anger," in Rom. i. 18, in the 32d verse is called "judgment."[2] Such is their second; and now follows the third argument:—

"When God forgives sins, it is attributed in Scripture to his justice. 'If we confess our sins, he is faithful and just to forgive us our sins, and to cleanse us from all unrighteousness.' 'Being justified freely by his grace through the redemption that is in Christ Jesus: whom God hath set forth to be a propitiation through faith in his blood, to de-

1 This point is treated at great length, and clearly proved, in the third chapter.—Tr.
2 The original word means a just sentence, or righteous judgment.—Tr.

clare his righteousness for the remission of sins that are past, through the forbearance of God; to declare, I say, at this time his righteousness: that he might be just, and the justifier of him which believeth in Jesus.'"[1] We answer, that we have already shown at great length that justice, universally taken, is the perfection and rectitude of God, and has various egresses, both in words and in deeds, according to the constitution of the objects about which it may be employed; hence effects distinct, and in some measure different, are attributed to the same divine virtue. But the justice on account of which God is said to forgive sins is the justice of faithfulness, which has the foundation of its exercise in this punitory justice: which being satisfied, God, who cannot lie, promises the forgiveness of sins through Jesus Christ; which promise, beyond all doubt, he will perform, because he is faithful and just.[2] And thus vanishes in smoke all that these unhappy catechists have scraped together against this divine truth.

CHAPTER IX.

Crellius taken to task—His first mistake—God doth not punish sins as being endowed with supreme dominion—The first argument of Crellius—The answer—The translation of punishment upon Christ, in what view made by God—Whether the remission of sins, without a satisfaction made, could take place without injury to any one—To whom punishment belongs—Whether every one can resign his right—Right twofold—The right of debt, what; and what that of government—A natural and positive right—Positive right, what—A description also of natural right—Concessions of Crellius.

JOHN CRELLIUS treats this subject at great length, and with his

[1] John i. 9; Rom. iii. 24–26.

[2] The argument from 1 John i. 9, which would resolve justice simply into a modification of benevolent feeling, and confound it with a disposition to forgive, is sufficiently met by the considerations urged by our author. The reply to the inference founded on the words "just," and "the justifier of him which believeth in Jesus," Rom. iii. 26, is not so clear. The question turns upon the import of δίκαιος. Two passages are quoted by Socinians in proof that it may denote *clemency* or *mercy;* and if in this sense exclusively the term were applicable to the Divine Being, no argument for the necessity of a proper atonement could be founded on the texts that speak of the justice of God. The passages urged by the Socinians with this view are Matt. i. 19 and Rom. iii. 26. Δίκαιος, however, in its primary meaning, signifies, "observant of rule and custom," "having a respect to order and decency;" as when Cheiron, in contrast with his ruder brethren (Il. xi. 832), is described as δικαιότατος κενταύρων. In this sense, the term admirably befits the state of mind in which Joseph must have been when he discovered the condition of Mary, and before the truth was supernaturally explained to him. In its secondary meaning, δίκαιος signifies *equal, just, fair,* every shade of meaning it bears coming under the category of *right* or *equity;* and in no instance of which we are aware can it be rendered as expressive of *clemency* or *mercy*. In the two passages to which an appeal is made, the adversative force of καὶ is overlooked, "just, *and yet* not willing," "just, *and yet* the justifier." That καὶ frequently conveys this antithetic meaning might be proved from several passages, such as John vii. 19, Mark xii. 12, etc. See Winer's "Idioms of the Greek Language," part iii. chap. v. s. 57.—ED.

usual artifice and acuteness, in his first book "Of the True Religion," prefixed to the works of Volkelius on the same subject.[1]

First, then, he asserts, "That God hath a power of inflicting and of not inflicting punishment, but that it is by no means repugnant to divine justice to pardon the sinner whom by his right he might punish."

But here Crellius (which is a bad omen, as they say) stumbles in the very threshold, supposing punishment to be competent to God as he hath, or is endowed with, an absolute and supreme dominion over the creatures. God never punisheth, or is said to punish, as using that power. It is the part of a governor or judge to inflict punishment; and the Scriptures furnish sufficient evidence that both these relations belong to him in the infliction of punishment: "There is one Lawgiver, who is able to save and to destroy." "He maintaineth right, and sitteth in his throne judging right." He is "judge of all the earth." He is the supreme "judge." "He hath prepared his throne for judgment; and he shall judge the world in righteousness, he shall minister judgment to the people in righteousness." He is "judge of the earth," who will "render a reward to the proud." He is "Jehovah, our judge, our lawgiver, and our king;" and "God the judge of all."[2] In all the acts of his absolute dominion and supreme power God is most free; and this the apostle openly asserts with regard to his decrees making distinctions among mankind in respect of their last end, and the means thereto conducing, according to his mere good pleasure: see Rom. ix. Moreover, in some operations and dispensations of providence concerning mankind, both the godly and ungodly, I acknowledge that God frequently asserts the equity and rectitude of his government from that supreme right which he possesseth and may exercise. "Behold, God is greater than man. Why dost thou strive against him? for he giveth not account of any of his matters. Yea, surely God will not do wickedly, neither will the Almighty pervert judgment. Who hath given him a charge over the earth? or who hath disposed the whole world? If he set his heart upon man, if he gather unto himself his spirit and his breath; all flesh shall perish together, and man shall turn again unto dust."[3]

But that God punishes omissions and avenges transgressions, as the supreme Lord[4] of all, and not as the Ruler of the universe and

[1] Chap. xxiii., title, "Of the Power of God," p. 181, etc.

[2] James iv. 12; Ps. ix. 4; Gen. xviii. 25; Ps. l. 6, ix. 7, 8, xciv. 2; Isa. xxxxiii. 22, Heb. xii. 23, etc.

[3] Job xxxiii. 12, 13, xxxiv. 12–15.

[4] As supreme Lord of the universe he exerciseth an uncontrolled dominion, doing "in the army of heaven, and among the inhabitants of the earth," whatsoever seemeth good unto him; but as the Ruler and Judge of the world he distributeth impartial justice, "giving to every one according to his works." The force of this argument, then, is this,—That in viewing God as punishing sin, we are not to consider him as supreme Lord, who may exercise an absolute and uncontrolled will, but as a righteous Judge, bound by a law to administer justice, and by a law founded in his nature, necessarily requiring him so to do.—Tr.

Judge of the world, is an opinion supported by no probable reason and by no testimony of Scripture. But let us hear what Crellius himself has to say. He thus proceeds:—

"He injures none, whether he punish or do not punish, if so be that the question is only respecting his right: for the punishment is not owing to the offending person, but he owes it, and he owes it to him upon whom the whole injury will ultimately redound; who in this matter is God. But if you consider the matter in itself, every one has it in his power to prosecute his right, and likewise not to prosecute it, or to yield up of it as much as he pleases; for this is the nature of a proper and sovereign right."

Ans. It is easy to be seen that the former fallacy diffuses its fibres through the whole of this reasoning; for the right, a dispensation with which he maintains to be lawful, he affirms to be a sovereign right, or the right of a lord and master. But this right is not the subject in question. It is a ruler and judge to whom punishment belongs, and who repays it. I would not, indeed, deny that God's supreme and sovereign right has a place in the matter of the satisfaction made by Christ in our stead: for although to inflict punishment be the office of a ruler and judge (that both these relations, namely, of a ruler and judge, are to be assigned to God, the Scriptures amply testify,—see chap. iii.), yet the very translation of guilt from us upon Christ, constituting him sin for us, is a most free act, and an act of supreme power; unless, perhaps, the acceptance of the promise made by the surety belong of right to him as ruler, and there be no other act to be assigned to God.

But let us consider these arguments of Crellius severally. "He injures no one," says he, "whether he punish or not." But an omission of the infliction of punishment, where it is due, cannot take place without injury to that justice on which it is incumbent to inflict the punishment.[1] For "he that justifieth the wicked is abomination to the LORD;" and a heavy woe is pronounced equally on them that "call evil good, and good evil."[2] It is true that God neither injures nor can injure any one, either in what he hath done or might do; for "who hath first given to him, and it shall be recompensed to him again?" Nor is it less true that he will not, yea, that he cannot, do injury to his own justice, which requireth the punishment of every sin. An earthly judge may oftentimes spare a guilty person without injury to another, but not without injustice in himself. Yea, Crellius asserts that God cannot forgive the sins of some sinners, namely, the contumacious, without injury to himself; for this, as he says, would be unworthy of God. But we are sure that every sin, without ex-

[1] The translation of the last clause is ambiguous. The words in the original are, "Justitiæ illius, cui pœnas irrogare incumbit,"—"That justice on which rests the obligation, which is bound, to inflict the punishment."—ED.

[2] Prov. xvii. 15; Isa. v. 20.

ception, setting aside the consideration of the redemption by Christ, would be attended with contumacy for ever. Were it not for that consideration, then, it would be unworthy of God to pardon the sins of any sinner.

Crellius adds: "Punishment is not owing to the sinner, but he owes it, and owes it to him on whom all the injury will ultimately redound; who is God." But because punishment is not owing to the sinner, but he owes it to the ruler, it doth not follow that the ruler may not inflict that punishment. Punishment, indeed, is not so owing to the sinner that an injury would be done him were it not inflicted. The debt of a sinner is not of such a kind that he can ask or enforce the payment of it; and a debt, properly speaking, implies such a condition.[1] But the sinner hath merited punishment in such a manner that it is just he should suffer it. But, again, the infliction of punishment belongs not to God as injured, as Crellius signifies, but as he is the ruler of all and the judge of sinners, to whom it belongs to preserve the *good of the whole,* and the dependence of his creatures on himself.

He thus proceeds: "But if you consider the thing in itself, every one has it in his power to prosecute his right, and likewise not to prosecute it, or to yield up of it as much as he pleases."

Ans. As Socinus himself, in his third book "Of the Saviour," chap. ii., hath afforded an opportunity to all our theologians who have opposed Socinianism of discussing this foolish axiom, "That every one may recede from his right," we shall answer but in few words to these positions of Crellius, and to the conclusions which he there draws as flowing from them.

There is, then, a double right;—in the first place, that of a *debt;* in the second place, that of *government.* What is purely a debt may be forgiven; for that only takes place in those things which are of an indifferent right, the prosecution of which neither nature nor justice obliges. There is also a debt, though perhaps improperly so called, the right of which it is unlawful to renounce; but our sins, in respect of God, are not debts only nor properly, but metaphorically[2] so called.

The right of government, moreover, is either *natural* or *positive.* The *positive* right of government, so to speak, is that which magistrates have over their subjects; and he who affirms that they can recede wholly from this right must be either a madman or a fool. But this right, as far as pertains to its exercise in respect of the in-

[1] The debt of a sinner is not any valuable consideration due to him, as a debt is to a creditor, but due by him as a debt is by a debtor; and in consequence of the failure of payment, punishment becomes due to him,—*i. e.*, is or may be inflicted in vindication of violated justice. But this is what he could not either claim or would wish to receive.—TR.

[2] Sin is most accurately defined by our Westminster divines, in that inimitable compendium of sound doctrine, the Shorter Catechism, to be "any want of conformity unto, or transgression of, the law of God."—TR.

fliction of punishment, either tends to the good of the whole republic, as in *ordinary* cases, or, as in some *extraordinary* cases, gives place to its hurt; for it is possible that even the exaction of punishment, in a certain condition of a state, may be hurtful. In such a situation of things, the ruler or magistrate has a power not to use his right of government in respect of particular crimes, or rather, he ought to use it in such a manner as is the most likely to attain the end; for he is bound to regard principally the good of the whole, and the safety of the people ought to be his supreme law. But he who affirms that, in ordinary cases, a magistrate may renounce his right, when that renunciation cannot but turn out to the hurt of the public good, is a stranger to all right. The same person may also affirm that parents may renounce their right over their children, so as not to take any care at all about them; and that they might do so lawfully,—that is, consistently with honour and decency. Yea, this is not a cessation from the *prosecution of right*, but from the *performance of a duty;* for the right of government supposes a duty: "For rulers are not a terror to good works, but to the evil. Wilt thou then not be afraid of the power? do that which is good, and thou shalt have praise of the same: for he is the minister of God to thee for good. But if thou do that which is evil, be afraid; for he beareth not the sword in vain: for he is the minister of God, a revenger to execute wrath upon him that doeth evil."[1] The question is not what magistrates do, but what, as the guardians and protectors of the law, they ought to do. See Ps. ci. 8.

There is also a *natural right* of government; such is the divine right over the creatures. The right, I say, of God over rational creatures is natural to him; therefore immutable, indispensable, and which cannot by any means be derogated. Thence, too, the debt of our obedience is natural and indispensable; nor is there any other kind of obligation to punishment. God, from the very nature of the thing, has dominion over us; and our subjection to him is either by obedience or a vicarious punishment, which comes in place of any omission or transgression on our part, as Crellius himself acknowledges. Those, then, who say that it is free to God to use this right or not, as he pleaseth, may as well say that it is free to God to be our God and Lord or not; for the demand of obedience and the exaction of punishment equally belong to God. But the Judge of the universe exercises his right; and his perpetual right, whence sinners are accounted worthy of death, he cannot but preserve unimpaired and entire.

The remaining objections, which are interspersed here and there in that book of his "Concerning God," against the vindicatory justice of God, either fall in with those which have been mentioned from

[1] Rom. xiii. 3, 4.

the Racovian Catechism, or shall be reduced to the order of those which follow.

We think proper, by way of conclusion, to annex some concessions of Crellius. "There is," says he, "a certain regard to honour, with which God himself cannot dispense."[1] Every transgression, then, of that regard hath a punishment coeval with itself, which, from the justice of God, must necessarily be inflicted. "Yea," says he, "neither the holiness nor majesty of God permits that his commands should, in any respect, be violated with impunity."[2] But the holiness of God is natural to him; an essential, then, and necessary attribute of God requires the punishment of sinners. But he himself farther adds, "It is unworthy of God to let the wickedness of obstinate sinners pass unpunished; for this is the first and perpetual effect of divine severity, not to pardon those who do not repent."[3] But we know for certain that all sinners would continue obstinate to all eternity, unless God be pleased, for Christ's sake, to renew them by his omnipotent grace to repentance. Crellius, then, grants that it is unworthy of God to let the sins of those pass unpunished for whom Christ hath not made satisfaction. He again testifies, also, that God hates and abhors all sin;[4] and grants that the mode of conducting the punishment of sin is derived from the divine justice.[5] But the thing itself is from that same Being from whom the mode or manner of it is derived. If the mode of punishment be from divine justice, the punishment itself can flow from no other source.

CHAPTER X.

The opinion of Socinus considered—What he thought of our present question,[6] namely, that it is the hinge on which the whole controversy concerning the satisfaction of Christ turns—His vain boasting, as if, having disproved this vindicatory justice, he had snatched the prize from his adversaries—Other clear proofs of the satisfaction of Christ—That it is our duty to acquiesce in the revealed will of God—The truth not to be forsaken—Mercy and justice not opposite—Vain distinctions of Socinus concerning divine justice—The consideration of these distinctions—His first argument against vindicatory justice—The solution of it—The anger and severity of God, what—Universal and particular justice, in what they agree—The false reasoning and vain boasting of the adversary.

WE come now to Socinus himself. In almost all his writings he opposes this *punitory justice*. We shall consider what he hath

[1] Book i. chap. xxiii., p. 180, "Of the True Religion."
[2] Chap. xxviii.
[3] Chap. xxii. 186, and chap. xxviii.
[4] Chap. xxx. 3, 9.
[5] Chap. i. p. 78, of his Answer to Grotius.
[6] Namely, Whether vindicatory justice be essential and natural to God, and the exercise of it, or the punishment of sin, consequently necessary?—TR.

written against Covetus, in that treatise of his entitled, "Of Jesus Christ the Saviour," and what he only repeats in other places, as occasion required. In the first book and first chapter, and also in the third book and first chapter, of that work, expressly, and of set purpose, he opposes himself vehemently and with all his might to the truth on this point. But because he very well understood that by the establishment of this justice a knife is put to the throat of his opinion, and that it cannot be defended (that is, that no reason can be given why Christ our Saviour is called Jesus Christ), he maintains that the whole controversy concerning the satisfaction of Christ hinges on this very question. The reader will perceive, from the arguments already used, that I am of the same opinion: for it being granted that this justice belongs to God, not even Socinus, though doubtless a man of a great, very artful, and fertile genius, could devise any way of obtaining salvation for sinners without a satisfaction; for had he either found out one, or even feigned it upon a supposition, he would not have wanted the effrontery of imposing it on the minds of the credulous and fanatic; which, however, he nowhere hath attempted.

But, on the other hand, gallantly supposing that he had removed this justice out of the way, as if the business were entirely settled, and the strong tower of his adversaries destroyed, he highly glories in the triumphs acquired for himself and his followers; "for," says he, "having got rid of this justice, had we no other argument, that human fiction of the satisfaction of Jesus Christ must be thoroughly detected, and totally vanish." This vain boasting of his the learned and pious have long ago sufficiently checked by innumerable testimonies from Scripture.

And forasmuch as the fact is abundantly clear that Christ bore our sins, God laying them upon him, and that by his satisfaction he purchased eternal salvation, though it had even pleased God to keep the causes and reasons of this infinitely wise transaction hid to all eternity in the abyss of his own goodness and wisdom, it would have been our duty to acquiesce in the infinite holiness and wisdom of his will. So, also, it is beyond any doubt that no helps of our faith are to be despised, and that no revelations of the divine nature and will are to be neglected, by which our merciful Father leads us into a more intimate and saving knowledge of this mystery of holiness.

We, also, to whom the most sacred deposit of this divine truth hath been committed, would immediately judge ourselves unworthy of it should we spontaneously betray any one point or jot of it, much less so strong a pillar of our faith and hope, to its adversaries. Though, then, we have other unanswerable proofs of the satisfaction of Christ, which the gates of hell shall in vain oppose, and numberless testimonies of the God who cannot lie, so that we may suppose Socinus is only idly insulting those who grant that God might forgive sin without any intervention of a satisfaction, but that he would not, (an expression which I by no means approve), we however think it necessary that this bulwark of punitory justice, a point, beyond all doubt, of the last importance to the cause, however it shall be disposed of, should be defended from the insults of adversaries.

In the first place, then, in the first chapter of the before-mentioned book, when going to dispute against this justice, he supposes that, according to our opinion, it is opposed to mercy, and that it is contrary to it, and builds upon this false supposition through the whole of his treatise, both in making his objections and answers. I acknowledge that he seized the opportunity of making this blunder from Covetus, against whom he is combating, who improperly and inaccurately hath said that this justice is opposed to mercy, because they have different effects; but we have formerly shown that they are neither *essentially*, nor *actually*, nor *effectively* opposite, as both of them are the very perfection of Deity itself, but that they are only distinguished as to their object, and not as to their subject. In all the sophisms, then, in which he afterward endeavours to prove that the Scripture acknowledges no such justice in God as is opposed to mercy, he trifles, through a perpetual mistake of the argument. But that justice which we mean, he says, is twofold in God. "The first," as he says, "is that by which he punishes and destroys the wicked and ungodly,—that is, those who obstinately persevere in wickedness, and who are not led, from a repentance of their sins, to have recourse to God. The second is that by which even those whom, in his great goodness, he approves as just, were he so to will it, could not stand in his presence."

But he again affirms, in the same chapter, "That the justice of God is twofold: that one kind he always uses when he punishes abandonedly wicked and obstinate sinners, sometimes, according to his law; the other kind, when he punishes sinners neither obstinate nor altogether desperate, but whose repentance is not expected." And of both these kinds of justice he brings some proofs from Scripture.

That punitory justice is one alone and individual, we affirm; but that it is variously exercised, on account of the difference of the objects about which it is employed, we acknowledge;—but this by no means proves it to be twofold; for he ought not, among men, to be said to be endowed with a twofold justice who renders different recompenses to those who merit differently. But his whole treatise, from beginning to end, is disgracefully built on a mistaken and falsely-assumed principle; for he supposes that "every sin shall not receive its just recompense of reward" from divine justice, but that God punishes some sins, and can punish others only if he please. From an exceeding desire to exclude all consideration of the satisfaction of Christ entirely in the matter of inflicting punishment for sins, he stumbled against this stone: for God most certainly will finally punish the impenitent to all eternity, because he is just, and because there is no sacrifice for their sins; nor is it less true that God casts out and destroys many who are strangers to the covenant of grace, not waiting for their repentance, but that he effectually leads others to repentance;—not because he exerciseth a twofold justice, but because his justice hath been satisfied for the sins of the latter by Christ, whereas it is not so with regard to the former. See Rom. iii. 24, 25. But because he would not acknowledge the foundation for that distinction, which may be seen in the acts or exercises of the divine justice concerning sinners, to be laid in the blood of Christ, he hath feigned a twofold justice, and a twofold mercy opposed to it, of which there is not the most distant mention made in the sacred Scriptures, and which ought not by any means to be ascribed to the divine nature, which is in itself most simple.

But coming to himself again, he denies that in the sacred writings there is any mention at all made of any kind of justice that is opposed to mercy. We, indeed, have never said that justice is opposed to mercy; but as it clearly appears that it is his wish to deny to God the whole of that kind of justice whence, in punishing sins, he is said, or may be said, to be just (which punishment is an effect different from the pardon of sin that flows from mercy), we choose not to contend about words. Let us see, then, what kind of arguments he produces to support his robbing God of this essential attribute. He says, "that the word 'justice,' when applied to God in the sacred writings, is never opposed to 'mercy,' but chiefly, and for the most part, means rectitude and equity."

It hath been already several times shown that justice and mercy are not opposite. We have likewise demonstrated, by many proofs adduced before, that the rectitude or supreme perfection of the divine nature is often called "justice" in Scripture; but this, I am sure, is by no means of advantage, but of much hurt, to the cause of Socinianism. Let him proceed, then.

"But that," says he, "which is opposed to 'mercy' is not named 'justice' by the sacred writers, but is called 'severity,' or 'anger,' or 'fury,' or 'vengeance,' or by some such name."

But our opponent avails himself nothing by this assertion; for that which is false proves nothing. By that which, he says, is opposed to mercy, he understands that virtue in God by which he punishes sins and sinners according as they deserve. But that this is never called "justice" in Scripture, or that God is not thence said to be "just," is so manifestly false that nobody would dare to affirm it but one determined to say any thing in support of a bad cause. Let the reader but consult the passages adduced on this head in the third chapter, and he will be astonished at the impudence of the man. But all are agreed that anger, fury, and words denoting such troubled affections, ought not properly to be ascribed to God, but only in respect of their effects,—though analogically and reductively[1] they belong to corrective justice,—because, in exercising his judgments, God is said to use them, but they do not denote any perfection inherent in God any farther than they can be reduced to justice, but only a certain mode of certain divine actions; for God doth not punish sins because he is angry, but because he is just, although in the punishment of them, according to our conception of things, he discovers anger.

He next proceeds to produce some passages, in order to prove that the justice of God in the sacred writings,—namely, that universal justice which we have before described,—is often used for the infinite rectitude of the divine nature (what nobody ever denied), where, in mentioning the justice of faithfulness and remunerative justice, agreeably to his faithfulness, which always hath respect to the covenant of grace ratified and established in the blood of Christ, God is said to pardon sins, and to reward those that believe, according to his justice; and thence he concludes, "that a justice opposed to mercy, by which God must punish sin, is not inherent in God." "For what," says he, "is more agreeable to the divine nature, and consequently more equitable and just, than to do good to the wretched and despised race of mankind, though unworthy, and freely to make them partakers of his glory?"

This surely is trifling in a serious matter, if any thing can be so called; for even novices will not bear one to argue from a position of universal justice to a negation of particular justice; much less shall we readily assent to him, who maintain that that particular justice is by no means distinguished from the universal rectitude of the divine nature, but that that rectitude is so called in respect of the egresses that it has, in consequence of the supposition of sin. But it is consonant with sound doctrine, "that that which is agreeable to the divine nature should be considered also as righteous and just;" and this Socinus acknowledges. We agree that it is agreeable to the divine nature to do good to sinners, but at the same time we dare not deny that the right of God is, that those who transgress are worthy of death; both which properties of his nature he hath very clearly demonstrated in the satisfaction of Christ, "whom he hath set forth to be a propitiation through faith in his blood, to declare his righteousness for the remission of sins;" whom, while the heretic rejecteth, he walketh in darkness, a stranger to the true and saving knowledge of God, and engaged wholly in his own vain imaginations.

But Socinus, as if having achieved some great exploit, at length

[1] That is, by consequence.—Tr.

thus concludes: "That punitory justice is not a virtue inherent in God, or a divine quality or property, but the effect of his will; and that that justice by which God always punishes impenitent sinners is so called, not properly, but by accident, namely, because it is agreeable to true justice or rectitude." We have already considered the arguments that he has produced in support of this opinion; whether they be of such weight that they should induce us to deny this justice, and whether to punish sinners be essential and proper to God or only accidental, let the reader, from what hath been said on the subject, determine. So much for our first skirmish with Socinus.

CHAPTER XI.

The arguments of Socinus against punitory justice weighed—A false hypothesis of his—Sins, in what sense they are debts—The first argument of Socinus, in which he takes for granted what ought to have been proved—A trifling supposition substituted for a proof—Whether that excellence by virtue of which God punishes sins be called justice in the Scriptures—The severity of God, what—Our opponent's second argument—It labours under the same deficiency as the first—It is not opposite to mercy to punish the guilty—The mercy of God, what—There is a distinction between acts and habits—Our opponent confounds them—The mercy of God infinite, so also his justice—A distinction of the divine attributes—In pardoning sins through Jesus Christ, God hath exercised infinite justice and infinite mercy—The conclusion of the contest with Socinus.

In the third part and first chapter of his treatise, being determined to contend to his utmost against the satisfaction of Christ, he maintains "That God, consistently with his right, could pardon our sins without any real satisfaction received for them;" and he endeavours to support the assertion chiefly by the following argument,—namely, "That God is our creditor, that our sins are debts which we have contracted with him, but that every one may yield up his right, and more especially God, who is the supreme Lord of all, and extolled in the Scriptures for his liberality and goodness." Hence, then, it is evident that God can pardon sins without any satisfaction received; and that he is inclined to do so, he uses his best endeavours afterward to prove.

But because he foresaw that his first supposition, the foundation of his whole future reasoning, was too much exposed and obnoxious to the divine justice, he labours hard in the first chapter to remove that out of the way entirely. Let us attend, then, to his reasoning, and follow him step by step: for if he have not insuperably, and beyond all confutation, proved that God can forgive sins without a satisfaction, what he afterward argues concerning the will, liberality, and mercy of God will become of no weight or consideration; yea, the foundation being destroyed, the whole edifice or Babylonish tower must instantly tumble to the ground. He thus proceeds:—

"But you will say, 'It is necessary that God should take care to satisfy his justice, which he cannot even himself renounce, unless he in a manner deny himself.'"

Ans. You are right, Socinus. We do affirm, agreeably to the holy Scriptures, that the justice of God is in such a manner natural to him, that if it be necessary that he should preserve the glory of his essential attributes undiminished, he cannot but indispensably exact the punishment of every sin and transgression of his law, and render a just recompense of reward to all sinners, or to their surety; and, therefore, we contend that without a satisfaction made no one could obtain the remission of sins and eternal salvation. Let us see, Socinus, what you have to oppose to this.

"All along, from the beginning of this answer," says he, "I have sufficiently shown that that justice which you contend ought at all events to be satisfied is not inherent in God, but is the effect of his own will; for when God punishes sinners, that we may call this work of his by some worthy name, we say that he then exerciseth justice: wherefore, there is no need that God should either provide for the satisfaction of that justice or renounce it."

Ans. We have already considered what Socinus says in the beginning of his treatise against the justice of God. If I mistake not, we have shown that the heretic has lost his labour, and that it is far beyond his power to dethrone the Deity; for "he sitteth in the throne judging righteously."[1] But we, diminutive beings, have not first, or of our own accord, maintained that God is just, and that he exerciseth justice in the punishment of sinners, "that we might call his work by some worthy name." But the Judge of all the earth himself, the God of truth, in almost innumerable places, gives this testimony of himself in the sacred records; and these ought always to be the only, as they are the infallible, guide of our judgments.

Distrusting, then, what he had formerly asserted (or it being manifestly of no weight), he attempts again by other sophisms to establish the reasoning which he had formerly begun. And he thus proceeds:—

"But besides the arguments which I have already used to prove that that justice is not inherent in God, it chiefly appears from this, that were it naturally resident in God, he could never pardon not even the least transgression to any one; for God never doth any thing, nor can do any thing, that is opposite to the qualities inherent in him. As, for instance, as wisdom and equity are naturally inherent in God, that justice never doth or can do any thing contrary to wisdom and equity, as we have seen above," etc.

[1] Ps. ix. 4.

The intelligent reader can easily perceive that Socinus proves nothing by this argument, but that he even absurdly adds heap upon heap to his own supposition; or that with a bold effrontery, he takes for granted the thing to be determined. It is indeed our opinion, that God cannot pass the smallest sin unpunished; and that he cannot, because he can do nothing that is opposite to the qualities inherent in him. But this our opponent brings forward as a great absurdity, that must bear against us in support of his own cause; but without even any appearance of a proof. But we have before demonstrated the state of the matter to be thus,—That God neither actually pardons any sin without a satisfaction made, nor can pardon it, without an infringement of his justice, by which he condemns sinners as worthy of death. So that as God never doth nor can do the things which are opposite to his equity and wisdom, so he neither doth nor can do those which are opposite to his justice. But to pardon the sins of believers on account of the satisfaction of Christ, "whom he hath set forth as a propitiation through faith in his blood, to declare his righteousness," is not opposite to his justice. But these seem absurdities to Socinus. And why should they not? for "we preach Christ crucified, unto the Jews a stumbling-block, and unto the Greeks foolishness." But "the preaching of the cross is to them that perish foolishness."[1]

Yea, in common equity, nothing could be mentioned more inequitable and unwise than this would be opposite to justice,—namely, not to pardon those sins for which that justice hath been amply satisfied. And must, then, this heretic, not only for nothing, substitute his own most absurd, yea, execrable opinion, namely, "That Jesus Christ hath not made satisfaction for our sins, nor borne their punishment,"—that is, that he was not "made sin for us, that we might be made the righteousness of God in him,"—an opinion neither proved, nor that will ever be proved to all eternity; but also insinuate it as a proof of another error, which that alone, it is evident, first begot in his mind? Indeed, I cannot sufficiently wonder that some, by the sophisms of such disputants, are so easily "removed unto another gospel," forsaking "him that called them into the grace of Christ."

"But that justice," says Socinus, "which, as we have seen before, in the sacred writings is not called 'justice,' but 'severity' or 'vengeance,' or by some such name, so far as it is opposed to mercy is nothing else but to punish sins; but to punish sins and to pardon sins are entirely opposite to one another."

A fine painter's show-board, but void of truth.

Ans. What the adversary so often yelps out is totally without foundation,—namely, that that justice is never called by its proper

[1] 1 Cor. i. 18, 23, 24.

name in the Scriptures. It is not only called by its own name, but is also called "purity" and "holiness," which are essential attributes of the Deity. It is called "severity," "vengeance," and "anger," but only improperly and analogically, and in respect of the effects which it produceth. What he asserts, too, of this justice, namely, that it is nothing else but to punish sin,—very improperly confounding a habit, an act, and an effect,—is altogether without foundation, and most absurd. "The LORD is just, and his judgments are righteous. The Judge of all the earth doeth right." And, in fine, it is false that this justice is opposed to mercy; for it is beyond any doubt that different operations and effects may, in different views, be ascribed to one and the same righteous principle. To punish sins and to pardon sins, unless spoken in the same point of view, are not opposed to one another. God, indeed, pardons to us those sins which he punished in our surety: which "foolishness of God is wiser than men."

Our opponent thus proceeds:—"If that justice be inherent in God,—that is, if there be any property in God which is altogether inclined expressly to punish any sins of mankind whatsoever, whether penitent or impenitent,—he neither spares nor can spare any one; for as to what your teachers in the church have devised, that according to this justice he can punish sin, even though the sinner should not be punished, that is quite inconsistent with this and every other kind of justice."

Our opponent again idly fancies that we are hard pressed by this conclusion. We grant, yea, we solemnly believe and declare, that because of his justice God can never spare any sinner, unless he expressly punish his sins in another. But he artfully and shrewdly endeavours to load our opinion with prejudice, insinuating "that God then could not even spare the penitent." But we believe all repentance of sin to be founded in the satisfaction and blood of Christ; for "him hath God exalted with his right hand to be a Prince and a Saviour, for to give repentance to Israel, and forgiveness of sins."[1] God, then, both can spare the penitent, and, according to the promises of the gospel, most certainly will spare them,—those, namely, for whose sins satisfaction hath been made through the blood of Christ, "who gave himself a ransom for them;" but that to punish sin, without the delinquents being punished, is neither contrary to this nor to any other kind of justice, absolutely considered, through divine help, shall be demonstrated in its proper place.

Hitherto our opponent hath discovered nothing but mere fancies, vain repetitions, absurd allegations, and a shameful ignorance of the argument. He thus proceeds: "But should you say, that by the same reasoning it may be proved that mercy is not inherent in God; for if it were, he could never inflict punishment on any, as mercy is

[1] Acts v. 31.

nothing else but to pardon those who have offended;—I will answer, as I have slightly noticed before, that it is very true that mercy, so far as it is opposed to that justice, that is, to severity and vengeance, is not inherent in God, but is the effect of his will. When, then, the sacred Scriptures testify that God is merciful, they mean nothing more than that God very often and very easily pardoneth sin, if, at least, they speak of this mercy; for there is another kind of divine mercy, of which, according to the old translation, mention is frequently made in the sacred writings, which ought rather to be called goodness, and hath a more extensive signification, for it comprehends the whole divine beneficence, whether it be exercised in the pardon of sin or in communication of any other kind of benefit to mankind."

It hath been shown already that it is not proved by such reasoning as this that justice is not inherent in God; nor from the force of such an argument will it easily appear that the divine mercy suffers any degradation. What he supposes, in the first place, is altogether without foundation, namely, "That the divine mercy is nothing else than to forgive offenders;" whereas in this an external effect of that mercy only is shown, which is itself an essential property of the divine nature, for he pardoneth sins because he is merciful. The supposition, also, is groundless, "That if mercy were inherent in God he could never inflict punishment on any;" for to inflict punishment on the impenitent, and those for whose sins the divine justice hath in no manner been satisfied, is not opposite to mercy. For mercy in God is not a sympathy or condolence with the miseries of others, with an inclination of assisting them,—a virtue which ofttimes borders near upon vice,—but is that supreme perfection of the divine nature whereby it is naturally disposed to assist the miserable, and which, the proper suppositions[1] being made, and the glory of his other perfections preserved, he willingly exerciseth, and is inclined to exercise. But this is not "opposed to the justice of God;" neither is it an "effect of his free will" (which expression, concerning the exercise of justice, our opponent foolishly wrests to the virtue itself), but a natural attribute of the Deity. What he adds concerning a twofold mercy of God are idle fancies: for the sparing mercy of which we are discoursing by no means differs from that benignity, grace, or goodness of God, of which he makes mention; for that very benignity, with respect to the special egresses which it hath towards miserable sinners, from the free-will of God, is that very mercy itself. That assertion of his, too, must also be noticed by the way,—namely, "That God very easily pardoneth sin;" which as it is a very precious truth if a regard be had to the oblation and satisfaction of his Son, so, simply spoken of him who hath threatened death to every transgression, and whose right it is that sinners should be worthy of death,

[1] That is, the existence and misery of a rational creature being supposed.—TR.

all, whosoever shall be cited before his tribunal, aliens and strangers to Christ, will find to be without foundation, and an absolute falsehood.

"But it is evident," says he, "that neither the justice nor mercy of which we are treating is inherent in God, from what we read, namely, that he is 'The LORD God, merciful and gracious, long-suffering and abundant in goodness;'[1] which plainly shows that these two,—namely, his justice and mercy,—are the effects of his will, the one of which is surpassed in greatness by the other, and they cannot consist with one another, and they are limited; whereas those qualities which are truly inherent in God have no limit, and are all consistent with one another, and, in respect of their greatness, are all absolutely equal."

Our opponent again very improperly applies a comparison made between external acts to the internal habits themselves. That anger and compassion, which are only attributed to God effectively, are free effects of the divine will, limited as to their object, and unequal, which cannot be exercised about the same person, in their highest degree, we acknowledge;[2]

But there is no reason that what is applicable to acts, or rather to effects, should also be applicable to the perfections whence these flow. But in that promulgation of the glory or name of God which we have in Exod. xxxiv. 6, he shows what and of what kind his disposition is towards those whom, namely, he hath purchased as his peculiar people through Jesus Christ, and what patience, long-suffering, and compassion, he is disposed to exercise towards them;[3] but in respect of all other sinners, he concludes that he "will by no means clear the guilty," or deliver them from the guilt of sin; which, indeed, strikes at the very root of Socinianism. But to conclude from this that the divine perfections are opposite one to another, unequal, or surpassing one another in greatness, is only the extreme folly of one ignorant of the righteousness or justice of God, and going about to establish a righteousness or justice of his own. He proceeds thus:—

"Hence it is manifest how grievously they err who affirm both this justice and mercy of God to be infinite; for as to justice, being deceived by the appearance of the word, they see not that they say no more than this, that the severity and anger of God are infinite, contrary to the most express testimonies of the sacred Scriptures, which, as we have just now said, declare God to be 'slow to anger.' That divine justice which hath no limit is not this of which we are discoursing, but that which alone, as we have seen before, is distinguished by this illustrious name in Scripture, and which, by another

[1] See Exod. xxxiv. 6; Numb. xiv. 18.

[2] Omitted: "though it is plain from the holy Scriptures that God not unfrequently manifests some kind of anger, in his paternal chastisements, towards those who all the while are the objects of his supreme love and mercy."—ED.

[3] See 2 Pet. iii. 9, etc.

name, may be called rectitude and equity. This, indeed, is inherent in God, and is most conspicuous in all his works; and by virtue of this alone, as we shall see hereafter, even if we had no other proof, that human fiction of the satisfaction of Christ would be thoroughly detected, and vanish."

Our opponent here serves up again nothing but his old dish, variously dressed, and repeatedly refused. We declare justice to be infinite, not deceived by the show of a word, but being so taught by the express testimonies of the sacred Scriptures, and by the most convincing and unanswerable arguments,—and we solemnly maintain it, not only with regard to that universal justice which may be called rectitude (though improperly), but also concerning that particular sin-avenging justice, which we deny to differ, either essentially or subjectively,[1] from the former,—but that anger and severity, so far as they denote effects of divine justice, or punishment inflicted, are infinite only in duration: "Seeing it is a righteous thing with God to take vengeance on them who know him not, and that obey not the gospel of our Lord Jesus Christ; who shall be punished with everlasting destruction from the presence of the Lord, and from the glory of his power."[2] But in respect of that divine excellence which they point out, we affirm them to be in every respect infinite.

But it would be altogether superfluous here again to repeat what we have before clearly settled concerning this justice, or again to recite the texts of Scripture formerly adduced. The sum is this: Sin-avenging justice differs not in reality from that universal justice which our opponent does not deny to be perpetually inherent in God and a natural attribute. It is only distinguished from it in respect of its egress to its own proper object; for the egresses of justice against sin flow from the most holy perfection of Deity itself. But anger and severity, so far as they may be reduced to that justice which is manifested in them, are also infinite; in respect of their effects, they have their limits assigned them by the wisdom and justice of God. These things, however, have been proved before.

But let the pious reader judge whether our opponent, who hath presumed to call the highest mystery of the gospel, the alone foundation of the salvation of sinners, the darling jewel of our religion, the greatest testimony of the divine love, our victory over the devil, death, and hell, "a human fiction," had sufficient cause to annex so dreadful an omission to the conclusion of this so long continued debate. He adds, in the last place,—

"But as to mercy, that is, the pardon of sins, how dare they affirm that to be infinite, when it is evident from the whole of Scripture that God doth not always use it, but frequently exerciseth vengeance

[1] That is, as it relates to God, who is the subject of it.—TR.
[2] See 2 Thess. i. 6, 8, 9.

and severity? Why, but because they have so shockingly blundered, that they have not attended to this, that these are only different effects of the divine will, but are not any properties, and have persuaded themselves that both of them are inherent in God. But how could they ever entertain such a persuasion, when, as we have said, the one destroys the other? But this they deny, and maintain that God exercised both of them perfectly in the salvation procured for us by Christ; which will more clearly appear, from what follows, to be not only false but ridiculous. Meantime, let them tell us, pray, when God punishes the guilty, but especially when he doth not even grant them time to repent, what kind of mercy he exerciseth towards these? But if God do many things in which not even any trace of that mercy appears, although he be said to be 'merciful and full of compassion' in Scripture, must we not say that he doth many things in which that justice is by no means discernible, to which he is said to be exceeding slow? We must then conclude, according to our opinion, that there is no such justice in God as expressly dictates the necessary punishment of sin, and which he hath not a power to renounce. And since this is the case, it is abundantly evident that there is no reason why God cannot freely pardon the sins of whomsoever he may please, without any satisfaction received."

Ans. On these heads a few observations shall suffice:—1. It is affirmed, without any show of reason, that mercy in God is not *infinite,* because sometimes he exerciseth severity; that is, that God cannot be called merciful, if he punish any guilty and impenitent sinners. To prove mercy to be an essential property of God, it is sufficient that he exercises it towards any: for in this very matter, that ought to be set down as a natural perfection in God which is the proper and immediate source and ground of that operation: which attributes (mercy and justice) have no egress but towards objects placed in particular circumstances; nor have they any effects without some free act of the divine will intervening. See Rom. ix. 13. Nor does it any more follow that the effects of mercy ought to be infinite if it be itself infinite, than that the works of God ought to be immense because immensity is an essential property of his nature.

2. By what argument will our opponent prove that the relation between mercy and justice is in such a manner the same, that because God exerciseth no mercy towards some,—that is, so as to pardon their sins,—that therefore he should not account it necessary to exercise justice towards every sin? We have formerly mentioned in what view they are distinct,—namely, that God is bound to exercise mercy to none, but that he cannot but exercise his justice towards sinners (provided he be inclined to be just), if he would preserve his natural right and dominion over his creatures, and the holiness and purity of his nature uninjured and entire; for disobedience would

take away all dependence of the creature on God, unless a compensation were made to him by a vicarious punishment. But, according to the sacred Scriptures, we maintain that God exercised both the one and the other, both justice and mercy, in justly punishing Christ, in mercifully pardoning sins, which he laid upon him, to us, who deserved everlasting punishment; which things, though they may be ridiculous to Socinus (for "the things of the Spirit of God are foolishness" to him), no divine truth, however, of any kind whatever, is more frequently, more plainly, or more clearly declared in the sacred writings: "All have sinned, and come short of the glory of God; being justified freely by his grace through the redemption that is in Christ Jesus: whom God hath set forth to be a propitiation through faith in his blood, to declare his righteousness for the remission of sins that are past, through the forbearance of God; to declare, I say, at this time his righteousness: that he might be just, and the justifier of him which believeth in Jesus," Rom. iii. 23–26. But setting the consideration of Christ altogether aside, there is no doubt but that Socinus would carry off the prize in this contest. But while it is reckoned worth while to have any regard to him, it is easy to perceive that this heretic uses nothing but continued false reasonings and false conclusions; for it is made evident to us in Christ the Son, how and by what means God, infinitely merciful and infinitely just,—acting on the principles of strict justice with some, and of mere grace with others, but in exercising both the one and the other, both justice and mercy, in and through the Mediator, the one, indeed, in his own proper person, and the other towards those for whom he was surety,—hath declared himself.

But while Socinus despised and set at nought him and his grace, is it to be wondered at if he "became vain in his imaginations," and that his "foolish heart was darkened?"

For what need I say more? Doth not God exercise supreme and infinite mercy towards us, miserable and lost sinners, in pardoning our sins through Christ? Have we deserved any such thing, who, after doing all that we can do, even when roused and assisted by his grace, are still unprofitable servants? Did we appoint a sacrifice, that his anger might be averted, and that an atonement to his justice might be made from our own store-house, sheep-fold, or herd? Yea, when we were enemies to him, alienated from his life, without help and without strength, dead in trespasses and in sins, knowing of no such thing, wishing for or expecting no such thing, he himself "made Christ to be sin for us, who knew no sin," that he might "save us from the wrath to come;" that, an expiation being made for our sins, we might be presented blameless before him, to the praise and glory of his grace. But whether he showed the strictest justice and severity towards our surety, over whom he exercised a most gracious care, both on his own account[1] and for our sakes, and whom he did not spare, shall afterward be considered.

Whether, then, when our opponent, relying on these subtleties of his, concludes, "That there is no justice in God which dictates the necessity of punishing sin, and that therefore there is no reason why God cannot freely pardon the sins of whomsoever he may please, without any satisfaction received," and then, as if he had accomplished a glorious achievement, triumphs over the cross of our Lord and Saviour Jesus Christ, be not acting the part of a most silly trifler and absurd heretic, let the reader determine. But, as all the arguments which he afterward uses against the satisfaction of Christ have their foundation in this most false supposition, which the Scriptures, as hath been shown, so often contradict, and on which he always depends in all his disputations, whether those have acted for the interest of the church of God who have voluntarily surrendered to him this impregnable tower of truth, which he hath in vain laid siege to, that he might with greater audacity carry on his attacks upon the gospel, is well known to God. We, as we hope, instructed by his word, entertain very different sentiments from theirs on this point.

But when our opponent has come to the conclusion of this dispute, he introduces many fictions about the mere good-will of God in pardoning sins, about his ceasing from his right without injury to any one, about the injustice of the substitution of a surety in the room of sinners;—all which arguments, as they depend on a false foundation, yea, on a most base error, it would be easy here to show how vain, false, inconclusive, and absurd they are, unless we had determined, with God's will, to explain the doctrine of the satisfaction of Jesus Christ, the greatest treasure of the gospel, and to defend and vindicate it from the unjust calumnies of heretics, in the proper place and time.

CHAPTER XII.

The progress of the dispute to the theologians of our own country—The supreme authority of divine truth—Who they are, and what kind of men, who have gone into factions about this matter—The Coryphæus of the adversaries, the very illustrious Twisse—The occasion of his publishing his opinion—The opinion of the Arminians—The effects of the death of Christ, what—Twisse acknowledges punitory justice to be natural to God—The division of the dispute with Twisse—Maccovius' answers to the arguments of Twisse—The plan of our disputation.

We come now to those, and the consideration of their opinion, who, agreeing with us concerning the satisfaction of Jesus Christ,

[1] "Behold my servant, whom I uphold; mine elect, in whom my soul delighteth."—Isa. xlii. 1.—Tr.

as revealed in the Scriptures, yet, it being supposed that God willed the salvation of sinners, contend that the whole necessity of it flowed from the most free will of God, though they by no means deny sin-avenging justice to be natural to God.[1]

But those who maintain this opinion are so numerous and respectable, and men who have merited so highly of the church of God, that although the freeman of Christ, and taught to call no man on earth master in matters of religion, unless I had on my side not fewer and equally famous men, I should have a religious scruple publicly to differ from them. I acknowledge that every, even the least particle of divine truth is furnished from heaven with authority towards every disciple of Jesus Christ, who is the way, the truth, and the life, of holding it fast in the love and admiration of it, and of enforcing its claim, defence, and declaration, even though the whole world should rise up against him; but, perhaps, it would be unbecoming in one who would cheerfully enter as a disciple to oppose such great, learned men, and those, too, so well trained to the field of dispute, unless supported by the dignity and suffrages of others not inferior even to those in merit.

But if modesty must be violated, all will agree that it ought to be violated in the cause of truth, and especially as I perceive that the authority of some theologians is of so great weight with many of our countrymen, that, not having duly weighed and pondered the matter, but relying on this, they go into the opinion contrary to that which we have undertaken to defend. Considering it of importance to weigh the arguments which these very illustrious men have used, although I know myself not only unequal to the task, but that, in marshalling the line for such a controversy, I am not deserving of even a third or fourth place from the van, having been only accustomed to the popular mode of declaiming; however, I do not fear to engage in this undertaking, whatever it be, nothing doubting but that from my attempt, though weak, the readers will easily perceive that the truth might triumph gloriously, were any one furnished with better abilities to come forward in its defence.

But here, first of all the antagonists, and who, indeed, is almost equal to them all, the very learned Twisse[2] opposes himself to us; concerning whose opinion in general a few things are to be premised before we come to the answers of objections.

The consideration of Arminius' opinion concerning the efficacy of the death of Christ and its immediate bearing, gave occasion to this learned man of publishing his own sentiments. Arminius contends,

[1] They agree that the satisfaction by Christ is the way of salvation revealed in the Scriptures, but that it is so because God willed it should be so, and deny that there was any necessity for such a satisfaction arising from the nature of divine justice.—TR.

[2] Twiss. Vind. Grat. lib. i. p. 2, sect. 25, digress. 8.

"That Christ by his satisfaction only accomplished this much, that God now, consistently with the honour of his justice (as it had been satisfied), might pardon sinners if he willed so to do."

This most absurd opinion, so highly derogatory to divine grace and the merit of the death of Christ, this illustrious man was inclined to differ from, so far that he maintained that that consideration, namely, "That God could forgive sins, his justice notwithstanding, as having been satisfied," had no place among the effects of Christ's death.

But Arminius is the only one, so far as I know, among our opponents of this opinion; and he himself, in asserting it, is scarcely uniform and self-consistent. I may venture to affirm that of his followers there are none, unless it be some mean skulker, who swears by the words of his master. The opinion of Corvinus, which Twisse afterward discusses, is plainly different. Episcopius, likewise, after Arminius, the Coryphæus of that cause, and by far its most noble champion, defends this very sentiment of this learned man. The Pelagian tribe have become reconciled with the Socinians, rather than brandish any more that very sharp-pointed weapon which cut the throat of their own desperate cause.

Nor can I at all see how this divine truth of ours should contribute to the support of Arminianism, as this illustrious writer seems to signify; for is he who says that Christ by his death and satisfaction effected this, that God might forgive sins, his justice not opposing, bound also to affirm that he accomplished nothing farther? God forbid. Yea, he who, without the consideration of the oblation of Christ, could not but punish sins, that oblation being made, cannot punish those sins for which Christ offered himself;[1] yea, that he is more bound, in strict right and in justice, in respect of Jesus Christ, to confer grace and glory on all those for whom he died, I have in its proper season elsewhere demonstrated.

The learned Twisse grants that punitory or sin-avenging justice is *natural* to God, or that it is an essential attribute of the divine nature. This he very eloquently maintains; and several times, when it is introduced by the adversaries[2] whom he selected to refute, he gives his suffrage in its favour. But what else is that justice but a constant will of punishing every sin, according to the rule of his right? The learned gentleman, then, grants that an immutably constant will of punishing every sin is natural to God: how, then, is it possible that he should not punish it? for who hath opposed his will?

There are two parts of the Twissian disputation. The first is contained in four principal arguments, supported by various reasons, in which he attacks this sentiment,—namely, "That God cannot without a satisfaction forgive sin." In the second, he endeavours to

[1] Rom. iii. 23–26.

[2] Namely, Piscator and Lubbertus.

answer the arguments of Piscator and Lubbertus in confirmation of this point; and he intersperses everywhere, according to his custom, a variety of new arguments on the subject. We shall briefly consider what this learned man hath done in both parts.

As to what relates to the first or introductory part, perhaps our labour may appear superfluous. The judicious Maccovius hath, with great success, performed this task, giving by no means trifling, but rather, for the most part, very solid answers to those four arguments, which Twisse calls his principal, and in a very plain and perspicuous manner; as was his general custom in all his writings.

But neither the plan of our work permits us to withdraw from this undertaking, though unequal to it, nor, perhaps, hath Maccovius satisfied his readers in every particular. Indeed, some things seem necessary to be added, that this controversy with Twisse may occasion no trouble to any one for the future. This veteran leader, then, so well trained to the scholastic field, going before and pointing us out the way, we shall, with your good leave, reader, briefly try these arguments by the rule of Scripture and right reason; and I doubt not but we shall clearly demonstrate, to all impartial judges of things, that this learned man hath by no means proved what he intended.

CHAPTER XIII.

Twisse's first argument—Its answer—A trifling view of the divine attributes—Whether God could, by his absolute power, forgive sins without a satisfaction—To let sins pass unpunished implies a contradiction; and that twofold—What these contradictions are—Whether God may do what man may do—Whether every man may renounce his right—Whether God cannot forgive sins because of his justice—The second argument—Its answer—Distinctions of necessity—God doth no work without himself from absolute necessity—Conditional necessity—Natural necessity twofold—God doth not punish to the extent of his power, but to the extent of his justice—God always acts with a concomitant liberty—An argument of the illustrious Vossius considered—God "a consuming fire," but an intellectual one—An exception of Twisse's—Whether, independent of the divine appointment, sin would merit punishment—In punishment, what things are to be considered—The relation of obedience to reward and disobedience to punishment not the same—The comparison between mercy and justice by Vossius improperly instituted.

THE first argument of this great man is this: "If God cannot forgive sins without a satisfaction, it is either because he cannot on account of his justice, or because he cannot by his power; but neither of these can be affirmed."

Ans. That enumeration of the divine attributes, as to the present cause, is mere trifling: for what God cannot do in respect of *one* attribute, he can do in respect of *none;* or, in other words, that which cannot be done because of any one essential property, cannot be done because of them all. As, for instance, if there be any thing which God cannot do in respect of *truth,* he cannot do that in any manner or in any respect. In the acts of the divine will, purely free, the case is otherwise; for, in a divided sense, God may do any thing (that is, he may create new worlds), which if a decree of creating this and no other be supposed, he could not do. But the objects presented to any attribute of the divine nature admit not of various respects, but are in their own kind absolutely necessary; therefore, we deny the minor. Neither in respect of justice nor in respect of power can this be done.

But our learned antagonist leads the proof of it through its parts; and, first, after a marginal animadversion on a certain oversight of Piscator, he affirms "That it cannot be maintained that God cannot forgive sins by his power, without a satisfaction."

"For," says he, "if God by his might or absolute power cannot pardon sin, then it is absolutely impossible for sin to be pardoned, or not to be punished; therefore, not to pardon sin consists of contradictory terms. The contradiction, then, ought to be shown, as none appears from the formal terms. And, on the other hand, it is evident that man not only can pardon, but that it is his duty to pardon his enemies when they transgress against him."

Ans. The non-punishment of sin implies a contradiction,—not, indeed, formally and in the terms, but virtually and eminently in respect of the thing itself: for, in the first place, it implies that God is the Lord of mankind by a natural and indispensable right, but that mankind are not subject to him, neither as to obedience nor as to punishment, which would be the direct case if sin should pass with impunity; for that natural and necessary dependence being cut off (which, also, in another respect is moral) which accords to a rational creature in respect of its Creator and supreme Lord, which really comes to pass by means of sin, it cannot be renewed or made amends for but by punishment. In the second place, to hate sin, that is, to will to punish it, and not to hate sin, to will to let it pass unpunished, are manifestly contradictory.

If you say that God hath it in his power not to hate sin, you say that he hath the contrary in his power,—that is, that he can love sin; for if he hate sin of his free will, he may will the contrary, for "the divine will is not so determinately inclined towards any secondary object by any thing in itself that can justly oppose its inclination to its opposite." This Scotus maintains, and Twisse agrees with him. But to will good and to love justice are not less natural to God than to be himself. Here is, then, a double contradiction in that assertion of this very learned man, namely, "That God can forgive sin absolutely, without any satisfaction received."

" But it is manifest," says he, " that man not only can pardon, but that it is his duty to pardon his enemies; and, therefore, this does not imply a contradiction."

Ans. The supposition is denied, that God may do what man may do. That learned man raises this objection himself, that man may sin, which God cannot do, and at great length, and with much erudition, explains away this example. But as this instance of Twisse's is not quite satisfactory to us, we think proper to proceed in a different manner.

I say, then, in the first place, that divine and human forgiveness are plainly of a different kind. The forgiveness of man only respects the *hurt;* the forgiveness of God respects the *guilt.* Man pardons sins so far as any particular injury hath been done himself; God pardons sin as the good of the universe is injured. Secondly, Neither is it in the power of every man to let sins pass unpunished, yea, of none absolutely to whom the right of punishing is competent; for although a *private person* may recede from his right, which for the most part is of charity, yet it is by no means allowed to a *public person* to renounce his right, which is a right of government, especially if that renunciation should in any way turn out to the hurt of the public. In the third place, then, I say that that instance is nothing to the purpose; for although a private person may, at certain times, renounce his right and dominion in certain cases, and ought to do so, it doth not follow from that that God, whose right and dominion is natural and indispensable, and which he cannot renounce unless he deny himself, can do the same. In the fourth place, the non-punishment of sin is an injury to the universe; for the glory of divine justice would be affronted with impunity.

Our celebrated antagonist proceeds to the consideration of divine justice. " But neither," says he, " can it be consistently said that God cannot do this because of his justice, if it be supposed that he can do it by his power. But Scotus reasons with more judgment and accuracy on this point. 'The divine will is not so inclined towards any secondary object by any thing in itself,' says he, 'that can oppose its being justly inclined towards its opposite in the same manner, as without contradiction it may will its opposite; otherwise, it may will absolutely and not justly, which is inconsistent with divine perfection.'"

Ans. We maintain that God from his nature cannot do this, and, therefore, that he cannot either by his power or his justice; and as our learned antagonist produces no argument to prove that God can do it without resistance from his justice, but what flows from this false supposition, that he can do it by his power, it is not necessary to give ourselves any trouble on this head. But to Scotus we answer: The divine will may incline to things opposite, in respect of the egresses of all those divine attributes which constitute and create objects to themselves, but not in respect of those attributes which have no egress towards their objects but upon a condition supposed. As, for instance: God may justly speak or not speak with man; but it being supposed that he wills to speak, the divine will cannot be indifferent whether he speak truth or not. So much for his first principal argument.

The second is this: "If God cannot let sin pass unpunished, then he must punish it from an absolute necessity; but this no one can maintain consistently with reason."

This consequence the learned doctor supposes, without any argument to support it; but we deny the consequence, nor will he ever be able to prove that there is no other kind of necessity but an absolute necessity. There is also a necessity arising from a supposed condition, and which deprives not the agent of a concomitant liberty. God could not but create the world; but God did not create the world from an absolute necessity, although it was necessary upon a supposition that it should be created. It is necessary that God should speak truly, but he doth not speak from an absolute necessity; but it being supposed that he wills to speak, it is impossible that he should not speak truly. We say, therefore, that God cannot but punish sin, or that he necessarily punishes sin; not, however, from an absolute necessity of nature, as the Father begets the Son, but upon the suppositions[1] before mentioned,—by a necessity which excludes an antecedent indifference but not a concomitant liberty in the agent, for in punishing sins he acts by volition and with understanding.

"But that necessity," you will say, "of what kind soever it be, flows from the nature of God, not his will or decree; but all necessity of nature seems to be absolute." I acknowledge, indeed, that all necessity of nature, considered in the first act and thing signified,[2] is absolute in its kind; but in the second act, and in its exercise, it is not so. The reader will easily perceive now that our very learned antagonist had no reason for freely supposing that consequence; which I reckon the very lowest of all the devices he has fallen upon. "If, then," says he, "God must punish sin from a natural necessity, he must necessarily punish it to the extent of his power;" but this, with great accuracy, he shows to be absurd, by a variety of arguments.

Ans. Maccovius hath, some time ago, very clearly answered this reasoning. We reject his consequence, as built upon a false supposition; for that necessity from which God punisheth sin does not require that he should punish it to the extent of his power, but so far as is just. We do not conceive God to be a senseless, inanimate

[1] Namely, That he willed to create a rational being, and to permit it to transgress the law of its creation.—Tr.

[2] "Actu primo et signato,"—"In its first and manifested act, its first act and manifestation."—Ed.

agent, as if he acted from principles of nature, after a natural manner, without a concomitant liberty; for he doth all things freely, with understanding and by volition, even those things which by supposition he doth necessarily, according to what his most holy nature requires.

The argument which the celebrated Vossius uses against our opinion is of no greater weight.[1] "Every agent," says that very learned man, "that acts naturally, acts upon an object naturally receptive of its action: wherefore, if to punish were natural, namely, in that acceptation which necessity carries with it, such action could not pass from the person of a sinner to another person."

But this learned man is mistaken when he imagines that we affirm God to be such a natural agent as must, without sense and immediately, operate upon the object that is receptive of it, in a manner altogether natural, and without any concomitant liberty,—that is, without any free act of understanding or volition; for although God be "a consuming fire," he is an intellectual one. Nor is a sinner alone an object properly receptive of the exercise of God's vindicatory justice, as he hath committed the transgressions in his own person; for antecedent to every act of that justice, properly so called, in respect of the elect, God appointed a surety, and this surety being appointed, and all the sins of the elect laid upon him, he in their room and stead is the proper object of this vindicatory justice, so far as relates to their sins. "For he hath made him to be sin for us, who knew no sin; that we might be made the righteousness of God in him," 2 Cor. v. 21.

But Twisse thus replies, "If God punish as far as he can with justice,—that is, as far as sin deserves,—then it must be either as far as sin deserves according to the free constitution of God, or without any regard to the divine constitution. If according to the divine constitution, this is nothing else but to assert that God punishes not so far as he can, but so far as he wills. If without any regard to the divine constitution, then without the divine constitution sin so deserves punishment that God ought to punish sin because of his justice. But I conclude this to be false in this manner: If disobedience deserve punishment in this manner,—that is, without the divine constitution,—therefore obedience will also, in like manner, deserve a reward without the divine constitution; for no reason can be shown that any one should maintain that even angels have merited, by their obedience, that God should reward them with celestial glory."

But although these arguments are specious, yet, strictly considered, they have no greater weight than those already discussed; for in the

[1] At the end of the "Defensio Fidei Catholicæ de Satisfactione Christi," by Grotius, there is appended "G. J. Vossii Responsio ad Herm. Ravenspergeri Judicium de eodem." It is in this "Responsio" that the sentiments refuted by Owen occur.—Ed.

punishment of sin two things are to be considered:—1. The punishment itself, so far as it is in its own nature something grievous and troublesome to the creature, and proper to recover the violated right of God. In this respect we say that sin merits punishment antecedently to every free act of the divine will, or to the divine constitution; or, if you would rather have it thus expressed, that it is just that God should inflict punishment, considered as such, on the transgressor, without regard to any free constitution: for if, without regard to such a constitution, sin be sin, and evil, evil,—and unless it be so, to hate the greatest and best of Beings may be the highest virtue, and to love him the greatest vice,—why may not punishment be due to it without regard to such a consideration? 2. In punishment, the mode, time, and degree are especially to be considered. In respect of these God punishes sin according to the divine constitution; for the justice of God only demanding punishment in general, as including in it the nature of punishment, nothing hinders but that God should freely appoint the mode and degree of it. He punishes them because it is just that he should do so, and consequently indispensably necessary. He punishes in one mode or in another, in one degree or in another, because, according to his wisdom, he hath determined freely so to do. What we understand by modes and degrees of punishment shall be afterward explained.

"But," says our celebrated antagonist, "if disobedience thus deserve punishment, why should not obedience in like manner deserve a reward, for no reason to the contrary can be assigned?" I wish this learned man had not so expressed himself, for he will never be able to prove that the relation of obedience to reward and disobedience to punishment is the same; for between obedience and the reward there intervenes no natural obligation. God is brought under an obligation to no one for any kind of obedience; for "after we have done all, we are still unprofitable servants." But God's right that rational creatures should be subject to him, either by obedience or a vicarious punishment, is indispensable. In a word, obedience is due to God in such a manner, that from the nature of the thing he can be debtor to none in conferring rewards; but disobedience would destroy all dependence of the creature upon God, unless a recompense be made by punishment.

The celebrated Vossius, again, reasons improperly, in the passage before quoted, from a comparison made between justice and mercy. "The question is not," says he, "whether it be just that a satisfaction be received? but whether it be unjust that it should not be received? for it doth not follow that if God be merciful in doing one thing or another, that he would be unmerciful in not doing it." I acknowledge that it does not follow: for although mercy be natural to God as to the habit, yet because there is no natural obligation between it and its proper object, it is as to all its acts entirely free; for the nature of the thing about which it is employed is not indispensable, as we have shown before to be the case with regard to justice. So much for the learned Twisse's second argument, with the consideration of it.

CHAPTER XIV.

Twisse's third argument—A dispensation with regard to the punishment of sin, what, and of what kind—The nature of punishment and its circumstances—The instance of this learned opponent refuted—The considerations of rewarding and punishing different—How long, and in what sense, God can dispense with the punishment due to sin—God the supreme governor of the Jewish polity; also, the Lord of all—The fourth argument of Twisse—The answer—Whether God can inflict punishment on an innocent person—In what sense God is more willing to do acts of kindness than to punish—What kind of willingness that assertion respects—The conclusion of the answer to Twisse's principal arguments.

THE third argument is this: "God can inflict a milder punishment than sin deserves; therefore, he can by his absolute power suspend the punishment altogether."

Ans. I answer, that the punishment which a sin deserves may be considered in a twofold point of view:—1. As by means of it God compels to order a disobedient creature, that hath cast off its dependence on his supreme and natural dominion, in such a manner that his will may be done with that creature, that is itself unwilling to do it; and in this point of view he cannot inflict a more mild punishment than sin deserves. Yea, properly speaking, in this respect it cannot be said to admit of degrees, either milder or more severe. And in this sense we simply deny the foregoing proposition. 2. It may be considered in this other point of view,—namely, as God, for the greater manifestation of his glory, hath assigned to it modes, degrees, and other circumstances. But if punishment be considered in this view, we deny the sequel;[1] for though it be granted that he exerciseth liberty as to the modes and degrees, as these flow from the free appointment of God, it doth not follow that the punishment itself, so far as the nature of punishment is preserved in it, and which takes its rise from the natural justice of God, can be altogether dispensed with.

What says our learned antagonist to this? He supposes the author of the supplement his opponent, and discusses his opinion in a variety of subtile reasonings, in his answer concerning the extent and dif-

[1] Namely, That God, by his absolute power, can suspend the punishment of sin altogether.—TR.

ferent degrees of justice. But he confesses that these have no relation to Piscator; and as they are of no avail to the argument, we therefore pass over the consideration of them.

But this learned gentleman has still something to oppose to our reasoning; for he thus proceeds, "God may reward beyond merit; therefore, he may punish less than what is merited." But this reason is evidently of no force; for besides that arguments from opposites do not hold always good in theology, as hath been shown in various instances by Maccovius, we have before demonstrated at large that the relation between remunerating grace and punitory justice is not the same.[1] Moreover, these considerations all along arise not from the nature of punishment, but from its degrees, about which we have no controversy, for we have never said that God in punishing sins acts without any concomitant liberty, which respects those degrees.

But forasmuch as Socinians[2] argue from the divine dispensation with regard to the punishment of sins to the free pardon of them without any satisfaction, we must say a few things in reply to this argument of our learned antagonist, as it seems pretty near akin to them, and as they are so very eager in wresting every thing to favour their own side of the question.

The divine dispensation, then, with the punishment of sins, respects either temporary or eternal punishment; but a temporary punishment may be considered either in respect of monitory threats or of a peremptory decree, and both in respect of the time of the infliction and of the degrees in the punishment to be inflicted. But God, as the avenger of sin, is considered in Scripture in a twofold point of view:—1. As the Legislator and supreme Lord of the Jews and their commonwealth; whose state, from that circumstance, Josephus calls a "theocracy:" or, 2. As the supreme Lord and just Judge of the universe. If these considerations be properly attended to, the subtleties of Crellius are easily dissolved: for God, as the Legislator and supreme Ruler of the Jewish republic, ofttimes dispensed with temporary punishments, as denounced in his threatenings, both as to the place, degree, and time of their execution; but God, as the supreme Lord and just Judge of the universe, doth not dispense with the eternal punishment of sin, to be inflicted at the proper and appointed time. The learned Twisse's fourth argument remains only to be considered.

"God is able," says he, "to inflict any torture, however great, even an infernal one, upon any person, without the consideration of

[1] That is, their relation to their objects, or their qualities considered in this point of view, is different. Divine justice necessarily operates towards its object to punish the sinner, otherwise it would not be justice; but as no creature can merit any thing of God, it depends on God's good pleasure whether he bestow rewards or not.—TR.

[2] Crellius, "Of the True Religion," p. 308.

any demerit; therefore, he is also able, notwithstanding the greatest demerit, to suspend the greatest punishment whatever. The antecedent hath been proved; the consequence from it is notorious, as God is more willing to do good than to punish."

Ans. 1. We have before observed that this mode of reasoning does not always hold good in theology; neither, however, in the second place, are these opposites, namely, to inflict torture and to suspend punishment, for torture and punishment are different. But to inflict an infernal punishment upon any innocent person is a thing impossible; for punishment supposes a transgression: and, therefore, not to inflict punishment upon a guilty person is also impossible; for transgression, from the very nature of the thing, requires punishment. But it is astonishing that this learned writer should insist on the proof of the sequel, namely, "That God is more willing to do good than to punish," as he hath many times, by very strong arguments, disallowed the natural inclination of the Deity towards the good of the creature; nor will he ever be able to prove that God is inclined to bestow such kind of benefits on a sinful creature as are opposite to the punishment due to sin, without regard to Christ and his satisfaction. But that difference respects a will commanding and exhorting according to morality, not decreeing or acting naturally.

And these are what this learned writer calls his "principal arguments;" in which he contends that God can let sin pass unpunished without any satisfaction. I hope that impartial judges, however great respect they may have for the name of Twisse, will not be offended that I have made these short answers to his arguments; as certainly they have been conducted without violence or sarcasm, and by no means from any weak desire of attacking so very illustrious a man, for whose many and great qualities none can have a greater respect. But I have engaged in this task from an earnest desire of preserving undiminished the glory of divine justice, and of establishing the necessity of the satisfaction of Christ, lest the Socinians should wrest to their purpose the arguments of this learned man, on the principal of which they place a principal dependence, and by which they acknowledge that they have been induced to adopt heretical opinions.

Our very learned antagonist adds other arguments to these; some of which have been satisfactorily answered by Maccovius; others belong not, according to our view of it, to the present controversy; and others will come to be considered in our vindication of the arguments of Piscator and Lubbertus, impugned by this celebrated writer, of which we shall take a short review, and, therefore, shall not now enter into any particular consideration of them.

CHAPTER XV.

The defence of Sibrandus Lubbertus against Twisse—The agreement of these very learned men in a point of the utmost importance—A vindication of his argument from God's hatred against sin—Liberality and justice different—The opinion of Lubbertus undeservedly charged with atheism—What kind of necessity of operation we suppose in God; this pointed out—The sophistical reasoning of this learned writer—How God is bound to manifest any property of his nature—The reasons of Lubbertus, and Twisse's objections to the same considered—That passage of the apostle, Rom. i. 32, considered and vindicated—His[1] mode of disputing rejected—The force of the argument from Rom. i. 32—The "righteous judgment of God," what—Our federal representative, and those represented by him, are one mystical body—An answer to Twisse's arguments, Exod. xxxiv. 6, 7—The learned writer's answer respecting that passage—A defence of the passage—Punitory justice a name of God—Whether those for whom Christ hath made satisfaction ought to be called guilty—Ps. v. 4–6, the sense of that passage considered—From these three passages the argument is one and the same—Lubbertus' argument from the definition of justice weighed—How vindicatory justice is distinguished from universal—The nature of liberality and justice evidently different—Punishment belongs to God—In inflicting punishment, God vindicates his right—Will and necessity, whether they be opposite—The end of the defence of Lubbertus.

THE learned Twisse, when about to reply to the arguments of Lubbertus,[2] brings forward two assertions of his, to the first of which he consents, but not to the latter. The first maintains "corrective justice to be essential to God," which he approves; and herein we congratulate this very learned man that thus far, at least, he assents to the truth, and in so doing hath given cause to the Socinians to grieve. But, that "it is natural to God to hate and punish sin," which is Lubbertus' second assertion, he denies. The nicety of his discrimination here is truly astonishing; for what is God's hatred against sin but this corrective justice? How, then, is it possible that that justice should be natural to God, and the hatred of sin not so likewise? I very well know that the learned man will not allow that there is any such affection as hatred in God, properly so called. What is it, then, else than the constant will of punishing sin? but that is the very vindicatory justice of which we treat. Besides, if to hate sin be not natural to God, then it is a thing free and indifferent to him; he may then not hate it; he may, according to the opinion of Scotus formerly mentioned, as approved by Twisse, will its contrary, —that is, he may love and approve of sin, though "he be of purer eyes than to behold iniquity." But, with good reason, he farther

[1] Namely, Twisse's.—TR.

[2] A learned protestant divine, who was born in Friesland, and lived 1556–1625. He wrote several works against Bellarmine, Socinus, Arminius, etc., but his best work is said to be "De Papâ Romanâ."—ED.

maintains that "mercy is essential to God, and yet that it is not necessary that he should show mercy to any one; but of his free good pleasure he showeth mercy to whomsoever he showeth mercy." We have again and again before shown that justice and mercy, in respect of their exercise, are different. God is under no obligation to exercise mercy towards any one, but he owes it to himself to preserve his own natural right and dominion over his rational creatures; and the learned gentleman cannot show that there is any such obligation, arising from the nature of the thing itself, between remunerating justice and liberality, on which he next insists, and their objects, as there is between corrective justice and its objects.

But he brings a grievous charge, no less than even that of atheism, against this sentiment of Lubbertus, and on a double account: for, first, he says that "hence it follows that God is a necessary and not a free agent;" and he calls that proposition a spreading gangrene. 1. But theologians agree, and without any risk of atheism, that God is, in respect of his operations within himself, a necessary agent. 2. If it be necessary that God should do any thing upon some condition supposed, is he therefore to be accounted a necessary and not a free agent? Perhaps never any one hath made God more a necessary agent than Twisse himself doth, for he everywhere maintains, that upon the supposition of a decree, it is necessary that God should do all things in conformity to it; which, however, I do by no means mention as finding fault with. Upon the supposition of a decree, for instance, God could not but create the world; but is he therefore to be called a necessary agent in the creation of the world? By no means. But you will say, "That necessity flows from the free will of God, but that which you dream of arises from the principles of his nature, and therefore how widely different!" I willingly grant, indeed, that the decree of creating the world flowed from the free will of God; but this being supposed, it was necessary to the divine nature, which is immutable, that it should be created. Nor do we ascribe any other kind of natural necessity to God in punishing sins. The decree of creating rational creatures bound to render him obedience, and so far liable to his right and dominion, and that he willed to permit these creatures to transgress the law of their creation, flowed merely from his free will; but these things being once supposed, it necessarily belongs to the divine nature, as it is just, to punish those who so transgress. But that God exerciseth a concomitant liberty in punishing them, we have several times allowed, and we have no doubt but, if this be atheism, it is also Christianity.

Secondly, "Is God at all bound," says our very learned antagonist, "or in any manner obliged, to manifest his justice, more than to manifest his mercy, munificence, and liberality? It is evident that God is not bound to exercise any one property whatever more than another. Wherefore, either all things must be said to be necessarily performed by God, and even that the world was not made of his free will, but from a natural necessity; or that all things have been, and still are, freely done by God." But besides that this reasoning is sophistical, it injures not our cause. The whole matter may be clearly explained in one word: God is not absolutely bound to manifest any property of his nature, much less one more than another, for this respects the free purpose of God; but upon a condition supposed, God may be more bound to exercise one property than another, for this relates to its exercise. But none of us have said that it is necessary that God should punish sin because he is necessarily bound to demonstrate his justice: in this very thing he demonstrates his justice indeed;[1] but it is necessary that he should punish sin because he is just. The learned writer then confounds the decree of manifesting the glory of the divine properties, to which God is absolutely bound by none of his properties, with the exercise of these properties upon a condition supposed; which we have endeavoured to prove to be necessary with respect to vindicatory justice.

In what sense all things are said to be done by God necessarily, though he be a free agent, hath been already explained. By these arguments, then, whereby he endeavours to weigh down our opinion with prejudices, it is evident that our antagonist hath nothing availed himself. Let us now see whether he hath been more successful in his replies to Lubbertus than in his system of opposition.

He briefly states five arguments of Lubbertus, each of which he answers in order.

That passage of the apostle to the Romans, chap. i. 32, "Who, knowing the judgment" (that is, the just right or righteous judgment) "of God, that they which commit such things are worthy of death," is quoted as a proof of this doctrine by Lubbertus. Twisse thus replies: "I acknowledge that they who commit such things are worthy of death. But it by no means follows from this that it is necessary that God should punish them; which I shall demonstrate by a twofold argument: For if that followed, it would follow that they who commit such things must necessarily be punished; but the elect, because of sin, are worthy of death, but they are not punished at all, much less necessarily. Will you say, because they who have committed such things are worthy of death, that therefore it is necessary, from an absolute necessity, that either they or others,—that is, that either they themselves, who are deserving of death, or some one else on their account, though innocent,—should be punished? Who can digest such a consequence as this? Again: If they are worthy of death, then they shall die the death; either, then, a temporal or eternal one. Beyond all doubt, he will answer an eternal

[1] Rom. i. 18.

death. It is necessary, therefore, that they should exist to all eternity, and by an absolute necessity, to the end that they may be punished to all eternity. And so, then, God cannot annihilate a creature."

But, with this great man's good leave, neither his mode of disputing,—namely, by substituting a double argument in the place of one solid and clear answer,—is at all satisfactory, nor are these arguments of any service to his cause, the first of which is captious and not at all solid, the other too nice and curious. For, first, Lubbertus does not contend that God cannot pardon sin without satisfaction, because simply, by some reason or other, sinners are worthy of death; but for this reason only, because the righteous judgment or just right of God is, that they who commit such things are worthy of death, and that, therefore, it would be unjust in God not to inflict that punishment,—namely, because, according to the justice of God, which Twisse himself acknowledges to be natural and essential to him, they are worthy of death, and therefore necessarily to be punished. But the arguments of Twisse do not prove the contrary; for the elect themselves are worthy of death, and therefore necessarily to be punished,—not from an absolute necessity in respect of the mode of acting in God the punisher, but in respect of a condition supposed, and which excludes not the liberty of the agent. That is to say, God may inflict the punishment due to one on another, after,—in consequence of his own right and the consent of that other,—he hath laid the sins upon that other on account of which he inflicts the punishment. He might punish the elect either in their own persons, or in their surety standing in their room and stead; and when he is punished, they also are punished: for in this point of view the federal head and those represented by him are not considered as distinct, but as one; for although they are not one in respect of personal unity, they are, however, one,—that is, one body in mystical union, yea, *one mystical Christ;*[1]—namely, the surety is the head, those represented by him the members; and when the head is punished, the members also are punished. Nor could even he himself be called a surety absolutely innocent: for although he was properly and personally innocent, he was imputatively and substitutively guilty; for "God made him to be sin for us;" He "laid on him the iniquity of us all."[2]

The second argument which this learned writer uses to confute the conclusion of Lubbertus is of no greater weight. We are not in the counsels of God, so that we can precisely pronounce with regard to his judgments and his ways. That God is able absolutely to reduce to nothing any creature that he hath created out of nothing,

[1] See 1 Cor. xii. 12, etc., "For as the body is one, and hath many members, and all the members of that one body, being many, are one body; so also is Christ," etc.—TR.
[2] 2 Cor. v. 21; Isa. liii. 6.

no one can doubt; but it being supposed that that creature is guilty of sin, and that that sin, according to the right and justice of God, deserves eternal death, we with confidence maintain that God, who cannot deny himself, cannot reduce it to nothing. Neither is there any thing absurd that can be inferred from this.

To the second proof brought from the word of God, declaring himself by that name of his, "Who will by no means clear the guilty," Exod. xxxiv. 6, 7, he answers: "It is true that God will by no means clear the guilty, yet it is evident that not a few are cleared by God. The guilty, then, whom he doth not clear, must be those who have neither repented nor believed in Christ. Hence it follows that every one hath either been punished or will be punished, either in himself or in Christ; which we do not at all deny. But it doth not at all follow hence that God doth this from a necessity of nature, for it is possible that it may proceed from the free will of God; neither doth it belong to him to exercise his mercy and bounty from a necessity of nature, but of his free will."

But, 1. It is of no service to his cause to urge that God does not punish some guilty sinners in their own persons, but clears them, when this learned man grants, yea, contends, that they have all been punished in Christ their head, by whom justice was fully satisfied. 2. It hath been several times shown before how God, from a necessity of nature, punishes sin, and yet with a concomitant liberty of will; and the difference between justice and mercy, in respect of their exercise and egress towards their proper objects, hath been shown; so that we do not think it proper to insist farther on these at present. These considerations, then, being set aside, it is evident that this learned man has not attended to the force of the argument: for it does not amount to this, that in respect of the event God clears none unpunished, either in themselves or in their surety,—an assertion which nobody but a Socinian speaks against; but rather to this, that as punitory justice is a natural attribute of God, a very considerable portion of his essential glory, yea, a well-known name of God, he can "by no means clear the guilty," unless he were to deny himself, and deliver up his glory to another,—than which nothing is farther from God. But those for whom the divine justice hath been satisfied by Christ ought not, in respect of the demand of that justice, to be called guilty, for their obligation to punishment, namely, the guilt of sin, is taken away; so that it is just with God to deliver them from the wrath to come, although it be free to him at what time he may will that that deliverance, in respect of them, should take place and be manifested to their consciences, that so "being justified by faith, they may have peace with God."

To those verses cited by Lubbertus from Ps. v. 4–6, he thus replies: "The prophet is testifying," says he, "that God hates all who work iniquity; however, it is sufficiently evident that God does not punish all who work iniquity, for he does not punish the elect. I acknowledge that God will in his own time destroy all the wicked out of Christ; but of his free will, and from no consideration of necessity, as he is an agent entirely free."

I am not altogether satisfied with this assertion, "That God doth not punish all who work iniquity;" neither does the instance of the elect confirm it, for even the learned gentleman does not deny that all their sins have been punished in Christ. We maintain alone that God cannot but punish every sin, because he is just; but whether he choose to do this in their own persons or in their surety rests entirely with himself: therefore, it doth not derogate from his justice that he transferred the sins of some upon Christ, and punished them in him. But they themselves, though personally guilty before Christ took their guilt upon himself, are not, however, punished, nor can be accounted guilty in respect of the judgment of God, their sins not being imputed to them; or, they ought to be said to have been punished in Christ their head, with whom they are now closely united. In the second place, we have shown before, and the learned gentleman acknowledges it, that a free act of the will may be consistent with some regard to necessity.

Allow me, then, from these three passages of Scripture cited by Lubbertus to collect one argument only; which, if I mistake not, no one of the various arguments of our very learned antagonist, nor even all of them, will be able to overthrow. It is to this purpose: If that just right or righteous "judgment of God" be essential,—namely, that which is made manifest and known to all by nature;[1] if his avenging justice be such that he "will by no means clear the guilty;"[2] if as he hates sin, so he will "destroy all the workers of iniquity,"[3]—then it is natural to God to punish sin, and he cannot let it pass unpunished, for he can do nothing contrary to his natural attributes, exercised about their proper objects. But the former part of the argument is true;[4] so also must the latter.

But Lubbertus likewise reasons by an argument taken from the common definition of justice, to which Twisse also refers. "Vindicatory justice," says he, "is the eternal will of God to give to every one his own; therefore, it belongs truly or naturally to God." Twisse cites these words from Lubbertus; for his writings against Vossius I have not by me at present. Now, although this justly celebrated man sometimes agrees to this conclusion, yet as he twitches[5] the argument various ways, we shall, as briefly as possible, bring it in

[1] See Rom. i. 32. [2] See Exod. xxxiv. 7. [3] Ps. v. 4–6.

[4] Being founded on the words of Scripture.—TR.

[5] "Objects to the argument on various grounds, which we shall, as briefly as possible, consider in succession."—ED.

regular order to a point. "First of all," says he, "allow me to put you in mind that that definition of justice holds good only with regard to justice in general, but not with regard to vindicatory justice in particular; for the whole of justice is employed in giving to every one his own." I have said before that that definition of the civilians was not quite agreeable to me, nor in every respect satisfactory. But the objection of Twisse is of no weight: for vindicatory justice is not distinguished from universal justice, or justice generally so called, as to its habit, but only in respect of its egress to its proper object; and, therefore, nothing ought to be included in the definition which is not found also in the thing itself. Although, then, the learned opponent throws obstacles in the way, he cannot deny that vindicatory justice is "a will to give to every one his own, or what is due to him."

"But let Lubbertus bethink himself," says Twisse, "whether the divine bounty is not likewise the eternal will of the Deity to give to some beyond what is their own. Would it not, then, justly follow that it is necessary, and even from absolute necessity, that he should exercise his bounty towards some?"

But neither is this comparison between things dissimilar of the smallest advantage to our adversary's cause: for,—1. The objects themselves about which these attributes are employed are very different; for who does not see that there cannot be any comparison formed between the giving to every one according to his right, and giving to some beyond their right? That to give to any one beyond his right is a most free act of the will, the thing itself declares; but to give to every one his own, or what is due to him, the very thing itself requires. All acknowledge that it depends on the mere good pleasure of the Deity whether he may will to be bounteous towards any; but who but an impious wretch would be bold enough to dispute whether he may will to be just towards any? But besides; supposing a constant will in the Deity of giving to some beyond their right, or of bestowing on them more than they deserve, in what respect it would not be necessary (the question does not respect absolute necessity) to him to exercise that bounty towards these some, I absolutely do not comprehend. But with regard to the divine bounty, and in what sense that is ascribed to God, and what kind of habitude of the divine will it denotes, this is not the place to inquire.

He again says: "If hence it follow that it is necessary that God should give to each his due, it will certainly be necessary that he should give to each of us eternal damnation."

That punishment belongs not to us, but to God himself, the learned gentleman will afterward acknowledge. But God may give to every one his own, or what is due to every one, in the infliction of punishment, although he do not inflict it on the sinners themselves, but on their surety, substituted in their room and stead. Thus he gives glory to his justice, and does no injury to us: for no one can demand it as his right to be punished; for no one hath a right to require punishment, which is an involuntary evil, but rather becomes subject to the right of another.

To these he replies: "If justice be only the *will* of giving to every one his own, it is not the *necessity* of giving it."

But here the learned gentleman trifles; for *will* and *necessity* are not opposed, as a thing itself may be prior, and the mode or affection of it posterior, to some other things, either in the first or second act.[1] Neither hath any one defined the justice of God by necessity, although from his justice it is necessary that he should act justly. Though it be the will of God, namely, "to give every one what is his due," yet it is a constant and immutable will, which, as it differs not in any respect from the divine essence itself, must exist necessarily; and a proper object for its exercise being supposed, it must necessarily operate, though it act freely.

In the last place, then, this celebrated writer denies that "punishment can properly be called ours, in such a sense that, from his will of giving to every one his own, it should be necessary that God should inflict it upon us sinners;" but he asserts that "it belongs to God, as having the full power either of inflicting or relaxing it." That punishment is ours, or belongs to us, cannot be said with propriety; it must be traced to the source whence it hath its rise,—that is, whence it is just that it should be inflicted upon sinners; but this is the just right or righteous judgment of God, Rom. i. 32. Thus far, then, it may be reckoned among the things that belong to God, as it is his justice that requires it should be inflicted. But it does not follow that God has a full power of inflicting it or relaxing it, because in this sense it may be accounted among the things which belong to him. God owes it to himself to have a proper regard to the honour of all his own perfections.

We choose not to enter any farther on the arguments which this learned writer advances, either in his disputations against Lubbertus, or in his answers to his arguments; partly as they coincide with those mentioned before, and have been considered in the vindication of the argument taken from the consideration of God's hatred against sin; and partly as they militate only against a natural and absolute necessity, which in the present case we do not assert.

[1] God's will of giving to every man his own was from everlasting, justice being an essential attribute of his unchangeable nature; but it is only after the supposition of a rational being that had sinned, that he must necessarily,—that is, from the very principles of his nature,—exercise that will towards sinners, and give them the wages of sin, namely, death.—TR. The Latin is :- "Cum prior res ipsa sit, posterior aliquarum rerum, vel in actu primo vel secundo, modus seu affectio,"—"Since the former is the thing itself, the latter a mode or affection of some things," etc.—ED.

CHAPTER XVI.

Piscator's opinion of this controversy—How far we assent to it—Twisse's arguments militate against it—How God punishes from a natural necessity—How God is a "consuming fire"—God's right, of what kind—Its exercise necessary, from some thing supposed—Whence the obligation of God to exercise it arises—Other objections of Twisse discussed.

THE consideration of what our justly celebrated antagonist hath advanced against Piscator,[1] whom he declares to hold the first place among the theologians of the present day, and to shine as far superior to the rest as the moon doth to the lesser stars, shall put an end to this dispute. He has chosen Piscator's notes upon his Collation of Vorstius,[2] as the subject of his consideration and discussion. In general we are inclined to give our voice in favour of the sentiments of Piscator; but as the disciples of Christ ought to call none on earth master in matters of religion, we by no means hold ourselves bound to support all the phrases, arguments, or reasons that he may have used in defence of his opinion. Setting aside, then, all anxious search after words, expressions, and the minutiæ of similes, which I could wish this distinguished writer had paid less attention to, we will endeavour to repel every charge brought against our common and principal cause, and to place this truth, which we have thus far defended, as we are now speedily hastening to a conclusion, beyond the reach of attacks and trouble from its adversaries.

The first argument, then, of Piscator, to which he replies, is taken from that comparison made in Heb. xii. 29, between God in respect of his vindicatory justice and a "consuming fire." From this passage Piscator concludes, "That as fire, from the property of its nature, cannot but burn combustible matter when applied to it, and that by a natural necessity; so God, from the perfection of his justice, cannot but punish sin when committed,—that is, when presented before that justice."[3] What he asserts, with regard to a natural and absolute necessity, we do not admit; for God neither exerciseth nor can exercise any act towards objects without himself in a natural manner, or as an agent merely natural. He, indeed, is a fire, but rational and intelligent fire. Although, then, it be no less necessary to him to punish sins than it is to fire to burn the combustible matter applied to it, the same manner of operation, however, accords not to him as to fire, for he worketh as an intelligent agent; that is, with a concomitant liberty in the acts of his will, and a consistent liberty in the acts of his understanding. We agree, then, with Piscator in his conclusion,

1 A learned professor of divinity at Herborn. He was born at Strasburg 1546, and died 1626. He was the author of several commentaries, controversial treatises, and a translation of the Bible into German.—ED.

2 "In Collationem Vorstii." The translation is not very intelligible. Vorstius wrote a work with this title, "Parasceue ad amicam collationem cum Jo. Piscatore," and Owen refers to Piscator's notes upon it.—ED.

though not in his manner of leading his proof.[1] The objections made to it by the learned Twisse we shall try by the standard of truth.

First, then, he maintains, and with many laboured arguments, that God doth not punish sin from a necessity of nature, which excludes every kind of liberty But whom do these kinds of arguments affect? They apply not at all to us; for Piscator himself seems to have understood nothing else by a "natural necessity" than that necessity which we have so often discussed, particularly modified: for he says, that "God doth some things by a natural necessity, because by nature he cannot do otherwise." That is, sin being supposed to exist, from the strict demands of that justice which is natural to him, he cannot but punish it, or act otherwise than punish it; although he may do this without any encroachment on his liberty, as his intellectual will is inclined to happiness by a natural inclination, yet wills happiness with a concomitant liberty; for it would not be a will should it act otherwise, as freedom of action is the very essence of the will. But the arguments of Twisse do not oppose this kind of necessity, but that only which belongs to inanimate, merely natural agents, which entirely excludes all sorts of liberty, properly so called.

Let us particularly examine some of this learned gentleman's arguments: "If," says he, "God must punish sin from a necessity of nature, he must punish it as soon as committed." Granted, were he to act by such a necessity of nature as denotes a necessary principle and mode of acting; but not if by a necessity that is improperly so called, because it is supposed that his nature necessarily requires that he should so act. As, for instance: suppose that he wills to speak, he must, by necessity of his nature, speak truly, for God cannot lie; yet he speaks freely when he speaks truly.

Again: "If," says he, "God punished from a necessity of nature, then, as often as he inflicted punishment, he would inflict it to the utmost of his power, as fire burns with all its force; but this cannot be said without blasphemy."

Here again this learned man draws absurd conclusions from a false supposition. The nature of God requires that he should punish as far as is just, not as far as he is able. It is necessary, sin being supposed to exist, that he should inflict punishment,—not the greatest that he is able to inflict, but as great as his right and justice require; for in inflicting punishment, he proceeds freely, according to the

[1] It is not Piscator's reasoning, but the kind of necessity implied in the reasoning, to which Owen takes exception. The words "nature" and "natural" also occasion considerable ambiguity. Justice is *natural* and *necessary*, according to Owen, in so far as it is not an act of the *will* merely; but he does not hold it to be natural in Piscator's sense, as operating by a blind and physical necessity, apart from the exercise of intelligence and volition, and the existence of an object requiring the manifestation of it. We might render the passage above as follows: "To this extent, then, I adopt Piscator's conclusion,—namely, in so far as he maintains the existence of a necessity, but not as regards the mode or kind of it."—ED.

rule of these. It is necessary that the glory of the divine holiness, purity, and dominion should be vindicated; but in *what manner*, at *what time*, in *what degree*, or *by what kind of punishment*, belongs entirely to God, and we are not of his counsels. But I am fully confident that the arguments last urged by this learned gentleman may be answered in one word. I say, then, God punishes according to what is due to sin by the rule of his right, not to what extent he is able. As, for instance: God does not use his omnipotence from an absolute necessity of nature; but supposing that he wills to do any work without himself, he cannot act but omnipotently. Neither, however, doth it hence follow that God acts to the utmost extent of his power, for he might have created more worlds. We do not, then, affirm that God is so bound by the laws of an absolute necessity that, like an insensible and merely natural agent, it would be impossible for him, by his infinite wisdom, to assign, according to the rule and demand of his justice, degrees, modes, duration, and extension of punishment, according to the degrees of the demerit or circumstances of the sin, or even to transfer it upon the surety, who has voluntarily, and with his own approbation, substituted himself in the room of sinners: but we only affirm that his natural and essential justice indispensably requires that every sin should have its "just recompense of reward;" and were not this the case, a sinful creature might emancipate itself from the power of its Creator and Lord. This very learned man having, according to his usual custom, introduced these preliminary observations, at length advances his answers to Piscator's argument, the nature and quality of which we shall particularly consider. That which he chiefly depends upon, which he forges from the Scripture, that asserts God, in respect of sin, to be a "consuming fire," we have examined in the proof of our second argument, and have shown of how little weight it is to invalidate the force of our argument.

To that asseveration of Abraham, "Shall not the Judge of all the earth do right?" he thus answers, "He will do right certainly, but his own right, and will exercise it according to his own free appointment. But without the divine appointment I acknowledge no right to the exercise of which God can be influenced by any kind of necessity."

Ans. That God exerciseth his right, or doeth right, according to his own free appointment, may be admitted in a sound sense; for in that exercise of his right he uses volition and understanding, or, more properly, he hath not appointed or determined so to act, for so to act is natural and essential to him concerning the things about which there is no free determination. It is, indeed, of the free determination of God that any right can be exercised, or any attribute manifested, for he freely decreed to create creatures, over which he hath a right, but he might not have decreed it so; and in every exercise of his right there are certain things, which we have mentioned before, which are not the objects of free determination. But that no right belongs to God without his divine appointment, to the exercise of which he is bound, is asserted without probability, and appears evidently false; for supposing that God willed to create rational creatures, does it depend upon his free determination that the right of dominion and the exercise of it should belong to him? If so, God might be neither the Lord nor God of his creatures, and a rational creature may be neither creature nor rational; for both its creation and reason suppose a dependence on and subjection to some Lord and Creator. If the right, then, of dominion depended on the free determination of God, then God might freely and justly determine that he would neither have nor exercise such right; for he might determine the contrary of that which he hath freely determined, without any injustice or any incongruity. From himself, then, and not from any one without himself,—that is, from his own nature,—he receives the obligation to exercise his right, both of dominion and of justice. Thus by nature he must speak truly, if he wills to speak.

"But I cannot," says this renowned man, "sufficiently express my astonishment at this very grave divine's assertion,[1]—namely, 'That God, without injury to his justice, may will evil antecedently to whomsoever he pleases;' for which I do not find fault with him, but that he does not assert that God, for the same or a better reason, might do good to a creature, notwithstanding its demerit, by pardoning its sin."

If by "willing evil antecedently" be understood his willing to inflict evil without regard to the demerit of sin, it is a point too intricate for me to determine. If the evil refer *to the infliction of it*, I must differ from this learned doctor. If it refer to the *willing*, the assertion avails not his cause; for if we suppose that God, without doing injury to any one, without dishonouring any of his own attributes, without regard to sin, hath decreed to punish a creature for the sin that it was to commit, would it not thence follow that God might let sin pass unpunished, in despite both of his own glory, and to the entire destruction of the dependence of rational creatures?[2] Nor is the following comment of our celebrated opponent of any greater weight,—namely, "That God would not be omnipotent if he necessarily punished sin, for thence it would follow that God cannot annihilate a sinful creature which he created out of nothing; which," says he, "is evidently contrary to omnipotence."

But how many things are there which this learned gentleman himself acknowledges that God, with respect to his decree, cannot do, without any disparagement to his omnipotence! He could not break the bones of Christ; but the person must be deprived of reason

[1] Namely, Piscator's.—TR.

[2] Because if he punished a creature for sin merely because he willed or determined so to do, and not because the nature of sin necessarily so required, he might as easily will the contrary; and, consequently, the subordination of the creature would be entirely subverted.—TR.

who would assert that this is any diminution of the divine omnipotence. If, then, there be many things which God cannot do, without any the smallest detraction from his omnipotence, because by a free determination he hath decreed not to do them, is he to be thought less omnipotent, so to speak, because he cannot, on account of his justice, let sins committed pass unpunished? Is God not omnipotent because, on account of his nature, he cannot lie? Yea, he would not be omnipotent if he could renounce his right and justice; for to permit a sinful creature to shake off his natural dominion is not a mark of omnipotence but of impotence, than which nothing is more remote from God.

After having brought the dispute thus far, and accurately weighed what remains of Dr Twisse's answer to Piscator, there seemed to me nothing that could occur to give any trouble to an intelligent reader. As there is no reason, then, either to give farther trouble to the reader or myself on this point, we here conclude the controversy; and this I do with entertaining the strongest hopes that no person of discretion, or who is unacquainted with the pernicious devices which almost everywhere abound, will impute it to me as a matter of blame, that I, a person of no consideration, and so very full, too, of employment, that I could devote only a few leisure hours to this disputation, should have attacked the theological digression of a man so very illustrious and renowned, not only among our own countrymen, but even in foreign nations, as the attack has been made in the cause of truth.

CHAPTER XVII.

Rutherford reviewed—An oversight of that learned man—His opinion of punitory justice—He contends that divine justice exists in God freely—The consideration of that assertion—This learned writer and Twisse disagree—His first argument—Its answer—The appointment of Christ to death twofold—The appointment of Christ to the mediatorial office an act of supreme dominion—The punishment of Christ an act of punitory justice—An argument of that learned man, easy to answer—The examination of the same—The learned writer proves things not denied—Passes over things to be denied—What kind of necessity we ascribe to God in punishing sins—A necessity upon a condition supposed—What the suppositions are upon which that necessity is founded—A difference between those things which are necessary by a decree and those which are so from the divine nature—The second argument of that learned man—His obscure manner of writing pointed out—Justice and mercy different in respect of their exercise—What it is to owe the good of punitory justice to the universe—This learned man's third argument—The answer—Whether God could forbid sin, and not under the penalty of eternal death—Concerning the modification of punishment in human courts from the divine appointment—The manner of it—What this learned author understands by the "internal court" of God—This learned author's fourth argument—All acts of grace have a respect to Christ—His fifth argument—The answer—A dissertation of the various degrees of punishment—For what reason God may act unequally with equals—Concerning the delay of punishment, and its various dispensations.

THE consideration of the arguments advanced by Mr Samuel

Rutherford[1] against this truth which we are now maintaining shall conclude this dissertation. He maintains, as I have observed before, "That punitory justice exists not in God by necessity of nature, but freely;" and he has said that Twisse hath proved this by a variety of arguments, one of which, in preference to the others, he builds on, as unanswerable.

But, with this great man's leave, I must tell him that Twisse hath never even said, much less proved, "That punitory justice exists freely in God, and not from a necessity of nature;" nor, indeed, can it be said by any one, with any show of reason, for punitory justice denotes the habit of justice, nor is it less justice because it is punitory. But be assured the accurate Twisse hath never maintained that any habit exists in God freely, and not from a necessity of nature. We have before accounted in what sense habits are ascribed to God. Even the more sagacious Socinians do not fall into such a blunder; but they deny such a habit to exist in God at all, and entirely divest him of this justice. Twisse, indeed, maintains that the exercise of that justice is free to God, but grants that justice itself is a natural attribute of God; the Socinians, that it is only a free act of the divine will. Which party this learned author favours appears not from his words. If by justice he mean the habit, he sides with the Socinians; if the act and exercise, he is of the same opinion with Twisse, although he expresses his sentiments rather unhappily. But let us consider this learned writer's arguments:—

The first, which he acknowledges to be taken from Twisse (the same thing may be said of most of his others), and which he pronounces unanswerable, is this: "God gave up his most innocent Son, our Lord Jesus Christ, to death, in consequence of his punitory justice, and it was certainly in his power not to have devoted him to death, for from no necessity of nature did God devote his Son to death; for if so, then God would not have been God, which is absurd, for of his free love he gave him up to death, John iii. 16; Rom. viii. 32."

As there is no need of a sword to cut this "indissoluble knot," as he calls it, let us try by words what we can do to untie it. I answer, then, The devoting of Christ to death is taken in a twofold sense:— 1. For the appointment of Christ to the office of surety, and to suffer the punishment of our sins in our room and stead. 2. For the infliction of punishment upon Christ, now appointed our surety, and our delivery through his death being now supposed.

The devoting of Christ to death, considered in the first sense, we deny to be an act of punitory justice, or to have arisen from that justice; for that act by which God destined his Son to the work of mediation, by which, in respect of their guilt, he transferred from us all our sins and laid them upon Christ, are acts of supreme dominion,

[1] In his book on Providence, chap. xxii. page 345, assert. 6.

and breathe love and grace rather than avenging justice. But the punishment of Christ, made sin for us, is an act of punitory justice; nor, upon the supposition that he was received in our room as our surety, could it be otherwise. And although, in drawing such consequences, I think we ought to refrain as to what might be possible, I am not, however, afraid to affirm that God could not have been God,—that is, just and true,—if he had not devoted to death his Son, when thus appointed our mediator.

What shall we say?—that even this learned man was aware of this twofold sense of the phrase, "The devoting of Christ to death?" He either had not thoroughly weighed that distinction, or else he is inconsistent with and shamefully contradicts himself; for in the beginning of the argument he asserts, that "the devoting of Christ to death had its rise from *punitory justice*," but in the end he says it was from "*free love.*" But certainly punishing justice is not free love. He must, then, either acknowledge a twofold appointment of Christ to death, or he cannot be consistent with himself. But the passages of Scripture that he quotes evidently mean the appointment of Christ to death, as we have explained it in the first sense of the phrase.

What reason this learned man had for so much boasting of this argument as unanswerable, let the reader determine; to me it appears not only very easily answerable, but far beneath many others that one disputing on such a subject must encounter.

But he introduces some as making answers to his argument, who affirm "That Christ was not innocent, but a sinner by imputation, and made sin for us; and that it was necessary from the essential justice of God, and his authority, as enjoining that he should make atonement for sin in himself and in his own person."[1]

I applaud the prudence of this learned man, who, from *no kind of necessity*, but *freely*, frames answers to his own arguments. Here he has exhibited such a one as nobody but himself would have dreamed of; for although what your crazy disputants, or this learned divine, fighting with himself, say be true, he must, however, be a fool who can believe that it has any relation to the present subject. To those adversaries who urge that "God freely punishes sin because he punished his Son who knew no sin," and who contend that "God may equally not punish the guilty as punish the innocent," we answer, that Christ, though *intrinsically* and *personally innocent*, yet as he was by *substitution*, and consequently legally, guilty, is no instance of the punishment of an innocent person; for he was not punished as the most innocent Son of God. Passing over these things, then,—and indeed they are of no import to the present subject,—he endeavours to prove, by several arguments, that God laid our sins upon Christ

1 "Necessary from the essential justice of God that he should suffer the punishment due to sinners, either in his own proper person, or in that of a surety."—ED.

by constituting him surety, and from no necessity of nature. But even this effort is of no service to his cause, for this we by no means deny; so that his labour is entirely superfluous. At length, however, in the progress of the dispute, this learned gentleman advances some arguments that seem suitable to his purpose.

"We readily grant," says he, "upon supposition that Christ was made our surety by the decree of God, that he could not be but punished by God, and yet freely, as God created the world of mere free will, though necessarily, in respect of his immutability; for it cannot be that a free action should impose on God a natural or physical necessity of doing any thing."

We have shown before what kind of a necessity we ascribe to God in punishing sins. It is not an inanimate or merely physical necessity, as if God acted from principles of nature, in a manner altogether natural,—that is, without any intervening act of understanding or will; for "he worketh all things according to the counsel of his will." But it is such a necessity as leaves to God an entire concomitant liberty in acting, but which necessarily, by destroying all antecedent indifference, accomplishes its object,—namely, the punishment of sin,—the justice, holiness, and purity of God so requiring. But this necessity, though it hindereth not the divine liberty, any more than that which is incumbent on God of doing any thing in consequence of a decree, from the immutability of his nature, yet it arises not from a decree, but from things themselves particularly constituted, and not as the other kind of necessity, from a decree only. And, therefore, in those things which God does necessarily, merely from the supposition of a decree, the decree respects the thing to be done, and affects it antecedently to the consideration of any necessity incumbent on him; but in those whose necessity arises from the demand of the divine nature, a decree only supposes a certain condition of things, which being supposed, immediately, and without any consideration of any respect to a decree, it is necessary that one or another consequence should follow. As, for instance: after God decreed that he would create the world, it was impossible that he should not create it, because he is immutable, and the decree immediately respected that very thing, namely, the creation of it. But the necessity of punishing sin arises from the justice and holiness of God, it being supposed that, in consequence of a decree, a rational creature existed, and was permitted to transgress; but he punishes the transgression which he decreed to permit because he is just, and not only because he decreed to punish it. The necessity, then, of creating the world arises from a decree; the necessity of punishing sin, from justice.

"But it is impossible," says Rutherford, "that a free action can impose a natural or physical necessity of doing any thing upon God."

But by a "free action" it can be proved that certain things may be placed in such a condition that God could not but exercise certain acts towards them, on account of the strict demand of some attribute of his nature, though not from a physical and insensible necessity, which excludes all liberty of action; for it being supposed that in consequence of a free decree God willed to speak with man, it is necessary from the decree that he should speak, but that he should speak truth is necessary from the necessity of his nature. Supposing, then, a free action, in which he hath decreed to speak, a natural necessity of speaking truth is incumbent on God, nor can he do otherwise than speak truth. Supposing sin to exist, and that God willed to do any thing with regard to sin (although perhaps this is not in consequence of a decree), it is necessary, by necessity of nature, that he should do justice,—that is, that he should punish it; for the righteous judgment of God is, "That they which commit such things," namely, who commit sin, "are worthy of death." There are certain attributes of the Deity which have no egress but towards certain objects particularly modified, for they do not constitute or create objects to themselves, as other divine attributes do; but these objects being once constituted by a free act of the divine will, they must necessarily,—for such is their nature and manner,—be exercised.

What this learned writer farther adds in support of his argument is founded on a mistaken idea of the subject in question; for as the necessity of punishing sin arises from the right and justice of God, it is by no means necessary that he should punish it in one subject more than in another, but only that he should punish it, and that thereby his right may be restored and his justice satisfied.

The second argument of this learned writer is this: "As God freely has mercy on whom he will,—for he is under obligation to none, and yet mercy is essential to him,—so God does not by any necessity of nature owe punishment to a sinner. Although, then, man owe obedience to God, or a vicarious compensation by means of punishment, from the necessity of a decree, yet those who say that God, by necessity of nature, owes the good of punitory justice to the universe, which were he not to execute he would not be God, —those, I say, indirectly deny the existence of a God."

Although any one may perceive that these assertions are unsubstantial, unfounded, and more obscure than even the books of the Sibyls, we shall, however, make a few observations upon them. In the first place, then, it must be abundantly clear, from what has been already said, that mercy and justice are different in respect of their exercise, nor need we now farther insist on that point. But how this learned man will prove that sparing mercy,—which, as not only the nature of the thing itself requires, but even the Socinians with the orthodox agree, ought to be viewed in the same light as punitory justice,—is essential to God, when he affirms punitory justice to exist in God freely, I cannot conjecture. But as there is no one who doubts but that God does all things for the glory and manifestation of his own essential attributes, why it should be more acceptable to him, in his administration respecting sin committed, to exercise an act of the will purely free, no excellence of his nature so requiring, than of an essential property,[1] to do in all respects whatsoever he pleaseth, and to spread abroad its glory, it will be difficult to assign a reason. God, I say, has a proper regard for the glory of his attributes; and as mercy earnestly and warmly urges the free pardon of sins, if no attribute of the divine nature required that they should be punished, it is strange that God, by an act of his will entirely free, should have inclined to the contrary. But we have shown before that the Scriptures lay a more sure foundation for the death of Christ.

Secondly, God does not owe to the sinner punishment from a necessity of nature, but he owes the infliction of punishment on account of sin to his own right and justice, for thence the obligation of a sinner to punishment arises; nor is the debt of obedience in rational creatures resolvable into a decree in any other respect than as it is in consequence of a decree that they are rational creatures.

In the third place, the conclusion of this argument would require even the Delian swimmer's abilities to surmount it. So very puzzling and harsh is the diction, that it is difficult to make any sense of it; for what means that sentence, "That God, by a necessity of nature, owes the good of punitory justice to the universe?" The good of the universe is the glory of God himself. To owe, then, "the good of punitory justice to the universe," is to owe the good of an essential attribute to his own glory. But, again, what is "the good of punitory justice?" Justice itself, or the exercise of it? Neither can be so called with any propriety. But if the learned author mean this, that God ought to preserve his own right and dominion over the universe, and that this is just, his nature so requiring him, but that it cannot be done, supposing sin to exist, without the exercise of punitory justice, and then that those who affirm this indirectly deny the existence of God,—this is easy for any one to assert, but not so easy to prove.

This learned author's third argument is taken from some absurd consequences, which he supposes to follow from our opinion; for he thus proceeds to reason: "Those who teach that sin merits punishment from a necessity of the divine nature, without any intervention of a free decree, teach, at the same time, that God cannot forbid sin to man without necessarily forbidding it under the penalty of eternal death. As if," says he, "when God forbids adultery or theft, in a human court he forbids them with a modification of the punishment,—namely, that theft should not be punished with death, but by a quadruple restitution,—he could not forbid them without any sanction of a punishment; and as he commands these to be

[1] Namely, mercy.—TR.

punished by men because they are sins, why cannot he for the same reason manage matters so in his own internal court,[1] and suspend all punishment, and nevertheless forbid the same transgressions?"

A fine show of reasoning; but there is no real solid truth in it, for all is false.

In what sense sin deserves punishment from the necessity of the divine nature, we have already shown at large. Neither, however, do we think ourselves bound to teach that God could not forbid sin but under the penalty of eternal death; for we hold that not one or another kind of punishment is necessary, but that punishment itself is necessary, and the punishment, according to the rule of God's wisdom and justice, is death. Moreover, a rational creature, conscious of its proper subjection and obediential dependence, being created and existing, God did not account it at all necessary to forbid it to sin by a free act of his will, under one penalty or another; for both these follow from the very situation of the creature, and the order of dependence,—namely, that it should not transgress by withdrawing itself from the right and dominion of the Creator, and if it should transgress, that it should be obnoxious and exposed to coercion and punishment. But it being supposed that God should forbid sin by an external legislation, the appointment of punishment, even though there should be no mention made of it, must be coequal with the prohibition.

"But God," says he, "in his human court forbids sin by a modification of the punishment annexed; as, for instance, theft, under the penalty of a quadruple restitution: why may he not do likewise in his own internal court, and consequently suspend all punishment?"

There is no need of much disputation to prove that there is nothing sound or substantial in these arguments. The modification of punishment respects either its appointment or infliction. Punishment itself is considered either in respect of its general end, which is the punishment of transgression, and has a regard to the condition of the creatures with respect to God; or in respect of some special end, and has a respect to the condition of the creatures among themselves. But whatever modification punishment may undergo, provided it attain its proper end, by accomplishing the object in view, the nature of punishment is preserved no less than if numberless degrees were added to it. As to the establishment of punishment, then, in a human court, as it has not primarily and properly a respect to the punishment of transgression, nor a regard to the condition of the creatures with respect to God, but with respect to one another, that degree of punishment is just which is fit and proper for accomplishing the proposed end.

The punishment, then, of theft by a quadruple restitution had in its appointment no such modification conjoined with it as could render it

[1] "Et moderari et suspendere,"—"In his own internal court both mitigate and suspend," etc.—Ed.

unfit and improper in respect of the end proposed, among that people to whom that law concerning retributions was given; but as the infliction of punishment, according to the sentence of the law, depended on the supreme Ruler of that people, it belonged to him to provide that no temporal dispensation with punishment exercised by him, in right of his dominion, should turn out to the injury of the commonwealth.

But hence this learned writer concludes, "That in his own internal court God may modify and suspend punishment."

We can only conjecture what he means by the "internal court" of God. From the justice of God the appointment of punishment is derived; but that is improperly called a court. How far God is at liberty, by this justice, to exercise his power in pardoning sins the Scriptures show. The just right of God is, "that they who commit sin are worthy of death." "But he may modify the punishment," says our author. But not even in a human court can any such modification be admitted as would render the punishment useless in respect of its end; nor, in respect of God, do we think any degree or mode of punishment necessary, but such as may answer the end of the punishment, so far as respects the state of the creatures with respect to God. Nor is any argument from a human court applied to the divine justice, nor from the modification to the suspension for a limited time, nor from a suspension to the total punishment, all which this learned author supposes, of any force.

The sum of the whole is this, as we have laid it down,—That God must necessarily, from his right and justice, inflict punishment on sin, so far as this punishment tends to preserve the state of the creature's dependence on its Creator and proper and natural Lord; so, whatever constitutions or inflictions of punishment, with any particular modification or dispensation, we have admitted, these do not, as the supreme judgment of all is reserved to the destined time, at all operate against our opinion.

The other reasons advanced by this learned author in support of this argument are not of sufficient weight to merit attention. It hath been clearly proved already that the supposition of the pardon of sin, without an intervening satisfaction, implies a contradiction, though not in the terms, in the very thing itself. Nor does it follow that God can without any punishment forgive sin,—to avoid which all rational creatures are indispensably bound from his natural right over them,—because any distinguished action among mankind, to the performance of which they are bound by no law, may be rewarded, there being no threatening of punishments for the neglect of it annexed, that has a respect to a privilege not due.[1] By such consequences, drawn from such arguments, the learned gentleman will neither establish his own opinion nor prejudice ours.

[1] See Suarez de Legib. Priv.

He proceeds, in the fourth place: "God," says he, "worketh nothing without himself from a necessity of nature." This objection hath been already answered by a distinction of necessity into that which is absolute and that which is conditional, nor shall we now delay the reader by repeating what has been said elsewhere. "But to punish sin," says he, "is not in any respect more agreeable to the divine nature than not to punish it; but this is an act of grace and liberty,—that is, an act which God freely exerciseth."

But, according to Rutherford, "it is much more disagreeable," to speak in his own words, "to the divine nature to punish sin than not to punish it; for not to punish it, or to forgive it, proceeds from that mercy which is essential, but to punish it from that justice which is a free act of the divine will. But such things as are natural and necessary have a previous and weightier influence with God than those which are free and may or may not take place." Our learned author means, that setting aside the consideration of his free decree, God is indifferent to inflict punishment or not inflict it. But by what argument will he maintain this absurd position? Does it follow from this, that God is said in Scripture to restrain his anger, and not to cut off the wicked? But surely he is not ignorant that such declarations of divine grace have either a respect to Christ, by whom satisfaction for sin was made, or only denote a temporal suspension of punishment, till the day of public and general retribution.

In the fifth place, he maintains "That a natural necessity will admit of no dispensation, modification, or delay; which, however, it is evident that God either uses, or may use, in the punishment of sin."

Ans. With respect to absolute necessity, which excludes all liberty, perhaps this is true; but with respect to that necessity which we maintain, which admits of a concomitant liberty in acting, it is altogether without foundation. Again: a dispensation with or delay of punishment regards either temporary punishment, with which we grant that God may freely dispense, when the immediate end of that punishment hath not a respect to the creatures in that state of subjection which they owe to God; or eternal punishment, and in respect of that, the time of inflicting it, etc., and freely to appoint it, belong entirely to God;—but that he should inflict the punishment itself is just and necessary.

Nor does that instance, brought from the various degrees of punishment, at all avail him,—namely, "That if God can add or take away one degree of punishment, then he may two, and so annihilate the whole punishment:" for we are speaking of punishment as it includes in it the nature of punishment, and is ordained to preserve God's right and dominion over his creatures, and to avenge the purity and holiness of God; not of it as, in consequence of the divine wisdom and justice, being this or that kind of punishment, or consisting of degrees. For thus far extends that liberty which we ascribe to God in the exercise of his justice, that it belongs to him entirely to determine, according to the counsel of his will, with regard to the degrees, mode, and time to be observed in the infliction of punishment; and no doubt but a proportion of the punishment to the faults is observed, so that by how much one sin exceeds another in quality, by so much one punishment exceeds another punishment in degree; and in the infliction of punishment, God has a respect to the comparative demerit of sins among themselves. We acknowledge, indeed, that God acts differently with persons in the same situation, but not without a respect to Christ and his satisfaction. The satisfaction of Christ is not, indeed, the procatarctic cause of that decree by which he determined such a dispensation of things; but the mediation of Christ, who was made sin for those to whom their sins are not imputed, is the foundation for the actual administration of the whole of that decree, respecting that part of it which consists in the dispensation of free grace and sparing mercy. What this learned writer adds, namely, "That not to punish is sometimes an act of severe justice, and that therefore God does not punish from a necessity of nature," is grossly sophistical: for not to punish denotes either the total removal of punishment altogether, as is the case with the elect, for whom Christ died, which, so far from being an act of severe justice, this learned man will not deny to proceed from the highest grace and mercy; or it denotes only a suspension of some temporal punishment, and for a short time, to the end that sinners may fill up the measure of their iniquity. But this is not, properly speaking, not to punish, but to punish in a different manner, and in a manner more severe, than that to which it succeeds.

What observations our learned author adds in the close of his arguments are either sophistical or very untheological. He says, namely, "That God, influenced by our prayers, averts even an eternal punishment after that we have deserved it." But what! is it to be imputed to our prayers that God averts from us the wrath to come? What occasion is there, pray, then, for the satisfaction of Christ? We have hitherto been so dull and stupid as to believe that the turning away from us of punishment, which has a respect to our faith and prayers, consisted in the dispensation of grace, peace, and the remission of the sins for which Christ made satisfaction, and that God averted from us no deserved punishment but what was laid upon Christ, "who hath redeemed us from the curse of the law, by being made a curse for us."

In his proofs of the sixth argument, which this learned author adds to his former from Twisse, he says, "There is neither reason nor any shadow of reason in it, that the delay of punishment, or a dispensation with it, as to time and manner, can be determined by the free good pleasure of God, either one way or other, if to punish, or punishment in itself and absolutely considered, be necessary."

We have explained before what were our sentiments as to what relates to the distinction between punishment simply considered, and attended with particular circumstances in the manner of its infliction. We affirm that a punishment proportioned to sin, according to the rule of the divine justice, from God's natural right, and from his essential justice and holiness, is necessarily inflicted, to vindicate his glory, establish his government, and preserve his perfections entire and undiminished: and God himself hath revealed to us that this just recompense of reward consists in death eternal; for "the righteous judgment of God is, that they who commit sin are worthy of death." It is just, then, and consequently necessary, that that punishment of death, namely, eternal, should be inflicted. But as God, though a consuming fire, is a rational or intellectual fire, who, in exercising the excellencies or qualities of his nature, proceeds with reason and understanding, it is free to him to appoint the time, manner, and suchlike circumstances as must necessarily attend that punishment in general, so as shall be most for his own glory and the more illustrious display of his justice. But when Rutherford says, somewhat dogmatically, that "there is neither any reason nor shadow of reason in this," let us see what solidity there is in the arguments by which he supports his assertion:—

"The determination of an infernal punishment, as to its manner and time, and consequently as to its eternal duration, will then depend on the mere good pleasure of God; therefore, God can determine the end and measure of infernal punishment; and therefore he is able not to punish, and to will not farther to punish, those condemned to eternal torments: therefore, it is not of absolute necessity that he punishes." But here is nothing but dross, as the saying is, instead of a treasure. The time concerning which we speak is of the infliction of punishment, not of its duration. He who asserts that an end may be put to eternal punishments expressly contradicts himself. We say that God hath revealed to us that the punishment due to every sin, from his right and by the rule of his justice, is eternal; nor could the thing in itself be otherwise, for the punishment of a finite and sinful creature could not otherwise make any compensation for the guilt of its sin. But as it is certain that God, in the first threatening, and in the curse of the law, observed a strict impartiality, and appointed not any kind of punishment but what, according to the rule of his justice, sin deserved; and as the apostle testifies, that "the righteous judgment of God is, that they who commit sin are worthy of death;" and we acknowledge that death to be eternal, and that an injury done to God, infinite in respect of the object, could not be punished, in a subject in every respect finite, otherwise than by a punishment infinite in respect of duration;—that the continuation or suspension of this punishment, which it is just should be inflicted, does not undermine[1] the divine liberty, we are bold to affirm, for it is not free to God to act justly or not. But we have shown before how absurd it is to imagine that the divine omnipotence suffers any degradation, because upon this supposition he must necessarily preserve alive a sinful creature to all eternity, and be unable to annihilate it.

CHAPTER XVIII.

The conclusion of this dissertation—The uses of the doctrine herein vindicated—The abominable nature of sin—God's hatred against sin revealed in various ways—The dreadful effects of sin all over the creation—Enmity between God and every sin—Threatenings and the punishment of sin appointed—The description of sin in the sacred Scriptures—To what great miseries we are liable through sin—The excellency of grace in pardoning sin through Christ—Gratitude and obedience due from the pardoned—An historical fact concerning Tigranes, king of Armenia—Christ to be loved for his cross above all things—The glory of God's justice revealed by this doctrine, and also of his wisdom and holiness.

LET us at length put an end to this dispute; and as all "acknowledging of the truth" ought to be "after godliness,"[2] we shall adduce such useful and practical evident conclusions as flow from this truth, which we have thus far set forth and defended, that we may not be thought to have spent our labour in vain.

First, then, Hence we sinners may learn *the abominable nature of sin.* Whatever there is in heaven or in earth that we have seen, or of which we have heard, whatever declares the glory of the Creator, also exposes this disgraceful fall of the creature. The genuine offspring of sin are death and hell; for "sin, when it is finished, bringeth forth death."[3] That the heavens cast out their native inhabitants, namely, "the angels which kept not their first estate, but left their own habitation,"[4] etc; that the earth is filled with darkness, resentments, griefs, malediction, and revenge,—is to be attributed entirely to this cankerous ulcer of nature. Hence "the wrath of God is revealed from heaven;"[5]—the earth, lately founded by a most beneficent Creator, is "cursed."[6] Hence, the old world having but just emerged from the deluge, "the heavens and the earth which are now, by the same word are kept in store, reserved unto fire against the day of judgment and perdition of ungodly men."[7]

[1] "Dei libertati non subjacere,"—"is not subject to."—ED. [2] Titus i. 5.
[3] James i. 15. [4] Jude 6. [5] Rom. i. 18. [6] Gen. iii. 17. [7] 2 Pet. iii. 7.

Yea, forasmuch as, in this state of things which we have described as being permitted by the will of God, "the creature was made subject to vanity,"[1] there is none of the creatures which, by its confusion, vanity, and inquietude, does not declare this detestable poison, with which it is thoroughly infected, to be exceeding sinful. This is the source and origin of all evils to sinners themselves. Whatever darkness, tumult, vanity, slavery, fearful looking for of judgment and fiery indignation to consume the adversaries, oppresses, tortures, harasses, vexes, burns, corrupts, or kills; whatever from without, penal, grievous, sad, dire, dreadful, even the last unavoidable calamity itself,—is all to be attributed to this prolific parent of miseries. Some one, perhaps, will wonder what this so great a plague is, which perverts the course of the creation; what crime, what kind of inexpiable wickedness, that it hath procured to creatures so very highly exalted, and created in the image of God to share in his glory, after being banished from heaven and paradise, an eternal deprivation of his glory, punishment to which no measure or end is appointed; what hath so incensed the mind of the most bountiful and merciful Father of all, and imbittered his anger, that he should bring eternal sorrows on the work of his own hands, and "kindle a fire that should burn to the lowest bottom, and inflame the foundations of the mountains." I will tell him in one word.

Is it to be wondered at, that God should be disposed severely to punish that which earnestly wishes him *not to be God,* and strives to accomplish this with all its might? Sin opposes the divine nature and existence; it is enmity against God, and is not an idle enemy; it has even engaged in a mortal war with all the attributes of God. He would not be God if he did not avenge, by the punishment of the guilty, his own injury. He hath often and heavily complained, in his word, that by sin he is robbed of his glory and honour, affronted, exposed to calumny and blasphemy; that neither his holiness, nor his justice, nor name, nor right, nor dominion, is preserved pure and untainted: for he hath created all things for his own glory, and it belongs to the natural right of God to preserve that glory entire by the subjection of all his creatures, in their proper stations, to himself. And shall we not reckon that sin is entirely destructive of that order, which would entirely wrest that right out of his hands, and a thing to be restrained by the severest punishments? Let sinners, then, be informed that every the least transgression abounds so much with hatred against God; is so highly injurious to him, and as far as is in its power brands him with such folly, impotence, and injustice; so directly robs him of all his honour, glory, and power,—that if he wills to be God, he can by no means suffer it to escape unpunished.

It was not for nothing that on that day on which he made man a

[1] Rom. viii. 20.

living soul, he threatened him with death, even eternal death; that in giving his law he thundered forth so many dread execrations against this fatal evil; that he hath threatened it with such punishment, with so great anger, with fury, wrath, tribulation, and anguish; that with a view to vindicate his own glory, and provide for the salvation of sinners, he made his most holy Son, who was "holy, harmless, undefiled, and separate from sinners," "sin" and a "curse,"[1] and subjected him to that last punishment, the death of the cross, including in it the satisfaction due to his violated law. All these things divine justice required as necessary to the preservation of his honour, glory, wisdom, and dominion. Let every proud complaint of sinners, then, be hushed, for we know that "the judgment of God is according to truth against them that do evil."[2]

But sin, in respect of the creature, is folly, madness, fury, blindness, hardness, darkness, stupor, giddiness, torpor, turpitude, uncleanness, nastiness, a stain, a spot, an apostasy, degeneracy, a wandering from the mark, a turning aside from the right path, a disease, a languor, destruction,—DEATH. In respect of the Creator, it is a disgrace, an affront, blasphemy, enmity, hatred, contempt, rebellion,—an injury. In respect of its own nature, it is poison, a stench, dung, a vomit, polluted blood, a plague, a pestilence, an abominable, detestable, cursed thing; which, by its most pernicious power of metamorphosing, hath transformed angels into devils, light into darkness, life into death, paradise into a desert, a pleasant, fruitful, blessed world into a vain, dark, accursed prison, and the Lord of all into a servant of servants; which hath rendered man, the glory of God, an enemy to himself, a wolf to others, hateful to God, his own destroyer, the destruction of others, the plague of the world, a monster, and a ruin. Attempting to violate the eternal, natural, and indispensable right of God, to cut the thread of the creature's dependence on the Creator, it introduced with it this world of iniquity.

First, then, to address you who live, or rather are dead, under the guilt, dominion, power, and law of sin, "how shall ye escape the damnation of hell?" The judgment of God is, that they who commit those things to which you are totally given up, and which you cannot refrain from, are "worthy of death." "It is a fearful thing to fall into the hands of the living God;"[3] since it is "a just thing with him to render to every one according to his works." And who shall deliver you out of his mighty hand? Wherewith can "the wrath to come" be averted? wherewithal can you make atonement to so great a judge? Sacrifices avail nothing; hence those words in the prophet, which express not so much the language of inquiry as of confusion and astonishment: "Wherewithal shall I come before the LORD, and bow myself before the high God? shall I come before him with

[1] Heb. vii. 26; 2 Cor. v. 21; Gal. iii. 13. [2] Rom. ii. 2. [3] Heb. x. 31.

burnt-offerings, with calves of a year old? Will the LORD be pleased with thousands of rams, or with ten thousands of rivers of oil? shall I give my first-born for my transgression, the fruit of my body for the sin of my soul?"[1] Would you attempt an obedience arduous and expensive beyond all credibility? By such dreadful propitiations, by such dire and accursed sacrifices, at the thought of which human nature shudders, would you appease the offended Deity? You are not the first whom a vain superstition and ignorance of the justice of God hath forced to turn away their ears from the sighs and cries of tender infants, breathing out their very vitals, your own blood, in vain. These furies, which now by starts agitate us within, will, by their vain attempts against the snares of death, torment us to all eternity: for God, the judge of all, will not accept of "sacrifice, or offering, or burnt-offerings for sin;" with these he is not at all delighted; for "the redemption of the soul is precious, and ceaseth for ever."[2] God cannot so lightly esteem or disregard his holiness, justice, and glory, to which your sins have done so great an injury, that he should renounce them all for the sake of hostile conspirators, unless there should be some other remedy quickly provided for us; —unless the judge himself shall provide a lamb for a burnt-offering; unless the gates of a city of refuge shall be quickly opened to you, exclaiming and trembling at the avenging curse of the law; unless you can find access to the horns of the altar. If God be to remain blessed for ever, you must doubtless perish for ever. If, then, you have the least concern or anxiety for your eternal state, hasten, "while it is called To-day," to "lay hold on the hope that is set before you." Give yourselves up entirely to him; receive him "whom God hath set forth to be a propitiation through faith in his blood, that he might declare his righteousness." But what and how bitter a sense of sin; how deep a humiliation, contrition, and dejection of heart and spirit; what self-hatred, condemnation, and contempt; what great self-indignation and revenge; what esteem, what faith in the necessity, excellence, and dignity of the righteousness and satisfaction of Christ, especially if God hath graciously condescended to bestow his holy Spirit, to convince men's hearts of sin, of righteousness, and of judgment (without whose effectual aid and heart-changing grace even the most apposite remedies applied to this disease will be in vain), and[3] to excite and work such sentiments concerning the transgression of the divine law, the nature of sin, or the disobedience of the creatures! A persuasion how fit and proper, those who have spiritual eyes will easily perceive.

[1] Mic. vi. 6, 7. [2] Ps. xlix. 8.

[3] From the figure of notation to the close of the paragraph, the sense of the author has been entirely misapprehended. Read, "must be excited and kept alive by such a fit and adequate view respecting the transgression of the divine law, the nature of sin, or the disobedience of the creature,—those who have spiritual eyes will easily perceive."—ED.

To those happy persons "whose sins are forgiven, and to whom God will not impute iniquity," because he hath laid their transgressions upon Christ, the knowledge of this divine truth is as a spur to quicken them to the practice of every virtue and to sincere obedience; for in what high, yea, infinite honour and esteem must God be held by him who, having escaped from the snares of death and the destruction due to him, through his inexpressible mercy, hath thoroughly weighed the nature of sin and the consequences of it, which we have mentioned before! for whosoever shall reflect with himself that such is the quality and nature of sin, and that it is so impiously inimical to God, that unless by some means his justice be satisfied by the punishment of another, he could not pardon it or let it pass unpunished, will ever acknowledge himself indebted to eternal love for the remission of the least transgression, because in inexpressible grace and goodness it hath been forgiven. And hence, too, we may learn how much beyond all other objects of our affection we are bound to love with our heart and soul, and all that is within us, our dear and beloved Deliverer and most merciful Saviour, Jesus Christ, "who hath delivered us from the wrath to come."

When Tigranes, son of the king of Armenia, had said to Cyrus that he would purchase his wife's liberty at the price of his life, and she was consequently set free by Cyrus, while some were admiring and extolling one virtue of Cyrus, and some another, she being asked what she most admired in that illustrious hero, answered, "My thoughts were not turned upon him." Her husband again asking her, "Upon whom, then?" she replied, "Upon him who said that he would redeem me from slavery at the expense of his life." Is not He, then, to be caressed and dearly beloved, to be contemplated with faith, love, and joy, who answered for our lives with his own,—devoted himself to punishment, and at the price of his blood, "while we were yet enemies," purchased us, and rendered us "a peculiar people to himself?" We, now secure, may contemplate in his agony, sweat, tremor, horror, exclamations, prayers, cross, and blood, what is God's severity against sin, what the punishment of the broken law and curse are. Unless God, the judge and ruler of all, after having thoroughly examined the nature, hearts, breasts, ways, and lives of us all, had thence collected whatever was contrary to his law, improper, unjust, and impure,—whatever displeased the eyes of his purity, provoked his justice, roused his anger and severity,—and laid it all on the shoulders of our Redeemer, and condemned it in his flesh, it had been better for us, rather than to be left eternally entangled in the snares of death and of the curse, never to have enjoyed this common air, but to have been annihilated as soon as born. "Wretched men that we are, who shall deliver us" from this most miserable state by nature? "Thanks be to God, which giveth us the victory through our Lord Jesus Christ." May we always, then, be "sick of love" towards our deliverer! may he always be our "beloved, who is white and ruddy, and the chiefest among ten thousand!"

The acknowledging of this truth has a respect not only to the manifestation of his justice, but also of the wisdom, holiness, and dominion of God over his creatures: for that justice which, in respect of its effect and egress, we call vindicatory, which, as we have before demonstrated, is natural to God and essential, and therefore absolutely perfect in itself, or rather perfection itself, this very truth, which we have thus far defended, evidently illustrates; as also his supreme rectitude in the exercise of it, "when he sits on his throne judging righteously;" and how severe a judge he will be towards impenitent sinners, whose sins are not expiated in the blood of Christ! That justice is not a free act of the divine will, which God may use or renounce at pleasure; nor is sin only a debt of ours, which, as we were unable to pay, he might forgive by only freely receding from his right: for what reason, then, could be assigned why the Father of mercies should so severely punish his most holy Son on our account, that he might, according to justice, deliver us from our sins, when, without any difficulty, by one act of his will, and that too a most free and holy act, he could have delivered both himself and us wretched sinners from this evil? But it exists in God in the manner of a habit, natural to the divine essence itself, perpetually and immutably inherent in it, which, from his very nature, he must necessarily exercise in every work that respecteth the proper object of his justice; for sin is that ineffable evil which would overturn God's whole right over his creatures unless it were punished. As, then, the perfection of divine justice is infinite, and such as God cannot by any means relax, it is of the last importance to sinners seriously and deeply to bethink themselves how they are to stand before him.

Moreover, the infinite wisdom of God, the traces of which we so clearly read in creation, legislation, and in the other works of God, is hereby wondrously displayed, to the eternal astonishment of men and angels; for none but an infinitely wise God could bring it about, that that which in its own nature is opposite to him, inimical, and full of obstinacy, should turn out to his highest honour, and the eternal glory of his grace. Yea, the divine wisdom not only had respect to God himself, and to the security of his glory, honour, right, and justice, but even provided for the good of miserable sinners, for their best interests, exaltation, and salvation, and from the empoisoned bowels of sin itself. "Out of the eater came forth meat, and out of the strong came forth sweetness." By interposing a surety and covenant-head between sin and the sinner, between the transgression of the law and its transgressor, he condemned and punished sin, restored the law, and freed the sinner both from sin and from the law. "He hath abounded toward us in all wisdom and prudence," Eph. i. 8, when he "made all men see what is the fellowship of the mystery, which from the beginning of the world hath been hid in God," chap. iii. 9; for "in Christ are hid all the treasures of wisdom and knowledge," Col. ii. 2, 3.

It will be for ever esteemed a miracle of God's providence, that he should have made the captivity or wicked sale of Joseph, by means of so many windings, perplexed mazes, and strange occurrences, issue at last in his own exaltation and the preservation of his brethren, who impiously sold him. But if any one, though endowed with the tongues of angels and of men, should attempt to describe this mystery of divine wisdom, whereby it is evident that God exalts his own name, and not only recovers his former honour, but even raises it, manifests his justice, preserves inviolable his right and dominion in pardoning sin, wherewith he is highly pleased and incredibly delighted (and unless this heavenly discovery, a truly God-like invention, had intervened, he could not have pardoned even the least sin), he must feel his language not only deficient, but the eye of the mind, overpowered with light, will fill him with awe and astonishment. That that which is the greatest, yea, the only disgrace and affront to God, should turn out to his highest honour and glory; that that which could not be permitted to triumph without the greatest injury to the justice, right, holiness, and truth of God, should find grace and pardon, to the eternal and glorious display of justice, right, holiness, and truth,—was a work that required infinite wisdom, an arduous task, and every way worthy of God.

Finally, Let us constantly contemplate in the mirror of this truth the holiness of God, whereby "he is of purer eyes than to behold evil," in "whose presence the wicked shall not stand," that we ourselves may become more pure in heart, and more holy in life, speech, and behaviour.

END OF VOL. X.